murach's
ASP.NET 4
web programming with
C# 2010

Anne Boehm   **Joel Murach**

MIKE MURACH & ASSOCIATES, INC.

1-800-221-5528 • (559) 440-9071 • Fax: (559) 440-0963
murachbooks@murach.com • www.murach.com

Author:	Anne Boehm
	Joel Murach
Editor:	Mike Murach
Cover Design:	Zylka Design
Production:	Cynthia Vasquez
	Ben Murach

Books for .NET 4 developers

Murach's C# 2010
Murach's ADO.NET 4 Database Programming with C# 2010
Murach's ASP.NET 4 Web Programming with C# 2010

Murach's Visual Basic 2010
Murach's ADO.NET 4 Database Programming with VB 2010
Murach's ASP.NET 4 Web Programming with VB 2010

Murach's C++ 2008

Murach's SQL Server 2008 for Developers

Books for web developers

Murach's HTML, XHTML, and CSS
Murach's JavaScript and DOM Scripting
Murach's PHP and MySQL

Books for Java developers

Murach's Java SE 6
Murach's Java Servlets and JSP (2nd Edition)
Murach's Oracle SQL and PL/SQL

For more on Murach books, please visit us at www.murach.com

10 9 8 7 6 5 4 3 2 1
ISBN: 978-1-890774-61-5

murach's
ASP.NET 4
web programming with
C# 2010

Contents

Expanded contents

Chapter 7   How to use the validation controls

Chapter 8   How to manage state

Section 3 ASP.NET database programming

Section 4 Professional ASP.NET skills

Chapter 21   How to use AJAX

Chapter 22   How to configure and deploy ASP.NET 4 applications

Introduction

Microsoft's ASP.NET is one of today's key technologies for developing web applications. As part of the .NET Framework, it allows you to use the Visual Studio IDE with its host of productivity tools and features to develop web applications more quickly and easily than you can with server-side languages that require intensive coding. In fact, if you've been using PHP or Java servlets and JSP for developing web applications, you'll soon see that ASP.NET offers many features that just aren't available on other platforms.

Before you can learn ASP.NET with this book, you need to know the basics of C# coding. If you do, this book will get you off to a fast start with ASP.NET 4. In fact, by the end of chapter 4, you'll know how to use Visual Studio and ASP.NET to develop and test multi-page database applications.

But this is much more than a beginning book. By the time you're done, you'll have all the skills you need for developing eCommerce web applications at a professional level.

What this book does

To be more specific about what this book presents, here is a brief description of each of its four sections:

* Section 1 is designed to get you off to a fast start. So the first three chapters show you how to use Visual Studio and ASP.NET to design and code both one-page and multi-page web applications that get data from a database. Then, chapter 4 shows you how to test and debug your web applications, and chapter 5 shows you what you need to know about HTML and CSS as you use ASP.NET. At that point, you're ready for rapid progress in the sections that follow.

* Section 2 presents the other skills that you're likely to use in every ASP.NET application that you develop. That includes how to use the server and validation controls, and more about managing the state of an application. Then, the last three chapters in this section present features that make it easier for you to develop professional-looking applications: master pages, site navigation, and themes.

* In section 3, you'll learn how to use the data access features of ASP.NET 4. That includes using SQL data sources, which reduce the amount of data access code that you need for an application. It includes bound controls that are designed to work with data sources, including the GridView, DetailsView, FormView, ListView, and DataPager controls. And it includes object data sources, which make it easier for you to separate presentation code from data access code.

* Section 4 completes the set of skills that you need for developing professional eCommerce web applications. Here, you'll learn how to secure data

transmissions between client and server, how to authenticate and authorize users, how to use email within your applications, how to use the AJAX feature of ASP.NET, how to configure and deploy your applications, and how to create and use WCF services.

To get the most from this book, we recommend that you start by reading the first section from start to finish. But after that, you can skip to any of the other sections to get the information that you need, whenever you need it. Since this book has been carefully designed to work that way, you won't miss anything by skipping around.

Why you'll learn faster and better with this book

Like all our books, this one has features that you won't find in competing books. That's why we believe you'll learn faster and better with our book than with any other. Here are some of those features.

- Because section 1 presents a complete subset of ASP.NET in just 5 chapters, you're ready for productive work much faster than you are when you use competing books. This section also uses a self-paced approach that lets experienced programmers move more quickly and beginners work at a pace that's comfortable for absorbing all of the new information.

- Because the next three sections present all of the other skills that you need for developing web applications at a professional level, you can go from beginner to professional in a single book.

- Unlike many ASP.NET books, this one shows you how to get the most from Visual Studio 2010 as you develop your applications. Because we've found that this IDE is one of the keys to development productivity, we're surprised that many books still ignore or neglect it.

- The exercises at the ends of the chapters in the first three sections let you practice what you've just learned. To help you get the most practice in the least time, these exercises start from applications that you download from our web site.

- If you page through this book, you'll see that all of the information is presented in "paired pages," with the essential syntax, guidelines, and examples on the right page and the perspective and extra explanation on the left page. This helps you learn faster by reading less...and this is the ideal reference format when you need to refresh your memory about how to do something.

- To make sure that you learn ASP.NET as thoroughly as possible, all of its features are presented in the context of complete applications. These applications include the web forms, the aspx code, and the C# code. As we see it, the best way to learn is to study applications like these, even though you won't find them in most competing books.

What software you need

To develop ASP.NET 4 applications, you can use any of the full editions of Visual Studio 2010, including the Professional Edition, Premium Edition, or Ultimate Edition. All of these editions come with everything you need, including the Visual Studio development environment, version 4 of the Microsoft .NET Framework, C# 2010 and Visual Basic 2010, a built-in web server that's ideal for testing ASP.NET applications, and a scaled-back version of SQL Server called SQL Server Express.

For a no-cost alternative to the commercial packages, you can download Visual Web Developer 2010 Express Edition and SQL Server Express from Microsoft's web site for free. Together, they provide all of the items listed above.

Keep in mind, though, that Web Developer 2010 is a scaled-back version of the full editions. That's why you'll find that some of its user interfaces are simpler than the ones in this book, which are from the Professional Edition. You'll also find that a few of the features in this book aren't available with Web Developer 2010. Nevertheless, it's is a terrific product for learning how to develop ASP.NET 4 applications. And both the applications and the skills that you develop with it will work with any of the full editions of Visual Studio.

How our downloadable files make learning easier

To help you get the most from this book, you can download the source code and databases for all of the applications presented in this book. Then, you can test and review these applications on your own to see how they work. And you can copy and paste the code that you want to use in your own applications.

The download also includes the starting applications for the exercises at the ends of the chapters. For more information about downloading and installing all the files for this book, please see appendix A.

3 companion books for ASP.NET programmers

As you read this book, you may discover that your C# skills aren't as strong as they ought to be. In that case, we recommend that you get a copy of *Murach's C# 2010*. It will get you up-to-speed with the language. It will show you how to work with the most useful .NET classes. And as a bonus, it will show you how to develop Windows Forms applications.

Another book that we recommend for all ASP.NET and C# programmers is *Murach's ADO.NET 4 Database Programming with C# 2010*. This book shows you how to write the ADO.NET code that you need for using object data sources in your applications. It gives you insight into what ADO.NET is doing as you use SQL data sources. And it shows you how to work with XML, create reports, and use LINQ and the Entity Framework. So, whether you're developing Windows or web applications with ADO.NET 4, this book should be on your desk.

The third companion is *Murach's SQL Server 2008 for Developers*. To start, it shows you how to write SQL statements in all their variations so you can code the right statements for your data sources. This often gives you the option of having Microsoft SQL Server do more so your applications do less. Beyond that, this book shows you how to design and implement databases and how to use advanced features like stored procedures.

2 books for every web developer

Although chapter 5 of this book presents a starting set of the HTML and CSS skills that you need for ASP.NET programming, every web developer should have a full set of these skills. For that, we recommend *Murach's HTML, XHTML, and CSS*. Beyond that, every web programmer should know how to use JavaScript for client-side programming. For that, we recommend *Murach's JavaScript and DOM Scripting*.

If you're new to these subjects, these books will get you started fast. If you have experience with these subjects, these books make it easy for you to learn new skills whenever you need them. And after you've used these books for training, they become the best on-the-job references you've ever used.

Support materials for trainers and instructors

If you're a corporate trainer or a college instructor who would like to use this book for a course, we offer an Instructor's CD that includes: (1) a complete set of PowerPoint slides that you can use to review and reinforce the content of the book; (2) instructional objectives that describe the skills a student should have upon completion of each chapter; (3) test banks that measure mastery of those skills; (4) the solutions to the exercises in this book; (5) projects that the students start from scratch; (6) solutions to those projects; and (7) the source code and databases for the book applications.

To learn more about this Instructor's CD and to find out how to get it, please go to our web site at www.murach.com and click on the Trainers link or the Instructors link. Or, if you prefer, you can call Kelly at 1-800-221-5528 or send an email to kelly@murach.com.

Please let us know how this book works for you

This is the fourth edition of our ASP.NET book. For each edition, we've added the new features of ASP.NET. But we've also tried to respond to the feedback that we've received and improve the content and structure of the book.

Now that we're done, we hope that we've succeeded in making this edition our best one ever. So, if you have any comments, we would appreciate hearing from you. If you like our book, please tell a friend. And good luck with your web programming.

Anne Boehm, Author
anne@murach.com

Mike Murach, Publisher
mike@murach.com

Section 1

The essence of ASP.NET web programming

This section presents the essential skills for designing, coding, and testing ASP.NET web applications. After chapter 1 introduces you to the concepts and terms that you need to know for web programming, chapters 2 and 3 teach you the essential skills for designing web forms and writing the C# code that makes them work. Then, chapter 4 shows you how to use the many features for testing and debugging ASP.NET applications. Finally, chapter 5 presents the essential HTML and CSS skills that you will need as an ASP.NET programmer.

When you finish all five chapters, you'll be able to develop real-world applications of your own. You'll have a solid understanding of how ASP.NET works. And you'll be ready to learn all of the other ASP.NET features and techniques that are presented in the rest of this book.

1

An introduction to ASP.NET web programming

This chapter introduces you to the basic concepts of web programming and ASP.NET. Here, you'll learn how web applications work and what software you need for developing ASP.NET web applications. You'll also see how the HTML code for a web form is coordinated with the C# code that makes the web form work the way you want it to. When you finish this chapter, you'll have the background you need for developing web applications of your own.

An introduction to web applications

A *web application* consists of a set of *web pages* that are generated in response to user requests. The Internet has many different types of web applications, such as search engines, online stores, auctions, news sites, discussion groups, games, and so on.

Two pages of a Shopping Cart application

Figure 1-1 shows two pages of a simple web application. In this case, the application is for an online store that lets users purchase a variety of Halloween products, including costumes, masks, and decorations. You'll see parts of this application throughout the book, so it's worth taking the time to become familiar with it in this chapter.

The first web page in this figure is used to display information about the various products that are available from the Halloween store. To select a product, you use the drop-down list that's below the banner at the top of the page. Then, the page displays information about the product including a picture, short and long descriptions, and the product's price.

If you enter a quantity in the text box near the bottom of the page and click the Add to Cart button, the second page in this figure is displayed. This page lists the contents of your shopping cart and provides several buttons that let you remove items from the cart, clear the cart entirely, return to the previous page to continue shopping, or proceed to a checkout page.

Of course, the complete Halloween Superstore application also contains other pages. For example, if you click the Check Out button in the second page, you're taken to a page that lets you enter the information necessary to complete a purchase.

An important point to notice about these pages is that they both contain controls that let the user interact with the page, like the drop-down list and buttons on the Order page. A page that contains controls like these is called a *web form*, and an ASP.NET application consists of one web form for each page in the application.

The Order page of a Shopping Cart application

The Cart page of a Shopping Cart application

Figure 1-1   Two pages of a Shopping Cart application

The hardware and software components for web applications

Figure 1-2 shows the basic hardware and software components that are required for a web application. To start, a web application is a type of *client/ server application*, which means that the functions of the application are split between a *client* computer and a *server* computer. The client and server computers are connected to one another via the Internet, and they communicate with each other using *HTTP*, or *Hypertext Transfer Protocol*.

To access a web application, you use a *web browser* that runs on a client computer. The most popular web browser is Microsoft's Internet Explorer, but two alternatives are Mozilla Firefox and Chrome.

The web application itself is stored on the server computer. This computer runs *web server* software that enables it to send web pages to web browsers. Although many web servers are available, the two most popular are Microsoft's *Internet Information Services* (or *IIS*) and The Apache Software Foundation's *Apache HTTP Server*, which is usually just called *Apache*. For ASP.NET applications, though, the server typically runs IIS. Although Apache can be configured to run ASP.NET applications, it doesn't support all of the features of ASP.NET.

Because most web applications work with data that's stored in a database, most server computers also run a *database management system* (or *DBMS*). Two popular database management systems for ASP.NET development are Microsoft SQL Server and Oracle. Note, however, that the database server software doesn't have to run on the same server computer as the web server software. In fact, a separate database server is often used to improve an application's overall performance.

Although this figure shows the client and server computers connected via the Internet, this isn't the only way a client can connect to a server in a web application. If the client and the server are on the same *local area network* (or *LAN*), they can connect via an *intranet*. Since an intranet uses the same protocols as the Internet, a web application works the same on an intranet as it does on the Internet.

Components of a web application

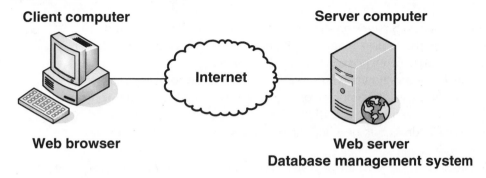

Client computer   **Server computer**

Web browser   **Web server**
                                        Database management system

Description

- Web applications are a type of *client/server application*. In that type of application, a user at a *client* computer accesses an application at a *server* computer. In a web application, the client and server computers are connected via the Internet or via an *intranet* (a local area network).

- In a web application, the user works with a *web browser* at the client computer. The web browser provides the user interface for the application. The most popular web browser is Microsoft's Internet Explorer, but other web browsers like Mozilla Firefox and Chrome may also be used.

- The application runs on the server computer under the control of *web server* software. For ASP.NET web applications, the server typically runs Microsoft's web server, called *Internet Information Services*, or *IIS*.

- For most web applications, the server computer also runs a *database management system*, or *DBMS*, such as Microsoft's SQL Server. The DBMS provides access to information stored in a database. To improve performance on larger applications, the DBMS can be run on a separate server computer.

- The user interface for a web application is implemented as a series of *web pages* that are displayed in the web browser. Each web page is defined by a *web form* using *HTML*, or *Hypertext Markup Language*, which is a standardized set of markup tags.

- The web browser and web server exchange information using *HTTP*, or *Hypertext Transfer Protocol*.

Figure 1-2   The hardware and software components for web applications

How static web pages work

Many of the web pages on the Internet are *static web pages* that don't change in response to user input. These pages are *HTML documents* that are defined by *HTML*, or *Hypertext Markup Language*.

Figure 1-3 shows how a web server handles static web pages. The process begins when a user at a web browser requests a web page. This can occur when the user enters a web address, called a *URL* (*Uniform Resource Locator*), into the browser's address box or when the user clicks a link that leads to another page.

In either case, the web browser uses HTTP to send an *HTTP request* to the web server. The HTTP request includes information such as the name and address of the web page being requested, the address of the browser making the request, and the address of the web server that will process the request.

When the web server receives an HTTP request from a browser, the server retrieves the requested HTML file from disk and sends the file back to the browser in the form of an *HTTP response*. The HTTP response includes the HTML document that the user requested along with the addresses of the browser and the web server.

When the browser receives the HTTP response, it formats and displays the HTML document. Then, the user can view the content. If the user requests another page, either by clicking a link or typing another web address in the browser's address box, the process begins again.

Figure 1-3 also shows the components of a URL. The first component is the protocol, in this case, HTTP. In most cases, you can omit the protocol and HTTP is assumed.

The second component is the *domain name*, which identifies your web site. The URL in this figure, for example, includes the domain name for our web site, www.murach.com. The browser uses the domain name to identify the server that's hosting the web site.

After the domain name, you specify the path where the file resides on the server. Notice that front slashes are used to separate the components of a path in a URL. After the path, you specify the name of the file you want to display in the browser. In this case, the file is a static web page named index.htm.

How a web server processes static web pages

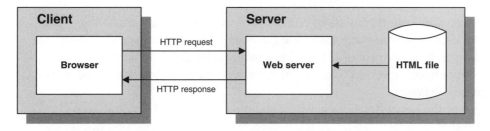

The components of an HTTP URL

Description

- A *static web page* is an HTML document that is the same each time it's viewed. In other words, a static web page doesn't change in response to user input. Everyone who views a static web page sees exactly the same content.

- Static web pages are usually simple HTML files that are stored on the web server. When a browser requests a static web page, the web server retrieves the file from disk and sends it back to the browser. Static web pages usually have a file extension of .htm or .html.

- A web browser requests a page from a web server by sending the server an HTTP message known as an *HTTP request*. The HTTP request includes, among other things, the name of the HTML file being requested and the Internet addresses of both the browser and the web server.

- A user working with a browser can initiate an HTTP request in several ways. One way is to type the address of a web page, called a *URL*, or *Uniform Resource Locator*, into the browser's address area and then press the Enter key. Another way is to click a link that refers to a web page.

- A web server replies to an HTTP request by sending a message known as an *HTTP response* back to the browser. The HTTP response contains the addresses of the browser and the server as well as the HTML document that's being returned.

Figure 1-3   How static web pages work

How dynamic web pages work

A web application consists of one or more web pages that are not static, but that can change in some way each time the page is displayed. Instead of being stored on disk in the form of HTML files, these pages are generated dynamically by the application. As a result, the generated pages are often referred to as *dynamic web pages*.

One of the key differences between static web pages and dynamic web pages is that dynamic web pages are web forms that contain one or more *server controls*, such as labels, text boxes, and buttons. Users work with these controls to interact with the application.

Figure 1-4 shows the basic processing for a dynamic web page. To start, the browser sends an HTTP request to the web server (IIS) that contains the address of the web page being requested, along with the information that the user entered into the form. When IIS receives this request, it determines that it's a request for a web form by looking up the extension of the requested page in a list of *application mappings*. These mappings indicate what program a file extension is associated with. Because an aspx file is associated with ASP.NET, the web server passes the request on to the ASP.NET *application server* for processing. ASP.NET, in turn, manages the execution of the web form that's requested.

By the way, you should realize that if you're using IIS 7, an HTTP request may be sent to ASP.NET for processing even if the request isn't for an aspx file. That's because IIS 7 provides a mode that integrates ASP.NET with the IIS server. One advantage of using integrated mode is that it lets you restrict access to static web pages as well as dynamic web pages using the ASP.NET authentication and authorization features you'll learn about in chapter 19. To determine whether or not an ASP.NET application uses integrated mode, you use *application pools*. You can learn more about using application pools with IIS 7 in appendix B.

When the web form is executed, it processes the information the user entered and generates an HTML document. If, for example, the web form displays data from a database, it queries the database to get the requested information. Then, it generates a page with that information, which is returned by ASP.NET to the web server. The web server, in turn, sends the page back to the browser in the form of an HTTP response, and the browser displays the page. This entire process that begins with the browser requesting a web page and ends with the page being sent back to the client is called a *round trip*.

When a user clicks on a control to start an HTTP request, it is called "posting back to the server," which is referred to as a *postback*. In the Order form in figure 1-1, for example, the user starts a postback by selecting an item in the drop-down list or by clicking on the Add to Cart button. Then, the web form for the Order page is processed using the new values that the user has entered into the page.

How a web server processes dynamic pages

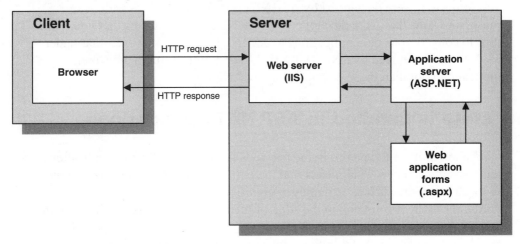

The URL for an ASP.NET web page

`http://www.microsoft.com/express/product/default.aspx`

Description

- A *dynamic web page* is an HTML document that's generated by a web form. Often, the web page changes according to information that's sent to the web form by the browser.

- When a web server receives a request for a dynamic web page, it looks up the extension of the requested file in a list of *application mappings* to find out which application server should process the request. If the file extension is aspx, the request is passed on to ASP.NET for processing.

- When the *application server* receives a request, it runs the specified web form. Then, the web form generates an HTML document and returns it to the application server, which passes it back to the web server and from there to the browser.

- The browser doesn't know or care whether the HTML was retrieved from a static HTML file or generated dynamically by a web form. Either way, the browser simply displays the HTML that was returned as a result of the request.

- After the page is displayed, the user can interact with it using its controls. Some of those controls let the user *post* the page *back* to the server, which is called a *postback*. Then, the page is processed again using the data the user entered.

- The process that begins with the user requesting a web page and ends with the server sending a response back to the client is called a *round trip*.

- If you omit the file name from the URL when you use your browser to request a page, IIS will look for a file with one of four names by default: Default.htm, Default.asp, index.htm, and iisstart.asp. (If you're using IIS 7, it will also look for a file with the name index.html or default.aspx.) If you want another page to be displayed by default, you can add the name of that page to this list. See appendix B (Windows 7 and Windows Vista) or C (Windows XP) for more information.

Figure 1-4   How dynamic web pages work

Incidentally, the application server for ASP.NET 4 can handle requests for web forms that were developed by ASP.NET 2.0, 3.0, and 3.5 as well as requests for forms that were developed by ASP.NET 4. That means that you don't have to convert your old applications to ASP.NET 4. Note, however, that under IIS 7, forms developed by ASP.NET 2.0, 3.0, or 3.5 must run in a different application pool than those developed by ASP.NET 4.

How state is handled in ASP.NET applications

Although it isn't apparent in the previous figure, an application ends after it generates a web page. That means that the current status of any data maintained by the application, such as variables or control properties, is lost. In other words, HTTP doesn't maintain the *state* of the application. This is illustrated in figure 1-5.

Here, you can see that a browser on a client requests a page from a web server. After the server processes the request and returns the page to the browser, it drops the connection. Then, if the browser makes additional requests, the server has no way to associate the browser with its previous requests. Because of that, HTTP is known as a *stateless protocol*.

Although HTTP doesn't maintain state, ASP.NET provides several ways to do that, as summarized in this figure. First, you can use *view state* to maintain the values of server control properties. For example, you can use view state to preserve the Text properties of label controls that are changed as a web form is processed or to maintain a list of items in a drop-down list. Because ASP.NET implements view state by default, you don't need to write any special code to use it.

Second, you can use *session state* to maintain data between executions of an application. To make this work, ASP.NET creates a *session state object* that is kept on the server whenever a user starts a new session. This session object contains a unique *session ID*, and this ID is sent back and forth between the server and the browser each time the user requests a page. Then, when the server receives a new request from a user, it can retrieve the right session object for that user. In the code for your web forms, you can add data items to the session object so their previous values are available each time a web form is executed.

Third, you can use an *application state object* to save *application state* data, which applies to all of the users of an application. For example, you can use application state to maintain global counters or to maintain a list of the users who are currently logged on to an application.

Fourth, you can use the *profile* feature to keep track of user data. Although a profile is similar to a session state object, it persists between user sessions because it is stored in a database. When you use profiles, for example, you can keep track of the last three products that a user looked at in his last session. Then, when the user starts a new session, you can display those products in a "Recently viewed items" list. Because profiles are used infrequently, I won't cover them in this book.

Why state is difficult to track in web applications

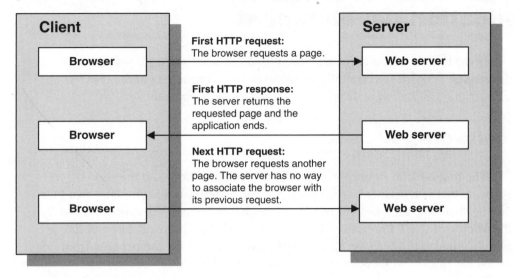

Concepts

- *State* refers to the current status of the properties, variables, and other data maintained by an application for a single user. The application must maintain a separate state for each user currently accessing the application.

- HTTP is a *stateless protocol*. That means that it doesn't keep track of state between round trips. Once a browser makes a request and receives a response, the application terminates and its state is lost.

Four ASP.NET features for maintaining state

- ASP.NET uses *view state* to maintain the value of form control properties that the application changes between executions of the application. Since view state is implemented by default, no special coding is required.

- When a user starts a new session, ASP.NET creates a *session state object* that contains a *session ID*. This ID is passed from the server to the browser and back to the server so the server can associate the browser with an existing session. To maintain *session state*, you can add program values to the session state object.

- When an application begins, ASP.NET creates an *application state object*. To maintain *application state*, you can add program values to the application state object. These values are available to all users of the application until the application ends.

- ASP.NET can also maintain a *profile* for each user of an application. Because profiles are stored in a database, the profile data is maintained from one user session to another. This makes it easier to personalize an application.

Figure 1-5   How state is handled in ASP.NET applications

An introduction to ASP.NET application development

In the three topics that follow, you'll find out what software you need for developing ASP.NET web applications, what the components of the .NET Framework are, and what development environments you can work in.

The software you need

The first table in figure 1-6 summarizes both the client and the server software that you need for developing ASP.NET applications. On your own PC, you need an operating system like Windows XP, Windows Vista, or Windows 7, the Microsoft .NET Framework 4, and a browser like Microsoft Internet Explorer. You also need Visual Studio 2010 if you want to get the benefits from using that Integrated Development Environment (IDE).

If you're using a server for your development, it will need a server operating system like Windows Server 2003 or later, Microsoft .NET Framework 4, and Internet Information Services. If you're going to develop applications from a remote computer, it will also need FrontPage Server Extensions. And if you're going to develop applications for the Internet, it will need an FTP server. In appendix A, you can get information about installing the software for both client and server.

Because most ASP.NET applications require database access, you also need a database server such as Microsoft SQL Server. For development work on your own PC, you can use SQL Server 2008 Express Edition, which is a scaled-back version of SQL Server that comes with Visual Studio 2010. But you'll probably need SQL Server itself on the server for a production application.

If you're developing production applications, you should also download and install other web browsers on your PC including Mozilla Firefox and Chrome. That way, you can test your applications with a variety of popular browsers.

The second table in this figure shows that Visual Studio 2010 is available in several editions. Most professional developers will work with either the Professional Edition or the Premium Edition. But large development teams may use the Ultimate Edition, which includes features designed for specialized development roles such as architects, developers, and testers.

A free alternative is Visual Web Developer 2010 Express Edition. This product is designed for individual developers, students, and hobbyists, and most of the features in this book will work with this edition.

Software requirements for ASP.NET 4 application development

Client	Server
Windows XP or later	Windows Server 2003 or later
Microsoft .NET Framework 4	Microsoft .NET Framework 4
A browser like Internet Explorer (6.0 or later)	Internet Information Services 6.0 or later
Visual Studio 2010	Microsoft SQL Server or equivalent database server
	FrontPage Server Extensions (for remote development only)

Visual Studio 2010 Editions

Edition	Description
Visual Web Developer 2010 Express Edition	Free, downloadable edition for Web development in Visual Basic or C#. There is also an Express Edition of SQL Server called SQL Server 2010 Express.
Visual Studio 2010 Professional Edition	Designed for individual developers who want to build a wide variety of Windows, Web, mobile, and Office-based solutions.
Visual Studio 2010 Premium Edition	Designed for individuals and teams who want to build scalable applications and includes standard testing tools, database deployment and change-management tools, and basic lifecycle management tools.
Visual Studio 2010 Ultimate Edition	Designed for teams and includes full testing, modeling, database, and lifecycle management tools.

Description

- To develop ASP.NET 4 applications, you need the client software shown above on your own PC. In addition, if a separate server isn't available to you, you will typically need IIS and a database server such as SQL Server 2008 Express Edition. For more information, see figure 1-8.

- Visual Studio 2010 comes in four different editions that provide all the basic features for developing ASP.NET applications. The edition you choose depends on the additional features you require.

Figure 1-6   The software you need for developing ASP.NET 4 applications

The components of the .NET Framework

Because you should have a basic understanding of what the *.NET Framework* does as you develop applications, figure 1-7 summarizes its major components. As you can see, this framework is divided into two main components, the .NET Framework Class Library and the Common Language Runtime, and these components provide a common set of services for applications written in .NET languages like Visual Basic or C#.

The *.NET Framework Class Library* consists of *classes* that provide many of the functions that you need for developing .NET applications. For instance, the ASP.NET classes are used for developing ASP.NET web applications, and the Windows Forms classes are used for developing standard Windows applications. The other .NET classes let you work with databases, manage security, access files, and perform many other functions.

Although it's not apparent in this figure, the classes in the .NET Framework Class Library are organized in a hierarchical structure. Within this structure, related classes are organized into groups called *namespaces*. Each namespace contains the classes used to support a particular function. For example, the System.Web namespace contains the classes used to create ASP.NET web applications, and the System.Data namespace contains the classes used to access data.

The *Common Language Runtime*, or *CLR*, provides the services that are needed for executing any application that's developed with one of the .NET languages. This is possible because all of the .NET languages compile to a common *Intermediate Language* (or *IL*). The CLR also provides the *Common Type System* that defines the data types that are used by all the .NET languages. That way, you can use the same data types regardless of what .NET language you're using to develop your application.

To run an ASP.NET application, the web server must have the .NET Framework installed. However, the client computers that access the web server don't need the .NET Framework. Instead, the client computers can run any client operating system with a modern web browser.

The .NET Framework

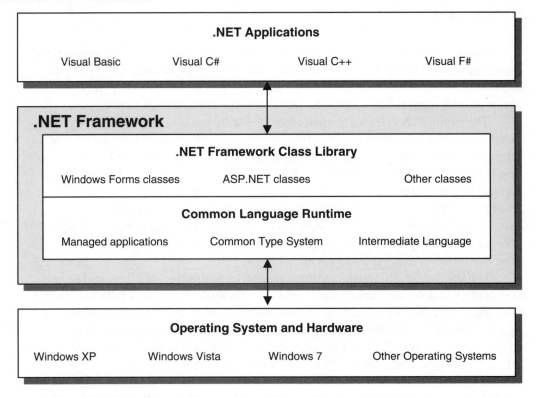

Description

- .NET applications work by using services of the *.NET Framework*. The .NET Framework, in turn, accesses the operating system and computer hardware.

- The .NET Framework consists of two main components: the .NET Framework Class Library and the Common Language Runtime.

- The *.NET Framework Class Library* provides pre-written code in the form of *classes* that are available to all of the .NET programming languages. These classes are organized into groups called *namespaces*. The classes that support ASP.NET web programs are stored in the System.Web namespace.

- The *Common Language Runtime*, or *CLR*, manages the execution of .NET programs by coordinating essential functions such as memory management, code execution, security, and other services.

- The *Common Type System* is a component of the CLR that ensures that all .NET applications use the same data types regardless of what programming languages are used to develop the applications.

- All .NET programs are compiled into *Microsoft Intermediate Language* (*MSIL*) or just *Intermediate Language* (*IL*), which is stored on disk in an assembly. This assembly is then run by the CLR.

Figure 1-7   The components of the .NET Framework

Three environments for developing ASP.NET applications

Figure 1-8 shows three common ways to set up a development environment for coding and testing ASP.NET applications. As you'll see, each setup has its advantages and disadvantages. The environment you choose will depend on your development needs and on the resources that are available to you.

The simplest development environment is a *standalone environment*. In this case, a single computer serves as both the client and the server. Because of that, it must run an operating system that supports ASP.NET development, and it must have the .NET Framework and Visual Studio 2010 installed. Because Visual Studio 2010 comes with its own *development server* for local testing, you don't have to install IIS when you use a standalone environment. Also, since Visual Studio comes with SQL Server 2008 Express Edition (or just *SQL Server Express*), you don't have to install a separate database product. This is the environment that I'll focus on in this book.

The second development environment works with separate client and server computers that are connected via a local area network. Here, the client computer has Windows, the .NET Framework, and Visual Studio 2010 installed, while the server runs Windows Server with the .NET Framework, IIS, and *FrontPage Server Extensions* (*FPSE*). FPSE provides the services that Visual Studio 2010 uses to communicate with a web site on a remote computer. In addition, the server uses SQL Server to handle database access. With this environment, more than one programmer can work on the same application, but all of the programmers are located at the same site.

With the third development environment, the client computers are connected to the server via the Internet rather than a LAN. This makes it possible to work with a web site that's hosted on another server. This environment requires an *FTP server*, which is used to copy the files in a web site between the client computer and the server. The FTP server uses *File Transfer Protocol* (*FTP*) to perform the copy operations, and IIS can be configured to act as an FTP server as well as a web server. So if a web site is hosted on a server that you have access to, you can configure the server so remote users can access it using FTP.

Standalone development

Windows XP or later
.NET Framework 4
Visual Studio 2010
Optional: IIS, SQL Server

Local area network development

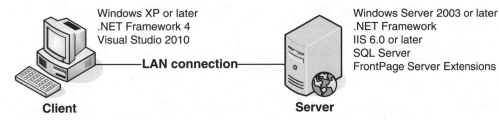

Windows XP or later
.NET Framework 4
Visual Studio 2010

LAN connection

Windows Server 2003 or later
.NET Framework
IIS 6.0 or later
SQL Server
FrontPage Server Extensions

Client   **Server**

Internet development

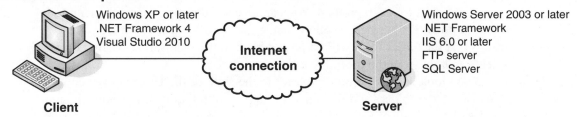

Windows XP or later
.NET Framework 4
Visual Studio 2010

**Internet
connection**

Windows Server 2003 or later
.NET Framework
IIS 6.0 or later
FTP server
SQL Server

Client   **Server**

Description

- When you use standalone development, a single computer serves as both the client and the server. Because Visual Studio comes with a scaled-back web server called the ASP.NET Development Server (or just *development server*), you don't need to use IIS for testing web applications on your own PC. However, you do need to use IIS to test certain features of web applications.

- When you use a *local area network* (*LAN*), a client computer communicates with a server computer over the LAN. With this setup, two or more programmers at the same site can work on the same application. This setup requires that *FrontPage Server Extensions* (*FPSE*) be installed on the server.

- When you use Internet development, a client computer communicates with a server computer over the Internet. With this setup, programmers at different locations can work on the same application. This setup requires an *FTP server* on the server. The FTP server uses *File Transfer Protocol* (*FTP*) to transfer files between the client computer and the server.

Figure 1-8   Three environments for developing ASP.NET applications

A quick preview of how an ASP.NET application works

With that as background, you're ready to learn more about how an ASP.NET application works. That's why this topic presents a quick preview of how the Order form in the Shopping Cart application works.

The files used by the Shopping Cart application

Figure 1-9 presents the Order form of the Shopping Cart application as it appears in the Web Forms Designer that you use when you develop web forms with Visual Studio 2010. In chapter 2, you'll learn how to use this Designer, but for now just try to get the big picture of how this form works.

If you look at the Designer window in the middle of the IDE, you can see the table that's used for this form as well as the label controls that are used to display the data for each product. You can also see that the smart tag menu for the drop-down list has been used to enable the AutoPostBack property. This means that the Order form will be posted back to the web server when the user selects an item from the drop-down list.

If you look at the Solution Explorer to the right of the Designer window, you can see the folders and files that this application requires. For now, though, just focus on the seven code files that are summarized in the table in this figure. The first three files in this table, which are in the App_Code folder, represent *business classes* named CartItem, CartItemList, and Product. All three of these files have cs as the extension, which means that they're C# files.

The next four files in the table are for the two web forms, Cart and Order, with two files for each form. The files with aspx as the extension (Cart.aspx and Order.aspx) contain the code that represents the design of the form. This code consists of standard HTML code plus asp tags that define the server controls used on the forms. We refer to this as *aspx code*, because the files that contain the code have the aspx extension.

The other two files, which have aspx.cs as the extension, contain the C# code that controls the operation of the forms. These are called *code-behind files* because they provide the code behind the web forms. For instance, the Order.aspx.cs file is the code-behind file for the Order form.

Before I go on, you should realize that it isn't necessary to store the aspx and C# code for a web form in separate files. Instead, ASP.NET lets you combine this code into a single aspx file. However, storing the aspx and C# code in separate files can simplify application development because it lets you separate the presentation elements for a page from its C# coding. This also makes it possible for HTML designers to work on the aspx files for an application, and then have C# programmers develop the code for the code-behind files.

The Order form in Design view

The aspx and C# files in the Shopping Cart application

Folder	File	Description
App_Code	CartItem.cs	A class that represents an item in the shopping cart.
App_Code	CartItemList.cs	A class that represents all the items in the shopping cart.
App_Code	Product.cs	A class that represents a product.
(root)	Cart.aspx	The aspx file for the Cart page.
(root)	Cart.aspx.cs	The code-behind file for the Cart page.
(root)	Order.aspx	The aspx file for the Order page.
(root)	Order.aspx.cs	The code-behind file for the Order page.

Description

- For each web form in an application, ASP.NET 4 keeps two files. The file with the aspx extension holds the HTML code and the asp tags for the server controls. The file with the aspx.cs extension is the *code-behind file* that contains the C# code for the form.

- If an ASP.NET 4 application requires other classes like *business classes*, they are kept in the App_Code folder.

Figure 1-9   The files used by the Shopping Cart application

The aspx code for the Order form

To give you some idea of how aspx code works, figure 1-10 shows some of the aspx code for the Order form. All of this code is generated by Visual Studio as you use the Web Forms Designer to design a form, so you don't have to code it. But you still should have a general understanding of how this code works.

The first set of tags for each web form defines a *page directive* that provides four *attributes*. Here, the Language attribute says that the language is C#, the CodeFile attribute says that the code-behind file is named Order.aspx.cs, and the Inherits attribute specifies the class named Order. In figure 1-12, you'll see how the Order.aspx class inherits the Order class.

The second set of tags defines a DOCTYPE declaration, which tells the browser what version of HTML the document uses. You can ignore this declaration for now, because you'll learn more about it in chapter 5.

The html tags mark the beginning and end of the HTML document, and the head tags define the heading for the document. Here, the title tags define the title that is displayed in the title bar of the browser when the page is run. In addition, the style tags define the styles used by the page. As you'll learn in chapter 5, this is just one way to define styles.

The content of the web page itself is defined within the div tags, which are within the body and form tags. Notice that the first form tag includes a Runat attribute that's assigned a value of "server." That indicates that the form will be processed on the server by ASP.NET. This attribute is required for all ASP.NET web forms and all ASP.NET server controls.

The asp tags within the div tags define the server controls that appear on the page. Since these controls include the Runat attribute with a value of "server," they will be processed on the server by ASP.NET. The last phase of this processing is *rendering* the controls, which means that the asp code is converted to standard HTML so the page can be displayed by a browser.

If you look at the asp code for the drop-down list, you can see that the AutoPostBack attribute has been set to True. That means that a postback will occur whenever the user selects an item from that list. Note that a postback will also occur whenever the user clicks the Add to Cart button. However, the AutoPostBack attribute isn't required for this control because performing a postback is the default operation of a button.

Although the asp code for the Add to Cart button doesn't include an AutoPostBack attribute, it does include an OnClick attribute. This attribute names the event handler that's executed when the user clicks the button and the form is posted back to the server.

Another attribute that you should notice is the PostBackUrl attribute for the last button in the aspx code. This attribute provides the path for the Cart.aspx file, which means that the Cart form will be requested when this button is clicked. That's one way to switch from one form to another as an application is run, and you'll see another in the next figure.

Although this has been a quick introduction to the aspx code for a web form, you should begin to see how this code defines a web page. In the next two chapters, though, you'll learn more about this code. And just in case you need it, chapter 5 presents a complete crash course in HTML.

The aspx file for the Order form (Order.aspx)

```
<%@ Page Language="C#" AutoEventWireup="true" CodeFile="Order.aspx.cs"
Inherits="Order" %>

<!DOCTYPE html PUBLIC "-//W3C//DTD XHTML 1.0 Transitional//EN"
"http://www.w3.org/TR/xhtml1/DTD/xhtml1-transitional.dtd">

<html xmlns="http://www.w3.org/1999/xhtml">
<head runat="server">
    <title>Chapter 3: Shopping Cart</title>
    <style type="text/css">
        .style1{
            width: 250px;
        }
        .style2{
            width: 20px;
        }
    </style>
</head>
<body>
    <form id="form1" runat="server">
    <div>
        <asp:Image ID="Image1" runat="server"
            ImageUrl="~/Images/banner.jpg" /><br /><br />
        <asp:Label ID="Label1" runat="server"
            Text="Please select a product:"></asp:Label> 
        <asp:DropDownList ID="ddlProducts" runat="server"
            DataSourceID="AccessDataSource1" DataTextField="Name"
            DataValueField="ProductID" Width="150px" AutoPostBack="True">
        </asp:DropDownList>
        <asp:AccessDataSource ID="AccessDataSource1" runat="server"
            DataFile="~/App_Data/Halloween.mdb"
            SelectCommand="SELECT [ProductID], [Name], [ShortDescription],
                [LongDescription], [ImageFile], [UnitPrice]
                FROM [Products] ORDER BY [Name]">
        </asp:AccessDataSource><br />
        <table>
            <tr>
                <td class="style1"><asp:Label ID="lblName" runat="server"
                    style="font-weight: 700; font-size: larger"></asp:Label>
                </td>
                <td class="style2" rowspan="4"></td>
                <td rowspan="4" valign="top">
                    <asp:Image ID="imgProduct" runat="server" Height="200px" />
                </td>
            </tr>
                .
                .    (Code for 3 more rows of a table)
                .
        </table><br />
        <asp:Label ID="Label3" runat="server" Text="Quantity:"
            Width="80px"></asp:Label>
        <asp:TextBox ID="txtQuantity" runat="server" Width="40px"></asp:TextBox>
        <br /><br />
        <asp:Button ID="btnAdd" runat="server" Text="Add to Cart"
            OnClick="btnAdd_Click" /> 
        <asp:Button ID="btnCart" runat="server" CausesValidation="False"
            PostBackUrl="~/Cart.aspx" Text="Go to Cart" />
    </div>
    </form>
</body>
</html>
```

Figure 1-10   The aspx code for the Order form

The C# code for the Order form

To give you some idea of how the C# code for a form works, figure 1-11 presents the code-behind file for the Order form. Here, I've highlighted the code that's specific to ASP.NET, and all of the other code is standard C# code.

The first highlighted line is a class declaration that names the class, which has the same name as the form. Because this statement uses the partial keyword, this is a partial class that must be combined with another partial class when it's compiled. The rest of this line of code indicates that this class inherits the System.Web.UI.Page class, which is the .NET class that provides all of the basic functionality of ASP.NET pages.

Each time the page is requested, ASP.NET initializes it and raises the Load event, which is handled by the Page_Load method. This method uses the IsPostBack property of the page to determine whether the page is being posted back to the server from the same page. If this property isn't True, the DataBind method of the drop-down list is used to bind the products that are retrieved from a database to the list. You will often see the IsPostBack property used like this in a Page_Load method to determine whether or not a page is being posted back by the user.

The btnAdd_Click method is executed when the user clicks on the Add to Cart button on the Order page, which starts a postback. This method starts by calling the GetCart method of the CartItemList class, which gets the current contents of the cart from session state. Then, it checks to see if the selected product is already in the cart. If it isn't, a new cart item is added to the cart. If it is, the quantity the user entered is added to the quantity in the cart. Finally, this method uses the Redirect method of the Response property of the page to transfer to the Cart page. This is a second way to switch from one page to another.

One coding point worth noting is that IsPostBack and Response are properties of the page. As a result, you could code them with Page as a qualifier as in

`Page.IsPostBack`

However, since Page is the default object within a code-behind file, you can omit this reference. This applies to Session as well, although it's not used by this page.

Although this is just a quick introduction to a code-behind file, I hope it gives you some insight into the way code-behind files are coded. Keep in mind, though, that all of this code will be explained in detail in the next two chapters. For now, you just need a general idea of how the events are processed, how the IsPostBack property is used, and how one web page can switch to another page.

The code-behind file for the Order form (Order.aspx.cs)

```csharp
using System;
using System.Collections.Generic;
using System.Linq;
using System.Web;
using System.Web.UI;
using System.Web.UI.WebControls;
using System.Data;

public partial class Order : System.Web.UI.Page
{
    private Product selectedProduct;

    protected void Page_Load(object sender, EventArgs e)
    {
        if (!IsPostBack)
            ddlProducts.DataBind();

        selectedProduct = this.GetSelectedProduct();
        lblName.Text = selectedProduct.Name;
        lblShortDescription.Text = selectedProduct.ShortDescription;
        lblLongDescription.Text = selectedProduct.LongDescription;
        lblUnitPrice.Text = selectedProduct.UnitPrice.ToString("c");
        imgProduct.ImageUrl = "Images/Products/" + selectedProduct.ImageFile;
    }

    private Product GetSelectedProduct()
    {
        DataView productsTable = (DataView)
            AccessDataSource1.Select(DataSourceSelectArguments.Empty);
        productsTable.RowFilter =
            "ProductID = '" + ddlProducts.SelectedValue + "'";
        DataRowView row = (DataRowView)productsTable[0];

        Product p = new Product();
        p.ProductID = row["ProductID"].ToString();
        p.Name = row["Name"].ToString();
        p.ShortDescription = row["ShortDescription"].ToString();
        p.LongDescription = row["LongDescription"].ToString();
        p.UnitPrice = (decimal)row["UnitPrice"];
        p.ImageFile = row["ImageFile"].ToString();
        return p;
    }

    protected void btnAdd_Click(object sender, EventArgs e)
    {
        CartItemList cart = CartItemList.GetCart();
        CartItem cartItem = cart[selectedProduct.ProductID];

        if (cartItem == null)
            cart.AddItem(selectedProduct, Convert.ToInt32(txtQuantity.Text));
        else
            cartItem.AddQuantity(Convert.ToInt32(txtQuantity.Text));

        Response.Redirect("Cart.aspx");
    }
}
```

Figure 1-11   The C# code for the Order form

How an ASP.NET application is compiled and run

The diagram in figure 1-12 shows what actually happens behind the scenes when a user requests a page of an ASP.NET 4 application. In step 1, the ASP.NET runtime reads the aspx file for the requested web page and generates a class and a partial class. The partial class contains the declarations for the form and the controls it contains and is given the same name as the partial class that's defined by the code-behind file for the page (Order in this example). In step 2, these partial classes are compiled to create a single class that provides all of the event-handling code for the page. The result is stored in a single *assembly* (dll file).

The class that's generated by the ASP.NET runtime contains the code that actually creates the ASP.NET page. This class gets its name from the aspx file for the web page plus _aspx, so its name is Order_aspx in this example. In step 3, this class is compiled and stored in another assembly. Because this class inherits the Order class, an object that is instantiated from the Order_aspx class will contain the code that creates the page, as well as the event-handling code provided by the Order class.

In step 4, after the page classes are compiled, the ASP.NET runtime calls the C# compiler to compile any class files that are in the application's App_Code folder. For the Shopping Cart application, this means that the CartItem, CartItemList, and Product classes are compiled and the result is saved in a single assembly.

After all the files are compiled into assemblies, ASP.NET creates an instance of the page and raises the appropriate events. Then, the events are processed by the event handlers for the page and the HTML for the page is rendered. To complete the round trip, the HTML document for the page is passed back to the web server and on to the user's browser.

Please note that the first four steps are done only the first time an aspx page is accessed. That's because ASP.NET caches the assemblies that are created by these steps. Then, when the page is accessed again, the saved assemblies are reused, so the application doesn't have to be recompiled. However, ASP.NET does compare the time stamps on the source files with the time stamps on the dll files. If any of the source files have been modified since they were last compiled, ASP.NET automatically recompiles them.

How an ASP.NET application is compiled

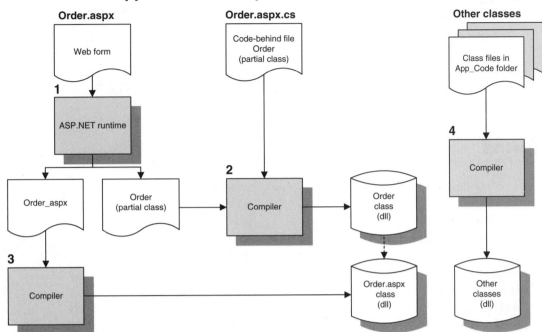

What happens when an ASP.NET page is requested

1. The ASP.NET runtime processes the .aspx file and generates a partial class (Order) that contains the declarations for the form and its controls, and a class (Order_aspx) that contains the code that will initialize the form, instantiate the controls, and generate the HTML for the web page.

2. The C# compiler compiles the partial class that contains the control declarations with the partial class defined by the code-behind file for the form into an *assembly* (.dll) that provides the event-handling code for the requested page.

3. The C# compiler compiles the Order_aspx class, which inherits the first compiled class (Order), and saves the result as an assembly that's executed when the page is requested.

4. If necessary, the C# compiler compiles any other class files that are stored in the application's App_Code folder. These classes are saved in a single assembly.

5. ASP.NET creates an instance of the page from the page's final assembly. Then, ASP.NET raises the appropriate events, which are processed by the event handlers for the page, and the page generates the HTML that's passed back to the web server for the response.

Description

*   The first four steps of this process are done only the first time the aspx page is requested. After that, the page is processed directly from the compiled assemblies.

*   The default name of a web form that you add to a web site is Default.aspx, and the name of the code-behind class for that form is _Default.

Figure 1-12   How an ASP.NET 4 application is compiled and run

Perspective

Now that you've read this chapter, you should have a general understanding of how ASP.NET applications work and what software you need for developing these applications. With that as background, you're ready to learn how to develop ASP.NET applications of your own. And that's what you'll learn to do in the next two chapters.

Terms

web application	session state
web page	session state object
web form	session ID
client/server application	application state
client	application state object
server	profile
HTTP (Hypertext Transfer Protocol)	.NET Framework
web browser	.NET Framework Class Library
web server	class
IIS (Internet Information Services)	namespace
DBMS (database management system)	CLR (Common Language Runtime)
LAN (local area network)	IL (Intermediate Language)
intranet	MSIL (Microsoft Intermediate
static web page	Language)
HTML document	Common Type System
HTML (Hypertext Markup Language)	standalone environment
URL (Uniform Resource Locator)	development server
HTTP request	SQL Server Express
HTTP response	FPSE (FrontPage Server Extensions)
domain name	FTP (File Transfer Protocol)
dynamic web page	FTP server
server control	business class
application server	aspx code
application mapping	code-behind file
round trip	page directive
postback	attribute
state	render
stateless protocol	assembly
view state	

About the book's applications

You can download all of the applications that are presented in this book from our web site (www.murach.com). Then, you can run the applications, review all of their code, and experiment with them on your own system. For more information about downloading and running these applications, please read appendix A.

About the exercises

If you're new to ASP.NET web programming, we recommend that you practice what you've learned after you finish each chapter in the first three sections of this book. To help you do that, we provide exercises for each of these chapters. Most of these exercises use directories and files that you can download from our web site. Before you start the exercises, then, you'll need to install these directories and files. When you do, they'll be placed in a directory named aspnet4_cs on your C drive.

Exercise 1-1   Use your web browser to run Internet applications

1. Open your web browser and type in this URL:

    `http://www.microsoft.com`

    Then, search for information about Visual Web Developer 2010 Express Edition. This of course is the site that you can use to download Visual Web Developer 2010 Express and SQL Server 2008 Express for free. As you move from page to page, note that most are dynamic aspx pages.

2. Type this URL into your web browser:

    `http://www.discountasp.net`

    Then, click on some of the links on the home page, and note which pages are static and which are dynamic.

Exercise 1-2   Use your web browser to run the Shopping Cart application on your PC

In this exercise, you'll use your web browser to run the Shopping Cart application that's illustrated in this chapter. This assumes that you've already installed IIS, Visual Studio 2010, and the files for these exercises as described in appendix A. When you get this application running, you'll know that you've got IIS and the application set up correctly on your PC. Note that if you're using Windows XP Home Edition, Windows Vista Home Basic or Starter Edition, or Windows 7 Home Basic or Starter Edition, you won't be able to do this exercise. That's because these editions don't come with IIS, or the version of IIS they come with doesn't support ASP.NET development.

Create a virtual directory for the Shopping Cart application

1. If you're using Windows 7 or Windows Vista, use the procedure in figure B-1 of appendix B to create an IIS application named Ch01Cart under the Default Web Site node for the application in C:\aspnet4_cs\Ch01Cart. If you're using Windows XP, use the procedure in figure C-1 of appendix C to create an IIS virtual directory named Ch01Cart under the Default Web Site node for the application in C:\aspnet4_cs\Ch01Cart.

Run the Shopping Cart application

2. Open your web browser, and type in the following URL, which uses the virtual directory as the path:

    `http://localhost/Ch01Cart/Order.aspx`

    This should start the Shopping Cart application that's shown in figure 1-1. If it doesn't, you need to make sure that IIS is installed and running, that the exercise files are installed, and that you did step 1 correctly.

3. Select a product from the drop-down list on the Order page that's displayed. Note that this starts a postback that returns the Order page with the data and image for the product that was selected.

4. Enter a quantity and click the Add to Cart button to display the Cart page. Then, click the Continue Shopping button to return to the Order page.

5. Continue to experiment with this application until you understand how it works. Note that because this application doesn't include data validation, you'll get an error if you click the Add to Cart button on the Order page without entering a quantity. When you're done, click the Close button in the upper right corner of the browser window to end the application.

2

How to develop a one-page web application

In the last chapter, you were introduced to the basic concepts of web programming and ASP.NET. Now, this chapter shows you how to develop a one-page web application using Visual Studio 2010. If you've used Visual Studio to develop Windows applications, you'll soon see that you develop web applications in much the same way. As a result, you should be able to move quickly through this chapter.

How to work with ASP.NET web sites

This chapter starts by presenting some basic skills for working with ASP.NET applications. Once you're comfortable with those skills, you'll be ready to learn how to build your first ASP.NET application.

How to start a new web site

In Visual Studio 2010, a web application is called a *web site*, and figure 2-1 shows the dialog box for starting a new web site. After you open the New Web Site dialog box, you select the language you want to use for the web site and the type of web site you want to create, and you specify the location where the web site will be created.

I started all the web sites for this book from the ASP.NET Empty Web Site template. When you use this template, the starting web site contains only a web.config file, which stores information about the web site. In contrast, if you start an application from the ASP.NET Web Site template, the starting web site contains numerous forms and files. You'll learn more about this template in the next chapter.

The Web Location drop-down list gives you three options for specifying the location of the web site. The simplest method is to create a *file-system web site*. This type of web site can exist in any folder on your local hard disk, or in a folder on a shared network drive. You can run a file-system web site using either Visual Studio's built-in development server or IIS.

You use the HTTP option to create a web site that runs under IIS on your local computer or on a computer that can be accessed over a local area network. To use this option, you must specify the IIS server where you want to create the web site. In addition, you must select or create the IIS directory that will contain the files for the web site, or you must select or create a virtual directory for the web site. You'll learn more about this option in chapter 4.

The third option, FTP, lets you create a web site on a remote server by uploading it to that server using FTP. To create this type of web site, you must specify at least the name of the FTP server and the folder where the web site resides. I won't present the FTP option in this book.

In addition to the language and location, Visual Studio 2010 lets you choose a *target framework* for a web site. By default, .NET Framework 4 is used, which is usually what you want. Then, you can use the features that this framework provides within your web applications. If you'll be deploying the application to a server that doesn't have .NET Framework 4, however, you may want to target .NET Framework 2.0, 3.0, or 3.5 instead. Then, you can be sure that you'll use only the features that these frameworks provide.

By default, Visual Studio 2010 creates a solution file for your web site in My Documents\Visual Studio 2010\Projects. This solution file is stored in this folder regardless of the location of the web site itself. To change the location where solutions are stored by default, choose Tools➔Options. Then, expand the

The New Web Site dialog box

Three location options for ASP.NET web sites

Option	Description
File System	A web site created in a folder on your local computer or in a shared folder on a network. You can run the web site directly from the built-in development server or create an IIS virtual directory for the folder and run the application under IIS.
HTTP	A web site created under the control of an IIS web server. The IIS server can be on your local computer or on a computer that's available over a local area network.
FTP	A web site created on a remote hosting server.

Description

- To create a new ASP.NET web application, called a *web site*, you use the File→New Web Site command.

- A *web project* is a project that's used for the development of a web site. In practice, web sites are often referred to as web projects, and vice versa. However, ASP.NET 4 web sites don't use project files. Instead, they use web.config files to store project information.

- When you start a new web site, Visual Studio creates a solution file for the web site in the default location for solution files, which is normally My Documents\Visual Studio 2010\Projects.

- By default, the web sites you create target .NET Framework 4 so you can use the features it provides. If you want to target a different version of the .NET Framework, you can select the version from the first drop-down list at the top of the dialog box.

- Visual Studio 2010 also provides for a type of web project called a *web application project*. With this type of project, you can create web applications that are similar in structure to applications created using Visual Studio 2003.

Figure 2-1   How to start a new web site

Projects and Solutions node, select the General category, and enter the location in the Projects Location text box.

In the dialog box in figure 2-1, I'm starting a new file-system web site named Ch02FutureValue in the aspnet4_cs folder on my own PC. Then, when I click the OK button, Visual Studio creates the folder named Ch02FutureValue and puts the web.config file for the web site in that folder. It also creates a solution file in the default folder for those files.

The folders and files that are used for developing a web site can be referred to as a *web project*. So in practice, web sites are often referred to as web projects, and vice versa. It's important to note, however, that ASP.NET 4 web sites don't use project files to store project information. Instead, they use web.config files.

How to add a web form to a web site

If you start a web site from the ASP.NET Empty Web Site template, the first thing you'll want to do is to add a *web form* to the web site. To do that, you use the Add New Item dialog box shown in figure 2-2. From this dialog box, you select the Web Form template. Then, you enter the name you want to use for the new form and click the Add button to add it to your web site.

When you add a new web form, be sure that the language setting is Visual C# and that the Place Code in Separate File box is checked. These settings are easy to overlook, but difficult to change manually if they're set wrong when you create the page.

If you select the Place Code in Separate File box, two files are added to your project. When I added the form shown in this figure, for example, files named Default.aspx and Default.aspx.cs were added. The Default.aspx file contains the HTML and asp code that defines the form, and the Default.aspx.cs file contains the C# code that determines how the form works. Then, Visual Studio displays the aspx file for the web form as you'll see in the next figure.

To add an existing web form from another web site, you can use the second procedure in this figure. You might want to do that if you need to create a form that's similar to a form in another web site. When you add the aspx file for a form, the code-behind file is added too. Then, you can modify the aspx and C# code so the form works the way you want it to in your new web site.

The Add New Item dialog box for adding a new web form

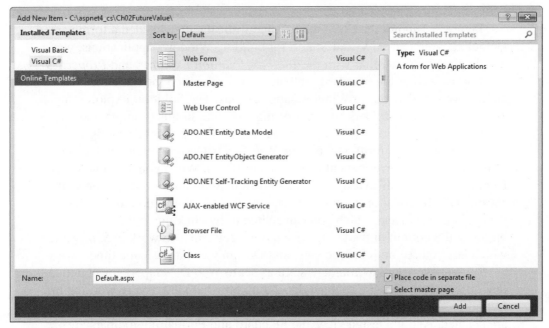

Two ways to open the Add New Item dialog box

- Right-click the project in the Solution Explorer, and then choose Add New Item from the shortcut menu.
- Click on the project in the Solution Explorer to select it, and then choose the Website→Add New Item command.

How to add a new web form to a project

- From the Add New Item dialog box, select the Web Form template, enter a name for the form, check the Place Code in Separate File box, and click the Add button.

How to add an existing web form to a project

- In the Solution Explorer, right-click the project and choose Add Existing Item. Then, locate the form you want to add, select it, and click the Add button.

Description

- If there's a form in another application that is like one that you're going to develop, you can copy that form into your web site. That copies both the web form and the code-behind file. Then, you can modify the aspx code and C# code so the form works the way you want it to.
- The drop-down list above the list of templates lets you change the order of the templates. The two buttons let you choose whether the templates are displayed as small icons or medium icons.

Figure 2-2   How to add a web form to a web site

How to work with the Visual Studio IDE

Figure 2-3 shows the Ch02FutureValue web site after I added a form named Default. If you've used Visual Studio for building Windows applications, you should already be familiar with the *Toolbox*, *Solution Explorer*, and *Properties window*, as well as the Standard toolbar. They work much the same for web applications as they do for Windows applications. The Solution Explorer, for example, shows the folders and files of the web site. In this example, the Solution Explorer shows two files for the web form and the web.config file.

To design a web form, you use the *Web Forms Designer* that's in the center of this Integrated Development Environment (IDE). When you add a new web form to a web site, this Designer is displayed in *Source view*, which shows the starting HTML code for the form. Normally, though, you'll do most of the design in *Design view*, which you can switch to by clicking on the Design button at the bottom of the Designer window. You can also work in *Split view*, which lets you see both Source view and Design view at the same time.

If you have your environment settings set to Web Developer, you'll notice that different toolbars are enabled depending on what view you're working in. In Source view, for example, the Standard and HTML Source Editing toolbars are enabled. And in Design view, the Standard and Formatting toolbars are enabled. This is typical of the way the Visual Studio IDE works. By the way, to change the environment settings, you use the Tools→Import and Export Settings command.

As you go through the various phases of building a web site, you may want to close, hide, or size the windows that are displayed. You'll see some examples of this as you progress through this chapter, and this figure presents several techniques that you can use for working with the windows.

After you've designed a web form, you'll need to switch to the Code Editor, which replaces the Web Forms Designer in the center of the screen. Then, you can write the C# code in the code-behind file for the form. One way to switch to the Code Editor is to double-click on the code-behind file in the Solution Explorer. If, for example, you double-click on the file named Default.aspx.cs, you'll switch to the Code Editor and the starting code for that file will be displayed. Later in this chapter, you'll learn other ways to switch between the Web Forms Designer and the Code Editor.

As you work with Visual Studio, you'll see that it commonly provides several ways to do the same task. Some, of course, are more efficient than others, and we'll try to show you the best techniques as you progress through this book. Often, though, how you work is a matter of personal preference, so we encourage you to review and experiment with the toolbar buttons, the buttons at the top of the Solution Explorer, the tabs at the top of the Web Forms Designer or Code Editor, the shortcut menus that you get by right-clicking on an object, and so on.

The starting screen for a new web site

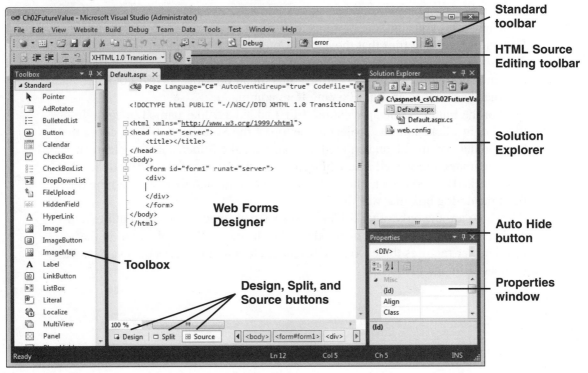

How to work with views and windows

- To change the Web Forms Designer from one view to another, click on the Design, Split, or Source button.

- To close a window, click on the close button in the upper right corner. To redisplay it, select it from the View menu.

- To hide a window, click on its Auto Hide button. Then, the window is displayed as a tab at the side of the screen, and you can display it by moving the mouse pointer over the tab. To restore the window, display it and click on the Auto Hide button again.

- To size a window, place the mouse pointer over one of its boundaries and drag it.

Description

- The primary window in the Visual Studio IDE is the Web Forms Designer window, or just *Web Forms Designer*. The three supporting windows are the *Toolbox*, the *Solution Explorer*, and the *Properties window*.

- You use the Web Forms Designer to design a *web form*. Later, to write the C# code for the form, you use the Code Editor as shown in figure 2-17.

- Visual Studio often provides several different ways to accomplish the same task. In this book, we'll try to show you the techniques that work the best.

Figure 2-3   How to work with the Visual Studio IDE

How to add folders and files to a web site

Right after you start a new web site, it often makes sense to add any other folders and existing files that the application is going to require. To do that, you can use the shortcut menus for the project or its folders in the Solution Explorer as shown in figure 2-4. As you can see, this menu provides a New Folder command as well as an Add Existing Item command.

For the Future Value application, I first added a folder named Images. To do that, I right-clicked on the project at the top of the Solution Explorer, chose the New Folder command, and entered the name for the folder. Then, I added an existing image file named MurachLogo.jpg to the Images folder. To do that, I right-clicked on the folder, chose Add Existing Item, and then selected the file from the dialog box that was displayed.

Those are the only other folders and files that I needed for the Future Value application, but often you'll need others. For instance, the application in the next chapter requires three existing business classes, an Access database, and a number of image files.

The Future Value project as a new folder is being added

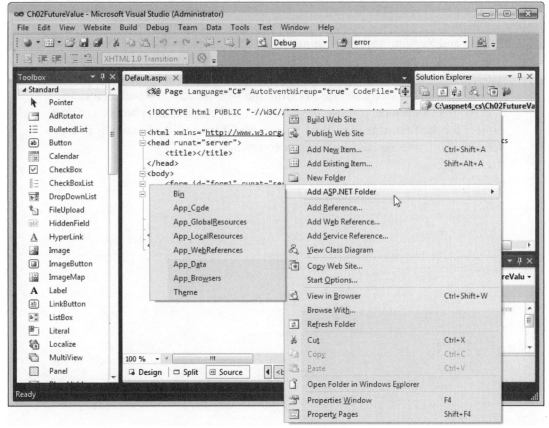

How to add a folder to a web site

- To add a standard folder, right-click on the project or folder you want to add the folder to in the Solution Explorer and choose New Folder. Then, type a name for the folder and press Enter.
- To add a special ASP.NET folder, right-click on the project in the Solution Explorer and choose Add ASP.NET Folder. Then, select the folder from the list that's displayed.

How to add an existing item to a web site

- In the Solution Explorer, right-click on the project or on the folder that you want to add an existing item to. Then, select Add Existing Item and respond to the resulting dialog box.

Description

- When you create a new web form, Visual Studio generates the starting HTML for the form and displays it in Source view of the Web Forms Designer.
- Before you start designing the first web form of the application, you can use the Solution Explorer to add any other folders or files to the web site.

Figure 2-4   How to add folders and files to a web site

How to open or close an existing web site

Figure 2-5 presents three ways to open an existing web site. The Open Project and Recent Projects commands are the easiest to use, but the Open Web Site command provides more flexibility. In the Open Web Site dialog box, you can use the icons on the left to identify the type of web site that you're opening so you can open a web site directly from the web server on which it resides.

To close a project, you use the Close Project command. After you close a project for the first time, you'll be able to find it in the list of projects that you see when you use the Recent Projects command.

The Open Web Site dialog box

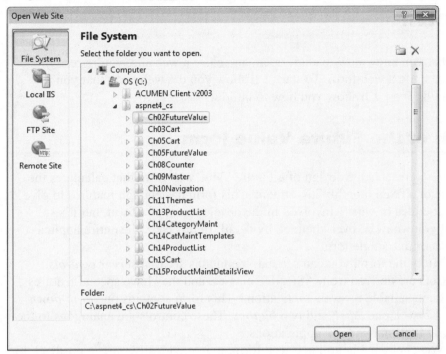

Three ways to open a web site

- Use the File→Open Project command.
- Use the File→Recent Projects command.
- Use the File→Open Web Site command.

How to use the Open Web Site dialog box

- To open a file-system web site, select File System on the left side of the dialog box, then use the File System tree to locate the web site.
- To open a web site that's managed by IIS on your own computer, you can click Local IIS and then select the web site from the list of available sites. Or, if you prefer, you can open it by using the File System tree. In that case, though, the web site won't run under IIS by default.
- The other icons on the left of the Open Web Site dialog box let you open web sites from an FTP site or from a remote IIS site.

How to close a project

- Use the File→Close Project command.

Note

- The Recent Projects list and the Open Project command are also available from the Start page.

Figure 2-5   How to open or close an existing web site

How to use Design view to build a web form

Now that you know how to start, open, and close a web site, you're ready to learn how to build a web form. To start, I'll show you the web form that you're going to build. Then, I'll show you how to build it.

The design of the Future Value form

Figure 2-6 presents the design of a Future Value web form that calculates the future value of a fixed monthly investment. This form has enough features to give you a realistic idea of what's involved in the development of a form, but it's so simple that you won't be overwhelmed by detail. In this case, the entire application consists of this single form.

If you study the form, you can see that it contains six *web server controls*. These controls are derived from ASP.NET classes, and they have special features that make them suitable for web applications. This form contains one *drop-down list*, two *text boxes*, one *label*, and two *buttons*. These controls are analogous to the ones that you use for Windows applications.

When you click on a button in a web form, it automatically starts a postback to the server. When you click the Calculate button, for example, the application calculates the future value based on the values in the drop-down list and two text boxes. The result is displayed in the label when the form is returned to the browser. When you click on the Clear button, the text boxes and label are cleared and the value in the drop-down list is reset to 50.

In contrast to the web server controls, the image at the top of this page (the Murach logo) is defined by a standard HTML element. Because you can't refer to standard HTML elements in code, you won't typically use them in web applications. Like the element in this application, though, they can occasionally be useful.

The arrangement of the web server controls on this web form is done through an HTML table. Note, however, that the preferred way to arrange the controls on a form is to use CSS. You'll learn more about that in chapter 5.

Above the table in this form, a heading has been entered and formatted. Then, in the first column of the first four rows of the table, text has been entered that describes the data in the second column. The fifth row of the table contains no text or controls. And the six row contains the two buttons.

In the rest of this chapter, you'll learn how to build this web form, how to validate the data the user enters in the form, and how to write the code for its code-behind file. Then, you'll learn how to test a web application. At the end of this chapter, you'll find exercises that will walk you through the development of this Future Value application and help you experiment with other features of Visual Studio.

Throughout this chapter, please note that the term *page* is sometimes used to refer to a web form. That's because a web form represents a page that's sent to a browser.

The Future Value web form in a browser

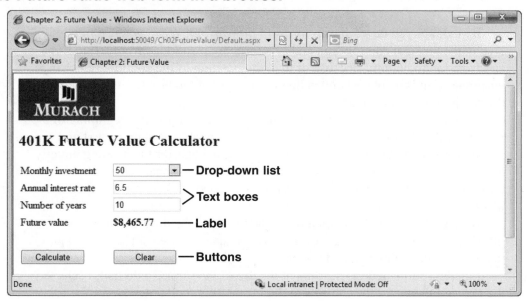

The six web server controls used by the Future Value form

- The *drop-down list* can be used to select a monthly investment value ranging from 50 to 500 in increments of 50.

- The two *text boxes* are used to enter values for the annual interest rate and the number of years that the monthly payments will be made.

- The *label* is used to display the future value that is calculated.

- The Calculate and Clear *buttons* are used to post the form back to the server and initiate the processing that needs to be done.

Description

- Besides the *web server controls*, the Future Value form uses a standard HTML element to display the image at the top of the form, and it uses text to display the heading below the image. It also uses an HTML table to align the text and web server controls below the image and heading.

- When the user clicks on the Calculate button, the future value is calculated based on the three user entries and the results are displayed in the label control.

- When the user clicks on the Clear button, the two text boxes and the label are cleared and the drop-down list is reset to a value of 50.

- To end the application, the user can click the Close button in the upper right corner of the browser window.

Figure 2-6   The design of the Future Value form

How to use flow layout

By default, you develop web forms in *flow layout*. When you use flow layout, the text and controls you add to a form are positioned from left to right and from top to bottom. Because of that, the position of the controls can change when the form is displayed depending on the size of the browser window and the resolution of the display.

To understand how flow layout works, figure 2-7 shows the beginning of a version of the Future Value form that doesn't use a table to align its text and controls. To create this form, I started by typing the text for the heading directly into the form. Then, I pressed the Enter key twice to add space between the heading and the text and controls that follow it. Next, I typed the text that identifies the first control, I pressed the space bar once to add some space after the text, and I added a drop-down list. When I added the drop-down list, it was placed immediately to the right of the text and space. I used similar techniques to enter the remaining text and text box.

Finally, I formatted the heading at the top of the form. To do that, I selected the text and then used the controls in the Formatting toolbar to change the font size to "x-large", to make the heading bold, and to change its color to blue.

You can see the results in the aspx code in this figure. Notice that a br element is inserted for each line break. In addition, span and strong elements are used to apply the formatting to the heading. As you can see, the span element includes a class attribute that names a style class. Although you can't see it here, this style class is defined within the head element for the page, and it specifies the font size and color. The strong element makes the heading bold.

The beginning of the Future Value form created using flow layout

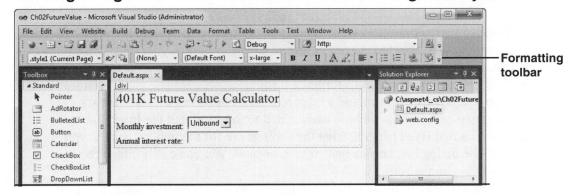

The aspx code for the Future Value form

```
<form id="form1" runat="server">
<div>
    <span class="style1"><strong>401K Future Value Calculator</strong>
    </span><br /><br />
    Monthly investment: 
    <asp:DropDownList ID="DropDownList1" runat="server">
    </asp:DropDownList><br />
    Annual interest rate: 
    <asp:TextBox ID="TextBox1" runat="server"></asp:TextBox>
</div>
</form>
```

How to use flow layout

- When you add controls to a form in *flow layout*, they will appear one after the other, from left to right and from top to bottom. Flow layout is the default for web forms in Visual Studio 2010.

- To make it easier to work with a form in Design view, Visual Studio places a border around the area defined by the div tags.

- To insert a line break after a control, press Enter. A <br /> tag is inserted into the aspx file.

- To insert literal text, type it directly into the designer window. Then, you can use the controls in the Formatting toolbar and the commands in the Format menu to change the font or font size; apply bold, italics, or underlining; or apply foreground or background color.

- When you apply formatting to literal text, Visual Studio usually creates a style class and applies that class to the text. Then, you can apply the same class to other literal text.

- To align text and controls when you use flow layout, you can use tables as described in the next figure. However, the preferred technique is to use CSS.

- See chapter 5 for more information on using the Formatting toolbar, style classes, and CSS.

Figure 2-7   How to use flow layout

How to add a table to a form

Because you're limited to what you can do with spaces and line breaks, you'll want to use other techniques to format a form in flow layout. In this chapter, I'll show you how to use a table to format a form. Then, in chapter 5, I'll show you how to use CSS to format a form.

Figure 2-8 shows how to add a table to a form. In this case, a table of six rows and two columns has already been added to the form, but the Insert Table dialog box is displayed to show what the settings are for that table. Usually, you can keep the dialog box entries that simple, because you can easily adjust the table once it's on the form.

The easiest way to resize a row or column is to drag it by its border. To change the width of a column, drag it by its right border. To change the height of a row, drag it by its bottom border. You can also change the height and width of the entire table by selecting the table and then dragging it by its handles. Note that when you make this type of change, Visual Studio creates style classes just like it does when you format text. Then, these classes are applied to the appropriate elements of the table.

You can also format a table in Design view by selecting one or more rows or columns and then using the commands in the Table menu or the shortcut menu that's displayed when you right-click the selection. These commands let you add, delete, or resize rows or columns. They also let you merge the cells in a row or column. If, for example, you want a control in one row to span two columns, you can merge the cells in that row.

How to add text to the cells of a table

In figure 2-8, you can see that text has been entered into the cells in the first four rows of the first column of the table. To do that, you just type the text into the cells. Then, you can format the text by selecting it and using the controls in the Formatting toolbar or the commands in the Format menu. If, for example, you want to bold the four text entries, you can select the four cells that contain the text and click on the Bold button.

The Future Value form with a table that has been inserted into it

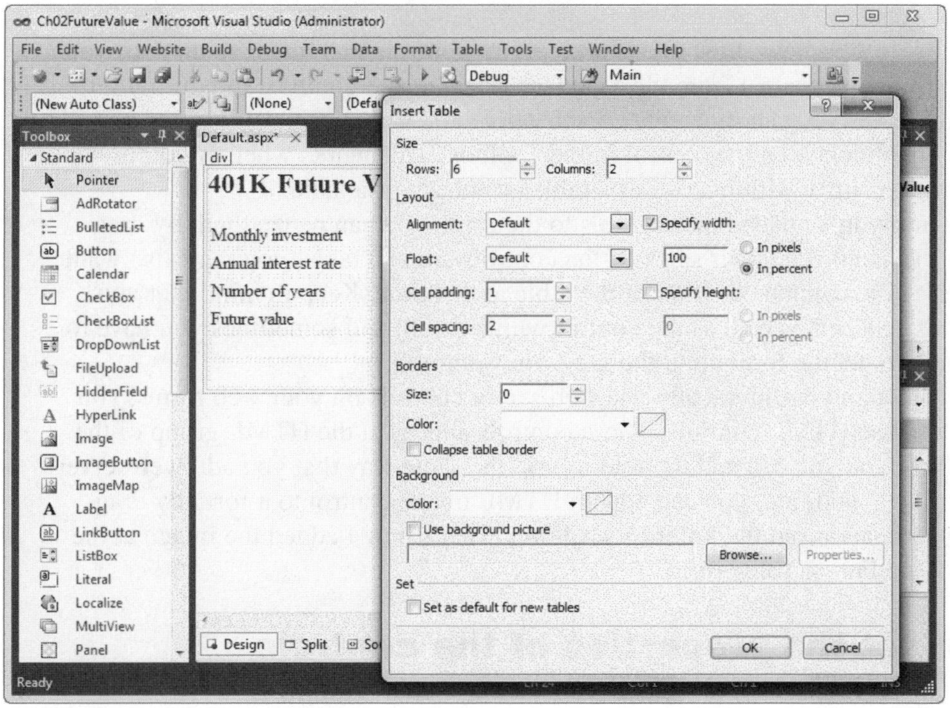

How to add a table to a form

- Use the Table→Insert Table command to display the Insert Table dialog box. Then, set the number of rows and columns that you want in the table, set any other options that you want, and click OK.

How to format a table after it has been added to a form

- To resize a row, drag it by its bottom border. To resize a column, drag it by its right border. To resize the entire table, select the table and then drag its handles.
- Select rows or columns and then use the commands in the Table menu or the shortcut menu to add, delete, resize, or merge the rows or columns.
- Some of the formatting that you apply to tables, rows, and columns is saved in style classes. Then, you can apply the same formatting to other tables, rows, and columns.

How to add and format text

- To add text to a table, type the text into the cells of the table.
- To format the text in a table, select the text, and then use the controls in the Formatting toolbar or the commands in the Format menu to apply the formatting.

Description

- To control the alignment of the text and controls on a web form in flow layout, you can use tables.

Figure 2-8   How to add a table to a form and text to a table

How to add server controls to a form

Figure 2-9 shows how to add web server controls to a form. To do that, you can just drag a control from the Standard group of the Toolbox and drop it on the form. Or, you can move the cursor where you want a control inserted and then double-click on the control in the Toolbox. This works whether you're placing a control within a cell of a table or outside of a table.

Once you've added the controls to the form, you can resize them by dragging the handles on their sides. If the controls are in a table, you may also want to resize the columns or rows of the table at this time. Keep in mind that you can resize a cell as well as the control within a cell, and sometimes you have to do both to get the formatting the way you want it.

Although you'll typically use web server controls on your web forms, you can also use HTML controls. These controls appear in the HTML group of the Toolbox, and you can add them to a form the same way that you add web server controls. In addition, you can add an HTML image control to a form by dragging an image from the Solution Explorer. That's how I added the image at the top of the Future Value form.

How to set the properties of the controls

After you have placed the controls on a form, you need to set each control's properties so the control looks and works the way you want it to when the form is displayed. To set those properties, you work in the Properties window as shown in figure 2-9. To display the properties for a specific control, just click on it in Design view.

In the Properties window, you select a property by clicking it. Then, a brief description of that property is displayed in the pane at the bottom of the window. To change a property setting, you change the entry to the right of the property name by typing a new value or choosing a new value from a drop-down list. In some cases, a button with an ellipsis (…) on it will appear when you click on a property. In that case, you can click this button to display a dialog box that helps you set the property.

Some properties are displayed in groups. In that case, a ▷ symbol appears next to the group name. This is illustrated by the Font property in this figure. To display the properties in a group, just click the ▷ symbol next to the group name.

To display properties alphabetically or by category, you can click the appropriate button at the top of the Properties window. At first, you may want to display the properties by category so you have an idea of what the different properties do. Once you become more familiar with the properties, though, you may be able to find the ones you're looking for faster if you display them alphabetically.

As you work with properties, you'll find that most are set the way you want them by default. In addition, some properties such as Height and Width are set interactively as you size and position the controls in Design view. As a result, you usually only need to change a few properties for each control. The only

The Future Value form after six web server controls have been added to it

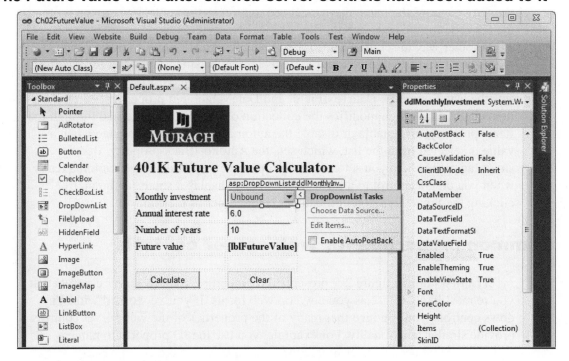

How to add a web server control to a web form

- Drag the control from the Standard group in the Toolbox to the form or to a cell in a table on the form. Or, move the cursor to where you want the control, and then double-click on the control in the Toolbox.

How to set the properties for a control

- Select a control by clicking on it, and all of its properties are displayed in the Properties window. Then, you can select a property in this window and set its value. When you select a property, a brief description is displayed in the pane at the bottom of the window.

- To change the Height and Width properties, you can drag one of the handles on a control. This also changes the Height and Width in the Properties window.

- You can use the first two buttons at the top of the Properties window to sort the properties by category or alphabetically.

- You can use the ▷ and ◢ symbols that are displayed in the Properties window to expand and collapse the list of properties. (If you're using Windows XP, + and – signs are used instead of these symbols.)

- Many web server controls have a *smart tag menu* that provides options for performing common tasks and setting common properties. To display a smart tag menu, click the Smart Tag icon in the upper right of the control.

Note

- The image on this form was created by dragging the MurachLogo.jpg file from the Solution Explorer to the form. This creates an HTML image control.

Figure 2-9   How to add web server controls to a form and set their properties

property that I set for the drop-down list, for example, is the ID property. This property contains the name that you'll use to refer to the control when you write the C# code for the code-behind file.

Another way to set properties for some controls is to use the control's *smart tag menu*. In figure 2-9, for example, you can see the smart tag menu for the drop-down list. You can use this menu to choose the data source for the control, which sets the DataSourceID, DataTextField, and DataValueField properties; edit the items in the list, which modifies the collection of items that's accessed through the Items property; and enable or disable the automatic posting of the page when a value is selected from the list, which sets the AutoPostBack property. Because smart tag menus help you set common properties, they're displayed automatically when you drag a control to a form. You can also display a smart tag menu by clicking the Smart Tag icon in the upper right corner of the control.

Common properties for web server controls

The first table in figure 2-9 presents the properties for web server controls that you're most likely to use as you develop web forms. If you've worked with Windows controls, you'll notice that many of the properties of the web server controls provide similar functionality. For example, you use the ID property to name a control that you need to refer to in code, and you can use the Text property to determine what's displayed in or on the control. However, the AutoPostBack, CausesValidation, EnableViewState, and Runat properties are unique to web server controls. Since you already know the purpose of the Runat property, I'll focus on the other three properties here.

The AutoPostBack property determines whether the page is posted back to the server when the user changes the value of the control. Note that this property is only available with certain controls, such as check boxes, drop-down lists, and radio buttons. Also note that this property isn't available with button controls. That's because button controls always either post a page back to the server or display another page.

The CausesValidation property is available for button controls and determines whether the validation controls are activated when the user clicks the button. This lets you check for valid data before the page is posted back to the server. You'll learn more about validation controls a few figures from now.

The EnableViewState property determines whether a server control retains its property settings from one posting to the next. For that to happen, the EnableViewState property for both the form and the control must be set to True. Since that's normally the way you want this property set, True is the default.

The second table in this figure lists four more properties that are commonly used with drop-down lists and list boxes. However, you don't need to set these at design time. Instead, you use them when you write the C# code for the code-behind file. For instance, you use the Items collection to add, insert, and remove ListItem objects. And you use the SelectedValue property to retrieve the value of the currently selected item. You'll learn more about these properties when you review the code-behind file for the Future Value form.

Common web server control properties

Property	Description
AutoPostBack	Determines whether the page is posted back to the server when the value of the control changes. Available with controls such as a check box, drop-down list, radio button, or text box. The default value is False.
CausesValidation	Determines whether the validation that's done by the validation controls occurs when you click on the button, link button, or image button. The default value is True. (You'll learn how to use two common validation controls later in this chapter.)
EnableViewState	Determines whether the control maintains its view state between HTTP requests. The default value is True.
Enabled	Determines whether the control is functional. The default value is True.
Height	The height of the control.
ID	The name that's used to refer to the control.
Runat	Indicates that the control will be processed on the server by ASP.NET.
TabIndex	Determines the order in which the controls on the form receive the focus when the Tab key is pressed.
Text	The text that's displayed in the control.
ToolTip	The text that's displayed when the user hovers the mouse over the control.
Visible	Determines whether a control is displayed or hidden.
Width	The width of the control.

Common properties of drop-down list and list box controls

Property	Description
Items	The collection of ListItem objects that represents the items in the control. Although you can set the values for these list items at design time, you normally use code to add, insert, and remove the items in a drop-down list or list box.
SelectedItem	The ListItem object for the currently selected item.
SelectedIndex	The index of the currently selected item. If no item is selected in a list box, the value of this property is -1.
SelectedValue	The value of the currently selected item.

Note

- When buttons are clicked, they always post back to the server. That's why they don't have AutoPostBack properties.

Figure 2-10   Common properties for web server controls

How to work in Source and Split views

As you design a form in Design view, HTML and asp tags are being generated in Source view. This is the code that's used to render the web page that's sent to the user's browser. What you see in Design view is just a visual representation of that code. In many cases, you'll need to work in Source view to get a page to look just the way you want it to. When you work in Source view, you can also use a new feature of Visual Studio for ASP.NET called code snippets. You may also want to work in Split view so you can see both Design view and Source view at the same time.

How to use Source view to modify the design

As you saw in the last chapter, HTML consists of tags. For instance, the <form> and </form> tags mark the start and end of the HTML code for a web form. And the <table> and </table> tags mark the start and end of the HTML code for a table.

In addition to the HTML tags, ASP.NET adds asp tags for the web server controls that are added to the form. In figure 2-11, you can see some of the asp tags for the Future Value form. For instance, the <asp:DropDownList> and </asp:DropDownList> tags mark the start and end of the code for a drop-down list. Within these tags, you'll find the code for the property settings of the controls. Note, however, that all of this asp code is converted to HTML before the page can be sent to a browser, because a browser can only interpret HTML.

Because the file that contains the source code for a web form has an aspx extension, we refer to the source code for a form as *aspx code*. This also indicates that the code contains both HTML and asp tags.

In case you need it, chapter 5 presents a crash course in HTML. In the meantime, though, you may be surprised to discover how easy it is to modify the design of a form by adjusting the aspx code using the *HTML Editor*.

To start, you can enter a title for the form between the <title> and </title> tags near the top of the source code. This is the title that's displayed in the title bar of the browser when the form is run (see figure 2-6). In this example, the title is "Chapter 2: Future Value." As you will see, all of the applications in this book have titles that indicate both the chapter number and the type of application.

You can also change the text that has been entered into a form or some of the settings for HTML elements. If, for example, you want to change the text in the first row of the table from "Monthly investment" to "Investment amount," you can just edit the text in Source view. And if you want to modify the color for the heading, you can do that too. As you edit, just follow the syntax of the other entries, which will be easier to do after you read chapter 5.

To change the properties of a server control, you can click in the starting asp tag to select the control. Then, you can use the Properties window just as if you were in Design view. When you change a property, the *attribute* that represents the property in the asp tag for the control is changed. You can also change the

The design of the Future Value form in Source view

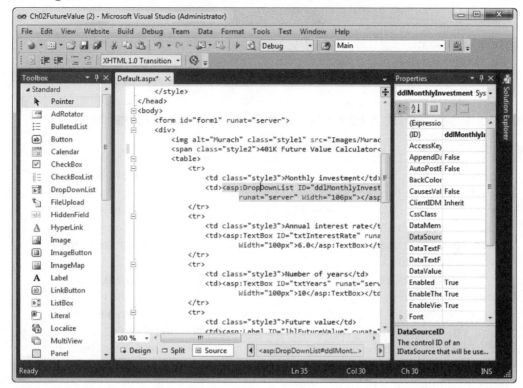

How to enter a title for the form

- Enter text between the <title> and </title> tags.

How to change the HTML and text for the form

- Change the source code itself.

How to change the property settings for a control

- To select a control, move the insertion point into the asp tag for the control. Then, use the Properties window to change the property settings for the control. Or, you can modify the property settings in the source code itself.

How to add a control

- Drag the control from the Toolbox to the location where you want it to appear.

Description

- Design view presents a visual representation of the code that you see in Source view.
- The source code includes HTML tags and asp tags. Before the form is sent to a browser, the asp tags are converted to HTML because browsers can only run HTML.
- The properties you set for a control appear as *attributes* in the asp tag for the control.
- We refer to the source code as *aspx code*, because the source files have aspx extensions.

Figure 2-11   How to use Source view to modify the design of a form

attributes directly in the source code whenever the syntax is obvious. That's often the fastest way to make an adjustment.

In addition to changing the properties of an existing control in Source view, you can add a new control. To do that, you just drag the control from the Toolbox and drop it in the location where you want it to appear. Then, you can set the control's properties using standard techniques.

How to use Split view to work with the design

In addition to Design view and Source view, you can work in Split view. Figure 2-12 shows how the Future Value form appears in Split view. When you use this view, you can see the aspx code for the form and the visual representation of that code at the same time. This is particularly helpful when you need to make minor adjustments to the appearance of a form. Then, you can check that the changes you make in Source view look the way you want them to without having to switch to Design view.

Note that when you make a change in Source view, the change isn't automatically reflected in Design view. Instead, a bar is displayed at the top of the Design view window that indicates that the two views are out of sync. In this figure, this bar was displayed when I changed the text in the first cell of the table. To synchronize the two views, you can click on this bar or anywhere in the Design view window. In contrast, if you make a change in Design view, it's reflected immediately in Source view.

The design of the Future Value form in Split view

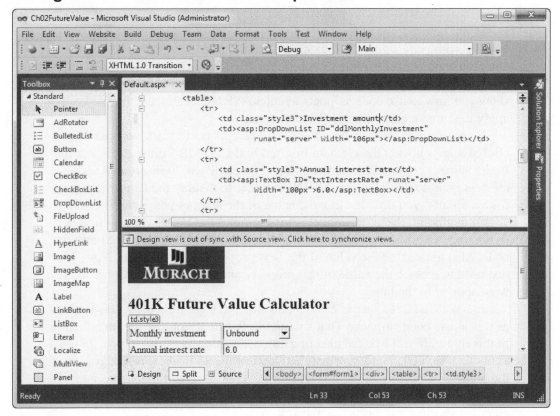

Description

- You can use Split view to display a form in Source view and Design view at the same time. This eliminates the need to switch back and forth between these two views.

- By default, the designer window is split horizontally as shown above. Then, the top half of the window displays the form in Source view, and the bottom half of the window displays the form in Design view.

- You can also split the designer window vertically. To do that, use the Tools→Option command to display the Options dialog box. Then, expand the HTML Designer node, select the General group, and check the Split Views Vertically option.

- If you make a change in Design view, it's reflected immediately in Source view. If you make a change in Source view, however, a bar is displayed at the top of the Design view window that indicates that Design view is out of sync with Source view. Then, you can click this bar or anywhere in the Design view window to synchronize the views.

Figure 2-12   How to use Split view to work with the design of a form

How to use code snippets

If you've used Visual Studio to do any C# coding, you may already be familiar with *code snippets*. You can use them in the Code Editor to enter common code patterns. With Visual Studio 2010, you can also use code snippets in the HTML editor to enter ASP.NET and HTML elements. In this topic, I'll show you how to use code snippets to enter ASP.NET elements, but you can apply the same techniques to HTML elements.

Figure 2-13 shows you how to use code snippets. To start, you can right-click where you want the element inserted in the HTML Editor and select the Insert Snippet command from the shortcut menu. Then, to insert an ASP.NET element, you double-click the ASP.NET folder to display the snippets in that folder. Finally, you double-click the name of the snippet you want to insert.

At that point, the code snippet is inserted into the HTML Editor. In this figure, for example, you can see that a label control has been inserted into the code. Also notice that the value of the Text property is highlighted. Now, you just need to replace the value of this property and add any other properties you want applied to the label.

In most cases, it's just as easy to add ASP.NET controls using the Toolbox as it is to use code snippets. That's particularly true if you use the menus shown in this figure. If you like the idea of using code snippets, though, you should know that each one has a shortcut that you can use to insert it instead of using the menus. For example, the shortcut for the code snippet that creates a label control is just "label". To insert this code snippet using its shortcut, you just enter the shortcut and press the Tab key.

If you use code snippets frequently, you should be aware that it's possible to add or remove snippets from the default list. To do that, you can choose the Code Snippets Manager command from the Tools menu. Then, you can use the resulting dialog box to remove code snippets that you don't use or to add new code snippets. Be aware, however, that writing a new code snippet requires creating an XML file that defines the code snippet. To learn how to do that, you can consult the documentation for Visual Studio.

The list that's displayed for code snippets

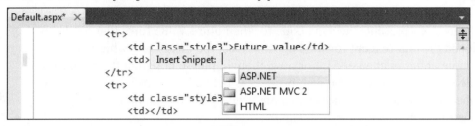

The list that's displayed for ASP.NET code snippets

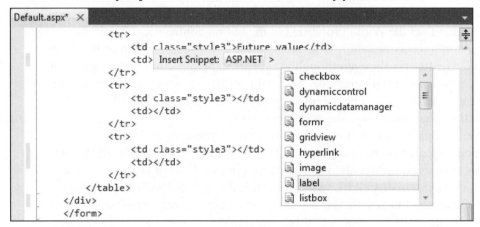

The snippet that's inserted for the label control

```
        <tr>
            <td class="style3">Future value</td>
            <td>
                <asp:Label Text="text" runat="server" /></td>
        </tr>
```

Description

- To insert a *code snippet*, right-click in the HTML Editor and select the Insert Snippet command from the resulting menu. Then, double-click the type of snippet you want to insert from the list that's displayed. Finally, double-click the snippet or highlight it and press the Tab or Enter key.

- Once a snippet has been inserted into your code, you can replace the highlighted property values with your own values and add any other required properties. To move from one highlighted value to the next, you can press the Tab key.

- You can use the Tools→Code Snippets Manager command to display a dialog box that you can use to edit the list of available code snippets and to add custom code snippets. This dialog box also lists shortcuts that you can use to insert a snippet.

- To insert a snippet using a shortcut, enter the shortcut and then press the Tab key.

Figure 2-13   How to use code snippets

The aspx code for the Future Value form

Figure 2-14 presents the aspx code for the Future Value form that has been developed thus far (except for the Page and Doctype directives, which you'll learn more about in chapter 5). For now, though, please note that the code for the title that's displayed in the web browser is between the <head> tags, along with the code for the style classes that are used by the form, and the code for the form design is between the <div> tags.

Within the <div> tags, I've highlighted the code for the HTML image control and the code for the six web server controls. If you study this code, you can see how the properties are set for each of these controls. For instance, you can see that I set the Width properties of the button controls to 100 pixels so they are both the same width. You can also see that I set the width of the drop-down list to 106 pixels, even though it appears to be the same width as the text boxes, which are 100 pixels wide. My point is that the sizing properties in the aspx code aren't always consistent, so you often have to fiddle with these properties to get the design the way you want it.

Before I go on, I want to point out that when you drag an image from the Solution Explorer, an Accessibility Properties dialog box is displayed that lets you set two properties for the HTML image control. First, it lets you set the Alternate Text property (Alt), which specifies the text that's displayed if for some reason the image can't be displayed. Because the version of HTML that Visual Studio 2010 uses requires this property, you'll want to be sure to enter a value for it.

Second, it lets you specify the Long Description property (LongDesc), which provides a *Uniform Resource Indicator* (*URI*) to a more extensive description of the image. A URI can be the address of a web page (a URL) or a name that identifies a resource or a unit of information (a *URN*, or *Uniform Resource Name*). The Long Description property isn't required, and in most cases you'll leave it blank.

The aspx code for the Future Value form

```
<html xmlns="http://www.w3.org/1999/xhtml">
<head runat="server">
    <title>Chapter 2: Future Value</title>
    <style type="text/css">
        .style1 {
            color: #0000FF;
            font-size: x-large;
        }
        .style2 {
            width: 100%;
        {
        .style3 {
            width: 140px;
            height: 23px;
        }
        .style4 {
            width: 150px;
            height: 65px;
        }
    </style>
</head>
<body>
  <form id="form1" runat="server">
  <div>
    <img alt="Murach" class="style4" src="Images/MurachLogo.jpg" /><br /><br />
    <span class="style1"><strong>401K Future Value Calculator</strong></span><br /><br />
    <table class="style2">
      <tr>
        <td class="style3">Monthly investment</td>
        <td><asp:DropDownList ID="ddlMonthlyInvestment"
        runat="server" Width="106px"></asp:DropDownList></td></tr>
      <tr>
        <td class="style3">Annual interest rate</td>
        <td><asp:TextBox ID="txtInterestRate" runat="server"
            Width="100px">6.0</asp:TextBox></td></tr>
      <tr>
        <td class="style3">Number of years</td>
        <td><asp:TextBox ID="txtYears" runat="server"
            Width="100px">10</asp:TextBox></td></tr>
      <tr>
        <td class="style3">Future value</td>
        <td><asp:Label ID="lblFutureValue" runat="server"
            Font-Bold="True"></asp:Label></td></tr>
      <tr>
        <td class="style3"> </td>
        <td> </td></tr>
      <tr>
        <td class="style3"><asp:Button ID="btnCalculate" runat="server"
                        Text="Calculate" Width="100px"
                        OnClick="btnCalculate_Click"/></td>
        <td><asp:Button ID="btnClear" runat="server"
            Text="Clear" Width="100px" OnClick="btnClear_Click"/></td></tr>
    </table>
  </div>
  </form>
</body>
</html>
```

Figure 2-14   The aspx code for the Future Value form

How to add validation controls to a form

A *validation control* is a type of ASP.NET control that's used to validate input data. The topics that follow introduce you to the validation controls and show you how to use two of the commonly used controls. Then, in chapter 7, you can learn all the skills that you need to master the use of these controls.

An introduction to the validation controls

Figure 2-15 shows the Validation group in the Toolbox. It offers five controls that can be called *validators*. These are the controls that you use to check that the user has entered valid data. You can use the last control in this group, the validation summary control, to display all the errors that have been detected by the validators on the form.

The easiest way to add a validation control to a web form is to drag it from the Toolbox. In this example, four validators have been added to the form: two required field validators and two range validators. In this case, the controls have been added below the table so ASP.NET will use flow layout to position the controls. However, these controls could have been added to a third column of the table. Although these controls aren't displayed when the form is displayed, the messages in their ErrorMessage properties are displayed if errors are detected.

In this case, the first required field validator checks that a value has been entered in the text box for the interest rate, and the first range validator checks that this value ranges from 1 to 20. Similarly, the second required field validator checks that a value has been entered in the text box for the number of years, and the second range validator checks that this value ranges from 1 to 45.

Validation tests are typically done on the client before the page is posted to the server. That way, a round trip to the server isn't required to display error messages if any invalid data is detected.

In most cases, client-side validation is done when the focus leaves an input control that has validators associated with it. That can happen when the user presses the Tab key to move to the next control or clicks another control to move the focus to that control. Validation is also done when the user clicks on a button that has its CausesValidation property set to True.

To perform client-side validation, a browser must support *Dynamic HTML*, or *DHTML*. Because most browsers in use today support DHTML, validation can usually be done on the client. However, validation is always done on the server too when a page is submitted. ASP.NET does this validation after it initializes the page.

When ASP.NET performs the validation tests on the server, it sets the IsValid property of each validator to indicate if the test was successful. In addition, after all the validators are tested, it sets the IsValid property of the page to indicate if all the input data is valid. You can test this property in the event handler for the event that causes the page to be posted to the server. You'll see how this works when you review the code-behind file for this form.

The validation controls on the Future Value form

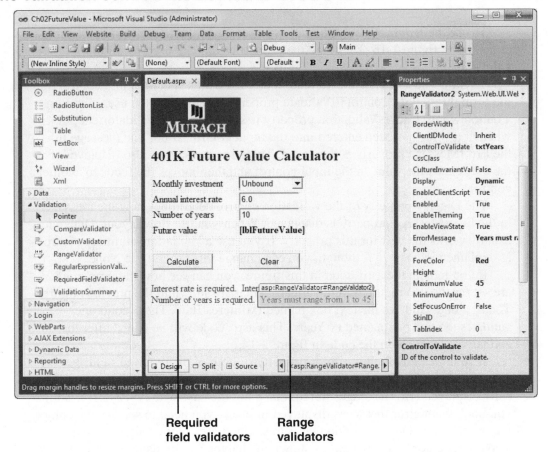

**Required
field validators**

**Range
validators**

Description

- You can use *validation controls* to test user input and produce error messages. The validation is typically performed when the focus leaves the control that's being validated and also when the user clicks on a button whose CausesValidation property is set to True.

- Each validation control is associated with a specific server control, but you can associate one or more validation controls with a single server control.

- The validation controls work by running client-side scripts. Then, if the validation fails, the page isn't posted back to the server. However, the validation is also performed on the server in case the client doesn't support scripts.

- If the client doesn't support scripts, you can test whether validation has been successful on the server by testing whether the IsValid property of the page is True.

Figure 2-15   An introduction to the validation controls

How to use the required field validator

To use the *required field validator*, you set the properties shown in the table at the top of figure 2-16. These are the properties that are used by all the validators.

To start, you associate the validation control with a specific input control on the form through its ControlToValidate property. Then, when the user clicks on a button whose CausesValidation property is set to True, the validator checks whether a value has been entered into the input control. If not, the message in the ErrorMessage property is displayed. The error message is also displayed if the user clears the value in the input control and then moves the focus to another control.

The Display property of the validation control determines how the message in the ErrorMessage property is displayed. When you use flow layout, Dynamic usually works the best for this property. If you use a validation summary control as explained in chapter 7, though, you can change this property to None.

If you look at the aspx code in this figure, you can see how the properties are set for the two required field validators that are shown in the previous figure. The first one validates the text box named txtInterestRate. The second one validates the text box named txtYears. This aspx code will be added after the end tag for the table in the code in figure 2-14.

Also notice that the ForeColor property of both of the required field validators is set to "Red". Although previous versions of ASP.NET automatically displayed error messages in red, that's not the case with ASP.NET 4. So if you don't want error messages displayed in black, you need to specify the color you want to use. One way to do that is to set the ForeColor property. You can also set the color by using CSS as shown in chapter 5 or by using skins as shown in chapter 11.

How to use the range validator

The *range validator* lets you set the valid range for an input value. To use this control, you set the properties in the first table in figure 2-16, plus the properties in the second table. In particular, you set the minimum and maximum values for an input value.

For this control to work correctly, you must set the Type property to the type of data you're testing for. Because the interest rate entry can have decimal positions, for example, the Type property for the first range validator is set to Double. In contrast, because the year entry should be a whole number, the Type property for the second range validator is set to Integer. You can see how all of the properties for the two range validators are set by reviewing the aspx code.

Common validation control properties

Property	Description
`ControlToValidate`	The ID of the control to be validated.
`Display`	Determines how an error message is displayed. Specify Static to allocate space for the message in the page layout, Dynamic to have the space allocated when an error occurs, or None to display the errors in a validation summary control.
`ErrorMessage`	The message that's displayed in the validation control when the validation fails.

Additional properties of a range validator

Property	Description
`MaximumValue`	The maximum value that the control can contain.
`MinimumValue`	The minimum value that the control can contain.
`Type`	The data type to use for range checking (String, Integer, Double, Date, or Currency).

The aspx code for the validation controls on the Future Value form

```
<asp:RequiredFieldValidator ID="RequiredFieldValidator1" runat="server"
    ControlToValidate="txtInterestRate" Display="Dynamic"
    ErrorMessage="Interest rate is required." ForeColor="Red">
</asp:RequiredFieldValidator> 
<asp:RangeValidator ID="RangeValidator1" runat="server"
    ControlToValidate="txtInterestRate" Display="Dynamic"
    ErrorMessage="Interest rate must range from 1 to 20."
    MaximumValue="20" MinimumValue="1" Type="Double" ForeColor="Red">
</asp:RangeValidator><br />
<asp:RequiredFieldValidator ID="RequiredFieldValidator2" runat="server"
    ControlToValidate="txtYears" Display="Dynamic"
    ErrorMessage="Number of years is required." ForeColor="Red">
</asp:RequiredFieldValidator> 
<asp:RangeValidator ID="RangeValidator2" runat="server"
    ControlToValidate="txtYears" Display="Dynamic"
    ErrorMessage="Years must range from 1 to 45."
    MaximumValue="45" MinimumValue="1" Type="Integer" ForeColor="Red">
</asp:RangeValidator>
```

Description

- The *required field validator* is typically used with text box controls, but can also be used with list controls.

- The *range validator* tests whether a user entry falls within a valid range.

- If the user doesn't enter a value into the input control that a range validator is associated with, the range validation test passes. Because of that, you should also provide a required field validator if a value is required.

Figure 2-16   How to use the required field and range validators

How to add code to a form

To add the functionality required by a web form, you add C# code to its code-behind file. This code responds to the events that the user initiates on the form. This code also responds to events that occur as a form is processed.

How to use the Code Editor

To create and edit C# code, you use the *Code Editor* shown in figure 2-17. The easiest way to display the Code Editor window is to double-click outside the body of the form or on a control in the Web Forms Designer window. That displays the code-behind file for the form.

If you double-click outside the body of the form in Design view, an *event handler* for the Load event of the page is generated. If you double-click a control, an event handler for the default event of the control is generated. If you double-click on a button control, for example, an event handler for the Click event of that control is created. Then, you can enter the code that you want to be executed within the braces of the event handler.

To create event handlers for other control events, you can use the Events button at the top of the Properties window. When you click this button, a list of all the events for the control that's currently selected is displayed. Then, you can double-click on any event to generate an event handler for that event.

When Visual Studio generates an event handler for a control, it also adds the appropriate event attribute to the asp code for that control. In figure 2-14, for example, you saw the OnClick event attributes that were generated for the Calculate and Clear buttons on the Future Value form. This is how events are wired to event handlers in ASP.NET, and you'll learn more about it in chapter 6.

You can also code methods other than event handlers by entering the code for the method directly into the Code Editor window. Then, you can call those methods from the event handlers for the form.

As you work with the Code Editor, you'll notice that it provides some powerful features that can help you code more quickly and accurately. One of the most useful of these features is the Auto List Members feature provided by IntelliSense. This feature displays a list of members that are available for an object when you type the object name and a period. Then, you can highlight the member you want by clicking on it, typing the first few letters of its name, or using the arrow keys to scroll through the list. In this figure, you can see the members that are listed for a drop-down list. When you press the Tab or Enter key, the member you select is inserted into your code.

You can also use the Text Editor toolbar to work with code in the Code Editor. You can use it to perform functions such as commenting or uncommenting several lines of code at once, increasing or decreasing the indentation of several lines of code, and working with bookmarks. If you experiment with this toolbar, you should quickly see how it works.

A project with the Code Editor window displayed

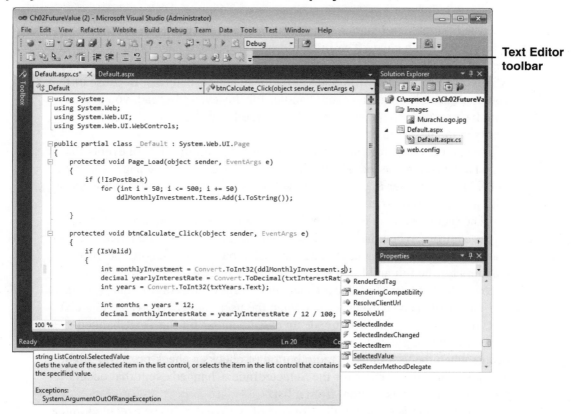

Text Editor toolbar

Three ways to open or switch to a file in the Code Editor window

- Select a web form in the Solution Explorer and click the View Code button at the top of the Solution Explorer. Double-click on a C# file (.aspx.cs or .cs) in the Solution Explorer. Or, click on a tab at the top of the Web Forms Designer (if the file is already open).

Three ways to start an event handler

- Double-click outside the body of a web form to start an event handler for the Load event of the page.
- Double-click on a control in the Web Forms Designer to start an event handler for the default event of that control.
- Select a control in the Web Forms Designer, click the Events button in the Properties window (the button with the lightening bolt), and double-click the event you want to create an event handler for.

Description

- The *Code Editor* includes powerful text editing features such as automatic indentation, syntax checking, and statement completion (as shown above).
- To enter a method other than an event handler, you type the method from scratch.

Figure 2-17   How to use the Code Editor

How to use page and control events

The first table in figure 2-18 presents some of the common events for working with web pages. The Init and Load events of a page occur whenever a page is requested from the server. The Init event occurs first, and it's used by ASP.NET to restore the view state of the page and its controls. Because of that, you don't usually create an event handler for this event. Instead, you add any initialization code to the event handler for the Load event. You'll see how this works in the next figure.

In contrast, the PreRender event is raised after all the control events for the page have been processed. It's the last event to occur before a page is rendered to HTML. In chapter 8, you'll see how this event can be useful when working with data in session state.

The second table in this figure lists some of the common events for web server controls. When the user clicks a button, for example, the Click event of that control is raised. Then, the page is posted back to the server, the event handlers for the Init and Load events of the page are executed, if present, followed by the event handler for the Click event of the control that was clicked.

The TextChanged event occurs when the user changes the value in a text box. In most cases, you won't code an event handler for the TextChanged event. However, you might code an event handler for the CheckedChanged event that occurs when the user clicks a radio button or checks a check box. You might also code an event handler for the SelectedIndexChanged event that occurs when the user selects an item from a list.

If you want the event handler for one of these events to be executed immediately when the event occurs, you can set the AutoPostBack property of the control to True. Then, the event handler will be executed after the Init and Load event handlers for the page. Note that if you don't set the AutoPostBack property to True, the event is still raised, but the event handler isn't executed until another user action causes the page to be posted to the server. Then, the event handlers for the Init and Load events of the page are executed, followed by the event handlers for the control events in the order they were raised.

In this figure, you can see the event handler for the Click event of the Clear button on the Future Value form. This event handler resets the value in the drop-down list to 50 and resets the text boxes and label to empty strings. Note that the name for this event handler is btnClear_Click, which is the ID of the button followed by the name of the event. If you look back to the aspx code for the Future Value form in figure 2-14, you'll see that this is the same name that's referenced in the OnClick event attribute that ASP.NET adds to the control when it generates the event handler.

Common ASP.NET page events

Event	Method name	Occurs when...
Init	Page_Init	A page is requested from the server. This event is raised before the view state of the page controls has been restored.
Load	Page_Load	A page is requested from the server, after all controls have been initialized and view state has been restored. This is the event you typically use to perform initialization operations such as retrieving data and initializing form controls.
PreRender	Page_PreRender	All the control events for the page have been processed but before the HTML that will be sent back to the browser is generated.

Common ASP.NET control events

Event	Occurs when...
Click	The user clicks a button, link button, or image button control.
TextChanged	The user changes the value in a text box.
CheckedChanged	The user selects a radio button in a group of radio buttons or selects or unselects a check box.
SelectedIndexChanged	The user selects an item from a list box, a drop-down list, a check box list, or a radio button list.

Code for the Click event of the btnClear button

```
protected void btnClear_Click(object sender, EventArgs e)
{
    ddlMonthlyInvestment.SelectedIndex = 0;
    txtInterestRate.Text = "";
    txtYears.Text = "";
    lblFutureValue.Text = "";
}
```

Description

- All of the events associated with an ASP.NET web page and its server controls are executed on the server. Because of that, the page must be posted back to the server to process any event for which you've coded an event handler.

- When a page is posted back to the server, the Init and Load events are always raised so any event handlers for those events are run first. Next, the event handlers for any control events that were raised are executed in the order they were raised. When these event handlers finish, the PreRender event is raised and any event handler for that event is run.

Figure 2-18   How to use page and control events

The C# code for the Future Value form

Figure 2-19 presents the complete C# code for the code-behind file of the Future Value form. It consists of three event handlers that handle the Load event for the page and the Click events of the Calculate and Clear buttons. This code also includes a method named CalculateFutureValue that is called by the event handler for the Click event of the Calculate button.

In this code, I've highlighted the two page properties that are commonly tested in the code for web forms. The first one is the IsPostBack property that's used in the Page_Load method. If it is True, it means that the page is being posted back from the user. If it is False, it means that the page is being requested by the user for the first time.

As a result, the statements within the if statement in the Page_Load method are only executed if the page is being requested for the first time. In that case, the values 50 through 500 are added to the drop-down list. For all subsequent requests by that user, the IsPostBack property will be True so the values aren't added to the drop-down list.

The other page property that's commonly tested is the IsValid property. It's useful when the user's browser doesn't support the client-side scripts for the validation controls. In that case, the application has to rely on the validation that's always done on the server. Then, if IsValid is True, it means that all of the input data is valid. But if IsValid is False, it means that one or more controls contain invalid input data so the processing shouldn't be done.

In the btnCalculate_Click method, you can see how the IsValid test is used. If it isn't True, the processing isn't done. But otherwise, this method uses the SelectedValue property of the drop-down list to get the value of the selected item, which represents the investment amount. Then, it gets the years and interest rate values from the text boxes and converts them to monthly units. Last, it calls the CalculateFutureValue method to calculate the future value, uses the ToString method convert the future value to a string with currency format, and puts the formatted value in the label of the form. When this method ends, the web form is sent back to the user's browser.

With the exception of the IsPostBack and IsValid properties, this is all standard C# code so you shouldn't have any trouble following it. But if you do, you can quickly upgrade your C# skills by getting our latest C# book.

The C# code for the Future Value form

```csharp
using System;
using System.Web;
using System.Web.UI;
using System.Web.UI.WebControls;

public partial class _Default : System.Web.UI.Page
{
    protected void Page_Load(object sender, EventArgs e)
    {
        if (!IsPostBack)
            for (int i = 50; i <= 500; i += 50)
                ddlMonthlyInvestment.Items.Add(i.ToString());
    }

    protected void btnCalculate_Click(object sender, EventArgs e)
    {
        if (IsValid)
        {
            int monthlyInvestment =
                Convert.ToInt32(ddlMonthlyInvestment.SelectedValue);
            decimal yearlyInterestRate =
                Convert.ToDecimal(txtInterestRate.Text);
            int years =
                Convert.ToInt32(txtYears.Text);

            int months = years * 12;
            decimal monthlyInterestRate = yearlyInterestRate / 12 / 100;

            decimal futureValue =
                this.CalculateFutureValue(monthlyInvestment,
                    monthlyInterestRate, months);

            lblFutureValue.Text = futureValue.ToString("c");
        }
    }

    protected decimal CalculateFutureValue(int monthlyInvestment,
    decimal monthlyInterestRate, int months)
    {
        decimal futureValue = 0;
        for (int i = 0; i < months; i++)
        {
            futureValue = (futureValue + monthlyInvestment)
                * (1 + monthlyInterestRate);
        }
        return futureValue;
    }

    protected void btnClear_Click(object sender, EventArgs e)
    {
        ddlMonthlyInvestment.SelectedIndex = 0;
        txtInterestRate.Text = "";
        txtYears.Text = "";
        lblFutureValue.Text = "";
    }
}
```

Figure 2-19   The C# code for the Future Value form

How to test a web application

After you design the forms and develop the code for a web application, you need to test it to be sure it works properly. Then, if you discover any errors in the application, you can debug it, correct the errors, and test it again.

In chapter 4, you'll learn all the skills you need to test and debug a web application. For now, I just want to show you how to run a web site with the built-in development server so you can test any applications that you develop for this chapter. Then, I'll show you the HTML code that's sent to the browser so you can see how that works.

How to run a web site with the built-in development server

When you run a file-system web site by using one of the techniques in figure 2-20, Visual Studio compiles the application. If the application compiles without errors, Visual Studio automatically launches the built-in ASP.NET Development Server and displays the starting page of the web site in your default browser. Then, you can test the application to make sure that it works the way you want it to.

However, if any errors are detected as part of the compilation, Visual Studio opens the Error List window and displays the errors. These can consist of errors that have to be corrected as well as warning messages. In this figure, three errors and one warning are displayed in the Error List window.

To fix an error, you can double-click on it in the Error List window. This moves the cursor to the line of code that caused the error in the Code Editor. By moving from the Error List window to the Code Editor for all of the messages, you should be able to find the coding problems and fix them.

As you're testing an application with the development server, exceptions may occur. If an exception isn't handled by the application, ASP.NET switches to the Code Editor window and highlights the statement that caused the exception. In this case, you can end the application by clicking on the Stop Debugging button in the Debug toolbar or using the Debug→Stop Debugging command. Then, you can fix the problem and test again.

In chapter 4, you'll learn all of the debugging skills that you'll need for more complex applications. For simple applications, though, you should be able to get by with just the skills you have right now.

An ASP.NET project with the Error List window displayed

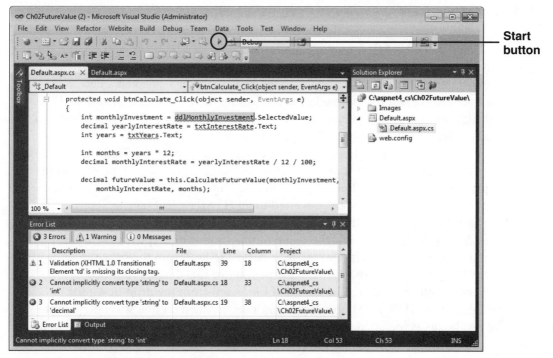

How to run an application

- Click on the Start button in the Standard toolbar or press F5. Then, the project is compiled and the starting page is displayed in your default browser.

- The first time you run an ASP.NET application, a dialog box will appear asking whether you want to modify the web.config file to enable debugging. Click the OK button to proceed.

How to stop an application

- Click the Close button in the upper right corner of the browser. Or, if an exception occurs, click the Stop Debugging button in the Debug toolbar or press Shift+F5.

How to fix syntax errors

- If any errors are detected when the project is compiled, an Error List window is opened and a list of errors is displayed along with information about each error. To display the source code that caused an error, double-click on the error in the Error List window.

- Syntax errors are also highlighted in the Code Editor window with a wavy underline.

- After you've fixed all the errors, run the application again and repeat this process if necessary. Note, however, that you don't have to fix the warnings.

Figure 2-20   How to run a web site with the built-in development server

How to review the HTML that's sent to the browser

To view the HTML for a page that's displayed in a browser, you can use the Source command in your browser's View menu. To illustrate, figure 2-21 presents the HTML that's sent back to the browser after I selected a new value from the drop-down list, entered new values into the text boxes, and clicked the Calculate button. Although you'll rarely need to view this code, it does give you a better idea of what's going on behind the scenes.

First, you'll see that this code doesn't include any asp tags. That's because these tags are rendered to standard HTML so the controls they represent can be displayed in the browser. For instance, the asp tag for the drop-down list in the first row of the table has been converted to an HTML select tag.

Second, you can see that the view state data is stored in a hidden input field named _VIEWSTATE. Here, the value of this field is encrypted so you can't read it. Because the data in view state is passed to and from the browser automatically, you don't have to handle the passing of this data in your code.

Third, you can see that the data that I selected from the drop-down list is included in the HTML. Although you can't see it, the data that was entered into the text boxes is included as well. This illustrates that you don't need view state to save the information that's entered by the user. Instead, view state is used to maintain the state of properties that have been set by code. For example, it's used to maintain the values that are loaded into the drop-down list the first time the user requests the form.

Keep in mind that this HTML is generated automatically by ASP.NET, so you don't have to worry about it. You just develop the application by using Visual Studio in the way I've just described, and the rest of the work is done for you.

The HTML for the Future Value form after a post back

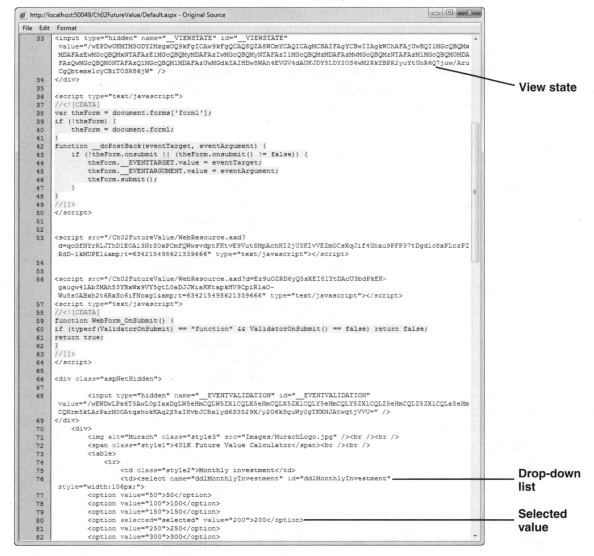

```
33  <input type="hidden" name="__VIEWSTATE" id="__VIEWSTATE"
       value="/wEPDwUKMTM5ODY2MzgxOQ9kFgICAw9kFgQCAQ8QZA8WCmCYCAQICAgMCBAIFAgYCBwIIAgkWChAFAjUwBQI1MGcQBQMx
       MDAFAzEwMGcQBQMxNTAFAzE1MGcQBQMyMDAFAzIwMGcQBQMyNTAFAzI1MGcQBQMzMDAFAzMwMGcQBQMzNTAFAzM1MGcQBQM0MDA
       FAzQwMGcQBQM0NTAFAzQ1MGcQBQM1MDAFAzUwMGdkZAIHDw8WAh4EVGV4dAUKUKJDY5LDY2OS4wM2RkZBPR2yuYtUnR6Q7juw/Aru
       CgQbtemeloyCBiTOSR86jW" />
34  </div>
35
36  <script type="text/javascript">
37  //<![CDATA[
38  var theForm = document.forms['form1'];
39  if (!theForm) {
40      theForm = document.form1;
41  }
42  function __doPostBack(eventTarget, eventArgument) {
43      if (!theForm.onsubmit || (theForm.onsubmit() != false)) {
44          theForm.__EVENTTARGET.value = eventTarget;
45          theForm.__EVENTARGUMENT.value = eventArgument;
46          theForm.submit();
47      }
48  }
49  //]]>
50  </script>
51
52
53  <script src="/Ch02FutureValue/WebResource.axd?
       d=qcGfNYrRLJThD1EOA13NrSOxPCmfQWwsvdptFKtvE9Vut8MpAchHIZjU3KIvVEZmOCsXqJif4Ghau9PFP37tDgd1c8xPLczPI
       RdD-1kMUPE1&amp;t=634215498621339666" type="text/javascript"></script>
54
55
56  <script src="/Ch02FutureValue/WebResource.axd?d=Ez9uOZRD6yQ5sXEI81YtDAcU3bdPkEK-
       gaugw41AbZMAh53YBxWx9VY5gtL0aDJJWiaKKtapkHV9CpiRla0-
       Wu8s0ABxh2t6RxSo6iFNoxg1&amp;t=634215498621339666" type="text/javascript"></script>
57  <script type="text/javascript">
58  //<![CDATA[
59  function WebForm_OnSubmit() {
60  if (typeof(ValidatorOnSubmit) == "function" && ValidatorOnSubmit() == false) return false;
61  return true;
62  }
63  //]]>
64  </script>
65
66  <div class="aspNetHidden">
67
68          <input type="hidden" name="__EVENTVALIDATION" id="__EVENTVALIDATION"
       value="/wEWDwLPx6T5AwL0pIaxDgLW5eHmCQLW5ZX1CQLX5eHmCQLX5ZX1CQLY5eHmCQLY5ZX1CQLZ5eHmCQLZ5ZX1CQLa5eHm
       CQKrm5kLArParM0OAtqshokKAq2S5aIKvbJCRx1yd6S3529X/y2O6kSguWy0gTKXNJAtwqtjVVU=" />
69  </div>
70      <div>
71          <img alt="Murach" class="style3" src="Images/MurachLogo.jpg" /><br /><br />
72          <span class="style1">401K Future Value Calculator</span><br /><br />
73          <table>
74              <tr>
75                  <td class="style2">Monthly investment</td>
76                  <td><select name="ddlMonthlyInvestment" id="ddlMonthlyInvestment"
       style="width:106px;">
77                  <option value="50">50</option>
78                  <option value="100">100</option>
79                  <option value="150">150</option>
80                  <option selected="selected" value="200">200</option>
81                  <option value="250">250</option>
82                  <option value="300">300</option>
```

View state → (line 33)

Drop-down list → (line 76)

Selected value → (line 80)

Description

- To view the HTML for a page, use the View→Source command in the browser's menu.
- The HTML that the browser receives consists entirely of standard HTML tags because all of the ASP.NET tags are converted to standard HTML when the page is rendered.
- View state data is stored in a hidden input field within the HTML. This data is encrypted so you can't read it.
- If the page contains validation controls and client scripting is enabled for those controls, the HTML for the page contains script to perform the validation on the client if the client supports DHTML.
- Values that the user enters into a page are returned to the browser as part of the HTML for the page.

Figure 2-21   How to review the HTML that's sent to the browser

Perspective

The purpose of this chapter has been to teach you the basic skills for creating one-page ASP.NET applications with Visual Studio. If you've already used Visual Studio and C# to develop Windows applications, you shouldn't have any trouble mastering these skills. You just need to get used to HTML and the properties and events for web server controls and validation controls.

Terms

web site
file-system web site
target framework
web project
web form
project
Web Forms Designer
Toolbox
Solution Explorer
Properties window
Source view
Design view
Split view
code snippets
web server control
drop-down list
text box
label
button

flow layout
HTML control
smart tag menu
HTML Editor
attribute
aspx code
validation control
validator
required field validator
range validator
Dynamic HTML (DHTML)
Code Editor
event handler
smart tag

Exercise 2-1   Build the Future Value application

This exercise guides you through the development of the Future Value application that's presented in this chapter.

Start, close, and open the application

1. Start an empty file-system web site as shown in figure 2-1 named Ch02FutureValue in the C:\aspnet4_cs directory.

2. Add a web form as shown in figure 2-2 using the default name. Be sure that the Place Code in Separate File option is selected.

3. Add a folder named Images to your project and add the Murach logo to it, as shown in figure 2-4. You can find the logo in the C:\aspnet4_cs directory. Note that you'll have to change the file type to All Files (*.*) to see this file.

4. Close the web site using the technique in figure 2-5, and reopen it using one of the three techniques in that figure. Then, switch to Design view.

Use Design view to build the form

5. Drag the logo from the Images folder in the Solution Explorer to the top of the web form. When the Accessibility Properties dialog box is displayed, enter "Murach" for the alternate text but leave the long description blank.

6. Enter the text for the heading as shown in figure 2-6. Then, select this text, and use the techniques in figure 2-7 to format it.

7. Use the techniques in figure 2-8 to add and format a table that provides for the six rows shown in figure 2-6. Then, add the text shown in figure 2-6 to the first four rows in the first column of the table.

8. Use the techniques in figure 2-9 to add the drop-down list, text boxes, label, and buttons shown in figure 2-6 to the table. Then, adjust the size of the columns, rows, and controls so the table looks the way it does in figure 2-6.

9. Switch to Source view and notice that when you changed the size of the controls, a Width attribute was added to the controls.

10. Switch back to Design view. Then, use the techniques of figure 2-9 and the summary in figure 2-10 to set the properties of the controls so they look like the ones in figure 2-6. When you do that, be sure to enter descriptive names for the ID property of each control.

Use Source view to modify the aspx code

11. Switch to Source view, and use the technique of figure 2-11 to enter "Future Value" for the title of the form.

12. Press F5 to run the application. When the dialog box asks whether you want to modify the web.config file to enable debugging, click the OK button. Now, test to see what works by clicking on the controls. Also, check to make sure that the web form looks the way it's supposed to when it's displayed in the default browser.

13. To end the application, click the Close button in the upper right corner of the browser. Depending on the browser you're using, this may or may not end debugging. If it doesn't, click the Stop Debugging button in the Debug toolbar. Then, switch to Split view, adjust the design of the form as necessary, and test it again.

Add the validation controls

14. Add the validation controls for the interest rate and years text boxes as shown in figures 2-15 and 2-16.

15. Press F5 to run the application. Then, test the field validators by leaving fields blank or entering invalid data. The validation will be done when the focus leaves a text box or when you click on a button.

16. To end the application, click the browser's Close button. Then, fix any problems and test again. If, for example, validation is done when you click the Clear button, you can fix that by setting its CausesValidation property to False.

Add the C# code and test as you go

17. Use one of the techniques in figure 2-17 to open the Code Editor for the form. Then, use the tab at the top of the window to switch to Design view.

18. Double-click outside the body of the form to switch to the Code Editor and start an event handler for the Load event. Next, write the code for this event handler, which should be like the code in figure 2-19. Then, press F5 to compile and test this event handler. If any errors are detected as you enter code or when the application is compiled, use the techniques in figure 2-20 to fix them.

19. Switch back to Design view, and double-click on the Clear button to start an event handler for the Click event of that button. Next, write the code for this event handler, which should be like the code in figure 2-19. Then, compile and test this code, and fix any errors.

20. Write the CalculateFutureValue method from scratch as shown in figure 2-19.

21. Switch back to Design view, and double-click on the Calculate button to start an event handler for the Click event of that button. Next, write the code for this event handler, which should use the CalculateFutureValue method and be like the code in figure 2-19. Then, compile and test, and fix any errors.

Do more testing and experimenting

22. Set the EnableViewState property of the drop-down list to False, and test the application to see what happens. When an exception occurs, click the Stop Debugging button in the Debugging toolbar. Then, reset the property.

23. Set the EnableClientScript property for the validators of the first text box to False so this validation will only be done on the server. Then, test the application to make sure that the validation still works.

24. Run the application again, and use the technique in figure 2-21 to review the HTML that's sent to the browser. When you're through, close the project.

3

How to develop a multi-page web application

In the last chapter, you learned how to develop a simple, one-page web application. Now, you'll learn how to develop a multi-page application, which requires several new skills. You'll also learn how to get the data for a web form from a database.

The Shopping Cart application

To illustrate the skills that you're going to learn, this chapter presents two pages of a Shopping Cart application. This application gets product data from a database, stores data in session state, and uses three business classes. So even though this is a simple application, it isn't trivial.

In the four topics that follow, you'll be introduced to the two web forms and the folders and files that this application requires. Then, you'll learn how to add the three business classes to this project.

The Order page

Figure 3-1 presents the first page of the Shopping Cart application. This page, named Order.aspx, includes a drop-down list from which the user can select a product. The products are retrieved from an Access database via an AccessDataSource control. Since the drop-down list is bound to the data source, the product names are displayed automatically.

Although it isn't apparent in this figure, the product data is retrieved from an Access database named Halloween.mdb. This database includes a table named Products. The Products table has these columns: ProductID, Name, ShortDescription, LongDescription, CategoryID, ImageFile, UnitPrice, and OnHand. All of these columns except CategoryID and OnHand are used by this application.

The AutoPostBack property of the drop-down list is set to True. That way, when the user selects a product, the page is posted back to the server. Then, the code for the page retrieves the data for the selected product from the data source, which has retrieved the data for all of the products from the Access database. The data for the selected product is displayed in several labels. In addition, the ImageFile column is used to set the ImageUrl property of an Image control so the product image is displayed in that control.

Once a product is selected, the user can enter a quantity and click the Add to Cart button. However, if the user clicks the Add to Cart button without entering a valid quantity, an error message is displayed. To accomplish that, two validation controls are included on the page. A required field validator makes sure that the user enters a quantity, and a range validator makes sure that the quantity is an integer that ranges from 1 to 500.

If the user enters a valid quantity, a list that contains the user's shopping cart is updated with the product information. If the product isn't already in the shopping cart, a new item is added to the list. But if the product already exists in the shopping cart, the quantity entered is added to the quantity for the product that's in the shopping cart. Because the shopping cart must be retrieved and updated each time a product is added or updated, the list that represents the shopping cart is saved in session state.

The design of the Order page

Description

- The Order page of this application accepts an order for any items in the online store.
- To order an item, the user selects the product from the drop-down list, enters a quantity in the text box, and clicks the Add to Cart button.
- When the user clicks the Add to Cart button, the selected product is added to the shopping cart. If the product is already in the shopping cart, the quantity is added to the quantity in the existing shopping cart item. Then, the Cart page is displayed.
- The product information is retrieved from an Access database by an AccessDataSource control that's bound to the drop-down list.
- The AutoPostBack property of the drop-down list is set to True so the page is posted when the user selects a product. Then, the information for the selected product is displayed.
- The shopping cart information is saved in session state so it can be retrieved and updated each time a product is ordered.
- Validation controls ensure that the user enters a positive integer for the quantity that ranges from 1 to 500.

Figure 3-1   The Order page of the Shopping Cart application

The Cart page

After the user selects a product from the Order page, enters a quantity, and clicks the Add to Cart button, the Cart page in figure 3-2 is displayed. This page lists all the items currently in the shopping cart in a list box. To do that, it must retrieve the shopping cart from session state.

To work with the items in the shopping cart, the user can use the two buttons to the right of the list box. To remove an item from the shopping cart, the user can select the item and click the Remove Item button. Or, to remove all the items from the shopping cart, the user can click the Empty Cart button.

If the user wants to add items to the shopping cart, he can click the Continue Shopping button to return to the Order page. Alternatively, the user can click the Check Out button to complete the order. However, the check out method hasn't yet been implemented in this version of the Shopping Cart application. So if the user clicks the Check Out button, a message is displayed to indicate that the check out feature isn't implemented. In a complete application, of course, clicking this button would cause additional pages to be displayed to complete the order.

Like most applications, there are several different ways to implement a shopping cart in ASP.NET. For instance, one design decision is how to save the shopping cart data. For this application, I decided to save the shopping cart data in session state. As an alternative, though, you could save the shopping cart data in a database table. Each approach has its advantages and disadvantages.

A second design decision for a shopping cart application is what type of ASP.NET control to use when you display the shopping cart. To keep this application simple, I used a list box. However, you can create a more advanced shopping cart by using the GridView control that's presented in chapter 14. With this control, you can display the shopping cart data in neatly arranged columns and include buttons or other controls in each row to let the user delete or modify the cart items.

The design of the Cart page

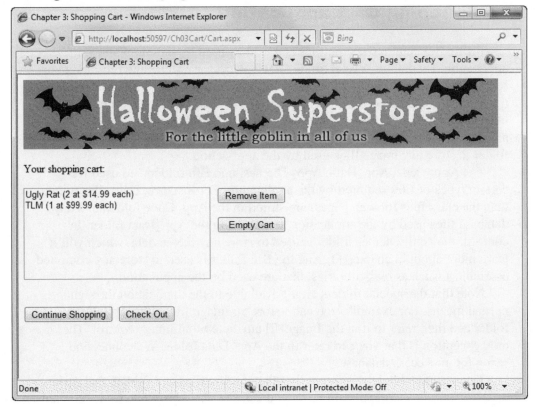

Description

- The Cart page displays the items in the shopping cart in a list box control. To load the list box, it uses the shopping cart information that's saved in session state by the Order page.
- The user can select any item in the shopping cart and then click the Remove Item button to remove the item from the cart. If the user clicks the Remove Item button without selecting an item, a message is displayed that asks the user to select the item to be removed.
- To remove all the items from the cart, the user can click the Empty Cart button.
- After reviewing the cart, the user can click the Continue Shopping button to return to the Order page and order additional products.
- If the user clicks the Check Out button, a message is displayed that indicates that the check out function hasn't been implemented yet.

Figure 3-2   The Cart page of the Shopping Cart application

The files and folders used by the Shopping Cart application

Figure 3-3 summarizes the files and folders used by the Shopping Cart application. By default, Visual Studio 2010 places new web page files and their related code-behind files in the application's root folder, but other files used by the application are placed in special folders. The first table in this figure lists the most commonly used special folders. Besides these folders, though, you can also create your own folders. For example, it's common to create an Images folder to store any image files used by the application.

The App_Code, App_Data, App_Themes, and Bin folders are used for certain types of files required by the application. For instance, class files (other than the class files for web pages) are stored in the App_Code folder, and any database files used by the application are stored in the App_Data folder. In contrast, the App_Themes folder is used to store any theme data, which you'll learn more about in chapter 11. And the Bin folder is used to store any compiled assemblies, such as class libraries, that are used by the application.

Note that the special folders aren't available to the application through normal means. For example, you can't store an image file in the App_Data folder and then refer to it in the ImageUrl attribute of an Image control. The only exception is that you can refer to the App_Data folder in a connection string for an Access database.

The second table in this figure lists the specific files and folders that make up the Shopping Cart application. As you can see, the App_Code folder contains three class files named CartItem.cs, CartItemList.cs, and Product.cs that define the CartItem, CartItemList, and Product classes required by the application. And the App_Data folder contains an Access database named Halloween.mdb.

The Shopping Cart application also includes a folder named Images. This folder includes just one image file, banner.jpg, which provides the banner that's displayed at the top of each page. However, this folder also includes a subfolder named Products, which includes a separate image file for each product in the Products table of the database. Because the Products table includes a column named ImageFile that provides the file name for each product's image, the application can display the correct image for each product.

Finally, the root folder for the application contains two files for each of the application's web pages: one for the page itself, the other for the code-behind file. For example, the Cart.aspx file contains the aspx code that defines the Cart page, and the Cart.aspx.cs file is the code-behind file that contains the C# code for the Cart page.

Please note that the root folder also contains a web.config file. This file is added automatically when you create an application.

The Solution Explorer for the Shopping Cart application

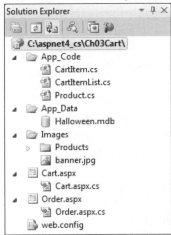

Special folders used in ASP.NET 4 applications

Folder	Description
App_Code	Non-page class files that are compiled together to create a single assembly.
App_Data	Database files used by the application.
App_Themes	Themes used by the application.
Bin	Compiled code used by the application.

Files in the Shopping Cart application

Folder	File	Description
App_Code	CartItem.cs	A class that represents an item in the shopping cart.
App_Code	CartItemList.cs	A class that represents the shopping cart.
App_Code	Product.cs	A class that represents a product.
App_Data	Halloween.mdb	The Access database file that contains the Halloween database.
Images	Banner.jpg	An image file that displays the banner used at the top of each page.
Images\Products	(multiple)	Contains an image file for each product in the database.
(root)	Cart.aspx	The aspx file for the Cart page.
(root)	Cart.aspx.cs	The code-behind file for the Cart page.
(root)	Order.aspx	The aspx file for the Order page.
(root)	Order.aspx.cs	The code-behind file for the Order page.
(root)	web.config	The application configuration file.

Description

- The Images folder is a custom folder that I created to hold the image files used by this application. The Products subfolder contains the image files for the products in the Products table of the Halloween database.

Figure 3-3   The files and folders used by the Shopping Cart application

How to add a class to a web site

As you just saw in the previous figure, the Shopping Cart application requires three business classes named Product, CartItem, and CartItemList. To use these classes with the web site, you can use the techniques presented in figure 3-4.

To add a new class to the web site, you use the Add New Item dialog box shown in this figure. From this dialog box, you select the Class template, enter the name for the class, and then click the Add button. When you do, Visual Studio will create a declaration for the new class. Then, you can complete the class by coding its properties and methods.

Before you create a new class, you'll typically add the special App_Code folder to the web site so that you can add the class directly to this folder. However, you can also add a new class without first adding the App_Code folder. To do that, just select Add New Item from the shortcut menu for the project. Then, when you click the Add button to add the class, Visual Studio will display a dialog box that indicates that the class should be placed in an App_Code folder and asks if you want to place the class in that folder. If you click the Yes button in this dialog box, Visual Studio will create the App_Code folder and place the new class in it.

To add an existing class to a web site, you use the Add Existing Item command as described in this figure. Then, the class file that you select is copied to your web site.

If the existing class you want to use is stored in a *class library*, you can use that class by adding a reference to the class library to your web site as described in this figure. One of the advantages of using class libraries is that the source code is stored in a single location. Then, if you need to modify a class, you can just modify the code in the class library and it will be available to any web sites that use that library. In contrast, if you copy a class to each web site that uses it, you have to modify the code in each web site.

The dialog box for adding a new class to the App_Code folder

Two ways to open the Add New Item dialog box

- Right-click the App_Code folder in the Solution Explorer if it already exists, and then choose Add New Item from the shortcut menu.
- Click on the App_Code folder in the Solution Explorer to select it, and then choose the Website→Add New Item command.

How to add a new class to a web site

- From the Add New Item dialog box, select the Class template, name the class, and click the Add button. Visual Studio will create the declaration for the class.
- If you try to add a class directly to the project instead of to the App_Code folder, Visual Studio will warn you that the class should be placed in the App_Code folder and ask you if you'd like to place the class in this folder. If you click the Yes button, Visual Studio will create the App_Code folder if necessary and place the class in this folder.

How to add an existing class to a web site

- To add a class from another project to a web site, right-click the App_Code folder in the Solution Explorer and select Add Existing Item. Then, locate the class file you want to add, select it, and click the Add button. The file is copied to your project.

How to use a class that's part of a class library

- Right-click the project in the Solution Explorer and select Add Reference from the shortcut menu. Click the Browse tab in the dialog box that's displayed, and then locate and select the dll file for the class library you want to use. The class library is added to the project's Bin folder, which is created if it doesn't already exist. To use the classes in the class library without qualification, add a using statement for the class library.

Figure 3-4   How to add a class to a web site

Six skills for working with multiple web forms

To create a multi-page web site, you need to learn some new skills like how to rename a web form, how to change the starting page for a web site, and how to transfer from one form to another. Before I present these skills, though, I want to show you how to create a web site that contains a number of folders and files by default.

How to create a web site with starting files and folders

Although I used the ASP.NET Empty Web Site template to create all of the web sites in this book, you should know about another template you can use to create a web site that contains a number of starting files and folders. This is the ASP.NET Web Site template, and the files it generates are shown in figure 3-5.

To start, you should notice that the root folder of the web site contains a file named Site.master. This file defines a type of form called a *master form*, and the contents of this form are displayed on each of the other forms in the web site. You'll learn more about working with master forms in chapter 9.

In addition to the master form, the root directory contains two forms named About.aspx and Default.aspx. It also contains a file named Global.asax. You'll learn how to use this file to work with application events in chapter 8.

Next, notice the four forms in the Account folder. These forms provide for adding a user account, logging in to the web site, and changing passwords. You'll see how forms like this work in chapter 19. This folder also contains a web.config file, which applies only to the forms in this folder. In contrast, the web.config file in the root folder applies to the entire web site.

This web site contains three folders in addition to the Account folder. The App_Data folder, as you know, is used to store data files used by the application, such as database files. The Scripts folder contains a JavaScript library called *jQuery* that lets you work with HTML elements. You'll learn more about JavaScript and jQuery in chapter 21. Finally, the Styles folder contains an external style sheet named Site.css. You'll learn more about using external style sheets in chapter 5.

A web site created using the ASP.NET Web Site template

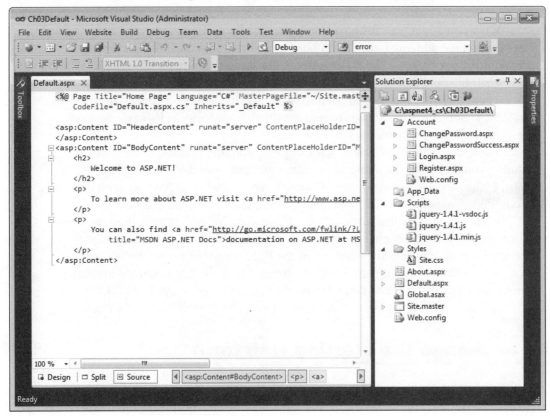

Some of the files used by the web site

Folder	File	Description
Account	ChangePassword.aspx	A form that lets users change their password.
Account	ChangePasswordSuccess.aspx	A form that indicates if a password has been successfully changed.
Account	Login.aspx	A form that lets users log in to an application.
Account	Register.aspx	A form that lets users creates new accounts.
Styles	Site.css	An external style sheet with styles used by the forms.
(root)	About.aspx	A form that lets you enter information about your web site, company, etc.
(root)	Default.aspx	The default form for the web site.
(root)	Global.asax	A file that lets you work with application data.
(root)	Site.master	The master page for the web site.

Description

- When you start a web site from the ASP.NET Web Site template, Visual Studio adds a number of folders and files to the web site. You'll learn how to work with many of the forms, the controls used on the forms, and the files later in this book.

Figure 3-5   How to create a web site with starting files and folders

How to rename a web form

When you add a web form to a web site, the form file is given the name you specify in the Add New Item dialog box. In addition, the partial class that contains the C# code for the form is given the same name, which is usually what you want. In some cases, though, you may need to rename the form file or the form class. In particular, if you use the technique in figure 3-5 to start an ASP.NET web site, you'll want to rename the default form so its name is more descriptive. Figure 3-6 shows you how.

When you change the name of a form file, you might think that Visual Studio would change the name of the class that contains the C# code for the form to the same name. However, it doesn't. To do that, you have to open the Code Editor window for the form and change the name in the class declaration.

When you change the name of a form file, the CodeFile attribute in the Page directive for the page is changed automatically. However, if you change the name of a class, the Inherits attribute in the Page directive is not changed unless you use the Rename command from the smart tag menu that becomes available when you change the class name. If you don't use this command, you'll have to change the Inherits attribute manually when you change the name of a class.

How to change the starting web form

If a web site consists of a single form, that form is displayed by default when you run the application. If a web site contains two or more forms, however, the current form—the one that's selected in the Solution Explorer—is displayed when you run the application. Or, if a form isn't currently selected, the form named Default.aspx is displayed. If the web site doesn't contain a form named Default, a directory listing of the application is displayed.

To make sure that the correct page is displayed when you run an application, you should set the start page for the application. To do that, just right-click on the form in the Solution Explorer and select the Set As Start Page command from the shortcut menu. Note that this only sets the start page that Visual Studio uses when you run an application. It doesn't set the page IIS displays by default when you run the application from a browser outside of Visual Studio. To do that, you have to use IIS. See appendix B (Windows 7 and Windows Vista) or appendix C (Windows XP) for more information.

A web form file being renamed in the Solution Explorer window

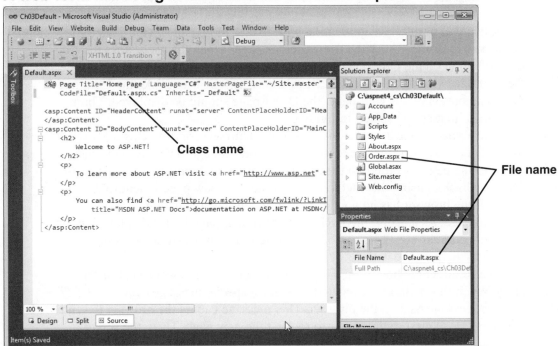

Two ways to rename a web form

- Right-click the form in the Solution Explorer, and then select the Rename command from the shortcut menu. Then, change the name directly in the Solution Explorer window.

- Click on the form in the Solution Explorer to select it. Then, click on it again and change the name directly in the Solution Explorer window.

How to rename the class that contains the C# code for a web form

- Display the code for the form in the Code Editor window. Then, change the name that's used for the form in the class declaration at the beginning of the file.

- Use the Rename command in the smart tag menu that becomes available to change the class name in the Inherits attribute of the Page directive. Alternatively, display the aspx code for the form and then change the Inherits attribute manually.

How to change the starting web form for a web site

- Right-click on the web form that you want to use as the starting form in the Solution Explorer. Then, choose Set As Start Page from the shortcut menu.

Note

- In most cases, you'll give a web form an appropriate name when you add it to the project. If you start a web site from the ASP.NET Web Site template, though, you may want to change the name of the web form that's added by default so it's more descriptive.

Figure 3-6   How to rename a web form and change the starting web form

How to redirect or transfer to another page

When you develop an application with two or more pages, you'll need to know how to display one page from another page. When the user clicks the Add to Cart button on the Order page of the Shopping Cart application, for example, the Cart page should be displayed. Similarly, when the user clicks the Continue Shopping button on the Cart page, the Order page should be displayed. Three ways to do that are presented in figure 3-7.

When you use the Transfer method of the HttpServerUtility class, ASP.NET immediately terminates the execution of the current page. Then, it loads and executes the page specified on the Transfer method and returns it to the browser. The drawback to using this method is that when the new page is sent to the browser, the browser has no way of knowing that the application returned a different page. As a result, the URL for the original page is still displayed in the browser's address box. This can be confusing to the user and prevents the user from bookmarking the page.

The Redirect method of the HttpResponse class works somewhat differently. When this method is executed, it sends a special message called an *HTTP redirect message* back to the browser. This message causes the browser to send a new HTTP request to the server to request the new page. Then, the server processes the page and sends it back to the browser.

Note that because of the way the Redirect method works, it requires an extra round trip to the browser. If this extra round trip will cause a performance problem, you may want to use the Transfer method instead. For most applications, however, the user friendliness of the Redirect method outweighs the small performance gain you get when you use the Transfer method.

Unlike the Transfer and Redirect methods, the RedirectPermanent method, which is new to ASP.NET 4, is typically used when a page is physically moved or renamed within a web site. For example, suppose you create a web site that includes a page named Products.aspx that's stored in the project folder. Later, suppose you decide to create a subfolder named Customer, and you move the Products page to this folder. Then, you can use the RedirectPermanent method as shown in the third example in this figure to redirect to the page. The main advantage of using this method is that search engines will store the new URL. That way, if the page is requested at the old location, it can be displayed from its new location.

The Transfer method of the HttpServerUtility class

Method	Description
`Transfer(URL)`	Terminates the execution of the current page and transfers control to the page at the specified URL.

The Redirect and RedirectPermanent methods of the HttpResponse class

Method	Description
`Redirect(URL)`	Redirects the client to the specified URL and terminates the execution of the current page.
`RedirectPermanent(URL)`	Permanently redirects to the specified URL and terminates the execution of the current page.

Code that transfers control to another page

```
Server.Transfer("Cart.aspx");
```

Code that redirects the client to another page

```
Response.Redirect("Cart.aspx");
```

Code that permanently redirects the client to another page

```
Response.RedirectPermanent("Customer/Products.aspx");
```

Description

- The Transfer method is a member of the HttpServerUtility class, which contains helper methods for processing web requests. To refer to this class, you use the Server property of the page.

- The Redirect and RedirectPermanent methods are members of the HttpResponse class, which contains information about the response. To refer to this class, you use the Response property of the page.

- All three of these methods cause the page specified by the URL to be displayed in the browser. See figure 3-9 for more information on coding URLs.

- When you use the Transfer method, the current page is terminated and a new page is processed in its place. This processing is efficient because it takes place on the server. However, the browser isn't updated to reflect the address of the new page.

- When you use the Redirect method, the server sends a special message called an *HTTP redirect message* to the browser. When the browser receives this message, it sends an HTTP request to the server to request the new page. The server then processes the new page and sends it back to the browser. Because this involves a round trip to the browser, it's less efficient than the Transfer method.

- In general, you should use the Redirect method to display another web page. You should use the Transfer method only if the application's performance is critical.

- If you change the name or location of a page, you can use the RedirectPermanent method to identify the new URL for the page. Then, search engines will store that URL and use it to display the page when they receive a request for the old URL.

Figure 3-7   How to redirect or transfer to another page

How to use cross-page posting

A fourth way to transfer to a different web page is to use *cross-page posting* as described in figure 3-8. To use cross-page posting, you specify the URL of another page in the PostBackUrl property of a button control. Then, when the user clicks the button, an HTTP Post message that contains the URL specified by the PostBackUrl property is sent back to the server. As a result, the page with that URL is loaded and executed instead of the page that was originally displayed.

For example, the Go to Cart button on the Order page uses cross-page posting to go to the Cart page. As a result, the PostBackUrl property of this button is set to Cart.aspx as shown in this figure. Then, when the user clicks the Go to Cart button, ASP.NET loads and executes the Cart.aspx page instead of the Order.aspx page.

Notice that the URL in the PostBackUrl property of this control starts with a tilde (~) operator. This operator is added automatically when you set the PostBackUrl property from the Properties window, and you'll learn more about it in the next topic.

If the user enters data into one or more controls on a page that uses cross-page posting, you can use the PreviousPage property to retrieve the data entered by the user. As the code example in this figure shows, you should first check to make sure that the PreviousPage property refers to a valid object. If this property doesn't refer to a valid object, it means that either the page isn't being loaded as the result of a cross-page posting, or the request came from another web site. In either case, no previous page is available.

If the PreviousPage property refers to a valid object, you can use the FindControl method to find a control on the previous page. Then, you can cast it to a text box (if the control is a text box). Finally, you can use the Text property to retrieve the data that the text box contains.

Because of the extra programming required to retrieve data entered by the user, cross-page posting is best used when no user input needs to be processed. For instance, since no data needs to be processed when the user clicks the Go to Cart button, I used cross-page posting instead of Response.Redirect or Server.Transfer. However, I used Response.Redirect for the Add to Cart button on the Order page so I could easily retrieve the selected product and the quantity entered by the user.

The PostBackUrl property of the Button control

Property	Description
PostBackUrl	Specifies the URL of the page that should be requested when the user clicks the button.

Members of the Page class used with cross-page posting

Property	Description
PreviousPage	Returns a Page object that represents the previous page.

Method	Description
FindControl(id)	Returns a Control object with the specified id. If the control is a text box, you can cast the Control object to TextBox, then use the Text property to access the data entered by the user.

The aspx code for a button that posts to a different page

```
<asp:Button ID="btnCart" runat="server" Text="Go to Cart"
    CausesValidation="False" PostBackUrl="~/Cart.aspx" />
```

Code that retrieves data from the previous page

```
protected void Page_Load(object sender, EventArgs e)
{
    if (PreviousPage != null)
    {
        TextBox txtQuantity =
            (TextBox) PreviousPage.FindControl("txtQuantity");
        lblQuantity.Text = txtQuantity.Text;
    }
}
```

Description

- *Cross-page posting* lets you use the PostBackUrl property of a button to specify the page that should be requested when the user clicks the button.

- When you post back to another page, the previous page is available via the PreviousPage property. Then, you can use the FindControl method to retrieve data entered by the user.

- In general, cross-page posting is more efficient than the Server.Transfer and Response.Redirect methods. However, cross-page posting makes it more difficult to retrieve data from the original page.

- If you don't need to retrieve data from the original page, cross-page posting is clearly better than the Server.Transfer and Response.Redirect methods.

Figure 3-8   How to use cross-page posting

How to code absolute and relative URLs

In chapter 1, you learned about the basic components of a URL. The URLs you saw in that chapter were all *absolute URLs*. An absolute URL includes the domain name of the web site. When coded within a Transfer or Redirect method, an absolute URL lets you display a page at another web site. For example, the first two statements in figure 3-9 display a page at the web site with the domain name www.murach.com. The first statement displays a page named Default.aspx in the root directory of the web site. The second statement displays a page named Search.aspx in the Books directory of the web site.

To display a page within the same web site, you can use a *relative URL*. This type of URL specifies the location of the page relative to the directory that contains the current page. This is illustrated by the third and fourth statements in this figure. The third statement displays a page that's stored in the same directory as the current page. The fourth statement displays a page in the Login subdirectory of the directory that contains the current page.

The next two statements show how you can use a relative URL to navigate up the directory structure from the current directory. To navigate up one directory, you code two periods followed by a slash as shown in the fifth statement. To navigate up two directories, you code two periods and a slash followed by two more periods and a slash as shown in the sixth statement. To navigate up additional directories, you code two periods and a slash for each directory.

To navigate to the root directory for the host, you code a slash as shown in the seventh statement. You can also navigate to a directory within the root directory by coding the path for that directory following the slash as shown in the eighth statement.

In addition to coding URLs on Transfer, Redirect, and RedirectPermanent methods, you can code them for the attributes of some server controls. This is illustrated in the last two examples in this figure. The next to last example shows how you might set the PostBackUrl attribute of a button control. And the last example shows how you might set the ImageUrl attribute of an image control.

Notice that both of these URLs start with a tilde (~) operator. This operator causes the URL to be based on the root directory of the web site. For example, the Cart.aspx file in the first URL is located directly in the root directory, and the banner.jpg file in the second URL is located in the Images subdirectory of the root directory.

Although I could have used relative URLs in these examples, it's easier to maintain URLs that use the tilde operator when you move pages or files from one folder to another. That's because it's easier to maintain a URL that's relative to the root directory of the web site than it is to maintain a URL that's relative to another page. So I recommend you use the tilde operator whenever you code a URL for an attribute of a server control.

Examples of absolute and relative URLs

Statements that use absolute URLs

```
Response.Redirect("http://www.murach.com/Default.aspx");
Response.Redirect("http://www.murach.com/Books/Search.aspx");
```

Statements that use relative URLs that are based on the current directory

```
Response.Redirect("Checkout.aspx");
Response.Redirect("Login/Register.aspx");
```

Statements that use relative URLs that navigate up the directory structure

```
Response.Redirect("../Register.aspx");
Response.Redirect("../../Register.aspx");
Response.Redirect("/Register.aspx");
Response.Redirect("/Login/Register.aspx");
```

Server control attributes that use URLs that are based on the root directory of the current web site

```
PostBackUrl="~/Cart.aspx"
ImageUrl="~/Images/banner.jpg"
```

Description

- When you code an *absolute URL*, you code the complete URL including the domain name for the site. Absolute URLs let you display pages at other web sites.

- When you code a *relative URL*, you base it on the current directory, which is the directory that contains the current page.

- To go to the root directory for the host, you code a slash. Then, you can code one or more directories after the slash.

- To go up one level from the current directory, you code two periods and a slash. To go up two levels, you code two periods and a slash followed by two more periods and a slash. And so on.

- If you're specifying a URL for the attribute of a server control, you can use the web application root operator (~) to base the URL on the root of the web site.

Figure 3-9   How to code absolute and relative URLs

How to create and use data sources

To connect to a database and work with its data, you can use an ASP.NET control called a *data source*. To illustrate how this works, the following topics show you how to create a data source that connects to a Microsoft Access database and bind it to a drop-down list. Keep in mind, though, that there's much more to working with data sources than these topics let on. That's why section 3 of this book is devoted to the use of data sources and databases.

How to create an Access data source

ASP.NET 4 provides several data source controls in the Data group of the Toolbox. The simplest of these controls is AccessDataSource, which is designed to retrieve data from a Microsoft Access database file. Figure 3-10 shows how to create this type of data source.

Before you can use an Access data source, though, you must first create an Access database and add it to the App_Data folder of the web site. As I've mentioned before, the Shopping Cart application for this chapter uses a database named Halloween.mdb.

To create an AccessDataSource control, open the Data group of the Toolbox, drag the AccessDataSource control, and drop it onto the form. Since the data source isn't displayed on the page when the application is run, it doesn't matter where you drop the data source on the page. However, if the data source is going to be bound to a web control, it makes sense to place it near that control.

When you drop the Access data source on the page, a smart tag menu will appear. Then, choose the Configure Data Source command to bring up the first page of the Configure Data Source wizard, which is shown in this figure. From this dialog box, select the Access database file you want to use for the data source.

Once you've selected the database file for the data source, you must configure the data source as described in the next figure. Then, you can bind it to the drop-down list as described in figure 3-12.

The first page of the Configure Data Source wizard

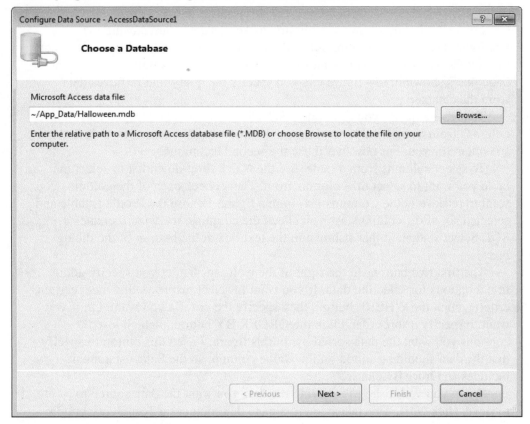

How to create an Access data source

1. In the Web Forms Designer, open the Data group of the Toolbox and drag the AccessDataSource control to the form.

2. Select Configure Data Source from the smart tag menu of the data source control to display the Configure Data Source dialog box.

3. Identify the Access database that you want to use in the App_Data folder and click Next. Then, complete the Configure Data Source wizard as described in the next figure.

Description

- Before you can create an Access *data source*, you must add the Access database file to the App_Data folder.

- The Shopping Cart application uses an AccessDataSource control to provide the list of products that's displayed in the drop-down list. This control reads data from a Microsoft Access database file.

- Although data source controls are visible in the Web Forms Designer, they don't render any HTML to the browser. As a result, they aren't visible when the application runs.

Figure 3-10   How to create an Access data source

How to configure an Access data source

Figure 3-11 shows how to configure an Access data source using the Configure Data Source wizard. After the first page of this wizard lets you select the Access database file you want to use (as in the previous figure), the second page that's shown in this figure lets you specify the query that retrieves data from the database.

To create a query, you can code a SQL Select statement. Or, you can choose columns from a single table or view and let the wizard generate the Select statement for you. For now, we'll use the second technique.

To select columns from a table, use the Name drop-down list to select the table you want to select the columns from. Then, check each of the columns you want to retrieve in the Columns list. In this figure, I chose the Products table and selected six of the columns. As you check the columns, the wizard creates a SQL Select statement that's shown in the text box at the bottom of the dialog box.

The first two buttons to the right of the Columns list let you specify additional options for selecting data. If you want to select just rows that meet certain criteria, click the WHERE button, then specify the criteria you want. Or, if you want to specify a sort order, click the ORDER BY button, then choose the columns you want the data sorted by. In this figure, I used this button to specify that the data should be sorted on the Name column, so the Select statement includes an Order By clause.

When you've finished specifying the data you want the data source to retrieve, click Next. This takes you to a page that includes a Test Query button. If you click this button, the wizard immediately retrieves the data that you have specified. You can then look over this data to make sure it's what you expected. If it isn't, click the Back button and adjust the query as needed.

The second page of the Configure Data Source wizard

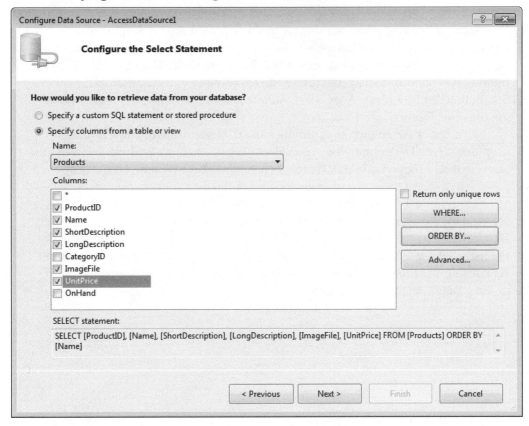

The aspx code for an Access data source control

```
<asp:AccessDataSource ID="AccessDataSource1" runat="server"
    DataFile="~/App_Data/Halloween.mdb"
    SelectCommand="SELECT [ProductID], [Name], [ShortDescription],
        [LongDescription], [ImageFile], [UnitPrice]
        FROM [Products] ORDER BY [Name]">
</asp:AccessDataSource>
```

Description

- The Configure Data Source wizard lets you create a query using SQL. You can specify the Select statement for the query directly, or you can let the wizard construct the Select statement from your specifications.

- You can click the WHERE button to specify one or more conditions that will be used to select the records.

- You can click the ORDER BY button to specify a sort order for the records.

- You can click the Advanced button to include Insert, Update, and Delete statements for the data source.

Figure 3-11   How to configure an Access data source

How to bind a drop-down list to a data source

Once you've created a data source, you can bind a drop-down list to it as shown in figure 3-12. To start, select the Choose Data Source command from the smart tag menu for the drop-down list. Then, when the Data Source Configuration Wizard is displayed, choose the data source in the first drop-down list. In this figure, I chose AccessDataSource1, the data source that I created in the previous figures.

Next, select the column that provides the data you want displayed in the drop-down list. The column that you select here is used for the drop-down list's DataTextField property. In this figure, I chose the Name column so the drop-down list displays the name of each product in the data source.

Finally, select the column that you want to use as the value of the item selected by the user. The column you select here is used for the list's DataValueField property, and the value of that column can be retrieved by using the list's SelectedValue property. In this figure, I selected the ProductID column. As a result, the program can use the SelectedValue property to determine the ID of the product selected by the user.

The Data Source Configuration Wizard dialog box

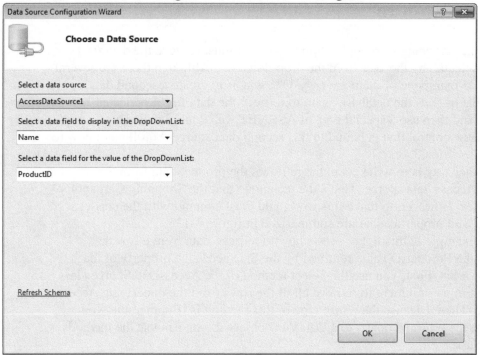

The aspx code for a drop-down list that's bound to a data source

```
<asp:DropDownList ID="ddlProducts" Runat="server" Width="150px"
    AutoPostBack="True" DataSourceID="AccessDataSource1"
    DataTextField="Name" DataValueField="ProductID" >
</asp:DropDownList>
```

Attributes for binding a drop-down list

Attribute	Description
DataSourceID	The ID of the data source that the drop-down list should be bound to.
DataTextField	The name of the data source field that should be displayed in the drop-down list.
DataValueField	The name of the data source field whose value should be returned by the SelectedValue property of the drop-down list.

Description

- You can bind a drop-down list to a data source so the list automatically displays data retrieved by the data source.
- You can use the Data Source Configuration Wizard dialog box to configure the data binding for a drop-down list. To display this dialog box, select the Choose Data Source command from the list's smart tag menu.
- Alternatively, you can use the Properties window or edit the aspx code directly to set the data binding attributes for a drop-down list.

Figure 3-12   How to bind a drop-down list to a data source

How to use C# code to get data from a data source

For the Shopping Cart application to work, it must retrieve the data for the product selected by the user from the drop-down list. Although there are several ways to do that, none of them are easy. One way is to create a second data source that queries the database again to retrieve the data for the selected product, and then use a special type of ASP.NET web control called a DetailsView control that is bound to this second data source. You'll learn how to do that in section 3.

Another way is to write code that retrieves the product data from the existing Access data source. That's the technique that the Shopping Cart application uses. However, to make this work, you must contend with the classes, methods, and properties that are summarized in figure 3-13.

The example in this figure shows how to retrieve data from a row that matches the ProductID value returned by the SelectedValue property of the drop-down list. First, you use the Select method of the AccessDataSource class with the Empty argument to retrieve all of the rows from the underlying Access database. Then, because the return type of this method is IEnumerable, you must cast the returned object to a DataView object so you can use the methods of that class.

Once you have the rows in a DataView object, you can use the RowFilter property to filter the rows so only the row selected by the user is available. To do that, you build a simple *filter expression* that lists the column name and value. For example, ProductID='jar01' filters the data view so only the row whose ProductID column contains jar01 is included.

Once you've filtered the DataView object so only the selected row is available, you can use two indexes to retrieve the data for a column. The first index identifies the only row that has been selected, so its value is 0, and this row is returned as a DataRowView object. Then, you can specify the index of the column you want to retrieve from the row, either as a string that provides the column name or as the index position of the column. In this example, column names are used for the columns that need to be retrieved. (Although using an index value is a little more efficient, specifying the column name makes the code more understandable.)

Once you establish the row and column index for each value, all that remains is to cast this value to the appropriate type. In this example, all of the columns except the UnitPrice column are cast to strings using their ToString methods, and the UnitPrice column is cast to a decimal type.

Please note that all six of the values that are retrieved are stored in the Product object that's instantiated by the fourth statement in this example. If you want to review the code for this class, you can look ahead to figure 3-16.

The Select method of the AccessDataSource class

Method	Description
`Select(selectOptions)`	Returns an IEnumerable object that contains the rows retrieved from the underlying Access database. To get all the rows, the selectOptions parameter should be DataSourceSelectArguments.Empty.

Members of the DataView class for retrieving rows

Property	Description
`RowFilter`	A string that is used to filter the rows retrieved from the Access database.

Indexer	Description
`[index]`	Returns a DataRowView object for the row at the specified index position.

Members of the DataRowView class for retrieving columns

Indexer	Description
`[index]`	Returns the value of the column at the specified index position as an object.
`[name]`	Returns the value of the column with the specified name as an object.

Code that gets product information for the selected product

```
DataView productsTable = (DataView)
    AccessDataSource1.Select(DataSourceSelectArguments.Empty);
productsTable.RowFilter =
    "ProductID = '" + ddlProducts.SelectedValue + "'";
DataRowView row = (DataRowView) productsTable[0];

Product p = new Product();
p.ProductID = row["ProductID"].ToString();
p.Name = row["Name"].ToString();
p.ShortDescription = row["ShortDescription"].ToString();
p.LongDescription = row["LongDescription"].ToString();
p.UnitPrice = (decimal)row["UnitPrice"];
p.ImageFile = row["ImageFile"].ToString();
```

Description

- The Select method of the AccessDataSource class returns an IEnumerable object that contains the rows retrieved from the Access database. To work with these rows, you must cast the IEnumerable object to a DataView object.

- The RowFilter property of the DataView class lets you filter rows in the data view based on a criteria string.

- You can use the indexer of the DataView class to return a specific row as a DataRowView object. Then, you can use the indexer of the DataRowView class to return the value of a specified column. The indexer for the column can be an integer that represents the column's position in the row or a string that represents the name of the column.

- The DataView and DataRowView classes are stored in the System.Data namespace.

Figure 3-13   How to use C# code to get data from a data source

How to use session state

In chapter 1, you learned that HTTP is a stateless protocol. You also learned that ASP.NET uses *session state* to keep track of each user session and that you can use session state to maintain program values across executions of an application. Now, you'll learn more about how session state works and how you use it.

How session state works

Figure 3-14 shows how session state solves the problem of state management for ASP.NET applications. As you can see, session state tracks individual user sessions by creating a *session state object* for each user's session. This object contains a session ID that uniquely identifies the session. This session ID is passed back to the browser along with the HTTP response. Then, if the browser makes another request, the session ID is included in the request so ASP.NET can identify the session. ASP.NET then matches the session with the session state object that was previously saved.

By default, ASP.NET sends the session ID to the browser as a *cookie*. Then, when the browser sends another request to the server, it automatically includes the cookie that contains the session ID with the request. In chapter 8, you'll learn more about how cookies work. You'll also learn how to implement session state by including the session ID in the URL for a page instead of in a cookie.

Although ASP.NET automatically uses session state to track user sessions, you can also use it to store your own data across executions of an application. This figure lists three typical reasons for doing that. First, you can use session state to maintain information about the user. After a user logs in to an application, for example, you can use the login information to retrieve information about the user from a file or a database. Then, you can store that information in the session state object so it's available each time the application is executed.

Second, you can use session state to save objects that the user is working with. For example, consider a maintenance application that lets the user change customer records. In that case, you can save the customer record that's currently being modified in the session state object so it's available the next time the application is executed.

Third, you can use session state to keep track of the operation a user is currently performing. If a maintenance application lets the user add or change customer records, for example, you can save an item in the session state object that indicates if the user is currently adding or changing a record. That way, the application can determine how to proceed each time it's executed.

How ASP.NET maintains the state of a session

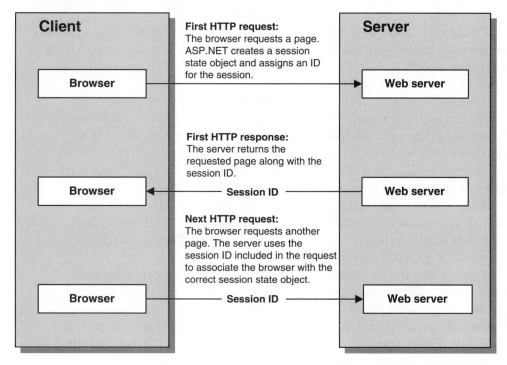

Description

- ASP.NET uses *session state* to track the state of each user of an application. To do that, it creates a *session state object*.
- The session state object includes a session ID that's sent back to the browser as a *cookie*. Then, the browser automatically returns the session ID cookie to the server with each request so the server can associate the browser with an existing session state object.
- If you want your application to work on browsers that don't support cookies, you can configure ASP.NET to encode the session ID in the URL for each page of the application. For more information, see chapter 8.
- You can use the session state object to store and retrieve items across executions of an application.

Typical uses for session state

- **To keep information about the user**, such as the user's name or whether the user has registered.
- **To save objects the user is working with**, such as a shopping cart or a customer record.
- **To keep track of pending operations**, such as what steps the user has completed while placing an order.

Figure 3-14   How session state works

How to work with data in session state

Figure 3-15 shows how you can use the session state object to store application data. To do that, you use the members of this object, which is created from the HttpSessionState class. To access this object from a web form, you use the Session property of the page.

The session state object contains a collection of items that consist of the item names and their values. One way to add an item to this collection is to use the indexer as shown in the first example. Here, an object named cart is assigned to a session state item named Cart. If the Cart item doesn't exist when this statement is executed, it will be created. Otherwise, the value of the Cart item will be updated.

Another way to add an item to the session state collection is to use the Add method, as illustrated in the second example. Just as when you use the indexer, if the item already exists, it's updated when the Add method is executed. Otherwise, it's added to the collection.

You can also use the indexer to retrieve the value of an item from the session state collection as shown in the third example. Here, the value of the Cart item is retrieved and assigned to the cart variable. Since the value of a session state item is stored as an Object type, you typically cast it to the appropriate type. In this example, the value of the Cart item is cast to a sorted list because the cart variable it's assigned to is defined as a sorted list.

Because the session state object uses valuable server memory, you should avoid using it to store large items. Or, if you must store large items in session state, you should remove the items as soon as you're done with them. To do that, you use the Remove method as illustrated in the fourth example in this figure.

The first four examples in this figure use the Session property of the page to access the session state object. Because Session is a property of the System.Web.UI.Page class, however, you can only use this property from a class that inherits the System.Web.UI.Page class. In other words, you can only use it from a code-behind file for a page. To access session state from a class that doesn't inherit the System.Web.UI.Page class, such as a database or business class, you use the Session property of the HttpContext object for the current request. To get this HttpContext object, you use the Current property of the HttpContext class as illustrated in the last example in this figure.

Common members of the HttpSessionState class

Property	Description
`SessionID`	The unique ID of the session.
`Count`	The number of items in the session state collection.

Indexer	Description
`[name]`	The value of the session state item with the specified name.

Method	Description
`Add(name, value)`	Adds an item to the session state collection.
`Clear()`	Removes all items from the session state collection.
`Remove(name)`	Removes the item with the specified name from the session state collection.

A statement that adds or updates a session state item

```
Session["Cart"] = cart;
```

Another way to add or update a session state item

```
Session.Add("Cart", cart);
```

A statement that retrieves the value of a session state item

```
SortedList cart = (SortedList) Session["Cart"];
```

A statement that removes an item from session state

```
Session.Remove("Cart");
```

A statement that retrieves the value of a session state item from a class that doesn't inherit System.Web.UI.Page

```
SortedList cart = (SortedList) HttpContext.Current.Session["Cart"];
```

Description

- The session state object is created from the HttpSessionState class, which defines a collection of session state items.

- To access the session state object from the code-behind file for a web form, use the Session property of the page.

- To access the session state object from a class other than the code-behind file for a web form, use the Current property of the HttpContext class to get the HttpContext object for the current request. This object contains information about the HTTP request. Then, use the Session property of the HttpContext class to get the session state object.

- By default, session state objects are maintained in server memory. As a result, you should avoid storing large items in session state.

Figure 3-15   How to work with data in session state

The code for the Shopping Cart application

Now that you've learned the basic skills for developing a multi-form application, you're ready to see all the aspx and C# code for the Shopping Cart application. Because you should be able to follow it without much trouble, I'll keep the descriptions to a minimum.

The code for the Product class

Figure 3-16 shows the C# code for the Product class. This class represents a product that the user can order from the Shopping Cart application. It has a property for each of the columns in the Products table except CategoryID and OnHand.

The code for the CartItem class

Figure 3-16 also shows the code for the CartItem class, which represents one item in the shopping cart. After the parameterless constructor, the next constructor for this class accepts two parameters that are used to initialize the Product and Quantity properties. These properties hold the Product object and quantity for the cart item.

In addition to the constructors and properties, the CartItem class includes two methods. The first one, AddQuantity, is used to add the quantity that's passed to it to the cart item. This method is called when the user adds a quantity to the cart for a product that's already in the cart. The second one, Display, returns a string that formats the data in a cart item so it can be displayed in one line of the list box on the Cart page.

The code for the Product class

```
public class Product
{
    public string ProductID { get; set; };
    public string Name { get; set; };
    public string ShortDescription { get; set; };
    public string LongDescription { get; set; };
    public decimal UnitPrice { get; set; };
    public string ImageFile { get; set; };
}
```

The code for the CartItem class

```
public class CartItem
{

    public CartItem() {}

    public CartItem(Product product, int quantity)
    {
        this.Product = product;
        this.Quantity = quantity;
    }

    public Product Product { get; set; };
    public int Quantity { get; set; };

    public void AddQuantity(int quantity)
    {
        this.Quantity += quantity;
    }

    public string Display()
    {
        string displayString =
            Product.Name + " (" + Quantity.ToString()
            + " at " + Product.UnitPrice.ToString("c") + " each)";

        return displayString;
    }
}
```

Description

- The Product class represents a product.
- The CartItem class represents a product that the user has added to the shopping cart plus the quantity ordered.
- For simplicity, the Product and CartItem classes are defined with auto-implemented properties. In a production application, however, they would most likely be defined with private fields that are accessible through standard properties.

Figure 3-16   The code for the Product and CartItem classes

The code for the CartItemList class

Figure 3-17 shows the code for the CartItemList class, which represents a list of CartItem objects. This list is defined in a private field named cartItems at the beginning of the class. Then, the constructor for this class initializes this field with a new List<CartItem> object.

Next, the Count property is a read-only property that simply returns a count of the items in the list. It's followed by an overloaded indexer. The first indexer gets and sets a cart item in the list using the index that's passed to it. This indexer is used to get the items in the cart when they're displayed in the list box on the Cart page. The second indexer is a read-only indexer that gets a cart item using the product ID that's passed to it. This indexer is used to determine if a product is already in the cart. Notice that if a product with the specified ID isn't found, this indexer returns a null value.

The first method, GetCart, gets the CartItemList object that's stored in session state. But first, it checks to see if a Session state item named "Cart" is equal to null. If it is, it means that a cart hasn't yet been created for the current user. Then, a new CartItemList object is created and added to Session state.

You should notice two things about this method. First, it's a static method. That makes sense because it simply retrieves the CartItemList object that's stored in session state. It doesn't work with the current CartItemList object. Second, because this code is not in a code-behind file, you can't use the Session property of the page to refer to the session state object. Instead, you have to refer to the session state object through the HttpContext object for the current request.

The next method, AddItem, adds a new cart item to the cart item list. It accepts a Product object and quantity as parameters. Then, it creates a CartItem object from these values and adds the cart item to the cart item list.

The last two methods, RemoveAt and Clear, should be easy to understand. The RemoveAt method simply removes the cart item at the given index from the list of cart items. And the Clear method removes all the cart items from the list.

Notice that the methods that add and remove items from the cart don't refer to session state directly. That's because session state is an object. So when you retrieve the cart from session state, you store it in a reference type variable. Then, when you use that variable to add and remove items from the cart, the session state object is updated automatically. This will make more sense when you see the code for the Order and Cart pages.

The code for the CartItemList class

```
using system;
using System.Collections.Generic;
using System.Web;

public class CartItemList
{
    private List<CartItem> cartItems;

    public CartItemList()
    {
        cartItems = new List<CartItem>();
    }

    public int Count
    {
        get { return cartItems.Count; }
    }

    public CartItem this[int index]
    {
        get { return cartItems[index]; }
        set { cartItems[index] = value; }
    }

    public CartItem this[String id]
    {
        get {
            foreach (CartItem c in cartItems)
                if (c.Product.ProductID == id) return c;
            return null;
        }
    }

    public static CartItemList GetCart()
    {
        CartItemList cart = (CartItemList) HttpContext.Current.Session["Cart"];
        if (cart == null)
            HttpContext.Current.Session["Cart"] = new CartItemList();
        return (CartItemList) HttpContext.Current.Session["Cart"];
    }

    public void AddItem(Product product, int quantity)
    {
        CartItem c = new CartItem(product, quantity);
        cartItems.Add(c);
    }

    public void RemoveAt(int index)
    {
        cartItems.RemoveAt(index);
    }

    public void Clear()
    {
        cartItems.Clear();
    }
}
```

Figure 3-17   The code for the CartItemList class

The aspx code for the Order page

Figure 3-18 shows the aspx code for the Order page, which is shown in its rendered form in figure 3-1. Since all of the code for this page is generated by the Web Forms Designer, you don't have to code any of it. To make it easier to follow this code, I highlighted the start tag and ID attribute for each of the server controls that appear on this page.

The first group of four controls defines an image that's used for the banner, a label with the text "Please select a product:", a drop-down list named ddlProducts, and the Access data source that the drop-down list is bound to. Here, the AutoPostBack attribute for the drop-down list is set to True so the page will be posted back to the server when the user selects a product. In addition, the DataSourceID, DataTextField, and DataValueField attributes specify how the drop-down list is bound to the Access data source.

The second group of server controls displays product information using several labels and an image control. A table is used to manage the layout of these controls so the image can be displayed to the right of the labels. To accomplish that, the rowspan attribute of the second and third cells of the first row is set to 4. That means that these cells span all four rows of the table. The second cell is used to add space between the first and third columns of the table and doesn't contain any data. The third cell contains the image for a product. In addition to the rowspan attribute, this cell includes a valign attribute that causes the image to be displayed at the top of the cell rather than in the middle of the cell.

The aspx file for the Order page (Order.aspx)   **Page 1**

```
<%@ Page Language="C#" AutoEventWireup="true" CodeFile="Order.aspx.cs"
Inherits="Order" %>

<!DOCTYPE html PUBLIC "-//W3C//DTD XHTML 1.0 Transitional//EN"
"http://www.w3.org/TR/xhtml1/DTD/xhtml1-transitional.dtd">

<html xmlns="http://www.w3.org/1999/xhtml">
<head runat="server">
    <title>Chapter 3: Shopping Cart</title>
    <style type="text/css">
        .style1 {
            width: 100%;
        }
        .style2 {
            width: 250px;
        }
        .style3 {
            width: 20px;
        }
    </style>
</head>
<body>
    <form id="form1" runat="server">
    <div>
        <asp:Image ID="Image1" runat="server"
            ImageUrl="~/Images/banner.jpg" /><br /><br />
        <asp:Label ID="Label1" runat="server"
            Text="Please select a product:"></asp:Label> 
        <asp:DropDownList ID="ddlProducts" runat="server"
            DataSourceID="AccessDataSource1" DataTextField="Name"
            DataValueField="ProductID" Width="150px" AutoPostBack="True">
        </asp:DropDownList>
        <asp:AccessDataSource ID="AccessDataSource1" runat="server"
            DataFile="~/App_Data/Halloween.mdb"
            SelectCommand="SELECT [ProductID], [Name], [ShortDescription],
                [LongDescription], [ImageFile], [UnitPrice]
                FROM [Products] ORDER BY [Name]">
        </asp:AccessDataSource><br />
        <table class="style1">
            <tr>
                <td class="style2">
                    <asp:Label ID="lblName" runat="server"
                        Font-Bold="True" Font-Size="Larger">
                    </asp:Label>
                </td>
                <td class="style3" rowspan="4">
                </td>
                <td rowspan="4" valign="top">
                    <asp:Image ID="imgProduct" runat="server" Height="200px" />
                </td>
            </tr>
```

Description

- The Order.aspx page displays a drop-down list that is bound to an Access data source.
- A table is used to specify the layout of the label and image controls that display information about the product selected by the user.

Figure 3-18   The aspx code for the Order page (part 1 of 2)

The third group of server controls defines a label with the text "Quantity:" followed by a text box named txtQuantity. Then, two validator controls provide data validation for the text box. Notice that both specify txtQuantity in the ControlToValidate attribute and Dynamic in the Display attribute. The range validator also provides MaximumValue, MinimumValue, and Type attributes, which specify that the quantity must be an integer in the range from 1 to 500.

The last group of controls for this page contains the two buttons. Here, the OnClick attribute names the event handler that will be executed when this button is clicked. In contrast, the btnCart button uses the PostBackUrl property to indicate that when the user clicks the button, the Cart.aspx page should be requested rather than the Order.aspx page. Since the CausesValidation attribute is set to False, the validation controls for the txtQuantity text box won't be executed when this button is clicked.

The aspx file for the Order page (Order.aspx)   **Page 2**

```
            <tr>
                <td class="style2">
                    <asp:Label ID="lblShortDescription" runat="server">
                    </asp:Label>
                </td>
            </tr>
            <tr>
                <td class="style2">
                    <asp:Label ID="lblLongDescription" runat="server">
                    </asp:Label>
                </td>
            </tr>
            <tr>
                <td class="style2">
                    <asp:Label ID="lblUnitPrice" runat="server"
                        Font-Bold="True" Font-Size="Larger">
                    </asp:Label>
                    <asp:Label ID="Label2" runat="server" Text="each"
                        Font-Bold="True" Font-Size="Larger">
                    </asp:Label>
                </td>
            </tr>
        </table>
        <br />
        <asp:Label ID="Label3" runat="server" Text="Quantity:"></asp:Label> 
        <asp:TextBox ID="txtQuantity" runat="server" Width="40px">
        </asp:TextBox>
        <asp:RequiredFieldValidator ID="RequiredFieldValidator1"
            runat="server" ControlToValidate="txtQuantity" Display="Dynamic"
            ErrorMessage="Quantity is a required field." ForeColor="Green">
        </asp:RequiredFieldValidator>
        <asp:RangeValidator ID="RangeValidator1" runat="server"
            ControlToValidate="txtQuantity" Display="Dynamic"
            ErrorMessage="Quantity must range from 1 to 500."
            MaximumValue="500" MinimumValue="1" Type="Integer" ForeColor="Green">
        </asp:RangeValidator><br /><br />
        <asp:Button ID="btnAdd" runat="server" Text="Add to Cart"
            OnClick="btnAdd_Click" /> 
        <asp:Button ID="btnCart" runat="server" CausesValidation="False"
            PostBackUrl="~/Cart.aspx" Text="Go to Cart" />
    </div>
    </form>
</body>
</html>
```

Description

- The txtQuantity text box lets the user enter the order quantity of the selected item. A RequiredFieldValidator and a RangeValidator are used to ensure that the user enters valid data in this text box.

- The OnClick attribute of the btnAdd button indicates that an event handler named btnAdd_Click will be executed when this button is clicked.

- The btnCart button uses cross-page posting to post to the Cart.aspx page.

Figure 3-18   The aspx code for the Order page (part 2 of 2)

The C# code for the Order page

Figure 3-19 presents the code for the Order page's code-behind file, Order.aspx.cs. This code starts by declaring a class-level variable that will hold a Product object that represents the item that the user has selected from the drop-down list. This variable is assigned a Product object by the second statement in the Page_Load method, which gets the Product object by calling the GetSelectedProduct method.

The Page_Load method starts by calling the DataBind method of the drop-down list if the page is being loaded for the first time (IsPostBack isn't True). This method binds the drop-down list to the Access data source, which causes the data specified in the SelectCommand property of the data source to be retrieved. Then, this method calls the GetSelectedProduct method, which gets the data for the selected product from the Access data source and returns a Product object. That object is stored in the selectedProduct variable, which is available to all of the methods in this class. Finally, the Page_Load method formats the labels and the image control to display the data for the selected product. At that point, the Order page is sent back to the user's browser.

For many applications, you don't need to call the DataBind method in the Page_Load method when you use data binding. Instead, you let ASP.NET automatically bind any data-bound controls. Unfortunately, this automatic data binding doesn't occur until after the Page_Load method has been executed. In this case, because the GetSelectedProduct method won't work unless the drop-down list has already been bound, I had to call the DataBind method to force the data binding to occur earlier than it normally would.

If the user clicks the Add to Cart button, the btnAdd_Click method is executed. After checking that the page is valid, this method calls the GetCart method of the CartItemList class to get the cart that's stored in session state. Remember that if a cart doesn't already exist in session state, this method creates a new CartItemList object and stores it in session state. Also remember that GetCart is a static method, so you call it from the class rather than an object created from the class.

Next, this method determines whether the cart already contains an item for the selected product. To do that, it uses the indexer of the CartItemList object to get the CartItem object with the product ID of the product. If an item isn't found with this product ID, the AddItem method of the CartItemList object is called to add an item with the selected product and quantity to the list. In contrast, if an item is found with the product ID, the AddQuantity method of the CartItem object is called to add the quantity to the item. Finally, this method uses Response.Redirect to go to the Cart.aspx page.

The code-behind file for the Order page (Order.aspx.cs)

```
using System;
using System.Web.UI;
using System.Data;

public partial class Order : System.Web.UI.Page
{
    private Product selectedProduct;

    protected void Page_Load(object sender, EventArgs e)
    {
        if (!IsPostBack)
            ddlProducts.DataBind();

        selectedProduct = this.GetSelectedProduct();
        lblName.Text = selectedProduct.Name;
        lblShortDescription.Text = selectedProduct.ShortDescription;
        lblLongDescription.Text = selectedProduct.LongDescription;
        lblUnitPrice.Text = selectedProduct.UnitPrice.ToString("c");
        imgProduct.ImageUrl = "Images/Products/" + selectedProduct.ImageFile;
    }

    private Product GetSelectedProduct()
    {
        DataView productsTable = (DataView)
            AccessDataSource1.Select(DataSourceSelectArguments.Empty);
        productsTable.RowFilter =
            "ProductID = '" + ddlProducts.SelectedValue + "'";
        DataRowView row = (DataRowView)productsTable[0];

        Product p = new Product();
        p.ProductID = row["ProductID"].ToString();
        p.Name = row["Name"].ToString();
        p.ShortDescription = row["ShortDescription"].ToString();
        p.LongDescription = row["LongDescription"].ToString();
        p.UnitPrice = (decimal)row["UnitPrice"];
        p.ImageFile = row["ImageFile"].ToString();
        return p;
    }

    protected void btnAdd_Click(object sender, EventArgs e)
    {
        if (Page.IsValid)
        {
            CartItemList cart = CartItemList.GetCart();
            CartItem cartItem = cart[selectedProduct.ProductID];
            if (cartItem == null)
            {
                cart.AddItem(selectedProduct, Convert.ToInt32(txtQuantity.Text));
            }
            else
            {
                cartItem.AddQuantity(Convert.ToInt32(txtQuantity.Text));
            }
            Response.Redirect("Cart.aspx");
        }
    }
}
```

Figure 3-19   The C# code for the Order page

The aspx code for the Cart page

Figure 3-20 shows the aspx code for the second page of the Shopping Cart application, Cart.aspx, which is rendered in figure 3-2. Once again, I've highlighted the start of each tag that defines a server control.

Here, the shopping cart is displayed in a ListBox control within an HTML table that allows the Remove and Empty buttons to be displayed to the right of the list box. These two buttons, as well as the CheckOut button, use an OnClick attribute to name the event handler that's executed when the button is clicked. The Continue button uses the PostBackUrl attribute to return to the Order.aspx page. And the lblMessage label is used to display messages to the user. Like the Order page, this page also contains an image control that defines the image that's displayed in the banner.

Notice here that the EnableViewState property of the label is set to False. That way, the value of this label isn't maintained between HTTP requests. So if an error message is displayed in this label, it won't be displayed again the next time the page is displayed.

The aspx file for the Cart page (Cart.aspx)

```
<%@ Page Language="C#" AutoEventWireup="true" CodeFile="Cart.aspx.cs"
Inherits="Cart" %>

<!DOCTYPE html PUBLIC "-//W3C//DTD XHTML 1.0 Transitional//EN"
"http://www.w3.org/TR/xhtml1/DTD/xhtml1-transitional.dtd">

<html xmlns="http://www.w3.org/1999/xhtml">
<head runat="server">
    <title>Chapter 3: Shopping Cart</title>
    <style type="text/css">
        .style1 {
            width: 100%;
        }
        .style2 {
            width: 285px;
            height: 155px;
        }
        .style3 {
            height: 155px;
        }
    </style>
</head>
<body>
    <form id="form1" runat="server">
    <div>
        <asp:Image ID="Image1" runat="server"
            ImageUrl="~/Images/banner.jpg" /><br /><br />
        Your shopping cart:<br /><br />
        <table class="style1" cellpadding="0" cellspacing="0">
            <tr><td class="style2" valign="top">
                    <asp:ListBox ID="lstCart" runat="server"
                        Height="135px" Width="275px"></asp:ListBox></td>
                <td class="style3" valign="top">
                    <asp:Button ID="btnRemove" runat="server" Text="Remove Item"
                        Width="100px" OnClick="btnRemove_Click" /><br /><br />
                    <asp:Button ID="btnEmpty" runat="server" Text="Empty Cart"
                        Width="100px" OnClick="btnEmpty_Click" /></td></tr>
        </table>
        <br />
        <asp:Button ID="btnContinue" runat="server"
            PostBackUrl="~/Order.aspx" Text="Continue Shopping" /> 
        <asp:Button ID="btnCheckOut" runat="server" Text="Check Out"
            OnClick="btnCheckOut_Click" /><br /><br />
        <asp:Label ID="lblMessage" runat="server" ForeColor="Green"
            EnableViewState="False"></asp:Label>
    </div>
    </form>
</body>
</html>
```

Description

- The Cart.aspx page uses a list box to display the shopping cart.
- The btnContinue button uses cross-page posting to post back to the Order.aspx page. The other buttons post back to the Cart page, where the event handler specified by the OnClick attribute of the the button is executed.

Figure 3-20   The aspx code for the Cart page

The C# code for the Cart page

Figure 3-21 presents the code-behind file for the Cart page. This code starts by declaring a class-level variable that will hold the CartItemList object for the shopping cart. Then, each time the page is loaded, the Page_Load method calls the GetCart method of the CartItemList class to retrieve the shopping cart from session state and store it in this variable.

If the page is being loaded for the first time, the Page_Load method also calls the DisplayCart method. This method starts by clearing the list box that will display the shopping cart items. Then, it uses a for loop to add an item to the list box for each item in the shopping cart list. Notice that this statement uses the Count property of the CartItemList object to get the number of items in the cart.

If the user clicks the Remove Item button, the btnRemove_Click method is executed. This method begins by making sure that the cart contains at least one item and that an item in the shopping cart list box is selected. If so, the RemoveAt method of the CartItemList object is used to delete the selected item from the shopping cart. Then, the DisplayCart method is called to add the cart items to the list box again, but without the deleted item.

If the user clicks the Empty Cart button, the btnEmpty_Click method is executed. This method calls the Clear method of the CartItemList object to clear the shopping cart. Then, it calls the Clear method of the Items collection of the list box to clear that list. Please note, though, that instead of using the Clear method to clear the list box, this method could call the DisplayCart method. Similarly, the btnRemove_Click method could use the Remove method of the Items collection of the list box to remove the item at the selected index instead of calling the DisplayCart method. This just shows that there is usually more than one way that methods like these can be coded.

Note that the Cart page doesn't contain a method for the Click event of the Continue Shopping button. That's because this button uses the PostBackUrl property to post directly to the Order.aspx page. As a result, the Cart page isn't executed if the user clicks the Continue Shopping button.

The code-behind file for the Cart page (Cart.aspx.cs)

```csharp
using System;

public partial class Cart : System.Web.UI.Page
{
    private CartItemList cart;

    protected void Page_Load(object sender, EventArgs e)
    {
        cart = CartItemList.GetCart();
        if (!IsPostBack)
            this.DisplayCart();
    }

    private void DisplayCart()
    {
        lstCart.Items.Clear();
        CartItem item;
        for (int i = 0; i < cart.Count; i++)
        {
            item = cart[i];
            lstCart.Items.Add(item.Display());
        }
    }

    protected void btnRemove_Click(object sender, EventArgs e)
    {
        if (cart.Count > 0)
        {
            if (lstCart.SelectedIndex > -1)
            {
                cart.RemoveAt(lstCart.SelectedIndex);
                this.DisplayCart();
            }
            else
            {
                lblMessage.Text = "Please select the item you want to remove.";
            }
        }
    }

    protected void btnEmpty_Click(object sender, EventArgs e)
    {
        if (cart.Count > 0)
        {
            cart.Clear();
            lstCart.Items.Clear();
        }
    }

    protected void btnCheckOut_Click(object sender, EventArgs e)
    {
        lblMessage.Text = "Sorry, that function hasn't been "
                        + "implemented yet.";
    }
}
```

Figure 3-21   The C# code for the Cart page

Perspective

The purpose of this chapter has been to get you started with the development of multi-page web applications. Now, if this chapter has worked, you should be able to develop simple multi-page applications of your own. Yes, there's a lot more to learn, but you should be off to a good start.

Frankly, though, much of the C# code in the Shopping Cart application is difficult, even in a simple application like this one. So if your experience with C# is limited, you may have trouble understanding some of the code. And you may have trouble writing the same type of code for your new applications.

If that's the case, we recommend that you get our latest C# book. It will quickly get you up to speed with the C# language. It will show you how to use dozens of the .NET classes, like the List<T> class. It will show you how to develop object-oriented Windows applications. It is a terrific on-the-job reference. And it is the perfect companion to this book, which assumes that you already know C#.

Terms

class library
master form
jQuery
HTTP redirect message
cross-page posting
absolute URL
relative URL

data source
session state
session state object
cookie

Exercise 3-1 Build the Shopping Cart application

This exercise guides you through the process of building a Shopping Cart application similar to the one that's presented in this chapter. This is good practice if you're relatively new to Visual Studio and ASP.NET 4, and you'll learn a lot by doing it. To help you get started fast, the images, database, and classes needed by the application are provided for you.

Start the web site

1. Start an empty file-system web site named Ch03Cart in the C:\aspnet4_cs directory.

2. Add a folder named App_Data to the web site as described in figure 2-4. Then, add the existing Access database named Halloween.mdb to this folder. You can find this file in the C:\aspnet4_cs\Ch01Cart\App_Data directory.

3. Add a folder named App_Code to the web site. Then, add an existing class named Product to this folder as described in figure 3-4. You can find the file for this class in the App_Code folder of the C:\aspnet4_cs\Ch01Cart directory.

4. Open the Product class in the Code Editor and review its code. This code should be similar to the code shown in figure 3-16.

Build a simple Order page

5. Add a form named Order to the web site and display it in Design view.

6. Add the Products drop-down list that lets the user select the product, along with the text that identifies it. Next, add an Access data source and configure it to get product data from the Halloween database as described in figures 3-10 and 3-11. Then, bind the drop-down list to the data source as described in figure 3-12.

7. Add the labels that are used to display the product's name, short description, long description, and unit price. Make sure to set the ID property for these labels appropriately. For example, use lblName for the label that will display the product's name. When you're done, the page should look something like this:

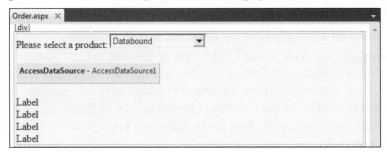

8. Run the application to see how the drop-down list works. At this point, you should be able to select a product from the list, but it won't change the text that's displayed by the labels.

9. Switch to the Code Editor and enter the code that displays the product that's selected in the drop-down list. To do that, you can code an event handler for the Load event of the page, and you can use a method named GetSelectedProduct as shown in part 1 of figure 3-19. When you add this code, don't forget to include a using statement for the System.Data namespace.

10. Set the AutoPostBack property of the Products drop-down list to True. Then, run the application and test the code. At this point, when you select a product from the list, the appropriate data for the product should be displayed on the page (but no image is displayed for the product yet).

Build a simple Cart page

11. Add existing classes named CartItem and CartItemList to the App_Code folder as described in figure 3-4. You can find the files for these classes in the C:\aspnet4_cs\ Ch01Cart\App_Code directory.

12. Open the CartItem and CartItemList classes in the Code Editor and review their code. The code for the CartItem class should be similar to the code shown in figure 3-16, and the code for the CartItemList class should be similar to the code shown in figure 3-17.

13. Add a second web form to the project named Cart. Then, set the Order form as the starting page as described in figure 3-6.

14. Add text and controls to the Cart page so it looks like the page shown in figure 3-2 without the image control at the top of the page. To help you align the controls, you can use a table. Make sure to set the ID property of the controls appropriately.

15. Set the PostBackUrl property of the Continue Shopping button so it displays the Order page.

16. Switch to Design view for the Order page and add the Add to Cart and Go to Cart buttons. Then, set the PostBackUrl property of the Go to Cart button so it displays the Cart page.

17. Run the application and use the Go to Cart and Continue Shopping buttons to switch between the two pages.

Modify the Cart and Order pages so the cart can store items

18. In the Order page, add code to the Click event of the Add to Cart button so it adds the selected product. To do that, you can use the GetCart and AddItem methods of the CartItemList class, the indexer of the CartItemList class, and the AddQuantity method of the CartItem class as shown in figure 3-19. However, since there isn't a text box for the quantity, you can assume that the quantity is always 1.

19. In the Cart page, add the code that displays the cart items in the list box. To do that, you can code an event handler for the Load event of the page as shown in figure 3-21. Within this event handler, you can use the GetCart method of the CartItemList class to get the cart from session state, and you can use a method named DisplayCart to display the cart items in the list box. When you add this code, don't forget to declare the cart variable outside of any methods.

20. Run the application and test this code. At this point, when you select a product and click the Add to Cart button, the application should add the item to the cart and display it in the Cart page. If the cart already contains the item, it should increase the quantity of the item by 1.

Modify the Cart page so it can remove items from the cart

21. In the Cart page, add the code that removes the selected item from the cart. To do that, you can code an event handler for the Click event of the Remove Item button as shown in figure 3-21. Note that because you didn't include the label for displaying an error message, you can omit the code that sets this label.

22. In the Cart page, add the code that clears all items from the cart. To do that, you can code an event handler for the Click event of the Empty Cart button as shown in figure 3-21.

23. Run the application and test this code. At this point, you should be able to use the Remove Item and Empty Cart buttons to remove items from the cart.

Exercise 3-2   Add another page to the Shopping Cart application

In this exercise, you'll add a third page to the Shopping Cart application that you developed in exercise 3-1. That will give you another chance to work with session state data.

Add a CheckOut page

1. Add a new form named CheckOut to your web site. This form should accept the first name, last name, and email address of the customer. In addition, it should have three required field validators (one for each text box) and two buttons that can be used to continue shopping or to cancel the order. Here's how this form should look in Design view:

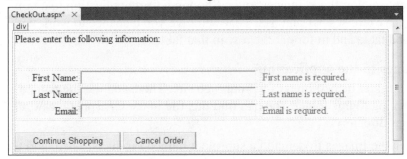

2. Add a new class named Customer to the App_Code folder. This class should define a customer that has a first name, last name, and email address.

3. Switch to the Cart page and add an event handler for the Click event of the Check Out button that displays the CheckOut page. This code should use the Redirect method of the HttpResponse class to transfer control.

4. Switch back to the CheckOut page and add an event handler for the Load event of the page. If the page is not being posted back, this event handler should get a Customer object from session state and store it in a variable that's declared outside the method. Then, if session state doesn't contain a Customer object, this variable will store a null value. If it doesn't store a null value, though, this method should display the customer information in the text boxes.

5. Code an event handler for the Click event of the Continue Shopping button. This event handler should create a Customer object if one doesn't already exist. Then, it should store the data in the text boxes in the Customer object, save that object in session state, and display the Order page.

6. Change the CausesValidation property of the Cancel Order button so validation isn't performed when this button is clicked. Then, code an event handler for the Click event of this button. This event handler should remove the customer and cart data from session state and display the Order page.

7. Run the application and test the CheckOut page. To do that, add one or more products to the cart and then click the Check Out button on the Cart page to display the CheckOut page. Click the Continue Shopping button to be sure that

the validators on this page work properly. Then, enter customer information in the text boxes and click the Continue Shopping button again. Add another item to the cart and click the Check Out button again. This time, the customer information should be displayed on the CheckOut page. Now, click the Cancel Order button to return to the Order page. Then, click the Go to Cart button to see that there isn't anything in the cart, and click the Check Out button to see that no customer information is displayed. If you encounter any problems, fix them.

Exercise 3-3   Add images and formatting to the Shopping Cart application

In this exercise, you'll add images to the Shopping Cart application that you developed in exercises 3-1 and 3-2. That will give you a chance to work with a more complicated table and to format the text in that table.

Add images to the application

1. Add a folder named Images to your web site. Then, add the file named banner.jpg to this folder. You can find this file in the C:\aspnet4_cs\Ch01Cart\ Images directory.

2. Within the Images folder, add a subfolder named Products. Then, add the jpg files for the products to this subfolder. You can find these files in the C:\aspnet4_cs\Ch01Cart\Images\Products directory.

3. Add the banner.jpg file to the top of all the pages in the Shopping Cart application.

Modify the Order page so it displays the images

4. Add a table and formatting to the Order page so it looks similar to the Order page shown in figure 3-1, but without the Quantity text box.

5. Add an Image control to the right column of the table, and set the ID property to imgProduct. Also, set the valign property of the cell that contains the image to "top".

6. Add code to the Order page to display the image for the selected product in the Image control. To do that, you can set the ImageUrl property of the Image control to the location of the image file relative to the page appended with the ImageFile property of the Product object for the selected product. Note that this works because the ImageFile property contains a string with the name of the image file.

7. Run the application and test the Order page. When it loads, it should display an image for the product that's selected in the drop-down list. When you select a new product, it should display that product in the Image control.

4

How to test and debug an ASP.NET application

If you've done much programming, you know that testing and debugging are often the most difficult and time-consuming phase of program development. Fortunately, Visual Studio includes an integrated debugger that can help you locate and correct even the most obscure bugs. And ASP.NET includes a Trace feature that displays useful information as your ASP.NET pages execute.

In this chapter, you'll learn how to use both of these powerful debugging tools. In addition, you'll learn how to create local IIS web sites so you can test them with that web server, and you'll learn how to test an application to determine if it works properly.

How to test an application using the ASP.NET Development Server

To test an ASP.NET application, you typically start by running it from within Visual Studio as a file-system web site so you can locate and correct any errors you encounter. This initial testing uses the default browser and the ASP.NET Development Server. Then, you test the application with other web browsers to make sure it works with them as well. You'll learn the techniques for performing both of these types of testing in the topics that follow. In addition, you'll learn how to use the Exception Assistant that's displayed if an error occurs while you're testing an application.

How to test an application with the default browser

Unless you've changed it, Windows uses Internet Explorer as its default browser. Figure 4-1 presents six different ways you can run a web application with the default browser. Three of these techniques start the debugger so you can use its features to debug any problems that might arise. The other three techniques do not start the debugger.

The first time you run a web application using one of the first three techniques, Visual Studio displays a dialog box indicating that debugging isn't enabled in the web.config file. From this dialog box, you can choose to enable debugging, or you can choose to run the application without debugging. In most cases, you'll enable debugging so that you can use the debugger with your application.

All of the techniques listed in this figure except the View in Browser command start the application and display the application's designated start page. However, the View in Browser command displays the selected page. For example, if you right-click the Cart page and choose View in Browser, the Cart page will be displayed. This command is most appropriate for making sure that the pages of an application look the way you want them to.

Notice that when you run an application using the ASP.NET Development Server, the URL for the page that's displayed identifies the server as "localhost:" followed by a number that's assigned by the server. In contrast, if you run an application under IIS as shown later in this chapter, the server is identified as just "localhost".

The Order page displayed in the default browser

Three ways to run an application with debugging
- Click the Start Debugging button in the Standard toolbar
- Press F5
- Choose the Debug→Start Debugging command

Three ways to run an application without debugging
- Press Ctrl+F5
- Choose Debug→Start Without Debugging
- Right-click a page in the Solution Explorer and choose View in Browser.

Three ways to stop an application that's run with debugging
- Press Shift+F5
- Click the Stop Debugging button in the Debug toolbar
- Choose Debug→Stop Debugging

Description
- If you run an application with debugging, you can use Visual Studio's built-in debugger to find and correct program errors.
- Unless you've changed the default browser for Windows, an application is run using Internet Explorer. See figure 4-2 for information on using a different browser. To end the application, close the browser.

Figure 4-1   How to test an application with the default browser

How to test an application with a browser other than the default

Once you've thoroughly tested your application with your default browser, you'll want to test it with other browsers to make sure it works as expected. Figure 4-2 describes two ways to do that. First, you can right-click the starting page for the application in the Solution Explorer and choose the Browse With command. This displays a Browse With dialog box like the one shown in this figure. From this dialog box, you can choose the browser you want to use and then click the Browse button.

Notice that the list of browsers in the Browse With dialog box includes the Internal Web Browser. If you choose this browser, the page is displayed in a Browse window within Visual Studio. You can test the application from this browser just as you would from any other browser. Then, when you're done with the browse operation, just close the Browse window.

You can also test an application with another browser by making that browser the default browser. To do that, right-click any page in the Solution Explorer and choose Browse With. Next, select the browser you want to designate as your default browser and click the Set As Default button. Then, click the Cancel button to close the Browse With dialog box. You can then use any of the techniques listed in figure 4-1 to start the application in the browser you selected. Note that setting a browser as the default is the only way to use the debugger with the browser. That's because the Browse With command runs an application without debugging.

Sometimes, the browser you want to test an application with doesn't appear in the Browse With dialog box even though it's installed on your computer. In most cases, that's because you installed the browser after installing Visual Studio. Then, you can add the browser by clicking the Add button in the Browse With dialog box to display the Add Program dialog box. This dialog box lets you locate the executable file for the browser you want to add and enter a "friendly" name that's used for the browser in the Browse With dialog box.

The Browse With dialog box

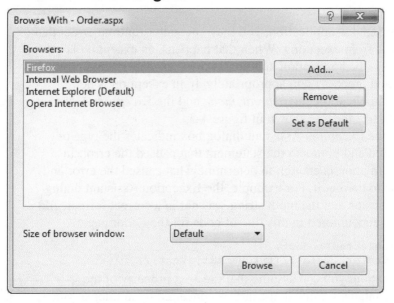

Two ways to test an application with a browser other than the default

- Right-click the starting page for the application in the Solution Explorer and choose Browse With from the shortcut menu. In the Browse With dialog box that's displayed, select the browser you want to use and click the Browse button.

- Select the browser you want to use in the Browse With dialog box and then click the Set as Default button to make that browser the default. The next time you run the application, it will be displayed in the browser you selected.

Description

- It's important to test an ASP.NET application in any browsers that might be used to run the application.

- If a browser isn't included in the list of available browsers, you can add it to the list by clicking the Add button in the Browse With dialog box and then using the Add Program dialog box that's displayed to add the desired browser.

- If you select the Internal Web Browser option, the page is displayed in a Browse window within Visual Studio. To end the browse operation from this window, just close the window.

- You'll need to change the default browser if you want to use the debugger with another browser, since the Browse With command starts the application without debugging.

- If you use a browser other than Internet Explorer to debug an application, the debugger may not end when you close the browser window. In that case, you can use one of the techniques in figure 4-1 to stop the application and end debugging.

Figure 4-2   How to test an application with a browser other than the default

How to use the Exception Assistant

As you test an ASP.NET application, you may encounter runtime errors that prevent an application from executing. When that happens, an exception is thrown. In many cases, the application anticipates these exceptions and provides code to catch them and process them appropriately. If an exception is not caught, however, the application enters *break mode* and the *Exception Assistant* displays a dialog box like the one shown in figure 4-3.

As you can see, the Exception Assistant dialog box indicates the type of exception that occurred and points to the statement that caused the error. In many cases, this information is enough to determine what caused the error and what should be done to correct it. For example, the Exception Assistant dialog box in this figure indicates that the input string was not in a correct format, and that the problem was encountered in this line of code for the Order page:

```
cart.AddItem(selectedProduct,
             Convert.ToInt32(txtQuantity.Text));
```

Based on that information, you can assume that the Text property of the txtQuantity control contains a value that can't be converted to an integer, since the AddItem method of the cart object accepts an integer as its second parameter. This could happen if the application didn't check that the user entered an integer value into this control. (To allow this error to occur, I disabled the range validator for the Quantity text box on the Order page.)

Many of the exceptions you'll encounter will be system exceptions like the one shown here. These exceptions apply to general system operations such as arithmetic operations and the execution of methods. If your applications use ADO.NET, you can also encounter ADO.NET and data provider exceptions. If the connection string for a database is invalid, for example, a data provider exception will occur. And if you try to add a row to a data table with a key that already exists, an ADO.NET error will occur.

In some cases, you won't be able to determine the cause of an error just by analyzing the information in the Exception Assistant dialog box. Then, to get more information about the possible cause of an exception, you can use the list of troubleshooting tips in this dialog box. The items in this list are links that display additional information in a Help window. You can also use the other links in this dialog box to search for more help online, to display the content of the exception object, and to copy the details of the exception to the clipboard.

If you still can't determine the cause of an error, you can use the Visual Studio debugger to help you locate the problem. You'll learn how to do that later in this chapter.

An Exception Assistant dialog box

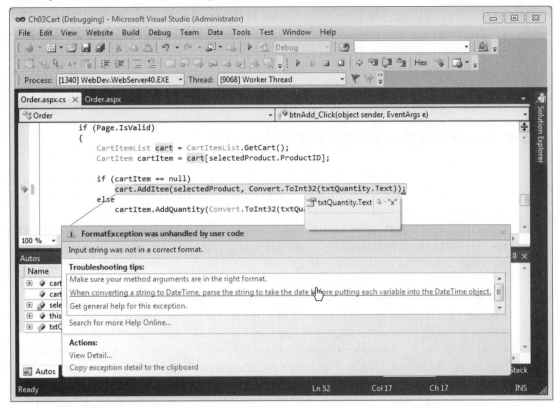

Description

- If an uncaught exception occurs in an ASP.NET application, the application enters *break mode* and the *Exception Assistant* displays a dialog box like the one shown above.

- The Exception Assistant provides the name and description of the exception, and it points to the statement in the program that caused the error. It also includes a list of troubleshooting tips. You can click on these tips to display additional information in the Help Viewer (see chapter 6).

- The information provided by the Exception Assistant is often all you need to determine the cause of an error. If not, you can close this window and then use the debugging techniques presented in this chapter to determine the cause.

- If you continue program execution after an exception occurs, ASP.NET terminates the application and sends a Server Error page to the browser. This page is also displayed if you run an application without debugging. It provides the name of the application, a description of the exception, and the line in the program that caused the error. It also includes a *stack trace* that indicates the processing that led up to the error.

Figure 4-3   How to use the Exception Assistant

How to test an application using IIS

In chapter 2, you learned how to create a file-system web site that runs under the ASP.NET Development Server. If you have access to an IIS web server, though, you may want to create a web site that runs under IIS so you can test the web site in that environment. Or, you may want to create and test a file-system web site with the ASP.NET Development Server first, and then test it under IIS later.

How to create a local IIS web site

A local IIS web site is a web site that resides on your local computer. To create a local IIS web site, then, you must have IIS installed on your computer. Please see appendix A for information on how to install IIS. In addition, Visual Studio must be running in the context of an administrator account. You don't need to be an administrator to do that, though. Instead, you can run Visual Studio as an administrator by right-clicking on it in the Start menu and choosing the Run As Administrator command.

Figure 4-4 illustrates how you create a local IIS web site. The easiest way to do that is to click the Browse button from the New Web Site dialog box to display the Choose Location dialog box shown in this figure. Then, you can click the Local IIS button at the left side of the dialog box to display the IIS web server, and you can select the directory where you want to create your web site. In this case, I selected the aspnet_2010 directory. Then, I clicked the Create New Web Application button to create a new web site named Ch03Cart in that directory.

By the way, when you create an IIS web site, a dialog box may be displayed indicating that the ASP.NET 4.0 Web extension is not enabled on the web server. To enable ASP.NET 4.0 on the web server, just click the Yes button.

When you use this technique, the files for the web site are stored within the directory you create. If that's not what you want, you can create a *virtual directory* that points to the directory where the files for the web site will be stored. To do that, just click the Create New Virtual Directory button in the Choose Location dialog box. Then, a dialog box is displayed that lets you enter a name for the virtual directory and the path where the files for the web site should be stored. In the dialog box shown in this figure, for example, the virtual directory will be named Ch03Cart, and the files will be stored in a directory with the same name within the aspnet4_cs directory on the C drive.

In addition to using the New Virtual Directory dialog box to create a virtual directory for a new web site, you can also use it to create a virtual directory for a file-system web site you've already created. To do that, just enter the path for the existing web site in this dialog box. Then, when you click the OK button in the New Web Site dialog box, Visual Studio will warn you that there is already a web site at the location you specified. To create a virtual directory that points to the existing web site, select the Open the Existing Web Site option. If you use this technique, be sure to set the starting page for the application. Also, if you're using Windows 7, be sure that the default application pool for IIS is set correctly before you create the virtual directory. For more information, see figure B-4 in appendix B.

The dialog box for selecting a local IIS web site

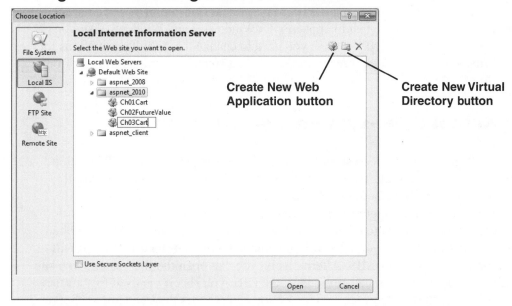

The dialog box for creating a virtual directory

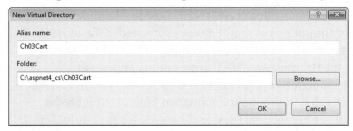

Description

- To create a web site that will run under IIS on your local computer, select HTTP for the location option in the New Web Site dialog box and then enter the path of the IIS directory where you want to create the web site. Or, click the Browse button to display the Choose Location dialog box.

- From the Choose Location dialog box, click the Local IIS button and expand the Default Web Site node. Then, select the directory where you want to create the web site from the default web site and click the Open button, or create a new directory or virtual directory.

- To create a new IIS directory for a web site, click the Create New Web Application button and then enter the name of the directory. The files for the web site will be stored in this directory.

- To create a *virtual directory* for the web site, click the Create New Virtual Directory button to display the New Virtual Directory dialog box. Enter a name for the directory and the path where you want to store the files for the web site. If the path you specify already contains a web site, you can open that web site from the virtual directory.

Figure 4-4   How to create a local IIS web site

Before I go on, you should realize that you can also create a virtual directory for a file-system web site using the IIS Management Console. If you're interested, you can learn how to do that in appendix B (Windows 7 and Windows Vista) or appendix C (Windows XP). Unless you need to change the default permissions for a virtual directory, though, I recommend that you create the virtual directory from within Visual Studio.

How to test a file-system web site with IIS

When you run a file-system web site, it runs under the ASP.NET Development Server by default. Because this server has limitations, however, you'll want to be sure to test a file-system web site under IIS as well as under the development server. Figure 4-5 describes how you do that.

To start, you need to create a virtual directory for the web site as described in figure 4-4. Then, if you open the web site from this virtual directory, it will automatically run under IIS. Alternatively, you can open the file-system web site directly and change its start options so the URL you specify is used to start the application. In this figure, for example, you can see that the Use Custom Server option has been selected and the URL for the web site's virtual directory has been entered in the Base URL text box.

This figure also lists the limitations of the ASP.NET Development Server. The most significant of these limitations is that it always runs under the current user's security context, but your own user account probably has stronger security privileges than the account IIS runs ASP.NET applications under. As a result, when you move the application to a production web server, you may have to contend with security issues that weren't apparent when you tested with the development server, especially if you access files or databases located in folders outside of the application's folder structure.

The dialog box for specifying a web server

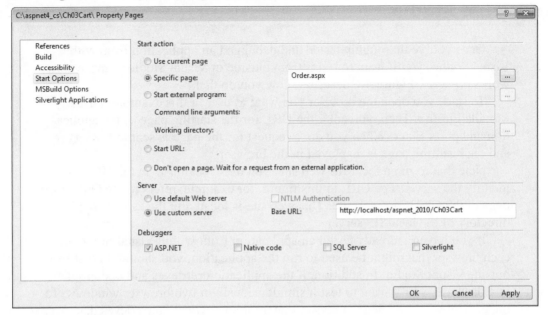

How to test a file-system web site with IIS

- Create a virtual directory for the web site as described in figure 4-4.
- Open the web site from its virtual directory, or open the file-system web site and then use the Property Pages dialog box shown above to specify the URL for the virtual directory.
- Run the application using one of the techniques in figure 4-1.

Limitations of the ASP.NET Development Server

- Can serve pages only to the local computer.
- Runs in the current user's security context, so it doesn't accurately test security issues.
- Uses a randomly chosen port rather than the standard HTTP port 80.

Description

- By default, a file-system web site is run using the ASP.NET Development Server. To run a file-system web site using IIS, you can use one of the techniques above.
- To open the Property Pages dialog box, right-click the project in the Solution Explorer and select Property Pages from the shortcut menu. Then, to change the server that's used to run the web site, click the Start Options node, select the Use Custom Server option, and enter the URL of the virtual directory for the web site.

Figure 4-5   How to test a file-system web site with IIS

How to test an application from outside of Visual Studio

Once you've thoroughly tested and debugged an application from within Visual Studio, you'll want to run it from outside of Visual Studio to make sure it works properly. Figure 4-6 describes how you do that.

To start, you open the browser you want to use. In this example, I used Mozilla Firefox. Then, you enter the URL for the starting page of the application and press Enter. When you do, a request for the page is sent to the server and the resulting page is displayed in the browser.

Note that to run a local IIS web site, you use "localhost" in the URL to identify the server. The URL in this figure, for example, refers to the Order.aspx page of the Ch03Cart web site. This web site is located in the aspnet_2010 directory of the local IIS server.

If you haven't already tested an application from within Visual Studio in each browser that might be used to run the application, you should do that from outside Visual Studio. In addition, if the application retrieves and updates data in a database, you'll want to test it simultaneously in two browser windows. To understand why, you need to realize that after an application retrieves data from a database, it closes the connection to the database. Because of that, two or more users can retrieve the same data at the same time. This is called *concurrency*, and it can cause *concurrency errors* when the data is updated.

In section 3 of this book, you'll learn more about concurrency and how you avoid concurrency errors. For now, you should just realize that you'll need to test your applications to be sure that they handle concurrency problems.

The Order page displayed in a Mozilla Firefox browser outside of Visual Studio

Description

- You can run any IIS application from outside of Visual Studio. To do that, open the browser you want to use, enter the URL for the starting page of the application as shown above, and press Enter.

- When you run an application from outside of Visual Studio, you can run it in two or more browser windows simultaneously. That way, you can be sure that the application provides for any *concurrency errors* that can occur.

- If you want to use the debugger while testing for concurrency errors, you can run one instance of the application from within Visual Studio with debugging, and you can run another instance from outside of Visual Studio.

Figure 4-6   How to test an application from outside of Visual Studio

How to use the debugger

The topics that follow introduce you to the basic techniques for using the Visual Studio *debugger* to debug an ASP.NET application. Note that these techniques are almost identical to the techniques you use to debug a Windows application. If you've debugged Windows applications, then, you shouldn't have any trouble debugging web applications.

How to use breakpoints

Figure 4-7 shows how to use *breakpoints* in an ASP.NET application. Note that you can set a breakpoint before you run an application or as an application is executing. Remember, though, that an application ends after it generates a page. So if you switch from the browser to Visual Studio to set a breakpoint, the breakpoint won't be taken until the next time the page is executed. If you want a breakpoint to be taken the first time a page is executed, then, you'll need to set the breakpoint before you run the application.

After you set a breakpoint and run the application, the application enters *break mode* before it executes the statement that contains the breakpoint. In this illustration, for example, the application will enter break mode before it executes the statement that caused the exception in figure 4-3 to occur. Then, you can use the debugging features described in the topics that follow to debug the application.

In some cases, you may want to set more than one breakpoint. You can do that either before you begin the execution of the application or while the application is in break mode. Then, when you run the application, it will stop at the first breakpoint. And when you continue execution, the application will execute up to the next breakpoint.

Once you set a breakpoint, it remains active until you remove it. In fact, it remains active even after you close the project. If you want to remove a breakpoint, you can use one of the techniques presented in this figure.

You can also work with breakpoints from the *Breakpoints window*. To disable a breakpoint, for example, you can remove the check mark in front of the breakpoint. Then, the breakpoint isn't taken until you enable it again. You can also move to a breakpoint in the Code Editor window by selecting the breakpoint in the Breakpoints window and then clicking on the Go To Source Code button at the top of this window, or by right-clicking the breakpoint in the Breakpoints window and choosing Go To Source Code from the shortcut menu.

You can also use the Breakpoints window to label and filter breakpoints. You use labels to group related breakpoints. To assign a label to one or more breakpoints, select the breakpoints in the Breakpoints window. Then, right-click on the breakpoints and select Edit Labels to display the Edit Breakpoint Labels dialog box. From this dialog box, you can enter the label you want to use or select a label you created previously.

To filter breakpoints, select the column you want to search from the In Column drop-down list or use the default to search all columns. To search just the

The Order page with a breakpoint

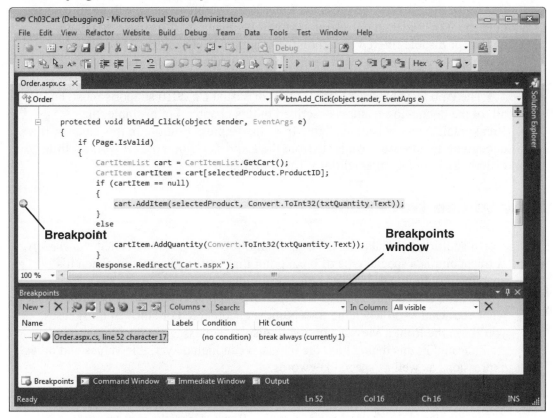

How to set and clear breakpoints

- To set a *breakpoint*, click in the margin indicator bar to the left of the statement where you want the break to occur. The statement will be highlighted and a breakpoint indicator (a large dot) will appear in the margin. You can set a breakpoint before you run an application or while you're debugging the application.

- To remove a breakpoint, click the breakpoint indicator. To remove all breakpoints at once, use the Debug→Delete All Breakpoints command.

- To disable all breakpoints, use the Debug→Disable All Breakpoints command. You can later enable the breakpoints by using the Debug→Enable All Breakpoints command.

- To display the *Breakpoints window*, use the Debug→Windows→Breakpoints command or the drop-down list for the rightmost button in the Debug toolbar. Then, you can use this window to go to, delete, enable, disable, label, or filter breakpoints.

Description

- When ASP.NET encounters a breakpoint, it enters *break mode* before it executes the statement on which the breakpoint is set. From break mode, you can use the debugger to determine the cause of an error.

- You can't set breakpoints on blank lines.

Figure 4-7   How to use breakpoints

Labels column, for example, choose Labels from this list. Then, enter the search text in the Search box and press the Enter key. The breakpoints will be filtered so only those that contain the search text will be displayed. You can also delete, enable, or disable filtered breakpoints using the Delete and Enable or Disable buttons, you can control the columns that are displayed using the Columns drop-down menu, and you can remove the filtering using the Reset button.

The Web Developer Express Edition of Visual C# 2010 supports most, but not all, of the debugging features described in this chapter. For example, the Breakpoints window isn't available from the Express Edition. In this chapter, if a debugging feature isn't available from the Express Edition or if it works a little differently than the other editions, I'll point that out.

How to use tracepoints

In addition to breakpoints, Visual Studio provides a feature called *tracepoints*. A tracepoint is a special type of breakpoint that performs an action when it's encountered. Figure 4-8 shows how tracepoints work.

To set a tracepoint, you use the When Breakpoint Is Hit dialog box to indicate what you want to do when the tracepoint is encountered or "hit." In most cases, you'll use the Print a Message option to display a message in the *Output window*. As indicated in this dialog box, the message can include variable values and other expressions as well as special keywords.

For example, the message shown here will include the value of the SelectedValue property of the ddlProducts control. You can see the output from this tracepoint in the Output window in this figure. Here, the first tracepoint message was displayed the first time the page was requested. The second message was displayed when a product was selected from the drop-down list. And the third message was displayed when a quantity was entered and the Add to Cart button was clicked.

Notice that the Output window is also used to display Visual Studio messages like the first one shown in this figure. Because of that, this window is displayed automatically when you run an application. If you ever close it and want to reopen it without running the application, however, you can do that by using the View→Output command.

To run a macro when a tracepoint is encountered, you select the Run a Macro option. Then, the drop-down list becomes available and you can select the macro you want to run from this list.

By default, program execution continues after the tracepoint action is performed. If that's not what you want, you can remove the check mark from the Continue Execution option. Then, the program will enter break mode when the tracepoint action is complete.

After you set a tracepoint on a statement, the statement will be highlighted and a breakpoint indicator will appear in the margin. If program execution will continue after the tracepoint action is performed, the indicator will appear as a large diamond. If the program will enter break mode, however, the same indicator is used as for a standard breakpoint.

The Order page with a tracepoint and the dialog box used to set it

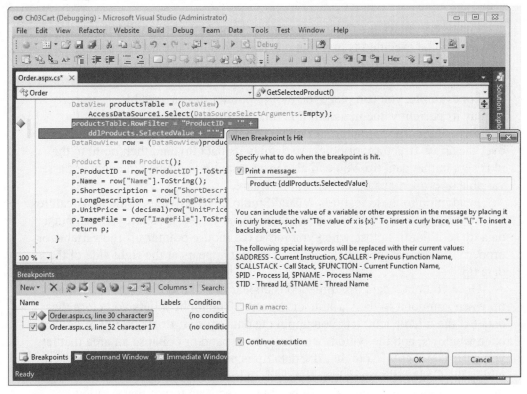

Output from the tracepoint in the Output window

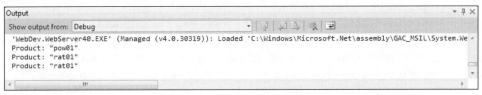

Description

- A *tracepoint* is a special type of breakpoint that lets you perform an action. When ASP.NET encounters a tracepoint, it performs the specified action and then continues execution if the Continue Execution option is selected or enters break mode if it isn't.

- You typically use tracepoints to print messages to the *Output window*. A message can include text, values, and special keywords. You can also use tracepoints to run macros.

- To set a tracepoint, right-click on the statement where you want it set and choose Breakpoint→Insert Tracepoint. Then, complete the When Breakpoint Is Hit dialog box and click OK. You can also convert an existing breakpoint to a tracepoint by right-clicking on its indicator and choosing When Hit.

- If program execution will continue after the tracepoint action is performed, the tracepoint will be marked with a large diamond as shown above. Otherwise, it will be marked just like any other breakpoint.

Figure 4-8   How to use tracepoints

How to work in break mode

Figure 4-9 shows the Order page in break mode. In this mode, the next statement to be executed is highlighted. Then, you can use the debugging information that's available to try to determine the cause of an exception or a logical error.

For example, you can place the mouse pointer over a variable or property to display its current value in a *data tip*. You can also display the values of the members of an array, structure, or object. To do that, place the mouse pointer over the array, structure, or object to display its data tip, and then point to the plus sign in that data tip. You can also use a data tip to change the value of a variable or property as described in this figure.

In addition to these features, Visual Studio 2010 provides some new features for working with data tips that make them easier to use. To start, you can pin a data tip so it doesn't close when you move the mouse pointer off the variable or property. To do that, you click the pin icon that appears at the right side of the data tip.

Once you pin a data tip, three icons appear in a bar to the right of the data tip when you point to the variable or property. The top icon lets you close the data tip, the middle icon lets you unpin the data tip so it floats on top of all the open windows, and the bottom icon lets you expand or collapse an area that lets you enter comments. Note that if a data tip is pinned, you can drag it anywhere within the Code Editor window. If a data tip is floated, however, you can drag it over any window and you will still be able to see it on top of that window.

In this figure, I displayed a data tip for the Text property of the Quantity text box. Then, I pinned the data tip so it remained displayed. Finally, I clicked the bottom icon to open a small text area where I could enter a comment.

You can also see the values of other properties and variables in the Autos window near the bottom left of the Visual Studio window. You'll learn more about the Autos window and some of the other debugging windows in a minute.

In addition to changing the values of variables and properties while in break mode, you can also make changes to the C# code. To do that, you use a Visual Studio feature called Edit and Continue. This feature lets you make changes to most statements within the methods of an application, and some statements outside the methods, in the Code Editor. Then, when you continue program execution using one of the techniques presented in this figure, the new code is compiled and debugging continues with the new code.

The Shopping Cart application in break mode

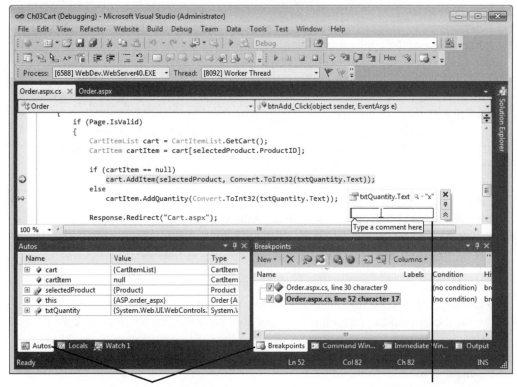

Debugging windows   **Pinned data tip**

Description

- When you enter break mode, the debugger highlights the next statement to be executed.
- You can use the debugging windows and the buttons in the Debug menu and toolbar to control the execution of the program and determine the cause of an exception.
- To display the value of a variable or property in a *data tip,* position the mouse pointer over the variable or property in the Code Editor window.
- To display the members of an array, structure, or object in a data tip, position the mouse pointer over it to display its data tip, and then point to the plus sign in the data tip.
- To change the value of a property or variable using a data tip, click on the value in the data tip and then enter the new value.
- You can use the icons to the right of a data tip to pin the data tip so it remains displayed, to unpin the data tip so it floats on top of all other open windows, to add, display, and hide the comment for a data tip, and to close the data tip.
- You can also make changes to your code while in break mode. These changes are applied when you continue program execution.
- To continue program execution, press F5 or click the Continue button in the Standard or Debug toolbar. For more on controlling program execution, see figure 4-10

Figure 4-9   How to work in break mode

How to control the execution of an application

Once you're in break mode, you can use a variety of commands to control the execution of the application. These commands are summarized in figure 4-10. As you can see, most of these commands are available from the Debug menu or the Debug toolbar, but three of them are available only from the shortcut menu for the Code Editor window. You can also use shortcut keys to start some of these commands.

To execute the statements of an application one at a time, you use the Step Into command. When you use this command, the application executes the next statement, then returns to break mode so you can check the values of properties and variables and perform other debugging functions. The Step Over command is similar to the Step Into command, but it executes the statements in called methods without interruption (they are "stepped over").

The Step Out command executes the remaining statements in a method without interruption. When the method finishes, the application enters break mode before the next statement in the calling method is executed.

To skip over code that you know is working properly, you can use the Run To Cursor or Set Next Statement command. You can also use the Set Next Statement command to rerun lines of code that were executed before an exception occurred. And if you've been working in the Code Editor window and have forgotten where the next statement to be executed is, you can use the Show Next Statement command to move to it.

If your application gets caught in a processing loop so it keeps executing indefinitely without generating a page, you can force it into break mode by choosing the Debug→Break All command. This command lets you enter break mode any time during the execution of an application.

Commands in the Debug menu and toolbar

Command	Toolbar	Keyboard	Function
Start/Continue	▶	F5	Start or continue execution of the application.
Break All	❚❚	Ctrl+Alt+Break	Stop execution and enter break mode.
Stop Debugging	■	Shift+F5	Stop debugging and end execution of the application.
Restart	◧	Ctrl+Shift+F5	Restart the entire application.
Show Next Statement	⇨		Display the next statement to be executed.
Step Into	⊑	F11	Execute one statement at a time.
Step Over	⊏	F10	Execute one statement at a time except for called methods.
Step Out	⊑	Shift+F11	Execute the remaining lines in the current method.

Commands in the Code Editor window's shortcut menu

Command	Function
Run to Cursor	Execute the application until it reaches the statement that contains the insertion point.
Set Next Statement	Set the statement that contains the insertion point as the next statement to be executed.
Show Next Statement	Move the insertion point to the next statement that will be executed.

Description

- Once the application enters break mode, you can use the Step Into, Step Over, Step Out, and Run To Cursor commands to execute one or more statements and return to break mode.

- To alter the normal execution sequence of the application, you can use the Set Next Statement command. Just place the insertion point in the statement you want to execute next, issue this command, and click the Continue button to continue application execution.

- To stop an application that's caught in a loop, switch to the Visual Studio window and use the Debug→Break All command.

Figure 4-10   How to control the execution of an application

How to use the Autos, Locals, and Watch windows to monitor variables

If you need to see the values of several application variables or properties, you can do that using the Autos, Locals, or Watch windows. By default, these windows are displayed in the lower left corner of the IDE when an application enters break mode. If they're not displayed, you can display them by selecting the appropriate command from the Debug➔Windows menu. Note that you can display up to four separate Watch windows. The exception is if you're using Web Developer Express Edition, in which case only one Watch window is available.

The content of the Autos, Locals, and Watch windows is illustrated in figure 4-11. The difference between the Autos and Locals windows is in the amount of information they display and the scope of that information.

The *Locals window* displays information about the variables within the scope of the current method. If the code in a form is currently executing, this window also includes information about the form and all of the controls on the form.

The *Autos window* is similar to the Locals window, but it only displays information about the variables used in the current statement and the previous statement. Although the information in this window can be more limited than the information shown in the Locals window, the Autos window helps you focus on the variables that are relevant to the current statement.

Unlike the Autos and Locals windows, the *Watch windows* let you choose the values that are displayed. The Watch window shown in this figure, for example, displays the Text property of the txtQuantity and lblUnitPrice controls, the cartItem object, and the Count property of the CartItemList object that's stored in the cart variable. The Watch windows also let you watch the values of expressions you specify. Note that an expression doesn't have to exist in the application for you to add it to a Watch window.

To add an item to a Watch window, you can type it directly into the Name column. Alternatively, if the item appears in the Code Editor window, you can highlight it in that window and then drag it to a Watch window. You can also highlight the item in the Code Editor or a data tip and then right-click on it and select the Add Watch command to add it to the Watch window that's currently displayed.

Besides displaying the values of variables and properties, you can use the Autos, Locals, and Watch windows to change these values. To do that, you simply double-click on the value you want to change and enter a new value. Then, you can continue debugging or continue the execution of the application.

The Autos window

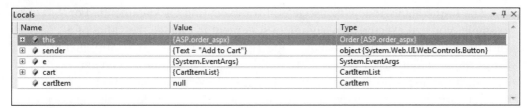

The Locals window

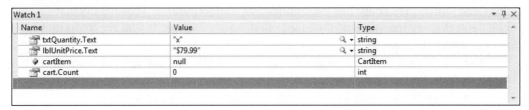

A Watch window

Name	Value		Type
txtQuantity.Text	"x"	🔍 ▾	string
lblUnitPrice.Text	"$79.99"	🔍 ▾	string
cartItem	null		CartItem
cart.Count	0		int

Description

- The *Autos window* displays information about variables in the current statement and the previous statement.

- The *Locals window* displays information about the variables within the scope of the current method.

- The *Watch windows* let you view the values of variables and expressions you specify, called *watch expressions*. You can display up to four Watch windows.

- To add a watch expression, type a variable name or expression into the Name column, highlight a variable or expression in the Code Editor window and drag it to the Watch window, or right-click on a variable, highlighted expression, or data tip in the Code Editor window and choose Add Watch.

- To delete a row from a Watch window, right-click the row and choose Delete Watch. To delete all the rows in a Watch window, right-click the window and choose Select All to select the rows, then right-click and choose Delete Watch.

- To display any of these windows, click on its tab if it's visible or select the appropriate command from the Debug→Windows menu.

- To change the value of a property or variable from any of these windows, double-click on the value in the Value column, then type a new value and press the Enter key.

Figure 4-11   How to use the Autos, Locals, and Watch windows to monitor variables

How to use the Immediate window to work with values

The *Immediate window*, shown in figure 4-12, is useful for displaying the values of variables or properties that don't appear in the Code Editor window. To display a value, you simply type a question mark followed by the name of the variable or property. The first line of code in this figure, for example, displays the Text property of the item selected from the Products drop-down list. You can see the result in the second line of this window.

The Immediate window is also useful for executing C# statements. For example, you can execute an assignment statement to change the value of a variable or property. After I displayed the Text property of the Quantity text box, for example, I assigned a value of "1" to this property. Similarly, you can execute a method. This can be useful for testing the result of a method with different arguments. If you execute a method that returns a value, you can also preface the method name with a question mark to display the value it returns.

When you enter commands in the Immediate window, they're executed in the same context (or scope) as the application that's running. That means that you can't display the value of a variable that's out of scope. If you try to do that, the debugger displays an error message.

The commands that you enter into the Immediate window remain there until you exit from Visual Studio or explicitly delete them using the Clear All command in the shortcut menu for the window. That way, you can use standard Windows techniques to edit and reuse the same commands from one execution of an application to another without having to reenter them.

To execute a command that you've already entered in the Immediate window, just use the Up and Down arrow keys to scroll through the commands. As you scroll, the commands are displayed at the bottom of the window. Then, you can change a command if necessary and press Enter to execute it.

The Immediate window

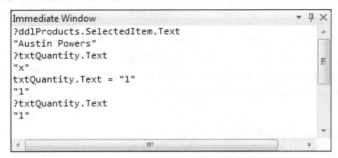

```
Immediate Window                                    ▼ ↟ ×
?ddlProducts.SelectedItem.Text                           ▲
"Austin Powers"
?txtQuantity.Text
"x"                                                      ▤
txtQuantity.Text = "1"
"1"
?txtQuantity.Text
"1"
                                                         ▼
◄          III                                    ►
```

Description

- You can use the *Immediate window* to display and assign values from a program during execution. To display this window, click on the Immediate Window tab or use the Debug➜Windows➜Immediate command.

- To display a value in the Immediate window, enter a question mark followed by the expression whose value you want to display. Then, press the Enter key.

- To assign a different value to a variable, property, or object, enter an assignment statement in the Immediate window. Then, press the Enter key.

- To execute a method from the Immediate window, enter its name and any arguments it requires. Then, press the Enter key. If you want to display the value that's returned by a method, precede the method call with a question mark.

- To reissue a command, use the Up and Down arrow keys to scroll through the commands until you find the one you want. Then, modify the command if necessary and press the Enter key to execute it.

- To remove all commands and output from the Immediate window, use the Clear All command in the shortcut menu for the window.

Figure 4-12   How to use the Immediate window to work with values

How to use the Trace feature

The *Trace feature* is an ASP.NET feature that displays some useful information that you can't get by using the debugger. Because the debugger works so well, you probably won't need to use the Trace feature very much, but you should at least be aware of the information that it can provide.

How to enable the Trace feature

To use the Trace feature, you must first enable tracing. To do that, you add a Trace attribute to the Page directive for the page, and you assign a value of True to this attribute. Then, when you run the page, trace information will be displayed at the end of the page output, as shown in figure 4-13.

When you enable the Trace feature, it is enabled only for the current page, which is usually what you want. To enable tracing for another page, you must modify the Page directive for that page too. Once this feature has been enabled for a page, ASP.NET adds trace output to the page whenever the page is requested.

How to interpret Trace output

In figure 4-13, you can see the start of the output for the Cart page after the user added an item to the shopping cart. After the request details, the trace information provides a list of trace messages that are generated as the application executes. Here, ASP.NET automatically adds Begin and End messages when major page events such as PreInit, Init, and InitComplete occur. If you scroll down to see all of these trace messages, you can see the variety of events that are raised during the life cycle of a page.

After the trace messages, you'll find information about the controls used by the page, the items in the session state object, the cookies that were included with the HTTP request, the HTTP request headers, and the server variables. In this figure, for example, you can see the session state and cookies data for the Cart page of the Shopping Cart application. In this case, an item named Cart has been added to the session state object. And a cookie named ASP.NET_SessionId is used to keep track of the user's session ID so the user's session state object can be retrieved.

The beginning of the trace output for the Cart page

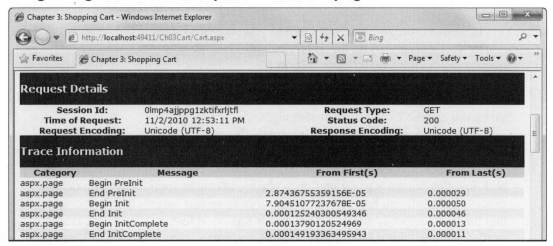

The session and cookies information for the Cart page

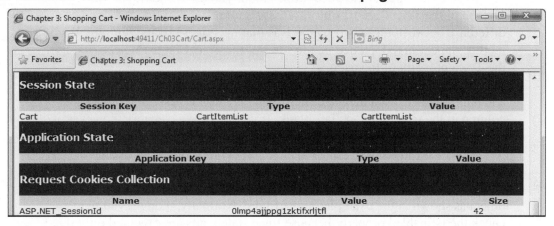

A Page directive that enables tracing for the Cart page

```
<%@ Page Language="C#" AutoEventWireup="true" CodeFile="Cart.aspx.cs"
Inherits="Cart" Trace="true" %>
```

Description

- The ASP.NET *Trace feature* traces the execution of a page and displays trace information and other information at the bottom of that page.

- To activate the trace feature for a page, you add a Trace attribute to the Page directive at the top of the aspx file for the page and set its value to True as shown above.

- The trace information is divided into several tables that provide specific types of trace information. For example, the Trace Information table provides information about how the page request was processed, and the Session State table provides information about the items currently stored in session state.

Figure 4-13   How to enable the Trace feature and interpret Trace output

How to create custom trace messages

In some cases, you may want to add your own messages to the trace information that's generated by the Trace feature. This can help you track the sequence in which the methods of a form are executed or the changes in the data as the methods are executed. Although you can also do this type of tracking by stepping through the methods of a form with the debugger, the trace information gives you a static listing of your messages.

Note, however, that you can also create this type of listing using tracepoints as described earlier in this chapter. The advantage to using tracepoints is that you can generate trace information without adding code to your application. In addition, this output is generated only when you run an application with debugging. In contrast, you have to add program code to add custom trace messages, and the trace output is generated whenever the Trace feature is enabled. Because of that, you may not need to create custom trace messages. But I've included it here in case you do.

To add messages to the trace information, you use the Write or Warn method of the TraceContext object. This is summarized in figure 4-14. The only difference between these two methods is that messages created with the Warn method appear in red. Notice that to refer to the TraceContext object, you use the Trace property of the page.

When you code a Write or Warn method, you can include both a category and a message or just a message. If you include just a message, the category column in the trace output is left blank. If you include a category, however, it appears as shown in this figure. In most cases, you'll include a category because it makes it easy to see the sequence in which the methods were executed.

If you want to determine whether tracing is enabled before executing a Write or Warn method, you can use the IsEnabled property of the TraceContext object as shown in the example in this figure. Normally, though, you won't check the IsEnabled property because trace statements are executed only if tracing is enabled.

Common members of the TraceContext class

Property	Description
`IsEnabled`	True if tracing is enabled for the page.

Method	Description
`Write(message)`	Writes a message to the trace output.
`Write(category, message)`	Writes a message to the trace output with the specified category.
`Warn(message)`	Writes a message in red type to the trace output.
`Warn(category, message)`	Writes a message in red type to the trace output with the specified category.

Code that writes a custom trace message

```
if (Trace.IsEnabled)
{
    Trace.Write("Page_Load", "Binding products drop-down list.");
}
```

A portion of a trace that includes a custom message

Trace Information

Category	Message	From First(s)	From Last(s)
aspx.page	Begin PreInit		
aspx.page	End PreInit	1.43718377679578E-05	0.000014
aspx.page	Begin Init	2.63483692412559E-05	0.000012
aspx.page	End Init	4.48264463714874E-05	0.000018
aspx.page	Begin InitComplete	5.44076715501259E-05	0.000010
aspx.page	End InitComplete	6.39888967287644E-05	0.000010
aspx.page	Begin PreLoad	7.28857486803573E-05	0.000009
aspx.page	End PreLoad	8.28091604725187E-05	0.000010
aspx.page	Begin Load	9.20481990376344E-05	0.000009
Page_Load	Binding products drop-down list.	0.00047837688570488	0.000386
aspx.page	End Load	0.0985302400575968	0.098052
aspx.page	Begin LoadComplete	0.0985559040536111	0.000026
aspx.page	End LoadComplete	0.0985675383984708	0.000012
aspx.page	Begin PreRender	0.098576777437036	0.000009
aspx.page	End PreRender	0.0986654037699384	0.000089

Custom trace message

Description

- You can use the TraceContext object to write your own messages to the trace output. The TraceContext object is available through the Trace property of a page.

- Use the Write method to write a basic text message. Use the Warn method to write a message in red type.

- Trace messages are written only if tracing is enabled for the page. To determine whether tracing is enabled, you use the IsEnabled property of the TraceContext object.

Figure 4-14   How to create custom trace messages

How to write information directly to the HTTP output stream

Another way to display information as a program executes is to write it directly to the HTTP output stream. To do that, you use the Write method of the HTTP Response object as shown in figure 4-15. When you use this technique, you'll want to be sure to remove any statements you've added when you finish testing your application.

At the top of this figure, you can see a Cart page that includes output that indicates the number of items that are currently in the shopping cart. To generate this output, I added a Response.Write method to the Page_Load method of the page. As you can see, this method uses the Count property of the cart object to determine the number of items that are in the cart.

Notice that the text you include on the Write method can include HTML tags. For example, the Write method shown here includes a <br /> tag so that the item count is followed by a blank line. Also note that the output you write to the output stream is always added to the beginning of the stream. Because of that, it always appears at the top of the browser window.

The Cart page with output generated by Response.Write

A Page_Load method that writes to the HTTP output stream

```
protected void Page_Load(object sender, EventArgs e)
{
    cart = CartItemList.GetCart();
    if (!IsPostBack)
    {
        this.DisplayCart();
        Response.Write("Items in cart = " + cart.Count + "<br />");
    }
}
```

Code that writes HTML output from another class

```
HttpContext.Current.Response.Write("Now updating file.<br />");
```

Description

- The Write method of the HttpResponse object provides a convenient way to write data directly to the HTTP output stream. The output can include any valid HTML.

- To access the HttpResponse object from the code-behind file for a web page, you use the Response property of the page. To access this object from a class that doesn't inherit the Page class, you use the Response property of the HttpContext object for the current request. To access this object, you use the Current property of the HttpContext class.

- The HTML output you add to the HTTP output stream using the Write method of the HttpResponse object appears at the beginning of the output stream. As a result, the output always appears at the top of the page in the browser window.

Figure 4-15   How to write information directly to the HTTP output stream

Perspective

As you can now appreciate, Visual Studio provides a powerful set of tools for debugging ASP.NET applications. For simple applications, you can usually get the debugging done just by using breakpoints, data tips, and the Autos window. You may also need to step through critical portions of code from time to time. For complex applications, though, you may discover the need for some of the other features that are presented in this chapter. With tools like these, a difficult debugging job becomes manageable.

Terms

virtual directory	breakpoint	Immediate window
browse location	break mode	Autos window
concurrency	Breakpoints window	Locals window
concurrency error	tracepoint	Watch window
stack trace	Output window	watch expression
debugger	data tip	Trace feature

Exercise 4-1   Use the Visual Studio debugger

In this exercise, you'll step through the Shopping Cart application that you developed in the exercises for chapter 3. In the process, you'll set breakpoints, use the Locals window, and use buttons in the Debug toolbar for controlling program execution.

1. Open the Ch04Cart web site in the aspnet4_cs directory. Then, display the code for the Order page, and set a breakpoint on the statement in the Load event handler that calls the GetSelectedProduct method.

2. Run the application in the default browser. When the application enters break mode, point to the IsPostBack property to display its value in a data tip. Then, point to the data tip and click the pin icon so the data tip remains open.

3. Press the F11 key to execute the next statement. Notice that this statement is in the GetSelectedProduct method. Press the F11 key two more times to see that only one statement is executed each time.

4. Click the Step Out button in the Debug toolbar to skip over the remaining statements in the GetSelectedProduct method. This should return you to the Page_Load method.

5. Click the Continue button in the Debug toolbar. This should execute the remaining statements in the Page_Load method and display the Order page.

6. Select another product from the combo box. This should cause the application to enter break mode again and stop on the statement that calls the GetSelectedProduct method. Notice that the data tip for the IsPostBack property is still displayed.

7. Press the F10 key to execute the Step Over command. This should step over all statements in the GetSelectedProduct method and enter break mode before the next statement in the Page_Load method is executed.

8. Point to the Text property of the labels to display these values. Then, point to the selected product to see the values that are stored in this object. Step through the statements that assign the product properties to the Text property of the labels and note how the values in the Text property change.

9. Note the values that are displayed in the Locals window. Click the plus sign next to the form object (this) to expand it and review the information that's available. When you're done, click the minus sign to collapse the information for this object.

10. Remove the breakpoint from the Page_Load method. Then, set another breakpoint on the statement in the GetSelectedProduct method that sets the value of the selected product's name, continue execution of the application, and select another product. When the application enters break mode again, notice the variables that are now displayed in the Locals window. That should include all of the variables that are in scope.

11. Display a Watch window. Add the Name column of the DataViewRow object to this window by dragging it from the Code Editor window. In the Watch window, it should look something like this:

```
row["Name"].ToString()
```

Then, enter an expression into the Watch 1 window that displays the Count property of the DataView object. In the Watch window, it should look something like this:

```
productsTable.Count
```

Note the value of the Count property. It should be 1.

12. Enter the same expression into the Immediate window, preceded by a question mark. Press the Enter key to see the value that's displayed. It should be 1.

13. Use the Immediate window to assign a new value to the Name column of the DataViewRow object. Check the value of this property in the Watch window and note that the new value is displayed.

14. Press F5 to continue program execution. This should display the Order page. Note that the Name value that you set in the previous step is displayed on the Order page.

15. Select another product from the combo box. This should cause the application to enter break mode again.

16. Click the Stop Debugging button in the Debug toolbar to end the application. Note that the breakpoint remains in the Code Editor even after you have stopped debugging.

Exercise 4-2   Use the Trace feature

In this exercise, you'll use the Trace feature of ASP.NET to display trace output on the Order page of the Shopping Cart application that you created in the exercises for chapter 3.

1. If it's not already open, open the Ch04Cart web site.

2. Display the Order page in the Web Forms Designer and switch to Source view. Then, enable tracing for the page by adding a Trace attribute to the Page directive as shown in figure 4-13.

3. Run the application and notice that the trace output is displayed below the controls on the Order page.

4. View the trace information. In particular, review the Session State information. When you're done, end the application.

5. Add a custom trace message to the GetSelectedProduct method that indicates that this method has created a new Product object. Use the method name as the category for this message. If you need help, you can refer to figure 4-14.

6. Add a custom trace message to the btnAdd_Click method that indicates that a product has been added to the cart. Use the method name as the category for this message. Also, comment out the statement that displays the Cart page. If you don't, you won't be able to see this trace message.

7. Run the application to see what messages are displayed. Then, click the Add to Cart button and see what messages are displayed this time.

8. End the application. Then, close and save the project.

Exercise 4-3   Test the Shopping Cart application with IIS and other browsers

In this exercise, you'll create a local IIS site for the Shopping Cart application that you created in the exercises for chapter 3, and you'll test this application using other browsers besides Microsoft's Internet Explorer.

1. If IIS isn't installed on your system, install it as described in figure A-2 (Windows 7 and Windows Vista) or figure A-3 (Windows XP) of appendix A.

2. Create a local IIS site for the Shopping Cart application as described in figure 4-4. In the Choose Location dialog box, click the Local IIS button and then select the Default Web Site node. Next, click the Create New Virtual Directory button and enter Ch04Cart as the alias that points to the web site in the C:\aspnet4_cs\Ch04Cart directory. This is the web site that you created in the exercises for chapter 3.

3. In the Web Site Already Exists dialog box, select the "Open the existing web site" option. Then, set the Order page as the start page.

4. Test the application with the default browser as described in figure 4-1. You can tell that the web site is using IIS instead of the ASP.NET Development Server because no port is specified in the URL.

5. If a browser other than the default is available to you, test the Shopping Cart application with that browser as described in figure 4-2. When you're done, end the application and close the project.

6. Launch a browser from outside of Visual Studio and run the Shopping Cart application as described in figure 4-6. When you're done, close the browser.

5

A crash course in HTML and CSS

As you know, a web form is defined by HTML and asp tags, and you'll learn how to code asp tags throughout this book. Although this book isn't intended to teach you HTML, you need to know some basic skills for coding HTML to use it with ASP.NET. That's particularly true when you use HTML to define the content and structure of a web page, and you use CSS, or cascading style sheets, to format the page. This is the technique professionals use to define web pages, and it's the technique you'll learn in this chapter.

If you already know how to code HTML and CSS, you should be able to go through this chapter quickly. However, you won't want to skip this chapter altogether because it presents some skills that are specific to Visual Studio .NET.

An introduction to HTML

HTML documents consist of *HTML elements* that define the content and structure of the page. In the topics that follow, you'll learn the basic rules for coding HTML elements, you'll learn how to work with HTML using Visual Studio, and you'll see how some of the basic web server controls are rendered to HTML.

Basic rules for coding HTML elements

Figure 5-1 presents the basic rules for coding HTML elements. To start, each HTML element is coded within a *tag* that starts with an opening bracket (<) and ends with a closing bracket (>). For example, <title>, </h1>, and <br /> are all examples of HTML tags.

Most HTML elements are made up of three parts. First, a *start tag* marks the start of the element. The start tag consists of the element name (such as title or h1) plus one or more optional *attributes* (such as id or class) that provide additional information for the tag. After the start tag is the *content*, which is the text or other data that makes up the element. After the content is the *end tag* that marks the end of the element. The end tag consists of a slash followed by the element's name. This is illustrated by the three lines of code in the first example in this figure.

It's important to realize that the content of an element can contain other elements. For example, consider this HTML code:

```
<h1>This is a <b>bold</b>heading</h1>
```

Here, the h1 element contains the text "This is a bold heading." Within this text, the b element indicates that the word "bold" should be boldfaced. You'll learn about these and other formatting elements later in this chapter.

Not all HTML elements have content and end tags. These tags are referred to as *self-closing tags*. For instance, the <br /> element shown in the second example in this figure is a self-closing tag that inserts a line break.

Notice that all of the tags shown in this figure are lowercase. This is a requirement of the XHTML version 1.0 standards. Although ASP.NET web pages currently use XHTML version 1.0 Transitional, which allows uppercase tags, you'll want to use lowercase tags so you won't need to change your HTML in the future.

Notice also that the <br /> tag includes a slash before the closing bracket. Although these slashes were optional in earlier HTML standards, they are required with XHTML version 1.0. As a result, you'll want to include them in your code.

You can also code *comments* within an HTML document as shown in the third example in this figure. That way, you can document sections of code that

Three HTML elements with start tags, content, and end tags

```
<title>Halloween Superstore</title>
<h1>About Us</h1>
<p id="product">Choose a product:</p>
```

An element that has no content or end tags

```
This line will break here<br />and continue on the next line.
```

A comment

```
<!-- This text will be ignored. -->
```

A line that has three consecutive spaces

```
Last name:   Wilson
```

Elements and tags

- An *HTML document* includes *HTML elements* that specify the content and structure of the page.

- Most HTML elements have three parts: a start tag, content, and an end tag. Each *tag* is coded within a set of brackets (< >).

- An element's *start tag* includes the name of the element. The *end tag* includes the element name preceded by a slash. And the *content* includes everything that appears between the start and end tags.

- Some HTML elements have no content or end tag. For example, the <br /> element, which forces a line break, consists of just one tag. This type of tag is called a *self-closing tag*.

- You should use lowercase letters for all your tags.

Attributes

- *Attributes* can appear within a start tag to supply optional values. For example, you can use the id attribute to specify an ID for any element.

- All attribute values should be enclosed in quotation marks.

- Use spaces to separate attributes from one another.

Comments and white space

- A *comment* is text that appears between the <!-- and --> characters. Web browsers ignore comments, so you can use them to document sections of your HTML code that might otherwise be confusing.

- *White space*, such as tabs, line returns, and consecutive spaces, is ignored by browsers. As a result, you can use space to indent lines of code and line breaks to separate elements from one another. Used properly, white space can make your HTML code easier to read.

- To force the browser to display two or more consecutive spaces, use the *character entity*   for each space.

Figure 5-1   Basic rules for coding HTML elements

might be confusing. In addition, you can use spaces, indentation, and blank lines to make your code easier to read. This is called *white space*, and web browsers ignore it.

If you want to include space within a line that the web browser doesn't ignore, you can use the special code   as shown in the last example in figure 5-1. This is just one of the *character entities* that you can use to display special characters in HTML. Later in this chapter, I'll present an example that uses two additional character entities. In that example, you'll see that each character entity starts with an ampersand (&) and ends with a semicolon (;).

How to work with HTML using Visual Studio

In chapter 2, you learned how to create a simple web form by dragging ASP.NET controls onto the design surface of the Web Forms Designer. You also learned some basic skills for modifying the design of a form from Source view. Now, figure 5-2 reviews some of these skills and presents some additional skills for working in Source view.

When you display a web form in Source view, you'll notice that Visual Studio uses different colors to identify various items of information. For example, element names are displayed in maroon, attribute names are displayed in red, and attribute values are displayed in blue. Visual Studio also makes syntax errors easy to locate by underlining them with a red wavy line.

Visual Studio also provides tools that help you enter and edit HTML code. One of the most useful is the statement completion feature. With this feature, a list of the available elements is displayed when you enter the opening bracket for a start tag. Then, you can select the element you want to add from this list and press the Tab or Enter key to add the element name to your document.

After you enter an element name followed by a space, Visual Studio displays a list of the available attributes for that element. In this figure, for example, you can see the list of attributes that's displayed for a p element. To add an attribute, you just select it from the list and press the Tab or Enter key. Then, you can type an equal sign and enter a value for the attribute. When you enter a value, be sure to enclose it in quotation marks or you'll get a syntax error. To enter additional attributes, type a space to redisplay the list. When you're finished entering the attributes for an element, you enter its closing bracket. Then, the end tag for that element, if it has one, is added automatically.

You can also use code snippets to enter HTML elements. This works the same as it does for entering ASP.NET elements. For more information, see figure 2-13 in chapter 2.

As you make changes in Source view, you'll frequently want to check the results of those changes in Design view. One way to do that is to switch back and forth between these two views. Another way is to use Split view. As you learned in chapter 2, Split view lets you see both Design view and Source view at the same time.

A web page in Source view with a completion list displayed

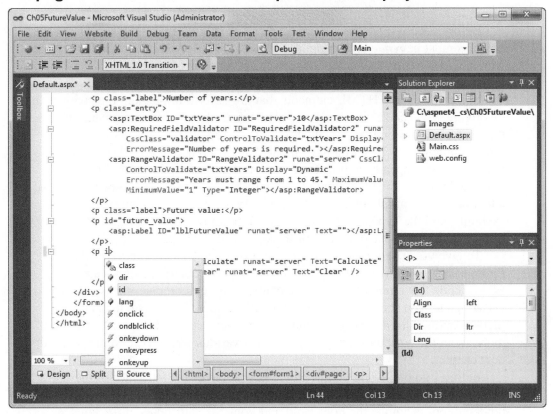

Description

- To edit the HTML for a web page in Visual Studio, display the page in Source view by clicking on the Source button at the bottom of the Web Forms Designer window.

- Visual Studio uses distinctive colors to identify various items in Source view. In addition, it highlights syntax errors with a red wavy underline so they're easy to locate.

- When you enter the opening bracket (<) for a start tag, Visual Studio displays a list of the available elements. To select an element, type one or more letters of the element or scroll to the element, and then press the Tab or Enter key.

- When you enter the name of an HTML element followed by a space, Visual Studio displays a list of the attributes you can use with that element. To select an attribute, type one or more letters of the attribute or scroll to the attribute, and then press the Tab or Enter key.

- When you enter the closing bracket (>) for a start tag, Visual Studio automatically adds the end tag.

- You can also enter HTML elements using code snippets as described in chapter 2.

- You can also add or modify element attributes using the Properties window. To do that, move the insertion point into the tag for the element to display its attributes in the Properties window and then change the attribute values as appropriate.

Figure 5-2   How to work with HTML using Visual Studio

How web server controls are rendered

Before a web page can be displayed in a browser, any web server controls it contains must be *rendered* to standard HTML. To help you understand how this works, figure 5-3 lists some common web server controls and describes the HTML elements they're rendered to.

If you review the HTML elements that are used to implement the controls in this figure, you can see that the same element can be used to implement more than one control. For example, the text box, button, and image button controls are all implemented by an Input element. The difference in how these controls appear and act depends on how their attributes are set. In this case, the Type attribute indicates the type of input control that's rendered. The Type attribute of a text box, for example, is set to "text," the Type attribute of a button is set to "submit," and the Type attribute of an image button is set to "image." Because of that, the browser handles each of these controls differently.

To give you a better idea of how web server controls are rendered, this figure also shows the aspx code for four web server controls along with the HTML code that's rendered for those controls. If you compare the aspx and HTML code, you should quickly see how it's related. Of course, the HTML that's generated for a control depends on how you set its attributes. You'll learn more about the attributes that you can set for various web server controls in the next chapter.

Before I go on, I want you to notice how some of the attributes of the controls in this example are included in the style attribute of the HTML that's rendered. For example, the Font-Bold and Font-Size attributes of the label control are rendered to the style attribute of a span element. Styles that are included within the HTML for an element are called *inline styles*, and you'll learn more about them later in this chapter.

For now, I just want you to realize that when an HTML element includes inline styles, they're passed between the client and the server along with the other information for the page. Because that can be inefficient, you'll want to avoid using control attributes that are rendered as inline styles. In general, these are the attributes that affect the appearance of the controls. Later in this chapter, you'll learn how to change the appearance of controls without using inline styles.

Some common web server controls and how they're rendered

Name	HTML element	Additional information
Label	`<span>`	The <span> element is typically used to apply special formatting to the text it encloses.
TextBox	`<input>`	The type="text" attribute identifies this element as a text box.
Button	`<input>`	The type="submit" attribute identifies this element as a button.
ImageButton	`<input>`	The type="image" attribute identifies this element as an image button.
LinkButton	`<a>`	This control is rendered as an Anchor element whose href attribute points to a function generated in JavaScript that posts the page back to the server.
HyperLink	`<a>`	This control is rendered as an Anchor element that links to another URL.
ListBox	`<select>`	Each item in the list is defined by an <option> element within the <select> element.
DropDownList	`<select>`	Each item in the list is defined by an <option> element within the <select> element.
Image	`<img>`	Displays the specified image.

The aspx code for four web server controls

```
<asp:Label ID="lblName" runat="server" Font-Bold="True" Font-Size="Larger"
    Text="Murach Books"></asp:Label>
<asp:TextBox ID="txtSearch" runat="server" Width="248px"></asp:TextBox>
<asp:Button ID="btnSearch" runat="server" Text="Search" />
<asp:ListBox ID="lstBooks" runat="server">
    <asp:ListItem Value="A4VB">ASP.NET 4 with VB 2010</asp:ListItem>
    <asp:ListItem Value="VB10">Visual Basic 2010</asp:ListItem>
    <asp:ListItem Value="SQL8">SQL Server 2008</asp:ListItem>
</asp:ListBox>
```

How the four web server controls are rendered in HTML

```
<span id="lblName" style="font-size:Larger;font-weight:bold;">Murach
Books</span>
<input name="txtSearch" type="text" id="txtSearch" style="width:248px;" />
<input type="submit" name="btnSearch" value="Search" id="btnSearch" />
<select size="4" name="lstBooks" id="lstBooks">
    <option value="A4VB">ASP.NET 4 with VB 2010</option>
    <option value="VB10">Visual Basic 2010</option>
    <option value="SQL8">SQL Server 2008</option>
</select>
```

Description

- All of the web server controls are *rendered* as standard HTML that can be interpreted by a browser.
- To view the HTML that's rendered for a web page, choose the View→Source command from the browser window. The HTML will be displayed in a separate Notepad window.

Figure 5-3   How web server controls are rendered

How to code HTML documents

Every HTML document for a web form must be structured in a certain way for it to be interpreted properly by ASP.NET. In the topics that follow, you'll learn about the basic structure of an HTML document. You'll also learn how to code the two basic types of elements that appear within an HTML document.

The basic structure of an HTML document

Figure 5-4 shows the code that's generated for a new ASP.NET web page. This code illustrates the overall structure of an HTML document. Because the elements that make up this structure are generated for you automatically, you don't have to worry about coding them yourself.

The first element is an ASP.NET Page directive. This directive supplies the information ASP.NET needs to process the web form. You'll learn more about this directive in the next figure.

The Page directive is followed by an HTML Doctype declaration. This declaration provides information the browser needs to display the page. You'll learn more about this element in the next figure too.

After the Page directive and the Doctype declaration is an html element. This element, known as the *root element*, contains all of the document's remaining elements. Prior to the XHTML version 1.0 standards, the start and end tags for the html element were optional. As a result, you'll sometimes see HTML documents without the <html> and </html> tags.

Within the html section, an HTML document contains two additional sections: a document head and a document body. The document head, defined by a head element, contains information about the document. As shown here, one element it contains by default is the title element. The value of this element determines what's displayed in the title bar of the browser window. Later in this chapter, you'll learn about two additional elements that you can add to the head element.

The document body, defined by a body element, contains the HTML content that's displayed when the document is viewed in a browser. For a web form, the document body consists of a form element with one or more div elements. As you've seen in previous chapters, the div element that's generated by default contains all of the asp and HTML elements for the form. This div element can also contain additional div elements that you define. This is common when you use CSS to format a web form.

Because the head and body elements are contained within an html element, the html element is called a *parent element* and the head and body elements are called *child elements*. The body element is also a parent element because it contains a form element. And the form element is a parent element because it contains a div element.

The code generated for a new ASP.NET web page

```
<%@ Page Language="C#" AutoEventWireup="true" CodeFile="Cart.aspx.cs"
Inherits="Cart" %>

<!DOCTYPE html PUBLIC "-//W3C//DTD XHTML 1.0 Transitional//EN"
"http://www.w3.org/TR/xhtml1/DTD/xhtml1-transitional.dtd">

<html xmlns="http://www.w3.org/1999/xhtml">
<head runat="server">
    <title></title>
</head>
<body>
    <form id="form1" runat="server">
    <div>

    </div>
    </form>
</body>
</html>
```

HTML elements generated for a new page

Element	Start tag	End tag	Description
Doctype declaration	`<!DOCTYPE ...>`		Identifies the type of HTML document. See figure 5-5 for details.
html element	`<html>`	`</html>`	Marks the beginning and end of an HTML document.
head element	`<head>`	`</head>`	Marks the beginning and end of the document head.
title element	`<title>`	`</title>`	Provides the title for the page.
body element	`<body>`	`</body>`	Marks the beginning and end of the document body.
form element	`<form>`	`</form>`	Marks the beginning and end of the form.
div element	`<div>`	`</div>`	Marks the beginning and end of a division within the form.

Description

- The html element contains the content of the document. This element is called the *root element* because it contains all the other elements in the document. Within this element, you code the head and body elements.

- The body element contains the form element that defines the form.

- The form element contains a div element that's used to provide formatting that applies to the entire page. Any elements you add to the page in the Web Forms Designer should be inserted within this div element. You can also add additional div elements within the outer div element to divide the contents of the page into smaller divisions.

- An element that's contained within another element is called a *child element*. The element that contains a child element is called the child's *parent element*.

- In addition to the HTML elements, a Page directive is generated. This directive supplies various options that are applied to the web page. See figure 5-5 for details.

Figure 5-4   The basic structure of an HTML document for an ASP.NET web page

The Page directive

Figure 5-5 shows the Page directive that appears at the beginning of all ASP.NET pages. Notice that the Page directive begins with the characters <%@ and ends with the characters %>. These special sequences of characters form a *directive block*. Because directive blocks aren't a part of standard HTML, they aren't included in the final HTML that's sent to the browser when the page is displayed. Instead, directive blocks are processed by ASP.NET when the page is compiled.

As you can see in this figure, the Page directive has several attributes. The first attribute, Language, specifies the programming language that's used for the page's code. For Visual C# projects, the value of this attribute is C#.

The next attribute is AutoEventWireup. For C# web forms created in Visual Studio, this attribute is set to True. That means that the event handlers for page events such as Init and Load must name the event handlers appropriately. For example, the event handlers for the Init and Load events must be named Page_Init and Page_Load. Then, C# automatically wires these handlers to the appropriate event.

The CodeFile and Inherits attributes work together to link the ASP.NET web page to the code-behind file. First, the CodeFile attribute provides the name of the code-behind file. Visual Studio uses this attribute to associate the partial class it generates for the page at runtime (the class that contains the control declarations) with the file that contains the C# code for the page. Then, the Inherits attribute provides the name of the compiled class that the page inherits at runtime. This is the name that's specified by the class declaration in the code-behind file.

Another attribute you can include in the Page directive is Trace. You learned about this attribute in chapter 4. It determines whether or not trace information that you can use for debugging is displayed on the web page.

The Doctype declaration

Figure 5-5 also shows the Doctype declaration. This declaration is used by a web browser to determine which version of HTML the document uses. The Doctype declaration generated by Visual Studio 2010 specifies XHTML version 1.0 Transitional, which includes some HTML elements that are expected to be phased out in the future. If you use these elements, error or warning messages are displayed in the Error List window.

A typical Page directive

```
<%@ Page Language="C#" AutoEventWireup="true" CodeFile="Cart.aspx.cs"
Inherits="Cart" %>
```

Common attributes of the Page directive

Attribute	Description
Language	Specifies the language used to implement the processing for the page. For C# applications, this attribute is set to C#.
AutoEventWireup	Indicates whether the event handlers for the page will be called automatically when the events occur for the page (True) or if you must bind event handlers to these events (False). For C# applications, Visual Studio sets this attribute to True when it creates a web form.
CodeFile	Specifies the name of the code-behind file. This file defines the partial class that is compiled with the partial class that ASP.NET generates from the page at runtime.
Inherits	Specifies the name of the compiled class (dll) that the page inherits at runtime. This name is typically the same as the name of the partial class defined in the CodeFile attribute.
Trace	Indicates whether tracing is enabled. The default is False.

A typical Doctype declaration

```
<!DOCTYPE html PUBLIC "-//W3C//DTD XHTML 1.0 Transitional//EN"
"http://www.w3.org/TR/xhtml1/DTD/xhtml1-transitional.dtd">
```

Description

- The Page directive is processed by ASP.NET when the page is compiled. It isn't included in the output that's sent to the browser.

- The Doctype declaration specifies that the root element of the document—that is, the first element after the Doctype declaration—is an HTML element.

- The Public attribute of the Doctype declaration and the string that follows it specify the version of HTML that the document complies with.

Figure 5-5   The Page directive and the Doctype declaration

How to code block elements

You use *block elements* to define the main structure of a web form. Figure 5-6 lists the most common block elements. Each of these elements begins on a new line when it's displayed in a browser.

I've already mentioned the div element. You use it to divide a form into logical divisions. The other block elements shown here are used to display various levels of headings and a standard paragraph.

If you review the example in this figure, you shouldn't have any trouble understanding how these elements work. Here, you can see that the content of the document is structured into three divisions. The first division contains the entire web page, and it's divided into two other divisions: one for the main portion of the web page and one for the footer. Note that each of these divisions has an id attribute. You can use this attribute to refer to the divisions from CSS as shown later in this chapter.

In addition to the div elements, this HTML uses h1, h2, and p elements to generate the text that's shown. When these elements are displayed by a browser, each element has a default font and size that's determined by the base font of the browser. This base font is typically Times New Roman in 16 pixels.

Although you might think that you would use the h1 through h6 elements to format headings, that's not the case. Instead, you should use them to provide a logical structure for your document. For example, the h1 element in this figure is used to mark the most important heading on the page, and the h2 element is used to mark the second most import heading. Then, you can use CSS to size and format the text in these elements.

Common block elements

Element	Description
div	Lets you structure a page into logical divisions that can be formatted and positioned with CSS. This element can contain text, inline elements, and other block elements.
h1	Creates a level-1 heading with content in bold at 200% of the base font size.
h2	Creates a level-2 heading with content in bold at 150% of the base font size.
h3	Creates a level-3 heading with content in bold at 117% of the base font size.
h4	Creates a level-4 heading with content in bold at 100% of the base font size.
h5	Creates a level-5 heading with content in bold at 83% of the base font size.
h6	Creates a level-6 heading with content in bold at 67% of the base font size.
p	Creates a paragraph of text at 100% of the base font size.

A page that uses block elements

```
<div id="page">
    <div id="main">
        <h1>Murach Books</h1>
        <h2>New! HTML, XHTML, and CSS</h2>
        <p>This book teaches you how to develop web pages the professional
        way, using HTML/XHTML to provide the content and structure of the
        elements on a page and CSS to format and lay out those elements.</p>
    </div>
    <div id="footer">
        <p>&copy; Copyright 2010 Mike Murach &amp; Associates, Inc.</p>
    </div>
</div>
```

The page displayed in a web browser

Murach Books

New! HTML, XHTML, and CSS

This book teaches you how to develop web pages the professional way, using HTML/XHTML to provide the content and structure of the elements on a page and CSS to format and lay out those elements.

© Copyright 2010 Mike Murach & Associates, Inc.

Description

- *Block elements* are the main building blocks of a web site and can contain other elements. Each block element begins on a new line.

- You can use div elements to define divisions within the body of a document. This can help indicate the overall structure of the page.

- The base font and font size for headings and paragraphs are determined by the browser. You can change these values using CSS.

Figure 5-6   How to code block elements

How to code inline elements

In contrast to a block element, an *inline element* doesn't start on a new line. Instead, an inline element appears within a block element. Figure 5-7 presents some of the most common inline elements and shows how to use them.

The first table in this figure presents some of the inline elements for formatting text. Then, the first six examples show you how to use some of these elements. Notice that each inline element is coded within a block element, in this case a p element. In addition, except for the br element, each element has both an opening and a closing tag. Then, the appropriate formatting is applied to the content between these tags.

As you review these elements, you'll notice that both the i and em elements cause the content to be displayed in italics. Similarly, both the b and strong elements cause the content to be displayed in bold. The difference is that the i and b elements don't assign any meaning to the content; they simply apply formatting. In contrast, the em element indicates that the content should be emphasized, and the strong element indicates that the content should be strongly emphasized.

Because of that, you should only use i and b when you don't need to associate any meaning with the content. In this figure, for example, you can see that the i element is used to italicize the term "Hypertext Markup Language", but the em element is used to emphasize the words "you won't pass the class". The examples for the b and strong elements are similar.

Please note that the way the i and b elements are used have changed since CSS has become available. Previously, these elements were commonly used to apply formatting. Now, it's more common to use em and strong and to use CSS to apply the appropriate formatting.

As you know, the last element in the first table, br, forces a new line of text. Note, however, that you shouldn't use this element to provide space between block elements; your CSS should do that. Instead, you should use it only to force a new line within a block element. In the sixth paragraph in this figure, for example, the br element is used to force a new line between two lines of poetry.

The second table in this figure presents an inline element for structuring text. The span element identifies text within a block element as shown in the last example in this figure. Then, you can refer to the span element from CSS to format the text that it contains.

Common inline elements for formatting text

Element	Description
i	Displays the content in italics.
em	Indicates that the content should be emphasized by being displayed in italics.
b	Displays the content in bold.
strong	Indicates that the content should be strongly emphasized by being displayed in bold.
code	Displays the content in a monospaced font.
sub	Displays the content as a subscript.
sup	Displays the content as a superscript.
br	Starts a new line of text.

An inline element for structuring text

Element	Description
span	Lets you identify text that can be formatted with CSS.

A page that uses inline elements

```
<p>If you don't get 78% on your final, <em>you won't pass the class.</em></p>
<p>Save a bundle at our <strong>big yearend sale</strong>.</p>
<p>HTML stands for <i>Hypertext Markup Language</i>.</p>
<p>Please be sure to boldface <b>Murach</b> in the company logo.</p>
<p>Your payment is due on the 4<sup>th</sup> of each month.</p>
<p>"To sleep, perchance to dream-<br />ay, there's the rub."</p>
<p><span id="hurry">Hurry!</span>The sale ends tomorrow.</p>
```

The page displayed in a web browser

If you don't get 78% on your final, *you won't pass the class.*

Save a bundle at our **big yearend sale**.

HTML stands for *Hypertext Markup Language*.

Please be sure to boldface **Murach** in the company logo.

Your payment is due on the 4th of each month.

"To sleep, perchance to dream-
ay, there's the rub."

Hurry! The sale ends tomorrow.

Description

- An *inline element* is coded within a block element and doesn't begin on a new line. Many of the inline elements, such as the ones in the first table above, are used to format text.

- The span element can also be used to format text. However, that formatting is specified using CSS.

Figure 5-7   How to code inline elements

Basic skills for using CSS

Until recently, most HTML documents were coded so the HTML not only defined the content and structure of the web page but also the formatting of that content. However, this mix of structural and formatting elements made it hard to edit, maintain, and reformat the pages.

Today, however, *cascading style sheets* (CSS) let you separate the formatting from the content and structure of a web page. As a result, most of the formatting that was once done in the HTML should now be done in the CSS. Note that in addition to CSS, you can use a feature of ASP.NET called skins to apply formatting to web server controls. As you'll learn in chapter 11, you can store style sheets and skins together in themes.

How to include CSS in a web page

The best way to apply a *style sheet* to an HTML document is to code the styles in a separate file called an *external style sheet*. When you do that, you must indicate what style sheet each page should use. To do that, you code a link element within the head element as shown in the first example in figure 5-8.

On the link element, you code three attributes. For a style sheet, the rel and type attributes should always be coded as shown here. Then, the href attribute specifies the URL of the style sheet. In this example, the style sheet is stored in the same directory as the other files for the project, so the URL is simply the name of the file. Note that a style sheet must have a file extension of *css*.

Instead of typing in the link element for a style sheet, you can have Visual Studio generate it for you. You can do that from either Design view or Source view as described in this figure. This is referred to as *attaching a style sheet*.

Although it isn't recommended, you can also use *internal style sheets* and *inline styles* to embed styles within an HTML document as shown by the second set of examples in this figure. When you use an internal style sheet, the CSS rule sets are coded in a style element. For instance, the internal style sheet in the first example in this group contains a rule set for the h1 element. You'll learn more about rule sets in the next figure.

When you use an inline style, you code a style attribute for the HTML element with a value that contains all the CSS declarations that apply to the element. For instance, the inline style in the second example in this group applies two CSS declarations to the span element. You'll learn more about declarations in the next figure too.

If you do use internal style sheets or inline styles, the styles in the embedded style sheets override the styles in the external style sheets, and the inline styles override the styles in the internal style sheet. If, for example, you code the internal style sheet in this figure, the declarations for the h1 element will override those in the external style sheet.

Remember, though, that using external style sheets is a best practice. When you use them, the CSS declarations are in a separate CSS file, which separates

How to include an external style sheet

```
<head runat="server">
    <title>Chapter 5: Future Value</title>
    <link href="Main.css" rel="stylesheet" type="text/css" />
</head>
```

How to embed styles in an HTML document (not recommended)

By including a style sheet in a style element

```
<head runat="server">
    <title>Chapter 5: Future Value</title>
    <style type="text/css">
        h1 {
            color: blue;
            font-size: 16pt;
        }
    </style>
</head>
```

By using the style attribute of an inline element

```
<span style="color: red; font-size: 14pt;">Warning!</span>
```

Part of a web page that uses two style sheets

```
<head runat="server">
    <title>Chapter 5: Shopping Cart</title>
    <link href="Styles/Main.css" rel="stylesheet" type="text/css" />
    <link href="Styles/Order.css" rel="stylesheet" type="text/css" />
</head>
```

Description

- It's a best practice to use *external style sheets* whenever possible. To do that, you code a link element within the head element.

- When you specify a relative URL for an external CSS file, the URL is relative to the current file.

- You can include two or more external style sheets in a single page. Then, the styles in the first style sheet are applied first, followed by the styles in the second style sheet, and so on.

- After you create an external style sheet, you can generate a link element for it from Design view for a page. To do that, choose the Format→Attach Style Sheet command and then select the style sheet from the Select Style Sheet dialog box that's displayed.

- You can also generate a link element in Source view by dragging the style sheet from the Solution Explorer to the head element for the page.

- If you use an internal style sheet, the styles appear within a style element in the document head.

- If you use inline styles, the styles appear in the style attribute of the inline element they're applied to.

Figure 5-8   How to include CSS in a web page

the formatting for a web page from its content. This also makes it possible for more than one web page to share the same CSS file, which has several benefits. First, the HTML files are smaller. Second, you can provide consistent formatting for all the pages that use the same style sheet. Third, you can modify the formatting for all those pages by modifying a single style sheet.

The last example in figure 5-8 shows that you can include more than one style sheet in a single document. You might do that if you want to store the basic formatting for all the pages of a web site in one style sheet, and you want to store the formatting that's specific to each page in a separate style sheet. For instance, you could use the two style sheets shown here, Main.css and Order.css, for the Order page of the Shopping Cart application. Then, you could use the Main.css style sheet, along with another style sheet named Cart.css, for the Cart page.

How to code CSS rule sets and comments

A CSS file consists of *rule sets*, also called *style rules*. As the diagram in figure 5-9 shows, a rule set consists of a *selector* followed by a set of braces. Within the braces are one or more *declarations*, and each declaration consists of a *property* and a *value*. Note that the property is followed by a colon and the value is followed by a semicolon.

In this diagram, the selector is h1 so it applies to all h1 elements. Then, the rule set consists of a single property named color that is set to the color navy. The result is that the content of all h1 elements will be displayed in navy blue.

In the CSS code that follows, you can see four other rule sets. The first two rule sets contain only one declaration (or *rule*), but the third and fourth rule sets contain three rules each. The rule set for the h2 element sets the font-style, color, and border-bottom properties, and the rule set for the p element sets the text-indent, margin-top, and margin-bottom properties. Although you won't learn about the individual properties in this chapter, you should be able to tell what most of them do from the property name and value.

Within a CSS file, you can also code *comments* that describe or explain what the CSS code is doing. For each comment, you start with /* and end with */, and anything between those characters is ignored. In the example in this figure, you can see how CSS comments can be coded on separate lines within a style sheet. You can also code a comment following the code on any line of a rule set.

You can also use comments to comment out portions of code that you want disabled. This can be useful when you're testing and debugging your CSS.

The parts of a CSS rule set

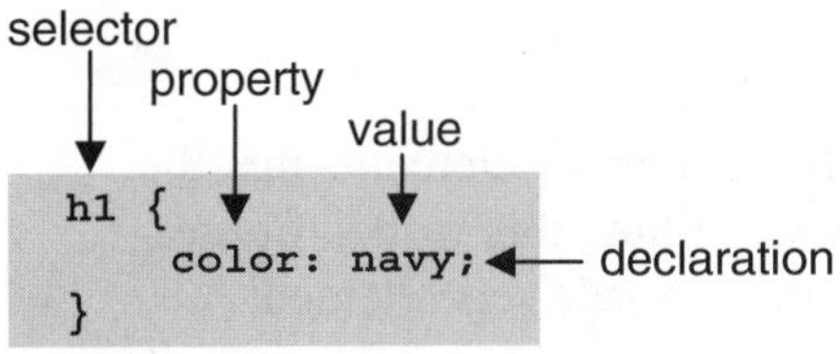

A simple style sheet

```
/* Adjust the styles for the body */
body {
    background-color: #F5F5F5;
}

/* Adjust the styles for the headings */
h1 {
    color: #FF0000;
}
h2 {
    font-style: italic;
    color: #00008B;
    border-bottom: 3px solid #00008B;
}

/* Adjust the styles for the paragraphs */
p {
    text-indent: 2em;
    margin-top: 0;
    margin-bottom: 5px;
}
```

Description

- A CSS *rule set* consists of a selector and a declaration block. In Visual Studio, a rule set is called a *style rule*.
- A CSS *selector* consists of the identifiers that are coded at the beginning of the rule set.
- A CSS *declaration block* consists of an opening brace, zero or more declarations, and a closing brace.
- A CSS *declaration* consists of a *property*, a colon, a *value*, and a semicolon. Although the semicolon for the last declaration in a block is optional, it's a best practice to code it.
- To make your code easier to read, you can use spaces, indentation, and blank lines within a rule set.
- CSS *comments* begin with the characters /* and end with the characters */. A CSS comment can be coded on a single line, or it can span multiple lines.
- Visual Studio provides a feature for generating rule sets. See figure 5-15 for details.

Figure 5-9   How to code CSS rule sets and comments

How to code selectors for elements, IDs, and classes

The selector of a rule set identifies the HTML element or elements that the rules should be applied to. To give you a better idea of how this works, figure 5-10 shows how to use the three basic selectors for CSS rule sets: element selectors, ID selectors, and class selectors.

An *element selector* identifies HTML elements like body, h1, or p elements. For instance, the selector in the first example applies to the h2 element shown in the HTML at the top of this figure. The first rule within this rule set sets the font to Arial if it's available or to a generic sans-serif font otherwise. Then, the second rule sets the margin above the h2 element to 5 pixels, and the third rule sets the margin below the h2 element to zero.

An *ID selector* starts with the pound sign (#) and applies to a single HTML element that's identified by an id attribute. For instance, #main applies to the HTML element that has an id attribute with a value of "main". As you can see, that's the first div element in the HTML code. Within this rule set, the first rule adds a solid black border that's two pixels wide around the division; the second rule puts a 10 pixel margin outside of the border; and the third rule puts 10 pixels of padding between the border and the content of the division.

A *class selector* starts with a period (.) and applies to all the HTML elements that are identified by the class attribute with the named value. For instance, .copyright applies to all elements with a class attribute that have a value of copyright. Here, the only element assigned to this class is the paragraph in the footer division. Then, the rules in this rule set right-align the text in the paragraph and reduce the font size to 80% of the base font size.

Note that because the copyright class is used only once in the example in this figure, I could have used an ID selector instead of a class selector. In fact, you'll typically use a class selector only if you need to apply formatting to more than one element. I used a class selector here only to illustrate how they work.

Although this figure only shows how to use rule sets with HTML elements, you can also use rule sets for ID and class selectors with server controls. To code an ID selector for a server control, you code a pound sign followed by the value of the control's id attribute just as you do for an HTML element. A class selector for a server control is similar to a class selector for an HTML element, except the class name must be coded on the control's CssClass attribute. That's because server controls don't have a class attribute. You'll see how the CssClass attribute is used in the application that's presented next.

It's important to note that the styles you specify for a server control are applied to the rendered HTML. For example, suppose I want to apply a style to a drop-down list. One way to do that is to code a rule set for it based on the control's ID or CssClass value. Another way, though, would be to code a rule set for the select element, since a drop-down list is rendered to a select element. Although you typically won't need to do this, you'll see one example where this can be useful in the next chapter.

HTML that can be selected by element, ID, or class

```
<div id="main">
    <h2>New! HTML, XHTML, and CSS</h2>
    <p>This book teaches you how to develop web pages the professional
    way, using HTML/XHTML to provide the content and structure of the
    elements on a page and CSS to format and lay out those elements.</p>
</div>
<div id="footer">
    <p class="copyright">&copy; Copyright 2010 Mike Murach &amp;
    Associates, Inc.</p>
</div>
```

CSS rule sets that select by element, ID, and class

Element

```
h2 {
    font-family: Arial, sans-serif;
    margin-top: 5px;
    margin-bottom: 0;
}
```

ID

```
#main {
    border: 2px solid black;
    margin: 10px;
    padding: 10px;
}
```

Class

```
.copyright {
    text-align: right;
    font-size: 80%;
}
```

The elements displayed in a browser

New! HTML, XHTML, and CSS

This book teaches you how to develop web pages the professional way, using HTML/XHTML to provide the content and structure of the elements on a page and CSS to format and lay out those elements.

© Copyright 2010 Mike Murach & Associates, Inc.

Description

- You code a selector for an HTML element simply by naming the element.
- You code a selector for an HTML element or ASP.NET server control with an id attribute by coding a pound sign (#) followed by the id value.
- You code a selector for an HTML element with a class attribute by coding a period followed by the class name. Then, the rule set applies to all elements with that class name.
- A class selector can also be applied to ASP.NET server controls. To do that, you code the class name on the CssClass attribute of the controls.

Figure 5-10 How to code selectors for elements, IDs, and classes

A Future Value page that uses CSS

Figure 5-11 presents the design of a Future Value page that uses an external style sheet. This page works just like the Future Value page you saw back in figure 2-6 of chapter 2. Before I present the HTML and CSS code for this page, then, you might want to compare the appearance of these two pages.

First, you can see that the page that uses CSS is centered in the browser window and displayed against a shaded background. Although you can't tell here, the page has a fixed width so the size of the page won't change if you change the size of the browser window. In contrast, the page that doesn't use CSS is always displayed on a white background at the left side of the browser window.

Another noticeable difference is that all of the text on the page that uses CSS is displayed in a sans-serif font. In contrast, the page that doesn't use CSS uses the default serif font. In addition, some of the spacing on the page that uses CSS has been improved.

The design of the Future Value page

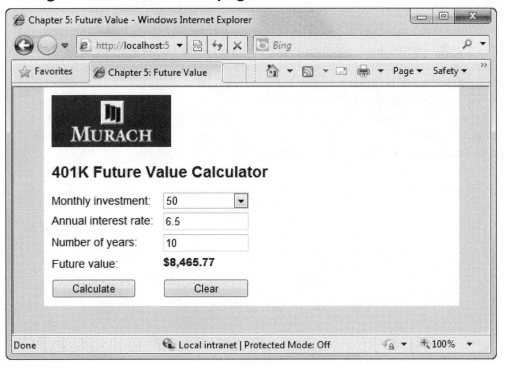

Description

- The Future Value page shown above is similar to the Future Value page you saw in chapter 2. However, this page uses an external style sheet for all formatting.
- The CSS for this page centers the page in the browser window; sets the font size, font family, and color for the text on the page; sets the size of the server controls; and sets the spacing for the elements.
- The CSS also positions the text to the left of the server controls and aligns the controls using a technique called floating.

Figure 5-11   A Future Value page that uses CSS

The aspx code for the Future Value form

Figure 5-12 presents the aspx code for the Future Value form. As you can tell from the link element for this form, it uses an external style sheet named Main.css. In a moment, you'll see that this style sheet contains rule sets for each element, ID, and class that's highlighted in this figure.

Notice here that this form doesn't use a table to lay out the text and controls like the form in chapter 2 did. Instead, the text and controls are coded within paragraphs. Then, CSS is used to format the paragraphs and lay them out on the page. In addition, CSS is used to format several of the controls.

The aspx code for the Future Value form

```
<head runat="server">
    <title>Chapter 5: Future Value</title>
    <link href="Main.css" rel="stylesheet" type="text/css" />
</head>
<body>
    <form id="form1" runat="server">
    <div id="page">
        <img id="logo" alt="Murach" src="Images/MurachLogo.jpg" />
        <h1>401K Future Value Calculator</h1>
        <p class="label">Monthly investment:</p>
        <p class="entry">
            <asp:DropDownList ID="ddlMonthlyInvestment" runat="server">
            </asp:DropDownList>
        </p>
        <p class="label">Annual interest rate:</p>
        <p class="entry">
            <asp:TextBox ID="txtInterestRate" runat="server">6.0
            </asp:TextBox>
            <asp:RequiredFieldValidator ID="RequiredFieldValidator1"
                runat="server" CssClass="validator"
                ErrorMessage="Interest rate is required."
                ControlToValidate="txtInterestRate" Display="Dynamic">
            </asp:RequiredFieldValidator>
            <asp:RangeValidator ID="RangeValidator1" runat="server"
                CssClass="validator" ControlToValidate="txtInterestRate"
                Display="Dynamic" MaximumValue="20" MinimumValue="1"
                ErrorMessage="Interest rate must range from 1 to 20."
                Type="Double"></asp:RangeValidator>
        </p>
        <p class="label">Number of years:</p>
        <p class="entry">
            <asp:TextBox ID="txtYears" runat="server">10</asp:TextBox>
            <asp:RequiredFieldValidator ID="RequiredFieldValidator2"
                runat="server" CssClass="validator"
                ControlToValidate="txtYears" Display="Dynamic"
                ErrorMessage="Number of years is required.">
            </asp:RequiredFieldValidator>
            <asp:RangeValidator ID="RangeValidator2" runat="server"
                CssClass="validator" ControlToValidate="txtYears"
                Display="Dynamic" MaximumValue="45" MinimumValue="1"
                ErrorMessage="Years must range from 1 to 45."
                Type="Integer"></asp:RangeValidator>
        </p>
        <p class="label">Future value:</p>
        <p id="future_value">
            <asp:Label ID="lblFutureValue" runat="server" Text=""
                CssClass="control"></asp:Label>
        </p>
        <p id="buttons">
            <asp:Button ID="btnCalculate" runat="server" Text="Calculate"
                OnClick="btnCalculate_Click" />
            <asp:Button ID="btnClear" runat="server" Text="Clear"
                OnClick="btnClear_Click" />
        </p>
    </div>
    </form>
</body>
```

Figure 5-12   The aspx code for the Future Value form

The CSS for the Future Value form

If you review the CSS for the Future Value form that's shown in figure 5-13, I think you'll find that most of it is easy to understand. Because of that, I'm going to focus on just a few aspects of this code.

To start, you'll notice that I coded a font family and font size for the body element of the form. These values will be used by all of the text paragraphs on the page unless a different font is specified. In addition, the margins and padding for the body are set to zero so the body starts at the outer edges of the browser window. This overrides the default for the browser. Finally, the background color for the body is set to a light gray (#D3D3D3).

Next, you can see that the division with an id attribute of "page" is given a width of 500 pixels, a background color of white, and padding of 10 pixels to provide space between the outer edge of the division and its contents. In addition, the top and bottom margins of the division are set to zero so the page starts at the top of the browser window. And the left and right margins are set to "auto", which causes the page to be centered in the browser window.

The most interesting rule set in this style sheet is the one for the class named label. This rule set uses the float property to cause the four paragraphs assigned to this class to be displayed to the left of the block elements that follow them. Notice that the width property is also coded on this rule set. This is required for floated elements, and it causes the controls to the right of the text to be left-aligned.

The CSS for the Future Value form   **Page 1**

```
/* The styles for the elements */
body
{
    font-family: Arial, Helvetica, sans-serif;
    font-size: 85%;
    margin: 0;
    padding: 0;
    background-color: #D3D3D3;
}
h1
{
    font-size: 140%;
    color: #0000FF;
    margin-top: 20px;
    margin-bottom: 15px;
}

/* The style for the page division */
#page
{
    width: 500px;
    margin: 0 auto;
    padding: 10px;
    background-color: White;
}

/* The style for the paragraphs that contain
the text that identifies the server controls */
.label
{
    float: left;
    width: 140px;
    margin-top: 2px;
    margin-bottom: 5px;
}
```

Notes

- Each browser can have its own defaults for font family and font size. Because of that, you'll want to set these properties explicitly in the style for the body element.

- You typically set the margins and padding for the body to zero so the body starts at the outer edges of the browser window. Then, if you set the left and right margins of the page division to auto, the page will be centered within the window.

- Each browser also has its own defaults for the spacing above and below headings and paragraphs. To control this spacing, you can set the margins and padding for these elements. The padding controls the space between the contents of the element and the border around it, if there is one, and the margins affect the space outside the border.

- You can use the float property to display a block element or image to the left or right of the block elements that follow it. This technique can be used to align the controls on a form without using a table.

Figure 5-13   The CSS for the Future Value form (part 1 of 2)

Another rule set of note is the one for the class named validator. If you look back at figure 5-12, you'll see that this name is coded on the CssClass attribute for each of the validation controls. This illustrates how you can apply CSS to a server control using a class.

The last five rule sets in this figure illustrate how you can apply CSS to a server control using an ID. In this case, the rule sets specify heights, widths, and margins, which is typical of the rule sets for controls. Notice that the rule sets for these controls look just like the ones for the paragraphs that are selected by ID.

You should also notice the different ways that you can code some of the properties and values. For example, the margin property for the body element specifies a single value to set all four margins to that value. In contrast, the margin property for the page division specifies two values to set the left and right margins to a different value than the top and bottom margins. You can also see two ways to set the background-color property in the body element and page division: using a color name and using a hexadecimal value. As you learn more about CSS, you'll see that there are a variety of ways to code property values.

The CSS for the Future Value form   **Page 2**

```
/* The styles for the paragraphs that contain
the server controls */
.entry
{
    margin-top: 0;
    margin-bottom: 5px;
}
.validator
{
    font-size: 95%;
    color: Red;
    margin-left: 5px;
}
#future_value
{
    height: 1em;
    font-weight: bold;
    margin-top: 0;
}
#buttons
{
    margin-top: 15px;
    margin-bottom: 0;
}

/* The styles for the server controls */
#logo
{
    width: 150px;
    height: 65px;
}
#ddlMonthlyInvestment
{
    width: 106px;
}
#txtInterestRate, #txtYears
{
    width: 100px;
}
#btnCalculate
{
    margin-right: 30px;
}
#btnCalculate, #btnClear
{
    width: 106px;
}
```

Figure 5-13   The CSS for the Future Value form (part 2 of 2)

Visual Studio features for working with CSS

Although the CSS you just saw may seem daunting, you should know that when you use Visual Studio, you don't have to keep track of all the CSS properties that are available. Instead, Visual Studio can generate rule sets for you using a visual interface. You'll see how that works in the next two topics. Then, you'll learn about some additional features that Visual Studio provides for working with style sheets.

How to work with styles from Design view

In chapter 2, you learned that you can use the Formatting toolbar to apply formatting to literal text. Now, figure 5-14 describes some additional ways to use the Formatting toolbar. It also shows how to work with margins and padding from Design view.

One way to use the Formatting toolbar is to enclose literal text within a block element. To do that, you select the text and then choose the element you want to use to format the text from the Block Format drop-down list. If a style is already defined for that element, the text is formatted according to that style. Otherwise, the default formatting for the element is applied. You can also use this technique to enclose one or more controls within a block element.

Many of the other controls on the Formatting toolbar let you apply formatting to a selected element or selected text. Depending on the selection you make and the formatting you apply, Visual Studio will either insert an inline style or add a class with a style rule that's defined in an internal style sheet. The exception is if you apply formatting to an element for which a style rule is already defined. Then, the formatting is added to that style rule whether it's in an internal or external style sheet. In this figure, for example, the first drop-down list (Target Rule) indicates that a style rule is defined for the h1 element in the Main.css style sheet. So any formatting that's applied to this element will be added to the h1 style rule.

If you want to change how this works, you can do that by selecting a different option from the Target Rule drop-down list. If you want formatting to be applied as an inline style, for example, you can select the (New Inline Style) option. Or, you can select the Apply New Style option to create a new style in an internal or external style sheet as described in the next figure.

In addition to applying basic formatting to an element in Design view, you can change its margins and padding. To do that, you start by clicking on the element to select it. Then, you click on the box that appears around the element to display the margins and padding that have been applied to the element. Finally, you drag the edge of a margin to change the margin, or you press the Shift key and drag a padding edge to change the padding. In this figure, for example, you can see that I'm dragging the bottom margin of the h1 element. If you experiment with this feature, you'll see how easy it is to use.

An h1 element with its margins displayed

Target Rule
drop-down
list

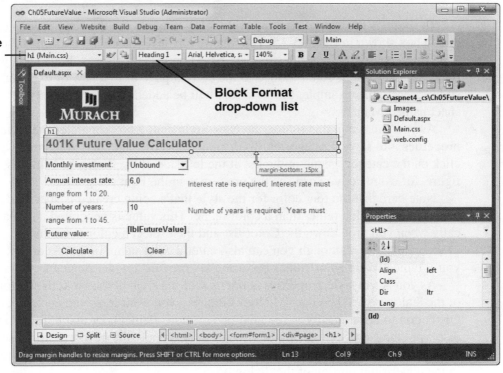

Description

- To enclose literal text or server controls within a block element, select the text or controls and then choose the block element from the Block Format drop-down list.

- To format selected text or a selected element, use the appropriate drop-down lists and buttons in the Formatting toolbar. When you do, Visual Studio typically adds a style rule with the appropriate styles to either an internal or an external style sheet.

- To display the margins and padding for an element, click on the element to select it and then click on the box that appears around it.

- To change an element's margin, just drag the edge of the margin. To change an element's padding, press the Shift key and drag its edge.

- You can use the Target Rule drop-down list to change where the formatting you select is defined. Two options are to define it in an inline style or to create a new style in an internal or external style sheet. See figure 5-15 for information on creating a new style.

Figure 5-14   How to work with styles from Design view

How to add style rules

To simplify the task of creating style rules, you can use the New Style dialog box shown in figure 5-15. This dialog box lets you create element-based style rules as well as style rules that are based on ids and classes. It also lets you select whether a style rule is added to the current page or to a new or existing style sheet. In this example, the style rule will be added to an external style sheet named Main.css.

As you can see in this figure, the New Style dialog box separates the style properties into several categories. To display a specific category, you simply click on the category name in the list at the left side of the dialog box. In this figure, for example, you can see the properties in the Font category.

Note here that the font color for the style that's being created is specified as a hexadecimal value rather than a color name. This value is generated automatically when you drop down the Color list and then select a color from the available palettes. Although you can also enter a color name in the Color box, you'll typically use color values because they provide a wider range of colors.

As you select style properties, a preview of the style is shown at the bottom of the dialog box. When the style looks the way you want it to, you can click the OK button to create it. If you selected one or more elements or text before you displayed the New Style dialog box, you can also apply the new style to those elements or that text when you create it. To do that, just select the Apply option in the upper right portion of the dialog box.

The New Style dialog box

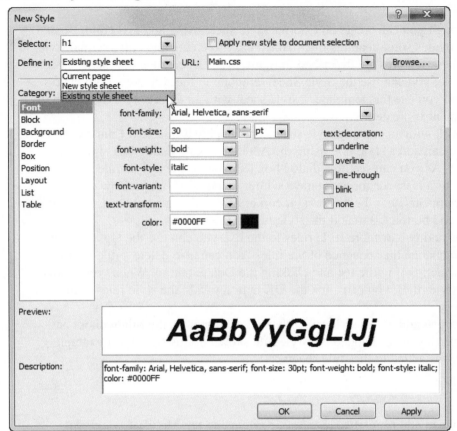

Description

- You can use the New Style dialog box to generate style rules from a page in Design view. To display the New Style dialog box, choose the Format→New Style command or select Apply New Style from the Target Rule drop-down list in the Formatting toolbar.

- The Selector drop-down list lets you select an element that you want the style rule to apply to or enter the name of an ID or class you want to create a style rule for.

- The Define In drop-down list lets you determine whether the style rule is added to the current page (an internal style sheet) or a new or existing external style sheet.

- If you choose to add a style rule to an existing external style sheet, the URL drop-down list and Browse button become available and you can use them to select a style sheet.

- If you choose to add a style rule to a new style sheet, a style sheet named StyleSheet.css is created and you're asked if you want to attach this style sheet.

- The Category list at the left side of the New Style dialog box lets you display different categories of style properties.

- If you want to apply the style rule you create to one or more elements or literal text, select those elements or text before you display the New Style dialog box. Then, select the Apply New Style To Document Selection option.

Figure 5-15   How to add styles from Design view

How to create and edit external style sheets

Although you can create an external style sheet using any text editor, Visual Studio provides some features that make it easy to create and edit external style sheets. These features are described in figure 5-16. To create a new style sheet, for example, you can use the Style Sheet template in the Add New Item dialog box. When you use this template, a style sheet with an empty style rule for the body element is created.

To work with an existing style sheet, you display it in a Text Editor window. Then, you can add a style rule using the Add Style Rule dialog box shown in this figure. As you can see, this dialog box lets you define a style rule for an element, for a class, or for an element with a specified ID. A preview of the style rule appears near the lower right corner of the dialog box. Then, you can click the add button (>) to add the style rule to the list box.

If you add two or more style rules to the list, you can use the Up and Down buttons to change the sequence of the rules. You can also delete a rule at any time by selecting it in the list and clicking the Delete button. When you're done creating style rules, you can click the OK button to add the style rules to the style sheet.

When you add a new style rule, Visual Studio creates the rule without any style properties. After I added the style rule shown in this figure, for example, this code was added to the style sheet:

```
.entry
{
}
```

Then, you can add properties to the style rule using the Modify Style dialog box. This dialog box is similar to the Add Style dialog box you saw in figure 5-15, but it doesn't include the options in the top portion of that dialog box. So you can only use it to change the properties for a style.

Note that if you create a style rule for a class, it's applied to any element with that class name by default. But you can also define a style rule that's only applied to a specific element with the class name. To do that, check the Optional Element option and then select the element from the drop-down list. Then, the selector for the class will be preceded by the element name and a period. For example, a style rule for the class shown in this figure that applies only to p elements would look like this:

```
p.entry
{
}
```

You should also notice the CSS Outline window that's displayed at the left side of the Visual Studio window when a style sheet is displayed. This window displays the style rules defined by the style sheet in a tree structure. You can use this tree to navigate to a specific style rule by expanding the folder that contains that rule and then clicking on the rule.

An external style sheet in Visual Studio

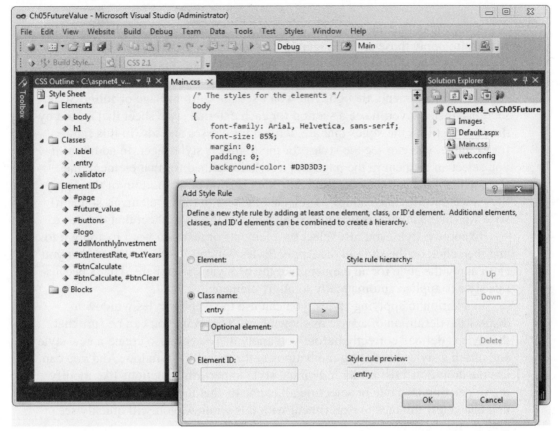

Description

- To create an external style sheet, choose the Web Site→Add New Item command. Then, select the Style Sheet template from the list of available templates, type the name you want to use for the new style sheet, and click Add.

- To edit an existing style sheet, double-click on it in the Solution Explorer to display it in a Text Editor window.

- To add a style rule to a style sheet, use the Add Style Rule dialog box. To display this dialog box, open the style sheet in an editor window and then choose Styles→Add Style Rule.

- You can also use the New Style dialog box to create a new style sheet or to add a style rule to an existing style sheet (see figure 5-15).

- To modify a style rule, click anywhere in the rule and choose the Styles→Build Style command to display the Modify Style dialog box.

- You can use the CSS Outline window (View→Document Outline) that's displayed at the left side of the Visual Studio window to navigate to the style rule you want.

Figure 5-16   How to create and edit external style sheets

How to use the Apply Styles window

After you define the styles for a web site, you can use the Apply Styles window to apply those styles. Figure 5-17 shows how to work with this window.

To start, you should realize that the main portion of this window can include any of the four sections listed in the table in this figure. If you use external style sheets as I recommend, though, you won't see the Current Page or Inline Style sections. Instead, you'll see a section for each external style sheet that's used by the page that lists the styles that are defined for classes and ids. In this figure, for example, you can see the styles for the Main.css style sheet. In addition, if you select an element in the page and a style is defined for that element, the style will appear in the Contextual Selectors section at the bottom of the Apply Styles window. In this example, I selected the text in the h1 element, so the h1 style was listed in this section under the name of the style sheet that defines it.

To apply a style, you just select the elements or text you want to apply it to and then click on the style in the Apply Styles window. Note, however, that you can't apply the style for an element like the h1 style shown here. That's because this style is applied automatically to all h1 elements.

In addition to applying styles, you can use the Apply Styles window to display the definition of a style as shown here. That way, you can be sure that the style is defined correctly before you apply it. You can also create a new style and attach a style sheet using the buttons at the top of the window. And you can use the drop-down list for an individual style to perform functions like modifying or deleting the style or selecting all elements that the style is applied to. If you take a few minutes to experiment with this window, you will quickly see how useful it can be.

The Apply Styles window

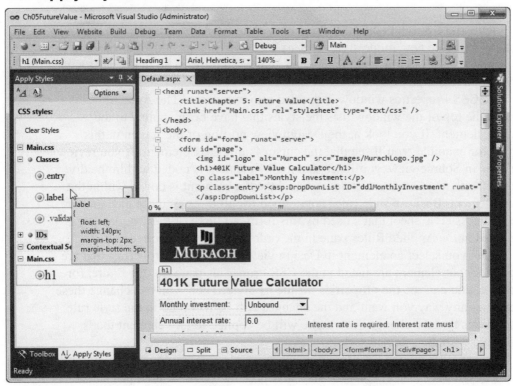

Sections that may appear in the Apply Styles window

Section	Description
Style sheet name	Class and ID styles that are defined in the style sheet with the specified name.
Current Page	Class and ID styles that are defined in the current page.
Contextual Selectors	The element style that's applied to the currently selected element, if any.
Inline Style	An inline style that's applied to the currently selected element, if any.

Description

- The Apply Styles window lets you work with the styles defined in both internal and external style sheets as well as inline styles. To display this window, use the View→Apply Styles command.

- To view the properties for a style, just point to the style in the Apply Styles window.

- To apply a style to an element or literal text, select the element or text and then click on the style in the Apply Styles window. To remove all class and inline styles, click Clear Styles.

- You can use the drop-down list for a style to perform a variety of functions, including applying the style, selecting all elements that the style is applied to, creating a new style from the existing style, modifying the style, and deleting the style.

- You can use the two buttons in the upper left corner of the Apply Styles window to create a new style and to attach a style sheet to the current page. You can use the menu that's displayed from the Options button to control the styles that are displayed in the window.

Figure 5-17   How to use the Apply Styles window to work with styles

How to use the CSS Properties window

Figure 5-18 presents the CSS Properties window. Although you can use this window to create new inline styles and style classes, it's most useful for working with the styles that have already been applied to a form. So that's what I'll focus on in this topic.

The CSS Properties window is divided into two panes. The Applied Rules pane at the top of the window lists the styles that have been applied to the current element. If you look at the Design view portion of the screen in this figure, for example, you'll see that the cursor is in the h1 element. If you review the code in Source view, you'll see that the h1 element is coded within the div element with an id attribute of "page", and the div element is coded within the body element. Because style rules are defined for all three of these elements in the Main.css style sheet that's used by this form, all three of these styles rules are listed in the Applied Rules pane in the order that they're applied.

When you select an element in Design view, all the style properties that are applied to that element are listed in the CSS Properties pane. In this figure, for example, you can see the properties for the h1 style. Then, you can change these properties any way you want and the changes will be recorded in the style rule. That means that the changes you make will be applied to any element that's formatted with the selected style.

You can also change the properties for any styles higher up in the hierarchy than the style rule that's applied to the current element. To do that, just select the style rule in the Applied Rules pane to display the style properties in the CSS Properties pane. Note that if a property of a style rule is overridden by another style rule that's applied to the current element, a red line will appear through the property name.

To make it easier to work with the style properties for an element, you can use the buttons at the top of the CSS Properties window. These buttons control whether the properties are displayed alphabetically or by category and whether the properties that are set by the style rule are displayed at the top. The default is to display the properties by category with the set properties at the top of each category. You can also click the Summary button to display just the properties that are set by the style rule.

The CSS Properties window

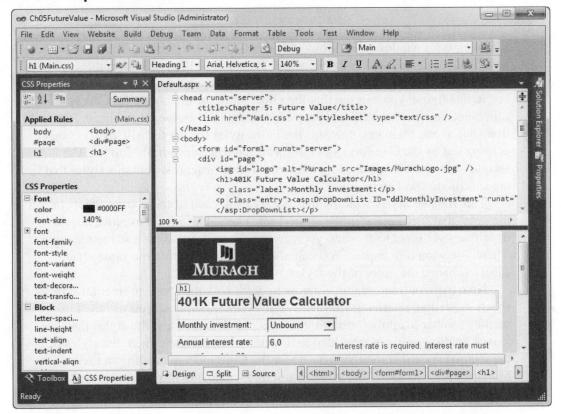

Description

- The CSS Properties window is most useful for reviewing and modifying the styles that have been applied to a page. To display this window, use the View→CSS Properties command.

- The Applied Rules pane of the CSS Properties window lists the style rules that have been applied to the currently selected element in the order in which they're applied. It also indicates if the style rule is defined by an inline style or an internal or external style sheet.

- The CSS Properties pane of the CSS Properties window lists the style properties that have been applied to the currently selected element. If you select a style rule from the Applied Rules pane, a red line will appear through any properties of that style rule that are overridden by the style rule for the currently selected element.

- To modify a style, select an element with that style in Design view, select the style in the Applied Rules pane, and then change its properties in the CSS Properties pane.

- You can use the buttons at the top of the CSS Properties window to sort the list of properties by category, alphabetically, or by the properties that have been applied. You can click the Summary button to display only the properties that are applied to the currently selected element.

Figure 5-18   How to use the CSS Properties window to work with styles

How to use the Manage Styles window

The last window Visual Studio provides for working with styles is the Manage Styles window. This window is most useful for working with a web form that uses more than one style sheet. Figure 5-19 illustrates how this window works.

In this figure, you can see that the Order form for the Shopping Cart application you saw in chapter 3 has been modified so it uses two style sheets. The first style sheet, Main.css, contains the basic styles for the form. This style sheet is also used by the Cart form so both forms have the same basic format. The second style sheet that's used by the Order form, Order.css, contains styles that are specific to this form.

The Manage Styles window lists the styles in each of these style sheets in the order that they appear in the style sheet. Then, if you want to move a style from one style sheet to another, you can simply click and drag it to the location where you want it to appear. You can also drag a style within the same style sheet to change the order of the styles.

Note that you can use this window to work with the styles in internal style sheets as well as external style sheets. For example, suppose you use the Formatting toolbar to apply formatting to selected elements, and the styles that Visual Studio generates are added to an internal style sheet. Then, the styles in the internal style sheet will appear under the Current Page heading in the Manage Styles window, and you can use this window to move those styles to an external style sheet.

The Manage Styles window

Description

- The Manage Styles window provides a convenient way to move the styles used by a page from one style sheet to another. That includes styles defined in both external and internal style sheets. To display this window, use the View→Manage Styles command.

- All styles in an external style sheet appear under the name of that style sheet. All styles in an internal style sheet appear under the Current Page heading.

- To move a style from one style sheet to another, simply drag and drop it. You can also drag and drop a style within a style sheet to change the order of the styles.

- If you select a style in the Manage Styles window, a preview of that style is displayed at the bottom of the window. If the preview isn't displayed, select the Display Selected Style Preview option from the menu that's displayed when you click the Options button.

- To view the properties for a style, just point to the style in the Manage Styles window.

- You can also use the Manage Styles window to apply styles, but that's best done using the Apply Styles window.

Figure 5-19   How to use the Manage Styles window to work with styles

Perspective

The goal of this chapter has been to teach you the HTML and CSS essentials that you need for ASP.NET programming. So at this point, you should feel qualified to modify the HTML that's generated by Visual Studio so it contains the content you need and so it's structured in a logical way that makes it easy to apply CSS. In addition, you should feel qualified to code some basic CSS for formatting and page layout.

Of course, there's a lot more to HTML and CSS than what's presented in this chapter. So if you want to learn more, we recommend our book *Murach's HTML, XHTML, and CSS*. This book teaches you everything you need to develop web pages from scratch. Of course, when you work in Visual Studio, much of the HTML is generated for you. In addition, as a programmer, you may not be responsible for coding the CSS for a page. Even so, it makes sense for you to have a solid understanding of how this code works.

Terms

HTML document	cascading style sheets (CSS)
HTML element	style sheet
tag	external style sheet
start tag	attach a style sheet
end tag	internal style sheet
content	inline style
self-closing tag	rule set
attribute	style rule
comment (HTML)	selector
white space	declaration block
character entity	declaration
render a control	property
root element	value
child element	rule
parent element	comment (CSS)
directive block	element selector
block element	ID selector
inline element	class selector

Exercise 5-1 Use Visual Studio to work with the HTML and CSS for a form

In this exercise, you'll use some of the features of Visual Studio that you learned about in this chapter to work with the HTML and CSS for a form.

Review and test the form

1. Open the Ch05InvoiceTotal web site in the C:\aspnet4_cs directory and review the HTML for the form.

2. Run the application to see how it looks in your web browser.

3. Enter a value in the Subtotal text box and then click the Calculate button to see how this application works. Then, close the browser.

Format the heading

4. With the form in Design view, select the text for the heading. Then, select Heading 1 from the Block Format drop-down list in the Formatting toolbar. This will enclose the text in an h1 element and apply the default formatting for an h1 element.

5. Use the Formatting toolbar to change the font size for the heading to large. This will add a class attribute with a value of "style1" to the h1 element and create a style for that class in an internal style sheet.

6. Use Design view to change the bottom margin for the h1 element to 20 pixels. Then, use the CSS Properties window to change the color property for the h1 element to red (Font category) and the text-align property to center (Block category). These properties will be added to the style in the internal style sheet.

Attach the external style sheet

7. Notice that this application includes an external style sheet named Main.css. Open this file and review the various selectors and properties.

8. Use one of the techniques in figure 5-8 to add a link element for the style sheet to the form.

9. Display the form in Design view, and notice that the background color, the font, and the space between the text and the edge of the window have changed because the style for the body element was applied.

Apply the style for the div element

10. Display the form in Source view and move the insertion point so it's after the "v" in the start tag for the div element.

11. Press the spacebar to display a completion list for the div element, select the id attribute, and press the Tab or Enter key to insert it into the element.

12. Type an equal sign followed by the value "page" enclosed in quotes. Review the results in Design view.

Modify a style and create new styles

13. Display the external style sheet. Then, right-click in the style for the #page style rule and select the Build Style command.

14. Select the Border category from the Modify Style dialog box. Then, use the drop-down lists to display a thin, solid black border around the page. Return to the form to see how this looks.

15. Choose the New Style command from the Format menu. Then, create a style in the Main.css style sheet for the Subtotal text box using the control's ID. Set the width property for this style (Position category) to 106 pixels. Repeat for the Calculate button. Review the styles that were generated.

Apply the remaining styles

16. Enclose each of the following within a paragraph element: the text that identifies the text box, the text box and its two validation controls, the text that identifies each label, each label control, and the button control. You can do this by using the Formatting toolbar or by entering the HTML directly into Source view.

17. Use the Apply Properties window to apply a style to each paragraph. The paragraphs that contain the text that identifies the text box and labels should be formatted with the .text style; the paragraph that contains the text box and validation controls should be formatted with the #entry style; the paragraphs that contain the labels should be formatted with the .label style; and the paragraph that contains the button should be formatted with the #button style. Notice the class and id attributes that are generated when these styles are applied.

    Note: After you apply these styles, the paragraphs may not appear to be aligned properly in Design view. In that case, you will need to run the application to determine if the page is formatted properly.

18. Use the Apply Properties window to apply the .validator style to the two validation controls, and notice the CssClass attributes that are generated.

19. Run the application. Because each line in the original HTML ended in a br element, there's now too much space between the lines. Close the browser.

20. Display the form in Source view and remove any unnecessary spaces and line breaks. Then, run the application again to see how it looks. Continue making adjustments until the spacing looks right.

Move the internal style to the external style sheet

21. Display the Manage Styles window and note that it lists the styles in the Main.css style sheet as well as the style in the internal style sheet.

22. Drag the style in the internal style sheet to the external sheet and drop it just below the style for the body element.

23. Switch to the Main.css file and change the selector for the style you just moved from the internal style sheet so it's applied to h1 elements.

24. Switch back to the form and delete the class attribute from the h1 element. In addition, delete the style element for the internal style sheet since it no longer contains any styles.

25. Run the application one more time to be sure it's displayed correctly. When it is, close the browser and then close the project.

Section 2

Basic ASP.NET skills

The six chapters in this section expand upon the essentials that you learned in section 1. To start, chapter 6 shows you how to work with the server controls that can be used for developing web pages. Then, chapter 7 shows you how to work with the validation controls, and chapter 8 presents the several ways that you can manage the state of an application or form.

The next three chapters present features of ASP.NET that make it easier to develop professional-looking web sites. Chapter 9 shows you how to use master pages to create pages with common elements; chapter 10 shows you how to use site navigation to make it easy for users to navigate through your site; and chapter 11 shows you how to use themes to customize the formatting that's applied to the elements on a page.

To a large extent, each of the chapters in this section is an independent unit. As a result, you don't have to read these chapters in sequence. If, for example, you want to know more about state management after you finish section 1, you can go directly to chapter 8. Eventually, though, you're going to want to read all six chapters. So unless you have a compelling reason to skip around, you may as well read the chapters in sequence.

6

How to work with server controls

So far in this book, you've learned the basic skills for working with some of the most common server controls: labels, text boxes, buttons, drop-down lists, and list boxes. Now, this chapter presents some additional skills for working with these controls. It also presents the skills for working with other common controls, like check boxes and radio buttons, and some advanced controls, like the file upload and image map controls. When you complete this chapter, you'll be able to create ASP.NET web forms that use any of the server controls.

An introduction to server controls

In chapter 2, you learned how to add server controls to a web form and set control properties. Now, you'll learn about the different types of server controls and how you use them. You'll also see a summary of the web server controls that are presented in this chapter, you'll learn two ways to handle control events, and you'll learn three additional techniques ASP.NET provides for working with web server controls.

Types of server controls

Figure 6-1 describes the six different types of server controls that you'll learn about in this book. These six categories correspond to groups in the Visual Studio Toolbox. For example, you'll find the standard controls in the Standard group of the Toolbox.

The controls you'll use most often are the standard controls, the data controls, and the validation controls. You'll learn how to use many of the standard controls in this chapter. Then, in chapter 7, you'll learn how to use the validation controls. And you'll learn how to use some of the data controls in chapters 13 through 17.

You'll use the next three types of controls only for special situations. For example, you can use the navigation controls to provide menus and path maps that let users navigate to various pages within your web site. You can use the login controls to manage access to your site. And you can use AJAX extension controls to design pages where only parts of a page are updated during a postback. You'll learn about these types of controls in later chapters.

In addition to the types of server controls shown here, ASP.NET also provides controls for working with web parts, dynamic data, and reports. You won't learn about these controls in this book. Together with the six control types shown in this figure, these controls are typically referred to as *web server controls*. As you know, a web server control is implemented by a class that you can use to work with the control from a web application that runs on a web server.

The last group of controls that's available from the Toolbox contains the HTML controls. In contrast to the web server controls, you can't work with the HTML controls from a web application. That's because these controls map directly to standard HTML elements. For example, the Text control maps directly to an Input element that has its Type attribute set to "Text".

If you want to work with an HTML control from a web application, you can convert it to a server control. To do that, just select the Run As Server Control command from the shortcut menu for the control. This adds a Runat attribute with the value "Server" to the HTML element. This attribute indicates that the element should be processed on the server. Then, you can work with the control using standard object-oriented techniques. Since *HTML server controls* don't provide the same functionality as the web server controls, however, you won't use them often.

Standard

- Commonly used user input controls such as labels, text boxes, and drop-down lists
- Many can be bound to a data source
- Described in this chapter

Data

- Databound user-interface controls that display data via a data source control
- Data source controls that access data from a variety of databases, XML data sources, and business objects
- Described in chapters 13 through 17

Validation

- Used to validate user input
- Work by running client-side scripts
- Can handle most validation requirements
- Described in chapter 7

Navigation

- Controls that provide menus and path maps for navigating a web site
- Described in chapter 10

Login

- Controls that provide user authentication
- Described in chapter 19

AJAX Extensions

- Controls that provide for updating selected parts of a page during a postback
- Described in chapter 21

Description

- The Toolbox contains several groups that contain more than 90 different controls. The headings in this figure correspond to the names of groups in the Toolbox.
- In addition to the groups listed above, the Toolbox includes groups for WebParts, Dynamic Data, Reporting, and HTML. These controls aren't covered in this book.

Figure 6-1 Types of server controls

The web server controls presented in this chapter

Figure 6-2 summarizes the web server controls that you'll learn about in this chapter. You'll find all of these controls in the Standard group of the Toolbox.

If you've developed Windows applications, you'll notice that many of these controls have Windows counterparts and operate similarly to the Windows controls. Because of that, you shouldn't have much difficulty learning how to use most of these controls. As you'll see in this chapter, however, some of the techniques you use to work with these controls are different from the techniques you use to work with their Windows counterparts. In addition, some of the functionality they provide is different. So you'll want to be sure to read about each control even if you're familiar with Windows controls.

Also, you should realize that there are other standard controls besides the ones shown in this figure. In fact, the Standard group of the Toolbox provides 29 different web server controls. Later in this chapter, you'll learn how to use the Visual Studio documentation to get information about the other controls so you can use them too.

The web server controls presented in this chapter

Control	Name	Suggested prefix	Description
A	Label	lbl	Displays descriptive information.
abl	TextBox	txt	Lets the user enter or modify a text value.
ab	Button	btn	Submits a page for processing.
ab	LinkButton	lbtn	Submits a page for processing.
	ImageButton	ibtn	Submits a page for processing.
A	HyperLink	hlnk	Lets the user move to another page in the application.
	DropDownList	ddl	Lets the user choose an item from a list that drops down from the control.
	ListBox	lst	Lets the user choose one or more items from a list.
	CheckBox	chk	Turns an option on or off.
	CheckBoxList	cbl	Turns options in a list of options on or off.
	RadioButton	rdo	Turns an option on or off. Only one radio button in a group can be on.
	RadioButtonList	rbl	Turns an option in a list of options on or off. Only one radio button in the list can be on.
	Image	img	Displays an image.
	ImageMap	imap	Displays an image with one or more clickable areas that submit the page for processing when clicked.
	BulletedList	blst	Displays a bulleted or numbered list.
	Calendar	cln	Displays a calendar and lets the user select one or more dates.
	FileUpload	upl	Displays a text box and a button that lets the user browse for a file to be uploaded.

Description

- The button, image button, and link button controls all provide the same functionality. They differ only in how they appear on the form.
- The check box list and radio button list controls serve as containers for a collection of check box or radio button items. They're typically used to create a list of check boxes or radio buttons that are bound to a data source.

Figure 6-2   The web server controls presented in this chapter

How to handle control events

Like other objects, server controls have events that are fired when certain actions are performed on them. When you click on a button control, for example, the Click event is fired. If your application needs to respond to an event, you code a method called an *event handler* as shown in figure 6-3.

When you generate an event handler from Visual Studio, an event attribute that names the event handler is added to the asp code for the control. Then, you enter the code you want to be executed when that event occurs within the event handler. This is illustrated by the first example in this figure. Here, the OnClick attribute of a button named btnCancel indicates that an event handler named btnCancel_Click will be executed when the Click event of the control is raised.

You can also use a single event handler to handle more than one event. To do that, you name the event handler on the appropriate event attribute of each control as illustrated in the second example. Here, the event handler will handle the Click event of two buttons named btnPrevious and btnNext. Notice in this example that I changed the name of the event handler to indicate that it processes more than one event.

This figure also lists some of the most common control events and their associated attributes. As I present each of the web server controls in this chapter, I'll illustrate how you can use these events.

Code that handles a Click event using the OnClick attribute

The asp tag for a button control

```
<asp:Button id="btnCancel" runat="server" Text="Cancel Order"
    OnClick="btnCancel_Click" />
```

The event handler for the Click event of the control

```
protected void btnCancel_Click(object sender, EventArgs e)
{
    Session.Remove("Cart");
    Response.Redirect("Order.aspx");
}
```

The asp tags for two button controls that use the same event handler

```
<asp:Button id="btnPrevious" runat="server" Text="Previous"
    OnClick="NavigationButtons_Click" />
<asp:Button id="btnNext" runat="server" Text="Next"
    OnClick="NavigationButtons_Click" />
```

Common control events

Event	Attribute	Controls
Click	OnClick	Button, image button, link button, image map
Command	OnCommand	Button, image button, link button
TextChanged	OnTextChanged	Text box
SelectedIndexChanged	OnSelectedIndexChanged	Drop-down list, list box, radio button list, check box list
CheckedChanged	OnCheckedChanged	Check box, radio button

Description

- An *event handler* is a method that's called when a specified event occurs. An event handler must be declared with public or protected scope.

- To wire an event to an event handler, you name the handler in the appropriate event attribute of the control. For example, you can use the OnClick attribute to name the event handler that's executed when the user clicks a control.

- A single event handler can be used to handle more than one event. To do that, you name the handler on each event attribute of each control you want it to handle.

Figure 6-3   How to handle control events

How to use access keys with web server controls

Access keys let the user select controls by using keyboard shortcuts. If, for example, you designate F as the access key for an input field that accepts a customer's first name, the user can move the focus directly to this field by pressing Alt+F. Figure 6-4 shows how to use access keys with ASP.NET.

To create an access key, you simply add the AccessKey attribute to the control you want to create the keyboard shortcut for. Since this attribute is defined by the System.Web.UI.WebControls.WebControl class, you can use it with any web control. Note, however, that the access keys you define for a form can conflict with the access keys that are defined for a browser. Because of that, you'll want to be sure to test them with all the modern browsers.

When you use access keys with text boxes and other controls that are identified by literal text, it's common to underline the access key in the literal text. To do that, you can use a Span element with a class attribute. This is illustrated by the text that identifies the two text boxes in this figure. Here, the class attribute has a value of "accesskey". Then, you can code a style rule for this class that sets the text-decoration property to underline.

If you use a label to identify a control instead of literal text, you can assign the access key to the label and then underline the appropriate letter of the label. In this case, you should also code the AssociatedControlID attribute to specify the control that should receive the focus when the user uses the access key.

You can also specify an access key for a button control as illustrated by the aspx code in this figure. However, you can't underline the access key in a button control. That's because buttons are rendered using the <input type="submit"> HTML element, and this element doesn't provide a way to format the text that's displayed by the button.

How to set the focus on a web server control

ASP.NET provides two features that let you set the focus to a specific control on a form. First, you can use the DefaultFocus attribute of the form to determine which control receives the focus when the page is first displayed. In figure 6-4, for example, this attribute is set to the txtName control.

Second, you can move the focus to a control at runtime. To do that, you use the Focus method of the control. The statement shown in this figure, for example, moves the focus to the txtEmail control.

How to set the default button control

ASP.NET also lets you set the button that's activated by default when you press the Enter key. To do that, you set the DefaultButton attribute of the form. In the example in this figure, this attribute is set to the btnNext button. Because of that, the form is posted back to the server when the Enter key is pressed, and the method for the Click event of the Next button is executed.

A form that uses access keys and default focus and button attributes

Please enter your contact information:

Name: [   ]

Email: [   ]

[Previous] [Next]

The aspx code for the form

```
<form id="form1" runat="server" defaultfocus="txtName" defaultbutton="btnNext">
<div id="page">
    <p>Please enter your contact information:</p>
    <p class="text"><span class="accesskey">N</span>ame:</p>
    <p class="entry"><asp:TextBox ID="txtName" runat="server" AccessKey="N">
                </asp:TextBox></p>
    <p class="text"><span class="accesskey">E</span>mail:</p>
    <p class="entry"><asp:TextBox ID="txtEmail" runat="server" AccessKey="E">
                </asp:TextBox></p>
    <p id="buttons">
        <asp:Button ID="btnPrevious" runat="server" AccessKey="P"
            Text="Previous" /> 
        <asp:Button ID="btnNext" runat="server" AccessKey="N" Text="Next" />
    </p>
</div>
</form>
```

The CSS for the accesskey class

```
.accesskey
{
    text-decoration: underline;
}
```

A statement that moves the focus to a control

```
txtEmail.Focus;
```

Description

- You can use the AccessKey attribute on a web server control to specify a keyboard shortcut for the control. To use the keyboard shortcut, the user holds down the Alt key and presses the *access key* to move the focus to the control.

- If you use literal text to identify another control, you can identify the access key used by that control by underlining the appropriate letter in the literal text as shown above.

- If you use a label to identify another control, you can set the AccessKey attribute for the label and then set the AssociatedControlID attribute to the other control. When the user presses the access key for the label, the focus will be moved to the associated control.

- You can set the control that receives the focus when a form is first displayed using the DefaultFocus attribute of the form. To move the focus to a control at runtime, use the Focus method of the control.

- You can set the button that causes a form to be posted back when you press the Enter key using the DefaultButton attribute of the form.

Figure 6-4   How to use access keys and set form defaults

How to work with button controls

Most web forms have at least one button control that the user can click to submit the form to the server for processing, commonly called a *submit button*. In the topics that follow, you'll learn how to use all three types of button controls that ASP.NET provides: buttons, link buttons, and image buttons.

How to work with buttons, link buttons, and image buttons

Figure 6-5 presents the three types of button controls. These controls differ only in how they appear to the user. This is illustrated by the three buttons shown at the top of this figure. As you can see, a *button* displays text within a rectangular area. A *link button* displays text that looks like a hyperlink. And an *image button* displays an image.

This figure also presents the asp tags for the three buttons that are illustrated. For the button and link button, the Text attribute provides the text that's displayed for the control. For the image button, the ImageUrl attribute provides the URL address of the image that's displayed on the button. In some cases, though, a browser may not be able to display the image. Because of that, you should also code the AlternateText attribute so it provides the text that's displayed if the browser isn't able to display the image.

When a user clicks one of the button controls, ASP.NET raises two events: Click and Command. You can see an event handler for the Click event of a button control in this figure. Notice that this event handler receives two arguments. The sender argument represents the control that was clicked. Because this argument has a type of object, you'll need to cast it to a button control if you want to access the properties and methods of the control. You might want to do that, for example, if you code a method that handles the processing for more than one button. Then, you can use the ID property of the control to determine which button was clicked. An easier way to do that, however, is to use the Command event. You'll see how to use this event in figure 6-7.

The second argument that's passed to the event handler of a Click event, e, contains event-specific information. You're most likely to use this argument with an image button control to determine where the user clicked on the image. You'll learn more about that in the next figure.

Of course, the Click and Command event handlers are executed only if the page posts back to itself. If a value is specified for the PostBackUrl attribute, however, the page at the specified URL is executed and displayed. This is the cross-page posting feature you learned about in chapter 3.

Incidentally, from this point on in this chapter and this book, the figures will often present the asp elements for the controls that are used. By studying the code for these controls, you can quickly see how their attributes are set. Please keep in mind, though, that you usually add a control to a form by using the Designer, and you set the attributes for a control by using the Properties window. Then, the code for the asp element in the aspx file is generated automatically.

A button, a link button, and an image button in a browser

Add to Cart   Check Out

The asp tags for the three buttons

```
<asp:Button ID="btnAdd" runat="server" Text="Add to Cart"
    OnClick="btnAdd_Click" />
    
<asp:LinkButton ID="lbtnCheckOut" runat="server"
    PostBackUrl="~/CheckOut1.aspx">Check Out</asp:LinkButton>
   
<asp:ImageButton ID="ibtnCart" runat="server" AlternateText="Cart"
    ImageUrl="~/Images/cart.gif" PostBackUrl="~/Cart.aspx" />
```

Common button attributes

Attribute	Description
Text	(Button and LinkButton controls only) The text displayed by the button. For a LinkButton control, the text can be coded as content between the start and end tags or as the value of the Text attribute.
ImageUrl	(ImageButton control only) The image to be displayed for the button.
AlternateText	(ImageButton control only) The text to be displayed if the browser can't display the image.
CausesValidation	Determines whether page validation occurs when you click the button. The default is True.
CommandName	A string value that's passed to the Command event when a user clicks the button.
CommandArgument	A string value that's passed to the Command event when a user clicks the button.
PostBackUrl	The URL of the page that should be requested when the user clicks the button.

An event handler for the Click event of a button control

```
protected void btnAccept_Click(object sender, EventArgs e)
{
    this.AddInvoice();
    Response.Redirect("Confirmation.aspx");
}
```

Description

- When a user clicks a *button*, *link button*, or *image button*, the page specified in the PostBackUrl attribute is loaded and executed. If this attribute isn't included, the page is posted back to the server and the Click and Command events are raised. You can code event handlers for either or both of these events.

- Two arguments are passed to the Click event handler: sender and e. Sender is the control that the user clicked, and e contains event-specific information. You can use the e argument with the image button control to determine where the user clicked in the image. See figure 6-6 for more information.

- See figure 6-7 for information on coding an event handler for the Command event.

Figure 6-5   How to work with buttons, link buttons, and image buttons

How to use the e argument
of an image button control

In some cases, the processing that's performed when the user clicks on an image button will depend on where within the button the user clicks. To illustrate, consider the image button shown at the top of figure 6-6 that represents four navigation buttons. (This image uses the standard icons for First (<<), Previous (<), Next (>), and Last (>>)). This image button could be used to let the user navigate through pages in a section of your web site or to different rows of a data table.

To process an image button like this, you can use the X and Y properties of the e argument that's passed to the Click event handler of the button. These properties indicate the x and y coordinates where the user clicked. The event handler shown in this figure illustrates how this works.

In this example, an if statement is used to determine the value of the X property. If it's between 0 and 23, it indicates that the user clicked the << icon. Then, the event handler executes the GoToFirstRow method. If it's between 24 and 47, it indicates that the user clicked the < icon, and the GoToPreviousRow method is executed. If it's between 48 and 71, it indicates that the user clicked the > icon, and the GoToNextRow method is executed. Last, if it's between 72 and 95, it indicates that the user clicked the >> icon, and the GoToLastRow method is executed. Notice that it's not necessary to check the y coordinate in this example. That's because all of the icons have the same y-coordinate range.

An image used for an image button control

The asp tag for the control

```
<asp:ImageButton ID="ibtnNavigate" runat="server"
    ImageUrl="~/Images/navbuttons.gif" Height="24px" Width="96px"
    OnClick="ibtnNavigate_Click" />
```

An event handler for the Click event of the control

```
protected void ibtnNavigate_Click(object sender, ImageClickEventArgs e)
{
    if (e.X >= 0 && e.X <= 23)
        this.GoToFirstRow();
    else if (e.X >= 24 && e.X <= 47)
        this.GoToPreviousRow();
    else if (e.X >= 48 && e.X <= 71)
        this.GoToNextRow();
    else if (e.X >= 72 && e.X <= 95)
        this.GoToLastRow();
}
```

Properties of the ImageClickEventArgs class

Property	Description
X	An integer that represents the x coordinate where the user clicked the image button.
Y	An integer that represents the y coordinate where the user clicked the image button.

Description

- When the user clicks an ImageButton control, ASP.NET calls the Click event handler for the control and passes the x and y coordinates where the user clicked the image as properties of the e argument.

- The e argument that's passed to a Click event handler for an image button is an ImageClickEventArgs object. This object includes properties that let you retrieve the x and y coordinates where the user clicked on the image. You can use these properties to determine the processing that's performed.

Figure 6-6   How to use the e argument of an image button control

How to use the Command event

Figure 6-7 shows how you can use the Command event to process a group of button controls using a single event handler. Like the Click event, this event receives both a sender argument and an e argument. In this case, the e argument represents a CommandEventArgs object.

The two properties of the CommandEventArgs class are shown in this figure. You can use these properties to get the CommandName and CommandArgument properties of a control. When you create a button control, you can set the CommandName and CommandArgument properties to any string value. Then, you can examine them in the Command event handler to determine how the application should respond when the user clicks the button.

The examples in this figure illustrate how this works. The first example shows the asp tags for four button controls. Notice that a different CommandName value is assigned to each one. However, the same event handler is named on the OnCommand attributes. That way, the same event handler will handle the Command event of all four controls. Although you can also assign CommandArgument values to each control, that's not necessary here.

The second example shows an event handler that processes the Command event of all four controls. To do that, it uses a switch statement to test the value of the CommandName property of the e argument. Since this value indicates the control that was clicked, it can be used to determine which method to call based on the button that was clicked. This is another way to do the processing you saw in figure 6-6 that used an image button control.

Four button controls that use the CommandName attribute

```
<asp:Button ID="btnFirst" runat="server" Text="<<" Width="25px"
    CommandName="First" OnCommand="NavigationButtons_Command" />
<asp:Button ID="btnPrevious" runat="server" Text="<" Width="25px"
    CommandName="Previous" OnCommand="NavigationButtons_Command" />
<asp:Button ID="btnNext" runat="server" Text=">" Width="25px"
    CommandName="Next" OnCommand="NavigationButtons_Command" />
<asp:Button ID="btnLast" runat="server" Text=">>" Width="25px"
    CommandName="Last" OnCommand="NavigationButtons_Command" />
```

An event handler for the Command events of the buttons

```
protected void NavigationButtons_Command(object sender, CommandEventArgs e)
{
    switch (e.CommandName)
    {
        case "First":
            this.GoToFirstRow();
            break;
        case "Previous":
            this.GoToPreviousRow();
            break;
        case "Next":
            this.GoToNextRow();
            break;
        case "Last":
            this.GoToLastRow();
            break;
    }
}
```

Properties of the CommandEventArgs class

Property	Description
CommandName	The value specified in the CommandName property for the control that generated the Command event.
CommandArgument	The value specified in the CommandArgument property for the control that generated the Command event.

Description

- The Command event is raised whenever a user clicks a button control. It's useful as an alternative to the Click event when you want to code a single event handler for a group of buttons that perform related functions.

- The e argument that's passed to a Command event handler is a CommandEventArgs object. This object includes properties that let you retrieve the values of the CommandName and CommandArgument properties of the control. You can use these values to determine which control raised the Command event.

Note

- If you code an event handler for both the Click event and the Command event, the Click event handler will be executed first.

Figure 6-7   How to use the Command event

How to work with text boxes, labels, check boxes, and radio buttons

Two controls you'll use frequently as you develop web forms are text boxes and labels. As you know, text boxes let you accept input from the user, and labels let you display information to the user. Since you already know the basic skills for working with these controls, the topic that follows presents some additional skills. After that, you'll learn how to use check boxes and radio buttons to let users select from one or more options.

How to work with text boxes and labels

At the top of figure 6-8, you can see part of a web page that contains a *text box* and a *label*. Unlike the text boxes you've seen up to this point, the text box shown here lets the user enter multiple lines of text. To accomplish that, the TextMode attribute of the text box is changed from its default of SingleLine to MultiLine. In addition, to indicate the number of lines that can be displayed in the text box at one time, the Rows attribute is set to 5. You can see these attributes in the asp tag for this control.

Another attribute you can use with a multi-line text box is Wrap. By default, this attribute is set to True, which means that text wraps automatically when it reaches the end of the text box. If you set this attribute to False, the user must press the Enter key to start a new line of text.

In addition to SingleLine and MultiLine, you can set the TextMode attribute to Password. Then, the characters the user enters are masked so they aren't displayed. Because ASP.NET provides a Login control that you can use to accept a user name and password from the user, you're not likely to use a text box to accept a password.

Although most text boxes are used to accept data from the user, you may occasionally need to restrict the user from entering data into a text box. To do that, you can set the ReadOnly attribute of the control to True. Then, the user can see the text in the control but can't change it.

You can use the MaxLength attribute to specify the maximum number of characters that can be entered into a text box. This is particularly useful if the data the user enters will be stored in a column of a database table. Then, you can limit the entry to the number of characters that are allowed for that column.

Although the width of a text box is set automatically as you size it in Design view, you can also set the width using the Columns attribute. This attribute specifies the width of the text box in characters. Note, however, that the width is approximate because it's based on the average width of a character for the font that's used.

Remember too that you can specify some attributes of a control, such as Width, using CSS. In this chapter, though, I'll show these attributes in the aspx code whenever that helps you understand how a control works.

A text box and a label displayed in a browser

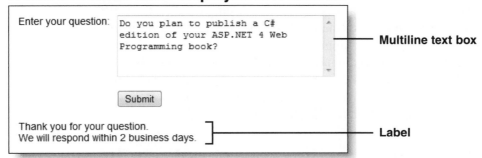

The asp element for the text box

```
<asp:TextBox ID="txtQuestion" runat="server" Rows="5" TextMode="MultiLine"
    Width="296px"></asp:TextBox>
```

Common text box attributes

Attribute	Description
TextMode	The type of text box. SingleLine creates a standard text box, MultiLine creates a text box that accepts more than one line of text, and Password causes the characters that are entered to be masked. The default is SingleLine.
Text	The text content of the text box.
MaxLength	The maximum number of characters that can be entered into the text box.
Wrap	Determines whether or not text wraps automatically when it reaches the end of a multi-line text box. The default is True.
ReadOnly	Determines whether the user can change the text in the text box. The default value is False, which means that the text can be changed.
Columns	The width of the text box in characters. The actual width is determined based on the font that's used for the text entry.
Rows	The height of a multi-line text box in lines. The default value is 0, which sets the height to a single line.

The asp element for the label

```
<asp:Label ID="lblConfirm" runat="server"></asp:Label>
```

Common label attribute

Attribute	Description
Text	The text displayed by the label.

Description

- *Text box controls* are typically used to accept input from the user. A text box can accept one or more lines of text depending on the setting of the TextMode attribute.

- *Label controls* provide an easy way to display text that can change from one execution of an ASP.NET page to the next. To display text that doesn't change, you typically use literal text.

Figure 6-8   How to work with text boxes and labels

The label control in figure 6-8 is also different from the ones you have seen so far in that it consists of two lines of text. To accomplish that, the text that's assigned to the Text property of the label includes HTML. You'll see the code that assigns this value in just a minute.

Before I go on, I want to remind you that you typically use labels only to display text that changes from one execution of the page to the next. To include text that doesn't change, you can use literal text. That's how I entered the text "Enter your question:" in the example shown here.

How to work with check boxes and radio buttons

In addition to entering text into a form, you may want to let users select from one or more options. To do that, you can use *check boxes* or *radio buttons*. The main difference between these two types of controls is that radio buttons in groups are mutually exclusive and check boxes operate independently. In other words, if the user selects one radio button in a group, all of the other radio buttons in the same group are automatically turned off. In contrast, when a user selects a check box, it has no effect on other check boxes.

Figure 6-9 presents part of a web page that includes four check box controls and a group of two radio button controls. The first check box lets the user indicate if he wants to be added to a mailing list. The other check boxes let the user select what he wants to be contacted about. The radio buttons let the user select how he wants to be contacted.

To create a group of radio buttons, you simply specify the same name for the GroupName attribute of each radio button in the group. If you want to create two or more groups of radio buttons on a single form, just use a different group name for each group. Note that if you don't specify a group name for a radio button, that button won't be a part of any group. Instead, it will be processed independently of any other radio buttons on the form.

If you've developed Windows applications, you'll realize that this is in contrast to how Windows radio buttons work. In a Windows application, any radio buttons on a form that aren't specifically included in a group are treated as part of the same group. As a result, if a form has only one group of radio buttons, you can let them default to the same group. Since the Web Server radio button controls don't work that way, however, you'll almost always specify a group name for them.

To determine whether or not a radio button or check box is selected when it's first displayed, you use the Checked attribute. If you look at the aspx code for the check boxes and radio buttons shown in this figure, for example, you'll see that the Checked attributes of the first check box and the first radio button are set to True. When the web page is first displayed, then, these options will be selected as shown. Note that since only one radio button in a group can be selected, you should only set the Checked attribute to True for one button. If you set this property to True for more than one button in a group, the last one will be selected.

Four check boxes and two radio buttons displayed in a browser

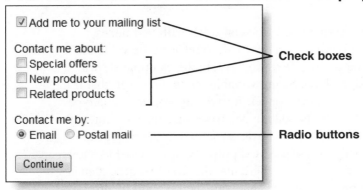

The aspx code for the check boxes and radio buttons

```
<asp:CheckBox ID="chkMail" runat="server" Checked="True"
    Text="Add me to your mailing list" /><br /><br />

Contact me about:<br />

<asp:CheckBox ID="chkSpecial" runat="server"
    Text="Special offers" /><br />
<asp:CheckBox ID="chkNew" runat="server"
    Text="New products" /><br />
<asp:CheckBox ID="chkRelated" runat="server"
    Text="Related products" /><br /><br />

Contact me by:<br />

<asp:RadioButton ID="rdoEmail" runat="server"
    Checked="True" GroupName="Contact" Text="Email" /> 
<asp:RadioButton ID="rdoPostal" runat="server"
    GroupName="Contact" Text="Postal mail" />
```

Common check box and radio button attributes

Attribute	Description
Text	The text that's displayed next to the check box or radio button.
Checked	Indicates whether the check box or radio button is selected. The default is False.
GroupName	The name of the group that the control belongs to (radio buttons only).

Description

- A *check box* displays a single option that the user can either check or uncheck. *Radio buttons* present a group of options from which the user can select just one option. All of the radio buttons in a group should have the same group name.

- If you want a check box or radio button to be selected when it's initially displayed, set its Checked attribute to True. If you set the Checked attribute of more than one radio button in the same group to True, only the last one will be selected.

Figure 6-9   How to work with check boxes and radio buttons

C# code for working with these controls

The examples in figure 6-10 show how you can work with text boxes, labels, check boxes, and radio buttons in code. First, to retrieve the value the user enters into a text box, you use the Text property. In the example shown here, the Text property is assigned to a String variable. Note, however, that if the text box contains numeric data, you can convert it to the appropriate data type and then assign it to a variable with that data type. To be sure the user enters the correct data type, you can use validation controls as shown in the next chapter.

To assign a value to a label, you use the Text property of the label as shown in the second example in this figure. Notice here that the first line of text ends with an HTML tag for a line break (<br />). That way, the text will be displayed on two lines as you saw in figure 6-8.

The third and fourth examples in this figure show two ways you can process check boxes and radio buttons. First, you can process these controls in the event handler for the Click event of the form's submit button. Then, you just use if statements to test the Checked properties of the check boxes and radio buttons.

You can also process check boxes and radio buttons by writing event handlers for their CheckedChanged events. For a check box, this event is raised whenever the checked status of the control changes. Then, you can use an if statement to test the Checked property of the control just as you do in the event handler for the Click event of a submit button.

The CheckedChanged event works a bit differently for a radio button. Instead of being raised any time the status of the control changes, it's raised only when the status changes to checked. Because of that, there's no need to test the Checked property within the event handler for the CheckedChanged event.

In addition to the check box and radio button controls shown here, ASP.NET provides check box list and radio button list controls. These controls can simplify the task of creating groups of controls. You'll learn about these controls and the other list controls next.

Code that retrieves the text entered by the user in figure 6-8

```
string question = txtQuestion.Text;
```

Code that changes the Text property of the label in figure 6-8

```
lblConfirm.Text = "Thank you for your question.<br />"
                + "We will respond within 2 business days.";
```

Code that processes the first check box and radio button in figure 6-9

```
protected void btnContinue_Click(object sender, EventArgs e)
{
    if (chkMail.Checked)
        customer.Mail = true;
    else
        customer.Mail = false;

    if (rdoEmail.Checked)
        customer.MailType = "Email";
    else
        customer.MailType = "Postal";
}
```

Another way to process the check box and radio buttons

```
protected void chkMail_CheckedChanged(object sender, EventArgs e)
{
    if (chkMail.Checked)
        customer.Mail = true;
    else
        customer.Mail = false;
}

protected void rdoEmail_CheckedChanged(object sender, EventArgs e)
{
    customer.MailType = "Email";
}

protected void rdoPostal_CheckedChanged(object sender, EventArgs e)
{
    customer.MailType = "Postal";
}
```

Description

- To determine whether a check box or radio button is selected, you test its Checked property.
- For a check box, the CheckedChanged event is raised whenever the checked status of the control changes. For a radio button, this event is raised only when the status of the control changes to checked.

Figure 6-10   C# code for working with these controls

How to work with list controls

ASP.NET provides several controls that are designed to present lists of information. You'll learn about all five of those controls here: the drop-down list, list box, radio button list, check box list, and bulleted list.

Basic skills for working with list boxes and drop-down lists

Figure 6-11 presents the basic skills for working with *list boxes* and *drop-down lists*. The list box shown here lets the user select from one of four colors. List boxes are typically used in cases like this where there are a small number of items to select from. In contrast, drop-down lists are typically used with larger lists so they don't take up as much space on the page. The drop-down list in this figure, for example, displays a list of the days of the week.

The aspx code for the list box and drop-down list is also shown in this figure. Here, you can see that the ListBox element has four ListItem elements that correspond to the four colors in the list. Similarly, the DropDownList element has seven ListItem elements that correspond to the days of the week. The easiest way to add elements like these to a list is to use the ListItem Collection Editor. You'll see how to do that in figure 6-14.

You can also add items to a list using C# code. In that case, the aspx code for the form won't include ListItem elements like those shown here. Instead, ASP.NET will generate the elements when the page is rendered. You'll learn two ways to add items to a list in figure 6-13.

A list box displayed in a browser

The aspx code for the list box

```
<asp:ListBox ID="lstColor" runat="server">
    <asp:ListItem Value="Black" Selected="True">Black</asp:ListItem>
    <asp:ListItem Value="Red">Red</asp:ListItem>
    <asp:ListItem Value="Blue">Blue</asp:ListItem>
    <asp:ListItem Value="Green">Green</asp:ListItem>
</asp:ListBox>
```

A drop-down list displayed in a browser

The aspx code for the drop-down list

```
<asp:DropDownList id="ddlDay" runat="server">
    <asp:ListItem Value="1">Sunday</asp:ListItem>
    <asp:ListItem Value="2">Monday</asp:ListItem>
    <asp:ListItem Value="3">Tuesday</asp:ListItem>
    <asp:ListItem Value="4">Wednesday</asp:ListItem>
    <asp:ListItem Value="5">Thursday</asp:ListItem>
    <asp:ListItem Value="6">Friday</asp:ListItem>
    <asp:ListItem Value="7">Saturday</asp:ListItem>
</asp:DropDownList>
```

Description

- *List boxes* and *drop-down lists* typically contain one or more list items. You can load list items by using C# code or the ListItem Collection Editor. See figures 6-13 and 6-14 for details.

- A list box lets a user choose one or more items from a list of items. A drop-down list lets a user choose an item from a drop-down list of items.

Figure 6-11   Basic skills for working with list boxes and drop-down lists

Properties for working with list boxes, drop-down lists, and list items

Figure 6-12 presents some common properties for working with list boxes and drop-down lists. As you just saw, these controls contain ListItem objects that define the items in the list. These objects are stored in a collection that you can refer to using the Items property of the control. You'll see examples that use this property in the next figure.

You can also get the selected item using the SelectedItem property of the control, you can get or set the index of the selected item using the SelectedIndex property, and you can get or set the value of the selected item using the SelectedValue property. By default, the SelectedIndex property of a drop-down list is set to zero, which means that the first item is selected. In contrast, the SelectedIndex property of a list box is set to -1 by default, which means that none of the items in the list are selected. Then, you can check if the user has selected an item using code like this:

```
if (lstColor.SelectedIndex > -1) ...
```

You can also select an item by default by setting the SelectedIndex property to the appropriate index value. And you can clear the selection from a list box by setting this property to -1. Finally, you can select an item by default by setting the SelectedValue property to the appropriate value.

The Rows and SelectionMode properties apply only to list box controls. The Rows property determines how many items are displayed at one time. The SelectionMode property determines whether the user can select more than one item from the list. Note that when multiple selections are allowed, the SelectedItem property gets the first selected item, the SelectedIndex property gets the index of the first selected item, and the SelectedValue property gets the value of the first selected item.

To work with an item in a drop-down list or list box, you use the properties shown in this figure. The Text property specifies the text that's displayed for the item. The Value property specifies a value that's associated with the item. And the Selected property indicates whether the item is selected.

This figure also shows three examples for working with a drop-down list or list box. In the first example, the SelectedValue property of a drop-down list is assigned to an int variable. Note that because the SelectedValue property contains a string, it is converted to an integer.

The second example uses the SelectedItem property to retrieve the ListItem object for the selected item. Then, it uses the Text property of the ListItem object to get the text that's displayed for the selected item.

The third example is an event handler for the SelectedIndexChanged event of the drop-down list. This event occurs any time the item that's selected changes between posts to the server. If you want the page to post immediately when the user selects an item, you should set the AutoPostBack property of the control to True.

Common properties of list box and drop-down list controls

Property	Description
Items	The collection of ListItem objects that represents the items in the control. This property returns an object of type ListItemCollection.
Rows	The number of items that are displayed in a list box at one time. If the list contains more rows than can be displayed, a scroll bar is added automatically.
SelectedItem	The ListItem object for the currently selected item, or the ListItem object for the item with the lowest index if more than one item is selected in a list box.
SelectedIndex	The index of the currently selected item, or the index of the first selected item if more than one item is selected in a list box. If no item is selected in a list box, the value of this property is -1.
SelectedValue	The value of the currently selected item, or the value of the first selected item if more than one item is selected in a list box. If no item is selected in a list box, the value of this property is an empty string ("").
SelectionMode	Indicates whether a list box allows single selections (Single) or multiple selections (Multiple).

Common properties of list item objects

Property	Description
Text	The text that's displayed for the list item.
Value	A string value associated with the list item.
Selected	Indicates whether the item is selected.

Code that retrieves the value of a selected item in a drop-down list

```
int dayNumber = Convert.ToInt32(ddlDay.SelectedValue);
```

Code that retrieves the text for a selected item in a drop-down list

```
string dayName = ddlDay.SelectedItem.Text;
```

Code that uses the SelectedIndexChanged event of a drop-down list

```
protected void ddlDay_SelectedIndexChanged(object sender, EventArgs e)
{
    int dayNumber = Convert.ToInt32(ddlDay.SelectedValue);
}
```

Description

- To work with the items in a drop-down list or list box, you use the Items property of the control. This property returns a ListItemCollection object that contains all of the items in the list.

- The SelectedIndexChanged event is raised when the user selects a different item from a drop-down list or list box.

Figure 6-12   Properties for working with drop-down lists, list boxes, and list items

Members for working with list item collections

Figure 6-13 presents some common members for working with a collection of list item objects. To get the item at a specific index, for example, you use the indexer. And to get a count of the number of items in the collection, you use the Count property.

All but two of the methods shown here let you add or remove items in the collection. The method you're most likely to use is Add, which adds an item to the end of the collection. The examples in this figure show two different ways you can use this method.

The first example contains the code that's used to load the colors into the list box you saw in figure 6-11. Here, the Add method is used to add an item with the specified string value. When you code the Add method this way, the value you specify is assigned to both the Text and Value properties of the item.

If you want to assign different values to the Text and Value properties of an item, you use the technique shown in the second example. Here, a new list item object is created with two string values. The first string is stored in the Text property, and the second string is stored in the Value property. Then, the Add method is used to add the new item to the list item collection of the drop-down list you saw in figure 6-11.

Notice in both of these examples that the Items property is used to refer to the collection of list item objects for the control. You can also use the SelectedIndex property of a control to refer to an item at a specific index. For example, you could use a statement like this to remove the selected item from a drop-down list:

```
ddlDay.Items.RemoveAt(ddlDay.SelectedIndex);
```

The last two methods let you locate a list item based on the value of its Text or Value property. These methods are useful when you need to access a list item and you don't know its index value.

Common members of list item collection objects

Property	Description
`Count`	The number of items in the collection.

Indexer	Description
`[integer]`	A ListItem object that represents the item at the specified index.

Method	Description
`Add(string)`	Adds a new item to the end of the collection, and assigns the specified string value to both the Text and Value properties of the item.
`Add(ListItem)`	Adds the specified list item to the end of the collection.
`Insert(integer, string)`	Inserts an item at the specified index location in the collection, and assigns the specified string value to the Text property of the item.
`Insert(integer, ListItem)`	Inserts the specified list item at the specified index location in the collection.
`Remove(string)`	Removes the item from the collection whose Text property is equal to the specified string value.
`Remove(ListItem)`	Removes the specified list item from the collection.
`RemoveAt(integer)`	Removes the item at the specified index location from the collection.
`Clear()`	Removes all the items from the collection.
`FindByValue(string)`	Returns the list item whose Value property has the specified value.
`FindByText(string)`	Returns the list item whose Text property has the specified value.

Code that loads items into a list box using strings

```
lstColor.Items.Add("Black");
lstColor.Items.Add("Red");
lstColor.Items.Add("Blue");
lstColor.Items.Add("Green");
```

Code that loads items into a drop-down list using ListItem objects

```
ddlDay.Items.Add(New ListItem("Sunday", "1"));
ddlDay.Items.Add(New ListItem("Monday", "2"));
ddlDay.Items.Add(New ListItem("Tuesday", "3"));
ddlDay.Items.Add(New ListItem("Wednesday", "4"));
ddlDay.Items.Add(New ListItem("Thursday", "5"));
ddlDay.Items.Add(New ListItem("Friday", "6"));
ddlDay.Items.Add(New ListItem("Saturday", "7"));
```

Description

- The ListItemCollection object is a collection of ListItem objects. Each ListItem object represents one item in the list.

- Items in a ListItemCollection object are numbered from 0. So the index for the first item in the list is 0, the index for the second item is 1, and so on.

- When you load items into a list box using strings, both the Text and Value properties of the list item are set to the string value you specify. To set the Text and Value properties of a list item to different values, you must create a list item object and then add that item to the collection.

Figure 6-13   Members for working with list item collections

How to use the ListItem Collection Editor

In the last figure, you saw how to use the Add method of a list item collection to load items into a drop-down list or list box control. If the items are static, however, you might want to use the ListItem Collection Editor to load them instead. Figure 6-14 shows you how to use this editor.

When you first display the ListItem Collection Editor, the list is empty. Then, you can use the Add button below the Members list to add items to the list. When you do, the item appears in the Members list and its properties appear in the Properties list. The first property lets you disable a list item so it doesn't appear in the list. The other three properties are the same properties you learned about in figure 6-12. Note, however, that when you set the Text property, the Value property defaults to the same value. If that's not what you want, you can change this value.

The ListItem Collection Editor dialog box

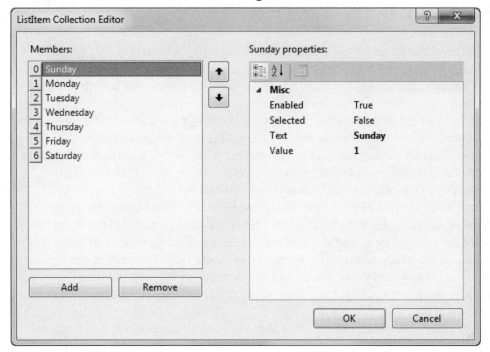

Description

- You can use the ListItem Collection Editor to add items to a drop-down list or list box. You'll typically use it to create a static list of items. Each item you add generates an asp:ListItem element in the aspx file.

- To display the Collection Editor dialog box, select Edit Items from the smart tag menu, or select the control and then click the ellipsis button that appears when you select the Items property in the Properties window.

- To add an item to the list, click the Add button and then enter the properties for the item in the Properties list. The item appears in the Members list.

- By default, the ListItem Collection Editor sets the Value property of a list item to the value you specify for the Text property.

- To remove an item, select it in the Members list and then click the Remove button.

- You can use the up and down arrow buttons to the right of the Members list to move the selected item up or down in the list.

Figure 6-14   How to use the ListItem Collection Editor

How to work with radio button lists and check box lists

Earlier in this chapter, you learned how to use radio buttons and check boxes. But ASP.NET also provides *radio button lists* and *check box lists* that you can use to create lists of radio buttons or check boxes. Figure 6-15 shows you how to use these controls.

As you can see from the aspx code for the check box list and radio button list, each control consists of a collection of ListItem objects. You can refer to this collection through the Items property of the control just as you can for drop-down lists and list boxes. These controls also have SelectedItem, SelectedIndex, and SelectedValue properties just like drop-down lists and list boxes.

Just like a group of radio buttons, only one item in a radio button list can be selected at one time. Then, you can use the SelectedValue property to get or set the value of the selected item, and you can use the SelectedIndex property to get or set the index of the selected item. This is illustrated by the first statement in this figure, which uses the SelectedValue property to get the value of the selected item. Note that this is much simpler than the code you use to get the value of the selected radio button in a group.

Like a list box, you can select more than one item in a check box list. Because of that, you'll usually determine whether an item in the list is selected using the Selected property of the item. This is illustrated in the second example in this figure. Here, the Items property of a check box list is used to get the item at index 0. Then, the Selected property of that item is used to determine if the item is selected. Notice here that you can't refer to individual check boxes by name when you use a check box list. Because of that, your code may not be as readable as it is when you use individual check box controls. That's why I recommend that you use check box lists only when they provide a distinct advantage over using individual controls.

To determine the layout of the items in a radio button or check box list, you use the attributes shown in this figure. The RepeatLayout attribute determines how ASP.NET aligns the buttons or check boxes in a list. In most cases, you'll use a table, which is the default. However, ASP.NET 4 also lets you use an ordered or an unordered list. If you use an ordered list, the control is rendered as an ol element with an li element for each item in the list. If you use an unordered list, the control is rendered as a ul element with li elements. Then, you can use CSS to format the ol or ul and li elements. Note that these are the same elements that are used to render numbered lists and bulleted lists as shown in the next figure.

The RepeatDirection attribute determines whether the controls are listed horizontally or vertically. For the radio button list in this figure, I set this attribute to Horizontal. In contrast, I left this attribute at its default of Vertical for the check box list.

The RepeatColumns attribute specifies the number of columns in the radio button or check box list. By default, the items are displayed in a single column. If a list contains more than just a few items, however, you may want to display the items in two or more columns to save space. The four check boxes in the list shown in this figure, for example, are displayed in two columns.

A check box list and a radio button list displayed in a browser

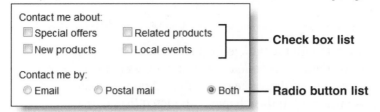

The aspx code for the check box list

```
<asp:CheckBoxList id="cblContact" runat="server" Width="305px"
    RepeatColumns="2">
    <asp:ListItem Value="Special">Special offers</asp:ListItem>
    <asp:ListItem Value="New">New products</asp:ListItem>
    <asp:ListItem Value="Related">Related products</asp:ListItem>
    <asp:ListItem Value="Events">Local events</asp:ListItem>
</asp:CheckBoxList>
```

The aspx code for the radio button list

```
<asp:RadioButtonList id="rblMail" runat="server" Width="346px"
    RepeatDirection="Horizontal">
    <asp:ListItem Value="Email">Email</asp:ListItem>
    <asp:ListItem Value="Postal">Postal mail</asp:ListItem>
    <asp:ListItem Value="Both" Selected="True">Both</asp:ListItem>
</asp:RadioButtonList>
```

Attributes for formatting radio button and check box lists

Attribute	Description
RepeatLayout	Specifies whether ASP.NET should use a table (Table), an unordered list (UnorderedList), an ordered list (OrderedList), or normal HTML flow (Flow) to format the list when it renders the control. The default is Table.
RepeatDirection	Specifies the direction in which the controls should be repeated. The available values are Horizontal and Vertical. The default is Vertical.
RepeatColumns	Specifies the number of columns to use when repeating the controls. The default is 0.

A statement that gets the value of the selected item in a radio button list

```
customer.MailType = rblMail.SelectedValue;
```

A statement that checks if the first item in a check box list is selected

```
if (cblContact.Items[0].Selected) ...
```

Description

- A *radio button list* presents a list of mutually exclusive options. A *check box list* presents a list of independent options. These controls contain a collection of ListItem objects that you refer to through the Items property of the control.

- These controls also have SelectedItem, SelectedIndex, and SelectedValue properties. These properties work just like they do for drop-down list and list box controls. See figure 6-12 for more information.

Figure 6-15   How to work with radio button lists and check box lists

How to work with bulleted lists and numbered lists

Figure 6-16 shows how to work with the bulleted list control. In spite of its name, this control can be used to create both *bulleted lists* and *numbered lists*. The type of list that's created depends on the value of the BulletStyle attribute.

Like the other list controls presented in this chapter, a bulleted list control contains a collection of ListItem objects. In this figure, for example, you can see the aspx code for the list items contained in the two controls shown at the top of this figure. Because the BulletStyle attribute of the first control is set to Disc, it's displayed as a bulleted list. In contrast, the BulletStyle attribute of the second control is set to Numbered, so it's displayed as a numbered list.

Unlike the other list controls, the bulleted list control is typically used only to display a list. In other words, it's not used to let the user make a selection. That's the case if the DisplayMode attribute is set to Text. If this attribute is set to Hyperlink, however, the user can click on the link to display the page at the URL specified by the Value attribute of the list item. This is illustrated by the numbered list in this figure.

If the DisplayMode attribute is set to LinkButton, the page is posted back to the server when the user clicks a link. Then, you can respond to the user clicking the link by coding an event handler for the Click event of the bulleted list control. Within that method, you can use the Selected property of a list item to determine if the item was clicked. This is illustrated by the statement in this figure. Alternatively, you can use the value of the e argument's Index property to determine which list item the user clicked.

A bulleted list and a numbered list displayed in a browser

Materials you will need:

- Styrofoam
- Gray and black latex paint
- Stone texture paint
- Rotary tool

Select a project type:

1. Costumes
2. Static props
3. Animated props

Common attributes of the bulleted list control

Attribute	Description
BulletStyle	Specifies the bullet style. For a bulleted list, allowable values are Disc, Circle, Square, or CustomImage. For a numbered list, allowable values are Numbered, LowerAlpha, UpperAlpha, LowerRoman, or UpperRoman.
BulletImageUrl	Specifies the URL of the image used to display the bullets if the BulletStyle attribute is set to CustomImage.
FirstBulletNumber	Specifies the starting number if numbers are displayed.
DisplayMode	Specifies how the text for each item should be displayed. Allowable values are Text, HyperLink, or LinkButton. Text is the default.

The aspx code for the bulleted list shown above

```
<asp:BulletedList ID="BulletedList1" runat="server" BulletStyle="Disc">
    <asp:ListItem>Styrofoam panel</asp:ListItem>
    <asp:ListItem>Gray and black latex paint</asp:ListItem>
    <asp:ListItem>Stone texture paint</asp:ListItem>
    <asp:ListItem>Rotary tool</asp:ListItem>
</asp:BulletedList>
```

The aspx code for the numbered list shown above

```
<asp:BulletedList ID="blstProjectTypes" runat="server" BulletStyle="Numbered"
    DisplayMode="HyperLink">
    <asp:ListItem Value="Costumes.aspx">Costumes</asp:ListItem>
    <asp:ListItem Value="StaticProps.aspx">Static props</asp:ListItem>
    <asp:ListItem Value="AnimatedProps.aspx">Animated props</asp:ListItem>
</asp:BulletedList>
```

A statement that checks if the first link button in a bulleted list was clicked

```
if (blstProjectTypes.Items[0].Selected) ...
```

Description

- The bulleted list control creates *bulleted lists* or *numbered lists*. This control contains a collection of ListItem objects that you refer to through the Items property of the control.

- If you set the DisplayMode attribute to Hyperlink, you can set the Value attribute of each ListItem object to the URL of the page you want to display when the link is clicked.

- If you set the DisplayMode attribute to LinkButton, you can use the Click event of the bulleted list to respond to the user clicking one of the links.

- Unlike the other list controls, the bulleted list control doesn't have SelectedItem, SelectedIndex, and SelectedValue properties.

Figure 6-16   How to work with bulleted lists and numbered lists

How to use other web server controls

As you learned earlier, ASP.NET provides many other controls besides those you've already seen in this chapter. So in the remaining topics of this chapter, I'll present several of those controls. But first, I want to show you how to get information about using a control that you haven't used before. You can also use this technique to get additional information about controls you have used.

How to get the information you need for using a control

The easiest way to get information about a web server control is to use the Help documentation that comes with Visual Studio. To access this documentation, you use the View Help command in the Help menu. When you select this command, the Help Viewer is displayed in your default browser as shown in figure 6-17.

The left pane of the Help Viewer lets you enter the text you want to look for in the Search text box. To look for information on a control, for example, you can enter the name of the control. Then, you can select a topic from the ones that are listed in the right pane of the Help Viewer.

In this figure, I entered "calendar control" in the Search text box and a list of Topics about this control was displayed. Then, I selected the topic shown here to display an overview of the control. This is usually a good place to start when you're learning how to use a control that you haven't used before.

Once you have a basic idea of how a control works, you can display other topics that describe specific features or functions of the control. You can do that by using the links that are available within a topic or by selecting topics from the table of contents in the left pane.

In addition to the topics that are listed for a control, you may want to review the members of the class that defines the control. If you display the topic for a class, you'll see that you can do that in one of two ways. First, you can select the "Members" topic from the table of contents to display all of the members of the class. Second, you can display each type of member separately by selecting the appropriate topic. For example, you can select the "Methods" topic to display all methods that are available from the Calendar class.

Some of the Help documentation for the calendar control

Description

- Visual Studio 2010 provides an abundance of information on the web server controls. To display this information in the Help Viewer, use the Help→View Help command.

- To start, you can review the information about the basic function and usage of the control. To do that, just enter the name of the control in the Search text box and then select the appropriate topic from those that are listed in the right pane.

- Most controls include a help topic that describes the control and a separate topic that describes the class for the control. To learn how to work with a control, you'll typically need to use both of these topics.

- The help information for most web server controls includes an "overview" topic like the one shown above that provides basic information about the control along with other related topics. Some of these topics describe specific features of the control.

- The help information for most control classes includes a topic that describes all members that are available from the control. To view this topic, you can select the "Members" topic. Or, you can select a more specific topic such as "Methods" to display a specific type of member.

- Because the Help documentation includes information on several versions of the .NET Framework, a topic you choose may be for a version other than .NET Framework 4. In that case, you can usually display the documentation for the correct version using the Other Versions drop-down list below the topic title.

Figure 6-17   How to get the information you need for using a control

How to use the image control

Figure 6-18 shows part of a web page that includes an *image control* that displays a graphic image. In this case, the graphic image is stored in a *JPEG* file. JPEG is a graphics format commonly used for photographs and scanned images. Graphic images are also frequently stored in *GIF* files and, more recently, in *PNG* files. These files are typically used for small images such as button images and icons.

You can also see some common attributes of an image control in this figure. The most important attribute is ImageUrl, which specifies the URL of the image file. As you can see in the asp tag for the image in this figure, the image file is located in the Images folder of the web site.

If you need to change the image that's displayed in an image control when a page is executed, you can do that by assigning a different value to the ImageUrl property. This is illustrated in the C# code example in this figure. Here, a URL that refers to an image named cat01.jpg in the Images\Products directory of the web site is assigned to the ImageUrl property of a control named imgProduct.

Since some browsers might not be able to display an image, you should also set the AlternateText attribute. Then, the text you specify will be displayed in place of the image if the image can't be displayed. If, for example, the image in this figure can't be displayed, the text "Murach Books" will be displayed instead.

The ImageAlign attribute determines how the image is aligned relative to the web page or other elements on the page. If you set this attribute to Left, for example, the image is aligned at the left side of the page and any text on the page will wrap around the right side of the image. Note that if you use CSS to format your web pages, you probably won't need to use the ImageAlign attribute.

The last two attributes, Width and Height, let you control the size of the displayed image. If you leave both of these attributes at their defaults, ASP.NET will display the image at its original size. If you specify just one of these attributes, ASP.NET will automatically set the other attribute so the proportions of the original image are maintained. If you set both attributes, the image will be distorted if necessary to fit the dimensions you specify. Because of that, you'll usually set just one of these attributes. You can also set the size of an image in CSS. Alternatively, you can use an image editor to size the image so it's appropriate for your application. Then, you won't need to specify the height or width of the image

How to use the hyperlink control

The web page in figure 6-18 also includes a *hyperlink control*. This control navigates to the web page specified in the NavigateUrl attribute when the user clicks the control. If you want to display text for a hyperlink control, you set the Text attribute or code the text as content between the start and end tags. Either way, the text appears with an underline as shown in this figure. Alternatively, you can display an image for this control. To do that, you set the ImageUrl attribute to the URL of an image you want to display.

An image control and a hyperlink control displayed in a browser

Image

Click here to order — Hyperlink

The asp tag for the image control

```
<asp:Image ID="Image1" runat="server" ImageUrl="~/Images/MurachLogo.jpg"
    AlternateText="Murach Books" />
```

Code that sets the URL of an image control

```
imgProduct.ImageUrl = "Images/Products/cat01.jpg";
```

Common image attributes

Attribute	Description
ImageUrl	The absolute or relative URL of the image.
AlternateText	The text that's used in place of the image if the browser can't display the image.
ImageAlign	The alignment of the image relative to the web page or other elements on the page. For more information, see online help.
Width	The width of the image.
Height	The height of the image.

The asp element for the hyperlink control

```
<asp:HyperLink ID="HyperLink1" runat="server"
    NavigateUrl="http://www.murach.com">Click here to order
</asp:HyperLink>
```

Common hyperlink attributes

Attribute	Description
NavigateUrl	The absolute or relative URL of the page that's displayed when the control is clicked.
Text	The text that's displayed for the control.
ImageUrl	The absolute or relative URL of the image that's displayed for the control.

Description

- An *image control* displays a graphic image, typically in *GIF* (*Graphic Interchange Format*), *JPEG* (*Joint Photographic Experts Group*), or *PNG* (*Portable Network Graphics*) format.

- If you don't specify the Height or Width attributes of an image control, the image will be displayed at full size unless the size is specified by CSS.

- A *hyperlink control* navigates to another web page when the user clicks the control. You can display either text or an image for the control.

Figure 6-18   How to use the image and hyperlink controls

How to use the file upload control

The *file upload control*, shown in figure 6-19, is designed for applications that let the user upload files to the web site. This control displays a text box that lets the user enter the path for the file to be uploaded, plus a Browse button that displays a dialog box that lets the user locate and select the file.

To upload the selected file, you must also provide a separate control that results in a postback, like the Upload button in this figure. When the user clicks this button, the page is posted and the file selected by the user is sent to the server along with the HTTP request.

The first example in this figure shows the aspx code that declares the file upload control and the Upload button shown at the top of this figure. Note here that the file upload control doesn't include an attribute that specifies where the file should be saved on the server. That's because the file upload control doesn't automatically save the uploaded file. Instead, you must write code that calls the SaveAs method of this control. The second example in this figure shows how to write this code.

Before you call the SaveAs method, you should test the HasFile property to make sure the user has selected a file. If the user has selected a valid file and it was successfully uploaded to the server, the HasFile property will be True. Then, you can use the FileName property to get the name of the selected file, and you can combine the file name with the path where you want the file saved. In this figure, the file is stored in the C:\Uploads directory.

To illustrate the use of the PostedFile.ContentLength property, the event handler in this figure uses this property to determine the size of the uploaded file. Then, if this value exceeds the limit set by the sizeLimit variable, the file isn't saved. Instead, an error message is displayed.

A file upload control displayed in a browser

File upload control

The aspx code used to implement the file upload

```
File upload:<br /><br />
<asp:FileUpload ID="FileUpload1" runat="server" /><br /><br />
<asp:Button ID="btnUpload" runat="server" Text="Upload"
    OnClick="btnUpload_Click" /><br /><br />
<asp:Label ID="lblMessage" runat="server"></asp:Label>
```

The Click event handler for the Upload button

```
protected void btnUpload_Click(object sender, EventArgs e)
{
    int sizeLimit = 5242880;    // 5,242,880 is 5MB
    if (FileUpload1.HasFile)
    {
        if (FileUpload1.PostedFile.ContentLength <= sizeLimit)
        {
            string path = "C:\\uploads\\" + FileUpload1.FileName;
            FileUpload1.SaveAs(path);
            lblMessage.Text = "File uploaded to " + path;
        }
        else
            lblMessage.Text = "File exceeds size limit.";
    }
}
```

Properties and methods of the FileUpload class

Property	Description
HasFile	If True, the user has selected a file to upload.
FileName	The name of the file to be uploaded.
PostedFile	The HttpPostedFile object that represents the file that was posted. You can use this object's ContentLength property to determine the size of the posted file.

Method	Description
SaveAs(string)	Saves the posted file to the specified path.

Description

- The *file upload control* displays a text box and a button that lets the user browse the client computer's file system to locate a file to be uploaded.

- Because the file upload control doesn't provide a button to upload the file, you must provide a button or other control to post the page. Then, in the button's Click event handler, you must call the SaveAs method of the file upload control to save the file on the server.

- To use the SaveAs method, the user must have write access to the specified directory.

Figure 6-19   How to use the file upload control

How to use the image map control

An *image map* is an image that has several clickable regions, called *hot spots*. Figure 6-20 shows how the *image map control* provides a simple way to create image maps in ASP.NET.

The image map control lets you create three types of hot spots: rectangles, circles, and polygons. The example in this figure displays two books with a polygon hot spot for each book. Each hot spot is defined by a PolygonHotSpot element, and the polygon shapes are defined on the Coordinates attribute using a list of x and y coordinates that indicate the corners of the hot spot.

You use similar techniques to define rectangle and circle hot spots. To create a rectangle hot spot, you specify the locations of its sides using the Top, Bottom, Left, and Right attributes. To create a circle hot spot, you specify the x and y coordinates of its midpoint and the length of its radius using the X, Y, and Radius attributes.

Unfortunately, Visual Studio doesn't provide a convenient point-and-click editor to define hot spots. As a result, you'll need to use a separate graphics program to determine the x and y coordinates for the map's hot spots, particularly for a polygon hot spot. Once you've determined those coordinates, you can return to Visual Studio to create the hot spot elements for the image map.

The HotSpotMode attribute of an image map indicates whether the page will link to another page (Navigate) or be posted back to the server (PostBack) when the user clicks a hot spot. If you set this attribute to Navigate, you should set the NavigateUrl attribute of each hot spot to the URL of the page you want to be displayed when the hot spot is clicked. If you set this attribute to PostBack, you should set the PostBackValue attribute of each hot spot to the value you want to be passed to the Click event handler of the image map when the hot spot is clicked. Then, you can use the PostBackValue attribute of the e argument in the Click event handler to determine which hot spot was clicked. This is illustrated in the code example in this figure.

Note that you can also specify the HotSpotMode attribute for each hot spot rather than for the whole image map. That way, you can perform a postback when some hot spots are clicked and link to other pages when other hot spots are clicked.

The new_books_2009.jpg image

The aspx code for the image map control

```
<asp:ImageMap ID="imapBooks2009" runat="server"
    ImageUrl="~/Images/new_books_2009.jpg" HotSpotMode="PostBack"
    OnClick="imapBooks2009_Click">
    <asp:PolygonHotSpot Coordinates="1, 19, 114, 0, 122, 53, 106, 143,
        26, 158, 24, 149" PostBackValue="C++" />
    <asp:PolygonHotSpot Coordinates="128, 21, 241, 42, 218, 178, 103, 159"
        PostBackValue="JavaScript" />
</asp:ImageMap>
```

The Click event handler for the image map

```
protected void imapBooks2009_Click(object sender, ImageMapEventArgs e)
{
    string book;
    if (e.PostBackValue.Equals("C++"))
        book = "C++ 2008";
    else
        book = "JavaScript and DOM Scripting";
}
```

Common image map attributes

Attribute	Description
ImageUrl	The URL of the image to be displayed.
HotSpotMode	Sets the behavior for the hot spots. PostBack causes the page to be posted and Navigate links to a different page. This attribute can also be specified for individual hot spot elements.

Description

- The *image map control* lets you display an *image map* with one or more *hot spots*. The page either posts back or links to another page when the user clicks a hot spot.
- To post the page back when the user clicks a hot spot, set the HotSpotMode attribute to PostBack, and set the PostBackValue attribute of the hot spot to the value you want passed to the Click event handler.
- To link to another page when the user clicks a hot spot, set the HotSpotMode attribute to Navigate and specify the URL of the page in the NavigateUrl attribute of the hot spot.
- To create a CircleHotSpot element, use the X, Y, and Radius attributes. To create a RectangleHotSpot element, use the Top, Bottom, Left, and Right attributes. To create a PolygonHotSpot element, use the Coordinates attribute.

Figure 6-20   How to use the image map control

How to use the calendar control

The *calendar control* provides an easy way for a user to select a date. Although this control can be used for more sophisticated purposes, this is its most common use. Figure 6-21 shows how you use this control.

The web page at the top of this figure illustrates one way to implement a calendar control. To start, the web page displays two drop-down lists that let the user select a month and day, plus an image button. If the user clicks the image button, the calendar control is displayed and the image button is hidden. Then, the user can use the controls at the top of the calendar to move to the previous or next month if necessary. Finally, when the user selects a date from the calendar, the drop-down lists are set to the selected month and day, the image button is displayed again, and the calendar is hidden.

By default, the calendar control lets the user select a single date. However, you can also let the user select an entire week or month by setting the SelectionMode property to the appropriate value. If you want the user to select entire weeks, set this property to DayWeek. If you want the user to select entire months, set it to DayWeekMonth. If you just want to display a calendar and not let the user make selections, you can set this property to None.

If you review the aspx code for the calendar control in this figure, you'll see that most of the attributes are used to apply styles to the calendar. For example, the BorderStyle and BorderColor attributes display a solid black border around the calendar. The attributes in the TodayDayStyle and TitleStyle elements cause the current date and the month heading to be displayed in white bold text on a blue background. And the ForeColor attribute in the NextPrevStyle element causes the symbols for going to the previous and next page to be displayed in white. In addition, the Visible attribute causes the control to be hidden when the page is first displayed.

When the user selects a date from the calendar, the SelectionChanged event is raised and the page is posted to the server. Then, you can use the SelectedDate property of the control within the event handler for this event to determine what date was selected. The event handler shown in this figure, for example, uses this property to select the appropriate values in the drop-down lists so they display the selected date.

If a calendar control lets the user select an entire week or month, you can use the SelectedDates property to retrieve the dates in the week or month the user selects. This property contains a collection of the selected dates, and you can use standard properties to work with this collection. For example, if you want to know how many dates were selected, you can use the Count property of this collection.

A web page with an image button that displays a calendar

The web page with the calendar displayed

The aspx code for the calendar control

```
<asp:Calendar ID="clnArrival" runat="server" Visible="False"
    OnSelectionChanged="clnArrival_SelectionChanged"
    BorderColor="Black" BorderStyle="Solid">
    <TodayDayStyle BackColor="Blue" Font-Bold="True" ForeColor="White" />
    <TitleStyle BackColor="Blue" Font-Bold="True" ForeColor="White" />
    <NextPrevStyle ForeColor="White" />
</asp:Calendar>
```

The SelectionChanged event handler for the calendar control

```
protected void clnArrival_SelectionChanged(object sender, EventArgs e)
{
    ddlMonth.SelectedValue = clnArrival.SelectedDate.Month.ToString();
    ddlDay.SelectedValue = clnArrival.SelectedDate.Day.ToString();
    clnArrival.Visible = false;
    ibtnCalendar.Visible = true;
}
```

Common properties of the Calendar class

Property	Description
SelectionMode	Specifies the type of selection that can be made. Acceptable values are Day, DayWeek, DayWeekMonth, and None.
SelectedDate	The currently selected date if a single date was selected, or the first selected date if multiple dates were selected.
SelectedDates	A collection that contains all of the selected dates in sequence. To determine the number of dates that were selected, use the Count property of this collection.

Description

- The *calendar control* is typically used to provide users with an easy way of selecting a date. Entire weeks and months can also be selected.

- When the user makes a selection from a calendar control, the SelectionChanged event is raised and the page is posted to the server.

Figure 6-21   How to use the calendar control

Perspective

In this chapter, you've learned how to use 17 of the standard web server controls that ASP.NET provides. In addition, you've learned how to use the Help documentation that Visual Studio provides to learn about any control. With that as background, you should be able to use any of the server controls.

Keep in mind, though, that you'll learn how to use many of the controls that weren't presented in this chapter later in this book. In the next chapter, for example, you'll learn how to use the validation controls. And in chapters 13 through 17, you'll learn how to use some of the data controls. If a control is presented in this book, then, you'll want to read about it here before you go to the Help documentation. Then, you can use the Help documentation to learn about any aspects of these controls that we may not present.

Terms

web server control
HTML server control
event handler
access key
submit button
button
link button
image button
text box
label
check box
radio button
list box
drop-down list
radio button list
check box list
bulleted list
numbered list
image control
JPEG (Joint Photographic Experts Group)
GIF (Graphic Interchange Format)
PNG (Portable Network Graphics)
hyperlink control
file upload control
image map
image map control
hot spot
calendar control

Exercise 6-1   Create a reservation form

In this exercise, you'll create a reservation form that uses many of the controls you learned about in this chapter. To make this form easier to develop, we'll give you a starting form that includes the required HTML and literal text. In addition, we'll give you style sheets that include all the styles for formatting the form. When you're done, the form should look like this:

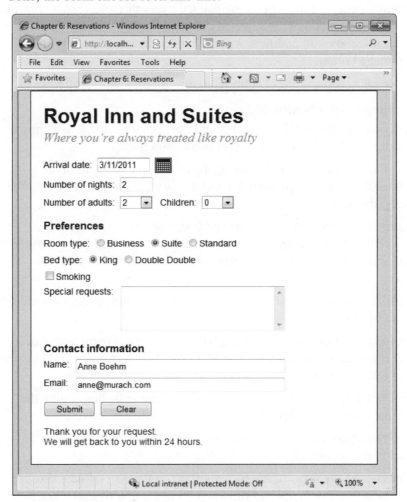

Open the web site and review the code

1. Open the Ch06Reservation web site in the C:\aspnet4_cs directory. Then, review the HTML for the Request.aspx web page and the Main.css and Request.css style sheets that are used to format this page.

Add the controls and code for the arrival date

2. Add the text box for the arrival date, followed by an image button that displays a calendar image. You'll find the image for this button in the Images folder. Be sure to add these controls to the same paragraph as the literal text that identifies them.

3. Start an event handler for the Load event of the form. Then, add code to display the current date in the format shown above if the form is not being posted back.

4. Add a calendar control to the next paragraph, and set its Visible property to False so it's hidden when the form is first displayed.

5. Code an event handler for the Click event of the image button. This event handler should hide the image button and display the calendar control.

6. Code an event handler for the SelectionChanged event of the calendar control. This event handler should get the selected date and display it in the text box in the format shown above. In addition, it should hide the calendar control and display the image button.

7. Run the application and test these controls to be sure they work correctly.

Add the remaining controls and code

8. Add the text box for the number of nights and the two drop-down lists for the number of adults and children in the appropriate paragraphs.

9. Add code to the Load event handler for the form that loads the numbers 1 through 4 into the Adults drop-down list and the numbers 0 through 4 into the Children drop-down list.

10. Add the radio buttons for the room type and bed type to the appropriate paragraphs, being sure to identify the radio button groups. Add code to the Load event handler for the form to set the default button in each group as shown above.

11. Add the check box to the paragraph that follows the paragraph that contains the second group of radio buttons.

12. Add the multiline text box to the paragraph that follows the paragraph that contains the literal text that identifies this text box. This text box should display four rows of text at a time.

13. Add the text boxes for the name and email to the paragraphs that follow the paragraphs that contain the literal text that identify these text boxes.

14. Add the two button controls to the paragraph with the ID "buttons", and add a label control to the paragraph with the ID "message".

15. Set the properties of the form so the focus will be on the Arrival date text box when the form is first displayed and the Submit button is activated when the Enter key is pressed.

16. Code an event handler for the Click event of the Submit button that displays the message shown above in the label at the bottom of the form.

17. Code an event handler for the Click event of the Clear button that returns all of the control values to their defaults.

18. Run the application and check that all of the controls look and work the way they should. Make any necessary corrections.

7

How to use the validation controls

In chapter 2, you learned the basic skills for using two of the validation controls: the required field validator and the range validator. Now, you'll learn more about using those controls as well as how to use the other validation controls. As you'll see, you can use the validation controls to perform the data validation required by most web forms.

An introduction to the validation controls

ASP.NET provides six *validation controls* that you can use to validate the data on a web form. You'll learn the basic skills for using these controls in the topics that follow.

How to use the validation controls

Figure 7-1 summarizes the validation controls that are available with ASP.NET. As you learned in chapter 2, the first five controls are called *validators*. These are the controls that you use to check that the user has entered valid data into the input controls on a web form. In contrast, you use the validation summary control to display a summary of all the errors on a page.

This figure also illustrates how the validation controls appear in the Web Forms Designer. Here, you can see the Order form for the Shopping Cart application that was presented in chapter 3. This form uses two validation controls. The first one is a required field validator that checks that the user entered a value into the Quantity text box, and the second one is a range validator that checks that the user entered an integer that ranges from 1 to 500.

In this example, the required field validator appears directly to the right of the text box, and the range validator appears to the right of the required field validator. As you will see later in this chapter, though, these validators are defined so the error message will be displayed directly to the right of the text box no matter which validator detects the error.

Validation controls on an Order form

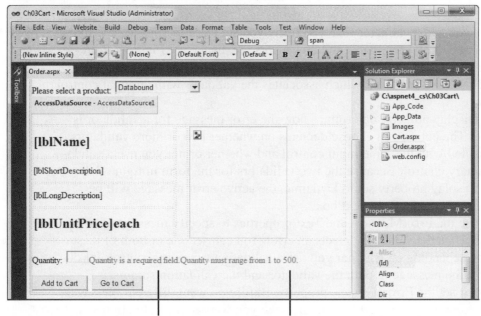

Required field validator   **Range validator**

The validation controls provided by ASP.NET

Control	Name	Description
	RequiredFieldValidator	Checks that an entry has been made.
	CompareValidator	Checks an entry against a constant value or the value of another control. Can also be used to check for a specific data type.
	RangeValidator	Checks that an entry is within a specified range.
	RegularExpressionValidator	Checks that an entry matches a pattern that's defined by a regular expression.
	CustomValidator	Checks an entry using validation code that you write yourself.
	ValidationSummary	Displays a summary of error messages from the other validation controls.

Description

- You can use the *validation controls* with any of the web server or HTML server input controls.

- Each *validator* is associated with a single input control, but you can associate two or more validators with the same input control.

Figure 7-1   How to use the validation controls

Common validator properties

After you add a validator to a web form, you set its properties to determine which input control it validates and how errors are displayed. Figure 7-2 presents the properties that you use to do that. The most important property is the ControlToValidate property, which associates the validator with an input control on the page.

The Display property determines how the error message for a validator is displayed. The option you choose depends on whether two or more validators are associated with the same input control and whether or not you use a validation summary control. Because the two validators for the form in figure 7-1 have the Display property set to Dynamic, the active error message will be displayed to the right of the text box.

You use the ErrorMessage and Text properties to specify messages that are displayed when the validator detects an error. You can set one or both of these properties depending on whether you use a validation summary control. If you want the same message in both the validator and the validation summary control, just set the ErrorMessage property. But if you want different messages, set the ErrorMessage property to the message you want in the validation summary control and the Text property to the message you want in the validator.

If the Enabled property of a validator is set to True, the validation test for the validator is performed. But if you want to skip the validation that's done by a validator, you can set this property to False. In contrast, the EnableClientScript property determines whether the client-side script for the validation is generated. If this property is set to False, the validation is only done on the server.

When ASP.NET performs the validation test specified by a validator, it sets the IsValid property of the validator to indicate whether or not the data is valid. Then, you can refer to this property in your C# code to test the result of the validation. In most cases, though, you won't test the result of individual validators. Instead, you'll test that all of the validators on the page passed their validation tests by checking the IsValid property of the page.

Common validator properties

Property	Description
ControlToValidate	The ID of the control to be validated.
Display	Determines how the error message is to be displayed. Specify Static to allocate space for the message in the page layout, Dynamic to have space allocated only when an error occurs, or None to display errors only in a validation summary control. The default is Static.
ErrorMessage	The message that's displayed in the validator and/or the validation summary control when the validation fails. To display one message in the validation summary and another in the validator, use the Text property for the validator message.
Text	The message that's displayed in the validator when you use the ErrorMessage property to display a message in the validation summary control.
Enabled	Indicates whether the validation control is enabled.
EnableClientScript	Indicates whether the validation will be done on the client.
ValidationGroup	Indicates which group the validation control is part of (see figure 7-8).
IsValid	Indicates whether the control specified in the ControlToValidate property passed the validation.

Description

- You typically set the Display property to Dynamic if you use two or more validators to validate the same control. Then, the validators that pass their validation tests don't take up space on the page.

- You can also format the error messages that are displayed by including HTML in the values you assign to the ErrorMessage and Text properties.

- In addition to the properties above, validators have properties that affect the appearance of the message that's displayed. However, you'll typically format validators using CSS as shown in chapter 5 or skins as shown in chapter 11.

- Each validator has an IsValid property that indicates whether its validation was successful. You typically use this property in the C# code-behind files only if you initiate validation manually using the Page.Validate method.

Note

- If you've used a previous version of ASP.NET, you should know that the error message for a validator is no longer displayed in red by default.

Figure 7-2   Common validator properties

How ASP.NET processes validation controls

To refresh your memory about how validation controls work, figure 7-3 summarizes the key points. To start, you should realize that the validation tests are typically done on the client before the page is posted to the server. That way, a round trip to the server isn't required to display error messages if any invalid data is detected.

In most cases, client-side validation is done when the focus leaves an input control that has validators associated with it. That can happen when the user presses the Tab key to move to the next control or clicks another control to move the focus to that control.

However, the required field validator works a bit differently. When you use this validator, the validation isn't done until the user clicks a button whose CausesValidation property is set to True. The exception is if the user enters a value into an input control and then tries to clear the value. In that case, an error will be detected when the focus leaves the control.

To perform client-side validation, a browser must support *Dynamic HTML*, or *DHTML*. Because most browsers today support DHTML, validation can usually be done on the client. In case the browser doesn't support DHTML, though, validation is always done on the server when a page is submitted. ASP.NET does this validation after it initializes the page.

When ASP.NET performs the validation tests on the server, it sets the IsValid property of each validator to indicate if the test was successful. In addition, it sets the IsValid property of the page to indicate whether all the input data is valid. You usually should test this property in the event handler for the event that caused the page to be posted to the server.

At the top of this figure, for example, you can see how this property is tested in the event handler for the Click event for the Add to Cart button in figure 7-1. You usually do this in case validation wasn't done on the client. That's especially true if the operations within the method perform critical tasks such as updating the database. If the validation is done on the client, of course, the page won't be posted if one or more controls contain invalid data so the IsValid test will always be True.

If you want to bypass client-side validation and just perform the validation on the server, you can set the EnableClientScript property of the validation controls to False. Then, the scripts that are typically used to perform the validation on the client aren't generated, and validation is done only on the server. This is useful in some applications.

Typical code for processing a page that contains validation controls

```
protected void btnAdd_Click(object sender, EventArgs e)
{
    if (Page.IsValid)
    {
        CartItemList cart = CartItemList.GetCart();
        CartItem cartItem = cart[selectedProduct.ProductID];
        if (cartItem == null)
        {
            cart.AddItem(selectedProduct,
                Convert.ToInt32(txtQuantity.Text));
        }
        else
        {
            cartItem.AddQuantity(Convert.ToInt32(txtQuantity.Text));
        }
        Response.Redirect("Cart.aspx");
    }
}
```

Description

- If a browser supports *DHTML (Dynamic HTML)*, the validation controls do their validation on the client using client-side script. That way, the validation is performed and error messages are displayed without the page being posted to the server.

- Validation is always done on the server too, right after the page is initialized, so the validation is done whether or not the browser supports DHTML. Although most browsers support DHTML, your code should still check that a page is valid in case a browser doesn't support DHTML.

- Validation is performed on the server when you click a button whose CausesValidation property is set to True. To create a button that doesn't initiate validation, you can set this property to False.

- Validation is performed on the client when the focus leaves the input control. The exception is a required field validator, which performs its validation only when you click a button whose CausesValidation property is set to True or when you enter a value into a control and then clear and leave the control.

- If a validation control indicates invalid data, the IsValid property of that control is set to False and the IsValid property of the page is set to False. These properties can be tested in your C# code.

- If you want to perform validation only on the server, you can set the EnableClientScript properties of the validation controls to False. Then, no client-side scripts are generated for validating the data.

Figure 7-3   How ASP.NET processes validation controls

How to use the basic validation controls

In the topics that follow, you'll learn about the three validation controls you'll use most often as you develop web applications. These are the required field validator, the compare validator, and the range validator.

How to use the required field validator

Figure 7-4 shows how to use the *required field validator*. This validator checks that the user entered a value into an input control. If the user doesn't enter a value, the validator's error message is displayed.

The three examples in this figure illustrate how you can use the required field validator. In the first example, this validator is used to check for a required entry in a text box. To do that, its ControlToValidate property is set to the ID property of the text box. Then, if the user doesn't enter anything into the text box, the text in the ErrorMessage property is displayed.

The second and third examples show how you can use the InitialValue property of the required field validator to check that the user changed the initial value of a control. By default, this property is set to an empty string, which is what you want if the input control is empty. If you specify an initial value for an input control, however, you'll want to set the InitialValue property of the required field validator to that value.

In the second example, this technique is used with a text box. Here, the initial value indicates the format for a date entry. If the user doesn't change this value, the validation test will fail.

The third example uses the InitialValue property with a list box. Here, the InitialValue property is set to None, which is the value of the first item in the list. That way, if the user doesn't select another item, the validation test will fail. You can also use this technique with a drop-down list or a radio button list.

Additional property of the required field validator

Property	Description
InitialValue	The initial value of the control that's validated. If this value isn't changed, the validation fails. The default is an empty string.

A required field validator that checks for a required entry

```
<asp:TextBox ID="txtName" runat="server"></asp:TextBox> 
<asp:RequiredFieldValidator ID="RequiredFieldValidator1" runat="server"
    ControlToValidate="txtName"
    ErrorMessage="You must enter a name.">
</asp:RequiredFieldValidator>
```

A required field validator that checks that an initial value is changed

```
<asp:TextBox ID="txtBirthDate" runat="server" Width="159px">mm/dd/yyyy
</asp:TextBox> 
<asp:RequiredFieldValidator ID="RequiredFieldValidator2" runat="server"
    ControlToValidate="txtBirthDate"
    InitialValue="mm/dd/yyyy"
    ErrorMessage="You must enter a birth date.">
</asp:RequiredFieldValidator>
```

A required field validator that forces an option to be chosen from a list box

```
<asp:ListBox ID="lstCardType" runat="server" Width="292px">
    <asp:ListItem Selected="True" Value="None">
        --Select a credit card--</asp:ListItem>
    <asp:ListItem Value="Visa">Visa</asp:ListItem>
    <asp:ListItem Value="MC">MasterCard</asp:ListItem>
    <asp:ListItem Value="AmEx">American Express</asp:ListItem>
</asp:ListBox> 
<asp:RequiredFieldValidator ID="RequiredFieldValidator3" runat="server"
    ControlToValidate="lstCardType"
    InitialValue="None"
    ErrorMessage="You must select a credit card type.">
</asp:RequiredFieldValidator>
```

How the input controls are initially displayed in a browser

Description

- The *required field validator* checks that the user entered data into an input control. It's typically used with text box controls, but can also be used with list controls.

Figure 7-4   How to use the required field validator

How to use the compare validator

Figure 7-5 shows how you use the *compare validator*. This validator lets you compare the value entered into an input control with a constant value or the value of another control. You can also use the compare validator to make sure that the value is a particular data type.

To define a compare validator, you use the four additional properties shown in this figure. To compare the input data with a constant value, you specify the value in the ValueToCompare property. Then, you set the Operator property to indicate the type of comparison you want to perform, and you set the Type property to the type of data you're comparing. The first example illustrates how this works. Here, the value entered into a text box is tested to be sure that it's an integer that's greater than zero. Then, if the user enters a value that isn't an integer, or if the user enters an integer that isn't greater than zero, the error message will be displayed.

To test for just a data type, you set the Type property to the type of data you're testing for, and you set the Operator property to DataTypeCheck. This is illustrated by the second example. Here, the value entered into a text box is tested to be sure that it's an integer.

The third example shows how to compare the value of an input control with the value of another control. To do that, you set the Operator and Type properties just as you do when you compare an input value with a constant. Instead of setting the ValueToCompare property, however, you set the ControlToCompare property to the ID of the control whose value you want to compare. This example tests that a date that's entered into one text box is after the date entered into another text box.

When you begin working with compare validators, you'll find that if the user doesn't enter a value into a control, the compare validator associated with that control will pass its validation test. Because of that, you must use a required field validator along with the compare validator if you want to be sure that the user enters a value into the input control.

You should also realize that if you compare the value of a control against the value of another control, the validation test will pass if the user doesn't enter a value into the other control or the value of the other control can't be converted to the correct type. To avoid that problem, you'll want to be sure that the other control is also validated properly.

Additional properties of the compare validator

Property	Description
ValueToCompare	The value that the control specified in the ControlToValidate property should be compared to.
Operator	The type of comparison to perform (Equal, NotEqual, GreaterThan, GreaterThanEqual, LessThan, LessThanEqual, or DataTypeCheck).
Type	The data type to use for the comparison (String, Integer, Double, Date, or Currency).
ControlToCompare	The ID of the control that the value of the control specified in the ControlToValidate property should be compared to.

A compare validator that checks for a value greater than zero

```
<asp:TextBox ID="txtQuantity" runat="server"></asp:TextBox> 
<asp:CompareValidator ID="CompareValidator1" runat="server"
    ControlToValidate="txtQuantity" Type="Integer"
    Operator="GreaterThan" ValueToCompare="0"
    ErrorMessage="Quantity must be greater than zero.">
</asp:CompareValidator>
```

A compare validator that checks for an integer value

```
<asp:TextBox id="txtQuantity" runat="server"></asp:TextBox> 
<asp:CompareValidator ID="CompareValidator2" runat="server"
    ControlToValidate="txtQuantity"
    Operator="DataTypeCheck" Type="Integer"
    ErrorMessage="Quantity must be an integer.">
</asp:CompareValidator>
```

A compare validator that compares the values of two text boxes

```
<asp:TextBox ID="txtStartDate" runat="server"></asp:TextBox><br /><br />
<asp:TextBox ID="txtEndDate" runat="server"></asp:TextBox> 

<asp:CompareValidator
    ID="CompareValidator3" runat="server"
    ControlToValidate="txtEndDate"
    Operator="GreaterThan" Type="Date"
    ControlToCompare="txtStartDate"
    ErrorMessage="End Date must be greater than Start Date.">
</asp:CompareValidator>
```

Description

- The *compare validator* compares the value entered into a control with a constant value or with the value entered into another control. You can also use the compare validator to check that the user entered a specific data type.

Figure 7-5   How to use the compare validator

How to use the range validator

The *range validator*, shown in figure 7-6, validates user input by making sure that it falls within a given range of values. To specify the valid range, you set the MinimumValue and MaximumValue properties. You must also set the Type property to the type of data you're checking. The first example in this figure, for instance, checks that the user enters an integer between 1 and 14 into a text box.

The second example in this figure shows how you can set the range for a range validator at runtime. Here, you can see that the MinimumValue and MaximumValue properties aren't set when the range validator is declared. Instead, they're set when the page is loaded for the first time. In this case, the MinimumValue property is set to the current date, and the MaximumValue property is set to 30 days after the current date.

Like the compare validator, you should realize that the range validator will pass its validation test if the user doesn't enter anything into the associated control. Because of that, you'll need to use a required field validator along with the range validator if the user must enter a value.

Additional properties of the range validator

Property	Description
MinimumValue	The minimum value allowed for the control.
MaximumValue	The maximum value allowed for the control.
Type	The data type to use for the comparison (String, Integer, Double, Date, or Currency).

A range validator that checks for a numeric range

```
<asp:TextBox ID="txtDays" runat="server"></asp:TextBox> 
<asp:RangeValidator ID="RangeValidator1" runat="server"
    ControlToValidate="txtDays" Type="Integer"
    MinimumValue="1" MaximumValue="14"
    ErrorMessage="Days must be between 1 and 14.">
</asp:RangeValidator>
```

How to set a range at runtime

A range validator that checks a date range that's set at runtime

```
<asp:TextBox ID="txtArrival" runat="server">01/01/12</asp:TextBox> 
<asp:RangeValidator ID="valArrival" runat="server"
    ControlToValidate="txtArrival" Type="Date"
    ErrorMessage="You must arrive within 30 days.">
</asp:RangeValidator>
```

Code that sets the minimum and maximum values when the page is loaded

```
protected void Page_Load(object sender, EventArgs e)
{
    if (!IsPostBack)
    {
        valArrival.MinimumValue
            = DateTime.Today.ToShortDateString();
        valArrival.MaximumValue
            = DateTime.Today.AddDays(30).ToShortDateString();
    }
}
```

Description

- The *range validator* checks that the user enters a value that falls within the range specified by the MinimumValue and MaximumValue properties. These properties can be set when the range validator is created or when the page is loaded.
- If the user enters a value that can't be converted to the correct data type, the validation fails.
- If the user doesn't enter a value into the associated input control, the range validator passes its validation test. As a result, you should also provide a required field validator if a value is required.

Figure 7-6   How to use the range validator

Validation techniques

Now that you're familiar with the basic validation controls, you're ready to learn some additional techniques for validating data. First, you'll learn how to use the validation summary control to display a summary of all the errors on a page. Then, you'll learn how to use validation groups.

How to use the validation summary control

The *validation summary control* lets you summarize all the errors on a page. The summary can be a simple message like "There were errors on the page," or a more elaborate message that includes information about each error. The summary can be displayed directly on the page, or, if validation is being performed on the client, in a separate message box.

Figure 7-7 shows how to use the validation summary control. The most difficult part of using this control is determining how to code the Text and ErrorMessage properties of a validator so the error messages are displayed the way you want. To display the same message in both the validator and the validation summary control, for example, you set the ErrorMessage property to that message.

To display different messages, you set the ErrorMessage property to the message you want to display in the validation summary control, and you set the Text property to the message you want to display in the validator. This technique is illustrated in the example in this figure. Here, the Text properties of two required field validators are set to "*" so those indicators appear next to the controls in error, and the ErrorMessage properties are set to more descriptive error messages. Notice that, unlike the ErrorMessage property, the Text property isn't stored in an attribute of the validator. Instead, it's stored as content between the opening and closing tags for the validator.

If you don't want to display individual error messages in the validation summary control, just set the HeaderText property of the control to the generic message you want to display. Then, leave the ErrorMessage property of each validator blank. Otherwise, you can set the HeaderText property to a value like the one shown in this figure, or you can leave it at its default so that no heading is displayed. Also, to display an error message in the validation summary control but not in a validator, set the Display property of the validator to None.

By default, the error messages displayed by a validation summary control are formatted as a bulleted list as shown in this figure. However, you can also display the errors in a simple list or paragraph format by setting the DisplayMode property accordingly. In addition, you can display the error messages in a message box rather than on the web page by setting the ShowMessageBox property to True and the ShowSummary property to False.

Properties of the validation summary control

Property	Description
DisplayMode	Specifies how the error messages from the validation controls are to be displayed. The available values are BulletList, List, or SingleParagraph. The default is BulletList.
HeaderText	The text that's displayed before the list of error messages.
ShowSummary	A Boolean value that determines whether the validation summary should be displayed on the web page. The default is True.
ShowMessageBox	A Boolean value that determines whether the validation summary should be displayed in a message box (client-side validation only). The default is False.

Two validators and a validation summary control that's displayed on the web page

```
<asp:RequiredFieldValidator ID="RequiredFieldValidator1" runat="server"
    ControlToValidate="lstCardType" InitialValue="None"
    ErrorMessage="You must select a credit card type."
    Display="Dynamic">*</asp:RequiredFieldValidator>

<asp:RequiredFieldValidator ID="RequiredFieldValidator2" runat="server"
    ControlToValidate="txtCardNumber"
    ErrorMessage="You must enter a credit card number."
    Display="Dynamic">*</asp:RequiredFieldValidator>

<asp:ValidationSummary ID="ValidationSummary1" runat="server"
    HeaderText="Please correct the following errors:"/>
```

How the controls appear on the web page

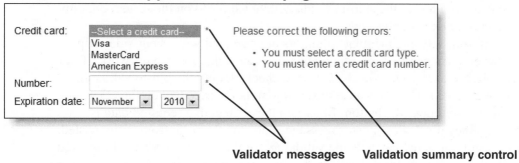

Validator messages   Validation summary control

Description

- The *validation summary control* displays a summary of the error messages that were generated by the page's validators. The summary can be displayed on the web page or in a separate message box.

- The error messages displayed in the validation summary control come from the ErrorMessage property of the page's validators. If you want to display a different message in the validator, set the Text property of the validator.

- If you don't want to display an error message in the validator, set its Display property to None.

Figure 7-7   How to use the validation summary control

How to use validation groups

The *validation group* feature of ASP.NET lets you group validation controls and specify which group should be validated when a page is posted. Figure 7-8 shows how to use these groups.

To illustrate, the web page in this figure provides for a bill-to address and an optional ship-to address, with a check box to indicate whether the ship-to address is the same as the bill-to address. Then, if the check box is checked, the ship-to address isn't required. As a result, the validators for the ship-to fields shouldn't be executed. To implement this type of validation, you can use two validation groups: one for the bill-to fields, the other for the ship-to fields.

The first example in this figure shows just one of the ship-to address text boxes and a validator that's assigned to a validation group named ShipTo. For the purpose of this example, though, you can assume that the other ship-to fields also have validators assigned to the ShipTo group. And you can assume that the bill-to fields have validators assigned to a group named BillTo.

The second example shows the button that submits the page. Here, the button specifies BillTo as its validation group. Because of that, the bill-to fields will be validated when the user posts the form, but the ship-to fields won't be. Note that for this to work, the CausesValidation property of the button must be set to True, which is the default.

The third example shows how you can invoke the ShipTo validators in your C# code if the check box is left unchecked. Here, the Validate method of the Page class is executed with the name of the validation group as its argument, which causes the Validate method of each validator in the ShipTo group to be executed. As a result, the ship-to fields will be validated on the server, but only if the check box isn't checked.

Unfortunately, the fact that validators are executed with client-side script whenever that's possible can complicate the way validation groups work. If, for example, the user leaves the check box unchecked, only the bill-to validations will be executed. That's because those validators are executed on the client side when the user clicks the button. But when they detect that required data is missing, they display their error messages and stop the page from being posted. As a result, the code that calls the validators for the ship-to fields isn't executed until all the bill-to fields are validated. (The only way around this limitation is to write your own client-side validation script to validate the ship-to fields if the check box is unchecked.)

Note that any validation controls that don't specify the ValidationGroup attribute are considered part of the *default group*. The validators in this group are executed only when the page is posted with a button or other control that causes validation but doesn't specify a validation group, or when the Page.Validate method is called without specifying a validation group.

Attributes that cause group validation when a button is clicked

Attribute	Description
CausesValidation	Specifies whether validation should be performed when the user clicks the button.
ValidationGroup	Specifies the name of the group to be validated if CausesValidation is True.

A web page that accepts a bill-to and a ship-to address

Bill-to address

Name: George Constantine

Address: 2050 N. Main Street

City, state, zip: Ann Arbor   MI   48103

Ship-to address ☑ Ship to same address

Name:

Address:

City, state, zip:

[Continue]

A text box with a validator that specifies a validation group

```
<asp:TextBox ID="txtShipToName" runat="server" />
<asp:RequiredFieldValidator ID="RequiredFieldValidator1" runat="server"
    ControlToValidate="txtShipToName"
    ErrorMessage="You must enter a ship-to name."
    ValidationGroup="ShipTo"></asp:RequiredFieldValidator>
```

A button that specifies a validation group

```
<asp:Button ID="btnContinue" runat="server" Text="Continue"
    ValidationGroup="BillTo" OnClick="btnContinue_Click" />
```

C# code that conditionally validates the ShipTo group

```
if (!chkShipToSameAsBillTo.Checked)
    Page.Validate("ShipTo");
```

Description

- A *validation group* is a group of validators that are run when a page is posted.

- To group validators, set the ValidationGroup attribute for each validator. Then, use the ValidationGroup attribute for each control that causes a postback (such as a button or a list box) to specify which group should be executed.

- You can use C# code to force the execution of a specific validation group by using the Page.Validate method with the validation group name as the argument.

- Any validators that don't specify the ValidationGroup attribute are part of the *default group*. This group is executed when started by a button or control that doesn't specify a validation group or when the Page.Validate method is used without an argument.

Figure 7-8   How to use validation groups

How to use the advanced validation controls

Besides the validation controls you've already learned about, ASP.NET provides two controls that provide advanced functionality. The regular expression validator lets you match data to a pattern you specify, and the custom validator lets you create your own validation routines.

How to use the regular expression validator

A *regular expression* is a string made up of special pattern-matching symbols. You can use regular expressions with the *regular expression validator* to make sure that an input control's data matches a particular pattern, such as a zip code, phone number, or email address. Figure 7-9 shows how to use the regular expression validator.

As you can see, the ValidationExpression property specifies the regular expression the input data must match. For instance, the code for the first regular expression validator in this figure specifies that the input data must contain five decimal digits (\d{5}). And the regular expression for the second validator specifies that the input data must be in the format of a U.S. phone number.

In the next topic, you'll learn how to create your own regular expressions. However, you should know that Visual Studio provides several standard expressions you can choose from. These expressions define patterns for validating phone numbers and postal codes for the U.S., France, Germany, Japan, and China; Social Security numbers for the U.S. and China; and Internet email addresses and URLs.

To use a standard expression, you simply select it from the Regular Expression Editor dialog box. You can also create a custom expression that's based on a standard expression by selecting the standard expression so its definition appears in the text box at the bottom of the Regular Expression Editor dialog box. Then, you can edit the regular expression any way you'd like.

An additional property of the regular expression validator

Property	Description
ValidationExpression	A string that specifies a regular expression. The regular expression defines a pattern that the input data must match to be valid.

A regular expression validator that validates five-digit numbers

```
<asp:TextBox ID="txtZipCode" runat="server"></asp:TextBox> 
<asp:RegularExpressionValidator ID="RegularExpressionValidator1"
    runat="server" ControlToValidate="txtZipCode"
    ValidationExpression="\d{5}"
    ErrorMessage="Must be a five-digit U.S. zip code.">
</asp:RegularExpressionValidator>
```

A regular expression validator that validates U.S. phone numbers

```
<asp:TextBox ID="txtPhone" runat="server"></asp:TextBox> 
<asp:RegularExpressionValidator ID="RegularExpressionValidator2"
    runat="server" ControlToValidate="txtPhone"
    ValidationExpression="((\(\d{3}\) ?)|(\d{3}-))?\d{3}-\d{4}"
    ErrorMessage="Must be a valid U.S. phone number.">
</asp:RegularExpressionValidator>
```

The Regular Expression Editor dialog box

Description

- The *regular expression validator* matches the input entered by the user with the pattern supplied by the ValidationExpression property. If the input doesn't match the pattern, the validation fails.

- The string you specify for the ValidationExpression property must use *regular expression* notation. For more information, see the next figure.

- ASP.NET provides several standard regular expressions that you can access using the Regular Expression Editor. To display its dialog box, select the validation control, select the ValidationExpression property in the Properties window, and click its ellipsis button.

- You can also use the Regular Expression Editor to create a custom expression that's based on a standard expression. To do that, select the standard expression and then edit it in the Validation Expression text box.

Figure 7-9   How to use the regular expression validator

How to create your own regular expressions

Figure 7-10 presents the basic elements of regular expressions. Although the .NET Framework provides many other elements that you can use in regular expressions, you can create expressions of considerable complexity using just the ones shown here. In fact, all of the standard expressions provided by ASP.NET use only these elements.

To start, you can specify any ordinary character, such as a letter or a decimal digit. If a character must be an A, for example, you just include that character in the expression. To include a character other than an ordinary character, you must precede it with a backslash. For example, \(specifies that the character must be a left parenthesis, \] specifies that the character must be a right bracket, and \\ specifies that the character must be a backslash. A backslash that's used in this way is called an *escape character*.

You can also specify a *character class*, which consists of a set of characters. For example, \d indicates that the character must be a decimal digit, \w indicates that the character must be a *word character*, and \s indicates that the character must be a *whitespace character*. The uppercase versions of these elements—\D, \W, and \S—match any character that is not a decimal digit, word character, or whitespace character.

To create a list of possible characters, you enclose them in brackets. For example, [abc] specifies that the character must be the letter a, b, or c, and [a-z] specifies that the character must be a lowercase letter. One fairly common construct is [a-zA-Z], which specifies that the character must be a lowercase or uppercase letter.

You can also use *quantifiers* to indicate how many of the preceding element the input data must contain. To specify an exact number, you just code it in brackets. For example, \d{5} specifies that the input data must be a five-digit number. You can also specify a minimum number and a maximum number of characters. For example, \w{6,20} specifies that the input data must contain from six to twenty word characters. You can also omit the maximum number to require just a minimum number of characters. For example, \w{6,} specifies that the input data must contain at least 6 word characters. You can also use the *, ?, and + quantifiers to specify zero or more, zero or one, or one or more characters.

If the input data can match one or more patterns, you can use the vertical bar to separate elements. For example, \w+|s{1} means that the input data must contain one or more word characters or a single whitespace character.

To create groups of elements, you use parentheses. Then, you can apply quantifiers to the entire group or you can separate groups with a vertical bar. For example, (AB)|(SB) specifies that the input characters must be either AB or SB. And (\d{3}-)? specifies that the input characters must contain zero or one occurrence of a three-digit number followed by a hyphen.

To help you understand how you can use each of these elements, this figure presents several examples. If you study them, you'll see the complex patterns that you can provide using these basic elements.

Common regular expression elements

Element	Description
Ordinary character	Matches any character other than ., $, ^, [, {, (, |,), *, +, ?, or \.
\	Matches the character that follows.
\d	Matches any decimal digit (0-9).
\D	Matches any character other than a decimal digit.
\w	Matches any word character (a-z, A-Z, and 0-9).
\W	Matches any character other than a word character.
\s	Matches any white space character (space, tab, new line, etc.).
\S	Matches any character other than a whitespace character.
[abcd]	Matches any character included between the brackets.
[^abcd]	Matches any character that is not included between the brackets.
[a-z]	Matches any characters in the indicated range.
{n}	Matches exactly *n* occurrences of the preceding element or group.
{n,}	Matches at least *n* occurrences of the preceding element or group.
{n,m}	Matches at least *n* but no more than *m* occurrences of the preceding element or group.
*	Matches zero or more occurrences of the preceding element.
?	Matches zero or one occurrence of the preceding element.
+	Matches one or more occurrences of the preceding element.
|	Matches any of the elements separated by the vertical bar.
( )	Groups the elements that appear between the parentheses.

Examples of regular expressions

Expression	Example	Description
\d{3}	289	A three digit number.
\w{8,20}	Frankenstein	At least eight but no more than twenty word characters.
\d{2}-\d{4}	10-3944	A two-digit number followed by a hyphen and a four-digit number.
\w{1,8}.\w{1,3}	freddy.jpg	Up to eight letters or numbers, followed by a period and up to three letters or numbers.
(AB)|(SB)-\d{1,5}	SB-3276	The letters AB or SB, followed by a hyphen and a one- to five-digit number.
\d{5}(-\d{4})?	93711-2765	A five-digit number, optionally followed by a hyphen and a four-digit number.
\w*\d\w*	arm01	A text entry that contains at least one numeral.
[xyz]\d{3}	x023	The letter x, y, or z, followed by a three-digit number.

Notes

- A regular expression can include elements other than those shown above. For more information, see the *Regular Expression Language Elements* topic in help.
- The standard regular expressions use only the elements shown above.

Figure 7-10 How to create your own regular expressions

How to use a custom validator

If none of the other validators provide the data validation your program requires, you can use a *custom validator*. Then, you can code your own validation routine that's executed when the page is submitted to the server. This technique is frequently used to validate input data that requires a database lookup.

Figure 7-11 shows how you use a custom validator. In this example, a custom validator is used to check that a value entered by the user is a valid product code in a table of products. To do that, the program includes an event handler for the ServerValidate event of the custom validator. This event occurs whenever validation is performed on the server.

When the ServerValidate event occurs, the event handler receives an argument named args that you can use to validate the data the user entered. The Value property of this argument contains the input value. Then, the event handler can perform the tests that are necessary to determine if this value is valid. If it is valid, the event handler assigns a True value to the IsValid property of the args argument so the validator passes its test. If it isn't valid, the event handler can assign a False value to the IsValid property of this argument so the validator doesn't pass its test. This causes the error message specified by the validator to be displayed.

In this figure, for example, the event handler calls the CheckProductCode method of the HalloweenDB class. Although you haven't seen this class or method before, all you need to know is that it checks the product code by looking it up in a database. If the product code exists, this method returns a value of True. Otherwise, it returns a value of False. In either case, the returned value is assigned to the IsValid property of the args argument.

Properties of the ServerValidateEventArgs class

Property	Description
Value	The text string to be validated.
IsValid	A Boolean property that you set to True if the value passes the validation test or to False otherwise.

Aspx code for a text box and a custom validator

```
<asp:TextBox ID="txtProductCode" runat="server"></asp:TextBox> 
<asp:CustomValidator id="valProductCode" runat="server"
    ControlToValidate="txtProductCode"
    ErrorMessage="Product code must be in database."
    OnServerValidate="valProductCode_ServerValidate">
</asp:CustomValidator>
```

C# code for the custom validator

```
protected void valProductCode_ServerValidate(object source,
    ServerValidateEventArgs args)
{
    args.IsValid = HalloweenDB.CheckProductCode(args.Value);
}
```

Description

- You can use a *custom validator* to validate input data using the validation tests you specify.

- You code the validation tests within an event handler for the ServerValidate event of the custom validator. This event is raised whenever validation is performed on the server. Because of that, the form must be submitted before the validation can be done.

- You can use the properties of the args argument that's passed to the ServerValidate event handler to test the input data (args.value) and indicate whether the data passed the validation test (args.IsValid). If you set the IsValid property of the args argument to False, the error message you specified for the custom validator is displayed.

- If the user doesn't enter a value into the associated input control, the custom validator doesn't perform its validation test. As a result, you should also provide a required field validator if a value is required.

Figure 7-11   How to use a custom validator

A validation routine that validates credit card numbers

To give you a better idea of what you can do with a custom validator, figure 7-12 shows the C# code for a custom validator that validates credit card numbers. To do that, it checks that the credit card number meets a mod-10 algorithm that all credit card numbers adhere to. This test often catches simple typographic errors before taking the time to actually authorize the card. Please note that this test doesn't establish that an account with the specified number exists or that credit is available on the account. It merely establishes that the number meets the required mod-10 algorithm.

To validate a credit card number, the event handler for the ServerValidate event calls a method named ValidateCreditCard and passes the card number to it. After this method declares three variables, it removes any spaces in the card number by using the Replace method of the String class. Then, it uses a for loop to store the digits in the credit card in reverse order in the reversedCardNumber variable. Next, it uses another for loop to double the digits in even-numbered positions. To determine if a digit is in an even-numbered position, it uses the modulus operator (%) to divide the position by 2 to see if there's a remainder. If not, it multiplies the number in that position by 2 and then concatenates it to the variable named digits. (Note that because the Substring method that gets the number returns a string, the string is converted to an integer before it's multiplied.) Otherwise, it just concatenates the number.

After the digits in the even-numbered positions have been multiplied, the method uses another for loop to add up all the digits. (Again, the result of the Substring method is converted to an integer.) The modulus operator is then used to determine if the result is evenly divisible by 10. If so, the credit card number is valid and a True value is returned to the calling method. Otherwise, a False value is returned and the error message associated with the custom validator is displayed.

C# code for a credit card validator

```
protected void valCreditCardNumber_ServerValidate(object source,
    ServerValidateEventArgs args)
{
    args.IsValid = ValidateCreditCard(args.Value);
}

private bool ValidateCreditCard(string cardNumber)
{
    int digitSum = 0;
    string digits = "";
    string reversedCardNumber = "";

    //Remove spaces and reverse string
    cardNumber = cardNumber.Replace(" ", null);
    for (int i = cardNumber.Length - 1; i >= 0; i--)
        reversedCardNumber += cardNumber[i];

    //Double the digits in even-numbered positions
    for (int i = 0; i < reversedCardNumber.Length; i++)
    {
        if ((i + 1) % 2 == 0)
            digits += Convert.ToInt32(reversedCardNumber.Substring(i, 1))
                    * 2;
        else
            digits += reversedCardNumber.Substring(i, 1);
    }

    //Add the digits
    for (int i = 0; i < digits.Length; i++)
        digitSum += Convert.ToInt32(digits.Substring(i, 1));

    //Check that the sum is divisible by 10
    if ((digitSum % 10) == 0)
        return true;
    else
        return false;
}
```

What the mod-10 validation algorithm does

1. Removes any spaces from the number.
2. Reverses the number.
3. Doubles the digits in even-numbered positions. If the original digit is 5 or greater, this will insert an additional digit into the number.
4. Adds up the individual digits.
5. Divides the result by 10. If the remainder is 0, the credit card number is valid.

Description

- This code can be used along with a custom validator to ensure that the user enters a credit card number that passes a standard mod-10 algorithm. If the card number passes this test, the program usually continues by checking that the account is valid and that the customer has available credit.

Figure 7-12   A validation routine that validates credit card numbers

Perspective

Now that you've completed this chapter, you should be able to create web forms that provide for most of the data validation that your applications will require. Keep in mind, though, that after you add validators to a form, you need to test them thoroughly to be sure that they detect all invalid entries. Although that can be time-consuming, particularly if you use regular expression validators that require complicated expressions or custom validators that require complicated validation routines, it's an essential part of developing professional web applications.

Terms

validation control	regular expression validator
validator	regular expression
DHTML (Dynamic HTML)	escape character
required field validator	character class
compare validator	word character
range validator	whitespace character
validation summary control	quantifier
validation group	custom validator
default group	

Exercise 7-1   Add validation to the Reservation form

In this exercise, you'll add validation to the Reservation form you created in exercise 6-1.

Add the required field validators

1. Open the Ch07Reservation web site in the C:\aspnet4_cs directory.

2. Add required field validators for the Arrival date, Number of nights, Name, and Email text boxes. Be sure to add these validators at the end of the paragraphs that contain the controls they validate. Enter a brief error message for each validator, and set the Display property to Dynamic.

3. Notice that the error messages for the validators are displayed in black. To fix this, add a style for a class named "validator" to the Main.css style sheet, and add a style property to set the color for this class to red. Then, set the CssClass property of each validator to this class.

4. Run the application and click the Submit button. The error messages for the Number of nights, Name, and Email text boxes should be displayed. To test the validator for the Arrival date text box, you'll need to delete the default value. Do that now, and then click the Submit button again. This time, the error message for the Arrival date text box should be displayed.

5. Enter valid values for all four text boxes and click the Submit button again to see that the error messages are no longer displayed.

6. Close the browser window and then run the application again. This time, click the Clear button to see that error messages are displayed when you click this button too. To fix that, you'll need to set the CausesValidation property of this button to False. You'll also need to set the CausesValidation property of the image button that displays the calendar control so it doesn't perform the validation. After you make these changes, run the application and test these buttons to be sure no errors are displayed.

7. Set the Text property of the Arrival date text box to "mm/dd/yyyy". Then, modify the code for the Form_Load event handler so it doesn't set this property to the current date. In addition, modify the event handler for the Click event of the Clear button so it sets this property to its initial value.

8. Set the InitialValue property of the required field validator for the Arrival date text box to the value that's displayed in this control by default. Then, run the application and click the Submit button. An error message should be displayed. Enter a valid date into the text box and click the Submit button again. This time, no error should be displayed for this text box.

Add the compare validators

9. Add a compare validator for the Arrival date text box. This validator should check that a date is entered into this text box.

10. Add a compare validator for the Number of nights text box. This validator should check that an integer greater than or equal to 1 is entered.

11. Run the application and click the Submit button without entering any data. Notice that the error messages for both validators associated with the Arrival date text box are displayed. That's because, as long as an entry is made in this text box, the compare validator will test it to be sure it's in the correct format.

12. Enter the value "11/31/2010" into the Arrival date text box, and enter the value "x" into the Number of nights text box. Click the Submit button. The error messages for both compare validators should be displayed because "11/31/2010" isn't a valid date and "x" isn't an integer.

13. Enter a valid date into the Arrival date text box, and enter the value "0" into the Number of nights text box. The error message for the number of nights should still be displayed because this value must be greater than or equal to one. Now, enter a valid value for this text box and click the Submit button to see that the error is no longer displayed.

Add a range validator

14. Add a range validator for the Arrival date text box. Because the date range will be set at runtime, you don't need to set the MinimumValue and MaximumValue properties.

15. Add code to the Load event handler for the page that sets the minimum value for the range validator to the current date and the maximum value to six months from the current date. This code will be similar to the code shown in figure 7-6.

16. Run the application, and enter or select a date that's before the current date. Click the Submit button. The error message for the range validator should be displayed.

17. Enter or select a date that's more than six months in the future, and click the Submit button again. The error message should still be displayed.

18. Enter or select a date within six months of the current date, and click the Submit button one more time. This time, the error message shouldn't be displayed.

Add a regular expression validator

19. Add a regular expression validator for the Email text box. Use the Regular Expression Editor dialog box as shown in figure 7-9 to set the ValidationExpression property to the Internet E-mail Address expression.

20. Run the application, and enter an email address that doesn't include an at sign (@). The error message for the regular expression validator should be displayed.

21. Enter another email address, this time without a period. The error message should still be displayed.

22. Enter an email address with both an at sign and a period, and then click the Submit button to see that the error message is no longer displayed.

Add a validation summary control

23. Add a new paragraph at the bottom of the page, and then add a validation summary control to the paragraph. Enter an appropriate value for the HeaderText property.

24. Run the application and click the Submit button to see how this looks. Notice that the error messages are displayed in both the validators and the validation summary control.

25. Set the Text property of each of the validators to an asterisk. Then, run the application again and click the Submit button to see how this looks.

26. Continue experimenting with the page until you're sure you understand how the validators work.

8

How to manage state

In chapters 2 and 3, you were introduced to the way that view state and session state are used. Now you'll learn more about using these states, and you'll also learn how to use application state. Beyond that, you'll learn how to use cookies and URL encoding to pass data between the server and the client. Because HTTP is a stateless protocol, these are essential skills for every web developer.

How to use view state

For the most part, *view state* is automatic. Because of that, you don't have to set any properties or write any code to use it. Nevertheless, you should at least understand how view state works and how to use it to your advantage. In some cases, you may even want to add your own data to view state.

How to work with view state

As the summary in figure 8-1 says, view state works by saving data in the HTML stream that's sent to the browser when a page is requested. This data is saved as a hidden input field named _VIEWSTATE. Because the field is hidden, it isn't displayed in the browser. And because the field is an input field, it's automatically sent back to the server when the user posts the page.

View state is used to retain the values of the form and control properties that you set in code. In the Future Value application of chapter 2, for example, the values in the drop-down list were set by code. As a result, these values don't need to be reset by code each time the page is posted back to the server. Instead, they're automatically reset by view state.

The EnableViewState property of a page and its controls determines if view state is enabled, which it is by default. Although this is usually what you want, you may occasionally want to disable view state. One reason for doing that is to get a control to work the way you want it to. Another reason is to improve performance when view state gets so large that it degrades performance.

If, for example, you change the value of a control property in code, but you want the initial value of that property restored each time the page is loaded, you can turn off view state to get the page to work right. Or, if a page is never posted back to itself, you can turn off view state to improve performance. In practice, though, you probably won't turn off view state until you discover that it's creating either a programming or performance problem.

With versions of ASP.NET before ASP.NET 4, you couldn't disable view state for a page and then enable view state for selected controls. That made it difficult to disable view state for most, but not all, of the controls on a page. But ASP.NET 4 makes this easy to do with its new ViewStateMode property. Note that this works only if the EnableViewState property of the page and the selected controls is set to True. Otherwise, the ViewStateMode property has no effect.

To determine the size of view state, you can enable the ASP.NET Trace feature as described in chapter 4. Then, you can scroll to the Control Tree section of the trace output to see which controls are using view state and how many bytes they're using. That way, you can tell whether it's worth the effort to turn view state off.

View state concepts

- *View state* is an ASP.NET feature that provides for retaining the values of page and control properties that change from one execution of a page to another.

- Before ASP.NET sends a page back to the client, it determines what changes the program has made to the properties of the page and its controls. These changes are encoded into a string that's assigned to the value of a hidden input field named _VIEWSTATE.

- When the page is posted back to the server, the _VIEWSTATE field is sent back to the server along with the HTTP request. Then, ASP.NET retrieves the property values from the _VIEWSTATE field and uses them to restore the page and control properties.

- ASP.NET also uses view state to save the values of the page properties it uses, such as IsPostBack.

- View state is *not* used to restore data entered by a user into a text box or any other input control unless the control responds to change events.

- If view state is enabled for a data-bound control, the control will not be rebound when the page is reposted. Instead, the control's values will be restored from view state.

Two cases when you may want to disable view state

- When restoring the control properties for a page affects the way you want the form to work, you may want to disable view state for one or more controls. Otherwise, you can modify your code so the page works without turning view state off.

- When the size of the view state field gets so large that it affects performance, you may want to disable view state for one or more controls or for an entire page.

How to disable view state

- To disable view state for a control, set the control's EnableViewState property to False.

- To disable view state for an entire page, set the EnableViewState property of the page (Page directive) to False. That disables view state for all the controls on the page.

How to enable view state for selected controls

- Set the EnableViewState property of the page and the controls whose view state you want to enable to True.

- Set the ViewStateMode property of the page (Page directive) to Disabled.

- Set the ViewStateMode property of the controls whose view state you want to enable to Enabled.

How to determine the size of view state for a page

- Enable the Trace feature for the page by setting the Trace attribute of the Page directive for the page to True as described in chapter 4. Then, scroll down to the Control Tree section of the trace output to see the number of bytes of view state used by the page and its controls.

Figure 8-1   How to work with view state

How to use view state for your own data

Although view state is designed to automatically save page and control property values across round trips to the browser, you can also add your own data to view state. To do that, you store the data in a *view state object* that's created from the StateBag class as shown in figure 8-2.

Like the session state object, the view state object contains a collection of key/value pairs that represent the items saved in view state. To access this object, you use the ViewState property of the page. Then, you can use the methods listed in this figure to work with the view state object.

To illustrate, the first two examples in this figure show how you can add or update a view state item named TimeStamp. The third example shows how to retrieve that item. And the last example shows how to remove it. Notice in the third example that because a view state item is stored as an object type, the code must cast the object to the DateTime data type.

Keep in mind that you usually use session state, not view state, to save data across round trips to the browser. Occasionally, though, it does make sense to use view state for passing small amounts of data, especially when you want to associate the data with a specific page. In chapter 20, you'll see an example of that.

Common members of the StateBag class

Indexer	Description
[name]	The value of the view state item with the specified name. If you set the value of an item that doesn't exist, that item is created.

Property	Description
Count	The number of items in the view state collection.
Keys	A collection of keys for all of the items in the view state collection.
Values	A collection of values for all of the items in the view state collection.

Method	Description
Add(name, value)	Adds an item to the view state collection. If the item you name already exists, its value is updated.
Clear()	Removes all items from the view state collection.
Remove(name)	Removes the item with the specified name from the view state collection.

A statement that adds or updates a view state item

```
ViewState.Add("TimeStamp", Now);
```

Another way to add or update a view state item

```
ViewState["TimeStamp"] = DateTime.Now;
```

A statement that retrieves the value of a view state item

```
DateTime timeStamp = (DateTime) ViewState["TimeStamp"];
```

A statement that removes an item from view state

```
ViewState.Remove("TimeStamp");
```

Description

- View state is implemented using a *view state object* that's defined by the StateBag class. This class defines a collection of view state items.
- Although the form and control properties are automatically saved in view state, you can also save other data in view state.
- To access the view state object for a page, you use the ViewState property of the page.

Figure 8-2   How to use view state for your own data

How to use session state

In chapter 3, you learned some basic skills for using session state to save data across round trips to the browser. The topics that follow review and expand on that information.

How to work with session state

As you have learned, ASP.NET uses *session state* to track the state of each user of an application. To do that, it creates a *session state object* that contains a unique *session ID* for each user's session. This ID is passed back to the browser as part of the response and then returned to the server with the next request. ASP.NET can then use the session ID to get the session state object that's associated with the request.

To manage a user session, you can store data in the session state object as shown in figure 8-3. Since you've already seen how session state is used in the Shopping Cart application, you shouldn't have any trouble understanding these examples. The first one adds or updates a session state item named EMail. The second one retrieves the value of the EMail item and stores it in a string variable. And the third one removes the EMail item from session state.

All three of these examples assume that session state is being accessed from the code-behind file of a web page. In that case, you refer to the session state object using the Session property of the page. To access session state from outside of a web page, however, you use the Session property of the HttpContext object for the current request as illustrated in the fourth example.

Common members of the HttpSessionState class

Indexer	Description
[name]	The value of the session state item with the specified name. If you set the value of an item that doesn't exist, that item is created.

Property	Description
SessionID	The unique ID of the session.
Count	The number of items in the session state collection.

Method	Description
Add(name, value)	Adds an item to the session state collection. If the item you name already exists, its value is updated.
Clear()	Removes all items from the session state collection.
Remove(name)	Removes the item with the specified name from the session state collection.

A statement that adds or updates a session state item

```
Session["EMail"] = email;
```

A statement that retrieves the value of a session state item

```
string email = Session["EMail"].ToString();
```

A statement that removes an item from session state

```
Session.Remove("EMail");
```

A statement that retrieves a session state item from a non-page class

```
string email = HttpContext.Current.Session["EMail"].ToString();
```

Description

- ASP.NET uses *session state* to track the state of each user of an application. To do that, it creates a *session state object* that contains a *session ID*. This ID is passed to the browser and then back to the server with the next request so the server can identify the session associated with that request.

- Because session state sends only the session ID to the browser, it doesn't slow response time. By default, though, session state objects are maintained in server memory so they can slow performance on the server side.

- To work with the data in session state, you use the HttpSessionState class, which defines a collection of session state items.

- To access the session state object from the code-behind file for a web form, use the Session property of the page.

- To access the session state object from a class other than a code-behind file, use the Current property of the HttpContext class to get the HttpContext object for the current request. Then, use the Session property to get the session state object.

Figure 8-3   How to work with session state

When to save and retrieve session state items

Most ASP.NET developers use session state in a consistent way. First, an application retrieves data from session state and stores it in variables. Then, the application uses these variables when it processes the user events. Finally, the application saves the updated variables back to session state so they can be retrieved the next time the page is posted back to the server.

If an item in session state is used within a single method in an application, you can retrieve, process, and save that item within that method. However, it's more common for an application to use a session state item in two or more methods. Because of that, it makes sense to retrieve the item when the application first starts and save it just before it ends. To do that, you can use the Load and PreRender events of the page as shown in figure 8-4.

The example in this figure illustrates how this works. To keep this simple, this application consists of a single page that contains a Post button that the user can click to post the page back to the server. Each time the user clicks this button, the program code updates the label on the page to indicate how many times the button has been clicked.

To implement this application, a session state item named Count is used to maintain a count of the number of times the user clicks the Post button. To start, the Page_Load method sets a count variable to zero if the session state item named Count hasn't been created yet. Otherwise, this method gets the value of the Count item from the session state object and assigns it to the count variable.

If the user clicked the Post button, the program executes the btnPost_Click method. This method adds one to the count variable and updates the label on the form to indicate how many times the button has been clicked.

Then, just before ASP.NET renders the HTML for the page, the Page_PreRender method is executed. This method saves the value of the count variable to session state so it's available the next time the user clicks the Post button. Because PreRender is a page event, it's raised each time the page is executed just like the Load event.

It's important to note that the variable that's used to store the value of the session state item in this example is a value-type variable. That means that the value is actually stored in the variable. Because of that, you have to explicitly update the session state item in the Page_PreRender method.

In contrast, if you use a reference-type variable such as a string or other object variable, the session state item is updated automatically when you update the variable that refers to it. That's because the variable contains a pointer to the object, not the data itself. As a result, you don't have to update the session state item explicitly. If you look back to the application in chapter 3, you'll see that the Cart item in the session state object is handled that way.

A Counter application that counts the times the user clicks the button

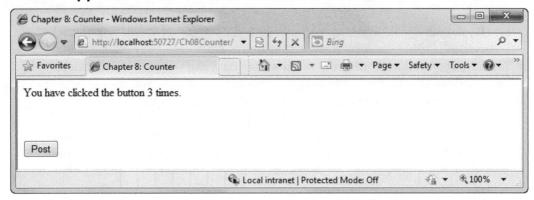

The code for the Counter application

```
int sessionCount;

protected void Page_Load(object sender, EventArgs e)
{
    if (Session["Count"] == null)
        sessionCount = 0;
    else
        sessionCount = Convert.ToInt32(Session["Count"]);
}

protected void btnPost_Click(object sender, EventArgs e)
{
    sessionCount++;
    lblSessionClicks.Text = "You have clicked the button "
                        + sessionCount + " times.";
}

protected void Page_PreRender(object sender, EventArgs e)
{
    Session["Count"] = sessionCount;
}
```

Description

- If a session state item is accessed from two or more event handlers, you usually code the application so it retrieves the value of that item in the Load event handler and saves the updated value back to session state in the PreRender event handler.

- Since the Load event is raised before any of the control events for the page, you can use its event handler to retrieve a session state item and store it in a class-level variable. Then, the item is available to all of the other methods.

- Since the PreRender event is raised after all the control events for the page have been processed, you can use its event handler to update the session state item.

- You only need to update a session state item explicitly if it's stored in a value-type variable. If it's stored in a reference-type variable, the session state item is updated automatically when the variable is updated.

Figure 8-4   When to save and retrieve session state items

Options for storing session state data

By default, ASP.NET stores session state data in server memory and tracks user sessions using cookies. However, as figure 8-5 shows, ASP.NET actually provides four options for storing session state data and two options for tracking session IDs. Although you typically use the default options, you should be familiar with these other options in case you ever need them.

The default for storing session state data is *in-process mode*. With this mode, session state data is stored in server memory within the same process that your ASP.NET application runs. This is the most efficient way to store session state data, but it only works for applications that are hosted on a single web server.

If your application has so many users that a single web server can't carry the load, you can deploy the application on two or more servers. When you do that, you need to store session state data in a location that can be accessed by all of the servers. Session state provides two options for doing that.

State Server mode stores session state data in server memory, but not in the same process as your application. Instead, session state is managed by the ASP.NET state service, which can be accessed by all of the servers that host the application. That's necessary because when two or more servers host an application, a different server can process the application each time it's executed. So if the session state data is stored on the server that processed the application the first time it was executed, that data won't be available if the application is processed by another server the next time it's executed.

Another way to make session state data available to two or more servers is to use *SQL Server mode*. With this mode, session state data is stored in a SQL Server database rather than in server memory. Although SQL Server mode is slower than in-process and State Server mode, it's also the most reliable. That's because if your web server goes down, the session state data will be maintained in the database. In contrast, session state data is lost if the server goes down when you're using in-process or State Server mode.

The last option for storing session state data is *custom mode*. With this mode, you create your own *session state store provider* that saves and retrieves session state data. You might use this option if you want to save session state data in a database, but your shop uses Oracle or some other database instead of Microsoft SQL Server.

Fortunately, the programming requirements for all four session state modes are identical. So you can change an application from one mode to another without changing any of the application's code. If you use the custom mode, however, you'll have to create the session state store provider.

Options for tracking session IDs

By default, ASP.NET maintains session state by sending the session ID for a user session to the browser as a cookie. Then, the cookie is returned to the server with the next request so the server can associate the browser with the

Four options for storing session state data

- *In-process mode* (the default) stores session state data in IIS server memory in the same process as the ASP.NET application. This is the session state mode that's used the most, but it's suitable only when a single server is used for the application.

- *State Server mode* stores session state data in server memory under the control of a separate service called the ASP.NET state service. This service can be accessed by other IIS servers, so it can be used when an application is hosted on a web farm that consists of more than one IIS server. In that case, each request for the application can be processed by a different server, so the session state information must be available to all the servers.

- *SQL Server mode* stores session state data in a SQL Server database. Like State Server mode, SQL Server mode is used for applications that require more than one IIS server. Although this mode is slower than In-process mode and State Server mode, it's also the most reliable.

- *Custom mode* lets you write your own *session state store provider* to read and write session state data.

Two options for tracking session IDs

- By default, ASP.NET uses *cookie-based session tracking* to keep track of user sessions. However, if a browser doesn't support cookies, this doesn't work.

- With *cookieless session tracking*, the session ID is encoded as part of the URL. As a result, cookieless session state works whether or not the browser supports cookies.

Description

- The programming requirements for all four session state modes are identical, so you don't have to recode an application if you change the mode. If you use custom mode, however, you do have to create a class that implements the session state store provider.

- Cookieless session tracking introduces security risks because the session ID is visible to the user. It also limits the way URL's can be specified in Response.Redirect, Response.RedirectPermanent, and Server.Transfer calls. For these reasons, most developers don't use cookieless sessions.

- You can control how session state data is stored and how session IDs are tracked by setting the attributes of the session state element in the application's web.config file. For more information, see the next figure.

- Custom mode is an advanced mode that isn't covered in this book. To learn more about how to create a session state store provider for use with custom mode, see the "Implementing a Session-State Store Provider" topic in the Help documentation.

Figure 8-5   Options for storing session state data and tracking session IDs

session. This is called *cookie-based session tracking*, and this is the most reliable and secure way to track sessions.

If a browser doesn't support cookies, however, session state won't work unless you switch to *cookieless session tracking*. Cookieless session tracking works by adding the session ID to the URL that's used to request the ASP.NET page. Unfortunately, because the URL is visible to the user and isn't encrypted, the use of cookieless session tracking creates a security risk.

Ideally, then, you should use cookie-based session tracking when cookies are supported and cookieless session tracking when they're not. As you can see in figure 8-6, ASP.NET lets you do just that.

How to set session state options

As you know, when you create an application, Visual Studio adds a web.config file to your web site. Then, you can add session state options to this file as shown in figure 8-6.

Although the web.config file is an XML file, you shouldn't have trouble editing it even if you aren't familiar with the details of XML syntax. To edit this file, just double-click on it in the Solution Explorer to display it in a Text Editor window. Then, add a sessionState element within the system.web element as shown in this figure. Within the sessionState element, you can code any of the attributes listed in the table in this figure. In the example shown here, I included the mode attribute to indicate that in-process mode should be used; I included the cookieless attribute to indicate that cookies should be used if they're supported, and URLs should be used if they're not; and I included the timeout attribute to increase the number of minutes that the session should be maintained without activity to 30.

If you use State Server mode, you'll need to set the stateConnectionString attribute to the server name or IP address and port number of the server that hosts the ASP.NET state service. If the name of the server is mma1, for example, the stateConnectionString attribute will look like this:

```
stateConnectionString="tcpip=mma1:42424"
```

Note that the port number is always 42424.

Similarly, if you use SQL Server mode, you'll need to set the sqlConnectionString attribute to the connection string for the instance of SQL Server that contains the database that's used to store the session state data. For instance, if the SQL Server instance is Murach, the attribute might look like this:

```
sqlConnectionString="Data Source=Murach;Integrated
Security=SSPI"
```

Note that the database isn't included in the connection string, which means that the default database named ASPState is used. If you want to use a different database to store session state data, you need to include the name of the database in the connection string, and you need to include the allowCustomSqlDatabase attribute with a value of True.

If you use any mode other than in-process, you can also compress the session state data by setting the compressionEnabled attribute to True. This is a new feature of ASP.NET 4 that can make it more efficient to pass the data to another server or a database.

Attributes of the session state element in the web.config file

Attribute	Description
Mode	The session state mode. Values can be Off, InProc, StateServer, SQLServer, or Custom. The default is InProc.
Cookieless	An HttpCookieMode value that specifies whether cookieless sessions are used. AutoDetect uses cookies if they're supported and a query string if they're not. UseUri uses a query string. The default is UseCookies.
Timeout	The number of minutes a session should be maintained without any user activity. The default is 20.
StateConnectionString	The server name or IP address and port number (always 42424) of the server that runs the ASP.NET state service. This attribute is required when State Server mode is used.
SqlConnectionString	A connection string for the instance of SQL Server that contains the database that's used to store the session state data. If the allowCustomSqlDatabase attribute is set to True, the connection string can also include the name of the database. This attribute is required when SQL Server mode is used.
AllowCustomSqlDatabase	A Boolean value that determines if the SqlConnectionString can specify the name of the database used to store state information. The default value is False, in which case the state information is stored in a database named ASPState.
CustomProvider	The name of the custom session state store provider.
CompressionEnabled	A Boolean value that determines if session state data that is not stored in-process is compressed. The default is False.

A sessionState element in the web.config file that uses in-process mode

```xml
<?xml version="1.0"?>
<configuration>
  <system.web>
    .
    .
    <sessionState mode="InProc"
      cookieless="AutoDetect"
      timeout="30"
    />
    .
    .
  </system.web>
</configuration>
```

Description

- The web.config file contains settings that affect how an ASP.NET web application operates. To change the default options for session state, you can add a sessionState element to the web.config file and then specify the attributes and values you want to use.

- Before you can use SQL Server mode, you must create the database that will be used to store session state data. For information on how to do that, see the "Session-State Modes" topic in the Help documentation.

- If you specify Custom mode, you must include additional information in the web.config file to identify the session state store provider. For more information, see the "Session-State Modes" topic in the Help documentation.

Figure 8-6   How to set session state options

How to use application state

In contrast to session state, which stores data for a single user session, application state lets you store data that is shared by all users of an application. In the topics that follow, you'll learn how to use application state.

How application state works

Figure 8-7 presents the concepts you need for working with *application state*. To start, an *application* is made up of all the pages, code, and other files that are located under a single directory in an IIS web server.

The first time a user requests a page that resides in an application's directory, ASP.NET initializes the application. During that process, ASP.NET creates an *application object* from the HttpApplication class. This object is represented by a special class file named global.asax, which you'll learn how to work with in figure 8-9.

The application object can be accessed by any of the application's pages. This object exists until the application ends, which normally doesn't happen until IIS shuts down. However, the application is automatically restarted each time you rebuild the application or edit the application's web.config file.

Each time ASP.NET starts an application and creates an application object, it also creates an *application state object* from the HttpApplicationState class. You can use this object to store data in server memory that can be accessed by any page that's part of the application.

Application state is typically used to store application-specific data that changes infrequently. For example, you might use application state to store discount terms and tax rates for an ordering system. Although you could retrieve this type of information from a database each time it's needed, it sometimes makes sense to retrieve it just once when the application starts and then store it in application state. That way, the data is more readily accessible as the application executes.

Although it's less common, application state can also be used to store information that changes each time a user visits a site or a page within a site. For example, you can use it to keep track of the users that are logged on to an application that provides a chat room or a forum. You can also use it to store hit counters that track how many times users have retrieved specific pages. For instance, the Counter application at the top of this figure tracks the number of times all of the users of the application have clicked the Post button. This is similar to the application you saw in figure 8-4, but that application used session state to track the count for a single user.

A Counter application that counts the number of times that all users click the button

Application concepts

- An ASP.NET *application* is the collection of pages, code, and other files within a single directory on a web server. In most cases, an ASP.NET application corresponds to a single Visual Studio web project.

- An application begins when the first user requests a page that's a part of the application. Then, ASP.NET initializes the application before it processes the request for the page.

- As part of its initialization, ASP.NET creates an *application object* from the HttpApplication class. This object exists for the duration of the application. You can use the global.asax file to work with the application object, as described in figure 8-9.

- Once an application has started, it doesn't normally end until the web server is shut down. If you rebuild the application or edit the web.config file, however, the application will be restarted the next time a user requests a page that's part of the application.

Application state concepts

- If you store items in *application state*, those items are available to all users of the application.

- To provide for the use of application state, ASP.NET creates an *application state object* for each application from the HttpApplicationState class and stores this object in server memory.

- Application state is typically used to store data that changes infrequently, but it can also be used to store data that changes as an application executes.

Figure 8-7   How application state works

How to work with application state data

Figure 8-8 presents the details for working with application state data. As you can see from the first three examples, the techniques you use to add items to and retrieve items from application state are similar to the techniques you use to work with items in session state. The main difference is that you use the Application property of the page to access the application state object from a code-behind file, and you use the Application property of the HttpContext object for the current request to access the application state object from a class other than a code-behind file.

When you're working with application state data, you'll want to lock the application state collection when you modify any of its data. This is illustrated in the last example in this figure, which increments an application state item named ClickCount by one. Here, the application state collection is locked before the ClickCount item is retrieved. Then, after the item is updated, the application state collection is unlocked. To minimize the length of time the application state object is locked, you should do as little processing as possible between the Lock and Unlock methods.

If you don't lock the application state collection while the count is updated, two or more users could access the count at the same time. To illustrate why that's a problem, let's assume that three users access the count item at the same time, and the starting count is 11. Then, when each of those users increment the count it becomes 12, and that's the value that each user stores in the application state collection. In this case, though, the correct count should be 14.

Common members of the HttpApplicationState class

Indexer	Description
[name]	The value of the application state item with the specified name. If you set the value of an item that doesn't exist, that item is created.

Property	Description
Count	The number of items in the application state collection.

Method	Description
Add(name, value)	Adds an item to the application state collection.
Clear()	Removes all items from the application state collection.
Remove(name)	Removes the item with the specified name from the application state collection.
Lock()	Locks the application state collection so only the current user can access it.
Unlock()	Unlocks the application state collection so other users can access it.

A statement that retrieves an item from application state

```
int applicationCount = Convert.ToInt32(Application["ClickCount"]);
```

A statement that adds an item to application state

```
Application.Add("ClickCount", 0);
```

A statement that retrieves the application state from a non-page class

```
int applicationCount = Convert.ToInt32
    (HttpContext.Current.Application["ClickCount"]);
```

Code that locks application state while retrieving and updating an item

```
Application.Lock();
int applicationCount = Convert.ToInt32(Application["ClickCount"]);
applicationCount++;
Application["ClickCount"] = applicationCount;
Application.UnLock();
```

Description

- You can use the application state object to store items that are common to all users of the application.

- To access the application state object from the code-behind file for an ASP.NET web form, use the Application property of the page.

- To access the application state object from a class other than a code-behind file, use the Current property of the HttpContext class to get the HttpContext object for the current request. Then, use the Application property of this object to get the application state object.

- Before you retrieve the value of an application state item that you intend to modify, you should lock the application state object so other users can't modify the application state data at the same time. As soon as you finish modifying the application state data, you should release the application state object so other users can access it.

Figure 8-8   How to work with application state data

How to work with application events

Now that you know how to work with application state data, you may be wondering how to initialize the values of application state items. To do that, you first add a Global.asax file to the project as described in figure 8-9. (If you started the project from the ASP.NET Web Site template, this file is already included.) By default, this file contains method declarations for five event handlers as shown in the example in this figure. Then, you can add code to any of these event handlers. This figure summarizes the four events you're most likely to use to work with application state data.

The example in this figure shows how you can initialize and update a session state item named HitCount that keeps track of the number of times a new session is started for an application. In this example, the Application_Start event handler retrieves the current hit count number from a database and adds an application state item named HitCount to the application state object. Similarly, the Application_End event handler saves the HitCount item to the database so it will be accurate when it's retrieved the next time the application starts. Although the HalloweenDB class that includes the methods that are used to retrieve and update the count isn't shown here, all you need to know is that the GetHitCount method retrieves the current hit count from the database as an integer value, and the UpdateHitCount method saves the integer value to the database.

The updating of the HitCount item takes place in the Session_Start event handler, which is raised whenever a new user session begins. This event handler starts by locking the application state object. Then, it increases the HitCount item by 1 and unlocks the application state object.

Four common application events

Event	Description
`Application_Start`	This event is raised when the first page of an application is requested by any user. It is often used to initialize the values of application state items.
`Application_End`	This event is raised when an application is about to terminate. It can be used to write the values of critical application state items to a database or file.
`Session_Start`	This event is raised when a user session begins. It can be used to initialize session state items, update application state items, or authorize user access.
`Session_End`	This event is raised when a user session is about to terminate. It can be used to free resources held by the user or to log the user off the application. It is raised only when in-process mode is used.

A Global.asax file that creates an object in application state

```csharp
<%@ Application Language="C#" %>
<script runat="server">

    void Application_Start(object sender, EventArgs e)
    {
        // Code that runs on application startup
        Application.Add("HitCount", HalloweenDB.GetHitCount());
    }
    void Application_End(object sender, EventArgs e)
    {
        //  Code that runs on application shutdown
        HalloweenDB.UpdateHitCount(Application["HitCount"]);
    }
    void Application_Error(object sender, EventArgs e)
    {
        // Code that runs when an unhandled error occurs

    }
    void Session_Start(object sender, EventArgs e)
    {
        // Code that runs when a new session is started
        Application.Lock();
        int hitCount = Convert.ToInt32(Application["HitCount"]) + 1;
        Application["HitCount"] = hitCount;
        Application.UnLock();
    }
    void Session_End(object sender, EventArgs e)
    {
        // Code that runs when a session ends.
    }
</script>
```

Description

- To create a Global.asax file, select the Website→Add New Item command, and then choose the Global Application Class template.

- The Global.asax file provides event handlers for application events. The event handlers are coded within a Script element that defines a code declaration block.

- To refer to the application state object from the Global.asax file, you use the Application property of the application.

Figure 8-9   How to work with application events

How to use cookies and URL encoding

Earlier in this chapter, you learned that view state data is stored in a hidden field on a page that's sent to the browser. But view state is just one of the client-based state management options that are available to you. Two others are cookies and URL encoding.

How to create cookies

A *cookie* is a name/value pair that is stored on the client's computer. For instance, the name of the first cookie in figure 8-10 is ASP.NET_SessionId, and its value is

`jsswpu5530hcyx2w3jfa5u55`

This is a typical session ID for a cookie that's generated by ASP.NET to keep track of a session. The other cookie examples are typical of cookies that you create yourself.

To create a cookie, you instantiate an object from the HttpCookie class. Then, you include it in the HTTP response that the server sends back to the browser, and the user's browser stores the cookie either in its own memory or in a text file on the client machine's disk.

A cookie that's stored in the browser's memory is called a *session cookie* because it exists only for that session. When the browser session ends, the contents of any session cookies are lost. Session cookies are what ASP.NET uses to track session ID's. In contrast, *persistent cookies* are written to disk, so they are maintained after the browser session ends. Whether session or persistent, though, once a cookie is sent to a browser, it's automatically returned to the server with each HTTP request.

Besides using cookies for session IDs, you can use cookies to save information that identifies each user so the users don't have to enter that information each time they visit your web site. You can also use cookies to store information that lets you personalize the web pages that are displayed for a user.

When you use cookies to store this type of information, you should keep in mind that some users may have disabled cookies on their browsers. In that case, you won't be able to save cookies on the user's computer. Unfortunately, ASP.NET doesn't provide a way for you to determine whether a user has disabled cookies. As a result, if you use cookies in an application, you may need to notify the user that cookies must be enabled to use it.

This figure also presents some properties of the HttpCookie class. Then, the first example shows how to create a session cookie. Here, both the cookie's name and value are specified on the constructor. Because the Expires property isn't set, it's given a default value of 12:00 a.m. on January 1, 0001. Because this value has already passed, the cookie is deleted when the session ends.

If you don't set the value of a cookie when you create it, you can use the Value property to set it later on. In addition, you can use the Expires property to set the expiration date for a persistent cookie. This is illustrated by the second example in this figure.

Examples of cookies

```
ASP.NET_SessionId=jsswpu5530hcyx2w3jfa5u55
EMail=Anne@Murach.com
user_ID=4993
password=opensesame
```

Two ways to create a cookie

```
New HttpCookie(name)

New HttpCookie(name, value)
```

Common properties of the HttpCookie class

Property	Description
Expires	A DateTime value that indicates when the cookie should expire.
Name	The cookie's name.
Secure	A Boolean value that indicates whether the cookie should be sent only when a secure connection is used. See chapter 18 for information on secure connections.
Value	The string value assigned to the cookie.

Code that creates a session cookie

```
HttpCookie nameCookie = new HttpCookie("UserName", userName);
```

Code that creates a persistent cookie

```
HttpCookie nameCookie = new HttpCookie("UserName");
nameCookie.Value = userName;
nameCookie.Expires = DateTime.Now.AddYears(1);
```

Description

- A *cookie* is a name/value pair that's stored in the user's browser or on the user's disk.

- A web application sends a cookie to a browser via an HTTP response. Then, each time the browser sends an HTTP request to the server, it attaches any cookies that are associated with that server.

- By default, ASP.NET uses a cookie to store the session ID for a session, but you can also create and send your own cookies to a user's browser.

- A *session cookie* is kept in the browser's memory and exists only for the duration of the browser session. A *persistent cookie* is kept on the user's disk and is retained until the cookie's expiration date.

- To create a cookie, you specify its name or its name and value. To create a persistent cookie, you must also set the Expires property to the time you want the cookie to expire.

Figure 8-10   How to create cookies

How to work with cookies

After you create a cookie, you work with it using the members of the HttpCookieCollection class shown in figure 8-11. This class defines a collection of HttpCookie objects. To refer to a cookie in a cookies collection, for example, you use the indexer of the collection. And to add a cookie to the collection, you use the Add method of the collection.

The key to working with cookies is realizing that you must deal with two instances of the HttpCookieCollection class. The first one contains the collection of cookies that have been sent to the server from the client. You access this collection using the Cookies property of the HttpRequest object. The second one contains the collection of cookies that will be sent back to the browser. You access this collection using the Cookies property of the HttpResponse object.

To send a new cookie to the client, you create the cookie and then add it to the collection of cookies in the HttpResponse object. This is illustrated in the first example in this figure. Here, a cookie named UserName is created and added to the HttpResponse object.

The second example shows you how to retrieve the value of a cookie that's sent from the browser. Here, the Request property of the page is used to refer to the HttpRequest object. Then, the indexer of the Cookies collection of the request object is used to get the cookie, and the Value property of the cookie is used to get the cookie's value.

The last example in this figure illustrates how you can delete a persistent cookie. To do that, you create a cookie with the same name as the cookie you want to delete, and you set its Expires property to a time in the past. In this example, I set the date to one second before the current time. Then, you add the cookie to the HttpResponse object so it's sent back to the browser. When the browser receives the cookie, it replaces the existing cookie with the new cookie. When the client's system detects that the cookie has expired, it deletes it.

Common members of the HttpCookieCollection class

Indexer	Description
`[name]`	The cookie with the specified name.

Property	Description
`Count`	The number of cookies in the collection.

Method	Description
`Add(cookie)`	Adds a cookie to the collection.
`Clear()`	Removes all cookies from the collection.
`Remove(name)`	Removes the cookie with the specified name from the collection.

A method that creates a new cookie and adds it to the HttpResponse object

```
private void AddCookie()
{
    HttpCookie nameCookie = new HttpCookie("UserName", txtUserName.Text);
    nameCookie.Expires = DateTime.Now.AddYears(1);
    Response.Cookies.Add(nameCookie);
}
```

A method that retrieves the value of a cookie from the HttpRequest object

```
protected void Page_Load(object sender, EventArgs e)
{
    if (!IsPostBack)
    {
        if (!(Request.Cookies["UserName"] == null))
            lblUserName.Text = "Welcome back "
                                + Request.Cookies["UserName"].Value + ".";
    }
}
```

A method that deletes a persistent cookie

```
private void DeleteCookie()
{
    HttpCookie nameCookie = new HttpCookie("UserName");
    nameCookie.Expires = DateTime.Now.AddSeconds(-1);
    Response.Cookies.Add(nameCookie);
}
```

Description

- Cookies are managed in collections defined by the HttpCookieCollection class.
- To access the cookies collection for a request or response, use the Cookies property of the HttpRequest or HttpResponse object. To refer to these objects, use the Request and Response properties of the page.
- To delete a persistent cookie, create a cookie with the same name as the cookie you want to delete and set its Expires property to a time that has already passed. Then, when the client's system detects that the cookie has expired, it deletes it.

Figure 8-11   How to work with cookies

How to enable or disable cookies

If an application relies on the use of cookies, you'll want to be sure that cookies are enabled in your browser as you test the application. Conversely, to test an application that's intended to work even if cookies have been disabled, you'll need to disable cookies in your browser. To do that, you can use the techniques presented in figure 8-12.

If you're using Internet Explorer, you use a slider control to determine what cookies are allowed. The default setting is Medium, which enables both session and persistent cookies. To disable both types of cookies, you can select a privacy setting that blocks all cookies as shown here. Alternatively, you can use the dialog box that's displayed when you click the Advanced button to override the default settings so your browser accepts session cookies but disables persistent cookies.

This figure also describes how to enable or disable cookies if you're using Mozilla Firefox. Although this technique is quite different from the technique for enabling or disabling cookies with Internet Explorer, you shouldn't have any trouble understanding how to use it. If you're using a browser other than Internet Explorer or Firefox, you can use the Help information for that browser to find out how to enable or disable cookies.

An Internet Explorer dialog box with disabled cookies

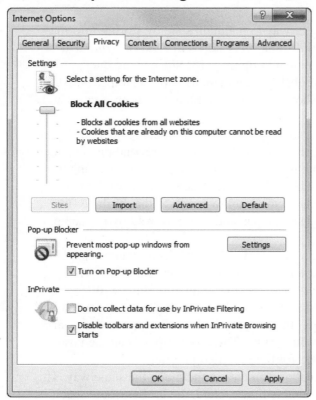

How to enable or disable cookies for Internet Explorer

1. Select the Tools→Internet Options command.
2. Select the Privacy tab.
3. Use the slider control to set the security level to accept or block cookies.

How to enable or disable cookies for Mozilla Firefox

1. Select the Tools→Options command.
2. Click the Privacy icon.
3. Select the Use Custom Settings for History option from the Firefox Will drop-down list.
4. Check or uncheck the Accept Cookies From Sites option, and select an item from the Keep Until drop-down list.

Description

- Internet Explorer also lets you enable or disable persistent cookies and session cookies separately. To do that, click the Advanced button and select from the advanced privacy settings that are displayed.

Figure 8-12   How to enable or disable cookies

How to use URL encoding

URL encoding provides another way to maintain state by storing information in a page on the client. This information is stored in a *query string* that's added to the end of the URL, as shown in figure 8-13. Since using query strings is a common technique, you've probably seen them used on search sites like Google (www.google.com) and shopping sites like Ebay (www.ebay.com) and Amazon (www.amazon.com).

At the top of this figure, you can see two URLs that include query strings. The first one includes a single attribute named cat, and the second one includes two attributes named cat and prod. As you can see, you add a query string by coding a question mark after the URL. Then, you code the name of the first attribute, an equal sign, and the value you want to assign to the attribute. To include another attribute, you code an ampersand (&), followed by the name and value of the attribute.

In most cases, you'll use query strings with hyperlinks or anchor elements (<a>) to pass information from one page of an application to another. The second example in this figure illustrates how to use query strings with hyperlinks. Here, the NavigateUrl attribute of the hyperlink indicates that it will link to a page named Product.aspx. In addition, the URL includes a query string that contains a category and a product value. The Product page can then use these values to display information for the specified product.

You use query strings with anchor elements in the much the same way. This is illustrated in the third example in this figure. Here, the href attribute specifies the URL with the query string. Note that because the hyperlink control provides the same functionality as the anchor element, you probably won't use the anchor element often. However, this element can be useful in some situations. For example, it's useful for creating menus in code.

To retrieve the values included in a query string, you use the QueryString property of the Request object as illustrated in the fourth example. The two statements in this example retrieve the two values passed by the query string in the second and third examples.

The fifth example shows that you can also use query strings in the URLs that you code for Redirect, RedirectPermanent, or Transfer methods. Here, the URL contains a query string with a single attribute that contains a category ID. You should also realize that you can code query strings in the PostBackUrl attribute of a button control, although you're not likely to do that.

Two URLs with query strings

```
Order.aspx?cat=costumes
Order.aspx?cat=props&prod=rat01
```

A hyperlink with a URL that includes a query string

```
<asp:HyperLink ID="HyperLink1" runat="server"
    NavigateUrl="~/Product.aspx?cat=fx&amp;prod=fog01">Fog machine
</asp:HyperLink>
```

An anchor element with a URL that includes a query string

```
<a href="product.aspx?cat=fx&prod=fog01">Fog machine</a>
```

Statements that retrieve the values of the query string attributes

```
string categoryID = Request.QueryString["cat"];
string productID = Request.QueryString["prod"];
```

Code that uses a URL with a query string in a Redirect method

```
Response.Redirect("Order.aspx?cat=" + categoryID);
```

Description

- When you use *URL encoding*, a *query string* that consists of attribute/value pairs is added to the end of a URL.

- Query strings are frequently used in hyperlinks and anchor elements (<a>) to pass information from one page of an application to another or to display different information on the same page.

- Query strings can also be used in the URLs that are specified for Response.Redirect, Response.RedirectPermanent, or Server.Transfer calls, and they can be used in the PostBackUrl property of a button control.

- When you use a hyperlink, an anchor element, or a Redirect or Transfer method that specifies a URL for the current page, the page is processed as if it's being requested for the first time.

- To code a query string, follow the URL with a question mark, the name of the attribute, an equal sign, and a value. To code two or more attributes, separate them with ampersands (&), and don't include any spaces in the query string.

- To retrieve the value of a query string attribute, use the QueryString property of the HttpRequest object and specify the attribute name. To refer to the HttpRequest object, use the Request property of the page.

- Different browsers impose different limits on the number of characters in a query string or on the total number of characters in a URL. Most browsers provide for a URL with at least 2000 characters, however.

Figure 8-13   How to use URL encoding

Perspective

If this chapter has succeeded, you should now be able to use view state, session state, and application state whenever they're required by your applications. You should also be able to use cookies and URL encoding whenever they're appropriate for your applications. Although this chapter doesn't present a complete application that illustrates the use of all these techniques, the exercise that follows will give you a chance to use some of them.

As you work with these techniques, please keep in mind that they aren't exclusive of one another. In fact, you'll often use two or more of these techniques in a single application. Most web applications, for example, use both view state and session state. And many applications also use application state, cookies, and URL encoding.

Terms

view state	cookieless session tracking
view state object	application
session state	application object
session state object	application state
session ID	application state object
in-process mode	cookie
State Server mode	session cookie
SQL Server mode	persistent cookie
custom mode	URL encoding
session state store provider	query string
cookie-based session tracking	

Exercise 8-1   Work with the view state of the Reservation application

In this exercise, you'll enable and disable view state for the Reservation form and its controls. That will give you a good idea of how view state works.

Disable view state for selected controls

1. Open the Ch08Reservation web site in the C:\aspnet4_cs directory.

2. Set the EnableViewState property of the drop-down list for the number of adults to False.

3. Run the application and note the values that have been loaded into the drop-down list. Now, click the calendar image button, and notice that the drop-down list no longer contains any values. That's because these values are loaded in code, so view state is required to maintain them.

4. Return to the form, set the EnableViewState property of the drop-down list back to True, and set the EnableViewState property of the label at the bottom of the form to False.

5. Run the application, complete the form, and click the Submit button to see the message that's displayed. Now, click the calendar image button and notice that this message is no longer displayed. In a case like this, this may be what you want since you'll submit the form again after you change the date.

Enable view state for selected controls

6. Display the form in Source view, and add a ViewStateMode attribute with a value of Disabled to the Page directive.

7. Return to Design view, and set the ViewStateMode of the two drop-down lists and the range validator for the arrival date to Enabled.

8. Run the application and test the form. In particular, make sure that the values in the drop-down lists are always displayed and that the range validator works correctly. When you're sure it works, close the browser.

Exercise 8-2 Use session state to store reservation information

In this exercise, you'll store data that's entered into the Request page of the Reservation application you worked on in exercise 8-1 in session state so it can be displayed on another page. To make that easier for you, you'll start from a project that contains the second page and the class that defines the session state object.

Review the new form and class

1. If it's not already open, open the Ch08Reservation web site that you worked on in exercise 8-1.

2. Display the Confirmation form in Design view so you can see what it looks like. Also, open the Reservation class in the Code Editor to see how it's defined.

Save the reservation request in session state

3. Modify the code for the Click event handler of the Submit button on the Request form so it creates a Reservation object, sets the properties of this object using the values the user entered on the form, saves the object to session state, and displays the Confirmation page. The statement that saves the object to session state should add the session state item if it doesn't already exist or update it if it does.

4. Delete any statements in the Click event handlers for the Submit and Clear buttons that refer to the message label at the bottom of the form. Then, delete the paragraph that contains this label from the form.

Retrieve the reservation request from session state and display it

5. Start an event handler for the Load event of the Confirmation page. This event handler should retrieve the Reservation object that was stored in session state by the Request form and display the properties of that object in the labels on the form. The label that indicates whether a smoking room is requested should be set to "Yes" or "No". The label that displays special requests should be set to "None" if no special requests are entered.

6.   Run the application, complete the Request form, and click the Submit button to display the Confirmation page. If the reservation data isn't displayed correctly, make the necessary corrections until it is.

7.   Click the Modify Request button to return to the Request form, and notice that the data is no longer displayed.

8.   Add code to the Load event handler for the Request page that checks if a Reservation object is stored in session state. This code should be executed only if the page is not being posted back. If a Reservation object is found, retrieve it and display its properties on the form. To get the number of nights, you can subtract the departure date from the arrival date and then use the Days property of the resulting TimeSpan object.

9.   Modify the code in the Load event handler so the two statements that initialize the radio buttons are executed only if a Reservation object isn't found. Otherwise, these radio buttons won't work correctly.

10. Run the application again, complete the Request form, and click the Submit button to display the Confirmation page. Click the Modify Request button to return to the Request page. This time, the data should still be displayed.

11. Make a change to the data and click the Submit button to be sure that the updated data is displayed on the Confirmation page. Continue testing until you're sure this works.

Exercise 8-3   Use cookies to store user information

In this exercise, you'll store the user name and email the user enters into the Request form of the Reservation application in cookies so they can be displayed the next time the application is run.

1.   If it's not already open, open the Ch08Reservation web site that you worked on in exercise 8-2.

2.   Add code to the Click event handler of the Confirm button on the Confirmation form that creates two persistent cookies with the user's name and email and adds them to the HttpResponse object. Set the expiration date for the cookies to six months from the current date.

3.   Add code to the Load event handler of the Request form that retrieves the two cookies and displays their values on the form. This code should be executed only if the page is not being posted back, a Reservation object is not found in session state, and the cookies exist.

4.   Run the application, complete the Request form, and submit and confirm the request. Close the browser window.

5.   Run the application again. This time, the user name and email that were saved in cookies should be displayed in the Request form.

9

How to use master pages

As you develop the pages of a web site, you'll often find pages that require some of the same elements. For example, both the Order and Cart pages of the Shopping Cart application you saw earlier in this book have an image displayed across the top of the page. The easiest way to create pages like these that have common elements is to use a master page. In this chapter, you'll learn the most important skills for creating and working with master pages.

How to create master pages

A *master page* is a page that provides a framework within which the content from other pages can be displayed. Master pages make it easy to include banners, navigation menus, and other elements on all of the pages in an application. In the topics that follow, you'll learn how to create master pages in your ASP.NET applications.

An introduction to master pages

Figure 9-1 shows the basics of how master pages work. As you can see, the page that's actually sent to the browser is created by combining elements from a master page and a *content page*. The content page provides the content that's unique to each page in the application, while the master page provides the elements that are common to all pages. In this example, the master page (Site.master) provides a banner at the top of each page, a simple navigation menu at the side of each page, and a message that indicates how many days remain until Halloween at the bottom of each page.

In addition, the master page contains a *content placeholder* that indicates where the content from each content page should be displayed. In this example, the content page is the Order.aspx page, and its content is displayed in the content placeholder in the central portion of the master page.

Notice that the name of the content page is Order.aspx, the same as the Order page that you saw in chapter 3. In other words, when you use master pages, the individual pages of your web application become the content pages. You'll learn how to create content pages or convert existing ASP.NET pages to content pages in figure 9-6.

The Shopping Cart application with a master page

Master page (Site.master)

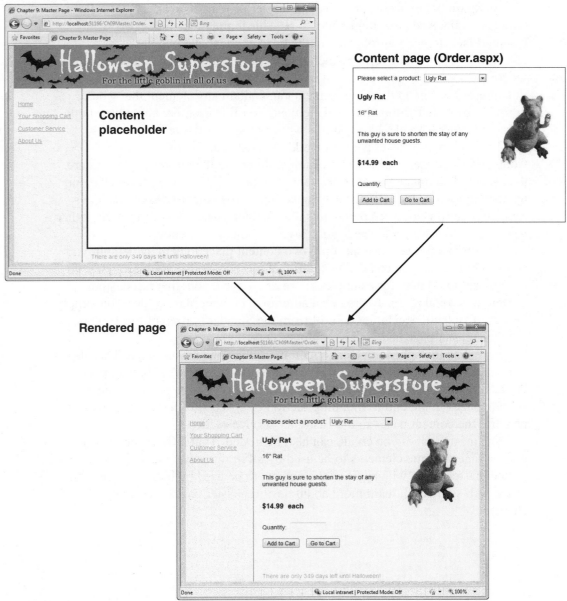

Content page (Order.aspx)

Rendered page

Description

- A *master page* provides a framework in which the content of each page on a web site is presented. Master pages make it easy to create pages that have a consistent look.
- The pages that provide the content that's displayed in a master page are called *content pages*.
- The content of each content page is displayed in the master page's *content placeholder*.

Figure 9-1   An application that uses a master page

How to create a master page

As figure 9-2 explains, you create a master page by using the Master Page template in the Add New Item dialog box. This template includes two ContentPlaceHolder controls: one in the head element and one in the form element. The one in the form element marks the location on the rendered page where the content from the content page is displayed, and it's the one shown in this figure. The one in the head element can contain any element that would normally be coded within the head element. You'll learn more about how both of these ContentPlaceHolder controls work in the next figure.

To develop the master page, you add elements outside of the ContentPlaceHolder controls. For example, to create the master page in figure 9-1, you add an image for a banner above the placeholder in the form element, navigation links to the left of this placeholder, and a label to display the days remaining until Halloween below this placeholder. Just as you can for any other form, you can use CSS to specify the layout of these elements.

Although a master page has only two content placeholders by default, you should realize that you can create additional placeholders if you need to. You might want to do that, for example, to create a page layout that has custom content in several areas. To create an additional content placeholder, you simply drag the ContentPlaceHolder control from the Standard group of the Toolbox onto the master page and give it a unique ID.

Note that an application can contain more than one master page. This allows you to create an application that has two or more sections with distinct page layouts. For example, you may want to use one master page for all of the content pages in the online shopping section of a web site, and another master page for the content pages in the customer service section.

The master pages you create can also be nested. That lets you create one master page with the elements to be used by all of the pages in a web site and nested master pages with additional elements to be used by individual sections of the web site. You'll learn more about nesting master pages later in this chapter.

A new master page in Design view

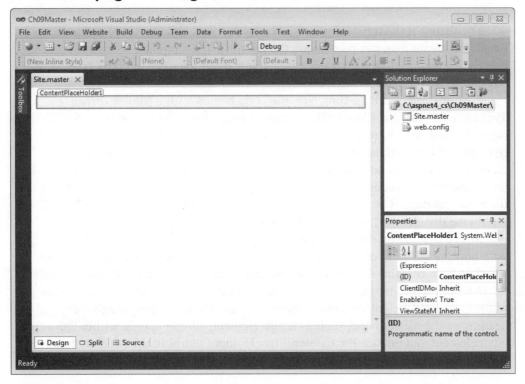

Description

- To add a master page to a project, choose the Website→Add New Item command. Then, in the Add New Item dialog box, select Master Page from the list of templates, specify the name of the master page you want to create in the Name text box (the default is MasterPage.master), and select the programming language. Then, click Add.

- The content placeholder in the form element of the page appears as a control in the Web Forms Designer. Although you can change the position of the content placeholder, you can't edit its contents from the master page. Instead, you add content to the master page by creating content pages as described later in this chapter.

- Any elements you add to the master page outside of the content placeholder will appear on every content page that uses the master page.

- Although most master pages have just one content placeholder in the form element, you can create more than one content placeholder if you need to. In that case, each placeholder displays a portion of the content of each content page.

- The head element of a master page also contains a content placeholder by default. See figure 9-3 for more information.

- An application can have more than one master page, and each content page specifies which master page should be used to display the content page.

- The aspx file for a master page uses the extension .master. The code-behind file uses .master.cs.

Figure 9-2   How to create a master page

The aspx code for a new master page

The listing at the top of figure 9-3 shows the aspx code that's generated when you create a master page using the Master Page template. As you can see, this code is similar to the aspx code that's generated for a regular ASP.NET web page, with two important differences.

First, instead of a Page directive, the code begins with a Master directive. This indicates that the file contains a master page rather than a regular ASP.NET page. Second, the master page contains two ContentPlaceHolder controls. The first one, which is contained within the head element, can be used for any element that can be coded within the head element. In most cases, you'll use this content placeholder for a link element that identifies an external style sheet for a content page. The second ContentPlaceHolder control, which is contained within the div element, is used for the main content of the page.

Notice that the master page file is itself a well-formed HTML document with html, head, and body elements. The body element includes a form element, which in turn contains a ContentPlaceHolder control. Any elements you add to the body of the master page should appear within the form element, but outside of the ContentPlaceHolder control. Similarly, any elements you add to the heading of the master page, such as a link element, should appear within the head element, but outside the ContentPlaceHolder control in the head element.

The aspx code for a new master page

```
<%@ Master Language="C#" AutoEventWireup="true" CodeFile="Site.master.cs"
Inherits="Site" %>

<!DOCTYPE html PUBLIC "-//W3C//DTD XHTML 1.0 Transitional//EN"
"http://www.w3.org/TR/xhtml1/DTD/xhtml1-transitional.dtd">

<html xmlns="http://www.w3.org/1999/xhtml">
<head runat="server">
    <title></title>
    <asp:ContentPlaceHolder id="head" runat="server">
    </asp:ContentPlaceHolder>
</head>
<body>
    <form id="form1" runat="server">
    <div>
        <asp:ContentPlaceHolder id="ContentPlaceHolder1" runat="server">
        </asp:ContentPlaceHolder>
    </div>
    </form>
</body>
</html>
```

Attributes of the Master page directive

Attribute	Description
Language	Specifies the language used for any code required by the page.
CodeFile	Specifies the name of the code-behind file.
Inherits	Specifies the name of the page class defined in the code-behind file.

Attributes of the ContentPlaceHolder control

Attribute	Description
ID	Specifies the name of the content placeholder.
Runat	Specifies that the control is a server-side control.

Description

- A master page must begin with a Master page directive and should include at least one ContentPlaceHolder control.

- By default, a master page contains two ContentPlaceHolder controls: one in the head element and one in the form element. The one in the head element is typically used for a link element that identifies an external style sheet. The one in the form element is used for the displayable elements of the content page.

- Any HTML or asp elements that you add to the master page will be displayed on every page that uses the master page, along with the content that's defined for the ContentPlaceHolder control in the form element.

Figure 9-3   The aspx code for a new master page

The aspx code for the Halloween Store master page

Figure 9-4 shows the complete aspx code for the master page in figure 9-1. To start, you should notice that the document head contains a link element. This element links the external style sheet named Main.css to the page. In addition, the document head contains the content placeholder that's added by default.

Next, notice that the main division for the page is divided into three additional divisions. The first division contains the image control that's used to display the banner at the top of the page. The second division contains four paragraphs, each containing a hyperlink. These hyperlinks are used to create the navigation menu at the left side of the form. The third division contains the content placeholder for the form.

Following the three divisions is a single paragraph. This paragraph contains a label control that will be used to display the number of days until Halloween.

Finally, notice that each division and paragraph on this page has either an id attribute or a class attribute. These attributes are used in the external style sheet to lay out the elements on the master page so they appear as shown in figure 9-1.

The aspx code for the master page

```
<%@ Master Language="C#" AutoEventWireup="true" CodeFile="Site.master.cs"
Inherits="Site" %>

<!DOCTYPE html PUBLIC "-//W3C//DTD XHTML 1.0 Transitional//EN"
"http://www.w3.org/TR/xhtml1/DTD/xhtml1-transitional.dtd">

<html xmlns="http://www.w3.org/1999/xhtml">
<head runat="server">
    <title>Chapter 9: Master Page</title>
    <link href="Styles/Main.css" rel="stylesheet" type="text/css" />
    <asp:ContentPlaceHolder id="HeadContent" runat="server">
    </asp:ContentPlaceHolder>
</head>
<body>
    <form id="form1" runat="server">
    <div id="page">
        <div id="header">
            <asp:Image ID="Image1" runat="server"
                ImageUrl="~/Images/banner.jpg" />
        </div>
        <div id="sidebar">
            <p class="link">
                <asp:HyperLink ID="HyperLink1" runat="server"
                    NavigateUrl="~/Order.aspx" ForeColor="DarkOrange">Home
                </asp:HyperLink>
            </p>
            <p class="link">
                <asp:HyperLink ID="HyperLink2" runat="server"
                    NavigateUrl="~/Cart.aspx" ForeColor="DarkOrange">
                    Your Shopping Cart</asp:HyperLink>
            </p>
            <p class="link">
                <asp:HyperLink ID="HyperLink3" runat="server"
                    NavigateUrl="~/Service.aspx" ForeColor="DarkOrange">
                    Customer Service</asp:HyperLink>
            </p>
            <p class="link">
                <asp:HyperLink ID="HyperLink4" runat="server"
                    NavigateUrl="~/About.aspx" ForeColor="DarkOrange">
                    About Us</asp:HyperLink>
            </p>
        </div>
        <div id="main">
            <asp:ContentPlaceHolder id="MainContent" runat="server">
            </asp:ContentPlaceHolder>
        </div>
        <p id="message">
            <asp:Label ID="lblMessage" runat="server"></asp:Label>
        </p>
    </div>
    </form>
</body>
</html>
```

Description

- Most master pages include elements like banners and navigation controls.
- You can use CSS to lay out the elements on a master page just as you can any other page.

Figure 9-4   The aspx code for the Halloween Store master page

The code-behind file for the master page

Master pages have events just like regular ASP.NET pages. So it's important to realize that most of these events are raised *after* the corresponding events for the content page are raised. For example, the Page Load event for the master page will be processed after the Page Load event for the content page. Likewise, any control events for the content page are processed before any control events for the master page. Note, however, that both the content page and the master page Load events are processed before any of the control events are processed.

Figure 9-5 shows the code-behind file for the master page in figure 9-4. This code-behind file includes a Page_Load method that's executed when the master page loads. As you can see, this method calls a method named DaysUntilHalloween, which calculates and returns the number of days remaining until October 31. Then, an appropriate message is assigned to the Text property of the lblMessage label.

The code-behind file for the master page

```
using System;
using System.Collections.Generics;
using System.Linq;
using System.Web;
using System.Web.UI;
using System.Web.UI.WebControls;

public partial class Site : System.Web.UI.MasterPage
{
    protected void Page_Load(object sender, EventArgs e)
    {
        int daysUntil = DaysUntilHalloween();
        if (daysUntil == 0)
            lblMessage.Text = "Happy Halloween!";
        else if (daysUntil == 1)
            lblMessage.Text = "Tomorrow is Halloween!";
        else
            lblMessage.Text = "There are only " + daysUntil
                + " days left until Halloween!";
    }

    private int DaysUntilHalloween()
    {
        DateTime halloween = new DateTime(DateTime.Today.Year, 10, 31);
        if (DateTime.Today > halloween)
            halloween = halloween.AddYears(1);
        TimeSpan ts = halloween - DateTime.Today;
        return ts.Days;
    }
}
```

Description

- Master pages have events just like regular ASP.NET pages. For this master page, the Load event is used to display the number of days remaining until Halloween.

- Most events for the content page are raised before the corresponding events for the master page. For example, the Load event for the content page is raised before the Load event for the master page. Similarly, events for controls in the content page are raised before events for controls in the master page.

Figure 9-5   The code-behind file for the master page

How to create and develop content pages

Once you create a master page, you can create and develop the content pages for the master page. The topics that follow show how.

How to create a content page

Figure 9-6 shows how to create a content page. In short, you use the same procedure to create a content page that you use to create a regular page, but you check the Select Master Page check box. Then, you can choose the master page you want to use for the content page from the Select a Master Page dialog box that's displayed.

Alternatively, you can select the master page you want to use in the Solution Explorer and then choose the Website→Add Content Page command. This creates a content page for the selected master page. Note that when you use this technique, the content page is automatically named Default.

The code example in this figure shows the code that's generated when you create a new content page named Order for the master page shown in figure 9-4. This code is quite different from the code that's generated when you create a regular ASP.NET page. Although the Page directive includes the same information as a regular ASP.NET page, it also includes a MasterPageFile attribute that specifies the master page you selected. And the rest of the content page is also different from a normal ASP.NET page.

Before I describe the other differences, you should know that the title you specify in the Title attribute of the Page directive of a content page overrides any title you specify in the master page. That way, you can display a different title for each content page. If you want to use the same title for each content page, however, you can specify the title in the master page and then delete the Title attribute from the content pages.

Unlike normal ASP.NET pages, content pages don't include a Doctype directive or any structural HTML elements such as html, head, body, or form. That's because those elements are provided by the master page. Instead, the content page includes one ASP.NET Content element for each content place-holder in the master page. In this case, because the master page contains two placeholders, the content page contains two Content elements. As you can see, the ContentPlaceHolderID attributes of these elements identify which place-holder they're associated with. Then, you place the content of the page between the start and end tags of the Content elements.

This figure also includes a procedure for converting a regular page to a content page. You'll need to follow this procedure if you start a web site without using master pages, and later decide to use master pages. Unfortunately, though, Visual Studio doesn't provide a way to automatically do this. As a result, you'll have to manually edit each of the pages to add the MasterPageFile attribute to

The aspx code for a new page that uses the master page in figure 9-4

```
<%@ Page Language="C#" MasterPageFile="~/Site.master" AutoEventWireup="true"
CodeFile="Order.aspx.cs" Inherits="Order" Title="Untitled Page" %>

<asp:Content ID="Content1" ContentPlaceHolderID="HeadContent" Runat="Server">
</asp:Content>
<asp:Content ID="Content2" ContentPlaceHolderID="MainContent" Runat="Server">
</asp:Content>
```

Two ways to create a new content page

- Choose the Website→Add New Item command. Then, select the Web Form template, enter the name for the form, check the Select Master Page check box, and click Add. When the Select a Master Page dialog box appears, select the master page you want and click OK.

- Select the master page in the Solution Explorer, then choose the Website→Add Content Page command.

How to convert a regular ASP.NET page to a content page

- First, add a MasterPageFile attribute to the Page directive that specifies the URL of the master page. Next, replace the div element that contains the actual content of the page with an ASP.NET Content element like the second one shown above. Then, if the head element contains other elements used by the page, replace the head element with a Content element like the first one shown above. Last, delete everything that's outside the Content elements except for the Page directive.

Two other ways to specify the master page

In the web.config file

```
<system.web>
    .
    <pages masterPageFile="Site.master" />
    .
</system.web>
```

In the Page_PreInit method

```
protected void Page_PreInit(object sender, EventArgs e)
{
    MasterPageFile = "Site.master";
}
```

Description

- The Page directive in the aspx code for a content page includes a MasterPageFile attribute that specifies the name of the master page.

- The aspx code for a content page includes Content elements that indicate the IDs of the content placeholders where the content for the page should be placed. Any content you create for the page should be coded between the start and end tags for these elements.

- You can also specify the master page in the web.config file or in the Page_PreInit method. However, the Web Forms Designer doesn't support either of these techniques, so you won't be able to view the content page in Design view.

Figure 9-6   How to create a content page

the Page directive, remove the Doctype directive and structural HTML elements (html, head, body, and form), and add one or more Content elements.

Because this conversion procedure is error prone, it pays to use master pages for all but the simplest of applications, even if each master page contains only the content placeholders. Then, when you're ready to provide a consistent look to the pages within the application, you can enhance the master pages.

Figure 9-6 also shows two other ways to specify which master page is used with a content page. First, you can add a MasterPageFile attribute that specifies the master page to be used with all pages that don't specify a master file to the pages element of the web.config file. Second, you can specify the master page at runtime by setting the MasterPageFile attribute of the page in the Page_PreInit method. Note, however, that the Web Forms Designer doesn't support either of these techniques. If you use them, then, you won't be able to view or edit your content pages in Design view.

How to add content to a page

Figure 9-7 shows how a content page appears in Design view. As you can see, the master page is displayed along with the Content control for the content placeholder in the form element of the master page. However, you can't edit any of the master page elements from this view. You can only edit the content of the page by adding text to the content area or by dragging controls from the Toolbox to the content area. Later, when you switch to Source view, any elements that you've added will appear between the Content element's start and end tags.

If you work with a master page that has more than one content placeholder in the form element, there will be a separate Content control for each placeholder. Then, you can edit the contents for each of those controls.

A content page in Design view

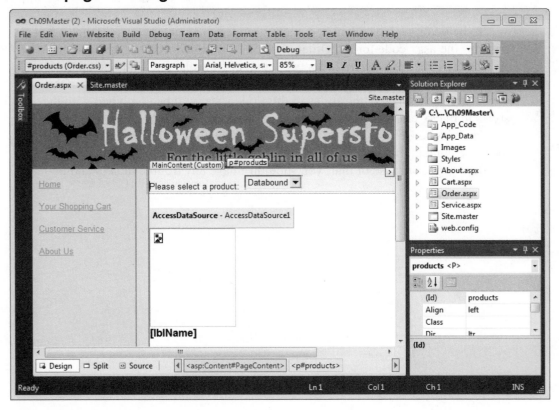

Description

- When you display a content page in Design view, the elements from the master page are displayed so you can see how they will affect the final appearance of the page.

- To add the content for a page, click the Content control. Then, you can type text or use the Toolbox to drag controls into the content area of the page. Any text or other elements you add will be placed between the start and end tags of the Content element in the aspx file.

- If you want to display only the master page's default content for a page, click the Smart Tag icon in the upper right corner of the Content control and choose Default to Master's Content. Then, you won't be able to edit the content of the content area. To edit the content again, choose Create Custom Content from the smart tag menu.

Figure 9-7   How to add content to a page

The aspx code for the Order content page

To help you understand how content is added to a content page, figure 9-8 presents the aspx code for the Order page of the Halloween Store application. As you can see, this code includes two Content controls. The first one includes a link element that identifies the external style sheet used by the page. When the Order page is displayed, the styles in this style sheet will be combined with the styles in the external style sheet identified by the master page.

The second Content control contains the main content for the page. This is the same content that would normally be included in the form element of a standard page. Because of that, you shouldn't have any trouble understanding it.

The aspx code for the content page

```
<%@ Page Language="C#" MasterPageFile="~/Site.master" AutoEventWireup="true"
CodeFile="Order.aspx.cs" Inherits="Order" %>

<asp:Content ID="HeaderContent" ContentPlaceHolderID="HeadContent"
    runat="server">
    <link href="Styles/Order.css" rel="stylesheet" type="text/css" />
</asp:Content>

<asp:Content ID="PageContent" ContentPlaceHolderID="MainContent" runat="server">
    <p id="products">
        <asp:Label ID="Label1" runat="server" Text="Please select a product:">
        </asp:Label> 
        <asp:DropDownList ID="ddlProducts" runat="server" AutoPostBack="True"
            DataSourceID="AccessDataSource1" DataTextField="Name"
            DataValueField="ProductID">
        </asp:DropDownList>
    </p>
    <asp:AccessDataSource ID="AccessDataSource1" runat="server"
        DataFile="~/App_Data/Halloween.mdb"
        SelectCommand="SELECT [ProductID], [Name], [ShortDescription],
            [LongDescription], [ImageFile], [UnitPrice]
            FROM [Products] ORDER BY [Name]">
    </asp:AccessDataSource>
    <asp:Image ID="imgProduct" runat="server" Width="135px" />
    <div id="product">
        <p id="name"><asp:Label ID="lblName" runat="server"></asp:Label></p>
        <p id="shortdesc">
            <asp:Label ID="lblShortDescription" runat="server"></asp:Label></p>
        <p id="longdesc">
            <asp:Label ID="lblLongDescription" runat="server"></asp:Label></p>
        <p id="unitprice">
            <asp:Label ID="lblUnitPrice" runat="server"></asp:Label> 
            <asp:Label ID="Label2" runat="server" Text="each"></asp:Label></p>
    </div>
    <div id="order">
        <p id="quantity">
            <asp:Label ID="Label3" runat="server" Text="Quantity:">
            </asp:Label> 
            <asp:TextBox ID="txtQuantity" runat="server"></asp:TextBox>
            <asp:RequiredFieldValidator ID="RequiredFieldValidator1"
                runat="server" CssClass="validator"
                ControlToValidate="txtQuantity" Display="Dynamic"
                ErrorMessage="Quantity is a required field.">
            </asp:RequiredFieldValidator>
            <asp:RangeValidator ID="RangeValidator1" runat="server"
                CssClass="validator"
                ControlToValidate="txtQuantity" Display="Dynamic"
                ErrorMessage="Quantity must range from 1 to 500."
                MaximumValue="500" MinimumValue="1" Type="Integer">
            </asp:RangeValidator>
        </p>
        <asp:Button ID="btnAdd" runat="server" Text="Add to Cart"
            OnClick="btnAdd_Click" />
        <asp:Button ID="btnCart" runat="server" Text="Go to Cart"
            PostBackUrl="~/Cart.aspx" CausesValidation="False" />
    </div>
</asp:Content>
```

Figure 9-8   The aspx code for the Order content page

How to nest master pages

In addition to creating content pages from a master page, you can create other master pages. When you nest master pages like this, you can create a *parent master page* that contains the elements used by all the pages in a web site. Then, you can create *child master pages* that add to the contents of the parent master page and that contain the elements used by different sections of the web site.

How to create nested master pages

To create a master page that's nested within another master page, you use a technique similar to the one in figure 9-2 for creating any master page. After you select the Master Page template and enter the name of the page, however, you check the Select Master Page check box. Then, you'll be asked to select the master page you want to use as the parent of the child master page.

The code example at the top of figure 9-9 shows the starting aspx code for a child master page. This page uses a parent master page that's similar to the one you saw in figure 9-4. The main difference is that I deleted the paragraph at the bottom of the page. As you may recall, this paragraph contained a label that displayed the number of days until Halloween.

Note that this code is almost identical to the code for a content page. The only difference is that it starts with a Master directive instead of a Page directive. Unlike the Master directive for a parent master page, though, the Master directive for a child master page includes MasterPageFile and AutoEventWireup attributes.

How to add content to a child master page

To add content to a child master page, you add elements to the Content controls. This is illustrated in the second code example in figure 9-9. Here, I added div and p elements to the second Content control. The div element contains a ContentPlaceHolder control that can be used by any content page that's created from this master page. And the p element contains the label that was originally included on the parent master page.

The first Content control contains a link element that identifies the external style sheet that's used by the page. In addition, it too contains a ContentPlaceHolder control. This control can be used by any content pages to include style and other heading information for the page.

Once you've created the parent and child master pages, you can create content pages that use either one of them. If you want a content page to include the label that indicates the number of days until Halloween, for example, you can create a page that uses the child master page. But if you don't want this label included on a content page, you can create a page that uses the parent master page.

The aspx code for a new child master page that uses a master page like the one in figure 9-4 as its parent

```
<%@ Master Language="C#" MasterPageFile="~/Site.master"
    AutoEventWireup="true" CodeFile="ChildMasterPage.master.cs"
    Inherits="ChildMasterPage" %>

<asp:Content ID="Content1" ContentPlaceHolderID="head" Runat="Server">
</asp:Content>
<asp:Content ID="Content2" ContentPlaceHolderID="Main" Runat="Server">
</asp:Content>
```

The aspx code after content has been added to the page

```
<%@ Master Language="C#" MasterPageFile="~/Site.master"
    AutoEventWireup="true" CodeFile="ChildMasterPage.master.cs"
    Inherits="ChildMasterPage" %>

<asp:Content ID="Content1" ContentPlaceHolderID="HeadContent" Runat="Server">
    <link href="Styles/Child.css" rel="stylesheet" type="text/css" />
    <asp:ContentPlaceHolder ID="HeadContent" runat="server">
    </asp:ContentPlaceHolder>
</asp:Content>
<asp:Content ID="Content2" ContentPlaceHolderID="MainContent" Runat="Server">
    <div id="main">
        <asp:ContentPlaceHolder ID="MainContent" runat="server">
        </asp:ContentPlaceHolder>
    </div>
    <p id="message">
        <asp:Label ID="lblMessage" runat="server"></asp:Label>
    </p>
</asp:Content>
```

Description

- When you create *nested master pages*, the *parent master page* is typically used to provide elements for every page in the web site. Then, different *child master pages* can be used to provide additional elements for different types of pages in the web site.

- To create a child master page, use the technique in figure 9-2 for creating a master page, but check the Select Master Page check box and then select the parent master page from the dialog box that's displayed.

- To add content to a child master page, place the content between the start and end tags of the Content elements. Use ContentPlaceHolder controls to identify areas where content can be added in content pages that use the master page.

- When you use nested master pages, you can create content pages for the parent master page or any of the child master pages.

Figure 9-9   How to nest master pages

How to access master page controls from a content page

In many applications, you need to access one or more of the controls in a master page from one of the application's content pages. For example, the master page shown earlier in this chapter has a label in the footer area that normally displays the number of days remaining until Halloween. But what if you want to display other information in this label when certain content pages are displayed?

For example, when the user is shopping for products with the Order.aspx page, you may want to display the number of items currently in the shopping cart instead of the number of days left until Halloween. To do that, you can expose a master page control as a public property, and then access the property from the content page.

How to expose a master page control as a public property

The easiest way to access a control on a master page from a content page is to create a public property that provides access to the control. Figure 9-10 illustrates a code-behind file for a master page that shows you how to do that.

First, you create a public property in the master page that identifies the control you want to be able to access. In this case, the property is a Label type, and the property is named MessageLabel. Then, you code get and set accessors for the property. Here, the get accessor returns the lblMessage label, and the set accessor assigns the property value to lblMessage.

Please notice that I also added another if statement to the Page_Load method for the master page. Now, the lblMessage label is set to the number of days left until Halloween only if the value of the label's Text property is empty. That way, if the content page has assigned a value to this label in its Page_Load method, the master page's Page_Load method won't overwrite the value. This works because the content page's Page_Load method is called before the master page's Page_Load method.

The code-behind file for a master page that provides a public property

```
using System;
using System.Collections.Generics;
using System.Linq;
using System.Web;
using System.Web.UI;
using System.Web.UI.WebControls;

public partial class Site : System.Web.UI.MasterPage
{
    public Label MessageLabel
    {
        get { return lblMessage; }
        set { lblMessage = value; }
    }

    protected void Page_Load(object sender, EventArgs e)
    {
        if (lblMessage.Text == "")
        {
            int daysUntil = DaysUntilHalloween();
            if (daysUntil == 0)
                lblMessage.Text = "Happy Halloween!";
            else if (daysUntil == 1)
                lblMessage.Text = "Tomorrow is Halloween!";
            else
                lblMessage.Text = "There are only " + daysUntil
                    + " days left until Halloween!";
        }
    }

    private int DaysUntilHalloween()
    {
        DateTime halloween = new DateTime(DateTime.Today.Year, 10, 31);
        if (DateTime.Today > halloween)
            halloween = halloween.AddYears(1);
        TimeSpan ts = halloween - DateTime.Today;
        return ts.Days;
    }

}
```

Description

- A content page can access a control in the master page if you expose the control as a public property in the master page. To do that, you code a property with get and set accessors.

Figure 9-10   How to expose a master page control as a public property

How to access a public property of the master page from a content page

Figure 9-11 shows how you can access a public property in a master page from a content page. As you can see in the top part of this figure, you use the MasterType directive in the aspx file of the content page to specify the name of the type used for the master page. The value you name in this directive specifies the type of the object returned by the content page's Master property. So in this example, the Master property will return an object of type Site. If you look at the class declaration in the previous figure, you'll see that Site is the name of the class that defines the master page.

The second part of this figure shows two methods from the code-behind file for the Order.aspx content page. As you can see, the Page_Load method calls a method named DisplayCartMessage. This method determines the number of items currently in the shopping cart and sets the Text property of the label exposed by the master page's MessageLabel property accordingly. But note that no value is assigned to the message label if the shopping cart is empty. In that case, the Page_Load method for the master page will set the label to the number of days remaining until Halloween.

Although using the MasterType directive in the content page's aspx file makes it easier to access the properties of the master page, you should realize that this directive isn't necessary. If you don't specify the MasterType directive, the Master property will return an object of type Master. You can then cast this object to the actual type of your master page to access any properties you've created.

For example, you could use code like this to assign text to the MessageLabel property:

```
MasterPage mp = (Site) this.Master;
if (cart.Count == 1)
    mp.MessageLabel.Text =
        "There is one item in your cart.";
else if (cart.Count > 1)
    mp.MessageLabel.Text =
        "There are " + cart.Count + " items in your cart.";
```

Here, the Master object is cast to a Site object so its MessageLabel property can be accessed. The purpose of the MasterType directive is to avoid this awkward casting.

A portion of the Order.aspx page

```
<%@ Page Language="C#" MasterPageFile="~/Site.master"
AutoEventWireup="true" CodeFile="Order.aspx.cs" Inherits="Order" %>

<%@ MasterType TypeName="Site" %>

<asp:Content ID="Content1" ContentPlaceHolderID="MainContent"
    runat="server">
    .
    .
    .
</asp:Content>
```

Two methods from the code-behind file for the Order.aspx page

```
protected void Page_Load(object sender, EventArgs e)
{
    if (!IsPostBack)
    {
        ddlProducts.DataBind();
        this.DisplayCartMessage();
    }
    selectedProduct = this.GetSelectedProduct();
    lblName.Text = selectedProduct.Name;
    lblShortDescription.Text = selectedProduct.ShortDescription;
    lblLongDescription.Text = selectedProduct.LongDescription;
    lblUnitPrice.Text = selectedProduct.UnitPrice.ToString("c");
    imgProduct.ImageUrl = "Images/Products/" + selectedProduct.ImageFile;
}

private void DisplayCartMessage()
{
    CartItemList cart = CartItemList.GetCart();
    if (cart != null)
    {
        if (cart.Count == 1)
            this.Master.MessageLabel.Text
                = "There is one item in your cart.";
        else if (cart.Count > 1)
            this.Master.MessageLabel.Text
                = "There are " + cart.Count + " items in your cart.";
    }
}
```

Description

- The MasterType directive in an aspx file specifies the name of the master page type. If you include this directive in a content page, you can use the Master property in the code-behind file to access the exposed property of the master page.

Figure 9-11   How to access a public property of the master page from a content page

Perspective

I hope this chapter has illustrated the power of master pages. In fact, I recommend that you use master pages for all but the simplest applications, even if you start out with nothing in your master pages but placeholders. Then, when you're ready to provide a professional look to your content pages, you can enhance the master pages, which will also enhance all of your content pages.

The alternative is to convert regular content pages so they use the master pages that you develop later on. But as figure 9-6 shows, that's a time-consuming and error-prone procedure. How much better it is to think ahead.

Terms

master page
content page
content placeholder
nested master pages
parent master page
child master page

Exercise 9-1   Create a master page for the Reservation application

In this application, you'll start by creating a simple master page for the Reservation application. Then, you'll add two content pages that use the master page, and you'll convert the two existing pages to content pages.

Create the master page

1. Open the Ch09Reservation application in the C:\aspnet4_cs directory.

2. Use the technique in figure 9-2 to add a master page named Site.master to the project. Review the aspx code for this page. In particular, notice the content placeholders in the head and body sections.

3. Switch to Design view and notice how the content placeholder in the body section is displayed.

4. Display the Request page in Source view and copy the h1 and h2 elements at the top of the page to the clipboard. Then, switch back to the master page and paste these elements within the div element but before the content placeholder. Notice that the h1 and h2 elements aren't formatted like they were on the Request page.

5. Display the master page in Source view, and add an id attribute with the value "page" to the div element. Then, attach the Main.css style sheet to this page. Now, the elements should be formatted properly.

6. Add a p element with the ID "links" below the h1 and h2 elements. Then, add three hyperlinks within this paragraph. Set the content of these links to "Home", "Reservation", and "About", and add a CssClass attribute to each hyperlink with a value of "hyperlink". Also, set the NavigateUrl property of the reservation link to Request.aspx, but don't set this property for the other links because the pages don't exist yet.

7. Display the master page in Design view to see how it looks. Notice that the first and third links aren't displayed as links because their NavigateUrl properties aren't set. Save the master page.

Create two new content pages

8. Use the first technique of figure 9-6 to create a new content page named Home.aspx. Notice the two Content controls that are added to the page that refer to the content placeholders in the master page.

9. Switch to Design view, and notice that the elements on the master page are displayed but they're grayed out so you can't change them.

10. Click in the Content control and type "The Home page is under development."

11. Set the Home page as the start page and then run the application to see how this page looks.

12. Use the second technique of figure 9-6 to create a new content page. Rename this page to About.aspx, and add the text "The About page is under development." to the Content control.

13. Switch back to the master page, and set the NavigateUrl property of the first and third hyperlinks to the Home.aspx and About.aspx pages.

14. Run the application again. When the Home page is displayed, click the About link to display the About page.

Convert the existing pages to content pages

15. Display the Request page in Source view, and add a MasterPageFile attribute to the Page directive. The value of this attribute should be the URL of the master page.

16. Replace the head element with an ASP.NET Content element like the first one shown in figure 9-6. Then, delete everything within this element except for the link element that attaches the Request.css style sheet.

17. Replace the div element with an ASP.NET Content element like the second one shown in figure 9-6. Then, delete the h1 and h2 elements from the Content element since they're included on the master page.

18. Delete the Doctype declaration and the html, body, and form elements.

19. Display the page in Design view to see how it looks. Now, run the application. When the Home page is displayed, click the Reservation link to display the Request page. This page should now display the contents of both the master page and the Request page.

20. Repeat steps 15 through 18 to convert the Confirmation page to a content page.

21. Run the application one more time. Click the Reservation link, complete the Request page, and click the Submit button to display the Confirmation page. Like the Request page, this page should now display the contents of both the master page and the Confirmation page.

10

How to use site navigation

The ASP.NET site navigation features make it easy for users to navigate to the various pages in your site. These features are valuable for both small and large web sites. This chapter shows you how to get the most from these features.

An introduction to site navigation

ASP.NET's *site navigation* features are designed to simplify the task of creating menus and other navigation features that let users find their way around your web site. To implement these features, ASP.NET provides a site map data source control and three navigation controls: TreeView, Menu, and SiteMapPath. The following topics introduce you to these controls.

An introduction to the navigation controls

Figure 10-1 shows a page from an application called the Navigation application. This application is a variation of the Halloween Store application you saw in the last chapter. It includes navigation features on the master page as well as a new page that displays a complete site map for the application. All three of the navigation controls are illustrated on this page.

The TreeView control displays the pages in a web site in a tree structure that's similar to a directory tree displayed by Windows Explorer. The user can expand or collapse a node by clicking the + or – icon that appears next to each node that has children. This control is most useful when you want to give users a complete view of the pages in a web site.

The Menu control creates dynamic menus that expand when you hover the mouse over a menu item that contains subitems. For example, if you were to hover the mouse over the Projects item in the menu in this figure, a submenu listing Costumes, Static Props, and Animated Props would appear.

The SiteMapPath control displays a list of links that lead from the web site's home page to the current page. This makes it easy for the user to quickly return to the home page or to a parent of the current page.

The TreeView and the Menu controls must be used with a SiteMapDataSource control, which binds the controls to a file named web.sitemap. This file contains XML that defines the structure of the pages that make up the web site. You'll learn how to create the web.sitemap file in the next two figures.

In most cases, you'll use either the Menu or the SiteMapPath control and possibly a TreeView control in a master page. That way, these navigation controls will be available from any page in the web site. If the site contains a large number of pages, though, you may want to use a separate Site Map page that includes a TreeView control. Then, the user can use the Site Map page to quickly locate any page within the web site.

A page with three site navigation controls

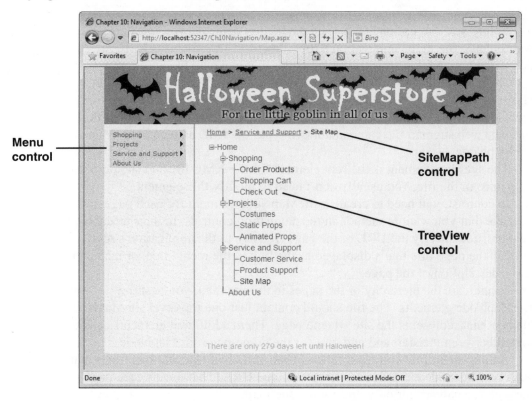

Menu control

SiteMapPath control

TreeView control

ASP.NET navigation controls

Control	Description
TreeView	Provides a hierarchical view of the site's structure. The user can click the + or – icon next to a node to expand or collapse the node. Must be bound to a SiteMapDataSource control. Located in the Navigation group of the Toolbox.
Menu	Creates a horizontal or vertical menu. Must be bound to a SiteMapDataSource control. Located in the Navigation group of the Toolbox.
SiteMapPath	Displays a list of links from the application's root page (the home page) to the current page. Doesn't need to be bound to a SiteMapDataSource control. Located in the Navigation group of the Toolbox.
SiteMapDataSource	Connects a navigation control to the site hierarchy specified by the web.sitemap file. Located in the Data group of the Toolbox.

Description

- ASP.NET provides three user-interface controls and a data source control designed to let the user navigate the pages in a web site.
- The navigation structure of a web site is defined by an XML file named web.sitemap located in the application's root folder. You must create this file before you can work with the navigation controls.

Figure 10-1   An introduction to site navigation

How to create a web.sitemap file

Before you can use one of the site navigation controls, you must create a web.sitemap file in the application's root directory. This file uses XML tags to define the hierarchical structure of the pages that make up the application.

As figure 10-2 shows, you can add a web.sitemap file to an application by choosing the Website→Add New Item command and selecting Site Map from the list of templates. Then, you use the Text Editor to edit the contents of this file. The web.sitemap file can contain two types of XML elements: siteMap and siteMapNode.

The siteMap element is the root element for the XML file and should occur only once in the file. You usually don't need to modify this element.

In contrast, you need to create a siteMapNode element for each page in the web site that you want to include in the navigation controls. In the siteMapNode element, you specify the URL of the page (relative to the application's root folder); the page title that's displayed as the link in the menu, tree, or map path; and a description of the page.

To indicate the hierarchy of the pages in the site map, you nest the siteMapNode elements. The file should contain just one top-level siteMapNode element that represents the site's home page. Then, additional elements can be nested between the start and end tags for the home-page siteMapNode.

An important rule you must follow when you create the sitemap file is that each siteMapNode element must have a unique URL. That means each page in the web site can appear only once in the site map.

Another important point is that you don't have to include all of the pages in the web site in the sitemap file. Instead, you should only include those pages that you want to make available via the site's navigation controls. If, for example, the site uses a two-page checkout process, you may not want to include the second check out page in the sitemap file. That way, the user will be able to access the first checkout page from a menu or tree view control, but not the second checkout page.

The web.sitemap file created from the Site Map template

```xml
<?xml version="1.0" encoding="utf-8" ?>
<siteMap xmlns="http://schemas.microsoft.com/AspNet/SiteMap-File-1.0" >
    <siteMapNode url="" title=""  description="">
        <siteMapNode url="" title=""  description="" />
        <siteMapNode url="" title=""  description="" />
    </siteMapNode>
</siteMap>
```

Attributes of the siteMapNode element

Attribute	Description
Url	The URL of the page. Each siteMapNode element must specify a unique value for this attribute.
Title	The text that will appear in the menu for the page.
Description	The tool tip text for the page.

Description

- To create a web.sitemap file, choose the Website→Add New Item command, select Site Map from the list of available templates, and click Add. You can then use the Text Editor to edit the web.sitemap file.

- The web.sitemap file contains an XML-based description of the navigation hierarchy of an ASP.NET application.

- Each siteMapNode element defines a page in the web site. You can nest siteMapNode elements within other siteMapNode elements to indicate the hierarchy of pages in the web site. But you don't have to include all of the pages in your web site in the site map.

Figure 10-2   How to create a web.sitemap file

The web.sitemap file for the Navigation application

Figure 10-3 shows the complete web.sitemap file for the Navigation application. The site navigation structure defined by this file corresponds to the structure shown in the TreeView control in figure 10-1.

If you compare the siteMapNode elements in this file with the items listed in the TreeView control in figure 10-1, you should see how the nesting of the siteMapNode elements specifies the site's hierarchical structure. For example, the siteMapNode elements for the Order.aspx, Cart.aspx, and Checkout1.aspx pages are contained within the start and end elements of the siteMapNode element for the Shopping.aspx page.

In this case, not all of the pages in the Navigation application are listed in the web.sitemap file. For example, there's a second checkout page and an order confirmation page that aren't in the sitemap file. That's because users shouldn't be allowed to navigate directly to these pages.

The web.sitemap file used for the controls in figure 10-1

```
<?xml version="1.0" encoding="utf-8" ?>
<siteMap xmlns="http://schemas.microsoft.com/AspNet/SiteMap-File-1.0" >

    <siteMapNode url="Default.aspx" title="Home"
        description="Home page.">

        <siteMapNode url="Shopping.aspx" title="Shopping"
            description="Shop for your favorite products.">
            <siteMapNode url="Order.aspx" title="Order Products"
                description="Order a product.">
            </siteMapNode>
            <siteMapNode url="Cart.aspx" title="Shopping Cart"
                description="View your shopping cart.">
            </siteMapNode>
            <siteMapNode url="Checkout1.aspx" title="Check Out"
                description="Finalize your purchase.">
            </siteMapNode>
        </siteMapNode>

        <siteMapNode url="Projects.aspx" title="Projects"
            description="Do-it-yourself Halloween projects.">
            <siteMapNode url="Costumes.aspx" title="Costumes"
                description="Costume projects.">
            </siteMapNode>
            <siteMapNode url="StaticProps.aspx" title="Static Props"
                description="Static props.">
            </siteMapNode>
            <siteMapNode url="AnimatedProps.aspx" title="Animated Props"
                description="Animated props.">
            </siteMapNode>
        </siteMapNode>

        <siteMapNode url="Service.aspx" title="Service and Support"
            description="Customer service and product support.">
            <siteMapNode url="CustService.aspx" title="Customer Service"
                description="Customer service.">
            </siteMapNode>
            <siteMapNode url="Support.aspx" title="Product Support"
                description="Product support.">
            </siteMapNode>
            <siteMapNode url="Map.aspx" title="Site Map"
                description="A map of all the pages on this web site.">
            </siteMapNode>
        </siteMapNode>

        <siteMapNode url="About.aspx" title="About Us"
            description="All about our company.">
        </siteMapNode>

    </siteMapNode>

</siteMap>
```

Figure 10-3   The web.sitemap file for the Navigation application

How to use the site navigation controls

Once you've created the sitemap file, you're ready to use the site navigation controls. The topics that follow show you how to do that.

How to use the TreeView control

Figure 10-4 shows how to use the TreeView control, which displays the pages in a web site as a hierarchical tree. Each node on the tree is a link that represents a page in the web site. You can click any of these links to go directly to that page. You can also click the + or – icons that appear next to the nodes to expand or collapse the nodes.

The table in this figure lists the attributes you're most likely to use with the TreeView control. The ID attribute provides a name for the TreeView control, and the DataSourceID attribute specifies the ID of the data source that provides the site map data. You'll learn how to create a site map data source in the next figure.

The other attributes let you customize the appearance and behavior of the TreeView control. For example, you can use the ExpandDepth attribute to set the number of levels that are initially expanded when the TreeView is first displayed. And you can use the ShowLines attribute to include lines that graphically show the tree's hierarchical structure. The best way to learn how these attributes affect the TreeView control is to experiment with them.

A TreeView control

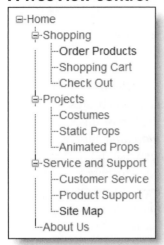

The aspx code for the TreeView control shown above

```
<asp:TreeView ID="TreeView1" runat="server"
              DataSourceID="SiteMapDataSource1"
              ShowLines="True">
</asp:TreeView>
```

Attributes of the TreeView control

Attribute	Description
ID	The ID of the control.
Runat	Must specify "server".
DataSourceID	The ID of the SiteMapDataSource control the tree should be bound to.
ExpandDepth	The number of levels to be automatically expanded when the tree is initially displayed. The default is FullyExpand.
MaxDepthDataBind	Limits the maximum depth of the tree. The default is -1, which places no limit.
NodeIndent	The number of pixels to indent each level. The default is 20.
NodeWrap	Set to True to word-wrap the text of each node. The default is False.
ShowExpandCollapse	Set to False if you want to hide the Expand/Collapse buttons. The default is True.
ShowLines	Set to True to include lines that show the hierarchical structure. The default is False.

Description

- The TreeView control is used to display the site map in a hierarchical tree.
- To display an application's navigation structure, the TreeView control must be bound to a SiteMapDataSource control as described in the next figure.

Figure 10-4   How to use the TreeView control

How to create a SiteMapDataSource control

Figure 10-5 shows two ways to create a SiteMapDataSource control. One way is to drag this control from the Data group of the Toolbox to a page. Then, you can set the properties for the control.

The other way is to click the Smart Tag icon for a TreeView or Menu control, and choose New Data Source from the menu that appears. This brings up the Data Source Configuration Wizard dialog box shown at the top of this figure. Then, you select Site Map and click OK to create a *site map data source*.

To customize the behavior of the site map data source, you can use the attributes listed in this figure. For example, the ShowStartingNode attribute determines whether the highest-level siteMapNode element in the web.sitemap file will be included in the tree or menu. Usually, you'll leave this attribute set to its default of True for TreeView controls and you'll set it to False for Menu controls.

The StartFromCurrentNode and StartingNodeUrl attributes let you bind a TreeView or Menu control to just a portion of the site map. If you specify True for the StartFromCurrentNode attribute, the tree or menu will start from the current page. As a result, only child pages of the current page will appear in the tree or menu. The StartingNodeUrl attribute lets you select any node in the site map as the starting node for the tree or menu.

The Data Source Configuration Wizard dialog box

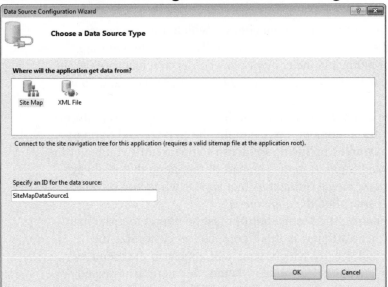

A default SiteMapDataSource control

```
<asp:SiteMapDataSource ID="SiteMapDataSource1" runat="server" />
```

A SiteMapDataSource control that specifies a starting level

```
<asp:SiteMapDataSource ID="SiteMapDataSource1" runat="server"
    StartingNodeUrl="Projects.aspx" />
```

Common attributes of the SiteMapDataSource control

Attribute	Description
ID	The ID of the control.
Runat	Must specify "server".
StartingNodeUrl	The URL of the node the SiteMapDataSource control should use as its starting node.
ShowStartingNode	Set to False to omit the starting node. The default is True.
StartFromCurrentNode	Set to True to start the navigation from the current node. The default is False, which starts the navigation from the root node specified in the web.sitemap file.

Two ways to create a SiteMapDataSource control

- Drag the control from the Data group of the Toolbox to a page.
- Click the Smart Tag icon in the upper-right corner of a TreeView or Menu control, then select New Data Source in the Choose Data Source drop-down list.

Description

- You use a SiteMapDataSource control to bind a TreeView or Menu control to the navigation structure defined by the web.sitemap file.

Figure 10-5   How to create a SiteMapDataSource control

How to use the Menu control

Figure 10-6 shows how to use the Menu control, which lets you create menus that are arranged either vertically or horizontally. *Vertical menus* are usually used in a sidebar alongside the content placeholder in a master page. In contrast, *horizontal menus* typically appear beneath a banner image and above the content placeholder.

Each item in a menu can contain a submenu that appears when you hover the mouse over the item for a moment. For example, the Service and Support submenu shown in the examples in this figure doesn't appear until you hover the mouse over the Service and Support item. The part of the menu that is always displayed is called the *static menu*. Submenus that appear when you hover the mouse over a menu item are called *dynamic menus*.

Like the TreeView control, the Menu control must be bound to a site map data source. Then, the other attributes in this figure let you customize the appearance of the menu and specify which items will appear in the menu. For example, the Orientation attribute determines whether the menu is arranged vertically or horizontally. And the MaximumDynamicDisplay attribute determines how many layers of dynamic submenus should be displayed.

The IncludeStyleBlock attribute is new with ASP.NET 4. The value of this attribute determines whether a style element with the CSS that's used to format the menu is generated. If you set the value of this attribute to False, you can then customize the appearance of the menu by coding your own CSS. The easiest way to do that is to display the page in a browser with the value of this attribute set to True. Then, you can display the HTML for the page, copy the generated CSS, paste it into an external style sheet, and modify it any way you like.

As you set the properties for a Menu control, you'll see that it includes many style properties that aren't listed in this figure. You can set these properties to control the formatting that's used to display the menu. The best way to do that is to define a skin for the control as shown in the next chapter.

Alternatively, you can automatically apply a predefined scheme to the menu by selecting Auto Format from the Menu control's smart tag menu. When you select a scheme, Visual Studio generates attributes and style elements that apply the formatting that you selected. Then, you can customize these attributes and elements any way you like. You'll see an example of this when I show you the aspx code for the master page of the Navigation application later in this chapter.

A menu with vertical orientation

A menu with horizontal orientation

Typical aspx code for a Menu control

```
<asp:Menu ID="Menu1" Orientation="Horizontal" runat="server"
    DataSourceID="SiteMapDataSource1">
</asp:Menu>
```

Common attributes of the Menu control

Attribute	Description
ID	The ID of the control.
Runat	Must specify "server".
DataSourceID	The ID of the SiteMapDataSource control the menu should be bound to.
IncludeStyleBlock	If True, the CSS that formats the menu is included in a style element in the rendered HTML. If False, no style element is generated. The default is True.
ItemWrap	If True, words in the menu items will be word-wrapped if necessary. The default is False.
MaximumDynamicDisplay	The number of levels of dynamic submenus to display.
Orientation	Horizontal or Vertical. The default is Vertical.
StaticDisplayLevels	The number of levels that should always be displayed. The default is 1.
StaticEnableDefaultPopOutImage	If True, an arrow graphic is displayed next to any menu item that has a pop-out submenu. If false, the arrow graphic is not displayed. The default is True.

Description

- The Menu control displays site navigation information in a menu. Submenus automatically appear when the user hovers the mouse over a menu item that has a submenu.

- To display an application's navigation structure, the Menu control must be bound to a SiteMapDataSource control.

- The Menu control has many formatting attributes that aren't listed in this figure. You can quickly apply a coordinated set of formatting attributes by clicking the Smart Tag icon for the Menu control and choosing Auto Format from the menu that appears. Then, you can select one of several predefined schemes for the menu.

Figure 10-6   How to use the Menu control

How to use the SiteMapPath control

Figure 10-7 shows how to use the SiteMapPath control, which creates a series of links that lead from the application's home page to the current page. These links are sometimes called *bread crumbs* because they let the user find his or her way back to the home page.

Unlike the TreeView and Menu controls, the SiteMapPath control doesn't need to be bound to a data source. Instead, it obtains the site navigation information directly from the web.sitemap file.

The attributes listed in this figure let you customize the appearance of the SiteMapPath control. In particular, you can indicate how many parent nodes to list, which direction the nodes are listed in, what text to use to separate the nodes, and whether the current page should be formatted as a link or just plain text.

Although this figure doesn't show it, the SiteMapPath control includes other attributes that let you completely customize the appearance of the site map path. Like the Menu control, you're more likely to use a skin to apply this formatting. Or, you can use the Auto Format command to apply a predefined scheme.

A SiteMapPath control

Home > Service and Support > Site Map

Aspx code for a SiteMapPath control

```
<asp:SiteMapPath ID="SiteMapPath1" runat="server">
</asp:SiteMapPath>
```

Common attributes of the SiteMapPath control

Attribute	Description
ID	The ID of the control.
Runat	Must specify "server".
ParentLevelsDisplayed	The maximum number of parent nodes to display. The default is -1, which displays all parent nodes.
PathDirection	Indicates the order in which nodes should be listed. Allowable values are RootToCurrent and CurrentToRoot. The default is RootToCurrent.
PathSeparator	The string displayed between each node of the path. The default is a greater-than sign.
RenderCurrentNodeAsLink	Set to True if you want the node that represents the current page to be rendered as a link. The default is False.

Description

- The SiteMapPath control displays a list of the links for each node in the site map from the root node to the current page.
- Unlike the TreeView and Menu controls, you don't need to bind the SiteMapPath control to a data source. Instead, it automatically uses the web.sitemap file to determine the current page's position within the web site's navigation structure.

Figure 10-7 How to use the SiteMapPath control

A master page for the Navigation application

To show you how the navigation controls work together, figure 10-8 presents the body of a master page that includes both a navigation menu and a site map path. This is the master page that was shown in figure 10-1.

Like the master page you saw in the last chapter, the content for this master page is divided into three divisions. The first division contains an Image control that displays a banner at the top of the page. Then, the second division contains a Menu control and a SiteMapDataSource control. Because of the way the CSS for this division is defined, it's displayed down the left side of the page below the banner. Finally, the third division contains a SiteMapPath control that's displayed below the banner, followed by a content placeholder. In figure 10-1, a Site Map page is displayed within the content placeholder.

Notice also that the asp:Menu element includes several style elements that specify the appearance of the menu. These elements were generated by Visual Studio when I selected a scheme for the menu. In the next chapter, you'll see how you can apply formatting like this using skins. In addition to these style elements, several attributes were added to the Menu control. However, I replaced these attributes with a CSS style rule that provides for the same formatting.

In addition, this master page uses a code-behind file named Site.master.cs that displays a message in the label at the bottom of the page. Since this code-behind file is the same as the one presented in chapter 9, it's not repeated here.

The body of the master page for the Navigation application

```
<body>
    <form id="form1" runat="server">
    <div id="page">
        <div id="header">
            <asp:Image ID="Image1" runat="server"
                ImageUrl="~/Images/banner.jpg" />
        </div>
        <div id="sidebar">
            <asp:Menu ID="Menu1" runat="server" DataSourceID="SiteMapDataSource1"
                DynamicHorizontalOffset="2" StaticSubMenuIndent="10px" >
                <StaticSelectedStyle BackColor="DarkOrange" />
                <StaticMenuItemStyle HorizontalPadding="5px"
                    VerticalPadding="2px" />
                <StaticHoverStyle BackColor="Gold" Font-Bold="True"
                    ForeColor="Black" />
                <DynamicHoverStyle BackColor="Gold" Font-Bold="True"
                    ForeColor="Black" />
                <DynamicMenuStyle BackColor="LightGrey" />
                <DynamicSelectedStyle BackColor="DarkOrange" />
                <DynamicMenuItemStyle HorizontalPadding="5px"
                    VerticalPadding="2px" />
            </asp:Menu>
            <asp:SiteMapDataSource ID="SiteMapDataSource1" runat="server"
                ShowStartingNode="False" />
        </div>
        <div id="main">
            <p id="map">
                <asp:SiteMapPath id="SiteMapPath1" runat="server">
                </asp:SiteMapPath>
            </p>
            <asp:ContentPlaceHolder id="MainContent" runat="server">
            </asp:ContentPlaceHolder>
        </div>
        <p id="message">
            <asp:Label ID="lblMessage" runat="server"></asp:Label>
        </p>
    </div>
    </form>
</body>
```

Figure 10-8   A master page that includes navigation controls

Perspective

This should give you a pretty good idea of how useful the navigation features can be. If you experiment with them, you should quickly see that they're also easy to use.

You'll also discover that the TreeView, Menu, and SiteMapPath controls include many attributes that weren't described in this chapter. However, most of these attributes are designed to let you alter the appearance of the navigation controls, not their behavior. So once you master the basics of using these controls, you shouldn't have any trouble learning how to tweak their appearance by using the other attributes.

Terms

site navigation
site map data source
vertical menu
horizontal menu
static menu
dynamic menu
bread crumbs

Exercise 10-1 Add site navigation to the Reservation application

In this application, you'll add site navigation to the Reservation application. To make that easier for you, you'll start from a project that contains all but one of the forms used by the application.

Create the web.sitemap file

1. Open the Ch10Reservation web site in the C:\aspnet4_cs directory.

2. Use the technique in figure 10-2 to create a web.sitemap file.

3. Modify the outermost siteMapNode element so it refers to the Home page, and modify the two nested elements so they refer to the Request and Accommodations pages. Use any titles and descriptions you want.

4. Add additional siteMapNode elements within the element for the Home page that refer to the Services, Activities, Specials, and About pages.

5. Add siteMapNode elements within the element for the Accommodations page that refer to the Standard Room, Business Room, and Suite pages. To do that, you'll need to replace the self-closing tag for the Accommodations page with start and end tags.

6. Add siteMapNode elements within the element for the Activities page that refer to the Restaurants, Shopping, Theaters, and Outdoor Activities pages.

7. Add siteMapNode elements within the element for the About Us page that refer to the History and Directions pages. The web.sitemap file should now include a siteMapNode element for each content page except for the Confirmation page.

Add a Menu control to the master page

8. Delete the paragraph that contains the three hyperlinks from the master page.

9. Add a Menu control below the h2 element, set its Orientation property to Horizontal, and set its StaticEnableDefaultPopOutImage property to False.

10. Add a SiteMapDataSourceControl to the page and bind it to the Menu control. Set the ShowStartingNode property to False.

11. Run the application to see how the menu looks, and display one of the menus with subitems to see how they look. Notice the tool tips that are displayed when you point to each item. Then, close the browser.

12. Display the smart tag menu for the Menu control and select the Auto Format command. Then, select "Classic" from the list of themes that are displayed and notice how the appearance of the menu changes.

13. Run the application again, and display one of the menus with subitems. Then, click one of these items to display the associated page. Continue experimenting with the menu until you're sure you understand how it works.

Add a SiteMapPath control to the master page

14. Add a paragraph with the ID "map" below the SiteMapDataSource control on the master page, and add a SiteMapPath control to that paragraph.

15. Run the application to see how this control looks. If you have the Home page set as the start page, this will be the only page displayed in the path.

16. Display other pages in the web site to see how the path changes.

17. Display the Request page, enter the required values, click the Submit button, and notice that the SiteMapPath control isn't displayed. That's because this page isn't include in the Web.sitemap file.

Add a TreeView control to a new page

18. Add a new page named Map to the web site, and add a TreeView control to the second Content control on the page.

19. Modify the web.sitemap file so it includes a siteMapNode element for this page. This element should be nested within the siteMapNode element for the About Us page.

20. Add a SiteMapDataSource control to the Map page and bind it to the TreeView control.

21. Display the smart tag menu for the TreeView control, select the Auto Format command, and select the "Arrows 2" scheme.

22. Run the application, and use the menu to display the Map page. Notice that the node for the Map page in the tree is displayed in a different color, is underlined, and is spaced differently than the other nodes.

23. Close the browser and display the Map page in Source view. Then, delete the SelectedNodeStyle element that's subordinate to the TreeView control.

24. Run the application again and display the Map page to see that the node for that page now looks just like the other nodes. This illustrates one way to customize a predefined scheme.

25. Click one of the ▼ symbols in the tree to collapse the nodes subordinate to that node. Then, click the ▷ symbol to redisplay the subordinate nodes.

26. Click on any node in the tree to display the page associated with that node. Continue experimenting until you're sure you understand how the TreeView control works.

11

How to use themes

When you develop a web site, you usually want to apply consistent formatting to all of its pages so the entire site has a cohesive look and feel. In addition, it's generally considered a good programming practice to separate the formatting of the web pages from the content of the web pages whenever that's possible. That way, web designers can focus on making the site look good, and programmers can focus on making the site work the way it should.

To make this easy and flexible, ASP.NET includes a feature known as *themes* that builds upon formatting technologies such as cascading style sheets (CSS). This feature allows you to create multiple themes for a web site, and it makes it easy to switch between themes. If you want, you can even write code that allows a user to customize a web site by choosing a preferred theme.

An introduction to themes

When you work with standard HTML, it's a common practice to store the global formatting information for a web site in an external style sheet as described in chapter 5. Then, you can apply the styles in this style sheet to all pages of the application. Although this works well for HTML elements, it can be tricky to get this to work correctly with ASP.NET server controls because it requires that the programmer and web designer understand how server controls are rendered to HTML. The solution to this problem is the use *themes*, which let you specify the formatting for both HTML elements and server controls.

A page before and after a theme has been applied

Figure 11-1 shows the Order page for the Halloween Store application before and after a theme has been applied to it. As you can see, these pages look quite different. In particular, the second page uses a different font, and it uses different font sizes and colors for some of the elements and controls. In addition, the buttons that are defined on the second page look different than the buttons on the first page because they have square corners and a different background color. Finally, a background color has been added outside the second page.

This Order page includes both HTML elements and ASP.NET server controls. To start, this page includes two HTML tags that define the heading and subheading for the page like this:

```
<h1>Halloween Superstore</h1>
<h2>For the little goblin in all of us</h2>
```

The custom formatting for these tags is stored in the external style sheet for the theme. Then, this page uses ASP.NET tags to define the server controls that are on the rest of the page. However, the custom formatting for these server controls isn't stored in the Order page. Instead, this formatting is stored in an external file as described in the next figure.

Before: The Order page without a theme

After: The Order page with a theme

Figure 11-1   A page before and after a theme has been applied

How themes work

Figure 11-2 gives an overview of how themes work. To start, it shows the Solution Explorer for an application that contains an App_Themes folder. This folder can contain multiple subfolders with each subfolder defining one theme. For example, the App_Themes folder in this figure contains two folders that define themes. The first folder contains a theme named BasicBlue, and the second folder contains a theme named Halloween.

The Halloween folder shows the three types of files a theme can include. First, a theme folder can include a file for the *cascading style sheet (CSS)* that contains the styles that define the appearance of the HTML elements. You code these styles as shown in chapter 5. Like the CSS files shown in that chapter, the CSS file for a theme must have an extension of css. In addition, it typically has the same name as the theme folder, although that's not required.

Second, a theme folder can contain files for the *skins* that define the appearance of the ASP.NET server controls. A skin specifies the formatting attributes for a server control, and a file that contains skins must have an extension of skin. In addition, if the theme only has one skin file, this file typically has the same name as the theme folder, although that's not required. In fact, as you'll see later in this chapter, it's possible to store skin definitions in multiple skin files within a theme folder.

Third, a theme folder can contain the files for any images or other resources that are used by the CSS and skins included in the theme. For example, the bullet.gif file shown here could be used in the BulletImageUrl attribute of a BulletedList control, and the bats.gif file could be used in the background-image property of a style. These files can be stored in the theme folder or any subfolder of the theme folder. In this case, the two GIF files are stored in the Images subfolder of the Halloween folder.

When you use themes, you should realize that ASP.NET provides for two different types of themes. The difference between these two types has to do with when they're applied. If you use a *customization theme*, its styles are applied after any styles specified outside the theme. Similarly, its control attributes are applied after the attributes specified by individual controls. Because of that, you can't override the styles or attributes that are applied by a customization theme.

In contrast, the styles and attributes in a *style sheet theme* are applied before the styles specified by any external, internal, or inline styles and before the attributes specified by individual controls. That means that you can override the styles that are applied by a style sheet theme. You'll learn how to work with both customization themes and style sheet themes in this chapter.

How to create themes

To create a theme, you start by creating an App_Themes folder as described in figure 11-2. When you do, a theme folder named Theme1 is added and you can change the name of this folder to anything you like. Finally, you add any css, skin, image, and other resource files you want to include in the theme to the theme folder using standard techniques.

The directory structure for a theme

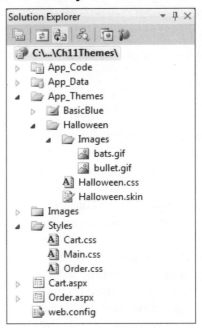

The order in which styles and control attributes are applied

1. Style sheet theme styles and control attributes

2. External, internal, and inline styles and control attributes

3. Customization theme styles and control attributes

Description

- The App_Themes folder can contain multiple subfolders with each subfolder defining one *theme*.

- Each theme folder can contain a file that contains the *cascading style sheet* (CSS) that defines the appearance of the HTML elements, files that define the *skins* that control the appearance of the ASP.NET server controls, and files for any images or other resources that are used by the cascading style sheet or the skins.

- ASP.NET provides for both *style sheet themes* and *customization themes*. The difference between the two has to do with when the styles and control attributes they contain are applied, as shown above.

- To create the App_Themes folder, you can right-click on the root folder, select the Add ASP.NET Folder submenu, select the Theme item, and enter a name for the theme folder. To create another folder, right-click the App_Themes folder instead of the root folder.

Figure 11-2   How themes work

How to work with skins

In the topics that follow, you'll learn the basic skills for creating and using skins. You'll also learn about two different ways that you can store skins.

How to create and use skins

Before you can create the skins for a theme, you must create the skin file. Then, you can add skins to the file by entering the opening tag for the control, entering a RunAt attribute, and entering the closing tag. This is illustrated by the start of the Halloween skin file at the top of figure 11-3.

Once you've entered the basic tag, you can set other attributes to control the formatting for the control. To do that, you can use the same techniques you use to set control attributes in an aspx file.

When you use themes, you typically define one skin for each type of control that you use in your application. In this figure, for example, you can see the skins for the Label, TextBox, Button, and DropDownList controls used by the Order page shown in figure 11-1. For a more robust application, you'd need to include skins for many more types of controls. Otherwise, a control that doesn't have a skin might not look like the rest of the controls.

Notice that the first four skins in this skin file don't include a SkinID attribute. As a result, they're the *default skins* that are used when a control of that type doesn't include a SkinID attribute. For example, the default skin for a label is applied to the first Label control that's shown in this figure.

If you need to supply multiple skins with different formatting for a control, you can code a *named skin* with a SkinID attribute that uniquely identifies the skin. For example, the named skin in this figure provides a second skin for the Label control with a SkinID of Error. This skin sets the font color to green, which is the color that's used to display error messages. To apply this skin to a Label control, you can set the control's SkinID attribute to Error as shown by the second Label control in this figure.

Before I go on, you should realize that it may not be necessary to include some of the attributes shown in this figure. For example, because the default font color is black (#000000) and because that color isn't changed by the style sheet for the theme or by individual controls, it's not necessary to include the ForeColor attribute for the default Label or Button controls. If you want to be sure that the font is always black, though, you should include this attribute.

The start of a skin file

A skin file that defines four default skins and one named skin

```
<asp:Label
    runat="server"                  ForeColor="#000000" />

<asp:DropDownList
    runat="server"                  ForeColor="#FF8C00"
    BorderColor="#000000"           BorderStyle="Solid"
    BorderWidth="1px" />

<asp:TextBox
    runat="server"                  ForeColor="#FF8C00"
    BorderColor="#000000"           BorderStyle="Solid"
    BorderWidth="1px" />

<asp:Button
    runat="server"                  ForeColor="#000000"
    Font-Bold="true"                BackColor="#FFA500"
    BorderColor="#000000"           BorderWidth="1px" />

<%-- a named skin for labels --%>
<asp:Label
    runat="server"                  ForeColor="#008000"
    SkinID="Error" />
```

A Label control that uses the default skin

```
<asp:Label ID="Label3" runat="server" Text="Quantity:"></asp:Label>
```

A Label control that specifies a named skin

```
<asp:Label ID="lblMessage" runat="server" SkinID="Error"></asp:Label>
```

Description

- To add a new .skin file to a theme, you can right-click on the folder for the theme, and select the Add New Item command. Then, you can use the Add New Item dialog box to select the Skin File template and enter the name for the .skin file.

- To specify a comment within a skin file, you must use the <%-- and --%> tags.

- To create a *default skin*, don't specify the SkinID attribute for the skin. Then, the skin will automatically be applied to any control of that type whose SkinID property isn't set.

- To create a *named skin*, specify the SkinID attribute for the skin. Then, you can use the SkinID attribute to apply the skin to a control of that type.

Figure 11-3   How to create and use skins

Another way to store skins

In figure 11-3, all of the skins for the application were stored in a single skin file. However, it's also possible to split skins up into multiple files. For example, figure 11-4 shows how you can store the skins in figure 11-3 in separate files. Here, both of the skins for the Label control are stored in a file named Label.skin, the skin for the DropDownList control is stored in a file named DropDownList.skin, and so on.

The choice of how to store your skins depends on your preferences and on the number of skins used by your application. If you have a large number of skins with multiple skins for each type of control, you may find it easier to organize and manage them by splitting them into separate files. This can make it easier to find skins and to copy them from one application to another. On the other hand, you might find that the additional skin files create a file management headache. As a result, you might prefer to keep all skins in a single file even if that file becomes very long.

A theme that uses multiple skin files

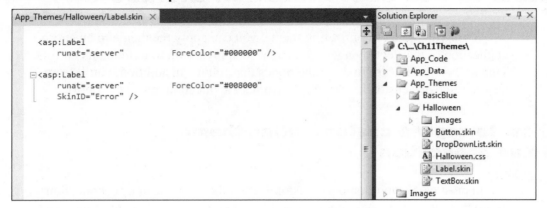

The Label.skin file

```
<asp:Label
    runat="server"              ForeColor="#000000" />

<asp:Label
    runat="server"              ForeColor="#008000"
    SkinID="Error" />
```

The DropDownList.skin file

```
<asp:DropDownList
    runat="server"              ForeColor="#FF8C00"
    BorderColor="#000000"       BorderStyle="Solid"
    BorderWidth="1px" />
```

The TextBox.skin file

```
<asp:TextBox
    runat="server"              ForeColor="#FF8C00"
    BorderColor="#000000"       BorderStyle="Solid"
    BorderWidth="1px" />
```

The Button.skin file

```
<asp:Button
    runat="server"              ForeColor="#000000"
    Font-Bold="true"            BackColor="#FFA500"
    BorderColor="#000000"       BorderWidth="1px" />
```

Description

- Skins can be stored in a single file as shown in the previous figure or in separate files as shown in this figure.

Figure 11-4   Another way to store skins

How to use customization themes

When you use a customization theme, you can apply the theme to an entire application or to selected pages. You can also apply a skin to individual controls. That's what you'll learn to do in the topics that follow. In addition, you'll learn how to remove a customization theme from an application, page, or control.

How to apply a customization theme to an application

In most cases, you'll apply a customization theme to the entire application. To do that, you add a pages element within the system.web element of the web.config file as shown in figure 11-5. Then, you code a theme attribute within the pages element that specifies the name of the theme.

Remember that when you apply a customization theme to an entire application, the formatting it specifies overrides any formatting that's specified for individual elements and controls. If an attribute isn't specified by the theme, though, you can use that attribute in an individual element or control to format that element or control. Because the Halloween theme specifies only the ForeColor attribute for the Label control, for example, you can apply any other formatting to individual labels.

How to apply a customization theme to a page

Figure 11-5 also shows how to apply a customization theme to a page. To do that at design time, you can use the Theme attribute of the Page directive. To do that at runtime, you use the Theme property of the Page class.

Note that the code that applies the theme at runtime must be executed before the HTML elements or ASP.NET controls are added to the page. Because the elements and controls are added during the Init event, the theme is typically applied during the PreInit event as shown in this figure. This event occurs just before the Init event.

In this example, the code that applies the theme sets the Theme property for the Page equal to a string for a theme that has been stored in the Session object. That way, if the user has selected a theme earlier in the session, the theme for this page will be changed to the theme selected by the user. However, unless you store this theme in a persistent data store, it will be lost when the user ends the current session.

How to apply a skin to a control

In figure 11-3, you saw how to use the SkinID attribute to apply a named skin to a server control at design time. Now, figure 11-5 reviews this skill, and it shows how to use the SkinID property of a server control to apply a named skin

How to apply a customization theme to all pages of an application

```
<configuration>
  <system.web>
    <pages theme="Halloween" />
  </system.web>
</configuration>
```

How to apply a customization theme to a page

At design time

```
<%@ Page Language="C#" Theme="Halloween" %>
```

At runtime

```
protected void Page_PreInit(object sender, EventArgs e)
{
    Page.Theme = Session["MyTheme"].ToString();
}
```

How to apply a skin to a control

At design time

```
<asp:Label ID="lblMessage" runat="server" SkinID="Head1"></asp:Label>
```

At runtime

```
protected void Page_PreInit(object sender, EventArgs e)
{
    lblName.SkinID = Session["MySkinID"].ToString();
}
```

Description

- To apply a customization theme to the current application, you can edit the web.config file for the application. Within the web.config file, you can use the theme attribute of the pages element to specify the name of the theme.

- When you use the theme attribute of the pages element to apply a theme to a page, any formatting it specifies overrides the formatting specified by individual elements and controls.

- To apply a customization theme to a single page, you can use the Theme attribute of the Page directive or the Theme property of the Page class.

- To apply a skin to a control, you can use the SkinID attribute or property of the control.

- The code that applies a theme or skin at runtime should be coded in the event handler for the PreInit event of the page so the code is executed before the HTML elements and ASP.NET controls are added to the page.

Figure 11-5   How to apply customization themes and skins

at runtime. To do that, you can use the PreInit event of the page to make sure that this skin is applied before the control is added to the page. This works the same as it does for applying a theme to a page.

How to remove a customization theme from an application

Although it isn't shown in this chapter, it's possible for a web site administrator to set a global theme that applies to all web applications running on the server. In that case, you may want to remove the global theme from all pages of your application. To do that, you can open the web.config file for your application and set the theme attribute of the pages element to an empty string as shown in figure 11-6.

How to remove a customization theme from a page

Figure 11-6 also shows how to remove a theme from a single page. You may need to do that if you want to apply formatting to that page that's different from the formatting that's used by the other pages of the application. To remove a customization theme from a page at design time, you can set the Theme attribute of the Page directive to an empty string. At runtime, you can set the Theme property of the Page class to an empty string. To do that, you can use the PreInit event of the page. This works the same as it does for applying a theme to a page.

How to remove a customization theme from a control

By default, the EnableTheming property is set to True for all controls. As a result, any themes that are applied to a page are applied to all controls on the page. In most cases, that's what you want. However, since an attribute that's set in a skin in a customization theme overrides the same attribute that's set at the control level, you may want to remove the theme from the control so the formatting that's specified by the control is applied instead. To do that, you can set the EnableTheming attribute for the control to False as shown in figure 11-6. Then, you can use standard ASP.NET formatting techniques to format that control. In this figure, for example, the ForeColor attribute is used to change the color of a label to red.

If you need to set the EnableTheming property at runtime, you can use the PreInit event of the page to make sure that this skin is removed before the HTML elements and controls are added to the page. This works the same as it does for applying a theme to a page.

How to remove a customization theme from all pages of an application

```
<system.web>
  <pages theme="" />
</system.web>
```

How to remove a customization theme from a page

At design time

```
<%@ Page Language="C#" Theme="" %>
```

At runtime

```
protected void Page_PreInit(object sender, EventArgs e)
{
    Page.Theme = "";
}
```

How to remove a customization theme from a control

At design time

```
<asp:Label ID="lblMessage" runat="server"
    EnableTheming="False" ForeColor="red">
</asp:Label>
```

At runtime

```
protected void Page_PreInit(object sender, EventArgs e)
{
    lblName.EnableTheming = false;
    lblName.ForeColor = System.Drawing.Color.Red;
}
```

Description

- To remove a customization theme from all of the pages in an application, you can set the theme attribute of the pages element in the web.config file to an empty string.

- To remove a customization theme from a single page, you can set the Theme attribute of the Page directive or the Theme property of the Page class to an empty string.

- To remove a customization theme from a control, you can set the EnableTheming attribute or property to False.

- The code that removes a theme at runtime should be coded in the event handler for the PreInit event of the page so the code is executed before the HTML elements and ASP.NET controls are added to the page.

Figure 11-6   How to remove customization themes and skins

How to use style sheet themes

If you want to be able to override the attributes specified by a theme, you can use style sheet themes instead of customization themes. Figure 11-7 shows how to use style sheet themes.

How to apply a style sheet theme

To apply a style sheet theme to an entire application, you add a pages element to the web.config file just as you do for a customization theme. Instead of adding a theme attribute, though, you add a styleSheetTheme attribute. This is illustrated in the first example in this figure.

To apply a style sheet theme to a page at design time, you set the StylesheetTheme attribute of the Page directive. To apply a style sheet theme at runtime, you don't use the PreInit event of the page like you do for a customization theme. Instead, you override the StyleSheetTheme property of the page to get and set the name of the theme. Then, when a page loads, it automatically calls the StyleSheetTheme property to set the style sheet theme. In this figure, for example, the StyleSheetTheme property for the page works with a theme that's stored in the Session object.

How to remove a style sheet theme

This figure also shows how to remove a style sheet them from a page. To do that at design time, you set the StylesheetTheme attribute of the Page directive to an empty string. To do that at runtime, you override the StyleSheetTheme property of the page just as you do to apply a theme at runtime. In this case, though, the get accessor can simply return an empty string, and the set accessor doesn't need to do anything. Note, though, that you can't omit the set accessor. That's because the StyleSheetTheme property of the page that this property overrides is defined with both get and set accessors.

Although you can also remove a style sheet theme from a control at design time by setting the control's EnableTheming property to False, you're not likely to do that. That's because any attributes you specify for individual controls are applied after the styles specified by the style sheet theme. So if you need to override an attribute that's set by a theme, you can simply include that attribute on the control. That's the main advantage of using style sheet themes.

How to apply a style sheet theme to all pages in the application

```
<system.web>
  <pages styleSheetTheme="Halloween" />
</system.web>
```

How to apply a style sheet theme to a single page

At design time

```
<%@ Page Language="C#" StylesheetTheme="Halloween" %>
```

At runtime by overriding the StyleSheetTheme property in the code-behind file

```
public override string StyleSheetTheme
{
    get
    {
        return Session["myTheme"].ToString();
    }
    set
    {
        Session["myTheme"] = value;
    }
}
```

How to remove a style sheet theme from a single page

At design time

```
<%@ Page Language="C#" StylesheetTheme="" %>
```

At runtime

```
public override string StyleSheetTheme
{
    get { return ""; }
    set { }
}
```

Description

- To apply or remove a style sheet theme at design time, you can use the StyleSheetTheme attribute. This works just like the Theme attribute does for customization themes.

- To apply or remove a style sheet theme at runtime, you can override the StyleSheetTheme property of the page.

Figure 11-7   How to use style sheet themes

Perspective

In this chapter, you learned how themes work and how they can be used to separate the formatting of an application from the code of an application. In particular, you learned how you can use skins to control the formatting of controls. Now, if you combine that knowledge with the information that was presented in chapter 5 on cascading style sheets, you should be able to work with a web designer to create a suitable theme for your application.

Terms

theme
cascading style sheet (CSS)
skin
default skin
named skin
customization theme
style sheet theme

Exercise 11-1   Create a theme for the Reservation application

In this exercise, you'll create a theme for the Reservation application. Then, you'll use different techniques to apply and remove that theme to see how this works.

Create a theme and add a skin file

1. Open the Ch11Reservation application in the aspnet4_cs directory.

2. Create an App_Themes folder and give the theme folder that's generated the name Basic.

3. Create a skin file named Basic within the Basic theme folder, and create a skin for each of the following controls: label, text box, button, drop-down list, radio button, check box, and calendar. To start, set the RunAt attribute for each of these controls to "server" and set the ForeColor attribute to "#000080" (navy).

4. Set the BorderColor attribute of the text box, drop-down list, and calendar controls so it's the same as the fore color, and set the BorderWidth attribute of these controls to "1px".

5. Set the BackColor attribute of the button control and the SelectedDayStyle-BackColor and TitleStyle-BackColor attributes of the calendar control to "B0C4DE".

6. Add a named skin for the Label control with the skin ID "Message". Set the ForeColor attribute of this skin to #800000 (maroon), and set the Font-Bold property to "true".

7. Display the Confirmation page and set the SkinId attribute of the label at the bottom of the page to "Message".

8. Open the web.config file, and add a pages element with a theme attribute that applies the Basic theme.

9. Run the application. The Request page should now look like this:

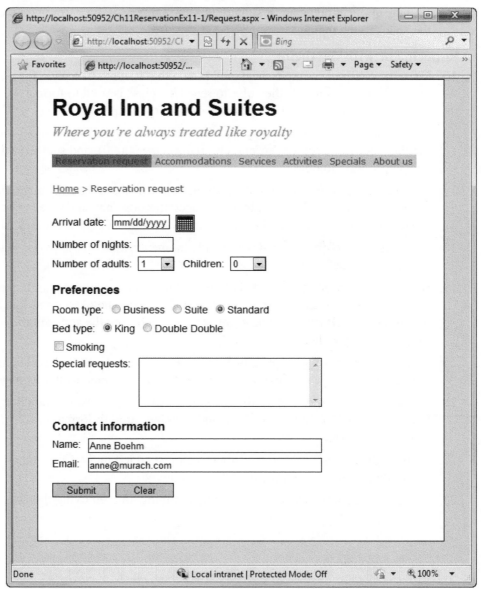

10. Complete the Request page and click the Submit button to see that the Confirmation page uses the same formatting.

11. Click the Confirm button to see that the message at the bottom of the page is displayed in a boldfaced maroon font instead of the font that's used by the other labels on the form.

Add a cascading style sheet to the theme

12. Create a style sheet named Basic within the Basic theme folder.

13. Display the Main.css style sheet in the Styles folder. Then, cut (not copy) the styles for the body, h1, h2, h3, and p elements, and paste them into the Basic.css style sheet.

14. Run the application again. It should look the same as it did before you moved the styles to the theme.

Experiment with the theme

15. Open the Request.css style sheet, and notice that it contains a style for a class named validator that sets the color to red. This class is used to format the validators and the validation summary control on the page.

16. Switch back to the Basic.css style sheet, and add a style for the validator class. Set the color property for this class to maroon (#800000), and set the font-weight property to bold.

17. Run the application, and click the Submit button without entering any data. The error text should be displayed in a boldfaced maroon font since the styles in the Basic.css style sheet are applied after the styles in the Request.css style sheet.

18. Open the web.config file, and replace the theme attribute in the pages element with a styleSheetTheme attribute.

19. Run the application again, and click the Submit button without entering any data. This time, the error text should be displayed in a boldfaced red font since the styles in the Basic.css style sheet are applied before the styles in the Request.css style sheet.

20. Display the Confirmation page in Source view, and add a StylesheetTheme attribute to the Page directive that removes the Basic theme from this page.

21. Run the application one more time, complete the Request page, and click the Submit button. Notice that the theme is no longer used to format the Confirmation page.

22. Remove the StylesheetTheme attribute you just added to the Confirmation page so this page is once again formatted by the theme.

23. If you'd like, continue experimenting by applying and removing themes.

Section 3

ASP.NET database programming

Since most ASP.NET applications store their data in databases, this section is devoted to the essentials of database programming. When you complete it, you should be able to develop database applications that use *SQL data sources* to access and update the data in the databases that your applications use. In addition, you should have at least a general understanding of how you can use *object data sources* to develop 3-layer database applications.

To start, chapter 12 introduces you to the concepts and terms you need to know for developing database applications. This chapter also presents an overview of the ADO.NET classes that do the database operations when you use SQL or object data sources. When you use SQL data sources, though, you don't use ADO.NET directly, even though the processing is done by ADO.NET.

Then, chapter 13 shows you how to use SQL data sources and the DataList control to get data from a database. Chapter 14 shows you how to use the GridView control to create more complex applications. Chapter 15 shows you how to use the DetailsView and FormView controls. And chapter 16 shows you how to use the ListView and DataPager controls. By using SQL data sources and the data controls, you'll be able to develop powerful applications with a minimum of code.

Finally, chapter 17 shows you how to use object data sources to develop 3-layer database applications. If you already know how to use ADO.NET directly, you should be able to use object data sources when you complete this chapter. Otherwise, you will at least understand the concepts and recognize the need for learning ADO.NET.

12

An introduction to database programming

This chapter introduces you to the basic concepts and terms that apply to database applications. In particular, it explains what a relational database is and describes how you work with it using SQL. It also presents an overview of the basic ADO.NET classes that are used to access the data in relational databases.

To illustrate these concepts and terms, this chapter presents examples that use *Microsoft SQL Server Express*. This is a scaled-back version of *Microsoft SQL Server 2008*, and SQL Server is the database you're most likely to use as you develop ASP.NET 4 database applications. Note, however, that the concepts and terms you'll learn in this chapter also apply to other databases.

An introduction to relational databases

In 1970, Dr. E. F. Codd developed a model for what was then a new and revolutionary type of database called a *relational database.* This type of database eliminated some of the problems that were associated with standard files and other database designs. By using the relational model, you can reduce data redundancy, which saves disk storage and leads to efficient data retrieval. You can also view and manipulate data in a way that is both intuitive and efficient. Today, relational databases are the de facto standard for database applications.

How a table is organized

The model for a relational database states that data is stored in one or more *tables.* It also states that each table can be viewed as a two-dimensional matrix consisting of *rows* and *columns.* This is illustrated by the relational table in figure 12-1. Each row in this table contains information about a single product.

In practice, the rows and columns of a relational database table are sometimes referred to by the more traditional terms, *records* and *fields.* In fact, some software packages use one set of terms, some use the other, and some use a combination. In this book, I've used the terms *rows* and *columns* for consistency.

If a table contains one or more columns that uniquely identify each row in the table, you can define these columns as the *primary key* of the table. For instance, the primary key of the Products table in this figure is the ProductID column. Here, the primary key consists of a single column. However, a primary key can also consist of two or more columns, in which case it's called a *composite primary key.*

In addition to primary keys, some database management systems let you define additional keys that uniquely identify each row in a table. If, for example, the Name column in the Products table contains a unique name for each product, it can be defined as a *non-primary key.* In SQL Server, this is called a *unique key,* and it's implemented by defining a *unique key constraint* (also known simply as a *unique constraint*). The only difference between a unique key and a primary key is that a unique key can contain a null value and a primary key can't.

Indexes provide an efficient way to access the rows in a table based on the values in one or more columns. Because applications typically access the rows in a table by referring to their key values, an index is automatically created for each key you define. However, you can define indexes for other columns as well. If, for example, you frequently need to sort the rows in the Products table by the CategoryID column, you can set up an index for that column. Like a key, an index can include one or more columns.

The Products table in a Halloween database

Primary key   Columns

ProductID	Name	ShortDescripti...	LongDescription	CategoryID	ImageFile	UnitPrice	OnHand
arm01	Freddie Arm	Life-size Freddy...	This arm will gi...	props	arm1.jpg	19.9500	200
bats01	Flying Bats	Bats flying in fr...	Bats flying in fr...	props	cool1.jpg	69.9900	25
bl01	Black Light (24")	24" Black light	Create that cree...	fx	blacklight1.jpg	24.9900	200
cat01	Deranged Cat	20" Ugly cat	This is one ugly...	props	cat1.jpg	19.9900	45
fog01	Fog Machine	600W Fog mac...	The perfect fog...	fx	fog1.jpg	34.9900	100
fogj01	Fog Juice (1qt)	1 qt Bottle of fo...	The drink your ...	fx	fogjuice1.jpg	9.9900	500
frankc01	Frankenstein	Frankenstein co...	It's alive!	costumes	frank1.jpg	39.9900	100
fred01	Freddie	Freddie Krueger...	The ultimate in ...	masks	freddy1.jpg	29.9900	50
head01	Michael Head	Mini Michael M...	For classic horr...	props	head1.jpg	29.9900	100
head02	Saw Head	Jigsaw head sca...	Perfect for getti...	props	head2.jpg	29.9900	100
hippie01	Hippie	Women's hippi...	Share the peace...	costumes	hippie01.jpg	79.9900	40
jar01	JarJar	Jar Jar Binks	Meesa happy t...	costumes	jarjar1.jpg	59.9900	25
martian01	Martian	Martian costume	Now includes a...	costumes	martian1.jpg	69.9900	100
mum01	Mummy	Mummy mask	All wrapped up ...	masks	mummy1.jpg	39.9900	30
pow01	Austin Powers	Austin Powers ...	Be the most sh...	costumes	powers1.jpg	79.9900	25
rat01	Ugly Rat	16" Rat	This guy is sure...	props	rat1.jpg	14.9900	75
rat02	Uglier Rat	20" Rat	Yuch! This one ...	props	rat2.jpg	19.9900	50
skel01	Life-size Skeleton	Life-size plastic ...	This blown plas...	props	skel1.jpg	14.9500	10
skullfog01	Skull Fogger	2,800 cubic foo...	This fogger put...	fx	skullfog1.jpg	39.9500	50
str01	Mini-strobe	Black mini stro...	Perfect for crea...	fx	strobe1.jpg	13.9900	200
super01	Superman	Superman cost...	Look, up in the ...	costumes	superman1.jpg	39.9900	100
tlm01	T&L Machine	Thunder & Lig...	Flash! Boom! Cr...	fx	tlm1.jpg	99.9900	10
vader01	Darth Vader Ma...	The legendary ...	OB1 has taught...	masks	vader1.jpg	19.9900	100

Rows

Concepts

- A *relational database* uses *tables* to store and manipulate data. Each table consists of one or more *records*, or *rows*, that contain the data for a single entry. Each row contains one or more *fields*, or *columns*, with each column representing a single item of data.

- Most tables contain a *primary key* that uniquely identifies each row in the table. The primary key often consists of a single column, but it can also consist of two or more columns. If a primary key uses two or more columns, it's called a *composite primary key*.

- In addition to primary keys, some database management systems let you define one or more *non-primary keys*. In SQL Server, these keys are called *unique keys*, and they're implemented using *unique key constraints*. Like a primary key, a non-primary key uniquely identifies each row in the table.

- A table can also be defined with one or more *indexes*. An index provides an efficient way to access data from a table based on the values in specific columns. An index is automatically created for a table's primary and non-primary keys.

Figure 12-1   How a table is organized

How the tables in a database are related

The tables in a relational database can be related to other tables by values in specific columns. The two tables shown in figure 12-2 illustrate this concept. Here, each row in the Categories table is related to one or more rows in the Products table. This is called a *one-to-many relationship*.

Typically, relationships exist between the primary key in one table and the *foreign key* in another table. The foreign key is simply one or more columns in a table that refer to a primary key in another table. In SQL Server, relationships can also exist between a unique key in one table and a foreign key in another table.

Although one-to-many relationships are the most common, two tables can also have a one-to-one or many-to-many relationship. If a table has a *one-to-one relationship* with another table, the data in the two tables could be stored in a single table. Because of that, one-to-one relationships are used infrequently.

In contrast, a *many-to-many relationship* is usually implemented by using an intermediate table, called a *linking table*, that has a one-to-many relationship with the two tables in the many-to-many relationship. In other words, a many-to-many relationship can usually be broken down into two one-to-many relationships.

The relationship between the Categories and Products tables

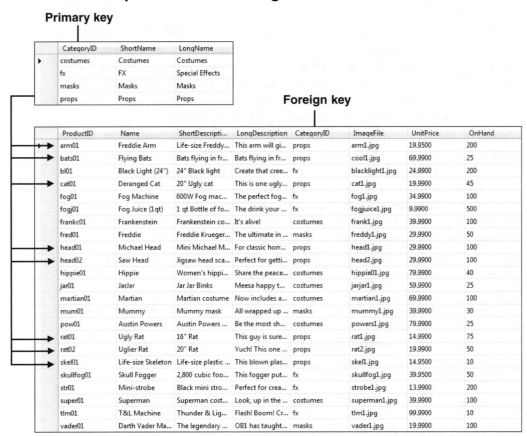

Primary key

Foreign key

CategoryID	ShortName	LongName
costumes	Costumes	Costumes
fx	FX	Special Effects
masks	Masks	Masks
props	Props	Props

ProductID	Name	ShortDescripti...	LongDescription	CategoryID	ImageFile	UnitPrice	OnHand
arm01	Freddie Arm	Life-size Freddy...	This arm will gi...	props	arm1.jpg	19.9500	200
bats01	Flying Bats	Bats flying in fr...	Bats flying in fr...	props	cool1.jpg	69.9900	25
bl01	Black Light (24")	24" Black light	Create that cree...	fx	blacklight1.jpg	24.9900	200
cat01	Deranged Cat	20" Ugly cat	This is one ugly...	props	cat1.jpg	19.9900	45
fog01	Fog Machine	600W Fog mac...	The perfect fog...	fx	fog1.jpg	34.9900	100
fogj01	Fog Juice (1qt)	1 qt Bottle of fo...	The drink your ...	fx	fogjuice1.jpg	9.9900	500
frankc01	Frankenstein	Frankenstein co...	It's alive!	costumes	frank1.jpg	39.9900	100
fred01	Freddie	Freddie Krueger...	The ultimate in ...	masks	freddy1.jpg	29.9900	50
head01	Michael Head	Mini Michael M...	For classic horr...	props	head1.jpg	29.9900	100
head02	Saw Head	Jigsaw head sca...	Perfect for getti...	props	head2.jpg	29.9900	100
hippie01	Hippie	Women's hippi...	Share the peace...	costumes	hippie01.jpg	79.9900	40
jar01	JarJar	Jar Jar Binks	Meesa happy t...	costumes	jarjar1.jpg	59.9900	25
martian01	Martian	Martian costume	Now includes a...	costumes	martian1.jpg	69.9900	100
mum01	Mummy	Mummy mask	All wrapped up ...	masks	mummy1.jpg	39.9900	30
pow01	Austin Powers	Austin Powers ...	Be the most sh...	costumes	powers1.jpg	79.9900	25
rat01	Ugly Rat	16" Rat	This guy is sure...	props	rat1.jpg	14.9900	75
rat02	Uglier Rat	20" Rat	Yuch! This one ...	props	rat2.jpg	19.9900	50
skel01	Life-size Skeleton	Life-size plastic ...	This blown plas...	props	skel1.jpg	14.9500	10
skullfog01	Skull Fogger	2,800 cubic foo...	This fogger put...	fx	skullfog1.jpg	39.9500	50
str01	Mini-strobe	Black mini stro...	Perfect for crea...	fx	strobe1.jpg	13.9900	200
super01	Superman	Superman cost...	Look, up in the ...	costumes	superman1.jpg	39.9900	100
tlm01	T&L Machine	Thunder & Lig...	Flash! Boom! Cr...	fx	tlm1.jpg	99.9900	10
vader01	Darth Vader Ma...	The legendary ...	OB1 has taught...	masks	vader1.jpg	19.9900	100

Concepts

- The tables in a relational database are related to each other through their key columns. For example, the CategoryID column is used to relate the Categories and Products tables above. The CategoryID column in the Products table is called a *foreign key* because it identifies a related row in the Categories table.

- Usually, a foreign key corresponds to the primary key in the related table. In SQL Server, however, a foreign key can also correspond to a unique key in the related table.

- When two tables are related via a foreign key, the table with the foreign key is referred to as the *foreign key table* and the table with the primary key is referred to as the *primary key table*.

- The relationships between the tables in a database correspond to the relationships between the entities they represent. The most common type of relationship is a *one-to-many relationship* as illustrated by the Categories and Products tables. A table can also have a *one-to-one relationship* or a *many-to-many relationship* with another table.

Figure 12-2   How the tables in a database are related

How the columns in a table are defined

When you define a column in a table, you assign properties to it as indicated by the design of the Products table in figure 12-3. The two most important properties for a column are Column Name, which provides an identifying name for the column, and Data Type, which specifies the type of information that can be stored in the column. With SQL Server, you can choose from *system data types* like the ones in this figure, and you can define your own data types that are based on the system data types. As you define each column in a table, you generally try to assign the data type that will minimize the use of disk storage because that will improve the performance of the queries later.

In addition to a data type, you must indicate whether the column can store a *null value*. A null represents a value that's unknown, unavailable, or not applicable. The Products table, for example, allows nulls in its ImageFile column.

You can also assign a *default value* to each column. Then, that value is assigned to the column if another value isn't provided. If a column doesn't allow nulls and doesn't have a default value, you must supply a value for the column when you add a new row to the table. Otherwise, an error will occur.

Each table can also contain a numeric column whose value is generated automatically by the DBMS. In SQL Server, a column like this is called an *identity column*, and you establish it using the Identity, Identity Seed, and Identity Increment properties. Identity columns are often used as the primary key for a table.

A *check constraint* defines the acceptable values for a column. For example, you can define a check constraint for the Products table in this figure to make sure that the UnitPrice column is greater than zero. A check constraint like this can be defined at the column level because it refers only to the column it constrains. If the check constraint for a column needs to refer to other columns in the table, however, it can be defined at the table level.

After you define the constraints for a database, they're managed by the DBMS. If, for example, a user tries to add a row with data that violates a constraint, the DBMS sends an appropriate error code back to the application without adding the row to the database. The application can then respond to the error code.

Another alternative is to validate the data that is going to be added to a database before the program tries to add it. That way, the constraints shouldn't be needed and the program should run more efficiently. In many cases, both data validation and constraints are used. That way, the programs run more efficiently if the data validation routines work, but the constraints are there in case the data validation routines don't work or aren't coded.

The Server Explorer design view window for the Products table

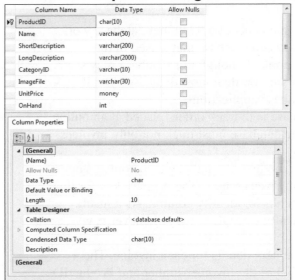

Common SQL Server data types

Type	Description
bit	A value of 1 or 0 that represents a True or False value.
char, varchar, text	Any combination of letters, symbols, and numbers.
date, time, datetime, smalldatetime	Alphanumeric data that represents a date, a time, or both a date and time. Various formats are acceptable.
decimal, numeric	Numeric data that is accurate to the least significant digit. The data can contain an integer and a fractional portion.
float, real	Floating-point values that contain an approximation of a decimal value.
bigint, int, smallint, tinyint	Numeric data that contains only an integer portion.
money, smallmoney	Monetary values that are accurate to four decimal places.

Description

- The *data type* that's assigned to a column determines the type of information that can be stored in the column. Depending on the data type, the column definition can also include its length, precision, and scale.

- Each column definition also indicates whether or not the column can contain *null values*. A null value indicates that the value of the column is not known.

- A column can be defined with a *default value*. Then, that value is used for the column if another value isn't provided when a row is added to the table.

- A column can also be defined as an *identity column*. An identity column is a numeric column whose value is generated automatically when a row is added to the table.

- To restrict the values that a column can hold, you define *check constraints*. Check constraints can be defined at either the column level or the table level.

Figure 12-3   How the columns in a table are defined

The design of the Halloween database

Now that you've seen how the basic elements of a relational database work, figure 12-4 shows the design of the Halloween database that's used in the programming examples throughout this book. Although this database may seem complicated, its design is actually much simpler than most databases you'll encounter when you work on actual database applications.

The purpose of the Halloween database is to track orders placed at an online Halloween products store. To do that, the database must track not only invoices, but also products and customers.

The central table for this database is the Invoices table, which contains one row for each order placed by the company's customers. The primary key for this table is the InvoiceNumber column, which is an identity column. As a result, invoice numbers are generated automatically by SQL Server whenever new invoices are created.

The LineItems table contains the line item details for each invoice. The primary key for this table is a combination of the InvoiceNumber and ProductID columns. The InvoiceNumber column relates each line item to an invoice, and the ProductID column relates each line item to a product. As a result, each invoice can have only one line item for a given product.

The Products and Categories tables work together to store information about the products offered by the Halloween store. The Category table has just three columns: CategoryID, ShortName, and LongName. The CategoryID column is a 10-character code that uniquely identifies each category. The ShortName and LongName columns provide two different descriptions of the category that the application can use, depending on how much room is available to display the category information.

The Products table contains one row for each product. Its primary key is the ProductID column. The Name, ShortDescription, and LongDescription columns provide descriptive information about the product. The ImageFile column provides the name of a separate image file that depicts the product, if one exists. This column specifies just the name of each image file, not the complete path. In the applications in this book, the image files are stored in a directory named Images beneath the application's main directory, so the application knows where to find them. If an image isn't available for a product, this column contains a null value.

The Customers table contains a row for each customer who has purchased from the Halloween Store. The primary key for this table is the customer's email address. The other columns in this table contain the customer's name, address, and phone number. The State column relates each customer to a state in the States table. The primary key for the States table is the 2-character StateCode column.

The tables that make up the Halloween database

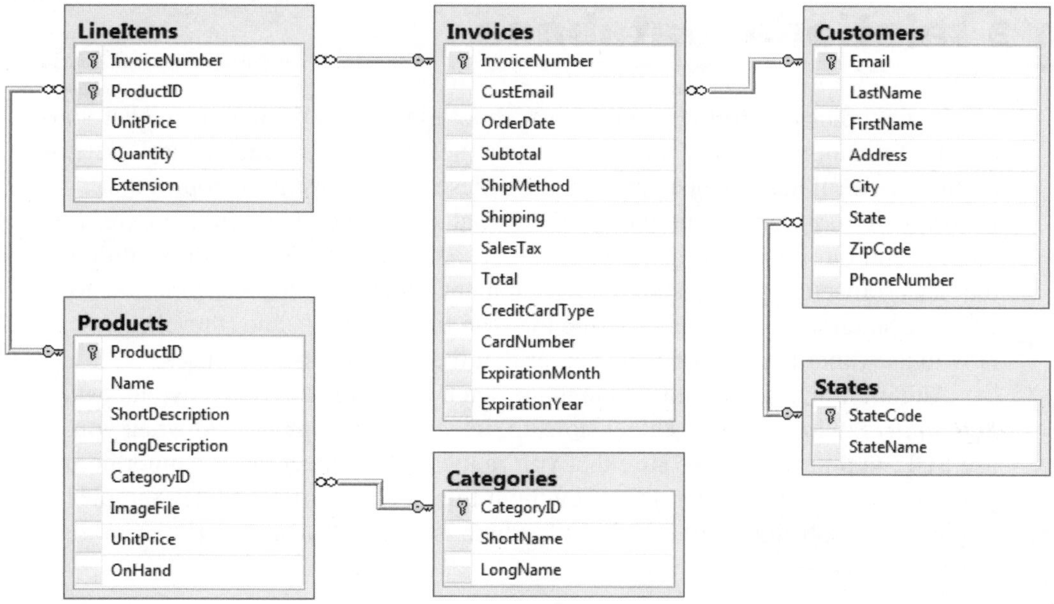

Description

- The Categories table contains a row for each product category. Its primary key is CategoryID, a 10-character code that identifies each category.

- The Products table contains a row for each product. Its primary key is ProductID, a 10-character code that identifies each product. CategoryID is a foreign key that relates each product to a row in the Categories table.

- The States table contains a row for each state. Its primary key is StateCode, a 2-character code that identifies each state.

- The Customers table contains a row for each customer. Its primary key is Email, which identifies each customer by his or her email address. State is a foreign key that relates each customer to a row in the States table.

- The Invoices table contains a row for each invoice. Its primary key is InvoiceNumber, an identity column that's generated automatically when a new invoice is created. CustEmail is a foreign key that relates each invoice to a row in the Customers table.

- The LineItems table contains one row for each line item of each invoice. Its primary key is a combination of InvoiceNumber and ProductID. InvoiceNumber is a foreign key that relates each line item to an invoice, and ProductID is a foreign key that relates each line item to a product.

- The relationships between the tables in this diagram appear as links, where the endpoints indicate the type of relationship. A key indicates the "one" side of a relationship, and the infinity symbol (∞) indicates the "many" side.

Figure 12-4   The design of the Halloween database

How to use SQL to work with the data in a relational database

In the topics that follow, you'll learn about the four SQL statements that you can use to manipulate the data in a database: Select, Insert, Update, and Delete. Although you'll learn the basics of coding these statements in the topics that follow, you may want to know more than what's presented here. In that case, we recommend our book, *Murach's SQL Server 2008 for Developers*. In addition to the Select, Insert, Update, and Delete statements, that book teaches you how to code the statements you use to define the data in a database, and it teaches you how to use other features of SQL Server that the top professionals use.

Although SQL is a standard language, each DBMS is likely to have its own *SQL dialect*, which includes extensions to the standard language. So when you use SQL, you need to make sure that you're using the dialect that's supported by your DBMS. In this chapter and throughout this book, all of the SQL examples are for Microsoft SQL Server's dialect, which is called *Transact-SQL*.

How to query a single table

Figure 12-5 shows how to use a Select statement to query a single table in a database. In the syntax summary at the top of this figure, you can see that the Select clause names the columns to be retrieved and the From clause names the table that contains the columns. You can also code a Where clause that gives criteria for the rows to be selected. And you can code an Order By clause that names one or more columns that the results should be sorted by and indicates whether each column should be sorted in ascending or descending sequence.

If you study the Select statement below the syntax summary, you can see how this works. Here, the Select statement retrieves three columns from the Products table. It selects a row only if the CategoryID column for the row has a value of "Props." And it sorts the returned rows by UnitPrice, so the least expensive products are listed first.

This figure also shows the *result table*, or *result set*, that's returned by the Select statement. A result set is a logical table that's created temporarily within the database. When an application requests data from a database, it receives a result set.

Although it's not shown here, you should realize that a result set can include columns that are calculated from other columns in the table. For example, you could create a column for the total value of each product in the Products table by multiplying the OnHand column in that table by the UnitPrice column. This type of column is called a *calculated column*, and it exists only in the results of the query.

Simplified syntax of the Select statement

```
Select column-1 [, column-2]...
From table-1
[Where selection-criteria]
[Order By column-1 [Asc|Desc] [, column-2 [Asc|Desc]]...]
```

A Select statement that retrieves and sorts selected columns and rows from the Products table

```
Select ProductID, Name, UnitPrice
From Products
Where CategoryID = 'props'
Order By UnitPrice
```

The result set defined by the Select statement

ProductID	Name	UnitPrice
skel01	Life-size Skeleton	14.9500
rat01	Ugly Rat	14.9900
arm01	Freddie Arm	19.9500
cat01	Deranged Cat	19.9900
rat02	Uglier Rat	19.9900
head01	Michael Head	29.9900
head02	Saw Head	29.9900
bats01	Flying Bats	69.9900

Concepts

- The result of a Select statement is a *result table*, or *result set*, like the one shown above. A result set is a logical set of rows that consists of all of the columns and rows requested by the Select statement.

- A result set can include *calculated columns* that are calculated from other columns in the table.

- To select all of the columns in a table, you can code an asterisk (*) in place of the column names. For example, this statement will select all of the columns from the Products table:

```
Select * From Products
```

Figure 12-5   How to query a single table

How to join data from two or more tables

Figure 12-6 presents the syntax of the Select statement for retrieving data from two tables. This type of operation is called a *join* because the data from the two tables is joined together into a single result set. For example, the Select statement in this figure joins data from the Categories and Products tables into a single result set.

An *inner join* is the most common type of join. When you use an inner join, rows from the two tables in the join are included in the result set only if their related columns match. These matching columns are specified in the From clause of the Select statement. In the Select statement in this figure, for example, rows from the Categories and Products tables are included only if the value of the CategoryID column in the Categories table matches the value of the CategoryID column in one or more rows in the Products table. If there aren't any products for a particular category, that category won't be included in the result set.

Notice that the Select clause in this statement doesn't indicate which table contains each column. That's because each of the columns exists in only one of the tables. If a column existed in both tables, however, you would need to indicate which table you wanted to retrieve the column from. If you wanted to retrieve the CategoryID column from the Categories table, for example, you would need to code that column like this:

```
Categories.CategoryID
```

Although this figure shows how to join data from two tables, you should know that you can extend this syntax to join data from additional tables. If, for example, you want to include data from the LineItems table in the results shown in this figure, you can code the From clause of the Select statement like this:

```
From Categories
    Inner Join Products
        On Categories.CategoryID = Products.CategoryID
    Inner Join LineItems
        On Products.ProductID = LineItems.ProductID
```

Then, in the column list of the Select statement, you can include any of the columns in the LineItems table.

The syntax of the Select statement for joining two tables

```
Select column-list
From table-1
    [Inner] Join table-2
    On table-1.column-1 {=|<|>|<=|>=|<>} table-2.column-2
[Where selection-criteria]
[Order By column-list]
```

A Select statement that joins data from the Products and Categories tables

```
Select ShortName, ProductID, Name, UnitPrice
From Categories Inner Join Products
    On Categories.CategoryID = Products.CategoryID
Order By Categories.CategoryID
```

The result set defined by the Select statement

ShortName	ProductID	Name	UnitPrice
Costumes	frankc01	Frankenstein	39.9900
Costumes	hippie01	Hippie	79.9900
Costumes	jar01	JarJar	59.9900
Costumes	martian01	Martian	69.9900
Costumes	pow01	Austin Powers	79.9900
Costumes	super01	Superman	39.9900
FX	tlm01	T&L Machine	99.9900
FX	fog01	Fog Machine	34.9900
FX	fogj01	Fog Juice (1qt)	9.9900
FX	skullfog01	Skull Fogger	39.9500
FX	str01	Mini-strobe	13.9900
FX	bl01	Black Light (24")	24.9900
Masks	fred01	Freddie	29.9900
Masks	mum01	Mummy	39.9900
Masks	vader01	Darth Vader Ma...	19.9900
Props	rat01	Ugly Rat	14.9900
Props	rat02	Uglier Rat	19.9900
Props	skel01	Life-size Skeleton	14.9500
Props	head01	Michael Head	29.9900
Props	head02	Saw Head	29.9900
Props	cat01	Deranged Cat	19.9900
Props	arm01	Freddie Arm	19.9500
Props	bats01	Flying Bats	69.9900

Concepts

- A *join* lets you combine data from two or more tables into a single result set.
- The most common type of join is an *inner join*. This type of join returns rows from both tables only if their related columns match.

Figure 12-6   How to join data from two or more tables

How to add, update, and delete data in a table

Figure 12-7 presents the basic syntax of the SQL Insert, Update, and Delete statements. You use these statements to add new rows to a table, to update the data in existing rows, and to delete existing rows.

To add a single row to a table, you use an Insert statement with the syntax shown in this figure. With this syntax, you specify the name of the table you want to add the row to, the names of the columns you're supplying data for, and the values for those columns. In the example, the Insert statement adds a row to the Categories table and supplies a value for each of the three columns in that table. If a table allows nulls or provides default values for some columns, though, the Insert statement doesn't have to provide values for those columns. In addition, an Insert statement never provides a value for an identity column because that value is generated by the DBMS.

To change the values of one or more columns in one or more rows, you use the Update statement. On this statement, you specify the name of the table you want to update, expressions that indicate the columns you want to change and how you want to change them, and a condition that identifies the rows you want to change. In the example, the Update statement changes the ShortName value for just the one row in the Categories table that has a CategoryID value of "food."

To delete one or more rows from a table, you use the Delete statement. On this statement, you specify the table you want to delete rows from and a condition that indicates the rows you want to delete. In the example, the Delete statement deletes just the one row in the Categories table whose CategoryID column is "food."

How to add a single row

The syntax of the Insert statement for adding a single row

```
Insert [Into] table-name [(column-list)]
    Values (value-list)
```

A statement that adds a single row to a table

```
Insert Into Categories (CategoryID, ShortName, LongName)
    Values ('food', 'Spooky Food', 'The very best in Halloween cuisine')
```

How to update rows

The syntax of the Update statement

```
Update table-name
    Set expression-1 [, expression-2]...
    [Where selection-criteria]
```

A statement that changes the value of the ShortName column for a selected row

```
Update Categories
    Set ShortName = 'Halloween cuisine'
    Where CategoryID = 'food'
```

How to delete rows

The syntax of the Delete statement

```
Delete [From] table-name
    [Where selection-criteria]
```

A statement that deletes a specified category

```
Delete From Categories
    Where CategoryID = 'food'
```

Description

- You use the Insert, Update, and Delete statements to maintain the data in a database table.

- The Insert statement can be used to add one or more rows to a table. Although the syntax shown above is for adding just one row, there is another syntax for adding more than one row.

- The Update and Delete statements can be used for updating or deleting one or more rows in a table using the syntax shown above.

Figure 12-7   How to add, update, and delete data in a table

An introduction to ADO.NET 4

ADO.NET 4 (ActiveX Data Objects) is the primary data access API for the .NET Framework. It provides the classes that are used when you develop database applications. The topics that follow introduce you to the important ADO.NET concepts.

How the basic ADO.NET components work

Figure 12-8 presents the primary ADO.NET objects that are used when you develop database applications. To start, the data used by an application is stored in a *dataset* that contains one or more *data tables*. To load data into a data table, you use a *data adapter*.

The main function of the data adapter is to manage the flow of data between a dataset and a database. To do that, it uses *commands* that define the SQL statements to be issued. The command for retrieving data, for example, typically defines a Select statement. Then, the command connects to the database using a *connection* and passes the Select statement to the database. After the Select statement is executed, the result set it produces is sent back to the data adapter, which stores the results in the data table.

To update the data in a database, the data adapter uses a command that defines an Insert, Update, or Delete statement for a data table. Then, the command uses the connection to connect to the database and perform the requested operation.

Although it's not apparent in this figure, the data in a dataset is independent of the database that the data was retrieved from. In fact, the connection to the database is typically closed after the data is retrieved from the database. Then, the connection is opened again when it's needed. Because of that, the application must work with the copy of the data that's stored in the dataset. The architecture that's used to implement this type of data processing is referred to as a *disconnected data architecture*. Although this is more complicated than a connected architecture, the advantages offset the complexity.

One of the advantages of using a disconnected data architecture is improved system performance due to the use of fewer system resources for maintaining connections. Another advantage is that it works well with ASP.NET web applications, which are inherently disconnected.

The ADO.NET classes that are responsible for working directly with a database are provided by the *.NET data providers*. These data providers include the classes you use to create data adapters, commands, and connections. The .NET Framework currently includes data providers for SQL Server, Oracle, OLE DB, and ODBC, although the Oracle data provider has been deprecated. Other third-party providers are also available.

Basic ADO.NET objects

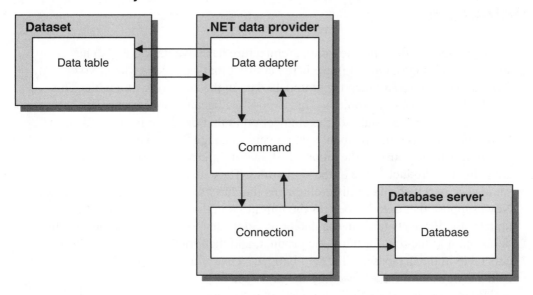

Description

- ADO.NET uses two types of objects to access the data in a database: *datasets*, which can contain one or more *data tables*, and *.NET data provider* objects, which include data adapters, commands, and connections.

- A dataset stores data from the database so it can be accessed by the application. The .NET data provider objects retrieve data from and update data in the database.

- To retrieve data from a database and store it in a data table, a *data adapter* object issues a Select statement that's stored in a *command* object. Next, the command object uses a *connection* object to connect to the database and retrieve the data. Then, the data is passed back to the data adapter, which stores the data in a table within the dataset.

- To update the data in a database based on the data in a data table, the data adapter object issues an Insert, Update, or Delete statement that's stored in a command object. Then, the command object uses a connection to connect to the database and update the data.

- The data provider remains connected to the database only long enough to retrieve or update the specified data. Then, it disconnects from the database and the application works with the data via the dataset object. This is referred to as a *disconnected data architecture.*

- All of the ADO.NET objects are implemented by classes in the System.Data namespace of the .NET Framework. However, the specific classes used to implement the connection, command, and data adapter objects depend on the .NET data provider you use.

Figure 12-8   How the basic ADO.NET components work

Concurrency and the disconnected data architecture

Although the disconnected data architecture has advantages, it also has some disadvantages. One of those is the conflict that can occur when two or more users retrieve and then try to update data in the same row of a table. This is called a *concurrency* problem. This is possible because once a program retrieves data from a database, the connection to that database is dropped. As a result, the database management system can't manage the update process.

To illustrate, consider the situation shown in figure 12-9. Here, two users are using the Products table at the same time. These users could be using the same page of a web site or different pages that have accessed the Products table. Now, suppose that user 1 modifies the unit price in the row for a product and updates the Products table in the database. Suppose too that user 2 modifies the description in the row for the same product, and then tries to update the Products table in the database. What will happen? That will depend on the *concurrency control* that's used by the programs.

When you use ADO.NET, you have two choices for concurrency control. By default, a program uses *optimistic concurrency*, which checks whether a row has been changed since it was retrieved. If it has, the update or deletion will be refused and a *concurrency exception* will be thrown. Then, the program should handle the error. For example, it could display an error message that tells the user that the row could not be updated and then retrieve the updated row so the user can make the change again.

In contrast, the *"last in wins"* technique works the way its name implies. Since no checking is done with this technique, the row that's updated by the last user overwrites any changes made to the row by a previous user. For the example above, the row updated by user 2 will overwrite changes made by user 1, which means that the description will be right but the unit price will be wrong. Since errors like this corrupt the data in a database, optimistic concurrency is used by most programs, which means that your programs have to handle the concurrency exceptions that are thrown.

If you know that concurrency will be a problem, you can use a couple of programming techniques to limit concurrency exceptions. If a program uses a dataset, one technique is to update the database frequently so other users can retrieve the current data. The program should also refresh its dataset frequently so it contains the recent changes made by other users.

Another way to avoid concurrency exceptions is to retrieve and work with just one row at a time. That way, it's less likely that two users will update the same row at the same time. In contrast, if two users retrieve the same table, they will of course retrieve the same rows. Then, if they both update the same row in the table, even though it may not be at the same time, a concurrency exception will occur when they try to update the database.

Two users who are working with copies of the same data

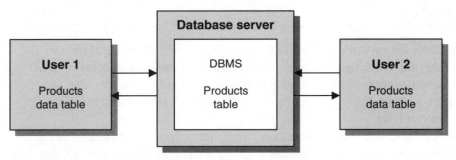

What happens when two users try to update the same row

- When two or more users retrieve the data in the same row of a database table at the same time, it is called *concurrency*. Because ADO.NET uses a disconnected data architecture, the database management system can't prevent this from happening.

- If two users try to update the same row in a database table at the same time, the second user's changes could overwrite the changes made by the first user. Whether or not that happens depends on the *concurrency control* that the programs use.

- By default, ADO.NET uses *optimistic concurrency*. This means that the program checks to see whether the database row that's going to be updated or deleted has been changed since it was retrieved. If it has, a *concurrency exception* occurs and the update or deletion is refused. Then, the program should handle the exception.

- If optimistic concurrency isn't in effect, the program doesn't check to see whether a row has been changed before an update or deletion takes place. Instead, the operation proceeds without throwing an exception. This is referred to as "*last in wins*" because the last update overwrites any previous update. And this can lead to errors in the database.

How to avoid concurrency errors

- For many applications, concurrency errors rarely occur. As a result, optimistic concurrency is adequate because the users will rarely have to resubmit an update or deletion that is refused.

- If concurrency is likely to be a problem, a program that uses a dataset can be designed so it updates the database and refreshes the dataset frequently. That way, concurrency errors are less likely to occur.

- Another way to avoid concurrency errors is to design a program so it retrieves and updates just one row at a time. That way, there's less chance that two users will retrieve and update the same row at the same time.

Figure 12-9   Concurrency and the disconnected data architecture

How to work with data without using a data adapter

When you want to work with two or more rows from a database at the same time, you typically use a data adapter to retrieve those rows and store them in a dataset as described earlier in this chapter. You should know, however, that you can also work with the data in a database without using a data adapter. Figure 12-10 shows you how.

As you can see, you still use command and connection objects to access the database. Instead of using a data adapter to execute the commands, though, you execute the commands directly. When you do that, you also have to provide code to handle the result of the command. If you issue a command that contains an Insert, Update, or Delete statement, for example, the result is an integer that indicates the number of rows that were affected by the operation. You can use that information to determine if the operation was successful.

If you execute a command that contains a Select statement, the result is a result set that contains the rows you requested. To read through the rows in the result set, you use a *data reader* object. Although a data reader provides an efficient way of reading the rows in a result set, you can't use it to modify those rows. In addition, it only lets you read rows in a forward direction. Once you read the next row, the previous row is unavailable. Because of that, you typically use a data reader to retrieve and work with a single database row at a time.

ADO.NET components for accessing a database directly

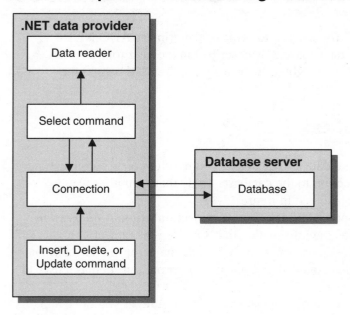

Description

- Instead of using a data adapter to execute commands to retrieve, insert, update, and delete data from a database, you can execute those commands directly.

- To retrieve data from a database, you execute a command object that contains a Select statement. Then, the command object uses a connection to connect to the database and retrieve the data. You can then read the results one row at a time using a *data reader* object.

- To insert, update, or delete data in a database, you execute a command object that contains an Insert, Update, or Delete statement. Then, the command object uses a connection to connect to the database and update the data. You can then check the value that's returned to determine if the operation was successful.

- If you use this technique in an application that maintains the data in a database, you typically work with a single row at a time. Because of that, the chance of a concurrency error is reduced.

Figure 12-10   How to work with data without using a data adapter

An introduction to the ADO.NET 4 classes

The topics that follow introduce you to some of the primary ADO.NET 4 classes. When you use SQL data sources as described in the next four chapters, though, you don't use these classes directly. Instead, they're used behind the scenes.

The SqlConnection class

Before you can access the data in a database, you have to create a connection object that defines the connection to the database. To do that, you use the SqlConnection class that's presented in figure 12-11.

The most important property of this class is ConnectionString. A *connection string* is a string that provides the information that's needed to connect to a database. That means it includes information such as the name of the database and the database server. It can also contain authentication information such as a user-id and password.

The two methods of this class that are shown in this figure let you open and close the connection. In general, you should leave a connection open only while data is being retrieved or updated. When you use a data adapter, though, the connection is opened and closed for you so you don't need to use these methods.

The SqlCommand class

To execute a SQL statement against a SQL Server database, you create a SqlCommand object that contains the statement. Figure 12-11 presents the SqlCommand class you use to create this object. Notice that the Connection property of this class associates the command with a SqlConnection object, and the CommandText property contains the SQL statement to be executed.

The CommandType property indicates how the command object should interpret the value of the CommandText property. Instead of specifying a SQL statement for the CommandText property, for example, you can specify the name of a stored procedure, which consists of one or more SQL statements that have been compiled and stored with the database.

Earlier in this chapter, you learned that you can use a data adapter to execute command objects. In addition, you can execute a command object directly by using one of the three Execute methods shown in this figure. If, for example, you use ExecuteReader for a Select statement, the results are returned as a DataReader object. If you use ExecuteScalar, only the value in the first column and row of the query results is returned.

If the command contains an Insert, Update, or Delete statement, you'll use the ExecuteNonQuery method to execute it. This method returns an integer value that indicates the number of rows that were affected by the command. If, for example, the command deletes a single row, the ExecuteNonQuery method returns 1.

Common members of the SqlConnection class

Property	Description
ConnectionString	Contains information that lets you connect to a SQL Server database, including the server name, the database name, and login information.

Method	Description
Open	Opens a connection to a database.
Close	Closes a connection to a database.

Common members of the SqlCommand class

Property	Description
Connection	The SqlConnection object used to connect to the database.
CommandText	The text of the SQL statement or the name of a stored procedure.
CommandType	A constant in the CommandType enumeration that indicates whether the CommandText property contains a SQL statement (Text) or the name of a stored procedure (StoredProcedure).
Parameters	The collection of parameters used by the command.

Method	Description
ExecuteReader	Executes a query and returns the result as a SqlDataReader object.
ExecuteNonQuery	Executes the command and returns an integer representing the number of rows affected.
ExecuteScalar	Executes a query and returns the first column of the first row returned by the query.

Common members of the SqlParameter class

Property	Description
ParameterName	The name of the parameter.
Value	The value assigned to the parameter.
SqlDbType	The SQL data type for the parameter.

Description

- A SqlConnection object is required to establish a connection to a SQL Server database.
- A SqlCommand object is used to execute a SQL command against a SQL Server database.
- A SqlParameter object is used to pass variable information to a SQL command.

Figure 12-11   The SqlConnection, SqlCommand, and SqlParameter classes

The SqlParameter class

The SqlParameter class, also shown in figure 12-11, lets you pass parameter values to a SQL command. Parameters are commonly used to limit the number of rows retrieved by a Select statement. For example, you can retrieve the Product row for a specific product by passing the ProductID as a parameter. Or, you can retrieve all of the products for a given category by passing the CategoryID as a parameter. Parameters are also commonly used to pass column values to Insert, Update, and Delete statements.

The SqlDataReader class

Figure 12-12 lists the most important members of the SqlDataReader class. You use this class to create a data reader object, which provides an efficient way to read the rows in a result set returned by a database query. In fact, when you use a data adapter to retrieve data, the data adapter uses a data reader to read through the rows in the result set and store them in a dataset.

The SqlDataAdapter class

As you have learned, the job of a data adapter is to provide a link between a database and a dataset. The four properties of the SqlDataAdapter class listed in figure 12-12, for example, identify the four SQL commands that the data adapter uses to transfer data from the database to the dataset and vice versa. The SelectCommand property identifies the command object that's used to retrieve data from the database. And the DeleteCommand, InsertCommand, and UpdateCommand properties identify the commands that are used to update the database based on changes made to the data in the dataset.

To execute the command identified by the SelectCommand property and place the data that's retrieved in a dataset, you use the Fill method. Then, the application can work with the data in the dataset without affecting the data in the database. If the application makes changes to the data in the dataset, it can use the data adapter's Update method to execute the commands identified by the DeleteCommand, InsertCommand, and UpdateCommand properties and post the changes back to the database.

Common members of the SqlDataReader class

Indexer	Description
[index]	Accesses the column with the specified index from the current row.
[name]	Accesses the column with the specified name from the current row.

Property	Description
IsClosed	Gets a Boolean value that indicates if the data reader is closed.

Method	Description
Read	Reads the next row. Returns True if there are more rows. Otherwise, returns False.
Close	Closes the data reader.

Common members of the SqlDataAdapter class

Property	Description
SelectCommand	A SqlCommand object representing the Select statement used to query the database.
DeleteCommand	A SqlCommand object representing the Delete statement used to delete a row from the database.
InsertCommand	A SqlCommand object representing the Insert statement used to add a row to the database.
UpdateCommand	A SqlCommand object representing the Update statement used to update a row in the database.

Method	Description
Fill	Executes the command identified by the SelectCommand property and loads the result into a dataset object.
Update	Executes the commands identified by the DeleteCommand, InsertCommand, and UpdateCommand properties for each row in the dataset that was deleted, added, or updated.

Description

- A data reader provides read-only, forward-only access to the data in a database. Because it doesn't require the overhead of a dataset, it's more efficient than using a data adapter. However, it can't be used to update data.
- When the Fill method of a data adapter is used to retrieve data from a database, the data adapter uses a data reader to load the results into a dataset.

Figure 12-12   The SqlDataReader and SqlDataAdapter classes

Perspective

This chapter has introduced you to the basic concepts of relational databases and described how you use SQL and ADO.NET classes to work with the data in a relational database. With that as background, you're now ready to learn how to develop ASP.NET database applications.

In the next four chapters, then, you'll learn how to use SQL data sources and five of the data controls to build database applications. After that, chapter 17 will show you how to use object data sources to build 3-layer database applications. Although you don't need to use ADO.NET directly when you use SQL data sources, you do need to use ADO.NET directly when you use object data sources.

Terms

Microsoft SQL Server Express	identity column
Microsoft SQL Server 2008	check constraint
relational database	SQL dialect
table	Transact-SQL
record	result table
row	result set
field	calculated column
column	join
primary key	inner join
composite primary key	ADO.NET
non-primary key	ActiveX Data Objects .NET
unique key	dataset
unique key constraint	data table
unique constraint	.NET data provider
index	data adapter
foreign key	command
foreign key table	connection
primary key table	disconnected data architecture
one-to-many relationship	concurrency
one-to-one relationship	concurrency control
many-to-many relationship	optimistic concurrency
linking table	concurrency exception
data type	last in wins
system data type	data reader
null value	connection string
default value	

13

How to use SQL data sources

In this chapter, you'll learn how to use the SqlDataSource control, which lets you access data from a SQL Server database with little or no programming. Along the way, you'll also learn how to use the DataList control, which lets you create lists of data.

How to create a SQL data source

In chapter 3, you learned the basics of using the AccessDataSource control to get data from an Access database. Now, in the topics that follow, you'll learn how to use a SqlDataSource control, which can be referred to as a *SQL data source,* to get data from a SQL Server database.

A Product List application that uses two SQL data sources

Figure 13-1 shows a simple one-page application that demonstrates the use of two SQL data sources. The drop-down list at the top of the page is bound to a SQL data source that gets the categories for the products that the company offers. Then, when the user selects a category from this list, the products for the selected category are retrieved from a second SQL data source, which is bound to a DataList control that's below the drop-down list. As a result, the products are displayed in the DataList control.

Since this application relies entirely on the data binding that's established in the Web Forms Designer, the code-behind file for this application contains no C# code. Although this is a simple application, even complicated applications that insert, update, and delete database data can often be written with little or no code.

That's not to say that most ASP.NET database applications are code-free. In chapters 14, 15, and 16, for example, you'll see applications that require database handling code. In particular, these applications require code to detect database errors and concurrency violations and display appropriate error messages. Also, as you'll learn in chapter 17, you can use object data sources to build 3-layer applications that require extensive amounts of database handling code.

The Product List application displayed in a web browser

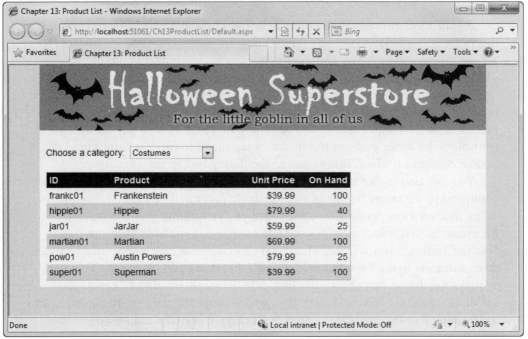

Description

- The Product List application uses two SqlDataSource controls to get category and product data from a SQL Server database and display it in two bound controls.
- The drop-down list near the top of the form displays the product categories. This control is bound to the first data source control.
- The DataList control, which is bound to the second data source control, displays the data for the products that are in the category that's selected in the drop-down list.
- This application requires no C# code in the code-behind file.

Figure 13-1   The Product List application

How to create a SqlDataSource control

Figure 13-2 shows how to create a SqlDataSource control. As you will see, this process is similar to the one for creating an AccessDataSource control. To get the process started, you can drag a SqlDataSource control onto the form you're developing.

Since a data source control isn't displayed on the page when the application is run, it doesn't matter where you drop this control. But it does make sense to place it near the control that it will be bound to. Once you've got the data source control on the form, you can use its smart tag menu to run the Configure Data Source command, which brings you to the dialog box in the next figure.

You can also create a SqlDataSource control using the Choose Data Source command in the smart tag menu of a bindable control. The exact technique for doing that varies depending on the control you're binding. For a drop-down list, for example, you select the Choose Data Source command to start the Data Source Configuration Wizard. Then, you can choose New Data Source from the drop-down list in the first dialog box that's displayed and click OK. That displays the dialog box shown in this figure. From this dialog box, you can select the Database icon and click OK, which drops the data source control onto the form next to the bindable control and brings you to the dialog box in the next figure.

The technique for creating a SQL data source from a DataList control is similar. The only difference is that the Choose Data Source command in the control's smart tag menu includes a drop-down list that lets you select New Data Source. When you do that, the Data Source Configuration Wizard dialog box shown in this figure is displayed just as it is for a drop-down list.

The starting dialog box of the Data Source Configuration Wizard

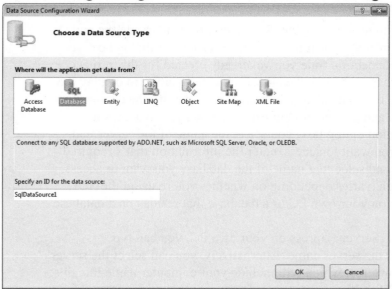

Aspx code generated for a basic SqlDataSource control

```
<asp:SqlDataSource ID="SqlDataSource1" runat="server"
    ConnectionString="<%$ ConnectionStrings:HalloweenConnectionString %>"
    SelectCommand="SELECT [CategoryID], [LongName] FROM [Categories]
        ORDER BY [LongName]">
</asp:SqlDataSource>
```

Basic SqlDataSource control attributes

Attribute	Description
ID	The ID for the SqlDataSource control.
Runat	Must specify "server."
ConnectionString	The connection string. In most cases, you should use a <%$ expression to specify the name of a connection string saved in the web.config file (see figure 13-4).
ProviderName	The name of the provider used to access the database. Values can be System.Data.Odbc, System.Data.Oledb, System.Data.OracleClient, or System.Data.SqlClient. The default is System.Data.SqlClient.
SelectCommand	The SQL Select statement executed by the data source to retrieve data.

Description

- To create a SqlDataSource control, drag the control from the Data group of the Toolbox onto the form. Then, choose Configure Data Source from the control's smart tag menu and proceed from there.

- You can also create a SQL data source using the Choose Data Source command in the smart tag menu of a bindable control. When you use this command, the dialog box shown above is displayed. Then, you can select the Database icon and proceed from there.

Figure 13-2   How to create a SqlDataSource control

How to define the connection

The first step in configuring a SqlDataSource control is to create the connection for the data source, as shown in figure 13-3. From this dialog box, you can select an existing connection (one you've already created for this project or for another project), or you can click the New Connection button to display the Add Connection dialog box. This dialog box helps you identify the database that you want to access and provide the information you need to access it.

In the Add Connection dialog box, you select the name of the server that contains the database you want to access, enter the information that's required to log on to the server, and select the name of the database you want to access. How you do that, though, varies depending on whether you're using the SQL Server Express Edition on your own PC or a database that resides on a database server.

If you're using SQL Server Express on your own PC, you can type localhost\sqlexpress for the server name. Alternatively, you can select the server name from the drop-down list, which will include your computer name like this: ANNE-PC\SQLEXPRESS. If you will be porting your applications from one computer to another, though, it's best to use localhost. That way, you won't have to change the server name to refer to the correct computer.

For the logon information, you can click on the Use Windows Authentication option. Then, SQL Server Express will use the login name and password that you use for your computer as the name and password for the database too. As a result, you won't need to provide a separate user name and password in this dialog box. Last, you select the name of the database that you want to connect to. When you're done, you can click on the Test Connection button to be sure that the connection works.

In contrast, if you're using a database on a server computer, you need to get the connection information from the network or database administrator. That will include the server name, logon information, and database name. Once you establish a connection to a database, you can use that connection for all of the other applications that use that database.

The first time you create a connection, Visual Studio displays the Change Data Source dialog box. You can use this dialog box, which isn't shown here, to select the data source and data provider you want to use. For a SQL Server database, you can select Microsoft SQL Server as the data source and the provider will default to .NET Framework Data Provider for SQL Server. This works for SQL Server 2005 and 2008 databases including SQL Server Express databases. If you ever need to access a different type of database, you can click the Change button in the Add Connection dialog box to display the Change Data Source dialog box again.

The dialog boxes for defining a connection

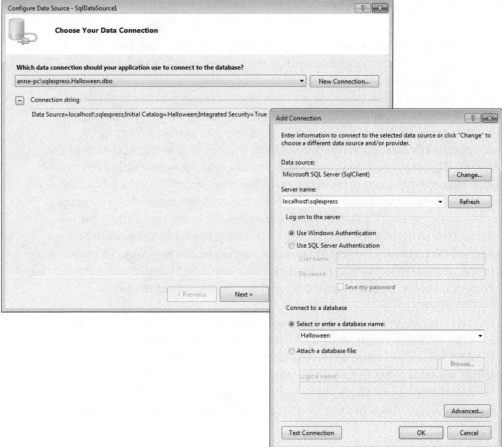

Description

- The Configure Data Source dialog box asks you to identify the data connection for the database you want to use. If you've previously created a connection for that database, you can select it from the drop-down list. To see the connection string for that connection, click the + button below the drop-down list.

- To create a new connection, click the New Connection button to display the Add Connection dialog box. Then, enter the name of the database server in the Server Name text box or select it from the drop-down list. For SQL Server Express, you can use localhost\sqlexpress as the server name.

- After you enter the server name, select the authentication mode you want to use (I recommend Windows Authentication). Then, select the database you want to connect to from the Select or Enter a Database Name drop-down list.

- To be sure that the connection is configured properly, you can click the Test Connection button.

Figure 13-3   How to define the connection

How to save the connection string in the web.config file

Although you can hard-code connection strings into your programs, it's much better to store connection strings in the application's web.config file. That way, if you move the database to another server or make some other change that affects the connection string, you won't have to recompile the application. Instead, you can simply change the connection string in the web.config file.

As figure 13-4 shows, ASP.NET can store connection strings in the web.config file automatically if you check the Yes box in the next step of the wizard. That way, you don't have to manually edit the web.config file or write code to retrieve the connection string. When you select this check box, the connection string will automatically be saved with the name that you supply.

This figure also shows the entries made in the web.config file when a connection string is saved. Here, the web.config file has a connectionStrings element that contains an add element for each connection string. In the example, the connection string is named HalloweenConnectionString, and the connection string refers to a database named Halloween on the server named localhost\sqlexpress.

Last, this figure shows how the aspx code that's generated for a data source can refer to the connection string by name. Here, the shaded portion of the example shows the value of the ConnectionString attribute. As you can see, it begins with the word ConnectionStrings followed by a colon and the name of the connection string you want to use. Note that this code is automatically generated by the Data Source Configuration Wizard, so you don't have to write it yourself.

The dialog box for saving the connection string in the web.config file

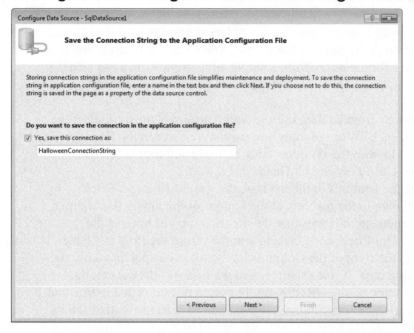

The ConnectionStrings section of the web.config file

```
<connectionStrings>
    <add name="HalloweenConnectionString"
      connectionString="Data Source=localhost\sqlexpress;
      Initial Catalog=Halloween;Integrated Security=True"
      providerName="System.Data.SqlClient" />
</connectionStrings>
```

Aspx code that refers to a connection string in the web.config file

```
<asp:SqlDataSource ID="SqlDataSource1" runat="server"
    ConnectionString="<%$ ConnectionStrings:HalloweenConnectionString %>"
    SelectCommand="SELECT [CategoryID], [LongName] FROM [Categories]
        ORDER BY [LongName]">
</asp:SqlDataSource>
```

Description

- ASP.NET applications can store connection strings in the web.config file.

- If you choose to save the connection string in the web.config file, the ConnectionString attribute of the data source control will include a special code that retrieves the connection string from the web.config file.

- If you choose not to save the connection string in the web.config file, the ConnectionString attribute of the data source control will specify the actual connection string.

- I recommend that you always save the connection string in the web.config file. Then, if the location of the database changes, you can change the connection string in the web.config file rather than in each data source that uses the connection.

Figure 13-4   How to save the connection string in the web.config file

How to configure the Select statement

Figure 13-5 shows how to configure the Select statement for a data source as you proceed through the steps of the wizard. The easiest way to do that is to choose the columns for the query from a single table or view. You can also specify a custom SQL statement or stored procedure as shown later in this chapter.

To select columns from a table, use the Name drop-down list to select the table. Then, check each of the columns you want to retrieve in the Columns list box. In this figure, I chose the Products table and selected four columns: ProductID, Name, UnitPrice, and OnHand.

As you check the columns in the list box, the wizard creates a Select statement that's shown in the text box at the bottom of the dialog box. In this case, the Select statement indicates that the data source will retrieve the ProductID, Name, UnitPrice, and OnHand columns from the Products table.

The buttons to the right of the Columns list box let you specify additional options for selecting data. If, for example, you want to sort the data that's retrieved, you can click on the ORDER BY button to display a dialog box that lets you select up to three sort columns. If you want to select rows that satisfy certain criteria, you can click on the WHERE button to display the dialog box that's described in the next figure. And if you want to use an advanced feature, you can click on the Advanced button to display the dialog box that's described in figure 13-16.

When you finish specifying the data you want the data source to retrieve, click Next. This takes you to a dialog box that includes a Test Query button. If you click this button, the wizard immediately retrieves the data that you specified. You can then look over this data to make sure the query retrieves the data you expected. If it doesn't, you can click the Back button and adjust the query as needed.

The dialog box for defining the Select statement

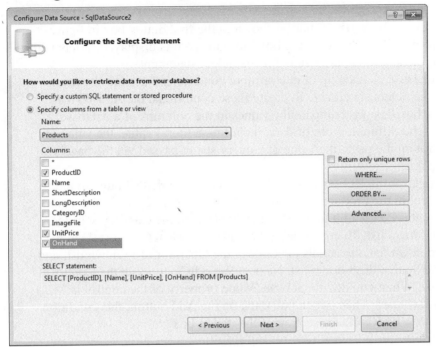

Description

- To configure the Select statement, you choose whether you want to use a custom SQL statement or specify the columns from a table or view in the database.

- If you choose to select the columns from a table or view, you can choose the table or view and columns you want retrieved. You can click the ORDER BY button to specify how the records should be sorted. And you can click the WHERE button to specify the selection criteria as shown in figure 13-6.

- If you choose to use custom SQL statements, the next dialog box lets you enter the SQL statements as shown in figure 13-8 or click the Query Builder button to build the query as shown in figure 13-9.

Figure 13-5   How to configure the Select statement

How to create a Where clause

If you click on the WHERE button shown in the first dialog box in figure 13-5, the Add WHERE Clause dialog box in figure 13-6 is displayed. It lets you create a Where clause and parameters for the Select statement.

A Where clause is made up of one or more conditions that limit the rows retrieved by the Select statement. To create these conditions, the Add WHERE Clause dialog box lets you compare the values in the columns of a database table with several different types of data, including a literal value, the value of another control on the page, the value of a query string passed via the page's URL, or a cookie.

For example, the Select statement for the data source that's bound to the DataList control in the Product List application uses a Where clause that compares the CategoryID column in the Products table with the category selected from the drop-down list. To create this Where clause, select CategoryID in the Column drop-down list, the equals operator in the Operator drop-down list, and Control in the Source drop-down list. Next, select ddlCategory in the Control ID drop-down list. When you do, the SelectedValue property of the control is automatically selected. Then, when you click on the Add button, this condition is shown in the WHERE clause section of the dialog box.

The Add WHERE Clause dialog box

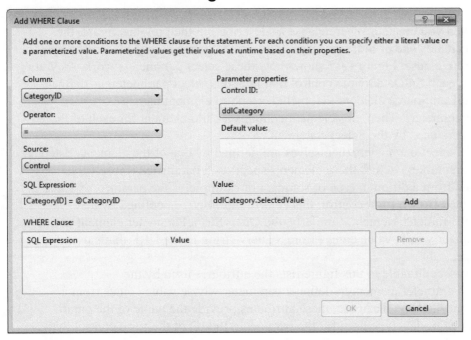

The WHERE clause section after a condition has been added

Description

- The Add WHERE Clause dialog box lets you specify a Where clause for the Select statement.
- The Where clause consists of one or more conditions that you construct by using the controls in this dialog box. To create a condition, you select the column you want to compare, the operator you want to use for the comparison, and the source of the data to use for the comparison. Then, you must click Add to add the condition to the list of Where clause conditions.
- The source of the data for the comparison can be a literal value, the value of another control on the form, a cookie, an HTML form field, a profile property, a query string in the URL for the page, or a value stored in session state.

Remember

- After you select the column, operator, and source for the comparison, be sure to click the Add button to add the condition to the generated Where clause. Otherwise, the condition won't be added to the Where clause.

Figure 13-6   How to create a Where clause

How select parameters work

When you create a Where clause as described in the previous figure, the wizard creates one or more *select parameters* that provide the values used by the Where clause. Figure 13-7 shows how these select parameters work. As you can see, each SqlDataSource control that includes select parameters is defined by a SqlDataSource element that includes a child element named SelectParameters. Then, this element contains a child element for each of the parameters used by the Select statement.

The select parameters themselves are defined by one of the elements listed in the first table. Each of these elements specifies a parameter whose value is obtained from a different type of source. For example, if the parameter's value is obtained from a form control, this *control parameter* is defined by a ControlParameter element. Similarly, the QueryStringParameter element defines a parameter whose value comes from a query string in the URL that's used for the page.

The second table in this figure lists the attributes used by the ControlParameter element to define a parameter whose value comes from a form control. As you can see, these attributes provide the name of the parameter, the SQL data type used for the parameter, the ID of the form control that provides the value, and the name of the property used to obtain the value.

The code example at the top of this figure shows the aspx code generated for the second SqlDataSource control used by the Product List application. Here, the Select statement uses one parameter named CategoryID. This parameter is defined by a ControlParameter element whose Name attribute is set to CategoryID. The SQL data type for this parameter is String, and the parameter's value is obtained from the SelectedValue property of the form control whose ID is ddlCategory.

Please note that the code in this example is generated by the Web Forms Designer when you configure the data source using the Data Source Configuration Wizard. As a result, you don't have to write this code yourself.

The aspx code for a SqlDataSource control that includes a select parameter

```
<asp:SqlDataSource ID="SqlDataSource2" runat="server"
    ConnectionString="<%$ ConnectionStrings:HalloweenConnectionString %>"
    SelectCommand="SELECT [ProductID], [Name], [UnitPrice], [OnHand]
        FROM [Products]
        WHERE ([CategoryID] = @CategoryID)
        ORDER BY [ProductID]">
    <SelectParameters>
        <asp:ControlParameter Name="CategoryID" Type="String"
            ControlID="ddlCategory" PropertyName="SelectedValue" />
    </SelectParameters>
</asp:SqlDataSource>
```

Elements used to define select parameters

Element	Description
SelectParameters	Contains a child element for each parameter used by the data source's Select statement.
Parameter	Defines a parameter with a constant value.
ControlParameter	Defines a parameter that gets its value from a control on the page.
QueryStringParameter	Defines a parameter that gets its value from a query string in the URL used to request the page.
FormParameter	Defines a parameter that gets its value from an HTML form field.
SessionParameter	Defines a parameter that gets its value from an item in session state.
ProfileParameter	Defines a parameter that gets its value from a profile property.
CookieParameter	Defines a parameter that gets its value from a cookie.

Attributes of the ControlParameter element

Attribute	Description
Name	The parameter name.
Type	The SQL data type of the parameter.
ControlID	The ID of the web form control that supplies the value for the parameter.
PropertyName	The name of the property from the web form control that supplies the value for the parameter.

Description

- The SelectParameters element defines the *select parameters* that are used by the Select statement of a data source. The aspx code that defines these parameters is generated automatically when you use the Add WHERE Clause dialog box to create parameters.

- A *control parameter* is a parameter whose value is obtained from another control on a web form, such as the value selected by a drop-down list. Control parameters are defined by the ControlParameter element.

- Once you understand how to use control parameters, you shouldn't have any trouble learning how to use the other types of parameters on your own.

Figure 13-7   How select parameters work

How to use custom statements and stored procedures

Earlier in this chapter, you learned how to configure the Select statement for a SQL data source by selecting columns from a table. If you need to code a Select statement that's more complex than what you can create using this technique, you can define your own custom statements. To do that, you can enter the statements directly, or you can use the Query Builder. You can also use stored procedures that have been defined within the database.

How to enter custom statements

If you select the first option from the dialog box shown in figure 13-5 and then click the Next button, the dialog box shown in figure 13-8 is displayed. As you can see, this dialog box includes tabs that let you enter Select, Update, Insert, and Delete statements for the data source. In this case, the Select statement is the same as the one that was generated by the wizard as shown earlier in this chapter. Because of that, you might think that you wouldn't need to enter a custom Select statement. Keep in mind, though, that when you create a Select statement by selecting columns from a table, you have no control over the Update, Insert, and Delete statements that are generated. So if you want to use statements other than those that are generated automatically, you can do that by entering custom statements.

How to select stored procedures

If the stored procedures you want to use to select, insert, update, and delete data have already been defined in the database, you can easily use them in a SQL data source. To do that, you select the Stored Procedure option from the appropriate tab of the dialog box shown in figure 13-8. Then, you select the stored procedure you want to use for the operation from the drop-down list that becomes available.

The dialog box for entering a custom Select statement

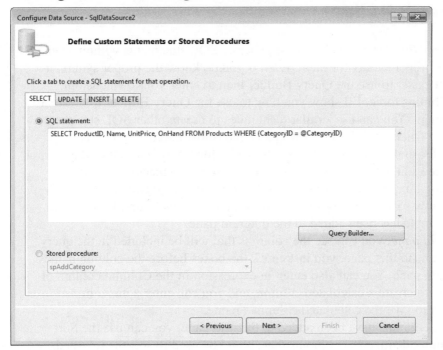

Description

- To use custom statements with a SQL data source, select the SQL Statement option and then enter the statement into the text box. You can enter Select, Update, Insert, and Delete statements by selecting the appropriate tab.

- You can also generate custom statements using the Query Builder as shown in figure 13-9.

- To use stored procedures with a SQL data source, select the Stored Procedure option and then select the stored procedure you want to use from the drop-down list that's displayed.

- When you use custom statements, Visual Studio doesn't generate Update, Insert, and Delete statements from the Select statement you enter. Because of that, you have to enter each of these statements yourself or use the Query Builder to generate them.

Figure 13-8   How to enter custom statements or select stored procedures

How to create a Select statement with the Query Builder

The *Query Builder* makes it easy to generate SQL statements without even knowing the proper syntax for them. Even if you do know the proper syntax, it can be much easier to use the Query Builder than to enter your own custom statements. In this topic, I'll show you how to use the Query Builder to create a Select statement. You can use similar techniques to create other SQL statements.

When the Query Builder window opens, the Add Table dialog box is displayed. This dialog box, which isn't shown in this figure, lists all of the tables and views in the database that the data source is connected to. You can use this dialog box to add one or more tables to the *diagram pane* of the Query Builder window so you can use them in your query. In this figure, for example, the Products table has been added to the diagram pane.

In the *grid pane*, you can see the columns that will be included in the query. To add columns to this pane, you just check the boxes before the column names in the diagram pane. You can also enter an expression in the Column column of the grid pane to create a calculated column, and you can enter a name in the Alias column to give the calculated column a name.

Once the columns have been added to the grid pane, you can use the Sort Type column to identify any columns that should be used to sort the returned rows and the Sort Order column to give the order of precedence for the sort if more than one column is identified. The Query Builder uses these specifications to build the Order By clause for the Select statement.

You can use the Filter column to establish the criteria to be used to select the rows that will be retrieved by the query. For the query in this figure, a parameter named @CategoryID is specified for the CategoryID column. As a result, only the products whose CategoryID field matches the value of the @CategoryID parameter will be retrieved.

Notice in this figure that the Output column for the CategoryID column in the grid pane isn't selected. That means that this column won't be included in the query output. However, it's included in the grid pane so it can be used to specify the filter criteria.

The Query Builder dialog box

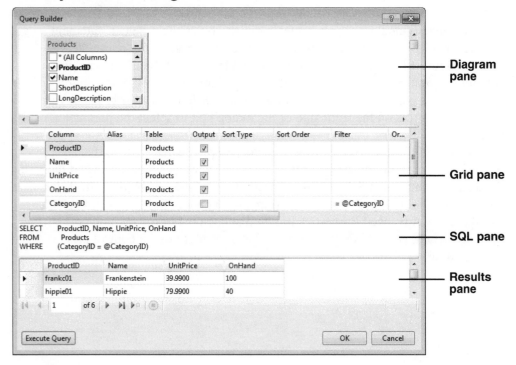

Diagram pane

Grid pane

SQL pane

Results pane

Description

- The *Query Builder* is displayed if you choose to enter a custom SQL statement, and then click the Query Builder button in the dialog box that follows.

- The Query Builder lets you build a Select statement by choosing columns from one or more tables and views and specifying the sort order and filter criteria for each column.

- When you first start the Query Builder, a dialog box is displayed that lets you select the database tables you want to include in the query. Each table you select is displayed in the *diagram pane* at the top of the Query Builder window.

- If you add two related tables to the diagram pane, the Query Builder automatically joins the two tables by including a Join phrase in the From clause.

- To include a column from a table, use the check box that appears next to the column in the diagram pane. This adds the column to the *grid pane*. Then, you can specify any sorting or filtering requirements for the column.

- You can use a parameter in an expression in the Filter column to create a parameterized query. If you use one or more parameters in the query, the Data Source Configuration Wizard lets you specify the source of each parameter value, as described in figure 13-10.

- As you select columns and specify sort and selection criteria, the Query Builder builds the Select statement and displays it in the *SQL pane*.

- To display the results of the query in the *results pane*, click the Execute Query button. If the query includes parameters, you will be asked to enter the value of each parameter.

Figure 13-9   How to create a Select statement with the Query Builder

How to define the parameters

If you specify one or more parameters when you create a Select statement with the Query Builder, the next dialog box lets you define those parameters as shown in figure 13-10. Here, the list box on the left side of the dialog box lists each of the parameters you created in the Query Builder. To define the source for one of these parameters, you select the parameter in this list box. Then, you can use the controls on the right side of the dialog box to select the parameter's source.

In this example, the source of the CategoryID parameter is set to the SelectedValue property of the control named ddlCategory. When I selected the ddlCategory control, the SelectedValue property was selected by default. If you want to use a different property as the source for a parameter, however, you can click the Show Advanced Properties link to display a list of the parameter properties. Then, you can set the PropertyName property to the control property you want to use.

The dialog box for defining parameters

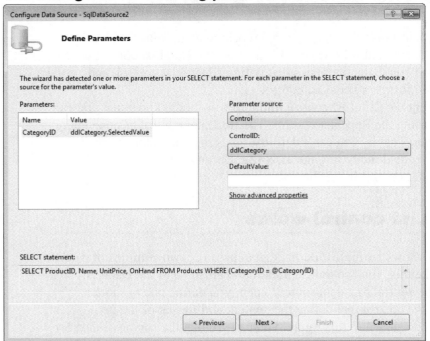

Parameter sources

Source	Description
Control	The parameter's value comes from a control on the page.
QueryString	The parameter's value comes from a query string in the URL used to request the page.
Form	The parameter's value comes from an HTML form field.
Session	The parameter's value comes from an item in session state.
Profile	The parameter's value comes from a profile property.
Cookie	The parameter's value comes from a cookie.

Description

- If you specify one or more parameters when you use the Query Builder to define a Select statement, the next dialog box lets you define those parameters.
- To define a parameter, you specify the source of the value for each parameter.

Figure 13-10   How to define the parameters

How to use the DataList control

A DataList control displays items from a repeating data source such as a data table. In the topics that follow, you'll learn how the DataList control works, you'll learn how to create the templates that define a DataList control, and you'll learn how to format a DataList control.

Before I present the DataList control, though, you should know that you can also create a list using the Repeater control. The Repeater control has one major drawback, however. That is, you can't define it using a visual interface. Instead, you have to enter code directly into the aspx file. Because of that, we won't present the Repeater control in this book.

How the DataList control works

Figure 13-11 shows a simple *data list* that consists of two columns of data. To create a list like this, you use the DataSourceID attribute of the DataList control to bind the control to a data source. Then, you define one or more *templates* within the control that define the content and format of the list.

In the aspx code shown in this figure, you can see that the source of data for the data list is a SQL data source control named SqlDataSource2. You can also see that a single Item template is used to create this list. This template includes two label controls that are bound to the Name and UnitPrice columns of the data source. You'll learn about the expressions you use to accomplish this binding later in this chapter.

A simple list displayed by a DataList control

Austin Powers $79.99
Frankenstein $39.99
Hippie $79.99
JarJar $59.99
Martian $69.99
Superman $39.99

The aspx code for the DataList control

```
<asp:DataList ID="DataList1" runat="server" DataSourceID="SqlDataSource2">
    <ItemTemplate>
        <asp:Label ID="lblName" runat="server"
            Text='<%# Eval("Name") %>'></asp:Label>
        <asp:Label ID="lblUnitPrice" runat="server"
            Text='<%# Eval("UnitPrice", "{0:C}") %>'></asp:Label>
    </ItemTemplate>
</asp:DataList>
```

Basic attributes of the DataList control

Attribute	Description
ID	The ID for the DataList control.
Runat	Must specify "server."
DataSourceID	The ID of the data source to bind the data list to.

Description

- A *data list* displays a list of items from the data source that it's bound to. To bind a data list to a data source, use the Choose Data Source command in the control's smart tag menu.

- To define the information to be displayed in a data list, you create one or more *templates*. Visual Studio provides a designer interface you can use to create the templates as shown in the next figure.

- To display the data from a column in the data source in a data list, you add a control to a template and then bind that control. See figure 13-14 for more information.

- You can use a DataList control for edit operations as well as display operations. However, you're more likely to use the GridView, DetailsView, FormView, and ListView controls for edit operations.

Figure 13-11   How the DataList control works

How to define the templates for a data list

Figure 13-12 shows you how to define the templates for a data list. The table in this figure lists the templates you're most likely to use. Although you can also create templates that let the user select and edit items in the list, you're not likely to use a DataList control for these functions. Instead, you'll use the GridView, DetailsView, FormView, or ListView controls as described in the next three chapters.

The only template that's required for a data list is the Item template, which defines how each item in the data source is displayed. Depending on the requirements of your application, though, you may need to use one or more of the other templates as well. For example, you'll typically use a Header template to create headings that are displayed in the first row of the data list.

To define the templates for a data list, you work in *template-editing mode*. At the top of this figure, for example, you can see the Item template for a list that includes four columns. This template is displayed by default when you enter template-editing mode. To display a different template, you can use the Display drop-down list in the smart tag menu for the control. You can also display a group of related templates by selecting the group name from this list. For example, you can display both the Header and Footer templates by selecting the Header and Footer Templates item.

If a data list consists of two or more columns, you'll want to place the text and controls in each template within a table. That way, you can set the width of each column in the data list by setting the widths of the columns in the table. In addition, if you add two or more templates to a data list, you can align the columns in the templates by setting the widths of the corresponding table columns to the same values. In this illustration, for example, I set the Width attributes of the corresponding columns in the Item template and the Header template to the same values.

Before I go on, you should realize that you use templates to define the content of a data list and not its appearance. For example, you use the AlternatingItem template to display different content for every other row in a data list, not to shade or highlight every other row. To format a data list, you use styles as shown in the next figure.

The Item template in template-editing mode

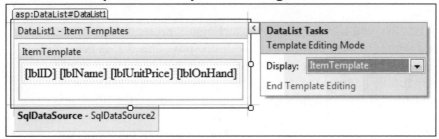

A Header template

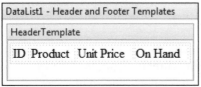

Common template elements for a data list

Element	Description
HeaderTemplate	Displayed before the first item in the data source.
FooterTemplate	Displayed after the last item in the data source.
ItemTemplate	Displayed for each item in the data source.
AlternatingItemTemplate	Displayed for alternating items in the data source.
SeparatorTemplate	Displayed between items.

Description

- The templates you define for a data list specify what content to display and what controls to use to display it. At the least, you must create an Item template that defines the items from the data source that you want to display.

- To create a template, choose Edit Templates from the smart tag menu for the control to display the control in *template-editing mode*. Then, select the template or group of templates you want to edit from the smart tag menu.

- To add text to a template, click in the template and begin typing. To add a control to a template, drag the control from the Toolbox onto the template, then use the Properties window or the control's smart tag menu to set its properties. When you're finished, choose End Template Editing from the smart tag menu.

- To line up the text and controls in two or more templates, place them in tables within the templates and set the column widths to the same values.

- When you set the data source for a DataList control, Visual Studio creates a default Item template. This template includes a text box for each column in the data source preceded by text that identifies the column.

Figure 13-12   How to define the templates for a data list

How to format a data list

To format a data list, you can use one of the techniques presented in figure 13-13. The easiest way is to use the Auto Format dialog box. This dialog box lets you select one of 17 predefined schemes that use different combinations of colors and borders for the items in the data list. To create the data list for the Product List application shown in figure 13-1, for example, I used the Black and Blue 1 scheme.

Another way to format a data list is to use the Format page of the Properties dialog box shown in this figure. This dialog box lets you set the colors, fonts, alignment, and other formatting options for the data list and each of its templates. Note that you can use this dialog box to customize an Auto Format scheme or to design your own scheme.

The Auto Format and Properties dialog boxes provide convenient ways to format a data list. However, you can also apply formatting directly from the Properties window. To do that, you use the properties in the Appearance and Style sections of this window, which are available when you display the properties by category. The properties in the Appearance section apply to the data list as a whole, and the properties in the Style section apply to the templates that make up the data list. To set the properties for the Item template, for example, you can expand the ItemStyle group, and to set the properties for the Header template, you can expand the HeaderStyle group.

This figure also presents the five style elements you're most likely to use with a data list. When you use one of the techniques in this figure to format the templates in a data list, the appropriate style elements are generated for you. In this figure, for example, you can see the HeaderStyle element that was generated when I applied the Black and Blue 1 scheme to the product list in figure 13-1. Of course, you can also format a data list by entering style elements directly into the aspx code. That's not usually necessary, however.

Instead of using the style elements shown here to format a data list, you can use CSS. Because a data list is rendered to nested HTML tables, though, that can be difficult to do. In most cases, then, you'll use the style elements instead.

The Format page of the Properties dialog box

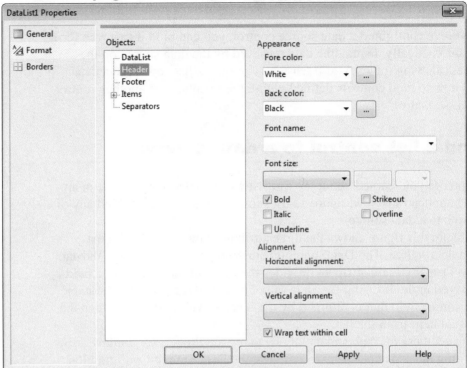

Common style elements for a data list

Element	Description
HeaderStyle	The style used for the header.
FooterStyle	The style used for the footer.
ItemStyle	The style used for each item in the data source.
AlternatingItemStyle	The style used for alternating items in the data source.
SeparatorStyle	The style for the separator.

The asp tag for a Header style

```
<HeaderStyle BackColor="Black" Font-Bold="True" ForeColor="White" />
```

Description

- You can format a data list by applying a predefined scheme, by using the Properties dialog box, by using the Properties window, or by editing the aspx code.

- To apply a scheme, choose Auto Format from the control's smart tag menu and then select the scheme you want to apply.

- To use the Properties dialog box, choose Property Builder from the control's smart tag menu and then set the properties for the data list and its templates.

- To use the Properties window to format a template, expand the style property for that template and then set its properties.

Figure 13-13   How to format a data list

How to use data binding

Once you've configured a data source control, you can bind it to a web form control to automatically display the data retrieved by the data source on the page. In the following topics, you'll learn how to bind a list control to a data source and how to bind controls defined within the templates of another control like a DataList control.

How to bind a list control to a data source

In chapter 6, you learned about the five list controls that you can use in an ASP.NET 4 application. Now, figure 13-14 shows you how you can bind any of these controls to a data source.

The table in this figure shows the three attributes you use to bind a list control to a data source. The DataSourceID attribute provides the ID of the data source. The DataTextField attribute provides the name of the data source field that's displayed in the list. And the DataValueField attribute provides the name of the data source field that is returned by the SelectedValue property when the user selects an item from the list.

You can set these attributes manually by using the Properties window or by directly editing the aspx code. Or, you can use the Data Source Configuration Wizard shown at the top of this figure to set these properties. To do that, display the smart tag menu for the list and select Choose Data Source. Then, use the wizard's controls to set the data source, display field, and value field.

The code example in this figure shows a drop-down list that's bound to a data source named SqlDataSource1. The field named LongName provides the values that are displayed in the drop-down list, and the field named CategoryID supplies the value that's returned by the SelectedValue property when the user selects an item from the list.

The Data Source Configuration Wizard for binding a drop-down list

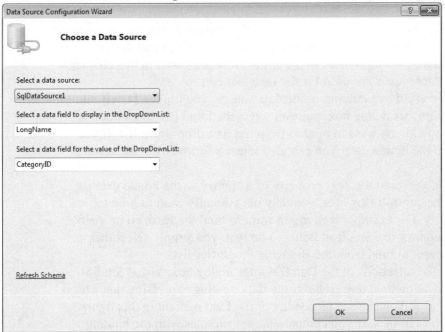

List control attributes for data binding

Attribute	Description
DataSourceID	The ID of the data source to bind the list to.
DataTextField	The name of the data source field that should be displayed in the list.
DataValueField	The name of the data source field whose value should be returned by the SelectedValue property of the list.

The aspx code for a drop-down list that's bound to a SQL data source

```
<asp:DropDownList ID="ddlCategory" runat="server"
    AutoPostBack="True"
    DataSourceID="SqlDataSource1"
    DataTextField="LongName"
    DataValueField="CategoryID">
</asp:DropDownList>
```

Description

- You can bind any of the controls that inherit the ListControl class to a data source. That includes the list box control, the drop-down list control, the check box list control, the radio button list control, and the bulleted list control.

- You can use the Data Source Configuration Wizard to select the data source for a list control, the data field to display in the list, and the data value to return for the selected item.

- You can also use the DataTextFormatString attribute of a list control to specify a format string you want to apply to the text that's displayed in the control.

Figure 13-14   How to bind a list control to a data source

How to bind the controls in a template

Figure 13-15 shows how you can bind the controls in a template to columns of a data source. This technique can be used with any control that uses templates and specifies a data source. In the application presented in this chapter, these binding techniques are used for the DataList control.

To bind a control to a column of the data source, you use the DataBindings dialog box. From this dialog box, you can select the Field Binding option and then select the field you want to bind to from the first drop-down list. If you want to format the bound data, you can also select a format from the second drop-down list.

By default, you bind the Text property of a control so the bound data is displayed in the control. However, you may occasionally want to bind to another property. For example, you might want to bind the Enabled or Visible property of a control to a Boolean field. To do that, you simply select the property you want to bind from the Bindable Properties list.

As you make selections in the DataBindings dialog box, Visual Studio generates an Eval method that contains the data binding expression that's used to bind the control. You can see the syntax of the Eval method in this figure along with two examples. If you compare these examples with the binding options in the DataBindings dialog box, you shouldn't have any trouble understanding how this method works.

Although the drop-down lists in the DataBindings dialog box make it easy to create a data binding expression, you can also create your own custom binding expressions. To do that, you just select the Custom Binding option and then enter the binding expression in the Code Expression text box. You might want to do that, for example, if you need to apply a custom format to the data. Or, you might want to code a custom expression that uses the Bind method instead of the Eval method.

Unlike the Eval method, which only provides for displaying bound data, the Bind method provides for both displaying and updating data. This method implements a feature that was introduced with ASP.NET 2.0 called *two-way binding*. You'll see an application that uses two-way binding in the next chapter.

The DataBindings dialog box for binding a control

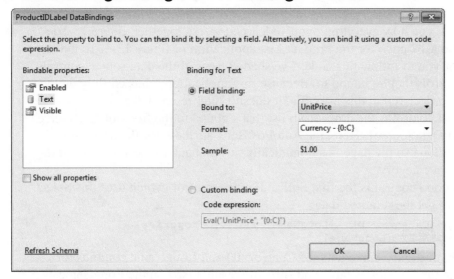

The syntax of the Eval and Bind methods

```
<%# {Eval|Bind}(NameString [, FormatString]) %>
```

Code examples

```
<%# Eval("Name") %>
<%# Eval("UnitPrice", "{0:C}") %>
<%# Bind("UnitPrice", "{0:C}") %>
```

Description

- To bind a control in a template, select the Edit DataBindings command from the smart tag menu for the control to display the DataBindings dialog box. Then, select the property you want to bind to (usually Text), select the Field Binding option, and select the field you want to bind to from the Bound To drop-down list.

- If you want to apply a format to the bound data, select a format from the Format drop-down list.

- As you specify the binding for a control, Visual Studio generates a data binding expression that uses the Eval method. You can see this method in the Code Expression box at the bottom of the DataBindings dialog box.

- You can also create a custom binding expression by selecting the Custom Binding option and then entering the expression in the Code Expression text box.

- The Eval method provides only for displaying data from a data source in a control. In contrast, the Bind method provides for *two-way binding*, which means that it can be used to display as well update data from a data source.

Note

- If the Field Binding option isn't enabled, you can click the Refresh Schema link and then click the OK button in the dialog box that's displayed to enable it.

Figure 13-15   How to bind the controls in a template

The aspx file for the Product List application

To show you how everything you've learned works together, figure 13-16 presents the aspx code for the Product List application of figure 13-1. To make it easier for you to follow this code, I've shaded parts of the data source controls and the controls they're bound to. Because this application relies entirely on the data binding declared in this aspx file, it doesn't require any C# code.

The first control is the drop-down list that's bound to the first SqlDataSource control, SqlDataSource1. Here, the AutoPostBack attribute for the drop-down list is set to True so the page is automatically posted back to the server when the user selects a category.

The second control is the first SqlDataSource control, which uses this Select statement to get the required data:

```
SELECT [CategoryID], [LongName] FROM [Categories]
    ORDER BY [LongName]
```

As a result, this data source gets the CategoryID and LongName columns for each row in the Categories table and sorts the result based on the LongName column. Then, these columns are used by the drop-down list that's bound to this data source.

The third control is a DataList control that's bound to the second SqlDataSource control, SqlDataSource2. The Header template for this control provides for a row of headings that are defined within a row of a table. Then, the Item template defines the table rows that display the data in the rows that are retrieved by the data source. As you can see, each column in the table contains a label whose Text attribute is bound to a column in the data source. Also notice that the columns in the Item template use the same style classes as the columns in the Header template. Although you can't see these style classes here, they specify the widths of the columns. Because of that, the columns in the two templates are aligned. In addition, the last two columns in each template are right aligned since they contain numeric data.

The last two elements for the DataList control define the styles for alternating items and for the header. You saw the Header style earlier in this chapter. It indicates that the header text should be displayed in a white, boldface font on a black background. The AlternatingItem style indicates that every other row in the data list should be displayed on a light gray background. Since no Item style is included, the other rows will be displayed on a white background.

The fourth control, SqlDataSource2, uses this Select statement:

```
SELECT [ProductID], [Name], [UnitPrice], [OnHand]
    FROM [Products]
    WHERE ([CategoryID] = @CategoryID)
    ORDER BY [ProductID]
```

Here, the Where clause specifies that only those rows whose CategoryID column equals the value of the CategoryID parameter should be retrieved. To make this work, the ControlParameter element specifies that the value of the CategoryID parameter is obtained from the SelectedValue property of the ddlCategory control.

The Default.aspx file

```
<body>
    <form id="form1" runat="server">
    <div id="page">
        <div id="header">
            <asp:Image ID="Image1" runat="server" ImageUrl="~/Images/banner.jpg" />
        </div>
        <div id="main">
            <p>Choose a category: 
                <asp:DropDownList ID="ddlCategory" runat="server"
                    DataSourceID="SqlDataSource1" DataTextField="LongName"
                    DataValueField="CategoryID" AutoPostBack="True">
                </asp:DropDownList></p>
            <asp:SqlDataSource ID="SqlDataSource1" runat="server"
             ConnectionString="<%$ ConnectionStrings:HalloweenConnectionString %>"
             SelectCommand="SELECT [CategoryID], [LongName] FROM [Categories]
                    ORDER BY [LongName]">
            </asp:SqlDataSource>
            <asp:DataList ID="ddlProducts" runat="server" DataKeyField="ProductID"
                    DataSourceID="SqlDataSource2" CellPadding="3" GridLines="Vertical">
                <HeaderTemplate>
                    <table><tr>
                        <td class="col1">ID</td>
                        <td class="col2">Product</td>
                        <td class="col3">Unit Price</td>
                        <td class="col4">On Hand</td></tr>
                    </table>
                </HeaderTemplate>
                <ItemTemplate>
                    <table><tr>
                        <td class="col1">
                            <asp:Label ID="lblID" runat="server"
                                Text='<%# Eval("ProductID") %>' /></td>
                        <td class="col2">
                            <asp:Label ID="lblName" runat="server"
                                Text='<%# Eval("Name") %>' /></td>
                        <td class="col3">
                            <asp:Label ID="lblUnitPrice" runat="server"
                                Text='<%# Eval("UnitPrice", "{0:C}") %>' /></td>
                        <td class="col4">
                            <asp:Label ID="lblOnHand" runat="server"
                                Text='<%# Eval("OnHand") %>' /></td></tr></table>
                </ItemTemplate>
                <AlternatingItemStyle BackColor="#CCCCCC" />
                <HeaderStyle BackColor="Black" Font-Bold="True"
                        ForeColor="White" />
            </asp:DataList>
            <asp:SqlDataSource ID="SqlDataSource2" runat="server"
             ConnectionString="<%$ ConnectionStrings:HalloweenConnectionString %>"
             SelectCommand="SELECT [ProductID], [Name], [UnitPrice], [OnHand]
                    FROM [Products] WHERE ([CategoryID] = @CategoryID)
                    ORDER BY [ProductID]">
                <SelectParameters>
                    <asp:ControlParameter ControlID="ddlCategory" Name="CategoryID"
                    PropertyName="SelectedValue" Type="String" />
                </SelectParameters>
            </asp:SqlDataSource>
        </div>
    </div>
    </form>
</body>
```

Figure 13-16   The aspx file for the Product List application

How to use the advanced features of a SQL data source

The SqlDataSource control provides several advanced features that you may want to use in your applications. These features are explained in the topics that follow.

How to create a data source that can update the database

Much like ADO.NET data adapters, a SQL data source can include Insert, Update, and Delete statements that let you automatically update the underlying database based on changes made by the user to bound data controls. To automatically generate these statements, you can check the first box in the dialog box shown in figure 13-17, which is displayed when you click on the Advanced button in the dialog box shown in figure 13-5. You can also check the box for optimistic concurrency, which enhances the generated statements so they check whether updated or deleted rows have changed since the data source retrieved the original data.

Note that for this to work, the primary key column of the table you're updating must be included in the Select statement. That's because this column is used to identify a row that's being updated or deleted. So if the Generate option in the Advanced SQL Generation Options dialog box isn't enabled, it's probably because you haven't selected the primary key column.

The code in this figure shows the aspx elements that are generated when you request Insert, Update, and Delete statements without using optimistic concurrency. Here, the InsertCommand, UpdateCommand, and DeleteCommand attributes provide the statements, and the InsertParameters, UpdateParameters, and DeleteParameters child elements define the parameters used by these statements. Because optimistic concurrency isn't used, these statements will update the database whether or not the data has changed since it was originally retrieved, which could lead to corrupt data.

If you check the Use Optimistic Concurrency check box, though, the update and delete commands will include Where clauses that compare the value of each column with the value originally retrieved. Because these values are passed as parameters, the generated aspx code will include additional elements that define these parameters. The SqlDataSource element will also include two additional attributes. The first one indicates that optimistic concurrency should be used, and the second one indicates the format that should be used for the names of the parameters that will hold the original column values. Then, if the value of any column has changed since it was originally retrieved, the update or delete operation will be refused, and your application needs to provide code that handles that situation. You'll see how that works in chapter 14.

The Advanced SQL Generation Options dialog box

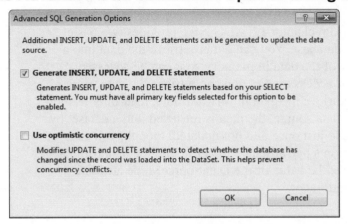

The aspx code for a SqlDataSource control that uses action queries

```
<asp:SqlDataSource ID="SqlDataSource1" runat="server"
    ConnectionString="<%$ ConnectionStrings:HalloweenConnectionString %>"
    SelectCommand="SELECT [CategoryID], [ShortName], [LongName]
                FROM [Categories]"
    InsertCommand="INSERT INTO [Categories] ([CategoryID], [ShortName],
                [LongName]) VALUES (@CategoryID, @ShortName, @LongName)"
    UpdateCommand="UPDATE [Categories] SET [ShortName] = @ShortName,
                [LongName] = @LongName WHERE [CategoryID] = @CategoryID"
    DeleteCommand="DELETE FROM [Categories]
                WHERE [CategoryID] = @CategoryID">
    <DeleteParameters>
        <asp:Parameter Name="CategoryID" Type="String" />
    </DeleteParameters>
    <UpdateParameters>
        <asp:Parameter Name="ShortName" Type="String" />
        <asp:Parameter Name="LongName" Type="String" />
        <asp:Parameter Name="CategoryID" Type="String" />
    </UpdateParameters>
    <InsertParameters>
        <asp:Parameter Name="CategoryID" Type="String" />
        <asp:Parameter Name="ShortName" Type="String" />
        <asp:Parameter Name="LongName" Type="String" />
    </InsertParameters>
</asp:SqlDataSource>
```

Description

- To automatically generate Insert, Update, and Delete statements for a data source, check the first box in the dialog box that you get by clicking on the Advanced button in the first dialog box in figure 13-5. To generate enhanced versions of the Update and Delete statements that use optimistic concurrency, check the second box too.

- The InsertCommand, UpdateCommand, and DeleteCommand attributes in the aspx code define the Insert, Update, and Delete statements used by a data source. If these statements require parameters, the InsertParameters, UpdateParameters, and DeleteParameters elements specify those parameters.

Figure 13-17   How to create a SQL data source that can update the database

How to change the data source mode

As you may remember from chapter 12, ADO.NET provides two basic ways to retrieve data from a database. You can either retrieve the data into a dataset, which retains a copy of the data in memory so it can be accessed multiple times and updated if necessary. Or, you can retrieve the data using a data reader, which lets you retrieve the data in forward-only, read-only fashion.

When you create a SQL data source, the data is retrieved into a dataset by default. If the data will be read just once and not updated, though, you can usually improve the application's performance by retrieving the data using a data reader. To do that, just set the value of the DataSourceMode attribute shown in figure 13-18 to DataReader.

How to use caching

ASP.NET's caching feature lets you save the data retrieved by a data source in cache memory on the server. That way, the next time the data needs to be retrieved, the cached data is used instead of getting it from the database again. Since this reduces database access, it often improves an application's overall performance.

To cache the data that's retrieved by a SQL data source, you use the attributes of the data source that are presented in figure 13-18. To enable caching, you simply set the EnableCaching attribute to True. Then, you can use the CacheDuration attribute to specify how long data should be kept in the cache. If, for example, the cached data rarely changes, you can set a long cache duration value such as 30 minutes or more. If the data changes more frequently, you can set a shorter cache duration value.

But what if the data in the database changes before the duration expires? In that case, the user will view data that is out of date. Sometimes, that's okay so you don't have to worry about it. Otherwise, you can minimize the chance of this happening by setting a shorter duration time.

The DataSourceMode attribute

Attribute	Description
DataSourceMode	DataSet or DataReader. The default is DataSet, but you can specify DataReader if the data source is read-only.

A SqlDataSource control that uses a data reader

```
<asp:SqlDataSource ID="SqlDataSource1" runat="server"
    ConnectionString="<%$ ConnectionStrings:HalloweenConnectionString %>"
    DataSourceMode="DataReader"
    SelectCommand="SELECT [CategoryID], [LongName]
        FROM [Categories]
        ORDER BY [LongName]"
</asp:SqlDataSource>
```

SqlDataSource attributes for caching

Attribute	Description
EnableCaching	A Boolean value that indicates whether caching is enabled for the data source. The default is False.
CacheDuration	The length of time in seconds that the cached data should be saved in cache storage.
CacheExpirationPolicy	If this attribute is set to Absolute, the cache duration timer is started the first time the data is retrieved and is not reset to zero until after the time has expired. If this attribute is set to Sliding, the cache duration timer is reset to zero each time the data is retrieved. The default is Absolute.
CacheKeyDependency	A string that provides a key value associated with the cached data. If you provide a key for the cached data, you can use the key value to programmatically expire the cached data at any time.

A SqlDataSource control that uses caching

```
<asp:SqlDataSource ID="SqlDataSource1" runat="server"
    ConnectionString="<%$ ConnectionStrings:HalloweenConnectionString %>"
    EnableCaching="True" CacheDuration="60"
    SelectCommand="SELECT [CategoryID], [LongName]
        FROM [Categories]
        ORDER BY [LongName]"
</asp:SqlDataSource>
```

Description

- The DataSourceMode attribute lets you specify that data should be retrieved using a data reader rather than being stored in a dataset. For read-only data, a data reader is usually more efficient.

- The data source caching attributes let you specify that data should be stored in cache storage for a specified period of time. For data that changes infrequently, caching can improve performance.

Figure 13-18   How to change the data source mode and use caching

Perspective

In this chapter, you've learned how to use the SqlDataSource control. However, we've only scratched the surface of what this data source can do. As you will see, the real power of a SQL data source lies in what it can do in combination with data controls like GridView, DetailsView, FormView, and ListView. As a result, all this chapter has really done is set the foundation for what you'll learn in chapters 14, 15, and 16.

I also want to point out what many developers feel is a weakness of the SQL data source control. Because this control can directly specify the SQL statements used to access and update a database, it violates one of the basic principles of good application design. That is, that the code that's used to manage the application's user interface should be separated from the code that's used to access the application's database and perform its business logic. Clearly, when you use the SqlDataSource control, the database code is mixed with the presentation code.

Fortunately, ASP.NET provides several ways to minimize or eliminate this problem. First, the SqlDataSource control can use stored procedures rather than SQL statements. That way, the SQL statements that access and update the database are placed in the database itself, separate from the presentation code.

Second, you can use ObjectDataSource controls rather than SqlDataSource controls. When you use ObjectDataSource controls, you can create and use separate database access classes, so the database access code isn't in the aspx file at all. In chapter 17, you'll learn how that works.

You can also use the LinqDataSource control or the EntityDataSource control. When you use one of these controls, you don't write any code for accessing the database. Instead, the SQL statements are generated and executed for you based on an object model that maps to the database. These controls aren't covered in this book.

Terms

SQL data source
select parameter
control parameter
Query Builder
diagram pane
grid pane
SQL pane
data list
template
template-editing mode
two-way binding

Exercise 13-1 Create an Invoice Line Item List application

In this exercise, you'll create an application that lists line items by invoice. To do that, you'll use two SqlDataSource controls and two bound controls. When you're done, the application should look like this:

Create a drop-down list and the data source it's bound to

1. Open the Ch13InvoiceLineItems application in the C:\aspnet4_cs directory. This application contains the starting page and the image and style sheet used by the page.

2. Enter the text shown above into the main division of the page, followed by a space. Add a drop-down list following the text. When the smart tag menu is displayed, select the Choose Data Source command and then select New Data Source from the first drop-down list in the Data Source Configuration Wizard dialog box that's displayed.

3. Continue configuring the data source as shown in figures 13-2 through 13-6. The data source should include the InvoiceNumber column from the Invoices table for all invoices whose Total column is greater than 300. To create the Where clause for the Select statement, select None from the Source drop-down list.

4. When the Data Source Configuration Wizard is displayed again, accept the defaults so the InvoiceNumber column is displayed in the drop-down list and stored as the value of the drop-down list.

5. Change the name of the drop-down list to ddlInvoice and set its AutoPostBack property to True. Then, review the aspx code that was generated. In particular, review the Select statement and the select parameter that were generated for the SqlDataSource control.

Create another data source and bind it to a data list

6. Add a second SqlDataSource control to the page. Configure this data source so it uses the connection string that's stored in the web.config file, so it selects the ProductID, UnitPrice, Quantity, and Extension columns from the LineItems table, and so it selects only the line items for the invoice that's selected from the drop-down list.

7. Add a DataList control to the form, and set its data source to the SqlDataSource control you just created.

8. Run the application to see how the data is displayed by default. Then, close the browser window.

Modify the templates for the data list

9. Display the smart tag menu for the DataList control, and select the Edit Templates command to display the Item template.

10. Delete the literal text for each column. Then, add a table at the bottom of the template that consists of one row and four columns and that has a width of 400 pixels.

11. Set the width of each column to 100 pixels, and right-align the second, third, and fourth columns. (You can do that by creating styles that use the width and text-align properties or by setting the Width and Align properties of the table cells.)

12. Move the labels for the four columns into the four cells of the table, and then delete the space above the table.

13. Select the label for the UnitPrice column, display its smart tag menu, and select Edit DataBindings. Then, use the DataBindings dialog box to apply the Currency format to that column. Do the same for the Extension column.

14. Use the drop-down list in the smart tag menu for the data list to display the header template for the control.

15. Add a table like the one you used for the Item template, but enter the values shown in the heading above. When you're done, exit from template-editing mode.

Format the data list

16. Display the smart tag menu for the data list, select the Auto Format command, and highlight one or more of the predefined schemes to see how they look.

17. Apply the Simple scheme. Then, review the aspx code for the DataList control to see the style properties and elements that were generated.

18. Run the application to make sure it's formatted properly. Select a different invoice from the drop-down list to make sure this works. Then, close the browser window.

14

How to use the GridView control

In this chapter, you'll learn how to use the GridView control. This control lets you display the data from a data source in the rows and columns of a table. It includes many advanced features, such as automatic paging and sorting. It lets you update and delete data with minimal C# code. And its appearance is fully customizable.

How to customize the GridView control

The GridView control is one of the most powerful user interface controls available in ASP.NET 4. It provides many options that let you customize its appearance and behavior. In the following topics, you'll learn how to define fields, customize the contents and appearance of those fields, enable sorting, and provide for custom paging.

How the GridView control works

As figure 14-1 shows, the GridView control displays data provided by a data source in a row and column format. In fact, the GridView control renders its data as an HTML table with one Tr element for each row in the data source, and one Td element for each column in the data source.

The GridView control at the top of this figure displays the data from the Categories table of the Halloween database. Here, the first three columns of the control display the data from the three columns of the table.

The other two columns of this control display buttons that the user can click to edit or delete a row. In this example, the user has clicked the Edit button for the masks row, which placed that row into edit mode. In this mode, text boxes are displayed in place of the labels for the short and long name columns, the Edit button is replaced by Update and Cancel buttons, and the Delete button is removed.

The table in this figure lists some of the basic attributes of the GridView control, and the aspx code in this figure is the code that creates the GridView control above it. By default, this control contains one column for each of the columns in the data source. These columns are defined by BoundField elements, which are coded within a Columns element. The GridView control in this figure, for example, contains a Columns element with three BoundField elements. Notice that all three BoundField elements contain ItemStyle elements that define the widths of the columns. The Columns element also contains two CommandField elements that define the button columns.

Most of the aspx code for a GridView control is created automatically by Visual Studio when you drag the control from the Toolbox onto the form and when you use the configuration wizard to configure the data source. However, you typically modify this code to customize the appearance and behavior of this control.

A GridView control that provides for updating a table

ID	Short Name	Long Name		
costumes	Costumes	Costumes	Edit	Delete
fx	FX	Special Effects	Edit	Delete
masks	Masks	Masks	Update Cancel	
props	Props	Props	Edit	Delete

The aspx code for the GridView control shown above

```
<asp:GridView ID="GridView1" runat="server" AutoGenerateColumns="False"
             DataSourceID="SqlDataSource1" DataKeyNames="CategoryID">
    <Columns>
        <asp:BoundField DataField="CategoryID" HeaderText="ID"
                       ReadOnly="True" SortExpression="CategoryID">
            <ItemStyle Width="100px" />
        </asp:BoundField>
        <asp:BoundField DataField="ShortName" HeaderText="Short Name"
                       SortExpression="ShortName">
            <ItemStyle Width="150px" />
        </asp:BoundField>
        <asp:BoundField DataField="LongName" HeaderText="Long Name"
                       SortExpression="LongName">
            <ItemStyle Width="200px" />
        </asp:BoundField>
        <asp:CommandField ButtonType="Button" ShowEditButton="True"
                         CausesValidation="False" />
        <asp:CommandField ButtonType="Button" ShowDeleteButton="True"
                         CausesValidation="False" />
    </Columns>
</asp:GridView>
```

Basic attributes of the GridView control

Attribute	Description
ID	The ID of the control.
Runat	Must specify "server."
DataSourceID	The ID of the data source to bind to.
DataKeyNames	The names of the primary key fields separated by commas.
AutoGenerateColumns	Specifies whether the control's columns should be automatically generated.
SelectedIndex	Specifies the row to be initially selected.

Description

- The GridView control displays data from a data source in a row and column format. The data is rendered as an HTML table.

- To create a GridView control, drag the GridView icon from the Data group of the Toolbox.

- To bind a GridView control to a data source, use the smart tag menu's Choose Data Source command.

Figure 14-1   How the GridView control works

How to define the fields in a GridView control

By default, a GridView control displays one column for each column in the data source. If that's not what you want, you can choose Edit Columns from the control's smart tag menu to display the Fields dialog box shown in figure 14-2. Then, you can use this dialog box to delete fields you don't want to display, change the order of the fields, add additional fields like command buttons, and adjust the properties of the fields.

The Available Fields list box lists all of the available sources for GridView fields, while the Selected Fields list box shows the fields that have already been added to the GridView control. To add an additional field to the GridView control, select the field you want to add in the Available Fields list box and click Add. To change the properties for a field, select the field in the Selected Fields list, and use the Properties list.

The table in this figure lists some of the properties you're most likely to want to change. For example, the HeaderText property determines the text that's displayed for the field's header row, the ItemStyle.Width property sets the width for the field, and the DataFormatString property specifies how you want a field formatted.

Instead of defining each bound field you want to include in a GridView control, you can have the control generate the fields for you automatically. To do that, you select the Auto-generate Fields option in the Fields dialog box. Then, a field will be automatically generated for each column in the data source. Because of that, you'll want to remove any bound fields that were added to the Selected Fields list by default. If you don't, these fields will appear in the GridView control twice.

Note that if you choose to have the bound fields generated automatically, the aspx code for those fields isn't generated until runtime. That means that you can't change the appearance or behavior of these fields at design time. Because of that, you're not likely to use auto-generated fields.

The Fields dialog box

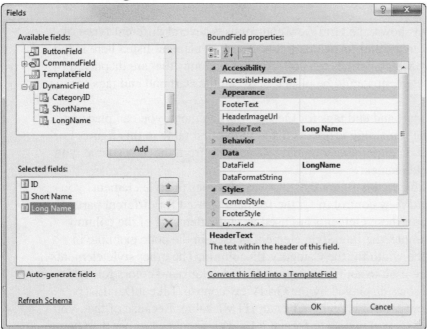

Commonly used field properties

Property	Description
DataField	For a bound field, the name of the column in the underlying data source that the field should be bound to.
DataFormatString	A format string used to format the data. For example, use {0:c} to format a decimal value as currency.
ItemStyle.Width	The width of the field.
ReadOnly	True if the field is used for display only.
NullDisplayText	The text that's displayed if the data field is null.
ConvertEmptyStringToNull	If True (the default), empty strings are treated as nulls when data is updated in the database. Set this property to False if the underlying database field doesn't allow nulls.
HeaderText	The text that's displayed in the header row for the field.
ShowHeader	True if the header should be displayed for this field.

Description

- By default, the GridView control displays one column for each column in the data source.

- To define the fields that you want to display in the GridView control, display the Fields dialog box by selecting the Edit Columns command in the control's smart tag menu.

- Another way to add a field to a GridView control is to use the Add New Column command in the smart tag menu. You'll see how to use this technique to add command buttons to a DetailsView control in the next chapter.

Figure 14-2   How to define the fields in a GridView control

Elements used to create and format fields

As figure 14-3 shows, the GridView control uses several different types of child elements to create and format its fields. The first element listed here is the Columns element, which defines the collection of columns that are displayed by the control. This element should be placed between the start and end tags for the GridView control.

Between the start and end tags for the Columns element, you can place any combination of the remaining elements listed in the first table in this figure. For example, to create a column that's bound to a column from the data source, you use the BoundField element.

The second table in this figure lists the various types of style elements you can use with a GridView control to set the formatting used for different parts of the control. Some of these elements are used as child elements of the column elements. For example, the ItemStyle element is used in the code example in this figure to set the width for the Category ID column. The other style elements in this example are used to set the foreground and background colors for different types of rows displayed by the GridView control. Like a DataList control, a GridView control is rendered as an HTML table. Because of that, you typically use these style elements to format a GridView control rather than using CSS.

Note that you don't have to create these elements yourself. Instead, these elements are created automatically when you use the Fields dialog box as described in the previous figure, when you use the Properties window to specify the styles for an element, or when you apply a scheme to the GridView control using the Auto Format command.

Column field elements

Element	Description
Columns	The columns that are displayed by a GridView control.
asp:BoundField	A field bound to a data source column.
asp:ButtonField	A field that displays a button.
asp:CheckBoxField	A field that displays a check box.
asp:CommandField	A field that contains Select, Edit, Delete, Update, or Cancel buttons.
asp:HyperlinkField	A field that displays a hyperlink.
asp:ImageField	A field that displays an image.
asp:TemplateField	Lets you create a column with custom content.

Style elements

Element	Description
RowStyle	The style used for data rows.
AlternatingRowStyle	The style used for alternating data rows.
SelectedRowStyle	The style used when the row is selected.
EditRowStyle	The style used when the row is being edited.
EmptyDataRowStyle	The style used when the data source is empty.
ItemStyle	The style used for an individual field.
HeaderStyle	The style used to format the header row.
FooterStyle	The style used to format the footer row.
PagerStyle	The style used to format the pager row.

The aspx code for a control that uses field and style elements

```
<asp:GridView ID="GridView1" runat="server" AutoGenerateColumns="False"
            DataKeyNames="CategoryID" DataSourceID="SqlDataSource1">
  <Columns>
    <asp:BoundField DataField="CategoryID" HeaderText="ID" ReadOnly="true" >
      <ItemStyle Width="100px" />
    </asp:BoundField>
    .
    .
  </Columns>
  <HeaderStyle BackColor="LightGray" ForeColor="White"
            Font-Bold="True" />
  <RowStyle BackColor="White" ForeColor="Black" />
  <SelectedRowStyle BackColor="Gray" ForeColor="White"
                  Font-Bold="True" />
  <FooterStyle BackColor="LightGray" ForeColor="Blue" />
  <PagerStyle BackColor="LightGray" ForeColor="Blue"
            HorizontalAlign="Center" />
</asp:GridView>
```

Description

- The GridView control uses several child elements to define the column fields in a row and the styles used to format the data.

Figure 14-3   Elements used to create and format fields

How to enable sorting

The GridView control has a built-in ability to let the user sort the rows based on any or all of the columns displayed by the control. As figure 14-4 shows, all you have to do to enable sorting is set the AllowSorting attribute to True and provide a SortExpression attribute for each column you want to allow sorting for. When sorting is enabled for a column, the user can sort the data by clicking the column header. The first time it's clicked, the data will be sorted in ascending sequence. The second time it's clicked, the data will be sorted in descending sequence. And so on.

Note that a SortExpression attribute is automatically generated for each BoundField column that's included by default or that you create with the Fields dialog box. As a result, instead of adding SortExpression attributes for the columns you want to allow sorting for, you must remove the SortExpression attributes for the columns you don't want to allow sorting for. You can use the Fields dialog box to do that by clearing the SortExpression properties. Or, you can use the HTML Editor to delete the SortExpression attributes.

The code example in this figure allows sorting for three of the five fields displayed by the GridView control. For the first two fields, the SortExpression attribute simply duplicates the name of the data source column the field is bound to. If, for example, the user clicks the header of the ProductID column, the data is sorted on the ProductID field.

In some cases, though, you may want the sort expression to be based on two or more columns. To do that, you just use commas to separate the sort field names. In this example, the sort expression for the Category ID column is "CategoryID, Name". That way, any rows with the same Category ID will be sorted by the Name column. Note that the first time the Category ID column header is clicked, the rows will be sorted by the Name column in ascending sequence within the CategoryID column in ascending sequence. If the Category ID column header is clicked again, the category IDs will remain in ascending sequence, but the names will be sorted in descending sequence.

It's important to note that the GridView control doesn't actually do the sorting. Instead, it relies on the underlying data source to sort the data. As a result, sorting will only work if the data source provides for sorting. For a SqlDataSource or AccessDataSource, this means that you need to use the default DataSet mode.

A GridView control with sorting enabled

ID	Name	Category	Unit Price	On Hand
pow01	Austin Powers	costumes	$79.99	25
frankc01	Frankenstein	costumes	$39.99	100
hippie01	Hippie	costumes	$79.99	40
jar01	JarJar	costumes	$59.99	25
martian01	Martian	costumes	$69.99	100
super01	Superman	costumes	$39.99	100
bl01	Black Light	fx	$19.99	200
fogj01	Fog Juice (1qt)	fx	$9.99	500
fog01	Fog Machine	fx	$34.99	100
str01	Mini-strobe	fx	$13.99	200
skullfog01	Skull Fogger	fx	$39.95	50
tlm01	T&L Machine	fx	$99.99	10

The aspx code for the control shown above

```
<asp:GridView ID="GridView1" runat="server" AllowSorting="True"
    AutoGenerateColumns="False" DataKeyNames="ProductID"
    DataSourceID="SqlDataSource1">
    <Columns>
        <asp:BoundField DataField="ProductID" HeaderText="ID"
            ReadOnly="True" SortExpression="ProductID">
            <HeaderStyle HorizontalAlign="Left" />
            <ItemStyle Width="75px" />
        </asp:BoundField>
        <asp:BoundField DataField="Name" HeaderText="Name"
            SortExpression="Name">
            <HeaderStyle HorizontalAlign="Left" />
            <ItemStyle Width="200px" />
        </asp:BoundField>
        <asp:BoundField DataField="CategoryID" HeaderText="Category"
            SortExpression="CategoryID, Name" />
        <asp:BoundField DataField="UnitPrice" DataFormatString="{0:c}"
            HeaderText="Unit Price">
            <ItemStyle Width="85px" HorizontalAlign="Right" />
            <HeaderStyle HorizontalAlign="Right" />
        </asp:BoundField>
        <asp:BoundField DataField="OnHand" HeaderText="On Hand">
            <ItemStyle Width="85px" HorizontalAlign="Right" />
            <HeaderStyle HorizontalAlign="Right" />
        </asp:BoundField>
    </Columns>
    <HeaderStyle BackColor="LightGray" />
</asp:GridView>
```

Description

- To enable sorting, set the AllowSorting attribute to True. Then, add a SortExpression attribute to each column you want to allow sorting for.
- For sorting to work, the DataSourceMode attribute of the data source must be set to DataSet mode.

Figure 14-4   How to enable sorting

How to enable paging

Paging refers to the ability of the GridView control to display bound data one page at a time, along with paging controls that let the user select which page of data to display next. As figure 14-5 shows, the GridView control lets you enable paging simply by setting the AllowPaging attribute to True.

When you enable paging, an additional row is displayed at the bottom of the GridView control to display the paging controls. If you want, you can provide a PagerStyle element to control how this row is formatted. In the example in this figure, the PagerStyle element specifies that the background color for the pager row should be light gray and the pager controls should be horizontally centered.

Unlike sorting, the GridView control doesn't delegate the paging function to the underlying data source. Like sorting, however, paging works only for data sources that are in DataSet mode.

A GridView control with paging enabled

ID	Name	Category	Unit Price	On Hand
arm01	Freddie Arm	props	$20.95	200
bats01	Flying Bats	props	$69.99	25
bl01	Black Light	fx	$19.99	200
cat01	Deranged Cat	props	$19.99	45
fog01	Fog Machine	fx	$34.99	100
fogj01	Fog Juice (1qt)	fx	$9.99	500
frankc01	Frankenstein	costumes	$39.99	100
fred01	Freddie	masks	$29.99	50
head01	Michael Head	props	$29.99	100
head02	Saw Head	props	$29.99	100

1 2 3

The aspx code for the control shown above

```
<asp:GridView ID="GridView1" runat="server" AllowPaging="True"
    AutoGenerateColumns="False" DataKeyNames="ProductID"
    DataSourceID="SqlDataSource1">
    <Columns>
        <asp:BoundField DataField="ProductID" HeaderText="ID"
            ReadOnly="True">
            <HeaderStyle HorizontalAlign="Left" />
            <ItemStyle Width="75px" />
        </asp:BoundField>
        <asp:BoundField DataField="Name" HeaderText="Name">
            <HeaderStyle HorizontalAlign="Left" />
            <ItemStyle Width="200px" />
        </asp:BoundField>
        <asp:BoundField DataField="CategoryID" HeaderText="Category" />
        <asp:BoundField DataField="UnitPrice" DataFormatString="{0:c}"
            HeaderText="Unit Price">
            <ItemStyle Width="85px" HorizontalAlign="Right" />
            <HeaderStyle HorizontalAlign="Right" />
        </asp:BoundField>
        <asp:BoundField DataField="OnHand" HeaderText="On Hand">
            <ItemStyle Width="85px" HorizontalAlign="Right" />
            <HeaderStyle HorizontalAlign="Right" />
        </asp:BoundField>
    </Columns>
    <HeaderStyle BackColor="LightGray" />
    <PagerStyle BackColor="LightGray" HorizontalAlign="Center" />
</asp:GridView>
```

Description

- To enable *paging*, set the AllowPaging attribute to True. Then, add a PagerStyle element to define the appearance of the pager controls. You can also add a PagerSettings element as described in the next figure to customize the way paging works.

- For paging to work, the DataSourceMode attribute of the data source must be set to DataSet mode.

Figure 14-5   How to enable paging

How to customize paging

Figure 14-6 shows how you can customize the way paging works with a GridView control. To start, the two attributes in the first table let you enable paging and specify the number of data rows that will be displayed on each page. The default setting for the second attribute is 10.

You can also customize the appearance of the pager area by including a PagerSettings element between the start and end tags of a GridView control. Then, you can use the attributes in the second table for the customization. The most important of these attributes is Mode, which determines what buttons are displayed in the pager area. If, for example, you set the mode to NextPrevious, only Next and Previous buttons will be displayed.

If you specify Numeric or NumericFirstLast for the Mode attribute, individual page numbers are displayed in the pager area so the user can go directly to any of the listed pages. You can then use the PageButtonCount attribute to specify how many of these page numbers should be displayed in the pager area. Note that if you specify NumericFirstLast, the first and last buttons are displayed only if the total number of pages exceeds the value you specify for the PageButtonCount attribute and the first or last page isn't displayed.

The remaining attributes in this table let you control the text or image that's displayed for the various buttons. By default, the values for the First, Previous, Next, and Last buttons use less-than and greater-than signs, but the example shows how you can change the text for these buttons.

Attributes of the GridView control that affect paging

Attribute	Description
AllowPaging	Set to True to enable paging.
PageSize	Specifies the number of rows to display on each page. The default is 10.

Attributes of the PagerSettings element

Attribute	Description
Mode	Controls what buttons are displayed in the pager area. You can specify NextPrevious, NextPreviousFirstLast, Numeric, or NumericFirstLast.
FirstPageText	The text to display for the first page button. The default is <<, which displays as <<.
FirstPageImageUrl	The URL of an image file used to display the first page button.
PreviousPageText	The text to display for the previous page button. The default is <, which displays as <.
PreviousPageImageUrl	The URL of an image file used to display the previous page button.
NextPageText	The text to display for the next page button. The default is >, which displays as >.
NextPageImageUrl	The URL of an image file used to display the next page button.
LastPageText	The text to display for the last page button. The default is >>, which displays as >>.
LastPageImageUrl	The URL of an image file used to display the last page button.
PageButtonCount	The number of page buttons to display if the Mode is set to Numeric or NumericFirstLast.
Position	The location of the pager area. You can specify Top, Bottom, or TopAndBottom.
Visible	Set to False to hide the pager controls.

Example

A PagerSettings element

```
<PagerSettings Mode="NextPreviousFirstLast"
               NextPageText="Next" PreviousPageText="Prev"
               FirstPageText="First" LastPageText="Last" />
```

The resulting pager area

First Prev Next Last

Description

- You can use the PageSize attribute of the GridView element to specify the number of rows to display on each page.
- You can also add a PagerSettings element to control the appearance of the pager area.

Figure 14-6   How to customize paging

A list application that uses a GridView control

Now that you've learned the basics of working with a GridView control, the following topics present the design and code for an application that uses a GridView control to list the rows of a data source. As you'll see, this application provides for sorting and paging and doesn't require a single line of C# code.

The Product List application

Figure 14-7 presents the Product List application. Here, the data from the Products table of the Halloween database is displayed in a GridView control. The data is displayed 8 rows at a time, and numeric page buttons are displayed at the bottom of the GridView control so the user can navigate from page to page. In addition, the user can sort the data by clicking the column headings for the ID, Name, and Category columns.

The Product List application

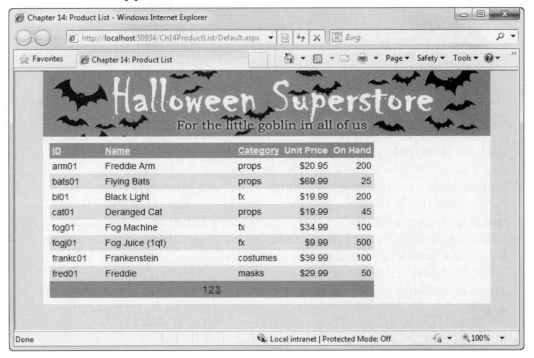

Description

- The Product List application uses a GridView control to display a list of all the products in the Products table. The GridView control is bound to a SqlDataSource control that works in DataSet mode.

- Sorting is enabled for the first three columns. That way, the user can sort the product data by ID, Name, or Category.

- Paging is enabled with 8 products displayed on each page.

- Currency formatting is applied to the Unit Price column.

Figure 14-7   The Product List application

The aspx file

Figure 14-8 shows the aspx code for this application, which is stored in the Default.aspx file. Because no code-behind methods are needed, the code-behind file isn't shown.

Because you've already been introduced to all of the code in the aspx file, you should be able to follow it without much trouble. So I'll just point out a few highlights.

The Columns element contains five BoundField child elements that define the fields displayed by the grid. All five columns are retrieved from the SQL data source. The first three of these BoundField elements include the SortExpression attribute to allow sorting. The fourth BoundField element includes the DataFormatString attribute to apply currency formatting. The ItemStyle elements for the first two fields set the width of the fields, and the ItemStyle elements for the last two fields set the alignment to right. Otherwise, the default formatting is used for the five fields.

A PagerStyle element is used to center the pager buttons in the pager area. Then, a PagerSettings element is used to specify the types of pager controls to display.

Finally, the SqlDataSource control uses this Select statement to retrieve data from the Halloween database:

```
SELECT [ProductID], [Name], [CategoryID],
    [UnitPrice], [OnHand] FROM [Products]
```

Because the DataSourceMode attribute isn't set, the default of DataSet mode is used, which means that sorting and paging can be enabled.

The Default.aspx file

```
<html xmlns="http://www.w3.org/1999/xhtml">
<head runat="server">
    <title>Chapter 14: Product List</title>
    <link href="Main.css" rel="stylesheet" type="text/css" />
</head>
<body>
    <form id="form1" runat="server">
    <div id="page">
        <div id="header">
            <asp:Image ID="Image1" runat="server"
                ImageUrl="~/Images/banner.jpg" />
        </div>
        <div id="main">
            <asp:GridView ID="GridView1" runat="server"
                AutoGenerateColumns="False" DataKeyNames="ProductID"
                DataSourceID="SqlDataSource1" AllowPaging="True" PageSize="8"
                AllowSorting="True" CellPadding="4" ForeColor="Black"
                GridLines="None">
                <Columns>
                    <asp:BoundField DataField="ProductID" HeaderText="ID"
                        ReadOnly="True" SortExpression="ProductID">
                        <HeaderStyle HorizontalAlign="Left" />
                        <ItemStyle Width="75px" />
                    </asp:BoundField>
                    <asp:BoundField DataField="Name" HeaderText="Name"
                        SortExpression="Name">
                        <HeaderStyle HorizontalAlign="Left" />
                        <ItemStyle Width="200px" />
                    </asp:BoundField>
                    <asp:BoundField DataField="CategoryID" HeaderText="Category"
                        SortExpression="CategoryID, Name" />
                    <asp:BoundField DataField="UnitPrice"
                        HeaderText="Unit Price" DataFormatString="{0:c}">
                        <ItemStyle HorizontalAlign="Right" />
                    </asp:BoundField>
                    <asp:BoundField DataField="OnHand" HeaderText="On Hand">
                        <ItemStyle HorizontalAlign="Right" />
                    </asp:BoundField>
                </Columns>
                <HeaderStyle BackColor="Gray" Font-Bold="True"
                    ForeColor="White" />
                <RowStyle BackColor="White" ForeColor="Black" />
                <AlternatingRowStyle BackColor="LightGray" ForeColor="Black" />
                <PagerStyle BackColor="Gray" ForeColor="Blue"
                    HorizontalAlign="Center" />
                <PagerSettings Mode="NumericFirstLast" />
            </asp:GridView>
            <asp:SqlDataSource ID="SqlDataSource1" runat="server"
              ConnectionString="<%$ ConnectionStrings:HalloweenConnectionString %>"
              SelectCommand="SELECT [ProductID], [Name], [CategoryID],
                [UnitPrice], [OnHand] FROM [Products]">
            </asp:SqlDataSource>
        </div>
    </div>
    </form>
</body>
</html>
```

Figure 14-8   The aspx file for the Product List application

How to update GridView data

Another impressive feature of the GridView control is its ability to update data in the underlying data source with little additional code. Before you can set that up, though, you must configure the data source with Update, Delete, and Insert statements, as described in the last chapter. Once you've done that, you can set up a GridView control so it calls the Update and Delete statements, which you'll learn how to do next. Then, you'll learn how to insert a row into a GridView control.

How to work with command fields

A *command field* is a GridView column that contains one or more command buttons. Figure 14-9 shows five of the command buttons that you can include in each row of a GridView control. Please note, however, that the Update and Cancel buttons are displayed only when a user clicks the Edit button to edit a row. You can't display these buttons in separate command fields.

When the user clicks a Delete button, the GridView control calls the data source control's Delete method, which deletes the selected row from the underlying database. Then, the GridView control redisplays the data without the deleted row.

When the user clicks the Edit button, the GridView control places the selected row in *edit mode*. In this mode, the labels used to display the editable bound fields are replaced by text boxes so the user can enter changes. Also, the row is formatted using the style attributes provided by the EditRowStyle element. Finally, the Edit button itself is replaced by Update and Cancel buttons. Then, if the user clicks the Update button, the GridView control calls the data source control's Update method, which updates the underlying database. But if the user clicks Cancel, any changes made by the user are discarded and the original values are redisplayed.

The Select button lets the user select a row. Then, the selected row is displayed with the settings in the SelectedRowStyle element. Also, the SelectedIndex and SelectedRow properties are updated to reflect the selected row. The Select button is most often used in combination with a FormView or DetailsView control to create pages that show the details for an item selected from the GridView control. You'll learn how this works in chapter 15.

The two tables in this figure show the attributes of a CommandField element. For instance, you can set the ShowEditButton attribute to True to display an Edit button in a command field. And you can use the EditText attribute to set the text that's displayed on that button.

Although a single command field can display more than one button, it's common to create separate command fields for Select, Edit, and Delete buttons. It's also common to set the CausesValidation attribute of the Select and Delete buttons to False since the operations these buttons perform don't require any data validation. On the other hand, you'll usually leave the CausesValidation attribute of the Edit button set to True so that validation is performed when the user clicks the Update button. Later in this chapter, you'll learn how to use validation controls with the Edit button by creating template fields.

The Fields dialog box for working with a command field

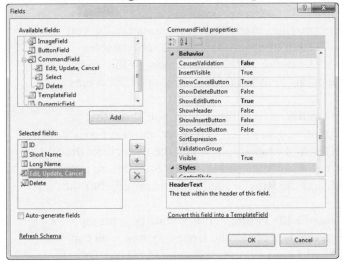

Typical code to define command fields

```
<asp:CommandField ButtonType="Button" ShowEditButton="True"
    CausesValidation="False" />
<asp:CommandField ButtonType="Button" ShowDeleteButton="True"
    CausesValidation="False" />
```

Attributes of the CommandField element

Attribute	Description
ButtonType	Specifies the type of button displayed in the command field. Valid options are Button, Link, or Image.
CausesValidation	Specifies whether validation should be performed if the user clicks the button.
ValidationGroup	Specifies the name of the group to be validated if CausesValidation is True.

Attributes that show buttons and set the text or images they display

Button	Show	Text	Image
Cancel	ShowCancelButton	CancelText	CancelImage
Delete	ShowDeleteButton	DeleteText	DeleteImage
Edit	ShowEditButton	EditText	EditImage
Select	ShowSelectButton	SelectText	SelectImage
Update	n/a	UpdateText	UpdateImage

Description

- A *command field* adds buttons that let the user edit, delete, or select data in a GridView control.
- The CommandField element also provides for an Insert button, but the GridView control doesn't directly support insert operations.

Figure 14-9   How to work with command fields

How to use events raised by the GridView control

Although the GridView control provides many features automatically, you still must write some code to handle such things as data validation, database exceptions, and concurrency errors. As figure 14-10 shows, most of this code will be in the form of event handlers that respond to one or more of the events raised by the GridView control.

If you look at the list of events in the table in this figure, you'll see that several of them come in pairs, with one event raised before an action is taken and the other after the action completes. For example, when the user clicks the Delete button in a GridView row, two events are raised. The RowDeleting event is raised before the row is deleted, and the RowDeleted event is raised after the row has been deleted.

The most common reason to handle the before-action events is to provide data validation. For example, when the user clicks the Update button, you can handle the RowUpdating event to make sure the user has entered correct data. If not, you can set the e argument's Cancel property to True to cancel the update.

In contrast, the after-action events give you an opportunity to make sure the database operation completed successfully. In most applications, you should test for two conditions. First, you should check for any database exceptions by checking the Exception property of the e argument. If this property refers to a valid object, an exception has occurred and you can notify the user with an appropriate error message.

Second, if optimistic concurrency is used, you should check to see if a concurrency violation has occurred. To do that, you can check the AffectedRows property of the e argument. If this property is zero, which means no rows have been changed, a concurrency error has probably occurred, and you can notify the user with an appropriate error message.

When you use optimistic concurrency, remember that the Where clause in an Update or Delete statement tries to find a row that has the same values as when the row was originally retrieved. If that row can't be found, which means that another user has updated one of the columns or deleted the row, the update or delete operation never takes place so no rows are affected.

When you try to update a row, one of the most common exceptions is caused by an attempt to store a null value in a database column that doesn't allow null values. This occurs when the user doesn't enter a value in one of the columns that's being updated. In this case, you can display an appropriate error message and set the e argument's ExceptionHandled property to True to suppress further processing of the exception. You can also set the KeepInEditMode property to True to leave the GridView control in edit mode. This is illustrated by the event handler that's coded in this figure.

Events raised by the GridView control

Event	Raised when ...
RowCancelingEdit	The Cancel button of a row in edit mode is clicked.
RowDataBound	Data binding completes for a row.
RowDeleted	A row has been deleted.
RowDeleting	A row is about to be deleted.
RowEditing	A row is about to be edited.
RowUpdated	A row has been updated.
RowUpdating	A row is about to be updated.
SelectedIndexChanged	A row has been selected.
SelectedIndexChanging	A row is about to be selected.

An event handler for the RowUpdated event

```
protected void GridView1_RowUpdated(object sender,
    GridViewUpdatedEventArgs e)
{
    if (e.Exception != null)
    {
        lblError.Text = "A database error has occurred. " +
            "Message: " + e.Exception.Message;
        e.ExceptionHandled = true;
        e.KeepInEditMode = true;
    }
    else if (e.AffectedRows == 0)
    {
        lblError.Text = "Another user may have updated that category. " +
            "Please try again.";
    }
}
```

Description

- The GridView control raises various events that can be handled when data is updated.

- The RowUpdating and RowDeleting events are often used for data validation. You can cancel the update or delete operation by setting the e argument's Cancel property to True.

- You can handle the RowUpdated and RowDeleted events to ensure that the row was successfully updated or deleted.

- To determine if a SQL exception has occurred, check the Exception property of the e argument. If an exception has occurred, the most likely cause is a null value for a column that doesn't accept nulls. To suppress the exception, you can set the ExceptionHandled property to True. And to keep the control in edit mode, you can set the KeepInEditMode property to True.

- To determine how many rows were updated or deleted, check the AffectedRows property of the e argument. If this property is zero and an exception has *not* been thrown, the most likely cause is a concurrency error.

Figure 14-10   How to use events raised by the GridView control

How to insert a row in a GridView control

You may have noticed that although the GridView control lets you update and delete rows, it has no provision for inserting new rows. When you use the GridView control in concert with a FormView or DetailsView control, though, you can provide for insert operations with a minimum of code. You'll learn how to do that in chapter 15. Another alternative is to create a page that lets you insert data into a GridView control by using the techniques described in figure 14-11.

To provide for insertions, you must first create a set of input controls such as text boxes into which the user can enter data for the row to be inserted. Next, you must provide a button that the user can click to start the insertion. Then, in the event handler for this button, you can set the insert parameter values to the values entered by the user and call the data source's Insert method to add the new row.

This is illustrated by the code in this figure. Here, if the insertion is successful, the contents of the text boxes are cleared. But if an exception is thrown, an error message is displayed. This message indicates that an exception has occurred and uses the Message property of the Exception object to display the message that's stored in the Exception object.

Notice in this example that a parameter is generated for each column in the Categories table. If a table contains an identity column, though, a parameter won't be generated for that column. That makes sense because the value of this column is set by the database when the row is inserted.

If you're using an Access data source instead of a SQL data source, you should realize that this works differently. In this case, a parameter is generated for an identity column (called an auto-incremented column in Access), and you have to set the value of that parameter. To set this value correctly, you have to get the maximum value that's stored in the column and then add one to that value. One way to do that is to use the ADO.NET classes you learned about in chapter 12 to retrieve the maximum value from the column. We won't present the specific coding techniques for doing that in this book, though.

Method and properties of the SqlDataSource class for inserting rows

Method	Description
Insert()	Executes the Insert command defined for the data source.

Property	Description
InsertCommand	The Insert command to be executed.
InsertParameters["name"]	The parameter with the specified name.

Property of the Parameter class for inserting rows

Property	Description
DefaultValue	The default value of a parameter. This value is used if no other value is assigned to the parameter.

Code that uses a SqlDataSource control to insert a row

```
protected void btnAdd_Click(object sender, EventArgs e)
{
    SqlDataSource1.InsertParameters["CategoryID"].DefaultValue
        = txtID.Text;
    SqlDataSource1.InsertParameters["ShortName"].DefaultValue
        = txtShortName.Text;
    SqlDataSource1.InsertParameters["LongName"].DefaultValue
        = txtLongName.Text;
    try
    {
        SqlDataSource1.Insert();
        txtID.Text = "";
        txtShortName.Text = "";
        txtLongName.Text = "";
    }
    catch (Exception ex)
    {
        lblError.Text = "A database error has occurred. " +
            "Message: " + ex.Message;
    }
}
```

Description

- The GridView control doesn't support insert operations, but you can use the GridView's data source to insert rows into the database. When you do, the new row will automatically be shown in the GridView control.

- To provide for inserts, the page should include controls such as text boxes for the user to enter data and a button that the user can click to insert the data.

- To use a SqlDataSource control to insert a database row, first set the DefaultValue property of each insert parameter to the value you want to insert. Then, call the Insert method.

- The Insert method may throw a SqlException if a SQL error occurs. The most likely cause of the exception is a primary key constraint violation.

Figure 14-11   How to insert a row in a GridView control

A maintenance application that uses a GridView control

To give you a better idea of how you can use a GridView control to update, delete, and insert data, the following topics present an application that maintains the Categories table in the Halloween database.

The Category Maintenance application

Figure 14-12 introduces you to the Category Maintenance application. It lets the user update, delete, and insert rows in the Categories table of the Halloween database. Here, a GridView control is used to display the rows in the Categories table along with Edit and Delete buttons. In this figure, the user has clicked the Edit button for the third data row, placing that row in edit mode.

Beneath the GridView control, three text boxes let the user enter data for a new category. Then, if the user clicks the Add New Category button, the data entered in these text boxes is used to add a category row to the database. Although it isn't apparent from this figure, required field validators are used for each text box. Also, there's a label control beneath the GridView control that's used to display error messages when an update, delete, or insert operation fails.

The Category Maintenance application

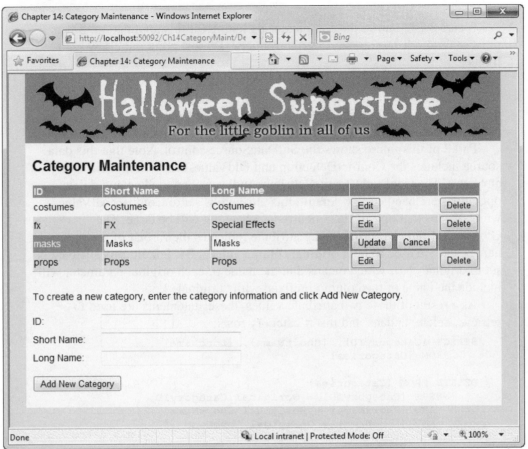

Description

- The Category Maintenance application uses a GridView control to let the user update or delete rows in the Categories table.

- To edit a category, the user clicks the Edit button. This places the GridView control into edit mode. The user can then change the Short Name or Long Name and click Update. Or, the user can click Cancel to leave edit mode.

- To delete a category, the user clicks the Delete button.

- The user can add a category to the table by entering data into the text boxes beneath the GridView control and clicking the Add New Category button.

- If the user attempts to update or add a row with a column that is blank, an error message is displayed.

Figure 14-12   The Category Maintenance application

The aspx file

Figure 14-13 shows the complete aspx listing for this application. Since most of this code has already been introduced, I'll just point out a few highlights.

Part 1 of this figure shows the aspx code for the GridView control. It specifies that the data source is SqlDataSource1 and the primary key for the data is CategoryID. The five columns defined in the Columns element display the three columns from the data source, an Edit button, and a Delete button.

Part 2 of this figure shows the SqlDataSource control. Note that this data source includes the ConflictDetection and OldValuesParameterFormatString attributes. The ConflictDetection attribute indicates how update and delete operations are handled. By default, this attribute is set to CompareAllValues, which means that optimistic concurrency checking will be done. The OldValuesParameterFormatString attribute indicates the format of the parameter names that are used to hold original column values. By default, this attribute is set to original_{0}, which means that the name of each original parameter will include the name of the column prefixed with "original_".

As a result of these two attribute values, these statements are used to retrieve, delete, update, and insert category rows:

```
SELECT [CategoryID], [ShortName], [LongName]
    FROM [Categories]

DELETE FROM [Categories]
    WHERE [CategoryID] = @original_CategoryID
      AND [ShortName] = @original_ShortName
      AND [LongName] = @original_LongName

UPDATE [Categories]
    SET [ShortName] = @ShortName,
        [LongName] = @LongName
    WHERE [CategoryID] = @original_CategoryID
      AND [ShortName] = @original_ShortName
      AND [LongName] = @original_LongName

INSERT INTO [Categories]
    ([CategoryID], [ShortName], [LongName])
    VALUES (@CategoryID, @ShortName, @LongName)
```

Here, the Where clauses implement optimistic concurrency by looking for rows that have the values originally retrieved. Then, the DeleteParameters, UpdateParameters, and InsertParameters elements in the aspx code define the parameters used by these statements.

Finally, part 3 of this figure shows the input controls used to enter the data for a new category. As you can see, each text box is validated by a required field validator that makes sure the user has entered data for the field. This validation is performed when the user clicks the Add New Category button. In addition, the MaxLength attribute is coded for each text box so the user can't enter more characters than are allowed by the associated column in the data source.

The Default.aspx file   **Page 1**

```
<%@ Page Language="C#" AutoEventWireup="true" CodeFile="Default.aspx.cs"
Inherits="_Default" %>

<!DOCTYPE html PUBLIC "-//W3C//DTD XHTML 1.0 Transitional//EN"
"http://www.w3.org/TR/xhtml1/DTD/xhtml1-transitional.dtd">

<html xmlns="http://www.w3.org/1999/xhtml">
<head runat="server">
    <title>Chapter 14: Category Maintenance</title>
    <link href="Main.css" rel="stylesheet" type="text/css" />
</head>
<body>
    <form id="form1" runat="server">
    <div id="page">
        <div id="header">
            <asp:Image ID="Image1" runat="server"
                ImageUrl="~/Images/banner.jpg" />
        </div>
        <div id="main">
            <h1>Category Maintenance</h1>
            <asp:GridView ID="GridView1" runat="server"
                AutoGenerateColumns="False" DataKeyNames="CategoryID"
                DataSourceID="SqlDataSource1" ForeColor="Black">
                <Columns>
                    <asp:BoundField DataField="CategoryID" HeaderText="ID"
                        ReadOnly="True" >
                        <HeaderStyle HorizontalAlign="Left" />
                        <ItemStyle Width="100px" />
                    </asp:BoundField>
                    <asp:BoundField DataField="ShortName" HeaderText="Short Name">
                        <HeaderStyle HorizontalAlign="Left" />
                        <ItemStyle Width="150px" />
                    </asp:BoundField>
                    <asp:BoundField DataField="LongName" HeaderText="Long Name">
                        <HeaderStyle HorizontalAlign="Left" />
                        <ItemStyle Width="200px" />
                    </asp:BoundField>
                    <asp:CommandField ButtonType="Button" CausesValidation="False"
                        ShowEditButton="True" />
                    <asp:CommandField ButtonType="Button" CausesValidation="False"
                        ShowDeleteButton="True" />
                </Columns>
                <HeaderStyle BackColor="Gray" Font-Bold="True" ForeColor="White" />
                <RowStyle BackColor="White" ForeColor="Black" />
                <AlternatingRowStyle BackColor="#F5F5F5" ForeColor="Black" />
                <EditRowStyle BackColor="#F46D11" ForeColor="White" />
            </asp:GridView>
```

Notes

- The GridView control is bound to the SqlDataSource1 data source.
- The Columns element includes child elements that define five columns. Three are for the bound fields; the other two are for the command buttons.

Figure 14-13   The aspx file for the Category Maintenance application (part 1 of 3)

The Default.aspx file

```
<asp:SqlDataSource ID="SqlDataSource1" runat="server"
  ConflictDetection="CompareAllValues"
  ConnectionString="<%$ ConnectionStrings:HalloweenConnectionString %>"
  OldValuesParameterFormatString="original_{0}"
  SelectCommand="SELECT [CategoryID], [ShortName], [LongName]
      FROM [Categories]"
  DeleteCommand="DELETE FROM [Categories]
      WHERE [CategoryID] = @original_CategoryID
        AND [ShortName] = @original_ShortName
          AND [LongName] = @original_LongName"
  InsertCommand="INSERT INTO [Categories]
      ([CategoryID], [ShortName], [LongName])
      VALUES (@CategoryID, @ShortName, @LongName)"
  UpdateCommand="UPDATE [Categories]
      SET [ShortName] = @ShortName,
          [LongName] = @LongName
      WHERE [CategoryID] = @original_CategoryID
        AND [ShortName] = @original_ShortName
        AND [LongName] = @original_LongName">
  <DeleteParameters>
    <asp:Parameter Name="original_CategoryID" Type="String" />
    <asp:Parameter Name="original_ShortName" Type="String" />
    <asp:Parameter Name="original_LongName" Type="String" />
  </DeleteParameters>
  <InsertParameters>
    <asp:Parameter Name="CategoryID" Type="String" />
    <asp:Parameter Name="ShortName" Type="String" />
    <asp:Parameter Name="LongName" Type="String" />
  </InsertParameters>
  <UpdateParameters>
    <asp:Parameter Name="ShortName" Type="String" />
    <asp:Parameter Name="LongName" Type="String" />
    <asp:Parameter Name="original_CategoryID" Type="String" />
    <asp:Parameter Name="original_ShortName" Type="String" />
    <asp:Parameter Name="original_LongName" Type="String" />
  </UpdateParameters>
</asp:SqlDataSource>
```

Notes

- The Select statement retrieves all rows in the Categories table.
- The Where clauses in the Delete and Update statements provide for optimistic concurrency.

Figure 14-13   The aspx file for the Category Maintenance application (part 2 of 3)

The Default.aspx file   **Page 3**

```
        <p id="new">To create a new category, enter the category information
            and click Add New Category.</p>
        <p>
            <asp:Label ID="lblError" runat="server"
                EnableViewState="False" CssClass="error">
            </asp:Label>
        </p>
        <p class="label">ID:</p>
        <p class="entry">
            <asp:TextBox ID="txtID" runat="server"
                Width="100" MaxLength="10">
            </asp:TextBox> 
            <asp:RequiredFieldValidator ID="RequiredFieldValidator1"
                runat="server" ControlToValidate="txtID" CssClass="error"
                ErrorMessage="ID is a required field.">
            </asp:RequiredFieldValidator>
        </p>
        <p class="label">Short Name:</p>
        <p class="entry">
            <asp:TextBox ID="txtShortName" runat="server"
                Width="200" MaxLength="15">
            </asp:TextBox> 
            <asp:RequiredFieldValidator ID="RequiredFieldValidator2"
                runat="server" ControlToValidate="txtShortName"
                CssClass="error"
                ErrorMessage="Short Name is a required field.">
            </asp:RequiredFieldValidator>
        </p>
        <p class="label">Long Name:</p>
        <p class="entry">
            <asp:TextBox ID="txtLongName" runat="server"
                Width="200" MaxLength="50">
            </asp:TextBox> 
            <asp:RequiredFieldValidator ID="RequiredFieldValidator3"
                runat="server" ControlToValidate="txtLongName"
                CssClass="error"
                ErrorMessage="Long Name is a required field.">
            </asp:RequiredFieldValidator>
        </p>
        <p>
            <asp:Button ID="btnAdd" runat="server" Text="Add New Category"
                OnClick="btnAdd_Click" />
        </p>
    </div>
    </div>
    </form>
</body>
</html>
```

Notes

- The text boxes are used to enter data for a new row.

- The required field validators ensure that the user enters data for each column of a new row.

Figure 14-13   The aspx file for the Category Maintenance application (part 3 of 3)

The code-behind file

Although it would be nice if you could create a robust database application without writing any C# code, you must still write code to insert data into a GridView control and to catch and handle any database or concurrency errors that might occur. Figure 14-14 shows this code for the Category Maintenance application.

As you can see, this code-behind file consists of just three methods. The first, btnAdd_Click, sets the values of the three insert parameters to the values entered by the user. Then, it calls the Insert method of the data source control. If an exception is thrown, an appropriate error message is displayed.

The second method, GridView1_RowUpdated, is called after a row has been updated. This method checks the Exception property of the e argument to determine if an exception has been thrown. If so, an error message is displayed, the ExceptionHandled property is set to True to suppress the exception, and the KeepInEditMode property is set to True to leave the GridView control in edit mode. If an exception hasn't occurred, the e argument's AffectedRows property is checked. If it's zero, it means that a concurrency error has occurred and an appropriate message is displayed.

The third method, GridView1_RowDeleted, is called after a row has been deleted. Like the method that's called after a row is updated, this method checks if an exception has been thrown or if a concurrency error has occurred. The only difference is that this method doesn't set the KeepInEditMode property to True, since the control isn't in edit mode when the Delete button is clicked.

The Default.aspx.cs file

```
public partial class _Default : System.Web.UI.Page
{
    protected void btnAdd_Click(object sender, EventArgs e)
    {
        SqlDataSource1.InsertParameters["CategoryID"].DefaultValue
            = txtID.Text;
        SqlDataSource1.InsertParameters["ShortName"].DefaultValue
            = txtShortName.Text;
        SqlDataSource1.InsertParameters["LongName"].DefaultValue
            = txtLongName.Text;
        try
        {
            SqlDataSource1.Insert();
            txtID.Text = "";
            txtShortName.Text = "";
            txtLongName.Text = "";
        }
        catch (Exception ex)
        {
            lblError.Text = "A database error has occurred.<br /><br />" +
                "Message: " + ex.Message;
        }
    }

    protected void GridView1_RowUpdated(object sender,
        GridViewUpdatedEventArgs e)
    {
        if (e.Exception != null)
        {
            lblError.Text = "A database error has occurred.<br /><br />" +
                "Message: " + e.Exception.Message;
            e.ExceptionHandled = true;
            e.KeepInEditMode = true;
        }
        else if (e.AffectedRows == 0)
        {
            lblError.Text = "Another user may have updated that category." +
                "<br />Please try again.";
        }
    }

    protected void GridView1_RowDeleted(object sender,
        GridViewDeletedEventArgs e)
    {
        if (e.Exception != null)
        {
            lblError.Text = "A database error has occurred.<br /><br />" +
                "Message: " + e.Exception.Message;
            e.ExceptionHandled = true;
        }
        else if (e.AffectedRows == 0)
        {
            lblError.Text = "Another user may have updated that category." +
                "<br />Please try again.";
        }
    }
}
```

Figure 14-14   The code-behind file of the Category Maintenance application

How to work with template fields

Although using bound fields is a convenient way to include bound data in a GridView control, the most flexible way is to use template fields. A *template field* is simply a field that provides one or more templates that are used to render the column. You can include anything you want in these templates, including labels or text boxes, data binding expressions, and validation controls. In fact, including validation controls for editable GridView controls is one of the main reasons for using template fields.

How to create template fields

Figure 14-15 shows how to create template fields. The easiest way to do that is to first create a regular bound field and then convert it to a template field. This changes the BoundField element to a TemplateField element and, more importantly, generates ItemTemplate and EditItemTemplate elements that include labels and text boxes with appropriate binding expressions. In particular, each EditItemTemplate element includes a text box that uses the Bind method to implement two-way binding (please see figure 13-15 for more information about this method).

Once you've converted the bound field to a template, you can edit the template to add any additional elements you want to include, such as validation controls. In the code example in this figure, you can see that I added a RequiredFieldValidator control to the EditItem template for the ShortName column. That way, the user must enter data into the txtGridShortName text box. I also changed the names of the label and the text box that were generated for the Item and EditItem templates from their defaults (Label1 and TextBox1) to lblGridShortName and txtGridShortName.

You can also edit the templates from Design view. To do that, you use the same basic techniques that you use to work with the templates for a DataList control. The main difference is that each bound column in a GridView control has its own templates. In this figure, for example, you can see the EditItem template for the ShortName column.

Although a text box is included in the EditItem template for a column by default, you should know that you can use other types of controls too. For example, you can use a check box to work with a Boolean column, and you can use a Calendar control to work with a date column. You can also use a drop-down list that lets the user select a value from the list. To do that, you must create a separate data source that retrieves the data for the list. Then, you can bind the drop-down list to this data source by setting the DataTextField and DataValueField attributes as shown in the last chapter, and you can bind the drop-down list to a column in the GridView's data source by setting its SelectedValue attribute using the DataBindings dialog box you saw in the last chapter.

How to edit templates

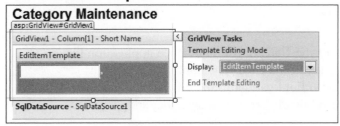

GridView template elements

Element	Description
ItemTemplate	The template used for an individual field.
AlternatingItemTemplate	The template used for alternate rows.
EditItemTemplate	The template used when the row is being edited.
HeaderTemplate	The template used for the header row.
FooterTemplate	The template used for the footer row.

A template field that includes a validation control

```
<asp:TemplateField HeaderText="Short Name">
    <ItemTemplate>
        <asp:Label ID="lblGridShortName" runat="server"
            Text='<%# Bind("ShortName") %>'></asp:Label>
    </ItemTemplate>
    <EditItemTemplate>
        <asp:TextBox ID="txtGridShortName" runat="server"
            width="125px" Text='<%# Bind("ShortName") %>'></asp:TextBox>
        <asp:RequiredFieldValidator
            ID="RequiredFieldValidator5" runat="server"
            ControlToValidate="txtGridShortName"
            ErrorMessage="Short Name is a required field."
            ValidationGroup="Edit">*</asp:RequiredFieldValidator>
    </EditItemTemplate>
    <HeaderStyle HorizontalAlign="Left" />
    <ItemStyle Width="150px" />
</asp:TemplateField>
```

Description

- *Template fields* provide more control over the appearance of the columns in a GridView control than bound fields. A common reason for using template fields is to add validation controls.

- To create a template field, first use the Fields dialog box to create a bound field. Then, click the Convert This Field into a TemplateField link.

- To edit a template, choose Edit Templates from the smart tag menu for the GridView control. Then, select the template you want to edit in the smart tag menu and edit the template by adding text or other controls. You may also want to change the names of the labels and text boxes that were generated when you converted to a template field. When you're finished, choose End Template Editing in the smart tag menu.

Figure 14-15   How to create template fields

The template version of the Category Maintenance application

Figure 14-16 shows a version of the Category Maintenance application that uses templates instead of bound fields in the GridView control. Then, each EditItem template includes a required field validator. In addition, the page uses a validation summary control to display any error messages that are generated by the required field validators.

The aspx code for the template version

Figure 14-17 shows the aspx code for the template version of the Category Maintenance application. Because this file is similar to the file shown in figure 14-13, this figure shows only the portions that are different. In particular, it shows the code for the GridView control and the ValidationSummary control. Because you've already been introduced to most of this code, I'll just point out a few highlights.

First, the GridView control uses template fields for the ShortName and LongName columns. These templates include required field validators to validate the text box input fields. Here, each validator is assigned to a validation group named Edit. Then, in the CommandField element for the Edit button, the CausesValidation attribute is set to True and the ValidationGroup attribute is set to Edit. As a result, when a row is displayed in edit mode, just the validators that belong to the Edit group will be invoked when the Update button is clicked.

Second, the ErrorMessage attribute of each of the Edit validators provides the error message that's displayed in the ValidationSummary control. For this control, you can see that the ValidationGroup is set to Edit so the right messages will be displayed. In addition, the content of each validator specifies that an asterisk will appear to the right of each field in the GridView control. If you look closely at the screen in the last figure, you can see that these asterisks are displayed in white on the dark column dividers.

Third, the text boxes in the EditItem templates for the Short Name and Long Name fields include the MaxLength attribute. That way, the user can't enter more characters than are allowed by the data source. This is another advantage of using templates with a GridView control.

Please note that there is one other difference between this version of the application and the previous version that isn't shown in this figure. Because this version uses a validation group for the validators in the GridView control, it must also use a validation group for the validators that are outside of the GridView control. As a result, the three validators for the text boxes as well as the Add New Category button all have a ValidationGroup attribute that assigns them to the New group.

The Category Maintenance application with template fields

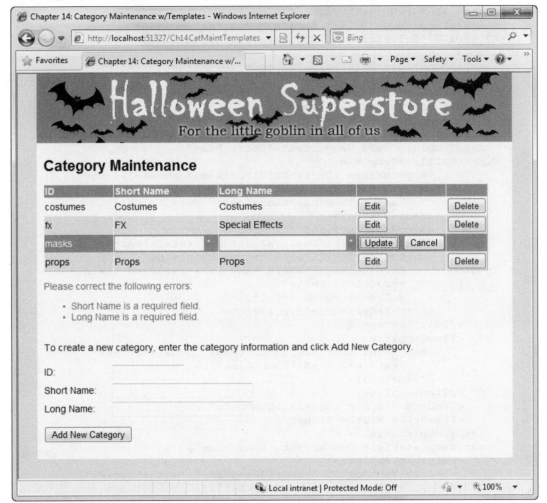

Description

- This version of the Category Maintenance application uses template fields in the GridView control, and the EditItem template for each editable field includes a required field validator.

- A ValidationSummary control is used to display the error messages generated by the required field validators.

- The text boxes in the EditItem templates for the Short Name and Long Name fields include the MaxLength attribute so the user can't enter more characters than are allowed by the data source.

Figure 14-16   The template version of the Category Maintenance application

The Default.aspx file

```
<asp:GridView ID="GridView1" runat="server"
    AutoGenerateColumns="False" DataKeyNames="CategoryID"
    DataSourceID="SqlDataSource1" ForeColor="Black">
    <Columns>
        <asp:BoundField DataField="CategoryID" HeaderText="ID"
            ReadOnly="True" >
            <HeaderStyle HorizontalAlign="Left" />
            <ItemStyle Width="100px" />
        </asp:BoundField>

        <asp:TemplateField HeaderText="Short Name">
            <EditItemTemplate>
                <asp:TextBox ID="txtGridShortName" runat="server"
                    Width="125px" MaxLength="15"
                    Text='<%# Bind("ShortName") %>'>
                </asp:TextBox>
                <asp:RequiredFieldValidator
                    ID="RequiredFieldValidator4" runat="server"
                    ControlToValidate="txtGridShortName"
                    ErrorMessage="Short Name is a required field."
                    ForeColor="White"
                    ValidationGroup="Edit">*
                </asp:RequiredFieldValidator>
            </EditItemTemplate>
            <ItemTemplate>
                <asp:Label ID="lblGridShortName" runat="server"
                    Text='<%# Bind("ShortName") %>'>
                </asp:Label>
            </ItemTemplate>
            <HeaderStyle HorizontalAlign="Left" />
            <ItemStyle Width="150px" />
        </asp:TemplateField>
        <asp:TemplateField HeaderText="Long Name">
            <EditItemTemplate>
                <asp:TextBox ID="txtGridLongName" runat="server"
                    Width="180px" MaxLength="50"
                    Text='<%# Bind("LongName") %>'>
                </asp:TextBox>
                <asp:RequiredFieldValidator
                    ID="RequiredFieldValidator5" runat="server"
                    ControlToValidate="txtGridLongName"
                    ErrorMessage="Long Name is a required field."
                    ForeColor="White"
                    ValidationGroup="Edit">*
                </asp:RequiredFieldValidator>
            </EditItemTemplate>
            <ItemTemplate>
                <asp:Label ID="lblGridLongName" runat="server"
                    Text='<%# Bind("LongName") %>'>
                </asp:Label>
            </ItemTemplate>
            <HeaderStyle HorizontalAlign="Left" />
            <ItemStyle Width="200px" />
        </asp:TemplateField>
```

Figure 14-17   The aspx code for the template version of the Category Maintenance application (part 1 of 2)

The Default.aspx file   **Page 2**

```
        <asp:CommandField ButtonType="Button" CausesValidation="True"
            ShowEditButton="True" ValidationGroup="Edit" />
        <asp:CommandField ButtonType="Button" CausesValidation="False"
            ShowDeleteButton="True" />
    </Columns>
    <HeaderStyle BackColor="Gray" Font-Bold="True" ForeColor="White" />
    <RowStyle BackColor="White" ForeColor="Black" />
    <AlternatingRowStyle BackColor="LightGray" ForeColor="Black" />
    <EditRowStyle BackColor="#F46D11" ForeColor="White" />
</asp:GridView>
.
.
<asp:ValidationSummary ID="ValidationSummary1" runat="server"
    HeaderText="Please correct the following errors:"
    ValidationGroup="Edit" CssClass="error" />
.
.
```

Description

- The EditItem templates for the Short Name and Long Name fields include required field validators, which are assigned to a validation group named Edit. This group is also referenced in the code for the Edit button and the ValidationSummary control so only the validators in this group are included.

- The text boxes in the EditItem templates for the Short Name and Long Name fields include the MaxLength attribute so the user can't enter more characters than are allowed by the data source.

- The aspx code that's not shown in this figure is identical to the code in figure 14-13, except that the required field validators for the text boxes for inserting a new category and the Add New Category button specify a validation group named New.

Figure 14-17   The aspx code for the template version of the Category Maintenance application (part 2 of 2)

Perspective

The GridView control is ideal for any application that displays a list of items retrieved from a database, and nearly all applications have that need. It's also ideal for displaying search results, such as product searches for an online catalog or document searches in an online customer support site. And it's ideal for maintaining simple tables that consist of just a few columns.

In the next chapter, you'll build on your knowledge of the GridView control by learning how to use it in combination with the FormView and DetailsView controls. Both are designed to display the details for an item that's selected from a GridView control or a list control. And the combination of a GridView control and a FormView or DetailsView control can be powerful.

Terms

paging	template
command field	field
edit mode	

Exercise 14-1   Create a Customer List application

In this exercise, you'll develop a page that displays customers in a GridView control that includes sorting and paging. When you're done, the page should look like this:

Chapter 14   How to use the GridView control   **481**

Create the GridView control and the SQL data source

1. Open the Ch14CustomerList application in the C:\aspnet4_cs directory. This application contains the starting page and the image and style sheet used by the page.

2. Add a GridView control to the main division of the page, and create a data source that retrieves the LastName, FirstName, State, and City columns from the Customers table sorted by LastName.

3. Use the AutoFormat dialog box to apply the Simple scheme to the control.

4. Use the Fields dialog box to left-align the header for each field and to set the column widths to 175, 150, 75, and 150 respectively.

5. Run the application to see how it looks. Notice that all the customers are displayed on a single page.

Add paging to the GridView control

6. Display the smart tag menu for the GridView control and check the Enable Paging option.

7. Set the Mode property in the PagerSettings group for the GridView control to NextPreviousFirstLast. In addition, set the BackColor property in the PagerStyle group so the background color of the pager area is the same as the background color of the header.

8. Run the application again, and use the paging controls to display different pages.

Add sorting to the GridView control

9. Display the smart tag menu for the GridView control and check the Enable Sorting option.

10. Remove the sort expressions from the FirstName and City fields, and set the sort expression for the State field so it sorts by city within state.

11. Run the application, and click the State heading. The rows should be sorted by city in ascending sequence within state in ascending sequence. Notice that the color of the sorted column changes.

12. Click the State heading again. This time, the rows should be sorted by city in descending sequence within state in ascending sequence, and the column should be displayed in a different color.

13. Close the browser, and delete the four Sorted style elements that were added to the GridView control when you applied the scheme. You can also delete any other style elements that aren't used by this application if you'd like.

14. Run the application one more time, and click the State heading. This time, the formatting shouldn't change. Continue experimenting if you want, and then close the browser.

Exercise 14-2   Create a Product Receipt application

In this exercise, you'll create a simple application that uses a GridView control to let the user update the on-hand quantity for products when a shipment is received. That will give you an idea of how to work with command fields and templates.

Create the GridView control using bound fields

1. Open the Ch14ProductReceipt application in the C:\aspnet4_cs directory. This application contains a page with a starting GridView control and its data source, a validation summary control that will be used to display error messages for validation controls you'll add later in this exercise, and a label that will be used to display database errors.

2. Display the Default page in Source view and review the code for the data source that's used by the GridView control.

3. Display the Fields dialog box, and set the ReadOnly property of the Name field to True so this field can't be changed.

4. Add a command field to the GridView control that provides for updating a row.

5. Add an event handler for the RowUpdated event of the GridView control. Add code like that shown in figure 14-10 that checks for database exceptions and displays error messages in the label near the bottom of the page. Don't check for concurrency errors, though, since the data source doesn't provide for concurrency checking.

6. Run the application. Click the Edit button for one of the products, change the on-hand amount, and click the Update button. If this works, click the Edit button again, clear the on-hand amount, and click the Update button. This time, an error message should be displayed indicating that a database error occurred. Click the Cancel button and close the browser.

Convert a bound field to a template field

7. Display the Fields dialog box for the GridView control, highlight the OnHand field, and click the Convert This Field into a Template Field link.

8. Display the EditItem template for the OnHand field, give the text box an appropriate name, and change its width to 75.

9. Add required field and compare validators after the text box. The compare validator should check that an integer greater than or equal to zero is entered. If an error occurs, display an asterisk in a white font following the text box, and display an error message in the validation summary control at the bottom of the page.

10. Run the application, click the Edit button for one of the products, clear the on-hand amount, and click the Update button to see that an asterisk is displayed to the right of the text box and the error message is displayed in the validation summary control. Now, try entering an invalid number to see what happens. When you're done experimenting, close the browser.

15

How to use the DetailsView and FormView controls

In this chapter, you'll learn how to use the DetailsView and FormView controls. Although both of these controls are designed to work with the GridView control to display the details of the item selected in that control, they can also be used on their own or in combination with other types of list controls such as drop-down lists or list boxes.

How to use the DetailsView control

The following topics present the basics of working with the DetailsView control. However, much of what you'll learn in these topics applies to the FormView control as well.

An introduction to the DetailsView control

As figure 15-1 shows, the DetailsView control is designed to display the data for a single item of a data source. To use this control effectively, you must provide some way for the user to select which data item to display. The most common way to do that is to use the DetailsView control in combination with another control such as a GridView control or a drop-down list. At the top of this figure, you can see how the DetailsView control works with a drop-down list, and you'll see how it works with a GridView control later in this chapter.

Alternatively, you can enable paging for the DetailsView control. Then, a row of paging controls appears at the bottom of the DetailsView control, and the user can select a data item using those controls. You'll learn how this works in figure 15-3.

As the code example in this figure shows, you use the DataSourceID attribute to specify the data source that a DetailsView control should be bound to. Then, the Fields element contains a set of child elements that define the individual fields to be displayed by the DetailsView control. This is similar to the way the Columns element for a GridView control works.

A DetailsView control can be displayed in one of three modes. In ReadOnly mode, the data for the current data source row is displayed but can't be modified. In Edit mode, the user can modify the data for the current row. And in Insert mode, the user can enter data that will be inserted into the data source as a new row.

A DetailsView control that displays data for a selected product

Choose a product:	Skull Fogger ▼

Product ID:	skullfog01
Name:	Skull Fogger
Short Description:	2,800 cubic foot fogger
Long Description:	This fogger puts out a whopping 2,800 cubic feet of fog per minute. Comes with a 10-foot remote control.
Category ID:	fx
Image File:	skullfog1.jpg
Unit Price:	39.9500
On Hand:	50

The aspx code for the DetailsView control shown above

```
<asp:DetailsView ID="DetailsView1" runat="server" AutoGenerateRows="False"
    DataKeyNames="ProductID" DataSourceID="SqlDataSource2" Width="450px">
    <Fields>
        <asp:BoundField DataField="ProductID" HeaderText="Product ID:"
            ReadOnly="True">
            <HeaderStyle Width="125px" />
            <ItemStyle Width="325px" />
        </asp:BoundField>
        <asp:BoundField DataField="Name" HeaderText="Name:" />
        <asp:BoundField DataField="ShortDescription"
            HeaderText="Short Description:" />
        <asp:BoundField DataField="LongDescription"
            HeaderText="Long Description:" />
        <asp:BoundField DataField="CategoryID" HeaderText="Category ID:" />
        <asp:BoundField DataField="ImageFile" HeaderText="Image File:" />
        <asp:BoundField DataField="UnitPrice" HeaderText="Unit Price:" />
        <asp:BoundField DataField="OnHand" HeaderText="On Hand:" />
    </Fields>
</asp:DetailsView>
```

Three modes of the DetailsView control

Mode	Description
ReadOnly	Used to display an item from the data source.
Edit	Used to edit an item in the data source.
Insert	Used to insert a new item into the data source.

Description

- The DetailsView control displays data for a single row of a data source. It is usually used in combination with a drop-down list or GridView control that is used to select the item to be displayed.

- The DetailsView element includes a Fields element that contains a BoundField element for each field retrieved from the data source.

- You can edit the fields collection by choosing Edit Fields from the smart tag menu of a DetailsView control.

Figure 15-1   An introduction to the DetailsView control

Attributes and child elements for the DetailsView control

The tables in figure 15-2 list the attributes and child elements you can use to declare a DetailsView control. The first table lists the attributes you're most likely to use for this control. You can use the DataKeyNames attribute to list the names of the primary key fields for the data source. And you can set the AutoGenerateRows attribute to True if you want the DetailsView control to automatically generate data fields. Then, you'll want to delete the Fields element that was added when you created the DetailsView control.

By the way, there are many other attributes you can use on the DetailsView element to specify the control's layout and formatting. For example, you can include attributes like Height, Width, BackColor, and ForeColor. To see all of the attributes that are available, you can use the HTML Editor's IntelliSense feature.

The second table in this figure lists the child elements that you can use between the start and end tags of the DetailsView element. Most of these elements provide styles and templates that control the formatting for the different parts of the DetailsView control. Like the DataList and GridView controls, the DetailsView controls is rendered as a table. So it's best to use the style elements to format the control rather than using CSS.

The Fields element can contain any of the child elements listed in the third table of this figure. These elements describe the individual fields that are displayed by the DetailsView control. Although this figure doesn't show it, these child elements can themselves include child elements to specify formatting information. For example, you can include HeaderStyle and ItemStyle as child elements of a BoundField element to control the formatting for the header and item sections of a bound field. Here again, you can use the HTML Editor's IntelliSense feature to see what child elements are available and what attributes they support.

How to define the fields in a DetailsView control

Just like when you create a GridView control, one BoundField element is created for each column in the data source when you create a DetailsView control. Then, you can work with those fields or create additional fields using the Fields dialog box you saw in figure 14-2 of chapter 14. To display this dialog box, you choose the Edit Fields command from the control's smart tag menu. You can also use the HTML editor to create these fields manually. Or you can use the Add Field dialog box as described later in this chapter.

Each BoundField element that's created for a DetailsView control includes a SortExpression attribute. However, these sort expressions are only meaningful if you enable paging for the control. Because of that, you can safely delete these attributes if you're not using paging.

DetailsView control attributes

Attribute	Description
ID	The ID of this control.
Runat	Must specify "server".
DataSourceID	The ID of the data source to bind the DetailsView control to.
DataKeyNames	A list of field names that form the primary key for the data source.
AutoGenerateRows	If True, a row is automatically generated for each field in the data source. If False, you must define the rows in the Fields element.
DefaultMode	Sets the initial mode of the DetailsView control. Valid options are Edit, Insert, or ReadOnly.
AllowPaging	Set to True to allow paging.

DetailsView child elements

Element	Description
Fields	The fields that are displayed by a DetailsView control.
RowStyle	The style used for data rows in ReadOnly mode.
AlternatingRowStyle	The style used for alternate rows.
EditRowStyle	The style used for data rows in Edit mode.
InsertRowStyle	The style used for data rows in Insert mode.
CommandRowStyle	The style used for command rows.
EmptyDataRowStyle	The style used for data rows when the data source is empty.
EmptyDataTemplate	The template used when the data source is empty.
HeaderStyle	The style used for the header row.
HeaderTemplate	The template used for the header row.
FooterStyle	The style used for the footer row.
FooterTemplate	The template used for the footer row.
PagerSettings	The settings used to control the pager row.
PagerStyle	The style used for the pager row.
PagerTemplate	The template used for the pager row.

Fields child elements

Element	Description
asp:BoundField	A field bound to a data source column.
asp:ButtonField	A field that displays a button.
asp:CheckBoxField	A field that displays a check box.
asp:CommandField	A field that contains command buttons.
asp:HyperlinkField	A field that displays a hyperlink.
asp:ImageField	A field that displays an image.
asp:TemplateField	A column with custom content.

Figure 15-2   Attributes and child elements for the DetailsView control

How to enable paging

Like the GridView control, the DetailsView control supports paging. As figure 15-3 shows, a row of paging controls is displayed at the bottom of the DetailsView control when you set the AllowPaging attribute to True. Then, you can specify the paging mode by including a PagerSettings element, and you can include PagerStyle and PagerTemplate elements to specify the appearance of the pager controls.

Note that if the data source contains more than a few dozen items, paging isn't a practical way to provide for navigation. In most cases, then, a DetailsView control is associated with a list control that is used to select the item to be displayed. You'll learn how to create pages that work this way in the next figure.

A DetailsView control that allows paging

Product ID:	bats01
Name:	Flying Bats
Short Description:	Bats flying in front of moon
Long Description:	Bats flying in front of a full moon make for an eerie spectacle.
Category ID:	props
Image File:	cool1.jpg
Unit Price:	69.9900
On Hand:	25
<< < > >>	

The aspx code for the DetailsView control shown above

```
<asp:DetailsView ID="DetailsView1" runat="server" AutoGenerateRows="False"
    DataKeyNames="ProductID" DataSourceID="SqlDataSource1"
    Width="450px" AllowPaging="True">
    <PagerSettings Mode="NextPreviousFirstLast" />
    <Fields>
        <asp:BoundField DataField="ProductID" HeaderText="ProductID"
            ReadOnly="True">
            <HeaderStyle Width="125px" />
            <ItemStyle Width="325px" />
        </asp:BoundField>
        <asp:BoundField DataField="Name" HeaderText="Name:" />
        <asp:BoundField DataField="ShortDescription"
            HeaderText="Short Description:" />
        <asp:BoundField DataField="LongDescription"
            HeaderText="Long Description:" />
        <asp:BoundField DataField="CategoryID"
            HeaderText="Category ID: " />
        <asp:BoundField DataField="ImageFile" HeaderText="Image File:" />
        <asp:BoundField DataField="UnitPrice" HeaderText="Unit Price:" />
        <asp:BoundField DataField="OnHand" HeaderText="On Hand:" />
    </Fields>
</asp:DetailsView>
```

Description

- The DetailsView control supports paging. Then, you can move from one item to the next by using the paging controls. This works much the same as it does for a GridView control, except that data from only one row is displayed at a time.

- For more information about paging, please refer to figure 14-6 in chapter 14.

Figure 15-3   How to enable paging

How to create a Master/Detail page

As figure 15-4 shows, a *Master/Detail page* is a page that displays a list of data items from a data source along with the details for one of the items selected from the list. The list of items can be displayed by any control that allows the user to select an item, including a drop-down list or a GridView control. Then, you can use a DetailsView control to display the details for the selected item. The page shown in figure 15-1 is an example of a Master/Detail page in which the master list is displayed as a drop-down list and a DetailsView control is used to display the details for the selected item.

A Master/Detail page typically uses two data sources. The first retrieves the items to be displayed by the control that contains the list of data items. For efficiency's sake, this data source should retrieve only the data columns necessary to display the list. For example, the data source for the drop-down list in figure 15-1 only needs to retrieve the ProductName and ProductID columns from the Products table in the Halloween database.

The second data source provides the data for the selected item. It usually uses a parameter to specify which row should be retrieved from the database. In the example in this figure, the data source uses a parameter that's bound to the drop-down list. That way, this data source automatically retrieves the data for the product that's selected by the drop-down list.

A Master/Detail page typically contains:

- A control that lets the user choose an item to display, such as a drop-down list or a GridView control.

- A data source that retrieves all of the items to be displayed in the list. The control that contains the list of data items should be bound to this data source.

- A DetailsView control that displays data for the item selected by the user.

- A data source that retrieves the data for the item selected by the user. The DetailsView control should be bound to this data source. To retrieve the selected item, this data source can use a parameter that's bound to the SelectedValue property of the control that contains the list of data items.

A SqlDataSource control with a parameter that's bound to a drop-down list

```
<asp:SqlDataSource ID="SqlDataSource2" runat="server"
    ConnectionString="<%$ ConnectionStrings:HalloweenConnection %>"
    SelectCommand="SELECT [ProductID], [Name], [ShortDescription],
        [LongDescription], [CategoryID], [ImageFile], [UnitPrice], [OnHand]
        FROM [Products]
        WHERE ([ProductID] = @ProductID)">
    <SelectParameters>
        <asp:ControlParameter ControlID="ddlProducts" Name="ProductID"
            PropertyName="SelectedValue" Type="String" />
    </SelectParameters>
</asp:SqlDataSource>
```

Description

- A *Master/Detail page* is a page that displays a list of items from a database along with the details of one item from the list. The DetailsView control is often used to display the details portion of a Master/Detail page.

- The list portion of a Master/Detail page can be displayed by any control that contains a list of data items, including a drop-down list or a GridView control.

- A Master/Detail page usually includes two data sources, one for the master list and the other for the DetailsView control.

Figure 15-4   How to create a Master/Detail page

How to update DetailsView data

Besides displaying data for a specific item from a data source, you can also use a DetailsView control to edit, insert, and delete items. You'll learn how to do that in the following topics.

An introduction to command buttons

Much like the GridView control, the DetailsView control uses command buttons to let the user edit and delete data. Thus, the DetailsView control provides Edit, Delete, Update, and Cancel buttons. In addition, the DetailsView control lets the user insert data, so it provides for two more buttons. The New button places the DetailsView control into Insert mode, and the Insert button accepts the data entered by the user and writes it to the data source. These command buttons are summarized in figure 15-5.

There are two ways to provide the command buttons for a DetailsView control. The easiest way is to use the AutoGenerate*xxx*Button attributes, which are listed in the second table and illustrated in the code example. However, when you use these attributes, you have no control over the appearance of the buttons. For that, you must use command fields as described in the next figure.

A DetailsView control with automatically generated command buttons

Product ID:	pow01
Name:	Austin Powers
Short Description:	Austin Powers costume
Long Description:	Be the most shagadelic guest at this year's party, baby.
Category ID:	costumes
Image File:	powers1.jpg
Unit Price:	79.9900
On Hand:	25

Edit Delete New

Command buttons

Button	Description
Edit	Places the DetailsView control in Edit mode.
Delete	Deletes the current item and leaves the DetailsView control in ReadOnly mode.
New	Places the DetailsView control in Insert mode.
Update	Displayed only in Edit mode. Updates the data source, then returns to ReadOnly mode.
Insert	Displayed only in Insert mode. Inserts the data, then returns to ReadOnly mode.
Cancel	Displayed in Edit or Insert mode. Cancels the operation and returns to ReadOnly mode.

Attributes that generate command buttons

Attribute	Description
AutoGenerateDeleteButton	Generates a Delete button.
AutoGenerateEditButton	Generates an Edit button.
AutoGenerateInsertButton	Generates a New button.

A DetailsView element that automatically generates command buttons

```
<asp:DetailsView ID="DetailsView1" runat="server"
    DataSourceID="SqlDataSource2" DataKeyNames="ProductID"
    AutoGenerateRows="False"
    AutoGenerateDeleteButton="True"
    AutoGenerateEditButton="True"
    AutoGenerateInsertButton="True">
</asp:DetailsView>
```

Description

- The DetailsView control supports six different command buttons.
- You can use the AutoGenerateDeleteButton, AutoGenerateEditButton, and AutoGenerateInsertButton attributes to automatically generate command buttons.
- To customize command button appearance, use command fields instead of automatically generated buttons as described in the next figure.

Figure 15-5   An introduction to command buttons

How to add command buttons

Like the GridView control, the DetailsView control lets you use
CommandField elements to specify the command buttons that should be displayed by the control. One way to do that is to use the Add Field dialog box
shown in figure 15-6 to add a command field to a DetailsView control. Of
course, you can also use the Edit Fields dialog box to add command fields, or
you can use the HTML Editor to code the CommandField elements manually.

To create a command button using the Add Field dialog box, you select
CommandField as the field type. When you do, four check boxes appear that let
you select which command buttons you want to show in the command field. In
addition, a drop-down list lets you choose whether the command buttons should
be displayed as buttons or hyperlinks.

When you first display the Add Field dialog box for a command field, you'll
notice that the Show Cancel Button check box is disabled. That's because this
button can only be used in conjunction with the New/Insert and Edit/Update
buttons. When you select one of these buttons, then, the Show Cancel Button
check box is enabled and it's selected by default. That makes sense because
you'll typically want to allow the user to cancel out of an insert or edit operation.

Note that the CommandField element includes attributes that let you specify
the text or image to be displayed and whether the button causes validation. For
more information about using these attributes, please refer back to chapter 14.

Before I go on, you should realize that you can use the Add Field dialog box
to create any of the elements shown in the third table in figure 15-2. To do that,
you just select the type of field you want to create from the drop-down list at the
top of the dialog box. Then, the appropriate options for that field type are
displayed. If you experiment with this, you shouldn't have any trouble figuring
out how it works.

The Add Field dialog box for adding a command field

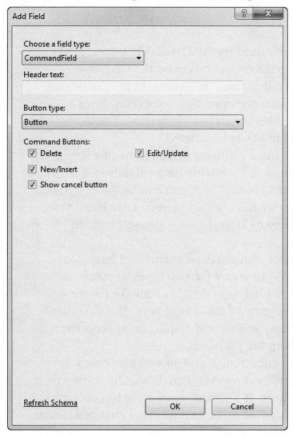

Code generated by the above dialog box

```
<asp:CommandField ButtonType="Button"
    ShowDeleteButton="True"
    ShowEditButton="True"
    ShowInsertButton="True" />
```

Description

- You can add command buttons to a DetailsView control to let the user update, insert, and delete data.

- The command buttons for a DetailsView control are similar to the command buttons for a GridView control. However, the DetailsView control doesn't provide a Select button, and it does provide New and Insert buttons. For more information about command buttons, please refer to figure 14-9 in chapter 14.

- To display the Add Field dialog box, choose Add New Field from the smart tag menu of the DetailsView control.

Figure 15-6   How to add command buttons

How to use events raised by the DetailsView control

Figure 15-7 lists the events that are raised by the DetailsView control. As you can see, these events are similar to the events raised by the GridView control. Most of these events come in pairs: one that's raised before an operation occurs, and another that's raised after the operation completes. For example, the ItemDeleting event is raised before an item is deleted, and the ItemDeleted event is raised after an item has been deleted.

As with the GridView control, the most common reason to handle the before events for the DetailsView control is to provide data validation. For example, when the user clicks the Update button, you can handle the ItemUpdating event to make sure the user has entered correct data. Then, you can set the e argument's Cancel property to True if the user hasn't entered correct data. This cancels the update.

The after-action events let you check that database operations have completed successfully. To do that, you need to check for two types of errors as illustrated in the example in this figure. First, you should check for database exceptions by testing the Exception property of the e argument. If it is not null, a database exception has occurred. Then, you should display an appropriate error message to let the user know about the problem.

If the data source uses optimistic concurrency, you should also check to make sure there hasn't been a concurrency error. You can do that by testing the AffectedRows property of the e argument. If a concurrency error has occurred, this property will be set to zero meaning that no rows have been changed. Then, you can display an appropriate error message.

If no errors occurred during the update operation, the ItemUpdated event shown in this figure ends by calling the DataBind method for the drop-down list control. This is necessary because view state is enabled for this control. As a result, this control will continue to display the old data unless you call its DataBind method to refresh its data. If view state were disabled for this control, the DataBind call wouldn't be necessary.

Events raised by the DetailsView control

Event	Description
`ItemCommand`	Raised when a button is clicked.
`ItemCreated`	Raised when an item is created.
`DataBound`	Raised when data binding completes for an item.
`ItemDeleted`	Raised when an item has been deleted.
`ItemDeleting`	Raised when an item is about to be deleted.
`ItemInserted`	Raised when an item has been inserted.
`ItemInserting`	Raised when an item is about to be inserted.
`ItemUpdated`	Raised when an item has been updated.
`ItemUpdating`	Raised when an item is about to be updated.
`PageIndexChanged`	Raised when the index of the displayed item has changed.
`PageIndexChanging`	Raised when the index of the displayed item is about to change.

An event handler for the ItemUpdated event

```
protected void DetailsView1_ItemUpdated(
    object sender, DetailsViewUpdatedEventArgs e)
{
    if (e.Exception != null)
    {
        lblError.Text = "A database error has occurred. " +
            "Message: " + e.Exception.Message;
        e.ExceptionHandled = true;
    }
    else if (e.AffectedRows == 0)
    {
        lblError.Text = "Another user may have updated that product. "
            + "Please try again.";
    }
    else
    {
        ddlProducts.DataBind();
    }
}
```

Description

- Like the GridView control, the DetailsView control raises events that you can use to test for database exceptions and concurrency errors.
- To determine if a SQL exception has occurred, test the Exception property of the e argument. If an exception has occurred, you can set the ExceptionHandled property to True to suppress the exception. You can also set the KeepInEditMode property to True to keep the DetailsView control in Edit mode. And you can set the KeepInInsertMode property to True to keep the control in Insert mode.
- If the AffectedRows property of the e argument is zero and an exception has not been thrown, a concurrency error has probably occurred.
- If the DetailsView control is used on a Master/Detail page, you should call the DataBind method of the master list control after a successful insert, update, or delete.

Figure 15-7   How to use events raised by the DetailsView control

How to create template fields

Like the GridView control, you can use template fields to control the appearance of the fields in a DetailsView control. You can do that to add validation controls or to use controls other than text boxes as described in the last chapter or to modify the text boxes that are displayed by default. Figure 15-8 illustrates how this works.

At the top of this figure, you can see two DetailsView controls displayed in Edit mode. The first control uses the default BoundField elements. Here, you can see that the text box for the long description isn't big enough to display all of the data in this column for the selected product, which makes it more difficult for the user to modify this field. In addition, to change the category, the user must enter the category ID. That makes it more likely that the user will enter a value that isn't valid.

The second DetailsView control illustrates how you can use templates to make it easier for the user to work with the data. Here, all of the text boxes have been resized so that they're appropriate for the data they will display. In particular, the text box for the long description has been changed to a multi-line text box. In addition, the text box for the category ID has been replaced by a drop-down list that displays the category name. This control is bound to a separate data source that retrieves the category IDs and category names from the Categories table.

To create template fields for a DetailsView control, you use the same techniques you use to create templates for a GridView control. That is, you convert bound fields to template fields, you switch to template-editing mode, and you select the template you want to edit. The table in this figure lists the five templates that are available for the template fields in a DetailsView control. In most cases, you'll define just the Item, EditItem, and InsertItem templates as shown in the code example in this figure.

The template field shown here is for the Name column of the Products table. Notice that in addition to setting the width of the text boxes for this column in the EditItem and InsertItem templates, I also set the MaxLength attribute. That way, the user can't enter more characters than are allowed by the Name column. As you'll see in the aspx code for the Product Maintenance application that's presented next, I used this same technique to restrict the number of characters that can be entered for the ProductID, ShortDescription, LongDescription, and ImageFile columns.

A DetailsView control in Edit mode without and with templates

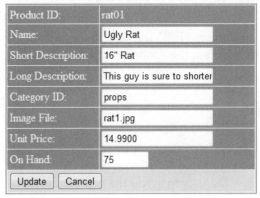 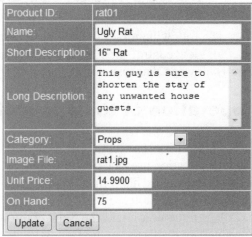

DetailsView template elements

Element	Description
ItemTemplate	The template used for an individual field.
AlternatingItemTemplate	The template used for alternating fields.
EditItemTemplate	The template used for a field in Edit mode.
InsertItemTemplate	The template used for a field in Insert mode.
HeaderTemplate	The template used for the header text for a field.

The aspx code for a custom template field

```
<asp:TemplateField HeaderText="Name:">
    <ItemTemplate>
        <asp:Label ID="Label8" runat="server" Text='<%# Bind("Name") %>'>
        </asp:Label>
    </ItemTemplate>
    <EditItemTemplate>
        <asp:TextBox ID="txtName" runat="server" Text='<%# Bind("Name") %>'
            Width="200px" MaxLength="50">
        </asp:TextBox>
    </EditItemTemplate>
    <InsertItemTemplate>
        <asp:TextBox ID="txtName" runat="server" Text='<%# Bind("Name") %>'
            Width="200px" MaxLength="50">
        </asp:TextBox>
    </InsertItemTemplate>
    <HeaderStyle HorizontalAlign="Left" Width="150px" />
    <ItemStyle Width="250px" />
</asp:TemplateField>
```

Description

- You can use template fields to control the appearance of the fields in a DetailsView control using the same techniques you use to work with template fields in a GridView control. See figure 14-15 in chapter 14 for more information.

Figure 15-8   How to create template fields

The Product Maintenance application

The following topics present an application that uses GridView and DetailsView controls in a Master/Detail page to maintain the Products table in the Halloween database.

The operation of the application

Figure 15-9 shows the operation of the Product Maintenance application. This application uses a GridView control to list the product records on the left side of the page. This control uses paging to allow the user to scroll through the entire Products table.

When the user clicks the Select button for a product, the details for that product are displayed in the DetailsView control on the right side of the page. Then, the user can use the Edit or Delete button to edit or delete the selected product. The user can also click the New button to insert a new product.

The aspx file

Figure 15-10 shows the Default.aspx file for the Product Maintenance application. In part 1, you can see the GridView control that displays the products as well as the data source for this control. Notice that the SelectedIndex attribute of the GridView control is set to 0. That way, the information for the first product will be displayed in the DetailsView control when the page is first displayed.

The DetailsView control is shown in parts 2 and 3 of the listing. Here, the DetailsView element includes the attributes that control the overall appearance of the control. I generated most of these attributes by applying a scheme to the DetailsView control, then editing the attributes to change the colors. You can also see that the scheme added RowStyle, EditRowStyle, and FooterStyle elements to the control. Since an InsertRowStyle element isn't included, this style will default to the EditRowStyle.

To make it easier for the user to work with the data in the DetailsView control, all of the bound fields have been converted to template fields. Then, the EditItem and InsertItem templates for these fields were modified so the fields are displayed as shown in the second DetailsView control in figure 15-8. In addition, required field validators were added for each field except for the category ID and image file fields, and compare validators were added for the unit price and on hand fields. Finally, a command field that provides for Edit, Delete, and New buttons was added.

The Product Maintenance application

Description

- The Product Maintenance application uses a GridView control and a DetailsView control to let the user update the data in the Products table.

- To select a product, the user locates the product in the GridView control and clicks the Select button. This displays the details for the product in the DetailsView control. Then, the user can click the Edit button to change the product data or the Delete button to delete the product.

- To add a new product to the database, the user clicks the New button in the DetailsView control. Then, the user can enter the data for the new product and click the Insert button.

Figure 15-9   The Product Maintenance application

The Default.aspx file

```
<%@ Page Language="C#" AutoEventWireup="true" CodeFile="Default.aspx.cs"
Inherits="_Default" %>

<!DOCTYPE html PUBLIC "-//W3C//DTD XHTML 1.0 Transitional//EN" "http://
www.w3.org/TR/xhtml1/DTD/xhtml1-transitional.dtd">

<html xmlns="http://www.w3.org/1999/xhtml" >
<head runat="server">
  <title>Chapter 15: Product Maintenance</title>
  <link href="Main.css" rel="stylesheet" type="text/css" />
</head>
<body>
  <form id="form1" runat="server">
  <div id="page">
    <div id="header">
      <asp:Image ID="Image1" runat="server" ImageUrl="~/Images/banner.jpg" />
    </div>
    <div id="main">
      <div id="gridview">
        <asp:GridView ID="GridView1" runat="server" AllowPaging="True"
            DataKeyNames="ProductID" DataSourceID="SqlDataSource1"
            AutoGenerateColumns="False" SelectedIndex="0"
            CellPadding="4" GridLines="None" ForeColor="Black" Width="320px">
          <Columns>
            <asp:BoundField DataField="ProductID" HeaderText="ID"
                ReadOnly="True">
              <HeaderStyle HorizontalAlign="Left" />
              <ItemStyle Width="75px" />
            </asp:BoundField>
            <asp:BoundField DataField="Name" HeaderText="Name">
              <HeaderStyle HorizontalAlign="Left" />
              <ItemStyle Width="150px" />
            </asp:BoundField>
            <asp:BoundField DataField="CategoryID" HeaderText="Category" >
              <HeaderStyle HorizontalAlign="Left" />
              <ItemStyle Width="95px" />
            </asp:BoundField>
            <asp:CommandField ButtonType="Button" ShowSelectButton="True" />
          </Columns>
          <HeaderStyle BackColor="Gray" Font-Bold="True" ForeColor="White" />
          <RowStyle BackColor="White" ForeColor="Black" />
          <AlternatingRowStyle BackColor="LightGray" ForeColor="Black" />
          <SelectedRowStyle BackColor="#F46D11" ForeColor="White" />
          <PagerStyle BackColor="Gray" ForeColor="White"
              HorizontalAlign="Center" />
        </asp:GridView>
        <asp:SqlDataSource ID="SqlDataSource1" runat="server"
            ConnectionString="<%$ ConnectionStrings:HalloweenConnectionString %>"
            SelectCommand="SELECT [ProductID], [Name], [CategoryID]
                FROM [Products] ORDER BY [ProductID]">
        </asp:SqlDataSource>
      </div>
```

Figure 15-10   The aspx file for the Product Maintenance application (part 1 of 4)

The Default.aspx file   **Page 2**

```
<div id="detailsview">
  <asp:DetailsView ID="DetailsView1" runat="server"
    DataSourceID="SqlDataSource2" DataKeyNames="ProductID"
    Height="50px" Width="350px" AutoGenerateRows="False"
    BackColor="White" BorderColor="White" BorderStyle="Ridge"
    BorderWidth="2px" CellPadding="3" CellSpacing="1"
    GridLines="None">
    <Fields>
      <asp:TemplateField HeaderText="Product ID:">
        <ItemTemplate>
          <asp:Label ID="Label4" runat="server"
            Text='<%# Bind("ProductID") %>'></asp:Label>
        </ItemTemplate>
        <EditItemTemplate>
          <asp:Label ID="Label1" runat="server"
            Text='<%# Eval("ProductID") %>'></asp:Label>
        </EditItemTemplate>
        <InsertItemTemplate>
          <asp:TextBox ID="txtID" runat="server"
            Text='<%# Bind("ProductID") %>' Width="100px"
            MaxLength="10">
          </asp:TextBox>
          <asp:RequiredFieldValidator
            ID="RequiredFieldValidator1" runat="server"
            ControlToValidate="txtID"
            ErrorMessage="Product ID is a required field.">*
          </asp:RequiredFieldValidator>
        </InsertItemTemplate>
        <HeaderStyle HorizontalAlign="Left" Width="130px" />
        <ItemStyle Width="220px" />
      </asp:TemplateField>
      .
      .
      <asp:TemplateField HeaderText="Category:">
        <ItemTemplate>
          <asp:Label ID="Label3" runat="server"
            Text='<%# Bind("CategoryID") %>'></asp:Label>
        </ItemTemplate>
        <EditItemTemplate>
          <asp:DropDownList ID="ddlCategory" runat="server"
            DataSourceID="SqlDataSource3"
            DataTextField="LongName" DataValueField="CategoryID"
            SelectedValue='<%# Bind("CategoryID") %>' Width="130px">
          </asp:DropDownList>
        </EditItemTemplate>
        <InsertItemTemplate>
          <asp:DropDownList ID="ddlCategory" runat="server"
            DataSourceID="SqlDataSource3"
            DataTextField="LongName" DataValueField="CategoryID"
            SelectedValue='<%# Bind("CategoryID") %>' Width="130px">
          </asp:DropDownList>
        </InsertItemTemplate>
        <HeaderStyle HorizontalAlign="Left" Width="130px" />
        <ItemStyle Width="220px" />
      .
      .
```

Figure 15-10   The aspx file for the Product Maintenance application (part 2 of 4)

In part 3 of this figure, you can see the aspx code for the data source that the DetailsView control is bound to. This data source includes Delete and Update statements that use optimistic concurrency.

A data source is also included for the drop-down lists that are used to display the categories in the EditItem and InsertItem templates for the CategoryID field. You can see this data source in part 4 of this figure. If you look back at the definitions of the drop-down lists, you'll see how they're bound to this data source.

The code-behind file

Figure 15-11 shows the code-behind file for the Default page of the Product Maintenance application. Even though this application provides complete maintenance for the Products table, only four methods are required. These methods respond to events raised by the DetailsView control. The first three handle database exceptions and concurrency errors for updates, deletions, and insertions.

Note that the error-handling code for the insert method is simpler than the error-handling code for the update and delete methods. That's because optimistic concurrency doesn't apply to insert operations. As a result, there's no need to check the AffectedRows property to see if a concurrency error has occurred.

The last method, DetailsView1_ItemDeleting, handles a problem that can occur when you apply a format to a control that's bound to the data source. In this case, the currency format is applied to the unit price field in the Item template. Because this application uses optimistic concurrency, the original values of each field are passed to the Delete statement as parameters to make sure that another user hasn't changed the product row since it was retrieved. Unfortunately, the DetailsView control sets the value of the unit price parameter to its formatted value, which includes the currency symbol. If you allow this value to be passed on to the Delete statement, an exception will be thrown because the parameter value is in the wrong format.

Before the Delete statement is executed, then, the DetailsView1_ItemDeleting method is called. This method removes the currency symbol from the parameter value so the value will be passed to the Delete statement in the correct format.

The Default.aspx file

```
            <asp:CommandField ButtonType="Button"
                ShowDeleteButton="True"
                ShowEditButton="True"
                ShowInsertButton="True" />
        </Fields>
        <RowStyle BackColor="LightGray" ForeColor="Black" />
        <EditRowStyle BackColor="Gray" ForeColor="White" />
        <FooterStyle BackColor="LightGray" />
    </asp:DetailsView>
    <asp:SqlDataSource ID="SqlDataSource2" runat="server"
        ConflictDetection="CompareAllValues"
        ConnectionString="<%$ ConnectionStrings:HalloweenConnectionString %>"
        OldValuesParameterFormatString="original_{0}"
        SelectCommand="SELECT [ProductID], [Name], [ShortDescription],
            [LongDescription], [CategoryID], [ImageFile],
            [UnitPrice], [OnHand]
            FROM [Products]
            WHERE ([ProductID] = @ProductID)"
        DeleteCommand="DELETE FROM [Products]
            WHERE [ProductID] = @original_ProductID
            AND [Name] = @original_Name
            AND [ShortDescription] = @original_ShortDescription
            AND [LongDescription] = @original_LongDescription
            AND [CategoryID] = @original_CategoryID
            AND (([ImageFile] = @original_ImageFile)
            OR (ImageFile IS NULL AND @original_ImageFile IS NULL))
            AND [UnitPrice] = @original_UnitPrice
            AND [OnHand] = @original_OnHand"
        InsertCommand="INSERT INTO [Products] ([ProductID], [Name],
            [ShortDescription], [LongDescription], [CategoryID],
            [ImageFile], [UnitPrice], [OnHand])
            VALUES (@ProductID, @Name, @ShortDescription,
            @LongDescription, @CategoryID, @ImageFile,
            @UnitPrice, @OnHand)"
        UpdateCommand="UPDATE [Products] SET [Name] = @Name,
            [ShortDescription] = @ShortDescription,
            [LongDescription] = @LongDescription,
            [CategoryID] = @CategoryID,
            [ImageFile] = @ImageFile,
            [UnitPrice] = @UnitPrice,
            [OnHand] = @OnHand
            WHERE [ProductID] = @original_ProductID
            AND [Name] = @original_Name
            AND [ShortDescription] = @original_ShortDescription
            AND [LongDescription] = @original_LongDescription
            AND [CategoryID] = @original_CategoryID
            AND (([ImageFile] = @original_ImageFile)
            OR (ImageFile IS NULL AND @original_ImageFile IS NULL))
            AND [UnitPrice] = @original_UnitPrice
            AND [OnHand] = @original_OnHand">
        <SelectParameters>
          <asp:ControlParameter ControlID="GridView1" Name="ProductID"
              PropertyName="SelectedValue" Type="String" />
        </SelectParameters>
```

Figure 15-10   The aspx file for the Product Maintenance application (part 3 of 4)

The Default.aspx file

```
        <DeleteParameters>
          <asp:Parameter Name="original_ProductID" Type="String" />
          <asp:Parameter Name="original_Name" Type="String" />
          <asp:Parameter Name="original_ShortDescription" Type="String" />
          <asp:Parameter Name="original_LongDescription" Type="String" />
          <asp:Parameter Name="original_CategoryID" Type="String" />
          <asp:Parameter Name="original_ImageFile" Type="String" />
          <asp:Parameter Name="original_UnitPrice" Type="Decimal" />
          <asp:Parameter Name="original_OnHand" Type="Int32" />
        </DeleteParameters>
        <UpdateParameters>
          <asp:Parameter Name="Name" Type="String" />
          <asp:Parameter Name="ShortDescription" Type="String" />
          <asp:Parameter Name="LongDescription" Type="String" />
          <asp:Parameter Name="CategoryID" Type="String" />
          <asp:Parameter Name="ImageFile" Type="String" />
          <asp:Parameter Name="UnitPrice" Type="Decimal" />
          <asp:Parameter Name="OnHand" Type="Int32" />
          <asp:Parameter Name="original_ProductID" Type="String" />
          <asp:Parameter Name="original_Name" Type="String" />
          <asp:Parameter Name="original_ShortDescription" Type="String" />
          <asp:Parameter Name="original_LongDescription" Type="String" />
          <asp:Parameter Name="original_CategoryID" Type="String" />
          <asp:Parameter Name="original_ImageFile" Type="String" />
          <asp:Parameter Name="original_UnitPrice" Type="Decimal" />
          <asp:Parameter Name="original_OnHand" Type="Int32" />
        </UpdateParameters>
        <InsertParameters>
          <asp:Parameter Name="ProductID" Type="String" />
          <asp:Parameter Name="Name" Type="String" />
          <asp:Parameter Name="ShortDescription" Type="String" />
          <asp:Parameter Name="LongDescription" Type="String" />
          <asp:Parameter Name="CategoryID" Type="String" />
          <asp:Parameter Name="ImageFile" Type="String" />
          <asp:Parameter Name="UnitPrice" Type="Decimal" />
          <asp:Parameter Name="OnHand" Type="Int32" />
        </InsertParameters>
      </asp:SqlDataSource>
      <asp:SqlDataSource ID="SqlDataSource3" runat="server"
        ConnectionString="<%$ ConnectionStrings:HalloweenConnectionString %>"
        SelectCommand="SELECT [CategoryID], [LongName] FROM [Categories]
            ORDER BY [LongName]">
      </asp:SqlDataSource>
      <asp:ValidationSummary ID="ValidationSummary1" runat="server"
        HeaderText="Please correct the following errors:"
        CssClass="error" />
      <p>
        <asp:Label ID = "lblError" runat="server" EnableViewState="False"
          CssClass="error"></asp:Label>
      </p>
    </div>
   </div>
  </div>
  </form>
</body>
</html>
```

Figure 15-10   The aspx file for the Product Maintenance application (part 4 of 4)

The Default.aspx.cs file

```
public partial class _Default : System.Web.UI.Page
{
    protected void DetailsView1_ItemUpdated(
        object sender, DetailsViewUpdatedEventArgs e)
    {
        if (e.Exception != null)
        {
            lblError.Text = "A database error has occurred. " +
                "Message: " + e.Exception.Message;
            e.ExceptionHandled = true;
            e.KeepInEditMode = true;
        }
        else if (e.AffectedRows == 0)
            lblError.Text = "Another user may have updated that product. " +
                "Please try again.";
        else
            GridView1.DataBind();
    }

    protected void DetailsView1_ItemDeleted(
        object sender, DetailsViewDeletedEventArgs e)
    {
        if (e.Exception != null)
        {
            lblError.Text = "A database error has occurred. " +
                "Message: " + e.Exception.Message;
            e.ExceptionHandled = true;
        }
        else if (e.AffectedRows == 0)
            lblError.Text = "Another user may have updated that product. " +
                "Please try again.";
        else
            GridView1.DataBind();
    }

    protected void DetailsView1_ItemInserted(
        object sender, DetailsViewInsertedEventArgs e)
    {
        if (e.Exception != null)
        {
            lblError.Text = "A database error has occurred. " +
                "Message: " + e.Exception.Message;
            e.ExceptionHandled = true;
            e.KeepInInsertMode = true;
        }
        else
            GridView1.DataBind();
    }

    protected void DetailsView1_ItemDeleting(
        object sender, DetailsViewDeleteEventArgs e)
    {
        e.Values["UnitPrice"]
            = e.Values["UnitPrice"].ToString().Substring(1);
    }
}
```

Figure 15-11   The code-behind file for the Product Maintenance application

How to use the FormView control

Besides the DetailsView control, ASP.NET also provides a FormView control. Like the DetailsView control, the FormView control is designed to display data for a single item from a data source. However, as you'll see in the following topics, the FormView control uses a different approach to displaying its data.

An introduction to the FormView control

Figure 15-12 presents an introduction to the FormView control. Although the FormView control is similar to the DetailsView control, it differs in several key ways. Most importantly, the FormView control isn't restricted by the HTML table layout of the DetailsView control, in which each field is rendered as a table row. Instead, the FormView control uses templates to render all of the fields as a single row by default. This gives you complete control over the layout of the fields within the row.

Because you have to use template fields with a FormView control, this control can be more difficult to work with than a DetailsView control that uses bound fields. As you learned earlier in this chapter, though, you can convert the bound fields used by a DetailsView control to template fields so you have more control over them. In that case, a FormView control is just as easy to work with.

When you create a FormView control and bind it to a data source, the Web Forms Designer will automatically create default templates for you, as shown in the first image in this figure. Then, you can edit the templates to achieve the layout you want. To do that, choose Edit Templates from the smart tag menu. This places the control in template-editing mode, as shown in the second image in this figure. Here, the drop-down list shows the various templates you can use with a FormView control. For most applications, you'll use just the Item, EditItem, and InsertItem templates.

A FormView control after a data source has been assigned

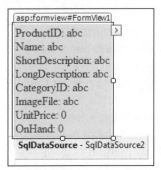

A FormView control in template-editing mode

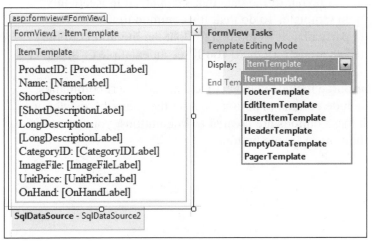

How the FormView control differs from the DetailsView control

- The DetailsView control can be easier to work with, but the FormView control provides more formatting and layout options.

- The DetailsView control can use BoundField elements or TemplateField elements with templates that use data binding expressions to define bound data fields. The FormView control can use only templates with data binding expressions to display bound data.

- The DetailsView control renders each field as a table row, but the FormView control renders all the fields in a template as a single table row.

Description

- A FormView control is similar to a DetailsView control, but its templates give you more control over how its data is displayed. To accomplish that, all the columns in the data source can be laid out within a single template.

- After you create a FormView control and assign a data source to it, you can edit the control's templates so the data is displayed the way you want.

Figure 15-12   An introduction to the FormView control

How to work with the Item template

When you use the Web Forms Designer to create a FormView control and bind it to a data source, the Web Forms Designer automatically generates basic templates for the FormView control. For instance, the code in figure 15-13 shows a typical Item template. This template is used to display the data from the data source in ReadOnly mode.

As you can see, the Item template consists of a literal header and a label control for each field in the data source. The Text attribute of each label control uses either the Bind or Eval method for data binding. The Eval method is used for columns that can't be modified. That's the case for the ProductID column in the Products table, since this is the key column.

To control the format and layout of the data that's displayed in ReadOnly mode, you can edit the Item template. To do that, it's common to use CSS as described in chapter 5. In particular, it's common to float the literal text to the left of the labels so the labels are left-aligned. You'll see an example of this later in this chapter.

Note that if the data source includes Update, Delete, and Insert commands, the Item template will include command buttons that let the user edit, delete, or add new rows. Although these buttons are created as link buttons, you can easily change them to regular buttons or image buttons.

The Item template generated for a FormView control

```
<asp:FormView ID="FormView1" runat="server" DataKeyNames="ProductID"
    DataSourceID="SqlDataSource2">
    <ItemTemplate>
        ProductID:
        <asp:Label ID="ProductIDLabel" runat="server"
            Text='<%# Eval("ProductID") %>' /><br />
        Name:
        <asp:Label ID="NameLabel" runat="server"
            Text='<%# Bind("Name") %>' /><br />
        ShortDescription:
        <asp:Label ID="ShortDescriptionLabel" runat="server"
            Text='<%# Bind("ShortDescription") %>' /><br />
        LongDescription:
        <asp:Label ID="LongDescriptionLabel" runat="server"
            Text='<%# Bind("LongDescription") %>' /><br />
        CategoryID:
        <asp:Label ID="CategoryIDLabel" runat="server"
            Text='<%# Bind("CategoryID") %>' /><br />
        ImageFile:
        <asp:Label ID="ImageFileLabel" runat="server"
            Text='<%# Bind("ImageFile") %>' /><br />
        UnitPrice:
        <asp:Label ID="UnitPriceLabel" runat="server"
            Text='<%# Bind("UnitPrice") %>' /><br />
        OnHand:
        <asp:Label ID="OnHandLabel" runat="server"
            Text='<%# Bind("OnHand") %>' /><br />
    </ItemTemplate>
        .
        .
        .
</asp:FormView>
```

Description

- When you bind a FormView control to a data source, the Web Forms Designer generates an Item template that includes heading text and a bound label for each column in the data source.

- The Item template is rendered whenever the FormView control is displayed in ReadOnly mode.

- The Item template uses the Eval and Bind methods to create binding expressions for the columns in the data source (see figure 13-15 in chapter 13).

- If the data source includes Update, Delete, and Insert commands, the generated Item template will include Edit, Delete, and New buttons.

- The Web Forms Designer also generates an EditItem template and an InsertItem template, even if the data source doesn't include an Update or Insert command. For more information, see the next figure.

- You can modify a generated template so you can use CSS to control the format and layout of the data that's rendered for that template.

Figure 15-13   How to work with the Item template

How to work with the EditItem and InsertItem templates

As figure 15-14 shows, the Web Forms Designer also generates an EditItem and InsertItem template when you bind a FormView control to a data source. These templates are used to display the fields in Edit and Insert mode, and they're generated even if the data source doesn't have an Update or Insert command. As a result, you can delete these templates if your application doesn't allow for edits and inserts. Although this figure only shows an EditItem template, the InsertItem template is similar.

One drawback to using the FormView control is that once you edit the Item template so the data is arranged the way you want, you'll usually want to provide similar layout code in both the EditItem template and the InsertItem template. That way, the layout in all three modes will be similar. One way to do that is to copy the code in one template and paste it into another. Then, you can make the necessary adjustments, such as replacing the labels that were generated for the Item template with the text boxes that were generated for the EditItem or InsertItem template.

Depending on the complexity of the layout, it may take considerable work to get the templates looking the way you want them. In addition, if you later decide to change that layout, you'll have to make the change to all three templates. Unfortunately, there's no escaping this duplication of effort.

A generated EditItem template as displayed in a browser window

ProductID: rat01
Name: Ugly Rat
ShortDescription: 16" Rat
LongDescription: This guy is sure to shorter
CategoryID: props
ImageFile: rat1.jpg
UnitPrice: 14.9900
OnHand: 75
Update Cancel

The aspx code for the EditItem template shown above

```
<EditItemTemplate>
    ProductID:
    <asp:Label ID="ProductIDLabel1" runat="server"
        Text='<%# Eval("ProductID") %>' />
    <br />
    Name:
    <asp:TextBox ID="NameTextBox" runat="server"
        Text='<%# Bind("Name") %>' />
    <br />
    ShortDescription:
    <asp:TextBox ID="ShortDescriptionTextBox" runat="server"
        Text='<%# Bind("ShortDescription") %>' />
    <br />
    .
    .
    .
    .
    .
    .
    <asp:LinkButton ID="UpdateButton" runat="server" CausesValidation="True"
        CommandName="Update" Text="Update" /> 
    <asp:LinkButton ID="UpdateCancelButton" runat="server"
        CausesValidation="False" CommandName="Cancel" Text="Cancel" />
</EditItemTemplate>
```

> The code generated for the LongDescription, CategoryID, ImageFile, UnitPrice, and OnHand columns is similar to the code generated for the ShortDescription column.

Description

- The EditItem template determines how the FormView control is rendered in Edit mode. It includes a text box for each editable bound column in the data source. The Text attribute for each text box uses a binding expression that binds the text box to its data source column.

- The EditItem template also includes Update and Cancel buttons.

- The InsertItem template is similar to the EditItem template. It determines how the FormView control is rendered in Insert mode.

Figure 15-14   How to work with the EditItem and InsertItem templates

A Shopping Cart application that uses a FormView control

To show the versatility of the FormView control, the following topics present a version of the Order page from the Shopping Cart application that was originally presented in chapter 3. That version of the application used simple label and image controls to display the information for the product selected by the user. Because data binding didn't work for those controls, C# code was required in the Page_Load method to set the values of the label and image controls. In contrast, this new version of the application takes advantage of the data binding ability of the FormView control, so no Page_Load method is required.

Because this application doesn't allow the user to update, delete, or insert product information, it doesn't illustrate the use of the EditItem or InsertItem templates or the use of command buttons with a FormView control. If you want to see an application that does use those features, though, you can download the applications for this book from our web site, www.murach.com.

The operation of the application

To refresh your memory, figure 15-15 shows the Order page displayed by the Shopping Cart application. As you can see, this page lets the user select a product from a drop-down list. When the user selects a product, the page displays the name, description, price, and an image of the selected product. Then, the user can order the product by entering a quantity and clicking the Add to Cart button.

This time, the product information is displayed within a FormView control, and the Item template is coded so CSS can be used to display the image to the right of the text. This demonstrates the layout flexibility of the FormView control. With a DetailsView control, it wouldn't be possible to display the image to the right of the text data, because the DetailsView control displays each column of the data source in a separate table row.

The Order page of the Shopping Cart application

Description

- This is the Shopping Cart application that was originally presented in chapter 3, but this time it's implemented with a FormView control that displays the data for the selected product.

- The Item template for the FormView control includes labels that are bound to the columns in the data source. It also includes an Image control whose ImageUrl property is bound to the ImageFile column in the data source.

- The Item template for the FormView controls contains HTML that's formatted using CSS.

Figure 15-15   The Shopping Cart application with a FormView control

The aspx file for the Order page

Figure 15-16 shows the aspx file for the Order page of the Shopping Cart application. Here, the FormView control includes an Item template that contains a division with four paragraphs. These paragraphs contain the labels that present the name, short description, long description, and price for the selected product. This division is followed by an image control that displays the product's image. A style sheet is used to format the image and paragraphs so they appear as shown in the previous figure.

Note that although the Web Forms Designer generated the EditItem and InsertItem templates, this application doesn't use them. As a result, I deleted those templates so they wouldn't clutter the listing.

There are two interesting things to notice about the format strings used in the binding expressions on this page. First, the format string used to bind the image control is this: "Images/Products/{0}". Since the ImageFile column in the Products table contains just the name of the image file for each product, not its complete path, this formatting expression prefixes the file name with the path Images/Products/ so the image file can be located.

Second, the format string used in the binding expression that displays the unit price is this: "{0:c} each". As a result, the price is displayed in currency format, followed by the word "each."

The code-behind file for the Order page

Figure 15-17 shows the code-behind file for the Order page. This code is similar to the code for the original version of this program that was presented back in chapter 3. However, there are only two substantial differences. First, this version doesn't include a Page_Load method because it doesn't need to do any data binding.

Second, the GetSelectedProduct method in this version is simpler than the one in the original version. Because the new application uses two data sources, a select parameter can be used to retrieve the selected product in the second data source. Then, because the second data source retrieves just a single row, a row filter isn't required. Instead, the index value 0 is used to retrieve data from the first and only row of the data source.

The Order.aspx file   Page 1

```
<%@ Page Language="C#" AutoEventWireup="true" CodeFile="Order.aspx.cs"
Inherits="Order" %>

<!DOCTYPE html PUBLIC "-//W3C//DTD XHTML 1.0 Transitional//EN"
"http://www.w3.org/TR/xhtml1/DTD/xhtml1-transitional.dtd">

<html xmlns="http://www.w3.org/1999/xhtml" >
<head runat="server">
    <title>Chapter 15: Shopping Cart</title>
    <link href="Styles/Main.css" rel="stylesheet" type="text/css" />
    <link href="Styles/Order.css" rel="stylesheet" type="text/css" />
</head>
<body>
    <form id="form1" runat="server">
    <div id="page">
      <div id="header">
        <asp:Image ID="Image1" runat="server"
            ImageUrl="~/Images/banner.jpg" />
      </div>
      <div id="main">
        <p id="products">
          <asp:Label ID="Label1" runat="server"
              Text="Please select a product:"></asp:Label> 
          <asp:DropDownList ID="ddlProducts" runat="server"
              AutoPostBack="True" DataSourceID="SqlDataSource1"
              DataTextField="Name" DataValueField="ProductID">
          </asp:DropDownList>
          <asp:SqlDataSource ID="SqlDataSource1" runat="server"
              ConnectionString="<%$ ConnectionStrings:HalloweenConnectionString %>"
              SelectCommand="SELECT [ProductID], [Name] FROM [Products]
                  ORDER BY [Name]">
          </asp:SqlDataSource>
        </p>
        <div id="formview">
          <asp:FormView ID="FormView1" runat="server"
              DataSourceID="SqlDataSource2">
            <ItemTemplate>
              <div id="product">
                <p id="name">
                  <asp:Label ID="lblName" runat="server"
                      Text='<%# Bind("Name") %>' >
                  </asp:Label>
                </p>
                <p id="shortdesc">
                  <asp:Label ID="lblShortDescription" runat="server"
                      Text='<%# Bind("ShortDescription") %>'>
                  </asp:Label>
                </p>
                <p id="longdesc">
                  <asp:Label ID="lblLongDescription" runat="server"
                      Text='<%# Bind("LongDescription") %>'>
                  </asp:Label>
                </p>
```

Figure 15-16   The aspx file for the Order page of the Shopping Cart application (part 1 of 2)

The Order.aspx file   **Page 2**

```
          <p id="unitprice">
            <asp:Label ID="lblUnitPrice" runat="server"
                Text='<%# Bind("UnitPrice", "{0:c} each") %>'>
            </asp:Label>
          </p>
        </div>
        <asp:Image ID="imgProduct" runat="server" width="135px"
            ImageUrl='<%# Bind("ImageFile", "Images/Products/{0}") %>' />
      </ItemTemplate>
    </asp:FormView>
    <asp:SqlDataSource ID="SqlDataSource2" runat="server"
        ConnectionString=
            "<%$ ConnectionStrings:HalloweenConnectionString %>"
        SelectCommand="SELECT [ProductID], [Name], [ShortDescription],
            [LongDescription], [ImageFile], [UnitPrice]
            FROM [Products]
            WHERE ([ProductID] = @ProductID)">
        <SelectParameters>
            <asp:ControlParameter ControlID="ddlProducts" Name="ProductID"
                PropertyName="SelectedValue" Type="String" />
        </SelectParameters>
    </asp:SqlDataSource>
    </div>
    <div id="order">
      <p id="quantity">
        <asp:Label ID="Label2" runat="server" Text="Quantity:"></asp:Label>
        <asp:TextBox ID="txtQuantity" runat="server"></asp:TextBox>
        <asp:RequiredFieldValidator
            ID="RequiredFieldValidator1" runat="server"
            ControlToValidate="txtQuantity" Display="Dynamic"
            ErrorMessage="Quantity is a required field."
            CssClass="validator">
        </asp:RequiredFieldValidator>
        <asp:RangeValidator ID="RangeValidator1" runat="server"
            ControlToValidate="txtQuantity" Display="Dynamic"
            ErrorMessage="Quantity must range from 1 to 500."
            MaximumValue="500" MinimumValue="1" Type="Integer"
            CssClass="validator">
        </asp:RangeValidator>
      </p>
      <asp:Button ID="btnAdd" runat="server" Text="Add to Cart"
          OnClick="btnAdd_Click" /> 
      <asp:Button ID="Button1" runat="server"  Text="Go to Cart"
          CausesValidation="False" PostBackUrl="~/Cart.aspx" />
    </div>
    </div>
    </div>
    </form>
</body>
</html>
```

Figure 15-16   The aspx file for the Order page of the Shopping Cart application (part 2 of 2)

The Order.aspx.cs file

```
using System;
using System.Collections.Generic;
using System.Linq;
using System.Web;
using System.Web.UI;
using System.Web.UI.WebControls;
using System.Data;

public partial class Order : System.Web.UI.Page
{
    protected void btnAdd_Click(object sender, EventArgs e)
    {
        if (Page.IsValid)
        {
            Product selectedProduct = this.GetSelectedProduct();
            CartItemList cart = CartItemList.GetCart();
            CartItem cartItem = cart[selectedProduct.ProductID];
            if (cartItem == null)
            {
                cart.AddItem(selectedProduct, Convert.ToInt32(txtQuantity.Text));
            }
            else
            {
                cartItem.AddQuantity(Convert.ToInt32(txtQuantity.Text));
            }
            Response.Redirect("Cart.aspx");
        }
    }

    private Product GetSelectedProduct()
    {
        DataView productsTable = (DataView)
            SqlDataSource2.Select(DataSourceSelectArguments.Empty);
        DataRowView row = (DataRowView)productsTable[0];
        Product p = new Product();
        p.ProductID = row["ProductID"].ToString();
        p.Name = row["Name"].ToString();
        p.ShortDescription = row["ShortDescription"].ToString();
        p.LongDescription = row["LongDescription"].ToString();
        p.UnitPrice = (decimal)row["UnitPrice"];
        p.ImageFile = row["ImageFile"].ToString();
        return p;
    }
}
```

Figure 15-17   The code-behind file for the Order page of the Shopping Cart application

Perspective

The DetailsView and FormView controls are ideal for any application that displays bound data one row at a time. The choice of whether to use a DetailsView or a FormView control depends mostly on how much control you want over the layout of the data. If you want to present a simple list of fields, the DetailsView control is usually the best choice because it can automatically present data in that format. But if you need more control over the layout of the data, you'll want to use the FormView control.

In the next chapter, you'll learn about two additional controls for working with the data in a data source: the ListView control and the DataPager control. The ListView control lets you work with the data in a data source much like the GridView control. Unlike the GridView control, though, the ListView control is highly customizable. In addition, it provides for insert operations, and it provides for paging using the DataPager control.

Term

Master/Detail page

Exercise 15-1   Create an application that uses a DetailsView control

In this exercise, you'll create an application that lets the user select a customer from a GridView control and maintain that customer in a DetailsView control. To make that easier for you, you'll start from an application with a page that contains a GridView control that lists customers and validation summary and label controls that will be used to display error messages.

Review the starting code for the application

1. Open the Ch15CustMaintDetailsView application in the C:\aspnet4_cs directory.

2. Review the aspx code for the SQL data source, and notice that it retrieves the Email, LastName, and FirstName columns from the Customers table.

3. Display the page in Design view, and notice that only the LastName and FirstName columns are displayed in the GridView control. That's because the Visible property of the Email column has been set to False. This column must be included in the data source, though, because it's the primary key of the Customers table, and it will be used to display the selected customer in a DetailsView control.

4. Run the application to see that you can page through the customers, but you can't select a customer.

Add a select function to the GridView control

5. Add a command field to the GridView control that will let the user select a customer.

6. Run the application again and click the Select button for any customer. Notice how the formatting for the selected row changes. That's because a SelectedRowStyle element is included for the control.

Add a default DetailsView control

7. Add a DetailsView control at the beginning of the division that contains the validation summary control, and set its width to 350 pixels.

8. Create a data source for the DetailsView control that retrieves each of the columns from the Customers table for the customer that's selected in the GridView control. Be sure to generate Insert, Update, and Delete statements and use optimistic concurrency.

9. Use the Add Field dialog box to add a command field that lets the user Edit, Delete, and Add rows.

10. Run the application, display the last page of customers in the GridView control, and select customer "Barbara White". The data for that customer should be displayed in the DetailsView control.

11. Click the Edit button to see that the text boxes that let you edit the data for a customer are all the same size, and the text box for the address is too small to display the full address for this customer.

12. Click the Cancel button to exit from Edit mode, and close the browser window.

Create templates for the DetailsView control

13. Use the Fields dialog box to convert each of the bound fields in the DetailsView control to a template field.

14. Modify the EditItem template for each field except the Email and State fields so the width of the text box is appropriate for the data, and so the user can't enter more characters than are allowed by the database. (LastName, FirstName, and PhoneNumber: 20 characters; Address: 40 characters; City: 30 characters; and ZipCode: 9 characters.)

15. Assign a meaningful name to each text box you just modified. Then, add a required field validator to each of these fields that displays an asterisk to the right of the text box and displays an error message in the validation summary control if a value isn't entered in the field.

16. Add another data source to the page below the data source for the DetailsView control. This data source should retrieve the StateCode and StateName columns from the States table and sort the results by the StateName column.

17. Replace the text box in the EditItem template for the State field with a drop-down list, and bind the list to the data source you just created so the state name is displayed in the drop-down list and the state code is stored in the list. Then, use the DataBindings dialog box (see chapter 13) to bind the SelectedValue property of the drop-down list to the State field of the Customers table.

18. Run the application and click the Edit button in the DetailsView control to make sure you have the controls in the EditItem template formatted properly.

19. Copy the text boxes, validation controls, and drop-down list you created for the EditItem templates to the InsertItem templates of the same fields. In addition, add a required field validator to the InsertItem template for the Email field, and modify the text box so it's wider and accommodates a maximum of 25 characters.

20. Run the application again and click the New button. The InsertItem template should look just like the EditItem template except that the email field is editable.

Add code to check for database and concurrency errors

21. Add event handlers for the ItemUpdated, ItemDeleted, and ItemInserted events of the DetailsView control. The ItemUpdated and ItemDeleted methods should check for both database and concurrency errors, but the ItemInserted method should check only for database errors. Display an appropriate error message in the label at the bottom of the page if an error is detected. Otherwise, bind the GridView control so it reflects the current data. If you need help, refer to figure 15-11.

22. Run the application and test it to make sure it works correctly.

Exercise 15-2   Format the data in a FormView control

In this exercise, you'll modify an application that uses a FormView control for maintaining customers. That will give you an idea of the flexible layouts you can create using this control.

1. Open the Ch15CustMaintFormView application in the C:\aspnet4_cs directory.

2. Run the application, and experiment with it until you understand how it works.

3. Display the page in Design view, and select the Edit Templates command from the smart tag menu for the FormView control. The Item template will be displayed with literal text and a label for each field on a separate line.

4. Change the text "City:" to "City, State, Zip:". Then, drag the State label so it follows the City label, and drag the ZipCode label so it follows the State label.

5. Exit from Template Editing mode, and display the page in Source view. Locate the Item template that you just modified, enter a comma and a space ( ) between the City and State labels, and enter a space between the State and ZipCode labels.

6. Delete the paragraphs from the Item template with the text "State:" and "Zip Code:", along with the paragraph that follows each of these paragraphs that previously contained the State and ZipCode labels.

7. Run the application to see that the city, state, and zip code are now displayed on a single line when the Item template is displayed.

16

How to use the ListView and DataPager controls

In this chapter, you'll learn how to use the ListView and DataPager controls. As you'll see, the ListView control works much like the GridView control you learned about in chapter 14. However, it provides features that make it much more versatile than the GridView control. For example, you can use the ListView control to insert rows into a data source, and you can use it to display items from the data source in groups as well as other customized formats. In addition, you can use the DataPager control in conjunction with the ListView control to implement paging.

How to use the ListView control

The ListView control is a highly customizable control that was introduced with ASP.NET 3.5. In the topics that follow, you'll learn the basic skills for defining the content and appearance of this control. In addition, you'll learn how to provide sorting and paging for this control.

An introduction to the ListView control

Figure 16-1 presents a ListView control that provides for updating the data in the Categories table of the Halloween database. As you can see, this control presents the data in a row and column format just like the GridView control. In fact, if you compare this control to the GridView control shown in figure 14-1 of chapter 14, you'll see that these controls look quite similar. The main difference is that the ListView control includes an additional row for inserting a new row into the table.

The first table in this figure lists some of the basic attributes of the ListView control. In most cases, these attributes are set the way you want them by default. If you want to change the location of the row that provides for insert operations, though, you can do that by changing the value of the InsertItemPosition attribute.

To define the layout of a ListView control, you use the templates listed in the second table in this figure. At the least, a ListView control typically contains a Layout template and an Item template. You use the Layout template to define the overall layout of the control, and you use the Item template to define the layout that's used for each item in the data source. You'll see how these and many of the other templates can be used as you progress through this chapter.

A ListView control that provides for updating a table

		CategoryID	ShortName	LongName
Delete	Edit	costumes	Costumes	Costumes
Delete	Edit	fx	FX	Special Effects
Delete	Edit	masks	Masks	Masks
Delete	Edit	props	Props	Props
Insert	Clear			

Basic attributes of the ListView control

Attribute	Description
ID	The ID of the control.
Runat	Must specify "server."
DataSourceID	The ID of the data source to bind to.
DataKeyNames	The names of the primary key fields separated by commas.
InsertItemPosition	The location within the ListView control where the InsertItem template is rendered. You can specify FirstItem, LastItem, or None.

Template elements used by the ListView control

Element	Description
LayoutTemplate	Defines the basic layout of the control.
ItemTemplate	The template used for each item in the data source.
ItemSeparatorTemplate	The template used to separate items in the data source.
AlternatingItemTemplate	The template used for alternating items in the data source.
EditItemTemplate	The template used when a row is being edited.
InsertItemTemplate	The template used for inserting a row.
EmptyDataTemplate	The template used when the data source is empty.
SelectedItemTemplate	The template used when a row is selected.
GroupTemplate	The template used to define a group layout.
GroupSeparatorTemplate	The template used to separate groups of items.
EmptyItemTemplate	The template used for empty items in a group.

Description

- The ListView control displays data from a data source using templates. It can be used to edit and delete data as well as insert data.

- The template elements define the formatting that's used to display data. These templates are generated automatically when you configure a ListView control. See figure 16-2 for information on configuring this control.

- The Layout template defines the overall layout of the control. This template includes an element that's used as a placeholder for the data. Then, the other templates are substituted for this placeholder as appropriate.

Figure 16-1   An introduction to the ListView control

How to configure a ListView control

The easiest way to configure a ListView control is to use the Configure ListView dialog box shown in figure 16-2. Before you do that, though, you have to add the ListView control to the page and bind it to a data source. Then, you can use the Configure ListView command in the control's smart tag menu to display this dialog box.

When you use the Configure ListView dialog box to configure a ListView control, Visual Studio generates templates based on the options you choose. If you want to generate templates that use a standard row and column format, for example, you can select the Grid layout as shown here. Then, if you want to add formatting to the templates, you can select a style. In this figure, for example, I selected the Professional style.

The other options in this dialog box let you enable editing, inserting, deleting, and paging. Note that if the data source isn't defined with Update, Insert, and Delete commands, the Enable Editing, Enable Inserting, and Enable Deleting options won't be available. Even so, EditItem and InsertItem templates are generated for the ListView control. If your application won't provide for updating and inserting data, then, you may want to delete these templates.

The Item template that's generated for a ListView control depends on the columns in the data source that the control is bound to and whether you enable editing and deleting. If you enable editing and deleting, Edit and Delete buttons are added to this template. You'll learn more about how these buttons and the other buttons used by the ListView control work later in this chapter.

If you select the Enable Paging option, a DataPager control is also added to the ListView control. The exact format of this control depends on the option you choose from the drop-down list. You'll learn more about this later in this chapter too.

As you select options in the Configure ListView dialog box, a preview of the control is displayed in the Preview window. That way, you can be sure that the ListView control is generated the way you want. And that will save you time later if you need to customize the control.

The Configure ListView dialog box

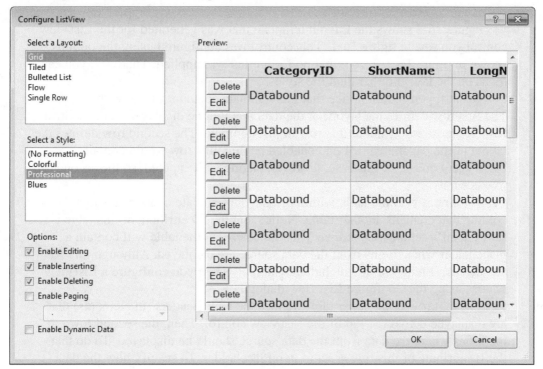

Description

- After you add a ListView control and bind it to a data source, you can configure it to generate many of the templates shown in figure 16-1. To do that, you use the Configure ListView dialog box.

- To display the Configure ListView dialog box, choose the Configure ListView command from the control's smart tag menu. Then, you can select a layout and style for the control, and you can enable editing, inserting, deleting, and paging.

- The EditItem and InsertItem templates are generated regardless of whether the data source provides for editing and inserting and whether editing and inserting are enabled for the ListView control.

- If you enable editing, an Edit button is added to the Item and AlternatingItem templates that lets the user switch to edit mode. If you enable deleting, a Delete button is added to the Item and AlternatingItem templates.

- If you enable inserting, the InsertItemPosition attribute is set to LastItem. This causes the InsertItem template to be displayed after the existing rows in the data source.

- If you enable paging, a DataPager control is added to the ListView control. See figures 16-6 and 16-7 for information on how to use this control.

Figure 16-2   How to configure a ListView control

How to work with the Layout template

Figure 16-3 shows the Layout template that was generated for the ListView control you saw in figure 16-1. This control was configured using the options shown in figure 16-2, except that no formatting was applied. That way, you can focus on the layout rather than the styles.

To start, you should notice that this template contains a table with two rows. The first row defines the layout of the data that will be displayed in the control. I'll have more to say about this row in just a minute. The second row defines the layout of the pager area. If I had enabled paging, this row would contain a DataPager control. In this case, however, paging isn't enabled, so the second row is empty.

The first row in the table within the Layout template contains a single column that contains another table. Notice that the ID attribute of this table is set to itemPlaceholderContainer. This indicates that the table will contain a placeholder where items from the data source are displayed. Although this attribute isn't required, it's included by default when you configure a ListView control using the Configure ListView dialog box.

The first row in the inner table defines the table headers (th elements) that are displayed across the top of the ListView control. Then, the second row identifies where the data from the data source should be displayed. To do that, the ID attribute of this row is set to itemPlaceholder. To specify how the data is displayed, you use the other templates of the ListView control. In the next figure, for example, you'll see the code for a basic Item template.

Before I go on, you should notice that each element within the Layout template has a Runat attribute set to "server". This is necessary for the table and tr elements that specify an ID attribute since only server controls can include this attribute. Although the Runat attribute isn't required for the other elements, it's added by default when you configure the control.

If you use the Configure ListView dialog box as shown in the previous figure, the ListView control that's generated always contains a Layout template. If you're creating a simple layout, though, you should know that you can omit this template. For example, suppose you want to create a list of names and addresses formatted like this:

FirstName LastName
Address
City, State ZipCode

Since the Layout template for this list would contain only the item placeholder, it can be omitted. This is a new feature of ASP.NET 4.

You should also realize that you can't modify the Layout template for a ListView control from Design view. Instead, you'll need to work with it in Source view. As you'll learn later in this chapter, though, you may be able to work with the other templates from Design view depending on what layout you use.

The Layout template for the ListView control in figure 16-1

```
<LayoutTemplate>
    <table runat="server">
        <tr runat="server">
            <td runat="server">
                <table ID="itemPlaceholderContainer" runat="server"
                    border="0" style="">
                    <tr runat="server" style="">
                        <th runat="server"></th>
                        <th runat="server">CategoryID</th>
                        <th runat="server">ShortName</th>
                        <th runat="server">LongName</th>
                    </tr>
                    <tr ID="itemPlaceholder" runat="server">
                    </tr>
                </table>
            </td>
        </tr>
        <tr runat="server">
            <td runat="server" style="">
            </td>
        </tr>
    </table>
</LayoutTemplate>
```

Description

- The Layout template that's generated for a ListView control that uses a grid layout consists of a table with two rows and one column. The first row defines the layout of the data that's displayed in the control, and the second row defines the layout of the DataPager control if paging is enabled.

- The column in the first row of the table for the Layout template contains another table with two rows. The first row defines the headers that are displayed for the columns of the data source as well as a header for any buttons that are displayed by the control. The second row defines a placeholder where the data defined by the other templates will be displayed.

- By default, the ID of the control that's used as a placeholder is set to itemPlaceholder. If you want to use a different name, you can set the ItemPlaceholderID attribute of the ListView control to the name you want to use.

- You can modify the Layout template any way you like. The only requirement is that it must contain a placeholder element that runs on the server.

- Design view doesn't support displaying the Layout template. Because of that, you must work with this template in Source view.

Figure 16-3   How to work with the Layout template

How to work with the Item template

You use the Item template to define how the items from a data source are displayed within a ListView control. To illustrate, figure 16-4 shows the Item template that was generated for the ListView control in figure 16-1. The first thing you should notice here is that this template contains a single tr element. That's necessary because the element that defines the item placeholder in the Layout template is a tr element. Then, at runtime, the tr element in the Item template is substituted for the tr element in the Layout template.

By default, the Item template for a ListView control with a grid layout contains one column for each column in the data source. As you can see, the data from each column is displayed in a label that's bound to the data source using the Eval method. In addition, if editing or deleting is enabled for the ListView control, an additional column is included in the Item template. This column contains the Edit and Delete buttons that can be used to perform edit and delete operations.

In addition to the Item template, an AlternatingItem template is generated for you when you configure a ListView control. Unless you apply a style to the control, though, this template is identical to the Item template, so each row in the control has the same appearance. If you want every other row to have a different appearance, you can modify the Item and AlternatingItem templates as appropriate. For example, you might want to set the background color for the AlternatingItem template so it's different from the background color for the Item template.

The Item template for the ListView control in figure 16-1

```
<ItemTemplate>
    <tr style="">
        <td>
            <asp:Button ID="DeleteButton" runat="server"
                CommandName="Delete" Text="Delete" />
            <asp:Button ID="EditButton" runat="server"
                CommandName="Edit" Text="Edit" />
        </td>
        <td>
            <asp:Label ID="CategoryIDLabel" runat="server"
                Text='<%# Eval("CategoryID") %>' />
        </td>
        <td>
            <asp:Label ID="ShortNameLabel" runat="server"
                Text='<%# Eval("ShortName") %>' />
        </td>
        <td>
            <asp:Label ID="LongNameLabel" runat="server"
                Text='<%# Eval("LongName") %>' />
        </td>
    </tr>
</ItemTemplate>
```

Description

- The Item template defines the layout of the data that's displayed in the ListView control. This template is substituted for the placeholder in the Layout template at runtime.

- The Item template that's generated for a ListView control with a grid layout consists of a single row with one column for each column in the data source. The data for each column is displayed in a label that's bound to the data source using the Eval method.

- If editing or deleting is enabled for the ListView control, an additional column that contains the buttons used to implement these operations is included in the Item template. See figure 16-13 for more information.

- You can modify the Item template any way you like to customize the layout that's used to display the data. To do that, you work in Source view since the Item template can't be displayed in Design view.

- The Item template is the only required template. If editing and inserting are enabled, however, you must also include EditItem and InsertItem templates. See figure 16-14 for more information on these templates.

Figure 16-4   How to work with the Item template

How to provide for sorting

Figure 16-5 shows how you provide sorting for a ListView control. To do that, you add a button to the Layout template for each column you want to sort by. The ListView control in this figure, for example, provides for sorting by using link buttons in the column headers for the first three columns.

To indicate that a button should be used for sorting, you set the CommandName attribute of the button to Sort. Then, you set the CommandArgument attribute of the button to the name of the column in the data source that you want to sort by. If the user clicks the Product ID button in the ListView control shown here, for example, the products will be sorted by the ProductID column. Similarly, if the user clicks the Name button, the products will be sorted by the Name column.

You can also sort by two or more columns in the data source. To do that, you separate the column names with commas. You can see how this works in the link button for the Category column in this figure. If you click this button, the products will be sorted by the Name column within the CategoryID column.

By the way, the sort sequence that's used for a ListView control is the same as the sequence that's used for a GridView control. That is, the first time you click a sort button, the column is sorted in ascending sequence. The second time you click the button, the column is sorted in descending sequence. If a sort button sorts by two or more columns, only the last column toggles between ascending and descending sequence. The other columns are always sorted in ascending sequence.

Also like the GridView control, the ListView control doesn't actually do the sorting. Instead, it relies on the underlying data source to sort the data. As a result, sorting will only work if the DataSourceMode attribute for the data source is set to DataSet.

A ListView control that provides for sorting

Product ID	Name	Category	Unit Price	On Hand
pow01	Austin Powers	costumes	$79.99	25
frankc01	Frankenstein	costumes	$39.99	100
hippie01	Hippie	costumes	$79.99	40
jar01	JarJar	costumes	$59.99	25
martian01	Martian	costumes	$69.99	100
super01	Superman	costumes	$39.99	100
bl01	Black Light (24")	fx	$24.99	200
fogj01	Fog Juice (1qt)	fx	$9.99	500
fog01	Fog Machine	fx	$34.99	100
str01	Mini-strobe	fx	$13.99	200
skullfog01	Skull Fogger	fx	$39.95	50
tlm01	T&L Machine	fx	$99.99	10

The Layout template for the ListView control

```
<LayoutTemplate>
    <table ID="itemPlaceholderContainer" runat="server"
        border="1" cellspacing="0" cellpadding="2">
        <tr id="head" runat="server">
            <th runat="server" class="left">
                <asp:LinkButton ID="LinkButton1" runat="server"
                    CommandName="Sort" CommandArgument="ProductID">
                    Product ID</asp:LinkButton></th>
            <th runat="server" class="left">
                <asp:LinkButton ID="LinkButton2" runat="server"
                    CommandName="Sort" CommandArgument="Name">
                    Name</asp:LinkButton></th>
            <th runat="server" class="left">
                <asp:LinkButton ID="LinkButton3" runat="server"
                    CommandName="Sort" CommandArgument="CategoryID, Name">
                    Category</asp:LinkButton></th>
            <th runat="server" class="right">Unit Price</th>
            <th runat="server" class="right">On Hand</th>
        </tr>
        <tr ID="itemPlaceholder" runat="server">
        </tr>
    </table>
</LayoutTemplate>
```

Description

- To sort the data in a ListView control, you add a button to the Layout template, set the button's CommandName attribute to Sort, and set its CommandArgument attribute to the name of the column you want to sort by. To sort by two or more columns, separate the column names with commas.

- For sorting to work, the DataSourceMode attribute of the data source must be set to DataSet.

Figure 16-5   How to provide for sorting

How to provide for paging

To provide paging for a ListView control, you use the DataPager control. Figure 16-6 presents the basic skills for using this control. The easiest way to create this control is to select the Enable Paging option from the Configure ListView dialog box. When you do that, a drop-down list becomes available that lets you choose whether you want to add a *next/previous pager* or a *numeric pager*.

The ListView control at the top of this figure shows the default next/previous pager, and the first code example shows the aspx code for this pager. Notice that the DataPager control contains a Fields element. Within this element, you can code one or more NextPreviousPagerField or NumericPagerField elements. In this case, the Fields element includes a single NextPreviousPagerField element. You'll learn more about the attributes that you can code on this element in the next figure.

The second pager in this figure is a simple numeric pager. The aspx code for this pager contains a NumericPagerField element with no attributes. Because of that, the default settings for this element are used. That means that five page buttons are displayed, along with an ellipsis button (...) if additional pages are available.

A ListView control that uses a next/previous pager

Product ID	Name	Category	Unit Price	On Hand
hippie01	Hippie	costumes	$79.99	40
jar01	JarJar	costumes	$59.99	25
martian01	Martian	costumes	$69.99	100
mum01	Mummy	masks	$39.99	30
pow01	Austin Powers	costumes	$79.99	25
rat01	Ugly Rat	props	$14.99	75
rat02	Uglier Rat	props	$19.99	50
skel01	Life-size Skeleton	props	$14.95	10
skullfog01	Skull Fogger	fx	$39.95	50
str01	Mini-strobe	fx	$13.99	200

First   Previous   Next   Last

The aspx code for the next/previous pager

```
<asp:DataPager ID="DataPager1" runat="server">
    <Fields>
        <asp:NextPreviousPagerField ButtonType="Button"
            ShowFirstPageButton="True"
            ShowLastPageButton="True" />
    </Fields>
</asp:DataPager>
```

A numeric pager

1 2 3 4 5 ...

The aspx code for the numeric pager

```
<asp:DataPager ID="DataPager1" runat="server">
    <Fields>
        <asp:NumericPagerField />
    </Fields>
</asp:DataPager>
```

Description

- To provide paging for a ListView control, you use a DataPager control. To add a DataPager control to a ListView control, you can select the Enable Paging option in the Configure ListView dialog box and then select Next/Previous Pager or Numeric Pager from the drop-down list that's displayed.

- The DataPager control contains a Fields element that can contain two types of pager elements. The NextPreviousPagerField element can display first, previous, next, and last buttons. The NumericPagerField element can display page numbers as well as an ellipsis button if additional pages are available.

- You can customize the appearance of a DataPager control by adding two or more pager elements to it. See figure 16-7 for more information.

- You can also create a DataPager control by dragging it from the Toolbox. When you do that, however, you have to add the Fields element and the pager elements manually.

Figure 16-6   How to provide for paging

How to customize paging

Figure 16-7 shows how you can customize a DataPager control. To do that, you use the attributes of the DataPager control and the NextPreviousPagerField and NumericPagerField elements shown in this figure. For example, to change the number of items that are displayed on each page, you set the PageSize attribute of the DataPager control.

Because the DataPager is a separate control, you don't have to place it inside the ListView control. Instead, you can place it anywhere you want on the page. If you do that, however, you need to set the PagedControlID attribute of the control. This attribute identifies the ListView control that it provides paging for.

By the way, the DataPager control can be used only with controls that implement the IPageableItemContainer interface. Currently, the ListView control is the only control that meets that criterion. In the future, however, I would expect other data-bound controls to implement this interface so their paging can be done from outside the controls.

The attributes of the NextPreviousPagerField element shown in this figure determine the type of buttons that are used in the pager and which buttons are displayed. The default is to display Previous and Next link buttons. Similarly, the attributes of the NumericPagerField element determine the type of buttons that are used and the number of buttons that are displayed. The default is to display five link buttons.

The code example in this figure shows a custom DataPager control that uses two next/previous pagers and one numeric pager. The resulting control is shown below this code. This should help you begin to see the flexibility that the DataPager control provides.

Attributes of the DataPager control

Attribute	Description
ID	The ID of the control.
Runat	Must specify "server."
PageSize	Specifies the number of items to be displayed on each page. The default is 10.
PagedControlID	The ID of the ListView control that the DataPager control provides paging for. Used only if the DataPager control is placed outside the ListView control.

Attributes of the NextPreviousPagerField element

Attribute	Description
ButtonType	The type of buttons to be used. You can specify Button, Image, or Link.
ShowFirstPageButton	Determines whether the first page button is displayed. The default is False.
ShowPreviousPageButton	Determines whether the previous page button is displayed. The default is True.
ShowNextPageButton	Determines whether the next page button is displayed. The default is True.
ShowLastPageButton	Determines whether the last page button is displayed. The default is False.

Attributes of the NumericPagerField element

Attribute	Description
ButtonCount	The maximum number of buttons to be displayed.
ButtonType	The type of buttons to be used. You can specify Button, Image, or Link.

Aspx code for a DataPager control that uses both types of pagers

```
<asp:DataPager ID="DataPager1" runat="server" PageSize="4">
    <Fields>
        <asp:NextPreviousPagerField ButtonType="Button"
            ShowFirstPageButton="True" ShowNextPageButton="False"
            ShowPreviousPageButton="False" />
        <asp:NumericPagerField ButtonCount="3" />
        <asp:NextPreviousPagerField ButtonType="Button"
            ShowLastPageButton="True" ShowNextPageButton="False"
            ShowPreviousPageButton="False" />
    </Fields>
</asp:DataPager>
```

The resulting DataPager control

First 1 2 3 ... Last

Description

- You can use the PageSize attribute of the DataPager control to specify the number of items to display on each page.
- You can place a DataPager control outside of the ListView control. Then, you must set the PagedControlID attribute of the DataPager control to the ID of the ListView control you want to use it with.
- The NextPreviousPagerField and NumericPagerField elements also have attributes that let you change the text or image for the buttons that are displayed.

Figure 16-7   How to customize paging

A list application that uses a ListView control

Now that you've learned the basic skills for working with a ListView control, the following topics present the design and code for an application that uses this control to display a list of products. If you compare this application with the list application in chapter 14 that uses a GridView control, you'll begin to see the flexibility that the ListView control provides.

The Product List application

Figure 16-8 presents the Product List application. Here, you can see that the first column in the ListView control contains the product name for each row in the Products table of the Halloween database. Then, the second column contains the headings for the other product columns that are included in the list, and the third column contains the data from each of the product columns. This type of layout wouldn't be possible with the GridView control.

You should also notice the DataPager control that's used with the ListView control. This control specifies that only four products should be displayed on each page. It's implemented using a next/previous pager with custom values for the text that's displayed on the buttons.

The Product List application

Description

- The ProductList application uses a ListView control to display a list of all the products in the Products table. The ListView control is bound to a SqlDataSource control that works in DataSet mode.

- The ListView control uses Item and AlternatingItem templates to display every other row with a different background color.

- A DataPager control is used within the ListView control to display four products on each page.

Figure 16-8   The Product List application

The aspx file

Figure 16-9 presents the aspx code for the Product List application. To generate the starting code for the ListView control used by this application, I selected flow layout from the Configure ListView dialog box. Unlike the code that's generated when you use grid layout, the code for flow layout doesn't use tables. That makes it easy to apply styles using CSS.

The first page of this listing shows the Layout template for the ListView control. The two divisions in this template were generated by default. The first division is used as the container for the item placeholder. In this case, the item placeholder is coded within a span element.

The second division contains the DataPager control that's used by the ListView control. By default, this division was generated with a style attribute, but I deleted that attribute and included an id attribute instead. That way, I was able to format the data pager using CSS.

As you can see, I set the PageSize attribute for the DataPager control to 4. Then, I used a NextPreviousPagerField element to implement the control. Here, I set the FirstPageText, PreviousPageText, NextPageText, and LastPageText attributes of this element so the buttons display less-than and greater-than signs as shown in the previous figure.

The only other change I made to this template was to add a paragraph before the two divisions. This paragraph contains the literal text that's displayed at the top of the ListView control. Like the division that contains the DataPager control, I included an id attribute for this paragraph so I could format it with CSS.

The second page of this listing shows the Item template for the control. I made considerable changes to the aspx code that was generated for this template to format the data so it looks as shown in the previous figure. To understand how this code works, you need to realize that the label that displays the name of a product is floated to the left of the remaining product information using CSS. Similarly, the literal text that identifies each of the remaining product columns is floated to the left of the label that displays the column value.

The third page of this listing shows the AlternatingItem template for the ListView control. This code is identical to the code for the Item template except that I gave the main division for this template a different value for the id attribute. That way, I was able to assign a different background color for alternate rows.

The SqlDataSource control is also shown on the third page of this listing. Notice here that the data source retrieves data from both the Products and Categories tables. The Categories table is included so the LongName column can be displayed instead of the CategoryID column from the Products table.

The Default.aspx file

```
<%@ Page Language="C#" AutoEventWireup="true" CodeFile="Default.aspx.cs"
Inherits="_Default" %>

<!DOCTYPE html PUBLIC "-//W3C//DTD XHTML 1.0 Transitional//EN"
"http://www.w3.org/TR/xhtml1/DTD/xhtml1-transitional.dtd">

<html xmlns="http://www.w3.org/1999/xhtml">
<head runat="server">
    <title>Chapter 16: Product List</title>
    <link href="Main.css" rel="stylesheet" type="text/css" />
</head>
<body>
    <form id="form1" runat="server">
    <div id="page">
        <div id="header">
            <asp:Image ID="Image1" runat="server"
                ImageUrl="~/Images/banner.jpg" />
        </div>
        <div id="main">
            <asp:ListView ID="ListView1" runat="server"
                DataKeyNames="ProductID" DataSourceID="SqlDataSource1">
            <LayoutTemplate>
                <p id="product">Product</p>
                <div ID="itemPlaceholderContainer" runat="server">
                    <span runat="server" id="itemPlaceholder" />
                </div>
                <div id="pager">
                    <asp:DataPager ID="DataPager1" runat="server"
                        PageSize="4">
                        <Fields>
                            <asp:NextPreviousPagerField
                                ButtonType="Button"
                                ShowFirstPageButton="True"
                                ShowLastPageButton="True"
                                FirstPageText="&lt;&lt;"
                                PreviousPageText="&lt;"
                                NextPageText="&gt;"
                                LastPageText="&gt;&gt;" />
                        </Fields>
                    </asp:DataPager>
                </div>
            </LayoutTemplate>
```

Figure 16-9   The aspx file for the Product List application (part 1 of 3)

The Default.aspx file   **Page 2**

```
<ItemTemplate>
    <div id="itemtemplate">
        <p class="name">
            <asp:Label ID="NameLabel" runat="server"
                Text='<%# Eval("Name") %>' />
        </p>
        <div class="info">
            <p class="label">Category:</p>
            <p class="control">
                <asp:Label ID="CategoryLabel" runat="server"
                    Text='<%# Eval("Category") %>' />
            </p>
            <p class="label">Short Description:</p>
            <p class="control">
                <asp:Label ID="ShortDescriptionLabel"
                    runat="server"
                    Text='<%# Eval("ShortDescription") %>' />
            </p>
            <p class="label"> Long Description:</p>
            <p class="control">
                <asp:Label ID="LongDescriptionLabel"
                    runat="server"
                    Text='<%# Eval("LongDescription") %>' />
            </p>
            <p class="label">Unit Price:</p>
            <p class="control">
                <asp:Label ID="UnitPriceLabel" runat="server"
                    Text='<%# Eval("UnitPrice", "{0:c}") %>' />
            </p>
            <p class="label">On Hand:</p>
            <p class="control">
                <asp:Label ID="OnHandLabel" runat="server"
                    Text='<%# Eval("OnHand") %>' />
            </p>
        </div>
    </div>
</ItemTemplate>
```

Figure 16-9   The aspx file for the Product List application (part 2 of 3)

The Default.aspx file   **Page 3**

```
            <AlternatingItemTemplate>
                <div id="alternatetemplate">
                    <p class="name">
                        <asp:Label ID="NameLabel" runat="server"
                            Text='<%# Eval("Name") %>' />
                    </p>
                    <div class="info">
                        <p class="label">Category:</p>
                        <p class="control">
                            <asp:Label ID="CategoryLabel" runat="server"
                                Text='<%# Eval("Category") %>' />
                        </p>
                        <p class="label">Short Description:</p>
                        <p class="control">
                            <asp:Label ID="ShortDescriptionLabel"
                                runat="server"
                                Text='<%# Eval("ShortDescription") %>' />
                        </p>
                        <p class="label"> Long Description:</p>
                        <p class="control">
                            <asp:Label ID="LongDescriptionLabel"
                                runat="server"
                                Text='<%# Eval("LongDescription") %>' />
                        </p>
                        <p class="label">Unit Price:</p>
                        <p class="control">
                            <asp:Label ID="UnitPriceLabel" runat="server"
                                Text='<%# Eval("UnitPrice", "{0:c}") %>' />
                        </p>
                        <p class="label">On Hand:</p>
                        <p class="control">
                            <asp:Label ID="OnHandLabel" runat="server"
                                Text='<%# Eval("OnHand") %>' />
                        </p>
                    </div>
                </div>
            </AlternatingItemTemplate>
        </asp:ListView>
        <asp:SqlDataSource ID="SqlDataSource1" runat="server"
            ConnectionString=
                "<%$ ConnectionStrings:HalloweenConnectionString %>"
            SelectCommand="SELECT Products.ProductID, Products.Name,
                Categories.LongName AS Category,
                Products.ShortDescription, Products.LongDescription,
                Products.UnitPrice, Products.OnHand
                FROM Products INNER JOIN Categories
                ON Products.CategoryID = Categories.CategoryID
                ORDER BY Products.Name">
        </asp:SqlDataSource>
    </div>
    </div>
    </form>
</body>
</html>
```

Figure 16-9   The aspx file for the Product List application (part 3 of 3)

How to group ListView data

One of the most exciting features of the ListView control is its ability to group data so it's displayed in two or more columns. In the topics that follow, you'll learn the basic skills for grouping data, and you'll see a simple application that uses groups.

How to define the templates for a group

Figure 16-10 shows how to define the templates for a ListView control that uses groups. This assumes that you started the ListView control from a layout that generates tables, such as the grid layout. If you started the control from a layout that doesn't generate tables, the procedure will be somewhat different.

To start, you change the ID attribute for the inner table in the Layout template to groupPlaceholderContainer, and you change the ID attribute for the row within that table to groupPlaceholder. You can also use a different value for the ID attribute of the group placeholder by setting the GroupPlaceholderID attribute of the ListView control to that value.

Next, you add a Group template to the control. In most cases, this template will contain a single row with its ID attribute set to itemPlaceholderContainer. Then, you can set the ID attribute for the single cell within that row to itemPlaceholder. When the application is run, the Item template will replace the item placeholder, and the group template will replace the group placeholder.

Finally, you set the GroupItemCount attribute of the ListView control to the number of items you want to include in each group. In this example, I set this attribute to 2. The result is shown at the top of this figure. Note that although the Item template for the ListView control isn't shown in this figure, you should be able to figure out its basic content by looking at the data for each product in the control. If you have trouble understanding how this works, however, it should become clearer when you see the complete application that's presented next.

Although you can modify a ListView control so it uses groups as I just described, you may find it easier to generate the basic code for the groups and then modify that code to customize the display. To do that, you can select the Tiled layout from the Configure ListView dialog box. Then, the ListView control is configured with Layout and Group templates like the ones shown here. In addition, the GroupItemCount attribute of the control is set to 3, and the Item template is formatted so it appears as shown in the ListView control at the top of this figure.

The beginning of a ListView control with two columns

Name: Austin Powers	Name: Black Light (24")
ShortDescription: Austin Powers costume	ShortDescription: 24" Black light
Category: Costumes	Category: Special Effects
UnitPrice: $79.99	UnitPrice: $24.99
OnHand: 25	OnHand: 200
Name: Darth Vader Mask	Name: Deranged Cat
ShortDescription: The legendary Darth Vader	ShortDescription: 20" Ugly cat
Category: Masks	Category: Props
UnitPrice: $19.99	UnitPrice: $19.99
OnHand: 100	OnHand: 45

The Layout and Group templates for the control

```
<asp:ListView ID="ListView1" runat="server" DataSourceID="SqlDataSource1"
    GroupItemCount="2">
    <LayoutTemplate>
        <table runat="server">
            <tr runat="server">
                <td runat="server">
                    <table ID="groupPlaceholderContainer" runat="server"
                        border="0" style="">
                        <tr ID="groupPlaceholder" runat="server"></tr>
                    </table>
                </td>
            </tr>
            .
            .
            .
        </table>
    </LayoutTemplate>
    <GroupTemplate>
        <tr ID="itemPlaceholderContainer" runat="server">
            <td ID="itemPlaceholder" runat="server">
            </td>
        </tr>
    </GroupTemplate>
    <ItemTemplate>
    .
    .
    .
    </ItemTemplate>
</asp:ListView>
```

Description

- You can use the Group template to display items in two or more columns. Then, the Group template replaces the element in the Layout template that has the ID "groupPlaceholder," and the Group template contains an element with the ID "itemPlaceholder" that's replaced by the Item template.

- To determine the number of columns in the group, you set the GroupItemCount attribute of the ListView control.

- The easiest way to create a Group template is to select the Tiled layout from the Configure ListView dialog box. Then, a group with three columns is created, and you can modify the aspx code to format the control any way you like.

Figure 16-10   How to define the templates for a group

A Product List application that uses groups

To illustrate how you can use groups, figure 16-11 presents a Product List application that uses groups. As you can see, this application displays the name and image for each product, and the products are displayed in three columns. Although this is a simple application, it should help you see how valuable using groups can be.

The aspx file for the grouped Product List application

Figure 16-12 presents the code for the grouped Product List application. The first thing you should notice here is that the GroupItemCount attribute of the ListView control is set to 3. This causes three items from the data source to be displayed in each row of the ListView control.

The second thing you should notice is that the Layout template includes a table row that acts as the group placeholder. This placeholder will be replaced by the Group template, which you can see at the bottom of the first page of this listing. The Group template, in turn, contains a single table row with a single cell that acts as the item placeholder.

The second page of this listing shows the Item template for the ListView control. Notice that because the item placeholder in the Group template is a table cell, the Item template must begin with a table cell. Then, two paragraphs are coded within this cell. The first paragraph contains a label that's bound to the Name column of the data source, and the second paragraph contains an image that's bound to the ImageFile column of the data source. Notice that the binding expression that's used for the image includes the path to the image file. That's necessary because the ImageFile column contains only the file name, not the path.

The SqlDataSource control that the ListView control is bound to is also shown on the second page of this listing. This data source simply retrieves the Name and ImageFile columns from the Products table and sorts the rows that are returned by the Name column.

The grouped Product List application

Description

- The grouped Product List application uses a ListView control to display the names and images of the products in the Products table. The products are grouped so that three products are displayed in each row.

- Although this application simply displays the product names and images, you could easily modify it to display additional information or to perform additional processing.

Figure 16-11   A Product List application that uses groups

The Default.aspx file

```
<%@ Page Language="C#" AutoEventWireup="true" CodeFile="Default.aspx.cs"
Inherits="_Default" %>

<!DOCTYPE html PUBLIC "-//W3C//DTD XHTML 1.0 Transitional//EN"
"http://www.w3.org/TR/xhtml1/DTD/xhtml1-transitional.dtd">

<html xmlns="http://www.w3.org/1999/xhtml">
<head runat="server">
    <title>Chapter 16: Grouped Product List</title>
    <link href="Main.css" rel="stylesheet" type="text/css" />
</head>
<body>
    <form id="form1" runat="server">
    <div id="page">
        <div id="header">
            <asp:Image ID="Image1" runat="server"
                ImageUrl="~/Images/banner.jpg" />
        </div>
        <div id="main">
            <asp:ListView ID="ListView1" runat="server"
                DataSourceID="SqlDataSource1" GroupItemCount="3">

                <LayoutTemplate>
                    <table runat="server">
                        <tr runat="server">
                            <td runat="server">
                                <table ID="groupPlaceholderContainer"
                                    runat="server" border="0">
                                    <tr ID="groupPlaceholder" runat="server">
                                    </tr>
                                </table>
                            </td>
                        </tr>
                        <tr runat="server">
                            <td runat="server" align="center">
                                <asp:DataPager ID="DataPager1" runat="server"
                                    PageSize="6">
                                    <Fields>
                                        <asp:NumericPagerField />
                                    </Fields>
                                </asp:DataPager>
                            </td>
                        </tr>
                    </table>
                </LayoutTemplate>

                <GroupTemplate>
                    <tr ID="itemPlaceholderContainer" runat="server">
                        <td ID="itemPlaceholder" runat="server">
                        </td>
                    </tr>
                </GroupTemplate>
```

Figure 16-12   The aspx file for the grouped Product List application (part 1 of 2)

The Default.aspx file   **Page 2**

```
            <ItemTemplate>
                <td runat="server">
                    <p class="name">
                        <asp:Label ID="NameLabel"
                            runat="server" Text='<%# Eval("Name") %>' />
                    </p>
                    <p class="image">
                        <asp:Image ID="ProductImage" runat="server"
                            height="190px"
                            ImageURL='<%#"~/Images/Products/" +
                                Eval("ImageFile") %>' />
                    </p>
                </td>
            </ItemTemplate>
        </asp:ListView>
        <asp:SqlDataSource ID="SqlDataSource1" runat="server"
            ConnectionString=
                "<%$ ConnectionStrings:HalloweenConnectionString %>"
            SelectCommand="SELECT [Name], [ImageFile]
                            FROM [Products]
                            ORDER BY [Name]">
        </asp:SqlDataSource>
    </div>
    </div>
    </form>
</body>
</html>
```

Figure 16-12   The aspx file for the grouped Product List application (part 2 of 2)

How to update ListView data

To update ListView data, you use the EditItem and InsertItem templates. I'll show you how to use these templates in just a minute. But first, I want to describe the various buttons you can use to work with data in a ListView control.

How to use buttons to perform update operations

You may recall that when you use a FormView control or a DetailsView control with templates to update data, the templates include buttons that let you insert, update, and delete data. You also use buttons to perform these operations using a ListView control. Although the buttons you need are generated automatically when you configure a ListView control, you will better understand how the ListView control works if you understand these buttons.

When the user clicks a button in a ListView control, the operation that's performed is determined by the value of the button's CommandName attribute. Figure 16-13 lists the predefined values for this attribute and describes their functions. For the most part, these values should be self-explanatory. For example, if the user clicks a button whose CommandName attribute is set to Edit, the row that contains that button is placed in edit mode. In that mode, the row is displayed using the EditItem template. As you'll see in a minute, the EditItem template contains buttons whose CommandName attributes are set to Update and Cancel. Then, if the user changes the data in that row and clicks the update button, the row in the database is updated. If the user clicks the cancel button instead, the original data is redisplayed using the Item template.

Notice that the ListView control can also contain a button whose CommandName attribute is set to Select. When this button is clicked, the selected row is displayed using the SelectedItem template. You can use a button like this to create a Master/Detail page like the one you saw in chapter 15 using a ListView control rather than a GridView control.

Buttons for working with the data in a ListView control

CommandName attribute	Description
Edit	Switches the ListView control to edit mode and displays the data using the EditItem template.
Update	In edit mode, saves the contents of the data-bound controls to the data source.
Cancel	Cancels the current operation. If a row is being edited, the original data is displayed using the Item template. If a row is being inserted, an empty InsertItem template is displayed.
Delete	Deletes the item from the data source.
Insert	Inserts the contents of the data-bound controls into the data source.
Select	Displays the contents of the data-bound controls using the SelectedItem template.

The aspx code for the Edit and Delete buttons in an Item template

```
<asp:Button ID="DeleteButton" runat="server"
    CommandName="Delete" Text="Delete" />
<asp:Button ID="EditButton" runat="server"
    CommandName="Edit" Text="Edit" />
```

Description

- To work with the data in a ListView control, you can use buttons whose CommandName attributes are set to predefined values. Then, when the user clicks these buttons, they perform the functions shown above.

- Although you must set the CommandName attribute to one of the values shown above to perform the associated function, you can set the Text attribute to anything you like.

- You can also create buttons that perform custom functions by setting the CommandName attribute to a custom value. Then, you can use the ItemCommand event of the ListView control to determine which button was clicked and perform the appropriate action.

Figure 16-13   How to use buttons to perform update operations

How to work with the EditItem and InsertItem templates

To help you understand how the EditItem and InsertItem templates work, figure 16-14 presents these templates for the ListView control you saw back in figure 16-1. This control was used to maintain the data in the Categories table of the Halloween database.

If you review the code for the EditItem template, you'll see that it includes two buttons whose CommandName attributes are set to Update and Cancel. Then, it includes a bound control for each of the three columns in the data source. The first column, CategoryID, is displayed in a label and is bound using the Eval method. That makes sense because this is the primary key for the table and shouldn't be changed. The other two columns, ShortName and LongName, are displayed in text boxes that are bound using the Bind method so they can be changed.

The InsertItem template is similar. Instead of update and cancel buttons, however, it includes insert and cancel buttons. Notice that although the CommandName attribute for the cancel button is set to Cancel just like it is for the cancel button in the EditItem template, the Text attribute is set to Clear instead of Cancel. That better describes what happens when this button is clicked. Also notice that all three columns in the data source are displayed in text boxes that are bound using the Bind method. That makes sense because all three values are required for a new category.

How to use events raised by the ListView control

The ListView control raises many of the same events as the DetailsView and FormView controls. For example, the ItemUpdating event is raised before an item is updated, and the ItemUpdated event is raised after an item has been updated. Similarly, the ItemInserting event is raised before an item is inserted, and the ItemInserted event is raised after an item has been inserted. And the ItemDeleting event is raised before an item is deleted, and the ItemDeleted event is raised after an item has been deleted. You'll typically use the before events to provide data validation, and you'll use the after events to check that the operation was successful. You'll see how some of these events are used in the maintenance application that follows.

The EditItem template for the ListView control in figure 16-1

```
<EditItemTemplate>
    <tr style="">
        <td>
            <asp:Button ID="UpdateButton" runat="server"
                CommandName="Update" Text="Update" />
            <asp:Button ID="CancelButton" runat="server"
                CommandName="Cancel" Text="Cancel" /></td>
        <td>
            <asp:Label ID="CategoryIDLabel1" runat="server"
                Text='<%# Eval("CategoryID") %>' /></td>
        <td>
            <asp:TextBox ID="ShortNameTextBox" runat="server"
                Text='<%# Bind("ShortName") %>' /></td>
        <td>
            <asp:TextBox ID="LongNameTextBox" runat="server"
                Text='<%# Bind("LongName") %>' /></td>
    </tr>
</EditItemTemplate>
```

The InsertItem template for the ListView control in figure 16-1

```
<InsertItemTemplate>
    <tr style="">
        <td>
            <asp:Button ID="InsertButton" runat="server"
                CommandName="Insert" Text="Insert" />
            <asp:Button ID="CancelButton" runat="server"
                CommandName="Cancel" Text="Clear" /></td>
        <td>
            <asp:TextBox ID="CategoryIDTextBox" runat="server"
                Text='<%# Bind("CategoryID") %>' /></td>
        <td>
            <asp:TextBox ID="ShortNameTextBox" runat="server"
                Text='<%# Bind("ShortName") %>' /></td>
        <td>
            <asp:TextBox ID="LongNameTextBox" runat="server"
                Text='<%# Bind("LongName") %>' /></td>
    </tr>
</InsertItemTemplate>
```

Description

- The EditItem template determines how an item in the ListView control is rendered in edit mode. By default, it includes a label for each column in the data source that can't be modified and a text box for each column in the data source that can be modified. These controls are bound to the columns of the data source using the Eval and Bind methods.

- The InsertItem template is similar to the EditItem template. It determines the content that's rendered for a new item that's being inserted.

- The EditItem template also includes update and cancel buttons by default, and the InsertItem template includes insert and cancel buttons.

Figure 16-14   How to work with the EditItem and InsertItem templates

A maintenance application that uses a ListView control

To give you a better idea of how you can use a ListView control to insert, update, and delete data, the topics that follow present an application that maintains the Categories table in the Halloween database. This application uses an enhanced version of the ListView control you saw in figure 16-1.

The Category Maintenance application

Figure 16-15 presents the Category Maintenance application. It uses a ListView control to display the rows in the Categories table using the Item and AlternatingItem templates, which include Edit and Delete buttons. Here, the user has clicked the button for the third category, so that row is displayed using the EditItem template. Then, the user can modify the data and click the Update button to save the changes to the database. Or, the user can click the Cancel button to cancel the changes and redisplay the original data.

The last row in the ListView control is displayed using the InsertItem template. This template lets the user enter the data for a new category into text boxes. Then, if the user clicks the Insert button, the new row is added to the database. If the user clicks the Clear button after entering data, though, the text boxes are cleared.

Note that required field validators are used for each text box in the EditItem and InsertItem templates. Then, if an error occurs, an asterisk is displayed to the right of the text box, and a message is displayed in the ValidationSummary control below the ListView control.

Before I go on, I want to point out that this application doesn't illustrate the formatting flexibility of the ListView control. In fact, except for the location of the buttons in this control, it looks almost identical to the GridView control used by the Category Maintenance application in chapter 14. However, it does illustrate the built-in capability to insert rows into a data source.

The Category Maintenance application

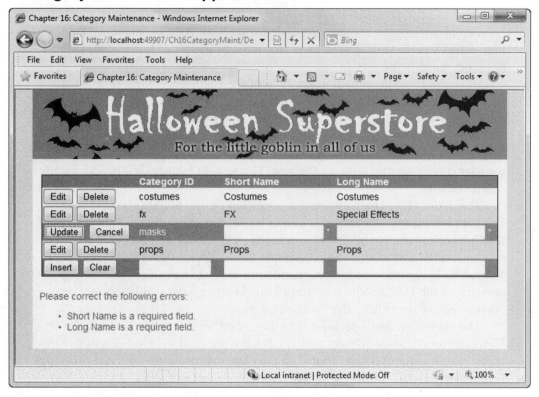

Description

- The Category Maintenance application uses a ListView control to let the user update, delete, or insert rows in the Categories table.

- To edit a category, the user clicks the Edit button for that category. This places the row for that category into edit mode. The user can then change the Short Name or Long Name and click the Update button. Or, the user can click the Cancel button to leave edit mode without performing the update.

- To delete a category, the user clicks the Delete button for that category.

- To add a category, the user enters a Category ID, Short Name, and Long Name into the last row of the ListView control and then clicks the Insert button. Or, the user can click the Clear button to clear the entries without adding the category.

- If the user attempts to update or add a row with a column that is blank, an error message is displayed in a ValidationSummary control.

Figure 16-15   The Category Maintenance application

The aspx file

Figure 16-16 presents the aspx code for the Category Maintenance application. Since you've already seen code like most of the code shown here, I'll just point out some highlights.

First, the InsertItemPosition attribute of the ListView control is set to LastItem. That causes the InsertItem template to be displayed at the bottom of the ListView control, as you saw in the previous figure.

Second, the Item and AlternatingItem templates contain two buttons. The first button, Edit, causes the row to be displayed using the EditItem template so the user can change the data for the row. The second button, Delete, lets the user delete the row.

Third, the MaxLength attribute is specified for the two text boxes in the EditItem template so the user can't enter more characters than are allowed by the Categories table. In addition, a required field validator is included for each text box so the user must enter values into them. Notice that the ValidationGroup attribute of these validators as well as the ValidationGroup attribute of the Update button is set to Edit. That way, the validation will be done when the user clicks the Update button.

The validation that's performed by the InsertItem template is similar. However, the ValidationGroup attribute for the required field validators and the Insert button is set to Insert. That way, only the validation for the controls in the InsertItem template will be done when the Insert button is clicked.

Fourth, this ListView control contains an EmptyData template. This template is displayed if no data is returned by the data source. Although it's not likely that the Categories table will be empty, this template is typically included for completeness.

Fifth, the SqlDataSource for this application doesn't use optimistic concurrency. Unfortunately, there appears to be a bug in the ListView control that doesn't let you use optimistic concurrency for delete operations. Hopefully, this bug will be corrected in an upcoming Service Pack for Visual Studio.

Finally, two ValidationSummary controls are included following the SqlDataSource control. Because the ValidationGroup attribute for the first control is set to Edit, it will be used to display errors that are detected when a row is being updated. In contrast, the ValidationGroup attribute for the second control is set to Insert, so it will be used to display errors that are detected when a row is being inserted.

The code-behind file

Figure 16-17 presents the code-behind file for the Category Maintenance application. This code is similar to the code for the maintenance applications you saw in the last two chapters, so you shouldn't have any trouble understanding how it works. Note that I've included the code that checks for optimistic concurrency, even though the data source doesn't provide for it. That way, this code will still work when the optimistic concurrency problem is fixed.

The Default.aspx file   **Page 1**

```aspx
<%@ Page Language="C#" AutoEventWireup="true" CodeFile="Default.aspx.cs"
Inherits="_Default" %>

<!DOCTYPE html PUBLIC "-//W3C//DTD XHTML 1.0 Transitional//EN"
"http://www.w3.org/TR/xhtml1/DTD/xhtml1-transitional.dtd">

<html xmlns="http://www.w3.org/1999/xhtml">
<head runat="server">
    <title>Chapter 16: Category Maintenance</title>
    <link href="Main.css" rel="stylesheet" type="text/css" />
</head>
<body>
  <form id="form1" runat="server">
  <div id="page">
    <div id="header">
      <asp:Image ID="Image1" runat="server" ImageUrl="~/Images/banner.jpg" />
    </div>
    <div id="main">
      <asp:ListView ID="ListView1" runat="server" DataKeyNames="CategoryID"
          DataSourceID="SqlDataSource1" InsertItemPosition="LastItem">
        <LayoutTemplate>
          <table runat="server">
            <tr runat="server">
              <td runat="server">
                <table ID="itemPlaceholderContainer" runat="server">
                  <tr id="listhead" runat="server">
                    <th runat="server"></th>
                    <th runat="server" class="left">Category ID</th>
                    <th runat="server" class="left">Short Name</th>
                    <th runat="server" class="left">Long Name</th>
                  </tr>
                  <tr ID="itemPlaceholder" runat="server"></tr>
                </table>
              </td>
            </tr>
          </table>
        </LayoutTemplate>
        <ItemTemplate>
          <tr id="item">
            <td class="buttons">
              <asp:Button ID="EditButton" runat="server" CommandName="Edit"
                  Text="Edit" CausesValidation="False" />
              <asp:Button ID="DeleteButton" runat="server"
                  CommandName="Delete" Text="Delete" /></td>
            <td class="catID">
              <asp:Label ID="CategoryIDLabel" runat="server"
                  Text='<%# Eval("CategoryID") %>' /></td>
            <td class="shortname">
              <asp:Label ID="ShortNameLabel" runat="server"
                  Text='<%# Eval("ShortName") %>' /></td>
            <td class="longname">
              <asp:Label ID="LongNameLabel" runat="server"
                  Text='<%# Eval("LongName") %>' /></td>
          </tr>
        </ItemTemplate>
```

Figure 16-16   The aspx file for the Category Maintenance application (part 1 of 4)

The Default.aspx file   **Page 2**

```
<AlternatingItemTemplate>
  <tr id="alternatingitem">
    <td class="buttons">
      <asp:Button ID="EditButton" runat="server" CommandName="Edit"
        Text="Edit" CausesValidation="False" />
      <asp:Button ID="DeleteButton" runat="server"
        CommandName="Delete" Text="Delete" /></td>
    <td class="catID">
      <asp:Label ID="CategoryIDLabel" runat="server"
        Text='<%# Eval("CategoryID") %>' /></td>
    <td class="shortname">
      <asp:Label ID="ShortNameLabel" runat="server"
        Text='<%# Eval("ShortName") %>' /></td>
    <td class="longname">
     <asp:Label ID="LongNameLabel" runat="server"
        Text='<%# Eval("LongName") %>' /></td>
  </tr>
</AlternatingItemTemplate>
<EditItemTemplate>
  <tr id="edititem">
    <td class="buttons">
      <asp:Button ID="UpdateButton" runat="server"
        CommandName="Update" Text="Update" ValidationGroup="Edit" />
      <asp:Button ID="CancelButton" runat="server"
        CommandName="Cancel" Text="Cancel" /></td>
    <td class="catID">
      <asp:Label ID="CategoryIDLabel1" runat="server"
        Text='<%# Eval("CategoryID") %>' /></td>
    <td class="shortname">
      <asp:TextBox ID="ShortNameTextBox" runat="server"
        Text='<%# Bind("ShortName") %>' Width="140px"
        MaxLength="15" />
      <asp:RequiredFieldValidator ID="RequiredFieldValidator1"
        runat="server" ControlToValidate="ShortNameTextBox"
        ErrorMessage="Short Name is a required field." Text="*"
        ValidationGroup="Edit" CssClass="validator">
      </asp:RequiredFieldValidator></td>
    <td class="longname">
      <asp:TextBox ID="LongNameTextBox" runat="server"
        Text='<%# Bind("LongName") %>' Width="215px"
        MaxLength="50" />
      <asp:RequiredFieldValidator ID="RequiredFieldValidator2"
        runat="server" ControlToValidate="LongNameTextBox"
        ErrorMessage="Long Name is a required field." Text="*"
        ValidationGroup="Edit" CssClass="validator">
      </asp:RequiredFieldValidator></td>
  </tr>
</EditItemTemplate>
```

Figure 16-16   The aspx file for the Category Maintenance application (part 2 of 4)

The Default.aspx file   Page 3

```
  <InsertItemTemplate>
    <tr id="insertitem">
      <td class="buttons">
        <asp:Button ID="InsertButton" runat="server"
            CommandName="Insert" Text="Insert"
            ValidationGroup="Insert" />
        <asp:Button ID="CancelButton" runat="server"
            CommandName="Cancel" Text="Clear" /></td>
      <td class="catID">
        <asp:TextBox ID="CategoryIDTextBox" runat="server"
            Text='<%# Bind("CategoryID") %>' Width="100px"
            MaxLength="10" />
        <asp:RequiredFieldValidator ID="RequiredFieldValidator3"
            runat="server" ControlToValidate="CategoryIDTextBox"
            ErrorMessage="Category ID is a required field." Text="*"
            ValidationGroup="Insert" CssClass="validator">
        </asp:RequiredFieldValidator></td>
      <td class="shortname">
        <asp:TextBox ID="ShortNameTextBox" runat="server"
            Text='<%# Bind("ShortName") %>' Width="140px"
            MaxLength="15" />
        <asp:RequiredFieldValidator ID="RequiredFieldValidator4"
            runat="server" ControlToValidate="ShortNameTextBox"
            ErrorMessage="Short Name is a required field." Text="*"
            ValidationGroup="Insert" CssClass="validator">
          </asp:RequiredFieldValidator></td>
      <td class="longname">
        <asp:TextBox ID="LongNameTextBox" runat="server"
            Text='<%# Bind("LongName") %>' Width="215px"
            MaxLength="50" />
        <asp:RequiredFieldValidator ID="RequiredFieldValidator5"
            runat="server" ControlToValidate="LongNameTextBox"
            ErrorMessage="Long Name is a required field." Text="*"
            ValidationGroup="Insert" CssClass="validator">
        </asp:RequiredFieldValidator></td>
    </tr>
  </InsertItemTemplate>
  <EmptyDataTemplate>
    <table id="emptydata" runat="server">
      <tr>
        <td>
          No data was returned.</td>
      </tr>
    </table>
  </EmptyDataTemplate>
</asp:ListView>
```

Figure 16-16   The aspx file for the Category Maintenance application (part 3 of 4)

The Default.aspx file

```
<asp:SqlDataSource ID="SqlDataSource1" runat="server"
    ConnectionString=
        "<%$ ConnectionStrings:HalloweenConnectionString %>"
    SelectCommand="SELECT [CategoryID], [ShortName], [LongName]
        FROM [Categories] ORDER BY [CategoryID]"
    DeleteCommand="DELETE FROM [Categories]
        WHERE [CategoryID] = @CategoryID"
    InsertCommand="INSERT INTO [Categories]
        ([CategoryID], [ShortName], [LongName])
        VALUES (@CategoryID, @ShortName, @LongName)"
    UpdateCommand="UPDATE [Categories]
        SET [ShortName] = @ShortName,
            [LongName] = @LongName
        WHERE [CategoryID] = @CategoryID">
    <DeleteParameters>
        <asp:Parameter Name="CategoryID" Type="String" />
    </DeleteParameters>
    <InsertParameters>
        <asp:Parameter Name="CategoryID" Type="String" />
        <asp:Parameter Name="ShortName" Type="String" />
        <asp:Parameter Name="LongName" Type="String" />
    </InsertParameters>
    <UpdateParameters>
        <asp:Parameter Name="ShortName" Type="String" />
        <asp:Parameter Name="LongName" Type="String" />
        <asp:Parameter Name="CategoryID" Type="String" />
    </UpdateParameters>
</asp:SqlDataSource>
<asp:ValidationSummary ID="ValidationSummary1" runat="server"
    HeaderText="Please correct the following errors:"
    ValidationGroup="Edit" CssClass="error" />
<asp:ValidationSummary ID="ValidationSummary2" runat="server"
    HeaderText="Please correct the following errors:"
    ValidationGroup="Insert" CssClass="error" />
<p>
    <asp:Label ID="lblError" runat="server"
        EnableViewState="False" CssClass="error"></asp:Label>
</p>
    </div>
  </div>
  </form>
</body>
</html>
```

Figure 16-16   The aspx file for the Category Maintenance application (part 4 of 4)

The Default.aspx.cs file

```csharp
using System;
using System.Collections.Generic;
using System.Linq;
using System.Web;
using System.Web.UI;
using System.Web.UI.WebControls;

public partial class _Default : System.Web.UI.Page
{
    protected void ListView1_ItemDeleted(object sender, ListViewDeletedEventArgs e)
    {
        if (e.Exception != null)
        {
            lblError.Text = "A database error has occurred.<br /><br />" +
                "Message: " + e.Exception.Message;
            e.ExceptionHandled = true;
        }
        else if (e.AffectedRows == 0)
        {
            lblError.Text = "Another user may have updated that category." +
                "<br />Please try again.";
        }
    }

    protected void ListView1_ItemInserted(object sender, ListViewInsertedEventArgs e)
    {
        if (e.Exception != null)
        {
            lblError.Text = "A database error has occurred.<br /><br />" +
                "Message: " + e.Exception.Message;
            e.ExceptionHandled = true;
        }
    }

    protected void ListView1_ItemUpdated(object sender, ListViewUpdatedEventArgs e)
    {
        if (e.Exception != null)
        {
            lblError.Text = "A database error has occurred.<br /><br />" +
                "Message: " + e.Exception.Message;
            e.ExceptionHandled = true;
            e.KeepInEditMode = true;
        }
        else if (e.AffectedRows == 0)
        {
            lblError.Text = "Another user may have updated that category." +
                "<br />Please try again.";
        }
    }
}
```

Figure 16-17   The code-behind file for the Category Maintenance application

Perspective

In this chapter, you've seen three different applications that demonstrate important features of the ListView control. The Product List application demonstrates its formatting capabilities. The grouped Product List application demonstrates its grouping capabilities. And the Category Maintenance application demonstrates its insert, update, and delete capabilities. In addition, both of the Product List applications demonstrate the use of the DataPager control. With these applications to guide you, you should now be able to use these controls in your own applications.

Up to this point, all of the database applications presented in this book have relied heavily on data binding that's defined in the aspx code, using C# code only for data validation and exception handling. However, ASP.NET also has powerful features for working with data access classes written with custom code. In the next chapter, then, you'll learn how the ObjectDataSource control lets you use data-bound controls such as the GridView, DetailsView, FormView, and ListView controls with custom data access classes.

Terms

next/previous pager
numeric pager

Exercise 16-1   Create a Customer List application

In this exercise, you'll use a ListView control to create a simple customer list that provides for sorting and paging.

1.   Open the Ch16CustomerList application in the C:\aspnet4_cs directory. This application contains the starting page and the image and style sheet used by the page.

2.   Add a ListView control to the main division of the page, and create a data source that retrieves the LastName, FirstName, State, City, and PhoneNumber columns from the Customers table, sorted by last name.

3.   Display the Configure ListView dialog box, make sure grid layout is selected, select the Professional style, enable paging, and select the Numeric Pager item from the drop-down list that becomes available.

4.   Run the application to see how the ListView control looks, and experiment with the buttons in the DataPager control to see how they work.

5.   Replace the literal text for the LastName, State, and City columns with link buttons. Add a CommandName attribute to each link button with the value "Sort", and add a CommandArgument attribute whose value is the name of the column to be sorted.

6. Run the application again, and make sure that the sorting works correctly.

7. Switch to Source view, and delete the EditItem, InsertItem, and SelectedItem templates since they aren't used by this application.

8. Locate the Layout template, and add a class attribute to each th element with the value "left". This will left-align the headers.

9. Locate the Item template, and change the widths of the columns to 135, 135, 70, 150, and 200 pixels respectively. The easiest way to do that is to add a style attribute with the width property. Do the same for the AlternatingItem template.

10. Run the application one more time to see how it looks.

Exercise 16-2   Create a grouped Customer List application

In this application, you'll create a Customer List application that displays customers in three columns.

1. Open the Ch16CustomerListGrouped application in the C:\aspnet4_cs directory. This application contains the starting page and the image and style sheet used by the page.

2. Add a ListView control to the main division of the page, and create a data source that retrieves the FirstName, LastName, Address, City, State, and ZipCode columns from the Customers table, sorted by last name.

3. Configure the ListView control so it uses a tiled layout. Enable paging and use a Next/Previous pager.

4. Display the smart tag menu for the ListView control, and select ItemTemplate from the CurrentView drop-down list.

5. Select the table cell within the Item template, and set its width to 230 pixels.

6. Delete the literal text that appears before each label. Then, adjust the template so the name and address will appear like this :

    FirstName LastName
    Address
    City, State ZipCode

7. Add another line break at the end of the Item template to provide for additional horizontal space between the items.

8. Repeat steps 5, 6, and 7 for the AlternatingItem template.

9. Select Runtime View from the CurrentView drop-down list to see how this looks.

10. Delete the templates that aren't used by this application. Then, run the application to see how it looks.

Exercise 16-3 Create a Product Maintenance application

In this exercise, you'll create an application that lets you maintain the products in the Products table.

1. Open the Ch16ProductMaint application in the C:\aspnet4_cs directory. This application contains the starting page with the validation summary and label controls that are used to display error messages, along with the image and style sheet used by the page.

2. Add a ListView control to the main division of the page above the validation summary control. Create a data source for the control that contains all of the rows from the Products table, sorted by the ProductID column. Be sure to generate Insert, Update, and Delete statements, but don't use optimistic concurrency.

3. Configure the ListView control so it uses flow layout and provides for deleting, editing, inserting, and paging.

4. Switch to Source view, and change the PageSize attribute of the DataPager control so that only two products are displayed at a time.

5. Modify the text boxes for each column in the EditItem and InsertItem templates except for the Category column so they're appropriate for the data. In addition, apply currency format to the unit price column in the Item template.

6. Use tables to align the labels and text boxes in the Item, EditItem, and InsertItem templates. This will take some work. If you're experienced with CSS, note that this could be done more easily with styles.

7. Add the appropriate validators for the text boxes in the EditItem and InsertItem templates. These validators should display a green asterisk to the right of the text box and display an error message in the validation summary control if an error is detected.

8. Add another data source to the page below the data source for the ListView control that retrieves the CategoryID and ShortName columns from the Categories table sorted by the ShortName column.

9. Replace the text boxes for the Category column in the EditItem and InsertItem templates with drop-down lists. Bind the lists by setting the DataSourceID attribute to the ID of the data source you just created, the DataTextField attribute to ShortName, the DataValueField attribute to CategoryID, and the SelectedValue attribute to the Bind expression that's used by the text boxes.

10. Add the C# code that's required to detect database errors when a row is updated, deleted, or inserted.

11. Run the application to see how it looks, and test it to be sure it works.

17

How to use
object data sources

This chapter is designed to introduce you to the use of object data sources as an alternative to the Access or SQL data sources that you've already learned about. The benefit of using object data sources is that they let you use a three-layer design in which the data access code is kept in data access classes. This lets you separate the presentation code from the data access code, but still lets you use the data binding features of ASP.NET.

To write the data access classes that are used with object data sources, you need to be able to use ADO.NET, which isn't presented in this book. But even if you don't understand ADO.NET, this chapter will show you how to use object data sources with existing data access classes. Then, you'll be able to decide whether you want to use object data sources in your applications and whether you want to learn how to use ADO.NET.

An introduction to object data sources

The following topics introduce you to object data sources and the 3-layer architecture that they let you implement.

How 3-layer applications work in ASP.NET

As you probably know, most development experts recommend a *3-layer architecture* for web applications that separates the presentation, business rules, and data access components of the application. The *presentation layer* includes the web pages that define the user interface. The *middle layer* includes the classes that manage the data access for those pages, and it may also include classes that implement business rules such as data validation requirements or discount policies. The *database layer* consists of the database itself.

In this chapter, you'll learn how to use *object data sources* to implement the 3-layer architecture. Figure 17-1 shows how this works. Here, you can see that the ObjectDataSource control serves as an interface between the data-bound controls in the presentation layer and the *data access classes* in the middle layer.

When you use an ObjectDataSource control, you must create a data access class to handle the data access for the control. This class provides at least one method that retrieves data from the database and returns it in a form that the ObjectDataSource control can handle. It can also provide methods to insert, update, and delete data. The data access class should be placed in the application's App_Code folder.

When you code a data access class, you can use any techniques you want to access the database. In this chapter, for example, you'll see data access classes that use ADO.NET. These classes can be used to get data from a SQL Server database, from other types of databases such as Oracle or MySQL databases, or from other sources such as XML or plain text files.

If you have already developed data access classes for the database used by your application, you may be able to use those classes with an object data source. Often, though, it's better to develop the data access classes specifically for the ObjectDataSource controls that you're going to use. That way, you can design each class so it works as efficiently as possible.

Incidentally, Microsoft uses both the term *business object class* and the term *data object class* to refer to a class that provides data access for an object data source. In this chapter, though, I used the term *data access class* for this type of class because if you use static methods to provide the data access functions, an object is never instantiated from the class.

The 3-layer architecture in ASP.NET

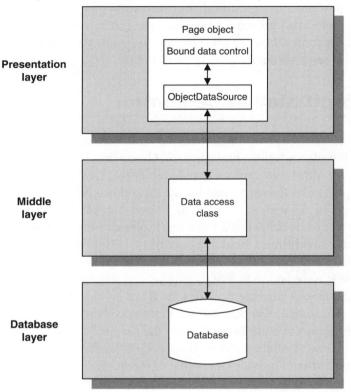

Presentation layer

Page object

Bound data control

ObjectDataSource

Middle layer

Data access class

Database layer

Database

The three layers

- The **presentation layer** consists of the ASP.NET pages that manage the appearance of the application. This layer can include bound data controls and ObjectDataSource objects that bind the data controls to the data.

- The **middle layer** contains the *data access classes* that manage the data access for the application. This layer can also contain business objects that represent business entities such as customers, products, or employees and that implement business rules such as credit and discount policies.

- The **database layer** consists of the database that contains the data for the application. Ideally, the SQL statements that do the database access should be saved in stored procedures within the database, but the SQL statements are often stored in the data access classes.

Description

- An *object data source* is implemented by the ObjectDataSource control, which lets you use data binding with the *3-layer architecture* for a database application.

- An object data source is similar to a SQL data source. However, instead of directly accessing a database, the object data source gets its data through a data access class that handles the details of database access.

Figure 17-1   How 3-layer applications work in ASP.NET

Also, you may be accustomed to using the term *3-tier architecture* for the *3-layer architecture* that's described in figure 17-1. Because some people use *3-tier* to refer to an architecture that puts the 3 layers on three different physical devices, though, I've used the term *3-layer* in this chapter. Although you could put each of the 3 layers on 3 separate devices, you don't have to.

How to use the ObjectDataSource control

Figure 17-2 presents the basics of working with the ObjectDataSource control. The image at the top of this figure shows how an ObjectDataSource control that's bound to a drop-down list appears in the Web Forms Designer. Then, the first code example shows the aspx code for the drop-down list and the object data source it's bound to. As with any other data source, you can add an object data source to a web page by dragging it from the Toolbox or by selecting the Choose Data Source command from a bindable control.

In the first code example, you can see that the drop-down list is bound to the object data source just as if it were bound to a SQL data source. The only difference is that the DataSourceID attribute provides the ID of an object data source rather than a SQL data source. You can also see that the code for the ObjectDataSource control has just two attributes besides the required ID and Runat attributes. The TypeName attribute provides the name of the data access class, and the SelectMethod attribute provides the name of the method used to retrieve the data. In this case, the data access class is ProductDB and the select method is GetAllCategories.

The second code example in this figure shows the GetAllCategories method of the ProductDB class. This method uses straightforward ADO.NET code to retrieve category rows from the Categories table and return a data reader that can be used to read the category rows. Notice, though, that the return type for this method is IEnumerable. Because the SqlDataReader class implements the IEnumerable interface, a data reader is a valid return object for this method. (You'll learn more about the return types that are acceptable for a select method in figure 17-8.)

A drop-down list bound to an ObjectDataSource control

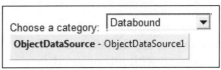

The code for the drop-down list and the ObjectDataSource control

```
<asp:DropDownList ID="ddlCategories" runat="server" AutoPostBack="True"
    DataSourceID="ObjectDataSource1"
    DataTextField="ShortName"
    DataValueField="CategoryID">
</asp:DropDownList>
<asp:ObjectDataSource ID="ObjectDataSource1" runat="server"
    TypeName="ProductDB"
    SelectMethod="GetAllCategories">
</asp:ObjectDataSource>
```

The GetAllCategories method of the ProductDB class

```
[DataObjectMethod(DataObjectMethodType.Select)]
public static IEnumerable GetAllCategories()
{
    SqlConnection con = new SqlConnection(GetConnectionString());
    string sel = "SELECT CategoryID, LongName "
        + "FROM Categories ORDER BY LongName";
    SqlCommand cmd = new SqlCommand(sel, con);
    con.Open();
    SqlDataReader dr = cmd.ExecuteReader(CommandBehavior.CloseConnection);
    return dr;
}
```

Basic attributes of the ObjectDataSource control

Attribute	Description
ID	The ID of the control.
Runat	Must specify "server."
TypeName	The name of the data access class.
SelectMethod	The name of the method that retrieves the data.
UpdateMethod	The name of the method that updates the data.
DeleteMethod	The name of the method that deletes the data.
InsertMethod	The name of the method that inserts the data.
DataObjectTypeName	The name of a class that provides properties that are used to pass parameter values.
ConflictDetection	Specifies how concurrency conflicts will be detected. CompareAllValues uses optimistic concurrency checking. OverwriteValues, which is the default, does no concurrency checking.

Description

- The ObjectDataSource control specifies the name of the data access class and the methods used to select, update, delete, and insert data.

Figure 17-2   How to use the ObjectDataSource control

How to configure an ObjectDataSource control

Figure 17-3 shows how you can use the Configure Data Source dialog boxes to configure an object data source control. As you can see, the first dialog box lets you choose the business object that will be associated with this object data source. The selection you make here will be used in the TypeName attribute of the ObjectDataSource control. (Notice that Microsoft refers to the data access class as a *business object* in this wizard. In other contexts, though, Microsoft refers to the data access class as a *data object* or a *data component*.)

The drop-down list in the first dialog box lists all of the classes that are available in the App_Code folder. If you check the "Show Only Data Components" box, only those classes that identify themselves as data components will be listed. In figure 17-10, you'll learn how to mark classes this way.

When you select a data access class and click Next, the second Configure Data Source dialog box is displayed. Here, you can select the method you want to use to retrieve data for the object data source. The one you select is specified in the SelectMethod attribute of the ObjectDataSource control. (In this step, the wizard uses a .NET feature called *reflection* to determine all of the available methods, and you'll learn more about reflection in a moment.)

If you select a select method that requires parameters, the Define Parameters step lets you specify the source for each of the required parameters. Then, Visual Studio generates the elements that define the parameters required by the ObjectDataSource control. This works the same as it does for a SQL data source.

As you can see in this figure, the second Configure Data Source dialog box also provides tabs that let you specify the methods for update, insert, and delete operations. Later in this chapter, you'll see an application that uses these methods. But for now, I'll just focus on how you can use an ObjectDataSource control to retrieve data.

How to work with bound controls

Although you can bind a control such as a drop-down list or GridView control to an object data source, you can't use the designer to select individual fields like you can when you use a SQL data source. That's because the fields are defined in the data access class and not directly in the data source. When you bind a drop-down list, for example, you have to manually enter the names of the fields you want to display and use for the value of the control. Similarly, when you bind a GridView control, you have to manually enter the name of each field you want to bind and, if the control provides for sorting, you have to enter the name of the field for each sort expression. In addition, you have to enter the appropriate field name or names for the DataKeyNames attribute of the control. The exception is if the select method returns a strongly-typed collection. You'll see an example like that later in this chapter. For now, just realize that because select methods that return a strongly-typed collection can make an object data source easier to work with, you should use them whenever that makes sense.

The dialog boxes for configuring a data source

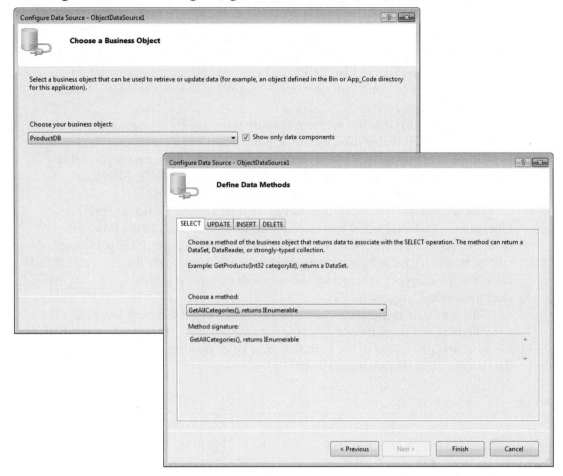

Description

- You can use the Configure Data Source dialog boxes to configure an ObjectDataSource control by choosing Configure Data Source from its smart tag menu.
- The Choose a Business Object step lets you select the data access class you want to use.
- The Define Data Methods step includes tabs that let you choose the methods you want to use for select, update, insert, and delete operations.
- If you choose a method that requires parameters, a Define Parameters step will appear. This step will let you choose the source of each parameter required by the method. For example, you can specify that a drop-down list should be used as the source for a parameter.
- If you create a new data source from a bound control, the Data Source Configuration Wizard asks you to choose a data source type. To create an object data source, select the Object option. Then, when you click the Next button, the first dialog box shown above is displayed.

Figure 17-3   How to configure an ObjectDataSource control

A Product List application

To illustrate the basics of working with the ObjectDataSource control, figure 17-4 presents a Product List application. This application is identical in appearance to the Product List application that was presented in chapter 13. However, instead of using SqlDataSource controls to retrieve the data, it uses ObjectDataSource controls.

This figure also lists the methods that are provided by the data access class named ProductDB that is used by this application. The first method, GetAllCategories, returns an IEnumerable object (actually, a data reader) that contains the data for all of the categories in the Categories table. This data includes just the category ID and long name for each category.

The second method, GetProductsByCategory, returns an IEnumerable object (again, a data reader) that includes all of the products in the Products table that have the category ID that's supplied by a parameter. This parameter will be bound to the SelectedValue property of the drop-down list. As a result, the ID of the category selected by the user will be passed to the GetProductsByCategory method.

This application illustrates how the use of object data sources lets you separate the presentation code from the data access code. As you will see, all of the presentation code is in the aspx file. And all of the data access code is in the data access class that's named ProductDB.

The Product List application

Methods of the ProductDB class

Method	Description
GetAllCategories()	Returns an IEnumerable object with the ID and long name of all the categories in the Categories table.
GetProductsByCategory(string CategoryID)	Returns an IEnumerable object with the ID, name, unit price, and on-hand quantity for all products in the Products table for the specified category.

Description

- The Category drop-down list is bound to an ObjectDataSource control that retrieves a list of categories from the Categories table.

- The DataList control is bound to a second ObjectDataSource control that uses a parameterized query to retrieve the products for a selected category. The CategoryID for the parameter is taken from the SelectedValue property of the drop-down list.

- Both ObjectDataSource controls use a data access class named ProductDB that contains the static methods that return a list of categories and the products for a specific category.

Figure 17-4   The Product List application

The aspx file

Figure 17-5 shows the main division of the Default.aspx page for the Product List application. If you compare this listing with the listing shown in figure 13-16, you'll discover that the only difference is that the SqlDataSource elements have been replaced by ObjectDataSource elements. In other words, the code for the drop-down list and DataList controls is identical whether the application uses a SQL data source or an object data source.

In the first ObjectDataSource control, the TypeName attribute specifies ProductDB, and the SelectMethod attribute specifies GetAllCategories. As a result, the GetAllCategories method in the ProductDB data access class will be called to retrieve the category data when the drop-down list is bound.

In the second ObjectDataSource control, a ControlParameter element within the SelectParameters element is used to declare the CategoryID parameter. This parameter is bound to the SelectedValue property of the drop-down list.

Because the data binding for this application is defined entirely in the aspx file, there is no code-behind file for this page. As a result, the only C# code for this application is in the ProductDB class, which is presented in the next figure.

The main division of the Default.aspx file

```
<div id="main">
    <p>
        Choose a category: 
        <asp:DropDownList ID="ddlCategory" runat="server"
            DataSourceID="ObjectDataSource1" DataTextField="LongName"
            DataValueField="CategoryID" AutoPostBack="True">
        </asp:DropDownList>
        <asp:ObjectDataSource ID="ObjectDataSource1" runat="server"
            SelectMethod="GetAllCategories" TypeName="ProductDB">
        </asp:ObjectDataSource>
    </p>
    <asp:DataList ID="dlProducts" runat="server" DataKeyField="ProductID"
        DataSourceID="ObjectDataSource2" CellPadding="3" GridLines="Vertical">
        <HeaderTemplate>
            <table>
                <tr>
                    <td class="col1">ID</td>
                    <td class="col2">Product</td>
                    <td class="col3">Unit Price</td>
                    <td class="col4">On Hand</td>
                </tr>
            </table>
        </HeaderTemplate>
        <ItemTemplate>
            <table>
                <tr>
                    <td class="col1">
                        <asp:Label ID="lblID" runat="server"
                            Text='<%# Eval("ProductID") %>' /></td>
                    <td class="col2">
                        <asp:Label ID="lblName" runat="server"
                            Text='<%# Eval("Name") %>' /></td>
                    <td class="col3">
                        <asp:Label ID="lblUnitPrice" runat="server"
                            Text='<%# Eval("UnitPrice", "{0:C}") %>' /></td>
                    <td class="col4">
                        <asp:Label ID="lblOnHand" runat="server"
                            Text='<%# Eval("OnHand") %>' /></td>
                </tr>
            </table>
        </ItemTemplate>
        <AlternatingItemStyle BackColor="#CCCCCC" />
        <HeaderStyle BackColor="Black" Font-Bold="True" ForeColor="White" />
    </asp:DataList>
    <asp:ObjectDataSource ID="ObjectDataSource2" runat="server"
        SelectMethod="GetProductsByCategory" TypeName="ProductDB">
        <SelectParameters>
            <asp:ControlParameter ControlID="ddlCategory" Name="CategoryID"
                PropertyName="SelectedValue" Type="String" />
        </SelectParameters>
    </asp:ObjectDataSource>
</div>
```

Figure 17-5   The aspx file for the Product List application

The ProductDB class

Figure 17-6 presents the C# code for the ProductDB class. To create this class, I used the Website→Add New Item command to add a class file to the App_Code folder. Then, I added the code for the public GetAllCategories and GetProductsByCategory methods. I also created a private method named GetConnectionString. This method is used by both of the public methods to retrieve the connection string for the Halloween database.

Before I explain the details of how these methods work, I want to point out the DataObject and DataObjectMethod attributes that appear in this class. These attributes are used to identify the class and methods as data objects, and you'll learn how to use them in figure 17-10. For now, just realize that they're used by the Data Source Configuration Wizard to determine which classes and methods to display when you configure an object data source.

The GetAllCategories method starts by creating a connection to the Halloween database. To get the connection for this database, it calls the GetConnectionString method. Next, this method creates a string that contains the Select statement that will be used to retrieve data from the Halloween database:

```
SELECT CategoryID, LongName
FROM Categories
ORDER BY LongName
```

Then, a SqlCommand object is created using the string that contains the Select statement and the connection object as parameters. Finally, the connection is opened, the ExecuteReader method of the command object is called to create a data reader object that contains the requested data, and the data reader is returned to the object data source.

The GetProductsByCategory method is slightly more complicated because it uses a parameter in its Select statement:

```
SELECT ProductID, Name, UnitPrice, OnHand
FROM Products
WHERE CategoryID = @CategoryID
ORDER BY ProductID
```

Here again, a SqlCommand object is created using this Select statement and the connection object. Then, a parameter named CategoryID is added to the command's Parameters collection before the connection is opened, and the command is executed so it returns a data reader with the requested data.

The GetConnectionString method uses the ConfigurationManager class to retrieve the connection string named "HalloweenConnectionString" from the web.config file. As a result, the connection string for the Halloween database must be stored in this file. To refresh your memory about how to store it, please refer to figure 13-4 in chapter 13.

The ProductDB class

```
using System;
using System.Collections;
using System.Configuration;
using System.Data;
using System.Data.SqlClient;
using System.ComponentModel;

[DataObject(true)]
public static class ProductDB
{
    [DataObjectMethod(DataObjectMethodType.Select)]
    public static IEnumerable GetAllCategories()
    {
        SqlConnection con = new SqlConnection(GetConnectionString());
        string sel = "SELECT CategoryID, LongName "
            + "FROM Categories ORDER BY LongName";
        SqlCommand cmd = new SqlCommand(sel, con);
        con.Open();
        SqlDataReader dr = cmd.ExecuteReader(CommandBehavior.CloseConnection);
        return dr;
    }

    [DataObjectMethod(DataObjectMethodType.Select)]
    public static IEnumerable GetProductsByCategory(string CategoryID)
    {
        SqlConnection con = new SqlConnection(GetConnectionString());
        string sel = "SELECT ProductID, Name, "
            + "UnitPrice, OnHand "
            + "FROM Products "
            + "WHERE CategoryID = @CategoryID "
            + "ORDER BY ProductID";
        SqlCommand cmd = new SqlCommand(sel, con);
        cmd.Parameters.AddWithValue("CategoryID", CategoryID);
        con.Open();
        SqlDataReader dr = cmd.ExecuteReader(CommandBehavior.CloseConnection);
        return dr;
    }

    private static string GetConnectionString()
    {
        return ConfigurationManager.ConnectionStrings
            ["HalloweenConnectionString"].ConnectionString;
    }
}
```

Note

- The DataObject and DataObjectMethod attributes are described in figure 17-10.

Figure 17-6   The ProductDB class for the Product List application

How to create a data access class

The most challenging aspect of using object data sources is developing the data access classes that they require. So the topics that follow explain how to design and implement these classes.

How to design a data access class

As figure 17-7 shows, the data access class used by an ObjectDataSource control can have four different types of methods that are used to select, insert, update, and delete data. You can use any method names that you want for these methods, and you can design the class so that it has more than one of each of these types of methods. For example, the ProductDB class used in the previous figure has two select methods that are named GetAllCategories and GetProductsByCategory.

The data access methods can be static methods or instance methods. If you define them as instance methods, the ObjectDataSource control will create an instance of the data access class before it calls the method, and then destroy the object after the method has been executed. For this to work, the data access class must provide a parameterless constructor. In C#, though, a parameterless constructor is provided by default if the class has no constructors.

Because creating and destroying a data access object can be time consuming, I suggest that you use static methods for the select, insert, update, and delete methods whenever possible. That way, the ObjectDataSource control won't have to create an instance of the data access class when it calls one of the data access methods.

Although you provide the names of the methods called by the ObjectDataSource control by using the SelectMethod, InsertMethod, UpdateMethod, and DeleteMethod attributes, the ObjectDataSource control doesn't generate the parameters that will be passed to these methods until runtime. Because of that, the ObjectDataSource control must use a .NET feature called *reflection* to determine if a method it calls contains the correct parameters. It also uses reflection to determine the return type of a select method. As you'll see in the next figure, this lets you design a select method that can return the selected data in a variety of forms.

In case you haven't encountered reflection before, it's a .NET feature that provides information about compiled classes at runtime. For example, reflection can determine what methods are provided by a particular class. In addition, it can determine what parameters each method requires and the type returned by the method.

Types of methods in a data access class

Method type	Description
Select	Retrieves data from a database and returns it as an IEnumerable object.
Insert	Inserts data for one row into the underlying database. The values for the new row are passed via one or more parameters.
Update	Updates the data for one row in the underlying database. The values for the updated row, along with any values that are used to implement optimistic concurrency, are passed via one or more parameters.
Delete	Deletes a row from the underlying database. The key or keys for the row to be deleted, along with any values that are used to implement optimistic concurrency, are passed via one or more parameters.

How an object data source determines which method to call

- The name of the method used for select, insert, update, and delete operations is specified by the SelectMethod, InsertMethod, UpdateMethod, or DeleteMethod attribute.

- The ObjectDataSource control determines what parameters need to be passed to the data access class methods based on the data fields to be inserted, updated, or deleted and whether or not optimistic concurrency is used.

- The ObjectDataSource control uses reflection to determine the parameter signatures for the insert, update, and delete methods provided by the data access class.

- At runtime, if the class doesn't provide a method with the correct name and parameters, an exception is thrown.

Description

- A data access class can declare public methods that select, insert, update, and delete data. These methods can be instance methods or static methods.

- You can use any method names you want for the select, insert, update, and delete methods.

- If the select, insert, update, and delete methods are static methods, the methods are used without creating an instance of the data access class.

- If the select, insert, update, and delete methods are instance methods, an instance of the data access class is created and destroyed for each data access operation. In this case, the data access class must provide a parameterless constructor.

- You can use parameters to pass selection criteria or other data to the select, insert, update, and delete methods. For more information on the parameters used with insert, update, and delete methods, see figure 17-9.

- *Reflection* is a .NET feature that provides information about compiled classes and methods at runtime.

Figure 17-7   How to design a data access class

How to create a select method

Figure 17-8 shows how to design and code a select method that can be used with an ObjectDataSource control. The table at the top of this figure lists the four different types of values that a select method can return. The simplest is the IEnumerable interface, which can return a data reader or a data view since the DataReader and DataView classes implement the IEnumerable interface. Also, the IEnumerable object can be a strongly-typed collection that's created by using the generics feature of C#.

The select method can also return a DataTable or DataSet object. Because a dataset can contain more than one table, the ObjectDataSource control simply uses the first table in the dataset. As a result, you must design the select method so the first table in the dataset contains the data you want to access.

The main advantage of returning a dataset rather than a data table or data view is that the object data source can cache a dataset. Then, to enable caching, you can set the EnableCaching attribute to True for the ObjectDataSource control. In that case, the select method will be called only the first time the data is requested. For more information on caching, which works the same as it does for a SqlDataSource control, please refer back to chapter 13.

You can also pass parameters to the select method. In that case, the ObjectDataSource control must include a SelectParameters element. This element is added automatically if you use the Data Source Configuration Wizard to create the control. Then, you can create a ControlParameter element that binds a parameter to a control such as a drop-down list. You saw an example of this in figure 17-5.

Allowable return types for a select method

Return type	Description
IEnumerable	A collection such as an ArrayList or HashTable or a strongly-typed collection such as System.Collections.Generic.List. (Because the DataReader and DataView classes implement IEnumerable, the select method can also return a data reader or a data view.)
DataTable	If the select method returns a data table, the ObjectDataSource control automatically extracts a data view from the table and uses the view for data binding.
DataSet	If the select method returns a dataset, the ObjectDataSource control extracts a data view from the first data table in the dataset and uses the view for data binding.
Object	If the select method returns an object, the ObjectDataSource control wraps the object in an IEnumerable collection with just one item, then does the data binding as if the method returned an IEnumerable object.

A select method that returns a data reader

```
public static IEnumerable GetAllCategories()
{
    SqlConnection con = new SqlConnection(GetConnectionString());
    string sel = "SELECT CategoryID, LongName "
        + "FROM Categories ORDER BY LongName";
    SqlCommand cmd = new SqlCommand(sel, con);
    con.Open();
    SqlDataReader dr = cmd.ExecuteReader(CommandBehavior.CloseConnection);
    return dr;
}
```

A select method that returns a dataset

```
public static DataSet GetAllCategories()
{
    SqlConnection con = new SqlConnection(GetConnectionString());
    string sel = "SELECT CategoryID, LongName "
        + "FROM Categories ORDER BY LongName";
    SqlDataAdapter da = new SqlDataAdapter(sel, con);
    DataSet ds = new DataSet();
    da.Fill(ds, "Categories");
    return ds;
}
```

Description

- The select method returns data retrieved from the underlying database. It can return the data in several forms, including a data reader or a dataset.

- If the select method returns a dataset, the object data source can cache the data.

- The select method can also return a strongly-typed collection using C#'s generics feature. See figure 17-15 for an example.

- If the select method accepts parameters, the parameters must be declared within the SelectParameters element of the ObjectDataSource control. Within this element, you can use the ControlParameter element to declare a parameter that's bound to another control on the page.

Figure 17-8   How to create a select method

How to create update, delete, and insert methods

Besides select methods, the data access class used by an object data source can provide methods that update, delete, and insert data in the underlying database. Before you can code these methods, you need to determine what parameters are required. Figure 17-9 summarizes how an object data source generates these parameters.

Any insert or delete method you create requires a single business object as its parameter. This business object must contain all the values required by the method, and you can give it any name you choose. If an update method doesn't provide for optimistic concurrency checking, it too requires a single business object as its parameter.

If an update method provides for optimistic concurrency checking, it requires two parameters as shown in the code at the top of this figure. One of the parameters must be a business object that provides the original values for the row to be updated, and the other parameter must be a business object that provides the new values for the row. Note that the name of the parameter for the business object that contains the new values can have any name you choose. However, the name of the parameter for the business object that contains the original values must be the same as the name of the parameter for the business object with the new values, preceded by the value of the OldValuesParameterFormatString attribute. In this example, the value of this attribute is original_, which is the default.

Two parameters are also required if the key column for a table is updatable. In that case, though, the object data source won't automatically generate two parameters. Because of that, you will need to set the ConflictDetection property of the object data source to CompareAllValues even if the update method doesn't provide for optimistic concurrency checking, and you will need to set the OldValuesParameterFormatString property accordingly. Then, you can use the property that contains the value for the key column of the object that contains the original values to identify the row to be updated.

This figure also lists the requirements for a business class that you can use to create the business objects. First, the class must provide a parameterless constructor. Since C# provides a parameterless constructor by default if a class isn't defined with any constructors, you may be able to omit this constructor. However, I prefer to include it for completeness.

Second, the class must define a public property for each bound field that's passed from the bound control to the object data source. If the object data source is bound to a GridView or DetailsView control that uses BoundField elements, the names of these properties must be the same as the names specified for the DataField attributes of those elements. In contrast, if the object data source is bound to a GridView or DetailsView control that uses TemplateField elements, or if the object data source is bound to a FormView or ListView control, the names of these properties must be the same as the names in the Eval and Bind methods of the bound controls.

A typical update method

```
public static int UpdateCategory(Category original_Category,
    Category category)
{
    SqlConnection con = new SqlConnection(GetConnectionString());
    string up = "UPDATE Categories "
        + "SET ShortName = @ShortName, "
        + "LongName = @LongName "
        + "WHERE CategoryID = @original_CategoryID "
        + "AND ShortName = @original_ShortName "
        + "AND LongName = @original_LongName";
    SqlCommand cmd = new SqlCommand(up, con);
    cmd.Parameters.AddWithValue("ShortName", category.ShortName);
    cmd.Parameters.AddWithValue("LongName", category.LongName);
    cmd.Parameters.AddWithValue("original_CategoryID",
        original_Category.CategoryID);
    cmd.Parameters.AddWithValue("original_ShortName",
        original_Category.ShortName);
    cmd.Parameters.AddWithValue("original_LongName",
        original_Category.LongName);
    con.Open();
    int updateCount = cmd.ExecuteNonQuery();
    con.Close();
    return updateCount;
}
```

How parameters are generated

- When the insert or delete method is called, one parameter of the business class type is generated and passed to the method. The parameter that's declared in the method can have any name you choose.

- One parameter of the business class type is also generated and passed to the update method when this method is called if optimistic concurrency isn't used. The parameter that's declared in the method can have any name you choose.

- If optimistic concurrency is specified, two parameters are generated and passed to the update method. One contains the original values, and the other contains the new values. The name of the parameter that contains the original values must be the same as the name of the parameter that contains the new values, preceded by the string that's specified by the OldValuesParameterFormatString attribute.

Requirements for the business class

- The class must provide a parameterless constructor.

- The class must have public properties with names that match the names of the bound fields that are passed to the object data source from the bound control.

- The public properties must have both get and set accessors.

Description

- To properly design an update, delete, or insert method, you must be aware of how the ObjectDataSource control generates the parameters passed to these methods.

Figure 17-9   How to create update, delete, and insert methods

Third, the property for each bound field must include both a get and a set accessor. The object data source uses the set accessors to set the values of the properties based on the values passed to it from the bound control. And the insert, update, and delete methods in the data access class use the get accessors to assign the values of the properties to parameters of command objects.

Once the ObjectDataSource control has determined what parameters need to be passed, it uses reflection to determine whether the data access class has a method that accepts the required parameters. If so, the method is called using these parameters. If not, an exception is thrown.

Before I go on, I want to point out that you don't have to use business objects as the parameters of insert, update, and delete methods. Instead, you can use a parameter for each bound field that's required by a method. This technique can be cumbersome, though, if more than just a few fields are required. In addition, it's more difficult to determine what parameters the object data source will generate. It's also more difficult to work with bound controls like the GridView control because you have to manually enter the name of each field you want to bind. That's because the fields are defined in the data access class and not directly in the data source. (When you use business objects, the business class is identified in the data source, and the properties of that class are made available to bound controls.) For these reasons, I recommend that you use business objects whenever possible.

How to use attributes to mark a data access class

Figure 17-10 shows how you can use *C# attributes* to identify a data access class and its methods. In case you haven't worked with attributes before, they are simply a way to provide declarative information for classes, methods, properties, and so on. Although some of these attributes have meaning at runtime, the attributes in this figure are used at design time. In particular, the Data Source Configuration Wizard uses these attributes to determine which classes in the App_Code folder are data access classes and which methods in the data access class are select, insert, update, and delete methods.

Note, however, that you don't need to use these attributes. The only reason to use them is to help the Data Source Configuration Wizard recognize the data access classes and methods. If you haven't marked your data access classes with these attributes, you can still access them from the wizard by clearing the Show Only Data Components check box in the Choose a Business Object step of the wizard (see figure 17-3).

Attributes for marking data access classes

To mark an element as...	Use this attribute...
A data object class	`[DataObject(true)]`
A Select method	`[DataObjectMethod(DataObjectMethodType.Select)]`
An Insert method	`[DataObjectMethod(DataObjectMethodType.Insert)]`
An Update method	`[DataObjectMethod(DataObjectMethodType.Update)]`
A Delete method	`[DataObjectMethod(DataObjectMethodType.Delete)]`

A marked data access class

```
using System;
using System.Collections;
using System.Data;
using System.Data.SqlClient;
using System.Configuration;
using System.ComponentModel;

[DataObject(true)]
public static class ProductDB
{
    [DataObjectMethod(DataObjectMethodType.Select)]
    public static IEnumerable GetAllCategories()
    {
        SqlConnection con = new SqlConnection(GetConnectionString());
        string sel = "SELECT CategoryID, LongName "
            + "FROM Categories ORDER BY LongName";
        SqlCommand cmd = new SqlCommand(sel, con);
        con.Open();
        SqlDataReader dr =
            cmd.ExecuteReader(CommandBehavior.CloseConnection);
        return dr;
    }
}
```

Description

- You can use DataObject and DataObjectMethod attributes to mark data access classes and methods. Visual Studio uses these attributes to determine which classes and methods to list in the drop-down lists of the Data Source Configuration Wizard.

- The DataObject and DataObjectMethod attributes are stored in the System.ComponentModel namespace.

Figure 17-10   How to use attributes to mark a data access class

A Category Maintenance application

To give you a better idea of how you can use an object data source to update, delete, and insert data, the following topics present an application that maintains the Categories table in the Halloween database. This application is a variation of the Category Maintenance application that was presented in chapter 14.

The design

Figure 17-11 presents the design for this version of the Category Maintenance application. It uses a GridView control to let the user update and delete category rows and a DetailsView control to insert new category rows. Both the GridView and DetailsView controls are bound to a single ObjectDataSource control. But the DetailsView control is used only in Insert mode so it isn't used to display, update, or delete existing category rows.

The table in this figure shows the public methods that are provided by the CategoryDB class. These four methods provide the select, update, delete, and insert functions. Since all of these methods are defined as static, an instance of the CategoryDB class doesn't have to be created to access the database.

The aspx file

The two parts of figure 17-12 show the Default.aspx file for this application. In part 1, you can see the aspx code for the GridView control that displays the category rows. Its Columns collection includes three BoundField columns, named CategoryID, ShortName, and LongName. (I didn't use templates or validation controls for this application so it would be easier to focus on how the ObjectDataSource control is used.)

In part 2, you can see the aspx code for the ObjectDataSource control. It names CategoryDB as the data access class and Category as the business class. It also provides the names of the select, insert, update, and delete methods that will be used to access the data. Notice that the ConflictDetection attribute is set to CompareAllValues so optimistic concurrency will be used. You'll see one way to implement optimistic concurrency with an object data source when you see the C# code for this application.

Also notice that parameters are included only for the update method. These parameters are included because the update method requires two parameters: an object that contains the original values and an object that contains the new values. Because these parameters must be given appropriate names as explained earlier, the object data source must include parameters that specify these names. In contrast, the names of the parameters in the insert and delete methods can be anything you like, so they don't have to be defined by the object data source.

You can also see the aspx code for the DetailsView control in part 2. Here, I set the DefaultMode attribute to Insert so this control is always displayed in Insert mode.

The Category Maintenance application

Methods of the CategoryDB class

Method type	Signature
Select	`public static IEnumerable GetCategories()`

Update	`public static int UpdateCategory(string ShortName,`
	`    string LongName, string original_CategoryID,`
	`    string original_ShortName, string original_LongName)`

Delete	`public static int DeleteCategory(string original_CategoryID,` `    string original_ShortName, string original_LongName)`
Insert	`public static int InsertCategory(string CategoryID,` `    string ShortName, string LongName)`

Description

- This version of the Category Maintenance application uses a GridView control to update and delete rows and a DetailsView control to insert rows. These controls are bound to an ObjectDataSource control that accesses the Categories table of the Halloween database.

- The data access class named CategoryDB provides the select, insert, update, and delete methods.

Figure 17-11   The Category Maintenance application

The Default.aspx file   Page 1

```
<%@ Page Language="C#" AutoEventWireup="true"  CodeFile="Default.aspx.cs"
Inherits="_Default" %>

<!DOCTYPE html PUBLIC "-//W3C//DTD XHTML 1.0 Transitional//EN"
"http://www.w3.org/TR/xhtml1/DTD/xhtml1-transitional.dtd">

<html xmlns="http://www.w3.org/1999/xhtml">
<head runat="server">
    <title>Chapter 17: Category Maintenance</title>
    <link href="Main.css" rel="stylesheet" type="text/css" />
</head>
<body>
    <form id="form1" runat="server">
    <div id="page">
        <div id="header">
            <asp:Image ID="Image1" runat="server"
                ImageUrl="~/Images/banner.jpg" />
        </div>
        <div id="main">
            <h1>Category Maintenance</h1>
            <asp:GridView ID="GridView1" runat="server"
                AutoGenerateColumns="False" DataKeyNames="CategoryID"
                DataSourceID="ObjectDataSource1" ForeColor="Black">
                <Columns>
                    <asp:BoundField DataField="CategoryID" HeaderText="ID"
                        ReadOnly="True" >
                    <HeaderStyle HorizontalAlign="Left" />
                    <ItemStyle Width="100px" />
                    </asp:BoundField>
                    <asp:BoundField DataField="ShortName"
                        HeaderText="Short Name"
                        SortExpression="ShortName" >
                    <HeaderStyle HorizontalAlign="Left" />
                    <ItemStyle Width="150px" />
                    </asp:BoundField>
                    <asp:BoundField DataField="LongName"
                        HeaderText="Long Name"
                        SortExpression="LongName" >
                    <HeaderStyle HorizontalAlign="Left" />
                    <ItemStyle Width="200px" />
                    </asp:BoundField>
                    <asp:CommandField ButtonType="Button"
                        ShowEditButton="True" />
                    <asp:CommandField ButtonType="Button"
                        ShowDeleteButton="True" />
                </Columns>
                <HeaderStyle BackColor="Gray" Font-Bold="True"
                    ForeColor="White" />
                <RowStyle BackColor="White" ForeColor="Black" />
                <AlternatingRowStyle BackColor="LightGray"
                    ForeColor="Black" />
                <EditRowStyle BackColor="#F46D11" ForeColor="White" />
            </asp:GridView>
```

Figure 17-12   The aspx file of the Category Maintenance application (part 1 of 2)

The Default.aspx file   **Page 2**

```
        <asp:ObjectDataSource ID="ObjectDataSource1" runat="server"
            DataObjectTypeName="Category" DeleteMethod="DeleteCategory"
            InsertMethod="InsertCategory"
            OldValuesParameterFormatString="original_{0}"
            SelectMethod="GetCategories" TypeName="CategoryDB"
            UpdateMethod="UpdateCategory"
            ConflictDetection="CompareAllValues">
            <UpdateParameters>
                <asp:Parameter Name="original_Category" Type="Object" />
                <asp:Parameter Name="category" Type="Object" />
            </UpdateParameters>
        </asp:ObjectDataSource>
        <p id="new">To create a new category, enter the category
            information and click Insert.</p>
        <p>
            <asp:Label ID="lblError" runat="server"
                EnableViewState="False" ForeColor="Green">
            </asp:Label>
        </p>
        <asp:DetailsView ID="DetailsView1" runat="server"
            Height="50px" Width="300px"
            AutoGenerateRows="False" CellPadding="4"
            DataSourceID="ObjectDataSource1"
            DefaultMode="Insert" GridLines="None">
            <Fields>
                <asp:BoundField DataField="CategoryID"
                    HeaderText="Category ID:"
                    SortExpression="CategoryID" />
                <asp:BoundField DataField="ShortName"
                    HeaderText="Short Name:"
                    SortExpression="ShortName" />
                <asp:BoundField DataField="LongName"
                    HeaderText="Long Name:"
                    SortExpression="LongName" />
                <asp:CommandField ButtonType="Button"
                    ShowInsertButton="True" />
            </Fields>
            <FieldHeaderStyle BackColor="Gray" Font-Bold="True"
                ForeColor="White" />
            <InsertRowStyle BackColor="LightGray" />
            <CommandRowStyle BackColor="#A9A9A9" />
        </asp:DetailsView>
    </div>
    </div>
    </form>
</body>
</html>
```

Figure 17-12   The aspx file of the Category Maintenance application (part 2 of 2)

The code-behind file

Figure 17-13 shows the code-behind file for the Default.aspx page of the Category Maintenance application. This file consists of five methods that handle the exceptions that might be raised and the concurrency errors that might occur when the object data source's update, delete, or insert methods are called.

The first method is executed after the data source is updated. This method retrieves the return value from the update method using the ReturnValue property of the e argument and assigns it to the AffectedRows property of the e argument. This is necessary because the AffectedRows property isn't set automatically like it is for a SQL data source. For this to work, of course, the update method must return the number of rows that were updated. You'll see the code that accomplishes that in figure 17-15.

The second method is executed after a row in the GridView control is updated, which happens after the data source is updated. This method checks the Exception property of the e argument to determine if an exception has been thrown. If so, an error message is displayed, the ExceptionHandled property is set to True to suppress the exception, and the KeepInEditMode property is set to True to leave the GridView control in edit mode.

If an exception didn't occur, this method continues by checking the AffectedRows property of the e argument. The value of this property is passed forward from the AffectedRows property of the object data source's Updated event. If the value of this property is zero, the row was not updated, most likely due to the concurrency checking code that was added to the SQL Update statement. As a result, an appropriate error message is displayed.

The next two methods are similar, except they handle the Deleted event of the ObjectDataSource control and the RowDeleted event of the GridView control. Like the Updated event handler of the ObjectDataSource control, the Deleted event handler sets the AffectedRows property of the e argument. And, like the RowUpdated event handler of the GridView control, the RowDeleted event handler checks for exceptions and concurrency errors.

The last method is executed after a row is inserted using the DetailsView control. It checks whether an exception has occurred and responds accordingly. Note that currency checking isn't necessary here because a concurrency error can't occur for an insert operation.

By the way, this code illustrates just one way that you can provide for concurrency errors. Another way is to write the update and delete methods so they throw an exception if a concurrency error occurs. Then, the RowUpdated and RowDeleted event handlers can test the e.Exception property to determine if this exception has been thrown. I prefer the technique illustrated here, though, because the code for the RowUpdated and RowDeleted event handlers is nearly the same as it is when you use a SQL data source. The only difference is that you have to use the InnerException property of the current Exception object to get the exception that caused the error. That's because a system exception occurs when a database exception isn't caught by the CategoryDB class, and the system exception is the one that's passed to the event handlers.

The Default.aspx.cs file

```csharp
using System;
using System.Web.UI.WebControls;

public partial class _Default : System.Web.UI.Page
{
    protected void ObjectDataSource1_Updated(object sender, ObjectDataSourceStatusEventArgs e)
    {
        e.AffectedRows = Convert.ToInt32(e.ReturnValue);
    }

    protected void GridView1_RowUpdated(Object sender, GridViewUpdatedEventArgs e)
    {
        if (e.Exception != null)
        {
            lblError.Text = "A database error has occurred.<br /><br />" +
                e.Exception.Message;
            if (e.Exception.InnerException != null)
                lblError.Text += "<br />Message: "
                    + e.Exception.InnerException.Message;
            e.ExceptionHandled = true;
            e.KeepInEditMode = true;
        }
        else if (e.AffectedRows == 0)
            lblError.Text = "Another user may have updated that category."
                + "<br />Please try again.";
    }

    protected void ObjectDataSource1_Deleted(object sender, ObjectDataSourceStatusEventArgs e)
    {
        e.AffectedRows = Convert.ToInt32(e.ReturnValue);
    }

    protected void GridView1_RowDeleted(object sender, GridViewDeletedEventArgs e)
    {
        if (e.Exception != null)
        {
            lblError.Text = "A database error has occurred.<br /><br />" +
                e.Exception.Message;
            if (e.Exception.InnerException != null)
                lblError.Text += "<br />Message: "
                    + e.Exception.InnerException.Message;
            e.ExceptionHandled = true;
        }
        else if (e.AffectedRows == 0)
            lblError.Text = "Another user may have updated that category. "
                + "<br />Please try again.";
    }

    protected void DetailsView1_ItemInserted(object sender, DetailsViewInsertedEventArgs e)
    {
        if (e.Exception != null)
        {
            lblError.Text = "A database error has occurred.<br /><br />" +
                e.Exception.Message;
            if (e.Exception.InnerException != null)
                lblError.Text += "<br />Message: "
                    + e.Exception.InnerException.Message;
            e.ExceptionHandled = true;
        }
    }
}
```

Figure 17-13   The code-behind file for the Category Maintenance application

The Category class

Figure 17-14 presents the Category business class that's used by the object data source for this application. If you've used business classes like this before, you shouldn't have any trouble understanding how it works. In this case, the class includes three public properties that correspond with the three columns of the Categories table. The values of these properties are stored in the three private fields declared by this class. As required for business classes that are used by an object data source, each property is defined with both a get and a set accessor. This class also includes a parameterless constructor that's called when the object data source creates an instance of the class.

The Category.cs file

```
public class Category
{
    private string categoryID;
    private string shortName;
    private string longName;

    public Category()
    {
    }

    public string CategoryID
    {
        get
        {
            return categoryID;
        }
        set
        {
            categoryID = value;
        }
    }

    public string ShortName
    {
        get
        {
            return shortName;
        }
        set
        {
            shortName = value;
        }
    }

    public string LongName
    {
        get
        {
            return longName;
        }
        set
        {
            longName = value;
        }
    }
}
```

Note

- Because auto-implemented properties automatically provide for both get and set accessors, you can use them in a business class instead of standard properties.

Figure 17-14   The Category class for the Category Maintenance application

The CategoryDB class

The two parts of figure 17-15 present the CategoryDB class that's used as the data access class for this application. This class uses the DataObject and DataObjectMethod attributes to mark the class as a data object class and to mark the methods as data object methods.

The four public methods in this class provide for the select, insert, delete, and update operations performed by this application. These methods use standard ADO.NET code to access the database. Since this code is straightforward, you shouldn't have any trouble understanding how it works. So I'll just describe it briefly here.

The GetCategories method retrieves all of the rows and columns from the Categories table in the Halloween database. This data is then stored in a List<Category> object. To do that, it creates an object from the Category class for each row that's retrieved by the data reader, and it assigns the values in that row to the appropriate properties of the object. Then, it adds that object to the List<Category> object. Finally, the List<Category> object is returned to the object data source, which uses it to populate the GridView control. Note that because List<Category> is a strongly-typed collection, the names of the properties that the Category class exposes were available from the Fields dialog box for the GridView control so I didn't have to enter them manually. You'll have a chance to experiment with this when you do exercise 17-2 at the end of this chapter.

To get a connection to the Halloween database, the GetCategories method calls the private GetConnectionString method. This method gets the connection string from the web.config file. The GetConnectionString method is also called by the other public methods.

When the user clicks the Insert button in the DetailsView control, the object data source executes the InsertCategory method. This method is declared with a single parameter for a Category object. When the object data source executes this method, it passes the values that the user entered into the DetailsView control to this object. Then, the method assigns the CategoryID, ShortName, and LongName properties of that object to the parameters that are defined in the Values clause of the Insert statement. When the Insert statement is executed, a new row with these values is inserted into the Categories table.

The CategoryDB.cs file   **Page 1**

```csharp
using System.Data;
using System.Data.SqlClient;
using System.Configuration;
using System.ComponentModel;
using System.Collections.Generic;

[DataObject(true)]
public static class CategoryDB
{
    [DataObjectMethod(DataObjectMethodType.Select)]
    public static List<Category> GetCategories()
    {
        List<Category> categoryList = new List<Category>();
        SqlConnection con = new SqlConnection(GetConnectionString());
        string sel = "SELECT CategoryID, ShortName, LongName "
            + "FROM Categories ORDER BY ShortName";
        SqlCommand cmd = new SqlCommand(sel, con);
        con.Open();
        SqlDataReader dr =
            cmd.ExecuteReader(CommandBehavior.CloseConnection);
        Category category;
        while (dr.Read())
        {
            category = new Category();
            category.CategoryID = dr["CategoryID"].ToString();
            category.ShortName = dr["ShortName"].ToString();
            category.LongName = dr["LongName"].ToString();
            categoryList.Add(category);
        }
        dr.Close();
        return categoryList;
    }

    private static string GetConnectionString()
    {
        return ConfigurationManager.ConnectionStrings
            ["HalloweenConnectionString"].ConnectionString;
    }

    [DataObjectMethod(DataObjectMethodType.Insert)]
    public static int InsertCategory(Category category)
    {
        SqlConnection con = new SqlConnection(GetConnectionString());
        string ins = "INSERT INTO Categories "
            + " (CategoryID, ShortName, LongName) "
            + " VALUES(@CategoryID, @ShortName, @LongName)";
        SqlCommand cmd = new SqlCommand(ins, con);
        cmd.Parameters.AddWithValue("CategoryID", category.CategoryID);
        cmd.Parameters.AddWithValue("ShortName", category.ShortName);
        cmd.Parameters.AddWithValue("LongName", category.LongName);
        con.Open();
        int i = cmd.ExecuteNonQuery();
        con.Close();
        return i;
    }
}
```

Figure 17-15   The CategoryDB class for the Category Maintenance application (part 1 of 2)

When the user clicks the Delete button in the GridView control, the object data source executes the DeleteCategory method. This method also accepts a single parameter for a Category object. This object contains the values that were originally retrieved from the Categories table. The CategoryID, ShortName, and LongName properties of this object are assigned to the parameters that are defined in the Where clause of the Delete statement.

Notice that this method returns an integer value. Then, when the command that contains the Delete statement is executed, the result is stored in an integer variable, which is returned to the object data source. Because this value indicates the number of rows that were deleted, it can be used as shown in figure 17-13 to check for a concurrency error.

The last method, UpdateCategory, is executed when the user clicks the Update button in the GridView control. It accepts two parameters for Category objects. The first one contains the values that were originally retrieved from the Categories table, and the second one contains the new values for the row. The CategoryID, ShortName, and LongName properties of the first object are assigned to the parameters that are defined in the Where clause of the Update statement, and the ShortName and LongName properties of the second object are assigned to the properties that are defined in the Set clause of the Update statement.

Like the DeleteCategory method, the UpdateCategory method returns an integer value that indicates the number of rows that were affected by the update operation. Then, this value can be used to check for a concurrency error.

The CategoryDB.cs file   **Page 2**

```csharp
[DataObjectMethod(DataObjectMethodType.Delete)]
public static int DeleteCategory(Category category)
{
    SqlConnection con = new SqlConnection(GetConnectionString());
    string del = "DELETE FROM Categories "
        + "WHERE CategoryID = @CategoryID "
        + "AND ShortName = @ShortName "
        + "AND LongName = @LongName";
    SqlCommand cmd = new SqlCommand(del, con);
    cmd.Parameters.AddWithValue("CategoryID", category.CategoryID);
    cmd.Parameters.AddWithValue("ShortName", category.ShortName);
    cmd.Parameters.AddWithValue("LongName", category.LongName);
    con.Open();
    int i = cmd.ExecuteNonQuery();
    con.Close();
    return i;
}

[DataObjectMethod(DataObjectMethodType.Update)]
public static int UpdateCategory(Category original_Category,
    Category category)
{
    SqlConnection con = new SqlConnection(GetConnectionString());
    string up = "UPDATE Categories "
        + "SET ShortName = @ShortName, "
        + "LongName = @LongName "
        + "WHERE CategoryID = @original_CategoryID "
        + "AND ShortName = @original_ShortName "
        + "AND LongName = @original_LongName";
    SqlCommand cmd = new SqlCommand(up, con);
    cmd.Parameters.AddWithValue("ShortName", category.ShortName);
    cmd.Parameters.AddWithValue("LongName", category.LongName);
    cmd.Parameters.AddWithValue("original_CategoryID",
        original_Category.CategoryID);
    cmd.Parameters.AddWithValue("original_ShortName",
        original_Category.ShortName);
    cmd.Parameters.AddWithValue("original_LongName",
        original_Category.LongName);
    con.Open();
    int updateCount = cmd.ExecuteNonQuery();
    con.Close();
    return updateCount;
}
}
```

Figure 17-15   The CategoryDB class for the Category Maintenance application (part 2 of 2)

How to use paging with object data sources

One complication that arises when you use an object data source is that it doesn't automatically provide for paging with controls like the GridView control. Because of that, you have to set the attributes of the object data source that provide for paging, and you have to provide for paging in the data access class. You'll learn how to do that in the two topics that follow.

How to create an ObjectDataSource control that provides for paging

To create an ObjectDataSource control that provides for paging, you set the four attributes shown in figure 17-16. The EnablePaging attribute simply indicates that the object data source supports paging. The StartRowIndexParameterName and MaximumRowsParameterName attributes specify the names of parameters that will be used by the select method in the data access class to determine which rows are returned by the method. You'll see an example of how that works in the next figure. For now, just realize that when you use a pager control to display another page of data in a bound control, the bound control passes the values that will be assigned to these two parameters to the ObjectDataSource control.

The last attribute, SelectCountMethod, names a method in the data access class that returns a count of the total number of rows that are retrieved by the select method. The control that's bound to the object data source uses this value to determine what pager controls to display. For example, if the bound control uses first, previous, next, and last pager controls, it will be able to determine when the first or last page is displayed so it can omit the first and previous or next and last pager controls. This is illustrated by the GridView control shown at the top of this figure, which is bound to the object data source shown here. In this case, the first page is displayed so the first and previous pager controls aren't included.

A GridView control that provides for paging

ID	Name	Category	Unit Price	On Hand
pow01	Austin Powers	costumes	$79.99	25
bl01	Black Light (24")	fx	$24.99	200
vader01	Darth Vader Mask	masks	$19.99	100
cat01	Deranged Cat	props	$19.99	45
bats01	Flying Bats	props	$69.99	25
fogj01	Fog Juice (1qt)	fx	$9.99	500
fog01	Fog Machine	fx	$34.99	100
frankc01	Frankenstein	costumes	$39.99	100
		≥≥≥		

Attributes of the ObjectDataSource control that are used for paging

Attribute	Description
EnablePaging	True if the ObjectDataSource control supports paging.
StartRowIndexParameterName	The name of the parameter in the select method of the data access class that receives the index of the first row to be retrieved. The default is startRowIndex.
MaximumRowsParameterName	The name of the parameter in the select method of the data access class that receives the maximum number of rows to be retrieved. The default is maximumRows.
SelectCountMethod	The name of a public method in the data access class that returns the total number of rows that are retrieved by the select method.

The aspx code for an ObjectDataSource control that provides for paging

```
<asp:ObjectDataSource ID="ObjectDataSource1" runat="server"
    SelectMethod="GetProductsByPage" TypeName="ProductDB"
    EnablePaging="True" StartRowIndexParameterName="startIndex"
    SelectCountMethod="SelectCount" MaximumRowsParameterName="maxRows">
</asp:ObjectDataSource>
```

Description

- To use paging with a control like a GridView control that's bound to an object data source, you must set the four attributes of the ObjectDataSource control shown above.

- When a pager control on a bound control is clicked, the index of the starting row to be displayed and the maximum number of rows to be displayed are passed to the ObjectDataSource control. The ObjectDataSource control then passes these values to the parameters of the select method specified by the StartRowIndexParameterName and MaximumRowsParameterName attributes of the control.

- In addition to the select method that's used to retrieve the rows to be displayed, the data access class must include a method that returns the total number of rows that are retrieved. This method is named on the SelectCountMethod attribute of the ObjectDataSource control, and it's used by the bound control to determine what pager controls to display.

Figure 17-16   How to create an object data source that provides for paging

How to create a data access class that provides for paging

Figure 17-17 shows the code for a data access class that's used by the object data source you saw in the last figure. This class uses a List<Product> object named productList to store the data that's retrieved by the select method. This list is declared at the class level so both the select method and the method that returns the count of rows have access to it. As you can see, the method that returns the count of rows, which is named SelectCount as specified by the SelectCountMethod property of the ObjectDataSource control, simply returns the number of items in this list.

The most difficult aspect of creating a data access class that provides for paging is determining what rows the select method should return. To do that, the select method uses the two parameters that are passed to it from the object data source. The names of these parameters are the same as the names specified by the StartRowIndexParameterName and MaximumRowsParameterName attributes of the ObjectDataSource control.

The body of the select method starts by retrieving all the rows specified by the Select statement just as any other select method does. In this case, the select method creates a data reader that contains the requested data from the Products table. Then, it retrieves each row of data from the data reader, stores it in a Product object, and adds the product object to the product list.

Next, this method gets a count of the rows in the list and stores the count in a variable named rowCount. Then, it checks to be sure that the rows specified by the values that were passed to the method aren't beyond the end of the list. That can happen if the total number of rows isn't evenly divisible by the number of rows on a page. For example, the Products table contains 23 rows, and 8 rows are displayed on each page (see figure 17-16). That means that the last page will contain only seven rows. In that case, the maximum number of rows must be adjusted so only those seven rows are returned. If you omit this code, an error will occur when you try to display the last page indicating that the index is out of range.

The last group of statements in this method retrieves the requested rows from the product list and stores them in another List<Product> object named pageList. To do that, it uses a for loop with a counter variable that varies from a value of 0 to the maximum number of rows minus 1. The first statement within the loop calculates the index of the item to be retrieved from the product list by adding the value of the starting index that was passed to the method to the counter variable. Then, the item at that index is added to the page list. Finally, after all the items have been added to the page list, the list is returned to the object data source.

By the way, if you use the wizard to create an ObjectDataSource control from a data access class that provides for paging, you should know that the wizard will ask you to define the two parameters used by the select method. Because these parameters are identified by attributes of the control, however, you can just click Finish when the Define Parameters step is displayed. Then, you'll need to delete the parameters that are generated by default.

The data access class used by the object data source

```
using System;
using System.Configuration;
using System.Data;
using System.Data.SqlClient;
using System.ComponentModel;
using System.Collections.Generic;

[DataObject(true)]
public static class ProductDB
{
    private static List<Product> productList;

    [DataObjectMethod(DataObjectMethodType.Select)]
    public static List<Product> GetProductsByPage(int startIndex, int maxRows)
    {
        productList = new List<Product>();
        SqlConnection con = new SqlConnection(GetConnectionString());
        string sel = "SELECT ProductID, Name, CategoryID, UnitPrice, OnHand "
            + "FROM Products ORDER BY Name";
        SqlCommand cmd = new SqlCommand(sel, con);
        con.Open();
        SqlDataReader dr = cmd.ExecuteReader(CommandBehavior.CloseConnection);
        Product product;
        while (dr.Read())
        {
            product = new Product();
            product.ProductID = dr["ProductID"].ToString();
            product.Name = dr["Name"].ToString();
            product.CategoryID = dr["CategoryID"].ToString();
            product.UnitPrice = (decimal) dr["UnitPrice"];
            product.OnHand = (int) dr["OnHand"];
            productList.Add(product);
        }
        dr.Close();

        int rowCount = productList.Count;
        if (startIndex + maxRows > rowCount)
            maxRows = rowCount - startIndex;

        List<Product> pageList = new List<Product>();
        int rowIndex;
        for (int i = 0; i <= maxRows - 1; i++)
        {
            rowIndex = i + startIndex;
            pageList.Add(productList[rowIndex]);
        }
        return pageList;
    }

    public static int SelectCount()
    {
        return productList.Count;
    }
    .
    .
    .
}
```

Figure 17-17   A data access class that provides for paging

Perspective

In this chapter, you've learned how to work with object data sources. As you've seen, object data sources take advantage of the time-saving data binding features of ASP.NET without sacrificing the basic principle of separating presentation code from data access code. Because of that, you may want to consider using object data sources instead of SQL or Access data sources.

If you decide that you do want to use object data sources in your applications, you will of course need to learn how to use ADO.NET in code. For that, we recommend our ADO.NET book for C# programmers, which provides a complete course in ADO.NET database programming. When you finish it, you'll be able to use ADO.NET with or without data sources.

Terms

3-layer architecture	business object class
presentation layer	data object class
middle layer	3-tier architecture
database layer	reflection
object data source	C# attribute
data access class	

Exercise 17-1   Create a Customer List application

In this exercise, you'll develop an application that uses two object data sources to display a list of customers in a selected state. To make that easier, you'll start from an application that contains the data access class that will be used by the object data sources, along with the starting page, the image and style sheet used by the page, and a web.config file that contains a connection string to the Halloween database.

Review the code in the data access class

1. Open the Ch17CustomerList application in the C:\aspnet4_cs directory.

2. Display the CustomerDB class in the App_Code folder, and notice that it contains three methods named GetAllStates, GetCustomersByState, and GetConnectionString. Also notice that the class is marked with a DataObject attribute and the GetAllStates and GetCustomersByState methods are marked with a DataObjectMethod attribute.

3. Review the code for the GetAllStates and GetCustomersByState methods to see that they both return an IEnumerable object. Specifically, the GetAllStates method returns a data reader object that contains the StateCode and StateName columns from the States table, and the GetCustomersByState method returns a data reader object that contains the LastName, FirstName, and PhoneNumber columns from the Customers table.

Add the drop-down list and its data source

4. Display the page in Design view, add a drop-down list to the main division, and select the Choose Data Source command from the smart tag menu to display the first step of the Data Source Configuration Wizard.

5. Select the option for creating a new data source, select Object from the second step of the wizard, and click OK to display the first Configure Data Source dialog box.

6. Display the drop-down list in this dialog box to see that it contains only the CustomerDB class. Select this class and then click Next to display the second Configure Data Source dialog box.

7. Display the drop-down list in this dialog box to see that that it contains both of the methods that are marked as data object methods. Select the GetAllStates method and then click Finish to return to the first step of the Data Source Configuration Wizard.

8. Display the drop-down lists in the wizard to see that they're both empty. Then, enter "StateName" in the first drop-down list and "StateCode" in the second drop-down list.

9. Enable auto postback for the drop-down list you just created, and change the ID attribute to an appropriate value.

Add the GridView control and its data source

10. Add a GridView control below the ObjectDataSource control, and bind it to a new object data source that gets its data from the GetCustomersByState method of the CustomerDB class. This method should get the value of its parameter from the drop-down list.

11. Run the application, display customers from different states, and notice that the widths of the columns in the GridView change depending on the data they contain.

12. Return to Design view, display the Fields dialog box for the GridView control, and notice that the Auto-generate Fields option is selected.

13. Remove the check mark from the Auto-generate Fields option, and then add three bound fields for the three columns that are returned by the GetCustomersByState method. To do that, you'll need to manually enter the column name for the DataField property, and you'll need to add a column header for the HeaderText property. In addition, set the width of each column to 150 pixels, and left-align the column headings.

14. Run the application again to see how this looks. Then, close the browser window.

Exercise 17-2   Modify the Product Receipt application

In this exercise, you'll modify the Product Receipt application you created in exercise 14-2 so it uses an object data source instead of a SQL data source. To make that easier, we'll include the code for the data access class and the business class that are used by the application.

Review the starting code

1. Open the Ch17ProductReceipt application in the C:\aspnet4_cs directory.

2. Review the aspx code for the Default page. Then, run the application to refresh your memory about how it works.

3. Review the code for the Product class in the App_Code folder to see that it defines three auto-implemented properties for the ProductID, Name, and OnHand columns.

4. Review the code for the ProductDB class. Notice that the GetProducts method returns a List<Product> objects. Also notice that the UpdateProduct method accepts a single Product object since it doesn't implement optimistic concurrency.

Add an ObjectDataSource control

5. Add an ObjectDataSource control to the Default page, and configure it so it retrieves data using the GetProducts method of the ProductDB class and updates a product using the UpdateProduct method.

6. Set the DataObjectTypeName property of the object data source to "Product".

7. Change the data source for the GridView control from the SQL data source to the object data source you just created. When a dialog box is displayed asking if you want to regenerate the GridView column fields and data keys, click No.

8. Delete the SqlDataSource control since it's no longer used by the page.

9. Run the application and test it to be sure it works correctly. When you're done, close the browser window.

Use the designer to review the bound fields

10. Display the smart tag menu for the GridView control and select the Edit Columns command.

11. Select the ID field, and scroll through the properties for that field until you can see the DataField property.

12. Display the drop-down list for the DataField property, and notice that you can see the names of all the available fields. That's because the select method returns a strongly-typed List<Product> collection.

Section 4

Professional ASP.NET skills

This section consists of six chapters that present ASP.NET skills that are often used in professional web applications. To start, chapter 18 shows you how to use a secure connection for an application, and chapter 19 shows you how to authenticate and authorize the users of an application using the Web Site Administration Tool and the login controls. These are essential skills for ecommerce applications.

Next, chapter 20 shows you how to use email and custom error pages as well as how to deal with the problems that can occur when users click the Back buttons in their browsers. These are useful skills for most professional applications.

Chapter 21 introduces you to AJAX and shows you how to use the AJAX server controls. Then, chapter 22 shows you how to configure and deploy an application, which you'll need to do for every application that you develop. At that point, you'll be able to develop and deploy ecommerce applications at a thoroughly professional level.

Finally, in chapter 23, you'll be introduced to WCF services. WCF services allow you to define operations that can be used by a variety of applications, including those built on other technologies and platforms. WCF is now the standard for developing services with ASP.NET.

Because each of the chapters in this section is written as an independent module, you can read these chapters in whatever sequence you prefer. If, for example, you want to learn how to send email from a web application, you can skip directly to chapter 20. Or, if you want to learn how to configure and deploy ASP.NET applications, you can skip to chapter 22. Eventually, though, you'll want to read all of the chapters because you should at least be aware of the capabilities that they offer.

18

How to secure a web site

Security is one of the most important concerns for any developer of ecommerce web sites. To secure a web site, you must make sure that private data that's sent between the client and the server can't be deciphered. To accomplish that, this chapter shows you how to use an Internet protocol called SSL.

An introduction to SSL

To prevent others from reading data that's transmitted over the Internet, you can use the *Secure Sockets Layer*, or *SSL*. SSL is an Internet protocol that lets you transmit data over the Internet using data encryption. The topics that follow explain how SSL works.

How secure connections work

Figure 18-1 shows a web page that uses SSL to transfer data between the server and the client over a *secure connection*. To determine if you're transmitting data over a secure connection, you can read the URL in the browser's address bar. If it starts with HTTPS rather than HTTP, then you're transmitting data over a secure connection.

With a regular HTTP connection, all data is sent as unencrypted text. As a result, if a hacker intercepts this data, it is easy to read. With a secure connection, however, all data that's transferred between the client and the server is encrypted. Although a hacker can still intercept this data, he won't be able to read it without breaking the encryption code.

Note that to test an application that uses a secure connection, you must run the application under IIS. Because of that, if you created the application as a file-system web site, you'll need to use one of the techniques described in chapter 4 to run it under IIS.

A page that was requested with a secure connection

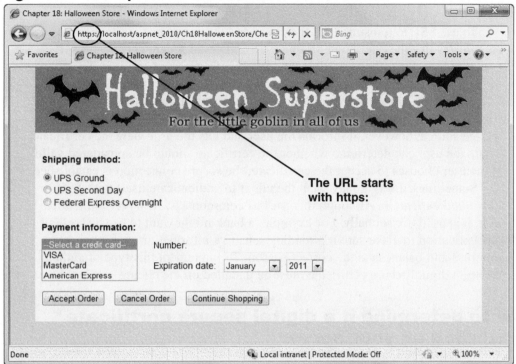

Description

- The *Secure Sockets Layer*, or *SSL*, is the protocol used by the World Wide Web that allows clients and servers to communicate over a *secure connection*.
- With SSL, the browser encrypts all data that's sent to the server and decrypts all data that's received from the server. Conversely, the server encrypts all data that's sent to the browser and decrypts all data that's received from the browser.
- SSL is able to determine if data has been tampered with during transit.
- SSL is also able to verify that a server or a client is who it claims to be.
- The URL for a secure connection starts with HTTPS instead of HTTP.

Notes

- To test an application that uses SSL, you must run the application under the control of IIS. For information on how to do that, see chapter 4.
- With some browsers, a lock icon is displayed when a secure connection is being used.

Figure 18-1   How secure connections work

How digital secure certificates work

To use SSL to transmit data, the client and the server use *digital secure certificates* like the one shown in figure 18-2. Digital secure certificates serve two purposes. First, they establish the identity of the server or client. Second, they provide the information needed to encrypt data before it's transmitted.

By default, browsers are configured to accept certificates that come from trusted sources. If a browser doesn't recognize a certificate as coming from a trusted source, however, it informs the user and lets the user view the certificate. Then, the user can determine whether the certificate should be considered valid. If the user chooses to accept the certificate, the secure connection is established.

Sometimes, a server may want the client to authenticate itself with *SSL client authentication*. Although this isn't as common as *SSL server authentication*, it is used occasionally. For example, a bank might want to use SSL client authentication to make sure it's sending sensitive information such as account numbers and balances to the correct person. To implement this type of authentication, a digital secure certificate must be installed on the client.

How to determine if a digital secure certificate is installed on your server

Before you learn how to obtain and use digital secure certificates, you may want to check if a certificate is already installed on your server. If IIS is running on your local machine, chances are that a certificate hasn't been installed. But if IIS is running on a server on a network, you can use the procedure in figure 18-2 to determine if a certificate has been installed and to view the certificate.

Please note that this procedure is for Windows 7, Windows Vista, and Windows Server 2008, which include IIS 7. If you're using Windows XP, which includes IIS 5.1, or Windows Server 2003, which includes IIS 6.0, the procedure for determining if a digital secure certificate is installed is somewhat different. In that case, you can refer to the topic later in this chapter on working with certificates using earlier versions of IIS.

The Certificate dialog box for a digital secure certificate

Types of digital secure certificates

Certificate	Description
Server certificate	Issued to trusted servers so client computers can connect to them using secure connections.
Client certificate	Issued to trusted clients so server computers can confirm their identity.

Concepts

- *Authentication* determines whether a server or client is who it claims to be.
- When a browser makes an initial attempt to communicate with a server over a secure connection that uses SSL, the server authenticates itself by sending its *digital secure certificate* to the browser.
- In some instances, the server may also request that a browser authenticate itself by presenting its own digital secure certificate. This is uncommon, however.

How to determine if a digital secure certificate is installed on your server

1. Display the IIS Management Console from the Control Panel by selecting the System and Security category, followed by the Administrative Tools category and then double-clicking on Internet Information Services (IIS) Manager.
2. Select the server in the Connections pane, and then double-click Server Certificates in the main window. If a certificate is installed, it will be listed in the Server Certificates window (see figure 18-4).
3. To display the certificate, select it and click View in the Actions pane.

Figure 18-2   How digital secure certificates work

How to get and use a digital secure certificate

In the topics that follow, you'll first learn the general procedure for getting a digital secure certificate. Then, you'll learn how to work with certificates under IIS 7. Finally, you'll learn how to work with certificates under IIS 5.1 or 6.0.

How to get a digital secure certificate

If you want to develop an ASP.NET application that uses SSL to secure client connections, you must first obtain a digital secure certificate from a trusted source such as those listed in figure 18-3. These *certification authorities*, or *CAs*, verify that the person or company requesting the certificate is a valid person or company by checking with a *registration authority*, or *RA*. To obtain a digital secure certificate, you'll need to provide a registration authority with information about yourself or your company. Once the registration authority approves the request, the certification authority can issue the digital secure certificate.

A digital secure certificate from a trusted source isn't free, and the cost of the certificate will depend on a variety of factors including the level of security. As a result, when you purchase a digital certificate, you'll want one that fits the needs of your web site. In particular, you'll need to decide what *SSL strength* you want the connection to support. SSL strength refers to the level of encryption that the secure connection uses when it transmits data.

Most certificates sold today provide for up to 128-bit SSL strength. It's nearly impossible to break the encryption code provided by this SSL strength, and the most popular browsers support it. If a browser doesn't support it, however, the browser will use the maximum strength it does support, which is either 40-bit or 56-bit. Most CAs also sell certificates that provide for 256-bit SSL strength, but this strength isn't currently supported by IIS.

In addition to SSL strength, you should consider whether a certificate is a single root certificate or a chained root certificate. A *single root certificate* is a certificate from a trusted source that has already been added to the most popular browsers. These certificates are stable and easy to install. In contrast, a *chained root certificate* is a certificate that inherits a certificate that browsers recognize. Although chained root certificates can be less expensive than single root certificates, they are less stable and more difficult to install.

Common certification authorities that issue digital secure certificates

```
www.verisign.com
www.geotrust.com
www.entrust.com
www.thawte.com
```

SSL strengths

Strength	Pros and cons
40-bit	Most browsers support it, but it's relatively easy to break the encryption code.
56-bit	It's thousands of times stronger than 40-bit strength and most browsers support it, but it's still possible to break the encryption code.
128-bit	It's over a trillion times a trillion times stronger than 40-bit strength, which makes it extremely difficult to break the encryption code, but it's more expensive and not all browsers support it.
256-bit	It's much stronger than 128-bit encryption, but it's not supported by all web servers and browsers.

Description

- To use SSL in your web applications, you must first purchase a digital secure certificate from a trusted *certification authority*, or *CA*. Once you obtain the certificate, you send it to the people who host your web site so they can install it on the server.

- A certification authority is a company that issues and manages security credentials. To verify information provided by the requestor of the secure certificate, a CA must check with a *registration authority*, or *RA*. Once the registration authority verifies the requestor's information, the certification authority can issue a digital secure certificate.

- Since SSL is built into all major browsers and web servers, installing a digital secure certificate enables SSL.

- *SSL strength* refers to the length of the generated key that is created during the encryption process. The longer the key, the more difficult it is to break the encryption code.

- The SSL strength that's used depends on the strength provided by the certificate, the strength supported by the web server, and the strength supported by the browser. If a web server or browser isn't able to support the strength provided by the certificate, a lesser strength is used.

- Most certificates are issued by trusted certification authorities who own and use their own certificates. These CAs are known to browser vendors, and their certificates have been added to many of the most popular browsers. This type of certificate is called a *single root certificate*.

- A *chained root certificate* is one that inherits the recognition of a trusted certification authority. This type of certificate is more difficult to install and some web servers and web applications can't use them.

Figure 18-3   How to get a digital secure certificate

How to work with certificates using IIS 7

Figure 18-4 shows you how to work with certificates using IIS 7, the version of IIS that comes with Windows 7, Windows Vista, and Windows Server 2008. At the top of this figure, you can see the IIS Management Console with the Server Certificates window displayed. Here, a self-signed certificate named Test certificate has been installed.

A *self-signed certificate* is simply a certificate that IIS creates for its own use, and you can use it to test security as you develop a web site. Then, if you deploy the web site to a server that doesn't already have a digital secure certificate installed, you can request a certificate from a certification authority and install it as described in this figure.

To use the HTTPS protocol with IIS 7, a *binding* must exist for that protocol. A binding defines how a web site can be accessed, and each web site is defined with a binding that uses the HTTP protocol by default. To use SSL with a web site, you must define a binding that uses the HTTPS protocol. When you define that binding, you must also select the certificate you want to use as described in this figure.

The IIS Management Console with a self-signed certificate installed

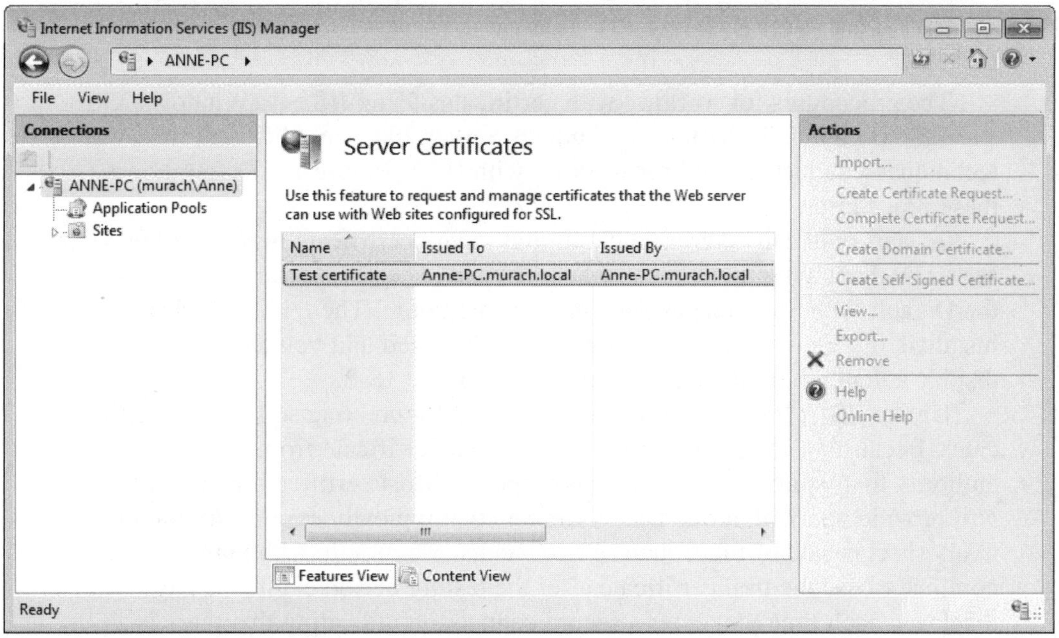

How to create and install certificates

- IIS 7 lets you create a *self-signed certificate* that can be used for testing purposes. To do that, display the Server Certificates window. Then, click Create Self-Signed Certificate in the Actions pane and complete the dialog box that's displayed.
- To create a certificate file that you can use to request a certificate from a certification authority, click Create Certificate Request in the Actions pane and complete the dialog boxes that are displayed.
- To install a certificate from a certification authority, click Complete Certificate Request in the Actions pane and complete the dialog box that's displayed.

How to create a binding for the HTTPS protocol

- Before you can use the HTTPS protocol, you must create a *binding* for that protocol. To do that, select the Default Web Site node in the Connections pane, click Bindings in the Actions pane, and click the Add button in the dialog box that's displayed. Then, select https from the Type drop-down list, select a certificate from the SSL Certificate drop-down list, and click the OK button.

Figure 18-4   How to work with certificates using IIS 7

How to work with certificates using earlier versions of IIS

The procedures for working with certificates using IIS 5.1 (Windows XP) and IIS 6.0 (Windows Vista and Windows Server 2003) are different from the techniques you just learned for working with IIS 7. Figure 18-5 summarizes these procedures.

To start, you can determine if a digital secure certificate in installed on your server by displaying the Directory Security tab of the Properties dialog box for the Default Web Site node as described in this figure. Then, if a certificate is installed, the View Certificate button will be enabled and you can click it to display a dialog box like the one you saw in figure 18-2.

Unlike IIS 7, IIS 5.1 and 6.0 don't provide for creating self-signed certificates. Because of that, you'll need to get a trial certificate from a certification authority that you can use for testing purposes. Most certification authorities will provide you with a free trial certificate that typically expires after a relatively short period of time, such as two weeks or a month. Although you can continue to use the trial certificate after the testing period expires, a page will be displayed each time you enter a secure connection indicating that there is a problem with the certificate. Then, you can click the "Continue to this website" link to proceed with the secure connection.

Of course, you shouldn't run an ASP.NET application in a production environment using an expired certificate. When you're ready to deploy your application, then, you should request a valid certificate from the certification authority. To do that, you can use the IIS Server Certificate Wizard as described in this figure.

After you select the option for creating a new certificate, the Wizard walks you through the steps needed to create a file that contains the information a certification authority needs to issue a certificate. Once you create this file, you'll need to go to the certification authority's web site for instructions on how to request a certificate. Then, when you receive the certificate, you can return to the Certificate Wizard to install it.

You can also use the Certificate Wizard to manage existing certificates for your IIS server. For example, you can use it to remove certificates or renew expired certificates. You can also use it to assign a certificate that was previously installed but has been removed or to import a certificate used by another server.

The IIS Certificate Wizard options if a certificate hasn't been requested or installed

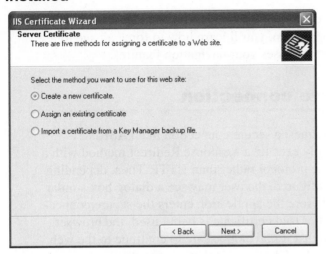

How to display the IIS Management Console

- Open the Control Panel, double-click on Administrative Tools, and then double-click on Internet Information Services.

How to determine if a digital secure certificate is installed on your server

- Expand the node for the server and the Web Sites node and then right-click on the Default Web Site node and select Properties to display the Properties dialog box. Click the Directory Security tab. If a digital secure certificate is installed, the View Certificate button will be enabled. Click this button to display the certificate.

How to get a trial certificate

- To test SSL connections in a local environment, you can request a free trial certificate from an established certification authority. The certificate typically expires in 14 to 30 days.

- The certification authority's web site will have detailed instructions you can follow to request, download, and install a trial certificate.

How to use the IIS Certificate Wizard

- The IIS Certificate Wizard manages the process of requesting certificates from certification authorities and installing certificates in IIS.

- To start the IIS Certificate Wizard, display the Directory Security tab of the Properties dialog box for the Default Web Site node as described above, and then click the Server Certificate button.

- The tasks that are available from the wizard depend on whether a certificate is already installed and whether you have requested a certificate but not installed it. To perform any of these tasks, select the appropriate option from the first IIS Certificate Wizard dialog box and then click the Next button and complete the remaining dialog boxes.

Figure 18-5   How to work with certificates using earlier versions of IIS

How to use a secure connection

In the topics that follow, you'll first learn how to request secure connections for the pages of your applications. Then, you'll learn how to force a page to use a secure connection when a user bypasses your navigation features.

How to request a secure connection

Figure 18-6 shows how to request a secure connection in an ASP.NET application. To do that, you simply execute a Response.Redirect method with a URL that specifies HTTPS as the protocol rather than HTTP. Then, depending on how the user's browser is configured, the user may see a dialog box similar to the one shown in this figure before the application enters the secure connection. In addition, if a self-signed or trial certificate is being used, the browser will display a page warning you that it may not be safe to continue to the web site. In that case, you can follow the directions on that page to display the requested page with a secure connection.

To request a secure connection using HTTPS, you must use an absolute URL. That means that the URL must include the complete application path, including the web server's domain name and the directory path that leads to the application. For example, the first URL in this figure specifies //localhost as the web server's domain name and /aspnet_2010/Ch18HalloweenStore as the directory path.

Rather than coding this information into each URL, you may want to store the application path in the web.config file as shown in the second coding example in this figure. As you can see, you store this information as an element within the appSettings section of this file. Then, you can use the AppSettings property of the ConfigurationManager class to retrieve the value of the element that contains the path. This is illustrated in the third coding example. If you use this technique, you'll only need to change the application path in the web.config file if you deploy the application to a different location.

Once your application has established a secure connection, it can navigate to other pages using relative URLs while maintaining the secure connection. To close the secure connection, the application must navigate to another page by specifying an absolute URL with HTTP rather than HTTPS as the protocol. This is illustrated in the last coding example in this figure.

A dialog box that may be displayed for secure connections

A URL that requests a secure connection

```
https://localhost/aspnet_2010/Ch18HalloweenStore/CheckOut1.aspx
```

A web.config file that defines the AppPath setting

```xml
<?xml version="1.0"?>
<configuration>
    <appSettings>
        <add key="AppPath"
            value="//localhost/aspnet_2010/Ch18HalloweenStore/" />
    </appSettings>
  <system.web>
    .
    .
```

Code that retrieves the application path from the web.config file

```
string url = "https:"
    + ConfigurationManager.AppSettings["AppPath"]
    + "CheckOut1.aspx";
Response.Redirect(url);
```

Code that returns to an unsecured connection

```
string url = "http:"
    + ConfigurationManager.AppSettings["AppPath"]
    + "Order.aspx";
Response.Redirect(url);
```

Description

- To request a secure connection, you must use an absolute URL that specifies HTTPS as the protocol. Once you establish a secure connection, you can use relative URLs to continue using the secure connection.

- To return to an unsecured connection after using a secure connection, you must code an absolute URL that specifies the HTTP protocol.

- Instead of coding the application's path into each URL, you can store it in the appSettings section of the web.config file. That way, if the path changes, you can change it in just one location.

- You can use the AppSettings property of the ConfigurationManager class within the application to access the elements in the appSettings section of the web.config file.

- Depending on the security settings in your browser, a dialog box may be displayed before a secure connection is established or before a secure connection is closed.

Figure 18-6   How to request a secure connection

How to force a page to use a secure connection

When you build a complete web application, you usually include navigation features such as menus or hyperlinks that guide the user from page to page. Unfortunately, users sometimes bypass your navigation features and access pages in your application directly. For example, a user might bookmark a page in your application and return to it later. Other users might simply type the URL of individual pages in your application into their browser's address bar. Some users do this innocently; others do it in an attempt to bypass your application's security features.

Because of that, a page that should use SSL to send or receive sensitive information shouldn't assume that a secure connection has been established. Instead, it should check for a secure connection and establish one if necessary. To do that, you can use the properties of the HttpRequest class shown in figure 18-7.

To check for a secure connection, you use the IsSecureConnection property. Then, if the connection isn't secure, you can use the Url property to retrieve the URL for the page and modify that URL so it uses the HTTPS protocol. After you do that, you can use the Redirect method to redirect the browser using the new URL. Notice that you typically include this code at the beginning of the Load method for the page. That way, you can be sure that no other code is executed until a secure connection is established.

Another way to force a page to use a secure connection is by setting a property of the page from IIS. When you use this technique, a user won't be able to access the page without using a secure connection. In other words, he won't be able to bypass the navigation features provided by your application. For more information on how to use this technique, please see appendix B (Windows 7 and Windows Vista) or appendix C (Windows XP).

Properties of the HttpRequest class for working with secure connections

Property	Description
IsSecureConnection	Returns True if the current connection is secure. Otherwise, returns False.
Url	The URL of the current request.

A Page_Load method that forces the page to use a secure connection

```
protected void Page_Load(object sender, EventArgs e)
{
    if (!Request.IsSecureConnection)
    {
        string url = Request.Url.ToString().Replace("http:", "https:");
        Response.Redirect(url);
    }
}
```

Description

- If a page requires the user to enter sensitive information, such as passwords or credit card data, it should make sure that it's operating on a secure connection. To do that, the page should check the IsSecureConnection property of the HttpRequest object in its Load event handler.

- If the page isn't using a secure connection, it should switch to a secure connection to protect the privacy of the user's data. To do that, it can replace the HTTP protocol in the URL to HTTPS and then redirect the browser to the new URL.

- You can also prevent a user from accessing a page without a secure connection by setting a property of the page from the Internet Information Services program. For more information, see appendix B (Windows 7 and Windows Vista) or appendix C (Windows XP).

Figure 18-7   How to force a page to use a secure connection

A Halloween Store application that uses SSL

To show how secure connections are used in a typical application, the next two topics present a version of the Halloween Store application that uses SSL.

The operation of the Halloween Store application

Figure 18-8 shows the five pages of the Halloween Store application. As you can see, this application lets the user select products and display the shopping cart without establishing a secure connection. When the user clicks the Check Out button from the Cart page, however, a secure connection is established. The secure connection is then maintained while the two Check Out pages and the Confirmation page are displayed. When the user clicks the Return to Order Page button, however, the Order page is redisplayed with an unsecured connection.

The code for the Halloween Store application

Figure 18-9 presents the code for using SSL in the Halloween Store application. At the top of the first page of this figure, you can see the code for the Click event of the Check Out button on the Cart page. (The code for the Click event of the Check Out button on the Order page is identical.) This code creates a URL that uses the HTTPS protocol and the path that's specified in the appSettings section of the web.config file. Then, it redirects the browser to the first Check Out page using a secure connection.

In the code for the first Check Out page, you can see that the Load event handler checks if a secure connection has been established. If not, the URL is retrieved from the request and the HTTP protocol is replaced with HTTPS. Then, the browser is redirected to that URL, which uses a secure connection.

If the user clicks the Continue Checkout button, a relative URL is used to display the second Check Out page, which means that the secure connection is maintained. If the user clicks the Cancel or Continue Shopping button, however, the browser is redirected to the Order page with an unsecured connection.

The code for the second Check Out page is shown in part 2 of this figure. Like the first Check Out page, its Load event handler makes sure that a secure connection is established before proceeding. In addition, if the user clicks the Cancel or Continue Shopping button, the Order page is redisplayed with an unsecured connection. If the user clicks the Accept Order button, however, the secure connection is maintained and the Confirmation page is displayed.

The code for the Confirmation page is also shown in this figure. As you can see, if the user clicks the Return to Order Page button on this page, the Order page is redisplayed with an unsecured connection.

How security is used by the Halloween Store application

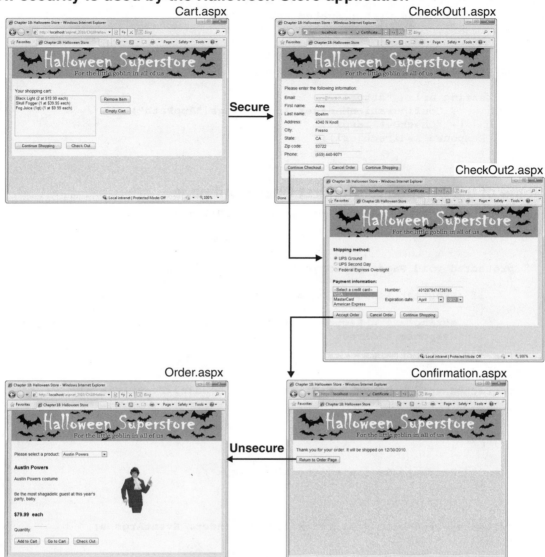

Description

- When the user clicks the Check Out button from the Cart page (or the Order page), the browser is redirected to the first Check Out page using a secure connection.
- When the user clicks the Continue Checkout button from the first Check Out page, the browser is redirected to the second Check Out page and remains in the secure connection.
- When the user clicks the Accept Order button from the second Check Out page, the browser is redirected to the Confirmation page and remains in the secure connection.
- When the user clicks the Return to Order Page button from the Confirmation page, the browser is redirected to the Order page in an unsecured connection.

Figure 18-8   The operation of the Halloween Store application with SSL

Some of the C# code for the Cart page

```csharp
public partial class Cart : System.Web.UI.Page
{
    .
    .
    protected void btnCheckOut_Click(object sender, EventArgs e)
    {
        string url = "https:"
            + ConfigurationManager.AppSettings["AppPath"]
            + "CheckOut1.aspx";
        Response.Redirect(url);
    }
}
```

Some of the C# code for the first Check Out page

```csharp
public partial class CheckOut1 : System.Web.UI.Page
{
    .
    .
    protected void Page_Load(object sender, EventArgs e)
    {
        if (!Request.IsSecureConnection)
        {
            string url = Request.Url.ToString().Replace("http:", "https:");
            Response.Redirect(url);
        }
    }

    protected void btnCheckOut_Click(object sender, EventArgs e)
    {
        if (Page.IsValid)
        {
            .

            .
            Response.Redirect("CheckOut2.aspx");
        }
    }

    protected void btnCancel_Click(object sender, EventArgs e)
    {
        Session.Remove("Cart");
        String url = "http:"
            + ConfigurationManager.AppSettings["AppPath"]
            + "Order.aspx";
        Response.Redirect(url);
    }

    protected void btnContinue_Click(object sender, EventArgs e)
    {
        string url = "http:"
            + ConfigurationManager.AppSettings["AppPath"]
            + "Order.aspx";
        Response.Redirect(url);
    }
}
```

Figure 18-9   The code for the Halloween Store application (part 1 of 2)

Some of the C# code for the second Check Out page

```csharp
public partial class CheckOut2 : System.Web.UI.Page
{
    .
    .

    protected void Page_Load(object sender, EventArgs e)
    {
        if (!Request.IsSecureConnection)
        {
            String url = Request.Url.ToString().Replace("http:", "https:");
            Response.Redirect(url);
        }
    }

    protected void btnAccept_Click(object sender, EventArgs e)
    {
        if (Page.IsValid)
        {
            .
            .

            Response.Redirect("Confirmation.aspx");
        }
    }

    protected void btnCancel_Click(object sender, EventArgs e)
    {
        Session.Remove("Cart");
        String url = "http:"
            + ConfigurationManager.AppSettings["AppPath"]
            + "Order.aspx";
        Response.Redirect(url);
    }

    protected void btnContinue_Click(object sender, EventArgs e)
    {
        String url = "http:"
            + ConfigurationManager.AppSettings["AppPath"]
            + "Order.aspx";
        Response.Redirect(url);
    }
}
```

Some of the C# code for the Confirmation page

```csharp
public partial class Confirmation : System.Web.UI.Page
{
    .
    .

    protected void btnReturn_Click(object sender, EventArgs e)
    {
        string url = "http:"
            + ConfigurationManager.AppSettings["AppPath"]
            + "Order.aspx";
        Response.Redirect(url);
    }
}
```

Figure 18-9   The code for the Halloween Store application (part 2 of 2)

Perspective

Now that you've completed this chapter, you should be able to use SSL encryption to secure the data transmissions between client and server. That's one part of securing an application. The other part is making sure that only authorized users are able to use your application, and you'll learn how to provide for that in the next chapter.

By the way, if you're interested in seeing the rest of the code for the Halloween Store application in this chapter, you should know that you can download all of the applications in this book from our web site (www.murach.com). See appendix A for details.

Terms

Secure Sockets Layer (SSL)
secure connection
authentication
server authentication
client authentication
digital secure certificate
certification authority (CA)
registration authority (RA)
SSL strength
single root certificate
chained root certificate
self-signed certificate
binding

19

How to authenticate and authorize users

In the last chapter, you learned how to secure the transmission of data between client and server. Now, you'll learn how to restrict access to some of the pages of an application, but let authorized users access those pages. To provide this functionality without writing a single line of code, you can use the Web Site Administration Tool and the login controls.

An introduction to authentication

If you want to limit access to all or part of your ASP.NET application to certain users, you can use *authentication* to verify each user's identity. Then, once you have authenticated the user, you can use *authorization* to check if the user has the appropriate privileges for accessing a page. That way, you can prevent unauthorized users from accessing pages that they shouldn't be able to access.

Three types of authentication

Figure 19-1 describes the three types of authentication you can use in ASP.NET applications. The first, called *Windows-based authentication*, requires that you set up a Windows user account for each user. Then, you use standard Windows security features to restrict access to all or part of the application. When a user attempts to access the application, Windows displays a login dialog box that asks the user to supply the user name and password of the Windows account.

To use *forms-based authentication*, you add a login page to your application that typically requires the user to enter a user name and password. Then, ASP.NET displays this page automatically when it needs to authenticate a user who's trying to access the application. ASP.NET automatically creates a database to store user data such as user names and passwords, and it includes login controls that automatically generate code that reads data from and writes data to this database. As a result, you can implement forms-based authentication without having to write a single line of code. That makes this type of authentication easy to use, and you'll see how this works as you progress through this chapter.

Windows Live ID authentication, previously called *Passport authentication*, relies on the *Windows Live ID* service to authenticate users. Windows Live ID is a centralized account management service that lets users access multiple web applications with a single user account. Before you can use Windows Live ID with a web site, you must register the web site with Microsoft. Then, you can download the Windows Live ID Web Authentication software development kit (SDK) and use it in your web site to authenticate users of the site. For more information, go to www.msdn.microsoft.com and search for Windows Live ID.

Windows-based authentication

- Causes the browser to display a login dialog box when the user attempts to access a restricted page.
- Is supported by most browsers.
- Is configured through the IIS management console.
- Uses Windows user accounts and directory rights to grant access to restricted pages.

Forms-based authentication

- Lets developers code a login form that gets the user name and password.
- The user name and password entered by the user are encrypted if the login page uses a secure connection.
- Doesn't rely on Windows user accounts. Instead, the application determines how to authenticate users.

Windows Live ID authentication

- *Windows Live ID* is a centralized authentication service offered by Microsoft.
- Windows Live ID lets users maintain a single user account that lets them access any web site that participates in Windows Live ID. The advantage is that the user only has to maintain one user name and password.
- To use Windows Live ID, you must register your web site with Microsoft to obtain an application ID and then download the Windows Live ID Web Authentication SDK.

Description

- *Authentication* refers to the process of validating the identity of a user so the user can be granted access to an application. A user must typically supply a user name and password to be authenticated.
- After a user is authenticated, the user must still be authorized to use the requested application. The process of granting user access to an application is called *authorization*.

Figure 19-1 Three types of authentication

How forms-based authentication works

To help you understand how forms-based authentication works, figure 19-2 shows a typical series of exchanges that occur between a web browser and a server when a user attempts to access a page that's protected by forms-based authentication. The authentication process begins when a user requests a page that is part of a protected application. When the server receives the request, it checks to see if the user has already been authenticated. To do that, it looks for a cookie that contains an *authentication ticket* in the request for the page. If it doesn't find the ticket, it redirects the browser to the login page.

Next, the user enters a user name and password and posts the login page back to the server. Then, if the user name and password are found in the database, which means they are valid, the server creates an authentication ticket and redirects the browser back to the original page. Note that the redirect from the server sends the authentication ticket to the browser as a cookie. As a result, when the browser requests the original page, it sends the cookie back to the server. This time, the server sees that the user has been authenticated and the requested page is sent back to the browser.

By default, the authentication ticket is sent as a session cookie. In that case, the user is authenticated only for that session. However, you also can specify that the ticket be sent as a persistent cookie. Then, the user will be authenticated automatically for future sessions, until the cookie expires.

HTTP requests and responses with forms-based authentication

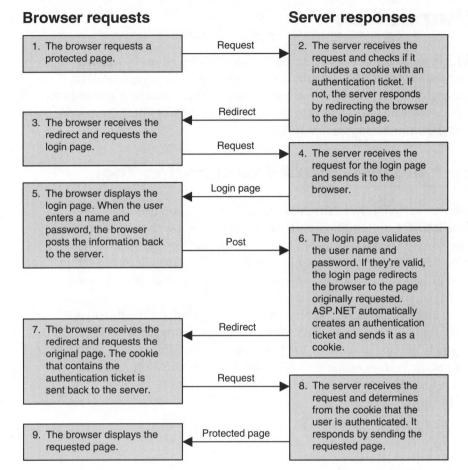

Browser requests

1. The browser requests a protected page.

3. The browser receives the redirect and requests the login page.

5. The browser displays the login page. When the user enters a name and password, the browser posts the information back to the server.

7. The browser receives the redirect and requests the original page. The cookie that contains the authentication ticket is sent back to the server.

9. The browser displays the requested page.

Server responses

2. The server receives the request and checks if it includes a cookie with an authentication ticket. If not, the server responds by redirecting the browser to the login page.

4. The server receives the request for the login page and sends it to the browser.

6. The login page validates the user name and password. If they're valid, the login page redirects the browser to the page originally requested. ASP.NET automatically creates an authentication ticket and sends it as a cookie.

8. The server receives the request and determines from the cookie that the user is authenticated. It responds by sending the requested page.

Request, Redirect, Request, Login page, Post, Redirect, Request, Protected page

Description

- When ASP.NET receives a request for a protected page from a user who has not been authenticated, the server redirects the user to the login page.

- To be authenticated, the user's computer must contain an *authentication ticket.* By default, this ticket is stored as a session cookie.

- ASP.NET automatically creates an authentication ticket when the application indicates that the user should be authenticated. ASP.NET checks for the presence of an authentication ticket any time it receives a request for a restricted page.

- The authentication ticket cookie can be made persistent. Then, the user will be authenticated automatically in future sessions, until the cookie expires.

Figure 19-2   How forms-based authentication works

How to set up authentication and authorization

By default, all pages of a web site can be accessed by all users whether or not they are authenticated. As a result, if you want to restrict access to all or some of the pages of the web site, you need to set up authentication and authorization. The easiest way to do that is to use the ASP.NET Web Site Administration Tool as shown in the topics that follow.

How to start the Web Site Administration Tool

To start the ASP.NET Web Site Administration Tool, you use the Website→ASP.NET Configuration command. This starts a web browser that displays the home page for this tool. Then, you can click on the Security tab to access a web page like the one shown in figure 19-3. This page lets you set up users, create groups of users known as *roles*, and create *access rules* that control access to parts of your application.

To set up authentication for the first time, you can click on the link that starts the Security Setup Wizard. This wizard walks you through several steps that allow you to set up the security for your application. Alternatively, you can use the links at the bottom of the page to select the authentication type and manage the users, roles, and access rules for your application.

The Security tab of the Web Site Administration Tool

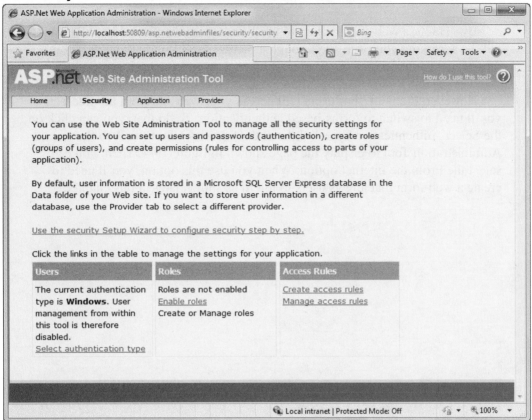

Description

- To start the ASP.NET Web Site Administration Tool, use the Website→ASP.NET Configuration command.

- You can use the ASP.NET Web Site Administration Tool to set up users, roles, and access rules.

Figure 19-3   How to start the Web Site Administration Tool

How to enable forms-based authentication

By default, a web site is set up to use Windows authentication. If all users will be accessing your web site through a private local Windows network (an intranet), this option may be the easiest to implement because it uses built-in Windows dialog boxes to allow users to log in.

However, if any of your users will access your web site from the Internet, you'll need to switch to forms-based authentication. To do that, you can click on the Select Authentication Type link from the Security tab of the Web Site Administration Tool to display the page shown in figure 19-4. Then, you can select the From the Internet option. When you use this option, you'll need to create a web form that allows users to log in as shown later in this chapter.

How to enable forms-based authentication

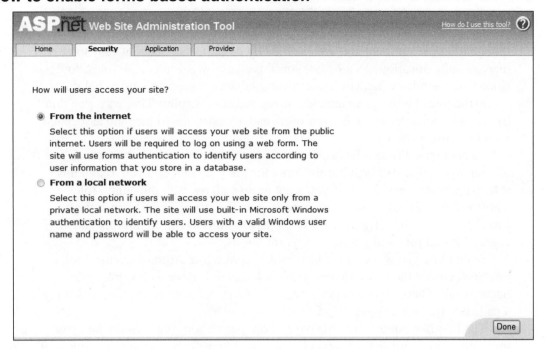

Description

- By default, a web site is set up to use Windows authentication. However, this option is only appropriate for accessing a web site through a local intranet.

- To switch to forms-based authentication, select the From the Internet option. This is the option that you'll need to use if you intend to deploy the application so it's available from the Internet.

- When you switch to forms-based authentication, Create User and Manage Users links become available from the main security page.

Figure 19-4   How to enable forms-based authentication

How to create and manage roles

Roles allow you to apply the same access rules to a group of users. Although roles are optional and are disabled by default, they make it easy to manage authentication. As a result, you'll typically want to enable roles. And since you use roles when you create users and access rules, it's often helpful to set up the roles before you create the users and access rules. That way, you don't have to go back later and edit your users and access rules so they are associated with the correct roles.

To understand how roles work, let's say you create a role named admin for all employees that will be administrators for the web site, and you assign this role to multiple users. Later, if you want to give all users in the admin role additional permissions, you don't have to give the permissions to each user. Instead, you can just give the additional permissions to the admin role and all users with that role will get the new permissions.

Before you can work with roles using the Web Site Administration Tool, you must enable them. To do that, you click on the Enable Roles link in the Security tab. Then, you can click on the Create or Manage Roles link to display a page like the one in figure 19-5.

The first two controls on this page allow you to add roles. To do that, you just enter a name for the role and click on the Add Role button, and the role will appear in the table at the bottom of the page. Then, you can click on the Manage link for the role to add users to the role or to remove users from the role. Or, you can click the Delete link for the role to delete the role entirely.

User names and roles

```
User name      Roles
anne           admin
joel           admin, custserv
kelly          custserv
```

How to create and manage roles

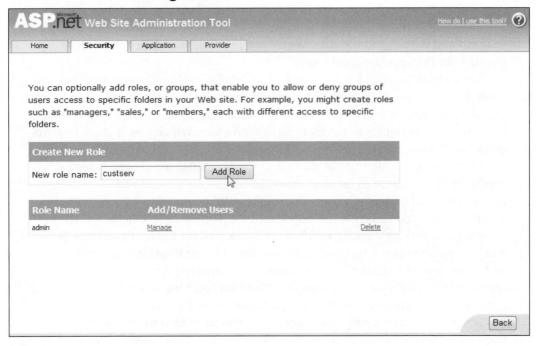

Description

- A *role* allows you to apply the same access rules to a group of users.

- Each user may be associated with one or more roles.

- By default, roles are disabled. To enable them, you need to click on the Enable Roles link in the Security tab.

- Once you enable roles, you can click on the Create or Manage Roles link in the Security tab to display the page shown above. This page lets you add roles, manage all users associated with a role, and delete roles.

Figure 19-5   How to create and manage roles

How to create and manage users

The first page displayed in figure 19-6 shows how to use the Web Site Administration Tool to create users. To do that, you start by entering all of the required information for a user. This information includes a user name, a password, an email address, and a security question and answer. If you want to associate the user with one or more roles, you can select the check box next to each role that you want to apply to the user. In this figure, for example, the user is associated with the admin role. When you're done, you can click on the Create User button to create the user.

The default password policy for an ASP.NET 4 application requires that you enter at least seven characters with one of them being a non-alphanumeric character. If that's too strict for your web site, though, you can relax this policy by adding two attributes to the membership provider, which you'll learn how to do in figure 19-8.

Once you've created one or more users, you can use the second screen displayed in this figure to manage them. To edit a user's email address, enter or change the description for a user, change the roles assigned to a user, or change a user's status, you can click the Edit User link. You can also change the roles assigned to a user by clicking on the Edit Roles link for the user and then working with the check boxes that are displayed in the Roles column of the table. And you can change a user's status by clearing the Active check box to the left of the user's name. This prevents the user from logging into your application but retains his or her information in your database.

If your application contains many users, you may need to use the Search For Users controls to search for users. When you use these controls, you can search by user name or email address. For example, to search by email address, you can select the E-mail option from the Search By drop-down list, enter the email address in the For text box, and click on the Find User button. If necessary, you can use the asterisk (*) wildcard for multiple characters, and you can use the question mark (?) wildcard for a single character. Alternatively, you can click on the letters displayed on this page to display all users whose user name or email address begins with the specified letter. Either way, you should be able to quickly find the user that you're looking for.

How to create a user

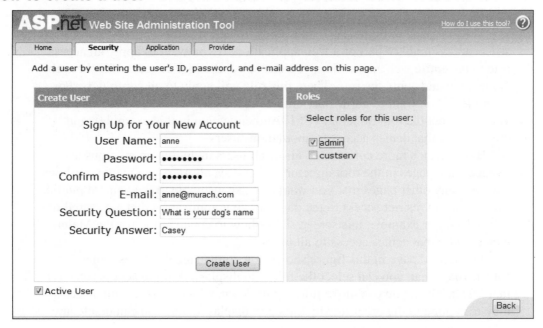

How to manage users

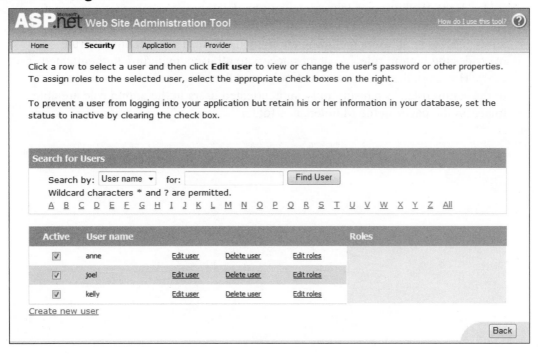

Figure 19-6   How to create and manage users

How to create and manage access rules

The first page in figure 19-7 shows how to create an *access rule* that restricts access to all or part of a web application. If you want to apply an access rule to the entire web application, you can select the root directory for the web application and apply the rule. Then, this rule will apply to all subfolders. For example, if you want to allow only authenticated users to access your web site, you can select the root directory (Ch19Authentication in this example), and create a rule that denies access to anonymous users.

However, it's more common to allow all users including anonymous users to access the pages in the root directory. That way, all users can view your home page and any other pages that you want to make available to the general public. Then, you can restrict access to the pages in your application that are stored in subfolders. For example, this screen shows how to create a rule for the Maintenance folder that denies access to all users.

The second page in this figure shows how to manage the access rules for a folder. To do that, you can select the folder to display all of the access rules for that folder. Then, you can move rules up or down, which is important since they're applied in the order in which they're displayed. Or, you can delete any rules that you no longer want to apply.

In this example, you can see the rules that restrict access to the Maintenance folder. Here, the bottom rule (which can't be deleted) is the rule that's automatically applied to all pages of a web site if you don't create new rules. This rule allows access to all users including anonymous users. Then, the middle rule overrides the bottom rule and denies access to all users including authenticated users. However, the top rule overrides the middle rule and allows access to users in the admin role. As a result, only authenticated users in the admin role are able to access the pages in the Maintenance folder.

How to create an access rule

How to manage access rules

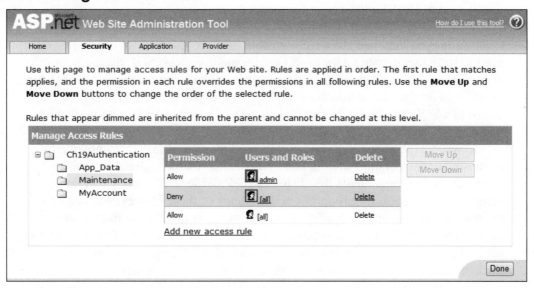

Description

- An *access rule* determines which users have access to portions of a web site.
- Each rule overrides the rules below it. As a result, for the Maintenance directory shown above, users in the admin role are allowed and all other users are denied.

Figure 19-7   How to create and manage access rules

How to modify the membership and role provider

When you add roles and users, a class known as a *data provider* contains the code that reads and writes the data for the users and roles. A data provider that works with membership data is often called a *membership provider*, and a data provider that works with roles data is often called a *role provider*. By default, a data provider named AspNetSqlProvider is used to store both membership and role data in a SQL Server Express database named AspNetDb.mdf that's stored in the App_Data folder of your web site. This database is created for you automatically, and it usually works the way you want, at least for prototyping.

However, the data provider architecture lets you use different data providers if you want to. If, for example, you want to use one data provider for the membership data and another for role data, you can use the Provider tab shown in figure 19-8 to select separate providers. The only provider for membership data is AspNetSqlMembershipProvider. Two providers are available for role data: AspNetSqlRoleProvider and AspNetWindowsTokenRoleProvider. If you use the Windows token provider, the role information will be based on Windows accounts. Because of that, you won't create roles and users as described in the previous topics. In addition, you won't use forms-based authentication. Instead, you'll need to use Windows-based authentication.

If the data providers that ship with ASP.NET 4 aren't adequate for your application, you may need to write a custom data provider. If, for example, you need to store membership data in an Oracle database, a MySQL database, or even on a midrange or mainframe computer, you can write a custom membership provider to do that. Or, if you need to work with existing membership data that's stored in a SQL Server database, you can write a custom provider to work with that data.

To write a membership provider, you need to code a class that implements the abstract MembershipProvider class. To write a role provider, you need to code a class that implements the abstract RoleProvider class. After you implement all of the necessary properties and methods of these classes, you can edit the machine.config or web.config file to add the providers to the list for all applications or the list for one application. Then, you can use the Provider tab to select the data providers for memberships and roles. Once you do that, the rest of the authentication features should work as described in this chapter.

This figure also shows how you can modify the attributes of a data provider to change the way that the data provider behaves. In particular, it shows how you can relax the strict password requirements for an application. To do that, you can copy the membership element from the machine.config file (which applies to all web applications) to the web.config file (which applies to your application). Then, you can edit the name attribute of the add element to create a unique name for the modified provider, and you can set the minRequiredPasswordLength and minRequiredNonAlphanumericCharacters attributes. In this case, these attributes are set so each password requires 6 characters and zero special characters. Last, you can add the defaultProvider attribute to the membership element so your application uses this provider.

The Provider tab of the Web Site Administration Tool

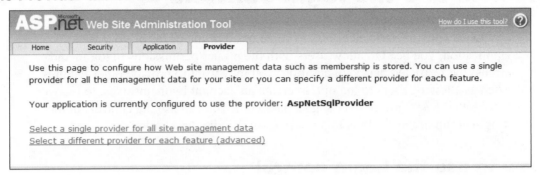

Elements in the web.config file that relax the default password policy

```
<membership defaultProvider="AspNetSqlMembershipProviderRelaxed">
  <providers>
    <add name="AspNetSqlMembershipProviderRelaxed"
         type="System.Web.Security.SqlMembershipProvider,
               System.Web, Version=2.0.0.0, Culture=neutral,
               PublicKeyToken=b03f5f7f11d50a3a"
         connectionStringName="LocalSqlServer"
         enablePasswordRetrieval="false"
         enablePasswordReset="true"
         requiresQuestionAndAnswer="true"
         applicationName="/"
         requiresUniqueEmail="false"
         passwordFormat="Hashed"
         maxInvalidPasswordAttempts="5"
         passwordAttemptWindow="10"
         passwordStrengthRegularExpression=""
         minRequiredPasswordLength="6"
         minRequiredNonalphanumericCharacters="0"/>
  </providers>
</membership>
```

Description

- By default, a *data provider* named AspNetSqlProvider is used to store both membership and role data in a SQL Server Express database named AspNetDb.mdf. However, you can use separate membership and role providers, and you can write your own custom providers.

- The definitions for the default membership and role providers can be found in the machine.config file. This file is stored in the Config folder subordinate to the .NET Framework 4 installation folder.

- To relax the password restrictions for a provider, you can change the attributes for password length and non-alphanumeric characters in the web.config file for an application.

Figure 19-8   How to modify the membership and role provider

How to use the login controls

Once you've restricted access to some or all of the pages of your web application, you need to allow users with the proper permissions to log in and access the restricted pages. In addition, you may want to provide other features such as allowing users to log out, to create an account by themselves, to recover a forgotten password, or to change a password. You can use the controls in the Login group of the Toolbox to automatically handle these tasks.

How to use the Login control

Figure 19-9 shows how to create a login page that contains a Login control. When you create a login page, you should name it Login.aspx. That's because ASP.NET looks for a page with this name when it attempts to authenticate a user. Also, since this page is used for the entire application, you usually want to use a simple format so it works equally well for all parts of the application.

Once you've created a page named Login.aspx, you can add all of the login functionality just by adding a Login control to the page. To do that, drag the Login control that's in the Login group of the Toolbox onto the page.

Like most login pages, the Login control includes two text boxes that let the user enter a user name and a password. In addition, it includes a check box that lets the users indicate whether or not they want to be logged in automatically the next time the application is accessed. If the user selects this check box, the application creates a persistent cookie that contains the authentication ticket.

When the user clicks the Log In button within the Login control, the code for the control tries to authenticate the user. It does that by checking to see whether the user name and password are in the membership data store. Then, if the user is authenticated, the code checks the role provider to see whether the user has the proper authorization for the requested page. If so, this code continues by redirecting the browser to that page.

If you want to automatically apply formatting to the Login control, you can select the Auto Format command from the control's smart tag menu. Then, you can use the resulting Auto Format dialog box to select a scheme that you like. When you do, Visual Studio will change many of the control's formatting properties. This feature works similarly for the CreateUserWizard, PasswordRecovery, and ChangePassword controls described in the pages that follow.

Although it's not shown in this figure, a login page should always force the page to use a secure connection. Then, if a hacker manages to intercept a user's user name and password, your application won't be compromised.

A Login control in the Web Forms Designer

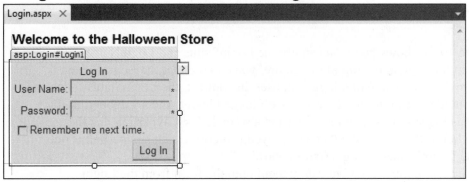

The aspx code for the Login control

```
<asp:Login ID="Login1" runat="server">
</asp:Login>
```

Common attributes of the Login control

Attribute	Description
DisplayRememberMe	Determines whether the Remember Me check box is displayed. By default, this is set to True.
RememberMeText	The text for the label of the RememberMe text box.
RememberMeSet	Determines whether a persistent cookie is sent to the user's computer, which is based on whether the RememberMe check box is selected.
FailureText	The text that's displayed when a login attempt fails.

Description

- When a user attempts to access a page that requires authentication, ASP.NET automatically redirects the user to the application's login page. This page must be named Login.aspx.
- To automatically apply formatting to the Login control, select the Auto Format command from the control's smart tag menu. Then, select a scheme from the dialog box that's displayed.

Figure 19-9   How to use the Login control

How to use the LoginStatus and LoginName controls

Figure 19-10 shows how you can use the LoginStatus and LoginName controls. In the page at the top of this figure, you can see that the LoginName control provides the name of a logged in user. In contrast, the LoginStatus control provides a Login link if a user hasn't logged in yet, and a Logout link if the user has logged in. Notice that this page also includes a hyperlink that the user can click if the user name that's displayed is incorrect. This hyperlink is not part of the LoginName or LoginStatus control.

To use these controls, you just drag them onto the form from the Login group of the Toolbox. Then, you can change the properties as needed. For instance, you can use the LoginText and LogoutText attributes of the LoginStatus control to change the text that's displayed by the links. And you can use the FormatString attribute of the LoginName control to add text before or after the placeholder for the user name.

When the user clicks on the Login link of a LoginStatus control, the user will be redirected to the login page and required to enter a user name and password. Then, after the user has been authenticated, the user will be redirected to the original page. Conversely, when the user clicks the Logout link, the user will be redirected to the login page (Login.aspx).

When a user has been authenticated, the LoginName control will display the user name. Otherwise, the control won't display the user name. However, it will display any other text that has been specified in the FormatString attribute.

The LoginName and LoginStatus controls displayed in a browser

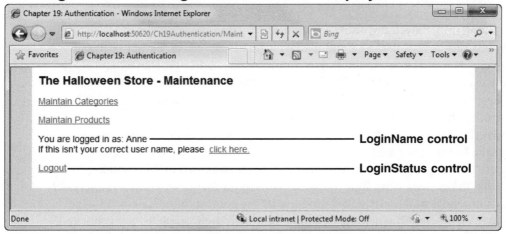

The LoginName and LoginStatus controls in the Web Forms Designer

The aspx code for the LoginName and LoginStatus controls

```
<asp:LoginName ID="LoginName1" runat="server"
    FormatString="You are logged in as: {0}" />

<asp:LoginStatus ID="LoginStatus1" runat="server" />
```

Common attribute of the LoginName control

Attribute	Description
FormatString	The text that's displayed with the user name. This string uses "{0}" to identify the User name parameter, and you can add text before or after this parameter.

Common attributes of the LoginStatus control

Attribute	Description
LoginText	The text that's displayed for the login link.
LogoutText	The text that's displayed for the logout link.

Figure 19-10 How to use the LoginStatus and LoginName controls

How to use the CreateUserWizard control

If you only have a few users for your application, you can use the Web Site Administration Tool to create and manage users as described earlier in this chapter. Then, you can use the Login, LoginStatus, and LoginName controls to allow users to log in and out. Often, though, you'll want to allow users to create user accounts for themselves. To do that, you can use the CreateUserWizard control as shown in figure 19-11.

By default, the CreateUserWizard control uses two steps to create a new user: the Create User step and the Complete step. To display these steps, you can use the drop-down list in the smart tag menu as shown in this figure. Usually, these steps work like you want them to. In that case, you can simply set the ContinueDestinationPageUrl property of the control to indicate what page the user is directed to when the Continue button in the Complete step is clicked.

If you need to modify the behavior of either of the steps, you can do that by selecting the Customize command for that step from the smart tag menu for the control. Then, you can customize that step by modifying the controls and properties of the step. If you modify the Complete step, note that you can specify the page that's displayed when the user clicks the Continue button by setting the PostBackUrl property of that button rather than by setting the ContinueDestinationPageUrl property of the CreateUserWizard control.

When you use the pages that result from the CreateUserWizard control, you should realize that the membership provider is being used to write the data to the appropriate data source. This works the same as it does for the Web Site Administration Tool.

The CreateUserWizard control with the smart tag menu shown

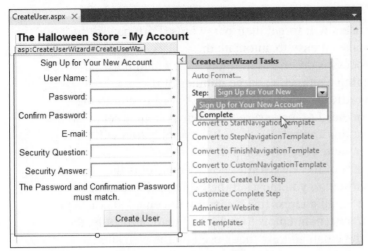

The two steps of a customized CreateUserWizard control in a browser

Description

- If you select the CreateUserWizard control in the Web Forms Designer, you can use the smart tag menu to switch between its two steps and customize or reset either step.

- To identify the page that the user is directed to when the Continue button in the Complete step is clicked, you can set the ContinueDestinationPageUrl property of the control. Or, if you've customized the Complete step, you can set the PostBackUrl property of the Continue button.

Figure 19-11   How to use the CreateUserWizard control

How to use the PasswordRecovery control

It's inevitable that some users will forget their passwords. Fortunately, the PasswordRecovery control makes it easy to automate the process of recovering forgotten passwords. This process is described in figure 19-12, and it's especially useful if you are managing a site with a large number of users.

When you use the PasswordRecovery control, the password is sent to the user via email. As a result, you need to make sure that your system is set up so it can send email before you test this control. By default, an application will try to send email to an SMTP server set to localhost on port 25.

The most important element of the PasswordRecovery control is the MailDefinition element. In particular, you must set the From attribute of the MailDefinition element to the email address that's sending the email message or an error will occur when your system attempts to send the email. Typically, the From email address is set to the email address that's used by the web site administrator. If you set this attribute correctly, a standard message will be sent to the user. To customize the subject line and message body, you can edit the other attributes of the MailDefinition element.

The PasswordRecovery control uses three views. In the Web Forms Designer, you can switch between these three views by using the smart tag menu, and you can edit the properties for any of these views as necessary.

When you display this control in a browser, the first view asks the user to enter a user name. Then, the second view requires the user to answer the security question. If the answer to this question is correct, the password is emailed to the address that's associated with the user name, and the third view is displayed. This view displays a message that indicates that the password recovery was successful and that the password has been sent to the user via email.

The PasswordRecovery control in the Web Forms Designer

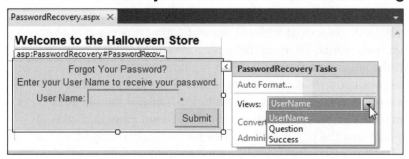

The first two views of the PasswordRecovery control

The aspx code for the PasswordRecovery control

```
<asp:PasswordRecovery ID="PasswordRecovery1" runat="server">
    <MailDefinition From="anne@murach.com">
    </MailDefinition>
</asp:PasswordRecovery>
```

Description

- After the second view is completed, the password is emailed to the user. For this to work, you need to edit the From attribute of the MailDefinition element to supply the from address for this email. In addition, the web server that you're using must be configured to work with an SMTP server.

- By default, an application will try to send email to an SMTP server set to localhost on port 25. For information on how to change these settings, see chapter 20.

Figure 19-12   How to use the PasswordRecovery control

How to use the ChangePassword control

Another common task associated with the authentication process is allowing users to change their passwords. To make that easy for you, ASP.NET provides the ChangePassword control, and figure 19-13 shows how to use it.

The ChangePassword control uses two views. The first view lets the user enter the current password and the new password twice. Then, if the old password is correct and the two new passwords match, the second view is displayed. This view tells the user that the password has been successfully changed.

Once you've placed the PasswordControl on the form, it usually works the way you want it to. However, you may need to edit the Url attributes so they point to the pages that you want to navigate to when the user clicks on the Cancel and Continue buttons.

The first view of the ChangePassword control in the Web Forms Designer

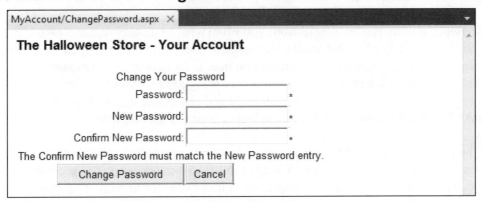

The second view of the ChangePassword control

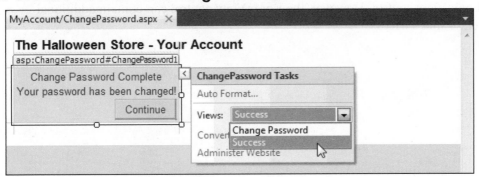

The aspx code for the ChangePassword control

```
<asp:ChangePassword ID="ChangePassword1" runat="server"
    CancelDestinationPageUrl="MyAccount.aspx"
    ContinueDestinationPageUrl="MyAccount.aspx">
</asp:ChangePassword>
```

Description

- The ChangePassword control uses two views to allow users to change their passwords. The first view lets the user change the password. The second view is displayed when the change has been successful.

- The CancelDestinationPageUrl and ContinueDestinationPageUrl attributes provide the URLs that are navigated to when the Cancel or Continue buttons are clicked.

Figure 19-13   How to use the ChangePassword control

How to use the LoginView control

If your web site uses authentication, you often need to display one message to users who are logged in and another message to users who aren't logged in. For example, when a user isn't logged in, you may want to display a message that asks the user to log in. Conversely, if a user is logged in, you may want to display a message that welcomes the user back and allows the user to log out. Figure 19-14 shows how to use the LoginView control to accomplish these tasks.

The LoginView control uses two views. The first view contains the controls that are displayed to users who aren't logged in (*anonymous users*). The second view contains the controls that are displayed to users who are logged in (*authenticated users*). In this figure, each view of the LoginView control contains a Label control followed by a LoginStatus control. This is a fairly typical use of the LoginView control. However, the LoginView control can contain additional content if that's necessary.

The LoginView control in the Web Forms Designer

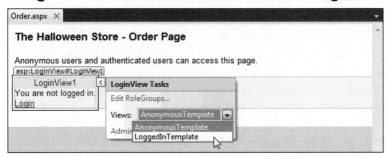

The aspx code for the LoginView control

```
<asp:LoginView ID="LoginView1" runat="server">
    <LoggedInTemplate>
        <asp:Label ID="Label2" runat="server"
            Text="You are logged in." Width="155px"></asp:Label><br />
        <asp:LoginStatus ID="LoginStatus2" runat="server" />
    </LoggedInTemplate>
    <AnonymousTemplate>
        <asp:Label ID="Label1" runat="server"
            Text="You are not logged in." Width="175px"></asp:Label><br />
        <asp:LoginStatus ID="LoginStatus1" runat="server" />
    </AnonymousTemplate>
</asp:LoginView>
```

The LoginView control displayed in a browser

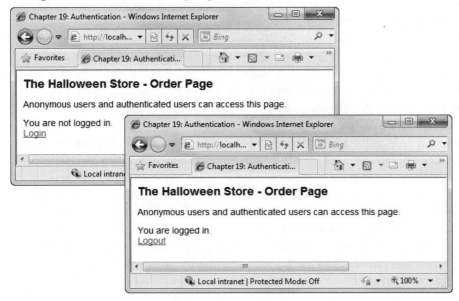

Description

- The LoginView control lets you change what's on the web page depending on whether the user isn't logged in (an *anonymous user*) or is logged in (an *authenticated user*).

Figure 19-14   How to use the LoginView control

The Authentication application

To show how to use forms-based authentication to restrict access to a web application, this topic presents part of a Halloween Store application that we'll refer to as the Authentication application. This application restricts access to all pages in the Maintenance folder to users with admin privileges. In addition, it restricts access to all pages in the MyAccount folder to users who have created an account and logged in.

As you review this application, please keep in mind that the authentication and authorization features don't require any code. That's why the figures that follow show only the pages, the directory structure, the access rules, and the web.config files.

The pages

Figure 19-15 shows just four pages of the Authentication application, but you can also think of the pages in figures 19-11 through 19-13 as part of this application. For instance, the Forgot Your Password link on the Login page goes to the page in figure 19-12, and the Need to Create a New Account link goes to the page in figure 19-11. Also, the Change Password link on the MyAccount page goes to a ChangePassword page like the one in figure 19-13.

To start this application, the Menu page in figure 19-15 contains three links that allow you to perform some tests to make sure that the authentication and authorization features are working correctly. The first link on this page lets the user access an Order page to begin placing an order. When the user clicks on this link, the system tries to authenticate the user by checking whether the user has a cookie with a valid authentication ticket. If so, the user will be authenticated automatically. If not, the user can view the Order page as an anonymous user. Either way, the Order page will be displayed. In other words, this page is available to both anonymous and authenticated users.

The second link on the Menu page lets the user access the MyAccount page where the user can edit settings for his or her personal account. To be able to access this page, the user must be authenticated. When the user clicks on this link, the system attempts to authenticate the user by checking if the browser has a cookie with a valid authentication ticket. If so, the user will be authenticated automatically and allowed to access the MyAccount page. If not, the user will be redirected to the Login page so he or she can log in. Once the user supplies a valid user name and password to the Login page, the browser will be redirected to the MyAccount page.

The Menu page

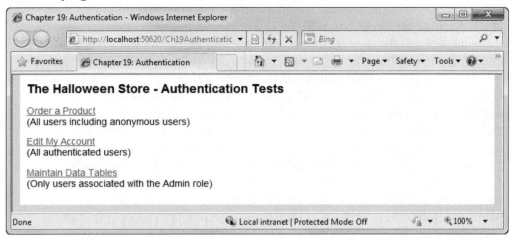

The Login page

Description

- The Menu page contains three links. The first lets anonymous users or authenticated users access the Order page. The second lets authenticated users access the MyAccount page. The third lets authenticated users who are associated with the admin role access the Maintenance page.

- The Login page is only displayed if the user clicks on the second or third link and the browser doesn't contain a cookie that authenticates the user.

- If the user clicks on the Forgot your Password link on the Login page, the PasswordRecovery page in figure 19-12 is displayed. If the user clicks on the Need to Create a New Account link, the CreateUser page in figure 19-11 is displayed.

Figure 19-15   The pages of the Authentication application (part 1 of 2)

The third link on the Menu page lets users access the Maintenance page that can be used to manage data that's stored in the Categories and Products tables of the database for the web site. To be able to access this page, the user must be authenticated and the user must be associated with the admin role. When the user clicks on this link, the system attempts to authenticate the user by checking if the browser has a cookie with a valid authentication ticket. If so, the user will be authenticated automatically and allowed to access the Maintenance page. If not, the user will be redirected to the Login page so he or she can log in. Once the user supplies a valid user name and password for a user with admin privileges, the browser will be redirected to the Maintenance page.

When using the MyAccount and Maintenance pages, the LoginStatus control on these pages allows the users to log out when they're done. This removes the authentication ticket from the browser. As a result, the application won't remember the user the next time the user attempts to access the application, even if the user has selected the Remember Me check box to store the authentication ticket in a persistent cookie.

The MyAccount page

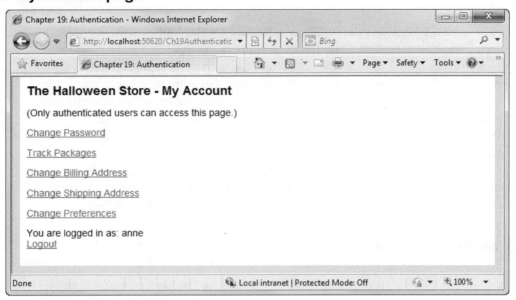

The Maintenance page

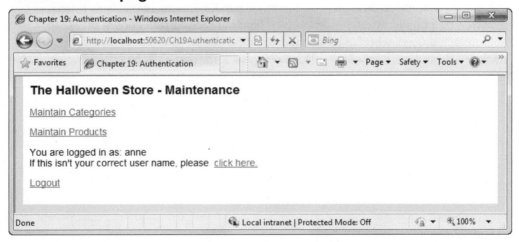

Description

- The MyAccount page lets a user edit account data. The user must be authenticated, but need not be associated with any role. When the user clicks on the Change Password link, a page like the one in figure 19-13 is displayed.

- The Maintenance page lets a user maintain data in the Categories and Products tables. The user must be authenticated and must be associated with the admin role.

- The LoginStatus control on these pages lets the user log out when done. This removes the authentication ticket from the browser. As a result, the application won't be able to remember the user the next time the user attempts to access the application.

Figure 19-15   The pages of the Authentication application (part 2 of 2)

The directory structure

Figure 19-16 shows the directory structure for the Authentication application. This shows the App_Data folder that stores the SQL Server Express database that's used to store the data about the web site's registered users and their roles. In addition, it shows two directories that store web pages that have restricted access. First, it shows the Maintenance directory, which contains the Maintenance page shown in the previous figure. Second, it shows the MyAccount directory, which contains the MyAccount page shown in the previous figure.

In addition, there are three web.config files for this application: one for the root directory, one for the Maintenance directory, and one for the MyAccount directory. The complete listings for these files are shown in figure 19-17.

The access rules

Figure 19-16 also shows the one access rule for the MyAccount directory. This rule denies access to anonymous users. As a result, only users who are authenticated can access the MyAccount directory.

The Maintenance directory, on the other hand, contains two access rules. The first rule denies access to all users. Then, the second rule allows access to authenticated users who are associated with the admin role. To refresh your memory about how this works, please refer back to figure 19-7.

The directory structure for the Authentication application

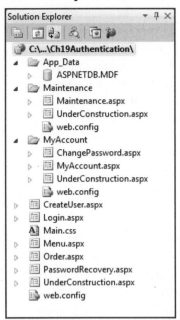

The access rules for the MyAccount directory

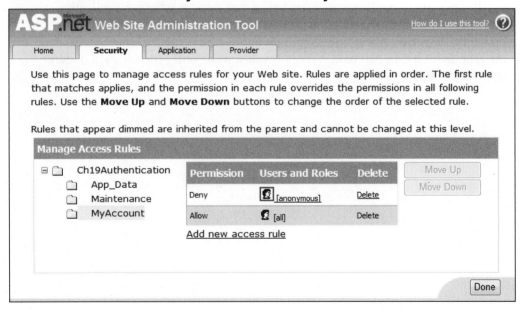

Description

- The MyAccount page lets a user edit personal account data. The user must be authenticated, but doesn't need to be associated with any role.

Figure 19-16   The directory structure and access rules for the Authentication application

The web.config files

Figure 19-17 shows the three web.config files for the Authentication application. When you use the Web Site Administration Tool to create access rules, it automatically creates and modifies these web.config files. As a result, you don't have to edit them manually. However, it's good to have an idea of what's going on under the hood as you use the Web Site Administration Tool.

In addition, once you become familiar with these files, you may find that you prefer to edit or review them manually. But first, you need to understand the XML code that's used by these files to store configuration settings.

To enable forms-based authentication, you can use the mode attribute of the authentication element. This attribute is set to Windows by default to use Windows authentication, but you can set it to Forms to enable forms-based authentication.

Once you've enabled forms-based authentication, you can use the authorization element to deny or allow access to specified users. To deny access to users, you can code a deny element within the authorization element and set the users and roles attributes. To allow access to users, you can code an allow element within the authorization element and set the users and roles attributes. Note that before you can use the roles attribute, you must enable role management. To do that, you set the enabled attribute of the roleManager element to True.

If you want to apply access rules to the root directory for the application, you can code an authorization element within the web.config file in the root directory. However, it's more common to apply access rules to subdirectories of the root directory. In that case, you can code a web.config file for each directory as shown in this figure.

The web.config files for the Authentication application

For the root directory

```xml
<?xml version="1.0"?>
<configuration>
    <system.web>
        <authentication mode="Forms"/>
        <roleManager enabled="True"/>
        ...
    </system.web>
</configuration>
```

For the MyAccount directory

```xml
<?xml version="1.0" encoding="utf-8"?>
<configuration>
    <system.web>
        <authorization>
            <deny users="?" />
        </authorization>
    </system.web>
</configuration>
```

For the Maintenance directory

```xml
<?xml version="1.0" encoding="utf-8"?>
<configuration>
    <system.web>
        <authorization>
            <allow roles="admin" />
            <deny users="*" />
        </authorization>
    </system.web>
</configuration>
```

Wildcard specifications in the users attribute

Wildcard	Description
*	All users, whether or not they have been authenticated.
?	All unauthenticated users.

Discussion

- When you use the Web Site Administration Tool, it automatically creates and modifies the web.config files for an application. If you prefer, you can manually edit these files and you can read them to quickly review the settings for an application.

- To enable forms-based authentication, set the mode attribute of the authentication element to Forms. This attribute is set to Windows by default.

- To enable role management, set the enabled attribute of the roleManager element to True.

- To deny access to users, you can code a deny element within the authorization element. To allow access to users, you can code an allow element within the authorization element. Then, you can set the users and roles attributes of these elements.

Figure 19-17   The web.config files for the Authentication application

Perspective

This chapter has presented the skills that you need for using forms-based authentication to restrict access to a web application. When you combine these skills with those of the previous chapter, you should have all of the skills you need for providing the security that an ecommerce application needs.

Terms

authentication
authorization
Windows-based authentication
forms-based authentication
Windows Live ID authentication
Passport authentication
Windows Live ID
authentication ticket
role
access rule
data provider
membership provider
role provider
anonymous user
authenticated user

20

How to use email, custom error pages, and back-button control

Once you've got an application working the way it's supposed to, you can add enhancements that make it work even better. In this chapter, you'll learn how to add three of the most useful enhancements. First, you'll learn how to send email from an ASP.NET application. Then, you'll learn how to create and use custom error pages. And last, you'll learn how to handle the problems that can occur when the user uses the Back button to access a page that has already been posted.

How to send email

When you create a web application, you often need to send email messages from the application. For instance, when a user makes a purchase from an ecommerce site, a web application usually sends an email to the customer that confirms the order. Or, if a serious error occurs, the web application often sends an email message to the support staff that documents the error. In the topics that follow, you'll learn how to send email from your ASP.NET applications.

An introduction to email

You're probably familiar with *mail client* software such as Microsoft Outlook or Outlook Express that allows you to send and retrieve email messages. This type of software communicates with a *mail server* that actually sends and retrieves your email messages. Most likely, your mail server software is provided by your Internet Service Provider (ISP) or through your company.

The diagram in figure 20-1 shows how this works. The two protocols that are commonly used to send email messages are *SMTP* and *POP*. When you send an email message, the message is first sent from the mail client software on your computer to your mail server using the SMTP protocol. Then, your mail server uses SMTP to send the mail to the recipient's mail server. Finally, the recipient's mail client uses the POP protocol to retrieve the mail from the recipient's mail server.

A third protocol you should know about is *MIME*, which stands for *Multi-purpose Internet Mail Extension*. Unlike SMTP or POP, MIME isn't used to transfer email messages. Instead, it defines how the content of an email message and its attachments are formatted. In this chapter, you'll learn how to send messages that consist of simple text as well as messages that use HTML format.

How email works

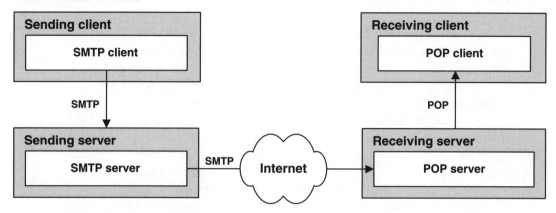

Three email protocols

Protocol	Description
SMTP	*Simple Mail Transfer Protocol* is used to send a message from one mail server to another.
POP	*Post Office Protocol* is used by mail clients to retrieve messages from mail servers. POP version 3, known as POP3, is the most widely used version, but a specification for POP version 4 has been developed.
MIME	The *Multipurpose Internet Mail Extension* specifies the type of content that can be sent as a message or attachment.

Three common reasons for sending email from an ASP.NET application

- **To confirm receipt of an order.** When the user completes an order, the application can email a confirmation of the order to the user.

- **To remind a registered user of a forgotten password.** If the user forgets his or her password, the application can email the password to the email address that's on file for the user. You can also accomplish this using the PasswordRecovery control presented in chapter 19.

- **To notify support personnel of a problem.** If a problem like an unhandled exception occurs, the application can email a message that summarizes the problem to the appropriate support person.

Description

- When an email message is sent, it goes from the sender's *mail client* to the sender's *mail server* to the receiver's mail server to the receiver's mail client.

- *SMTP* and *POP* are the protocols that are commonly used for sending and retrieving email messages. *MIME* is the protocol for defining the format of an email message.

Figure 20-1   An introduction to email

How to install an SMTP server

If you're using the Web Development Server to test your ASP.NET applications, they won't be able to send email. As a result, before you can test an ASP.NET application that sends email messages, you must install IIS and use it to run your web applications. In addition, before you can test an ASP.NET application that sends email messages, you must install an SMTP server.

If you're using Windows XP, you can use the SMTP server that's built into IIS. If you're using Windows 7 or Windows Vista, however, you should know that the version of IIS that comes with these operating systems doesn't include an SMTP server. Because of that, you'll need to get a separate SMTP server. Several servers can be downloaded for free from the Internet.

To start the SMTP service under Windows XP, you use the IIS Management Console as shown in figure 20-2. To display this program, open the Control Panel and then open Administrative Tools and double-click the Internet Information Services icon. Once you've opened the IIS Management Console, you can expand the tree to display the Default SMTP Virtual Server node. Then, you can start the SMTP service by selecting it in the tree and clicking the Start button in the toolbar.

Once you've started the SMTP service, you must configure it so that it allows your ASP.NET applications to send mail. To do that, you enable relaying for the local computer. This allows the mail server to accept mail from a specified computer and deliver it to the intended recipient. To configure the SMTP service to relay mail from the local computer, open the Relay Restrictions dialog box as described in this figure and add the localhost address (127.0.0.1) to the list of computers that the SMTP server will relay mail for.

How to make sure SMTP is running on your local server

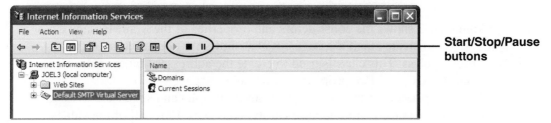

Start/Stop/Pause buttons

1. Open the Control Panel, double-click on Administrative Tools, and then double-click on Internet Information Services to open the IIS Management Console shown above.

2. Expand the tree to display your local computer's IIS server and the services running under it.

3. Select the Default SMTP Virtual Server service.

4. If the SMTP service is *not* running, the Stop button (■) will be disabled. In that case, click the Start button (▸) to start the SMTP service.

How to allow relaying for the local host

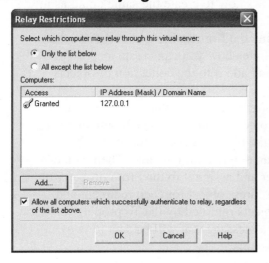
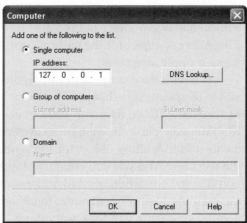

1. In the IIS Management Console, right-click the Default SMTP Virtual Server node and choose the Properties command.

2. Click the Access tab, then click the Relay button. This displays the Relay Restrictions dialog box shown above.

3. Click the Add button to display the Computer dialog box shown above. Then, select Single Computer, type 127.0.0.1 into the IP address field, click OK to close the Computer dialog box, and click OK again to close the Relay Restrictions dialog box.

Figure 20-2   How to configure the SMTP service in IIS under Windows XP

How to create an email message

Figure 20-3 shows the constructors and properties of the MailMessage class that you use to create email messages. It also shows the constructors of the MailAddress class. This class is used to create the addresses that are stored in the From, To, CC, and Bcc properties of a mail message.

The first example in this figure illustrates how you can use these classes to create a mail message that includes a carbon copy (cc). Here, all of the values needed to create the email message are passed to the method as arguments. Then, the first three statements of the method create MailAddress objects for the from, to, and cc addresses. Notice that the MailAddress object for the from address includes both an email address and a display name. When a display name is included, it's displayed in the mail client's email list instead of the email address.

The fourth statement in this method creates a MailMessage object using the to and from MailAddress objects. Then, the next two statements set the Subject and Body properties of the message. Finally, the last statement adds the cc MailAddress object to the collection of objects in the CC property.

The second example in this figure shows how to create the same email as in the first example without setting the display name for the sender. To do that, you simply create the MailMessage object using the from and to addresses and the subject and body. This example also illustrates how you can create a MailAddress object for the carbon copy and add it to the collection of objects using a single statement.

Although the examples in this figure create messages that will be sent to a single recipient, you should realize that you can send a message to any number of recipients. To do that, you need to use the first constructor for the MailMessage class shown here to create an empty mail message. Then, you can create a MailAddress object for the sender and assign it to the From property of the message. And you can create a MailAddress object for each recipient and add it to the collection of MailAddress objects returned by the To property of the mail message. For example, to create a message that will be sent to two people, your code will look something like this:

```
MailMessage msg = new MailMessage();
msg.From = new MailAddress("anne@murach.com");
msg.To.Add(new MailAddress("joel@murach.com"));
msg.To.Add(new MailAddress("kelly@murach.com"));
```

Constructors and properties of the MailMessage class

Constructor	Description
`MailMessage()`	Creates an empty mail message.
`MailMessage(from, to)`	Creates a mail message with the to and from addresses specified as strings or MailAddress objects.
`MailMessage(from, to, subject, body)`	Creates a mail message with the to address, from address, subject, and body specified as strings.

Property	Description
`From`	A MailAddress object for the message sender.
`To`	A collection of MailAddress objects for the message recipients.
`CC`	A collection of MailAddress objects for the copy recipients.
`Bcc`	A collection of MailAddress objects for the blind copy recipients.
`Subject`	The subject line for the message.
`Body`	The body of the message.
`IsBodyHtml`	A Boolean value that indicates if the body of the message contains HTML. The default is False.
`Attachments`	A collection of Attachment objects.

Constructors of the MailAddress class

Constructor	Description
`MailAddress(address)`	Creates an email address with the specified address string.
`MailAddress(address, displayName)`	Creates an email address with the specified address and display strings.

Code that creates an email message with a carbon copy

```
private void SendTextMessageCC(string fromAddress, string fromName,
    string toAddress, string subject, string body, string ccAddress)
{
    MailAddress fromAdd = new MailAddress(fromAddress, fromName);
    MailAddress toAdd = new MailAddress(toAddress);
    MailAddress ccAdd = new MailAddress(ccAddress);
    MailMessage msg = new MailMessage(fromAdd, toAdd);
    msg.Subject = subject;
    msg.Body = body;
    msg.CC.Add(ccAdd);
}
```

Another way to create a message

```
MailMessage msg = new MailMessage(fromAddress, toAddress, subject, body);
msg.CC.Add(new MailAddress(ccAddress));
```

Description

- To create an email message, you use the MailMessage and MailAddress classes that are in the System.Net.Mail namespace.

- To add an address to a collection of MailAddress objects, you use the Add method of the collection.

Figure 20-3   How to create an email message

How to send an email message

After you create an email message, you use the SmtpClient class shown in figure 20-4 to send the message. The technique you use to do that depends on the message you're sending and on whether you have set the SMTP configuration settings for the application. To set the SMTP configuration settings, you use the Web Site Administration Tool as shown in this figure. Then, these settings are saved in the web.config file.

Before I go on, you should realize that the server name shown here, localhost, doesn't necessarily refer to IIS. Instead, it refers to the SMTP server that's installed on your local machine. So if you're using an SMTP server other than the one that comes with older versions of IIS, localhost refers to that server.

The first example in this figure shows you how to send a message using settings in the web.config file. When you use this technique, you don't have to specify the name or port for the SMTP server when you create the SmtpClient object. Instead, these settings are taken from the Smtp section of the web.config file.

The first example also illustrates how to send a message that's been stored in a MailMessage object. To do that, you simply name the MailMessage object on the Send method.

If you haven't set the SMTP configuration options, or if you want to override these options, you can specify the domain name of the server when you create the SmtpClient object. This is illustrated in the second example in this figure. Here, the name "localhost" is specified so the SMTP server on the local machine will be used. Notice that when you use the local server, you don't have to specify a port number. That's because the default port number is 25, which is also the default port for an SMTP server. If you use a server at a different port, though, you'll have to specify the port number.

The second example also illustrates how you can send a mail message without creating a MailMessage object. To do that, you just pass the from and to addresses and the subject and body text to the Send method. Then, the Send method creates the MailMessage object for you and sends it. You can use this format of the Send method if the message is in simple text format, you don't need to send the message to more than one person, you don't need to send copies of the message to anyone, and you don't need to send attachments with the message.

If you've read chapter 19, you know that another way to send an email is to use the PasswordRecovery control. This control sends an email to a user that includes the user's password. Because you don't specify the server that's used to send the message when you use this control, you must set the server name (and port if necessary) in the web.config file for it to work. In addition, you should set a from address to appear in the email that's sent by this control.

How to set the SMTP configuration settings

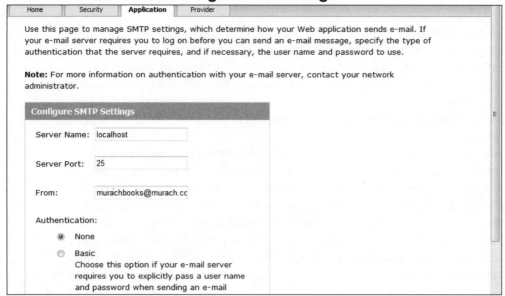

Constructors and methods of the SmtpClient class

Constructor	Description
`SmtpClient()`	Creates a client using the settings specified in the web.config file.
`SmtpClient(name)`	Creates a client that can send email to the specified SMTP server.
`SmtpClient(name, port)`	Creates a client that can send email to the specified SMTP server and port.

Method	Description
`Send(message)`	Sends the specified MailMessage object.
`Send(from, to, subject, body)`	Creates and sends an email message using the specified from, to, subject, and body strings.

Code that sends a message using settings in the web.config file

```
SmtpClient client = new SmtpClient();
client.Send(msg);
```

Code that creates and sends a message to a named server

```
SmtpClient client = new SmtpClient("localhost");
client.Send(fromAddress, toAddress, subject, body);
```

Description

- To send an email message, you use the SmtpClient class in the System.Net.Mail namespace.

- You can use the Web Site Administration Tool to specify the settings that will be used to send email messages. To do that, select the Website→ASP.NET Configuration command, display the Application tab, click the Configure SMTP E-mail Settings link, and enter the values on the page that's displayed.

Figure 20-4   How to send an email message

How to add an attachment to an email message

An *attachment* is a file that's sent along with an email message. The most common types of attachments are text files, word processing documents, spreadsheets, pictures, and other media files such as sound and video files.

Figure 20-5 shows how you can create an attachment and add it to an email message. After you create an attachment object using the Attachment class, you add the object to the mail message's Attachments collection. Then, you can send the message.

Since SMTP protocol is designed to send text messages, not binary files, any email attachment for a binary file must be converted to text format before it can be sent. Then, the text attachment must be converted back to a binary file when it's received. The most common format for converting attached binary files to text and back to binary is called *UUEncode*, and it's used by default. The other available format for converting binary files is called *Base64*. Since you shouldn't need to use this format, I haven't shown you how to create an attachment that uses it here.

The syntax for creating an attachment

```
new Attachment(fileName)
```

One way to create a new attachment and add it to a message

```
MailMessage msg = new MailMessage(fromAddress, toAddress, subject, body);
string fileName = "C:\\HalloweenStore\\Attachments\\ReturnPolicy.doc";
Attachment attach = new Attachment(fileName);
msg.Attachments.Add(attach);
```

Another way to create a new attachment and add it to a message

```
MailMessage msg = new MailMessage(fromAddress, toAddress, subject, body);
string fileName = "C:\\HalloweenStore\\Attachments\\ReturnPolicy.doc";
msg.Attachments.Add(new Attachment(fileName);
```

Description

- An *attachment* is a file that is sent along with an email message. When the recipient receives the email message, he or she can open or save the attachment.

- To add an attachment to an email message, you create the attachment using the Attachment class. Then, you add the attachment to the message using the Add method of the Attachments collection of the MailMessage class.

- If an email attachment contains a binary file, it must be converted to text before it can be sent, and it must be converted back to binary when it's received. By default, binary files are converted to a format called *UUEncode*. However, you can also use a format called *Base64*.

Figure 20-5   How to add an attachment to an email message

How to create an HTML message

By default, email messages consist of plain text with no formatting. However, you can create a formatted message by using HTML as the MIME type as described in figure 20-6. When you set the IsBodyHtml property of the MailMessage object to True, you can use HTML formatting tags in the body of the message.

The example in this figure calls a private method named GetConfirmationMessage that formats the HTML for the body of an order confirmation message. This method uses basic HTML formatting tags to create a message that includes an image and some text. Note that the text includes the customer's first and last names, which are retrieved from a data view that contains the customer data. Also note that if you refer to an image in the body by including an <img> tag, you must include the image file as an attachment as shown here. Otherwise, the recipient won't be able to see the image.

How an HTML message appears in an email client

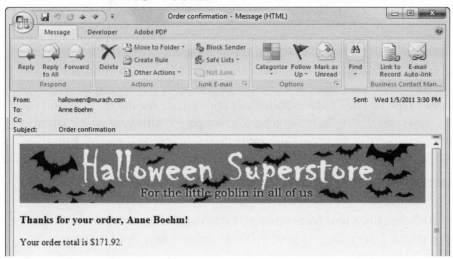

A method that creates and sends a simple HTML message

```
private void SendConfirmation()
{
    MailMessage msg = new MailMessage("halloween@murach.com", toAddress);
    msg.Subject = "Order Confirmation";
    msg.Body = this.GetConfirmationMessage();
    msg.IsBodyHtml = true;
    string file = "C:\\aspnet4_cs\\Ch20HalloweenStore\\Images\\banner.jpg";
    msg.Attachments.Add(new Attachment(file));
    SmtpClient client = new SmtpClient("localhost");
    client.Send(msg);
}

private string GetConfirmationMessage()
{
    string message = "<html><head><title>Order confimation</title></head>"
                + "<body><img src='banner.jpg' alt='Halloween Store' />"
                + "<br /><br /><h3>Thanks for your order, "
                + dvCustomer[0]["FirstName"].ToString() + " "
                + dvCustomer[0]["LastName"].ToString() + "!</h3>"
                + "<p>Your order total is " + total.ToString("c")
                + ".</p></body></HTML>";
    return message;
}
```

Description

- To create an email message in HTML format, set the IsBodyHtml property to True. Then, you can use HTML in the message that you assign to the Body property.

- An HTML email message can include links to your web site. However, you should avoid sending HTML that includes scripts or web form controls. Many mail servers will reject them because they might be malicious.

- If the HTML includes <img> tags, you should include the image files as attachments. Otherwise, recipients won't be able to see the images in your email.

Figure 20-6   How to create an HTML message

How to use custom error handling

When an error occurs in an ASP.NET application, an exception is thrown. Then, if the exception isn't handled by the application, an ASP.NET Server Error page is displayed. This page includes an error message, a portion of the source code that threw the unhandled exception, and other debugging information. Since this type of error page usually isn't appropriate for the users of an application, you typically replace the generic error pages with your own custom error pages after you're done testing the web site but before you go live with it.

An introduction to custom error handling

Figure 20-7 describes four techniques you can use to display your own custom error pages. Depending on your application, you may need to use one or more of these techniques.

The first technique is to enclose code that might generate exceptions in a try block of a try-catch statement. Then, you can redirect to a custom error page if an exception does occur.

The second technique is to code a Page_Error method in the code-behind file for a page. This method is called whenever an unhandled exception occurs on the page. Then, in the Page_Error method, you redirect the user to a custom error page.

The third technique is to code an Application_Error method in the global.asax file. This method is called whenever an unhandled exception occurs on a page that doesn't have a Page_Error method. Then, the Application_Error method can redirect the user to a custom error page.

The fourth technique is to use the customErrors element in the web.config file to designate custom error pages. This technique is used to display custom error pages when common HTTP errors such as a 404 – Not Found error occur.

A custom error page in a browser

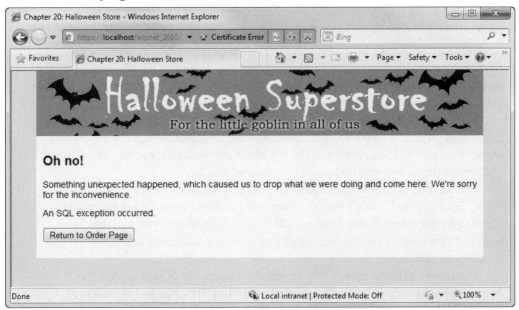

Four ways to display a custom error page when an exception occurs

- Use try-catch statements to catch exceptions as they occur, then redirect or transfer to a custom error page.
- Use the Page_Error method in a code-behind file to catch unhandled exceptions at the page level, then redirect or transfer to a custom error page.
- Use the Application_Error method in the global.asax file to catch unhandled exceptions at the application level, then redirect or transfer to a custom error page.
- Use the customErrors element of the web.config file to specify custom error pages that are displayed for specific types of HTTP errors.

Description

- If an unrecoverable error occurs, most applications display a custom error page to inform the user that a problem has occurred.
- Behind the scenes, the custom error page may also record the error in a log or send an email message to the application's support staff to notify them of the error.
- Custom error pages often use an Exception object to display a detailed message that describes the error.

Figure 20-7   An introduction to custom error handling

How to get and use the Exception object for an error

Figure 20-8 shows how you can use the properties and methods of the Exception and HttpServerUtility classes to get and use the Exception object for an error. This is the object that contains information about the exception that has occurred. The examples in this figure show how this works.

The first example shows how you can use a try-catch statement to get the Exception object. As you should know, the catch block catches the Exception object if any of the statements in the try block throw an exception. You can use this technique in any method of a code-behind file.

The second example shows how to get the Exception object within the Page_Error method. This method is executed automatically if an exception isn't handled by the other methods of a code-behind file. Here, you use the GetLastError method of the Server object, which you access using the Server property of the page.

The third example shows how to get the Exception object within the Application_Error method of the global.asax file. This method is executed automatically if an exception isn't handled by any of the methods in the code-behind file including the Page_Error method. In the Application_Error method, however, the GetLastError method doesn't return the correct Exception object. That's because a second exception called HttpUnhandledException is thrown if an exception occurs and the exception isn't handled by a try-catch statement or a Page_Error method. As a result, the GetLastError method returns the HttpUnhandledException exception, not the exception that originally caused the error. To access the original exception, you must use the InnerException property of the Exception object that's returned by the GetLastError method.

Although you might think that you could use the ClearError method to clear the HttpUnhandledException exception and then use GetLastError to get the original exception, that won't work. That's because you can only use GetLastError to get the Exception object for the last exception that occurred. In this case, that's the HttpUnhandledException exception.

The fourth example shows how you might use the properties of an Exception object as you test an application. Here, the Write method of the HttpResponse object is used to display the Message and Source properties on the page. Notice that before this method is executed, the ClearError method of the Server object is used to clear the error. That way, the ASP.NET Server Error page won't be displayed.

Common properties of the Exception class

Property	Description
Message	A message that describes the error.
Source	The name of the application or object that caused the error.
InnerException	The Exception object that caused the exception at the application level.

Methods of the HttpServerUtility class for working with exceptions

Method	Description
GetLastError()	Gets the most recent exception.
ClearError()	Clears the most recent exception.

Code that gets the Exception object at the method level

```
try
{
    statements that could throw an exception
}
catch (Exception ex)
{
    statements that use the Exception object named ex
}
```

Code that gets the Exception object at the page level

```
Exception ex = Server.GetLastError();
```

Code that gets the Exception object at the application level

```
Exception ex = Server.GetLastError().InnerException;
```

Code that displays the error message and source of the Exception object

```
Server.ClearError();
Response.Write(ex.Message + "<br />" + ex.Source);
```

Description

- You can use a try-catch statement in any method of a code-behind file to get the Exception object for an error.

- The Page_Error method is executed when an unhandled exception occurs. Within this method, you use the GetLastError method of the Server object to get the Exception object for the error.

- If you don't handle an exception with a try-catch statement or a Page_Error method, an HttpUnhandledException is thrown. Then, you can use the Application_Error method in the global.asax file to handle the exception. To do that, you use the GetLastError method of the Server object to get the Exception object for the HttpUnhandledException, and you use the InnerException property of that exception to get the Exception object that caused the error.

- During testing, you may want to use the Write method of the HttpResponse object to write information about the exception to the page. Before you do that, you need to clear the error from the Server object so the ASP.NET Server Error page isn't displayed.

Figure 20-8   How to get and use the Exception object for an error

How to code methods that redirect to a custom error page

Figure 20-9 shows three ways to redirect to a custom error page when an exception occurs in an ASP.NET application. The first example shows how you can redirect to a custom error page from a try-catch statement. Here, a call to the Insert method of a SQL data source is placed in a try block so any database exceptions can be handled in the catch block. If an exception occurs, the catch block adds the Exception object to session state and redirects to the error page. Then, the error page can use the Exception object to get information about the exception.

The second example shows how you can use a Page_Error method to catch all unhandled exceptions for a page and redirect to a custom error page. Here, the GetLastError method is used to get the Exception object. Then, the method adds the Exception object to session state and redirects to the custom error page.

The third example shows how you can use an Application_Error method in the global.asax file to catch all unhandled exceptions for an entire application. Here, the GetLastError method is used to get the Exception object, and the InnerException property of the Exception object is used to get the exception that caused the error. Then, the method adds the Exception object to session state and redirects to the custom error page.

A try-catch statement that redirects to a custom error page if an exception occurs during a database operation

```
try
{
    SqlDataSource1.Insert();
}
catch (Exception ex)
{
    Session["Exception"] = ex;
    Response.Redirect("ErrorPage.aspx");
}
```

A Page_Error method that redirects to a custom error page

```
private void Page_Error(object sender, EventArgs e)
{
    Exception ex = Server.GetLastError();
    Session["Exception"] = ex;
    Response.Redirect("ErrorPage.aspx");
}
```

An Application_Error method in the global.asax file that redirects to a custom error page

```
void Application_Error(object sender, EventArgs e)
{
    Exception ex = Server.GetLastError().InnerException;
    Session["Exception"] = ex;
    Response.Redirect("ErrorPage.aspx");
}
```

Description

- You can redirect to a custom error page from a try-catch statement, a Page_Error method, or an Application_Error method in the global.asax file.
- Before redirecting to a custom error page, the Exception object should be added to session state so it can be used by the error page.
- If you run an application with debugging and an unhandled exception occurs, Visual Studio enters break mode and displays a dialog box that describes the error and provides links you can use to get additional information on the error. To continue program execution when this dialog box is displayed, click the Continue button.

Figure 20-9   How to code methods that redirect to a custom error page

The code for a custom error page

Figure 20-10 shows the aspx code and the code-behind file for the custom error page that's shown in figure 20-7. Here, the aspx code should be self-explanatory because it simply displays a message and provides a button for returning to the Order page.

The code-behind file for the error page is more interesting, though, because it sends an email message to the support personnel that describes the error that has occurred. This assumes that the try-catch statement, Page_Error method, or Application_Error method that redirects to the error page has added the Exception object to session state. Then, the Load event handler for the error page gets the Exception object from session state and passes it to the SendEmail method, which sends the email message. After that, the Load event handler removes the Exception object from session state.

The aspx code for the body of the Error page

```
<body>
    <form id="form1" runat="server">
    <div id="page">
        <div id="header">
            <asp:Image ID="Image1" runat="server"
                ImageUrl="~/Images/banner.jpg" />
        </div>
        <div id="main">
            <h2>Oh no!</h2>
            <p>Something unexpected happened, which caused us to drop what we
                were doing and come here. We're sorry for the inconvenience.</p>
            <p>
                <asp:Button ID="btnReturn" runat="server"
                    Text="Return to Order Page" PostBackUrl="~/Order.aspx" />
            </p>
        </div>
    </div>
    </form>
</body>
```

The C# code for the Error page

```csharp
using System.Net.Mail;

public partial class ErrorPage : System.Web.UI.Page
{
    protected void Page_Load(object sender, EventArgs e)
    {
        if (!IsPostBack)
        {
            Exception ex = (Exception)Session["Exception"];
            this.SendEmail(ex);
            Session.Remove("Exception");
        }
    }

    private void SendEmail(Exception ex)
    {
        string body = "An exception occurred at "
                    + DateTime.Now.ToLongTimeString()
                    + " on " + DateTime.Now.ToLongDateString()
                    + "<br />" + ex.Message;
        MailMessage msg = new MailMessage("halloween@murach.com",
            "support@murach.com");
        msg.Subject = "Exception in Halloween application";
        msg.Body = body;
        msg.IsBodyHtml = true;
        SmtpClient client = new SmtpClient("localhost");
        client.Send(msg);
    }
}
```

Note

- This code assumes that the Exception object has been placed in session state.

Figure 20-10   The code for a custom error page

How to handle HTTP errors with the web.config file

Not all unrecoverable errors cause ASP.NET to throw an exception. As figure 20-11 shows, some error conditions result in HTTP errors that are handled by the web server itself. For these errors, you can use the customErrors element in the web.config file to specify custom error pages.

Although there are many different types of HTTP errors that can occur, the common types are listed in this figure. Of these, the most common is the 404 error. This error occurs when a user attempts to retrieve a page that doesn't exist. In some cases, a 404 error is caused by a missing page or a page that has been renamed. In other cases, a 404 error is caused by an error in your application's navigation controls, such as a hyperlink that uses an incorrect URL.

As this figure shows, you include an error element in the web.config file for each HTTP error that you want to redirect to a custom error page. In the example, this is done for two types of errors. The first error element specifies that the page named E404.aspx should be displayed if a 404 error occurs. The second element specifies that the page named E500.aspx should be displayed if a 500 error occurs.

You can also specify a default error page that's displayed if an HTTP error that isn't specifically listed in an error element occurs. In the example in this figure, the defaultRedirect attribute specifies that a page named DefaultError.aspx should be displayed if an HTTP error other than 404 or 500 occurs.

A customErrors element in the web.config file that designates custom error pages

```
<system.web>
    .
    .
    .
    <customErrors mode="On" defaultRedirect="DefaultError.aspx">
        <error statusCode="404" redirect="E404.aspx" />
        <error statusCode="500" redirect="E500.aspx" />
    </customErrors>
    .
    .
    .
</system.web>
```

Common HTTP error codes

Code	Description
401	Unauthorized request. The client must be authorized to access the resource.
403	Forbidden request. The client is not allowed to access the resource.
404	File Not Found. The resource could not be located.
500	Internal Server Error. This is usually the result of an unhandled exception.

Description

- The customErrors element in the web.config file lets you designate custom error pages that are automatically displayed when unrecoverable HTTP errors occur. You don't have to write any code to redirect or transfer to these pages.

- To enable custom error pages, add a customErrors element to the system.web element of the web.config file. Then, set the mode attribute to On, and set the defaultRedirect attribute to the name of the generic error page.

- To associate a custom error page with an HTTP error, add an error element that specifies the HTTP error code in the statusCode attribute and the name of the custom error page in the redirect attribute.

- You can also add a customErrors element to the web.config file using the Web Site Administration Tool. To do that, select the Website→ASP.NET Configuration command, display the Application tab, click the Define Default Error Page link, and then select the appropriate settings.

Note

- You shouldn't use a customErrors element if you use the Application_Error method to handle errors. If you do, the customErrors element will be ignored.

Figure 20-11   How to handle HTTP errors with the web.config file

How to handle the back-button problem

If the user clicks the Back button in the browser window to return to a previous ASP.NET form and then posts the form, the application's session state may not correspond to that form. In some cases, this can result in a problem that we refer to as the *back-button problem*. The topics that follow show you how to deal with this problem.

An introduction to the back-button problem

Figure 20-12 illustrates the back-button problem in a shopping cart application. Here, the contents of the user's shopping cart are stored in session state and displayed on the page. The user then deletes one of the two items, which changes the data in session state. At that point, the user changes his mind and clicks the Back button, which displays both items again, even though session state only includes one item.

If the user now proceeds to check out, the order is likely to show one item when the user thinks he has ordered two items. But that depends upon how the application is coded. In the worst cases, the back-button problem may cause an application to crash. In the best cases, clicking on the Back button won't cause a problem at all.

In general, there are two ways to handle the back-button problem. The first is to try to prevent pages from being saved in the browser's cache. Then, when the user clicks the Back button, the old page can't be retrieved and a new request for the page is sent to the server. As you will see in the next figure, ASP.NET provides four methods for doing that, but they don't work if the user's browser ignores the page cache settings that are sent with a response.

The second way is to code critical web forms so they detect when the user attempts to post a page that isn't current. To do that, a form can use timestamps or random numbers to track the use of pages. Because there's no reliable way to prevent a page from being cached and retrieved via the Back button, you should use this second technique whenever possible.

An example of a back-button problem in the Cart page of the Halloween Store application

1. The user adds two products to the shopping cart. The shopping cart data is stored in session state and currently contains two items: one Deranged Cat at $19.99 and one Flying Bats at $69.99. The shopping cart displayed in the browser window looks like this:

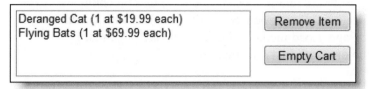

2. The user selects the Deranged Cat product and clicks the Remove Item button to delete it. The product is deleted from the shopping cart in session state and the updated page is sent to the browser:

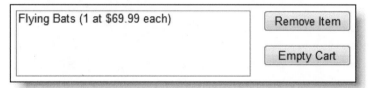

3. The user decides that he or she wants to purchase the Deranged Cat after all and clicks the browser's Back button, thinking this will undo the Delete action. The browser retrieves the previous page from its local cache:

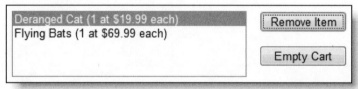

Because the browser redisplayed this page directly from its cache, the Deranged Cat was not added back to the shopping cart in session state. As a result, session state contains only one item even though the web page displays two items.

Two ways to handle the back-button problem

*   Disable browser page caching for user input forms.
*   Use timestamps or random numbers to track pages so you can detect when a page isn't current.

Description

*   When a user clicks the browser's Back button, the browser retrieves a locally cached copy of the previous page without notifying the server. As a result, the information stored in session state can become out of sync with the data displayed in the browser window.

Figure 20-12   An introduction to the back-button problem

How to disable browser page caching

Figure 20-13 shows how you can use four ASP.NET methods to prevent a user's browser from caching pages. All of these methods work by adding information to the HTTP headers that are sent to the browser along with the page.

Unfortunately, some browsers ignore these headers, so these techniques don't guarantee that a page won't be cached. Still, it's not a bad idea to add the code in this figure to the Page_Load method of any ASP.NET page that gets important data like customer or product information.

Methods that set page caching options

Method	Description
`Response.Cache.SetCacheability`	Indicates how the page should be cached. Specify HttpCacheability.NoCache to suppress caching.
`Response.Cache.SetExpires`	Specifies when the cached page should expire. Specify Now().AddSeconds(-1) to mark the page as already expired.
`Response.Cache.SetNoStore`	Specifies that the browser should not cache the page.
`Response.AppendHeader`	Adds a header to the HTTP response object. Specifying "Pragma" for the key and "no-cache" for the value disables caching.

Code that disables caching for a page

```
Response.Cache.SetCacheability(HttpCacheability.NoCache);
Response.Cache.SetExpires(Now.AddSeconds(-1));
Response.Cache.SetNoStore();
Response.AppendHeader("Pragma", "no-cache");
```

Description

- You can limit the effect of the Back button by directing the browser to not cache pages that contain state-sensitive data. Then, when the user attempts to return to a page using the Back button, the page may be reloaded or a warning message may be displayed indicating that the page has expired. If a warning message is displayed, the user can click the Refresh button to reload the page.

- You can place the code to disable browser page caching in the method that handles the Load event of the page. This code should be executed each time the page is loaded.

- Unfortunately, the technique described in this figure doesn't work with all browsers. As a result, you may want to use the technique in the next figure to prevent back-button problems.

Figure 23-13   How to disable browser page caching

How to use timestamps to avoid the back-button problem

Figure 20-14 illustrates the most reliable way to avoid the back-button problem. Here, you see the code for a web page that uses timestamps to determine whether the posted page is current. The basic technique is to record a timestamp in two places when a page is posted: view state and session state. Then, the view state stamp is sent back to the browser and cached along with the rest of the information on the page, while the session state stamp is saved on the server.

Later, when the user posts a page for the second time, the Page_Load method calls a private method named IsExpired. This method retrieves the timestamps from view state and session state and compares them. If they are identical, the page is current and IsExpired returns False. But if they are different, it indicates that the user has posted a page that was retrieved from the browser's cache via the Back button. In that case, the IsExpired method returns True. Then, the Page_Load method redirects to a page named Expired.aspx, which in turn displays a message indicating that the page is out of date and can't be posted.

Notice that before comparing the timestamp items in session state and view state, the IsExpired method checks that both of these items exist. If not, the method returns False so that current timestamps can be saved in both session state and view state.

For this to work, of course, the page must be posted back to the server. That means that you can't use the PostBackUrl property of a button to display another page if you first want to check that the current page hasn't expired. For example, suppose the user deletes an item from the cart and then uses the Back button to add it back as shown in figure 20-12. Then, if the user clicks either the Check Out button or the Continue Shopping button, you want the Expired page to be displayed so the user knows that the shopping cart isn't accurate. To do that, the Check Out and Continue Shopping buttons must post the Cart page back to the server, which doesn't happen if you use the PostBackUrl property.

Incidentally, this technique can also be used to deal with problems that occur when the user clicks the Refresh button. This posts the page to the server and gets a new response, which refreshes the page, so it has nothing to do with the browser's cache. However, this can cause problems like a user ordering a product twice without realizing it. Because most users tend to click the Back button far more than the Refresh button, though, the Refresh button causes far fewer errors. That's why most web developers ignore this problem.

A page that checks timestamps to avoid the back-button problem

```
public partial class Cart : System.Web.UI.Page
{
    private CartItemList cart;

    protected void Page_Load(object sender, EventArgs e)
    {
        if (IsExpired())
            Response.Redirect("Expired.aspx");
        else
            this.SaveTimeStamps();
        cart = CartItemList.GetCart();
        if (!IsPostBack)
            this.DisplayCart();
    }

    private bool IsExpired()
    {
        if (Session["Cart_TimeStamp"] == null)
            return false;
        else if (ViewState["TimeStamp"] == null)
            return false;
        else if (ViewState["TimeStamp"].ToString() ==
                 Session["Cart_TimeStamp"].ToString())
            return false;
        else
            return true;
    }

    private void SaveTimeStamps()
    {
        DateTime dtm = DateTime.Now;
        ViewState.Add("TimeStamp", dtm);
        Session.Add("Cart_TimeStamp", dtm);
    }
    .
    .
    .
}
```

Description

- One way to avoid back-button problems is to use timestamps. The page saves two copies of a timestamp obtained via the Now property: one in view state, the other in session state.

- The IsExpired method tests the view state and session state timestamps to make sure they are the same. If they aren't, the user has posted a page that has been retrieved from the browser's cache.

Note

- Some developers prefer to use random numbers rather than timestamps. Either technique will work.

Figure 20-14   How to use timestamps to avoid the back-button problem

Perspective

This chapter has presented three types of enhancements that you can add to an application once you've got the basic functions working right. In practice, most serious applications use both email and custom error pages to make an application more user friendly and less error prone.

In contrast, many serious applications ignore the back-button problem on the theory that the users should be smart enough to avoid that problem themselves. As a result, clicking on the Back button and re-posting a page will cause a problem on many e-commerce sites. That's why you may want to use the techniques in this chapter to handle that problem on your own web site.

Terms

Simple Mail Transfer Protocol (SMTP)
Post Office Protocol (POP)
Multipurpose Internet Mail Extension (MIME)
mail client
mail server
attachment
UUEncode
Base64 encoding
back-button problem

21

How to use AJAX

This chapter introduces you to the ASP.NET server controls that provide for building AJAX-enabled web pages. These controls let you develop web applications that are more responsive to users and that help reduce the load on the web server. It also introduces you to jQuery AJAX, another technique you can use to develop AJAX-enabled web pages.

An introduction to AJAX

Over the years, web sites have changed from collections of static web pages to complex, dynamic, data-driven web applications. As web applications started performing many of the same functions as traditional desktop applications, users wanted their web applications to perform in the same way. A *rich Internet application (RIA)* is a web application that provides users with an enhanced user interface, advanced functionality, and a quick response time like desktop applications.

There are many frameworks you can use to build a RIA, including Java applets, Adobe Flash player, and Microsoft Silverlight. For most frameworks to work, however, the user must install a plug-in into the web browser. Only one framework uses just the features that are built into all modern web browsers. That framework is known as *Asynchronous JavaScript and XML (AJAX)*.

AJAX concepts

AJAX is not a single technology. It is a collection of technologies that, when used together, enable developers to build a RIA. These technologies allow a web page to communicate with a web server and update the page after it's loaded without having to reload the entire page.

As you saw in chapter one, when a web browser sends an HTTP request to a web server, the server returns an HTTP response that contains the content to be displayed for the page. Whether the page is static or dynamic, once the page is returned, the connection to the server is closed. Even if state is maintained with application variables, session variables, or cookies, a full HTTP request and response cycle must take place to update the web page. This is illustrated in the first diagram in figure 21-1.

In contrast, if portions of a web page are AJAX-enabled, AJAX can update the web page after it's loaded without having to perform a full HTTP request and response cycle. This is illustrated in the second diagram in this figure. Here, AJAX initiates a request that sends just the data that's needed by the server to respond to the request. That can include information about what event triggered the request, as well as the contents of the relevant controls on the page. Then, when the server sends its response back to the browser, the browser can use the data in the response to update the contents of the web page without having to reload the entire page.

AJAX-initiated requests can be repeated as many times as necessary to update a page. For example, one common use for AJAX is to update information on a page at a given time interval. In that case, a full HTTP request and response cycle would only be performed when part of the page that is not AJAX-enabled needs to be updated or when a different page needs to be loaded.

Standard request and response cycle

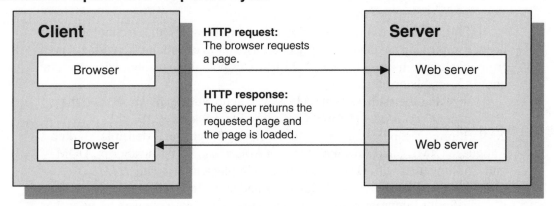

AJAX-enabled request and response cycle

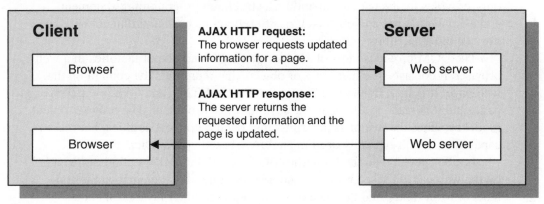

Description

- A *rich Internet application* (*RIA*) is an application that is displayed in a web browser, but has some of the features of a desktop application such as an enhanced user interface and quick response time.
- *Asynchronous JavaScript and XML* (*AJAX*) is one way to build a RIA. It lets you update part of a web page without having to reload the entire page. This can also reduce the load on the web server.
- Each time a standard HTTP request and response cycle is performed, the entire page is returned from the server and the page is loaded into the browser. This type of request and response is required the first time a page is requested even if the page is AJAX-enabled.
- With an AJAX HTTP request and response cycle, the browser can request just the information it needs to update the page. Then, the updated information that's returned from the server can be used to update the page without having to reload it.

Figure 21-1   AJAX concepts

How AJAX works

HTML by itself can only describe a static web page. Other technologies are needed to provide an enhanced user interface and to communicate with a server from within a web page. Figure 21-2 illustrates how these technologies work in an AJAX-enabled web page.

The technologies that enable AJAX web applications are *JavaScript*, the *Document Object Model* (*DOM*), Cascading Style Sheets (CSS), the XMLHttpRequest object, a server-side scripting language, Extensible Markup Language (XML), and *JavaScript Object Notation* (*JSON*). JavaScript, DOM, and CSS, together with HTML, are used to implement *Dynamic HTML* (*DHTML*), which provides for interactive and animated web pages.

JavaScript is a programming language that's built into the web browser that can read and write the properties of HTML tags on a web page. The JavaScript language has no built-in mechanisms for gathering input or displaying output. It only provides mathematical capabilities, structured programming statements, and a few data types and objects. It has to rely on its host environment to provide other facilities.

The DOM provides most of JavaScript's input and output facilities in a web browser. It consists of a hierarchy of objects that represents the content on the web page. It is built by the web browser from the HTML and CSS in the web page, and it is made available to the JavaScript environment. The browser object model provides the rest of JavaScript's input and output capabilities, but these capabilities aren't typically used in an AJAX-based web application.

JavaScript can read the properties of objects in the DOM to find out what's on the web page. These properties include the style of text elements, the contents of form fields, and the state of form controls. When JavaScript code updates an object in the DOM, the web browser updates the web page that's displayed to reflect the changes.

When an event occurs on an object in the DOM, JavaScript code can run to handle the event. These events include user actions such as when the user clicks the mouse, types on the keyboard, or changes elements on a form. They can also include events initiated by the web page, such as a timer expiring.

The XMLHttpRequest object is also provided by the web browser. It has methods that can initiate an HTTP request to the web server. The scripting language on the web server then processes the data in the request and generates a response that's sent back to the browser. When the browser receives the response, it stores it in the XMLHttpRequest object for JavaScript to use as a basis for updating the web page by manipulating the DOM.

Although the XMLHttpRequest object was designed to send and receive XML documents, any text-based format can be used. Because XML documents are hard to create and process in JavaScript, they're typically used only to send data to the server. Then, JSON, which provides a plain text representation of a JavaScript object, is used to send data back to the browser.

The architecture of AJAX

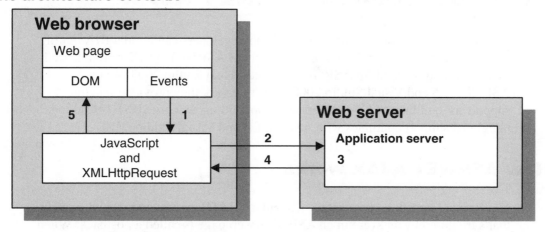

How AJAX updates the contents of a web page

1. An event happens on the web page. This can be the user moving the mouse, clicking a button, or changing a field. Or, this can be a timer going off. This event triggers JavaScript code to execute.

2. JavaScript prepares a request and sends it to the web server. The request contains information about the event and the current state of the controls on the web page.

3. The server receives the data and processes it. Although processing can take place on the client, some actions, such as database access, must happen on the server.

4. The server prepares a response and sends it back to the browser. The response contains the updated state of the controls on the web page.

5. JavaScript parses the response and uses the data it contains to update the contents of the web page by modifying objects in the DOM. The browser then updates the user's screen.

Description

- The web page that is downloaded from the web server contains HTML, CSS, and *JavaScript*. JavaScript is a programming language that's built into the web browser.

- The web browser uses the HTML and CSS to build the *Document Object Model* (*DOM*), which is an object-oriented representation of the content in the page. This content is displayed on the screen for the user. Whenever the objects in the DOM are modified, the web browser updates the content on the screen to display those changes.

- JavaScript is used to run code when events occur in the web page. JavaScript also has access to the DOM to determine the state of controls on the page and to make changes to the DOM that are shown to the user.

- The XMLHttpRequest object that's built into the web browser is used to communicate with the web server. JavaScript is used to access the functionality of the XMLHttpRequest object.

- When AJAX was first developed, it used XML to format the data that's sent between the web browser and web server. For most requests, *JavaScript Object Notation* (*JSON*) is now used to send data back to the web browser.

Figure 21-2   How AJAX works

An introduction to ASP.NET AJAX

Microsoft developed ASP.NET AJAX so developers can build a RIA out of standard ASP.NET controls. The components of ASP.NET AJAX were released as a separate download for ASP.NET 2.0 and Visual Studio 2005. When ASP.NET 3.5 and Visual Studio 2008 were released, they provided integrated support for building AJAX-enabled web applications using ASP.NET. And that integrated support continues with ASP.NET 4 and Visual Studio 2010.

How ASP.NET AJAX works

As you learned in chapter one, a standard HTTP request and response cycle that's triggered by an event in an ASP.NET web page is called a postback. When a postback occurs, the view state of the controls on the page is sent to the server as part of the request. Then, the server processes the request, updates the view state as necessary, and sends a response back to the browser that contains a new page with the new view state.

In contrast, ASP.NET AJAX enables a process known as an *asynchronous postback*. This is similar to a standard postback in that the view state of controls on the page is sent to the server in response to an event on the page. In an asynchronous postback, however, the XMLHttpRequest object is used to send the view state to the server. Then, the response that's returned by the server is used to update the controls on the page without having to reload the entire web page in the browser.

Figure 21-3 shows the three components of ASP.NET AJAX and illustrates how they work. The *ASP.NET AJAX client-side framework* is a JavaScript library that is loaded by the web browser when an AJAX-enabled ASP.NET page is displayed. It allows JavaScript code to interact with the ASP.NET application server through the XMLHttpRequest object it encapsulates.

ASP.NET AJAX also provides five server controls. They are used to AJAX-enable the ASP.NET web page so that other ASP.NET server controls can be updated in the web browser without having to reload the page. These controls render JavaScript code as part of the web page just as other controls render HTML and CSS. The code they render uses the ASP.NET AJAX client-side framework to process events in the web page, manage and update controls in the web page, and trigger an asynchronous postback to interact with the server.

The ASP.NET AJAX client-side framework and the ASP.NET AJAX server controls are built into ASP.NET 4 and Visual Studio 2010. In contrast, the *ASP.NET AJAX Control Toolkit* is not. Instead, it's available as a separate download for Visual Studio 2010. This toolkit consists of components and server control extensions that provide a variety of effects, animations, and interactive features.

The architecture of ASP.NET AJAX

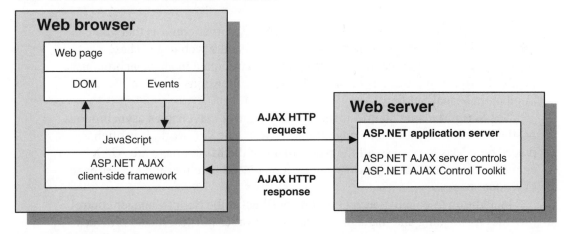

Components of ASP.NET AJAX

Component	Description
ASP.NET AJAX client-side framework	A JavaScript library that's loaded on the client to support the ASP.NET AJAX server controls.
ASP.NET AJAX server controls	Five server controls that encapsulate other ASP.NET controls on the web page to indicate that they will be controlled on the client by the ASP.NET AJAX client-side framework.
ASP.NET AJAX Control Toolkit	An open source project that provides more than 40 ASP.NET controls that you can use to build AJAX-enabled web applications.

Description

- Microsoft developed a set of extensions to ASP.NET code-named Atlas that provided AJAX support. These extensions were released as a fully supported extension of ASP.NET 2.0 in January of 2007. They have been included as built-in features of ASP.NET since the release of ASP.NET 3.5 and Visual Studio 2008.

- An *asynchronous postback* is the process used by ASP.NET to perform a partial-page update. During an asynchronous postback, the view state of the web page is sent to the server, which processes the request and sends back the new view state of the controls being updated.

- The ASP.NET AJAX server controls enclose other ASP.NET server controls to make them AJAX-enabled. These controls can then be updated using an asynchronous postback.

- A single page can have one or more groups of AJAX-enabled controls that can be updated independently or simultaneously. Server controls that are not AJAX-enabled still trigger a full postback that causes the entire page to be reloaded.

- The ASP.NET AJAX Control Toolkit adds animation and effects to standard server controls. It is not officially supported by Microsoft.

Figure 21-3   How ASP.NET AJAX works

The ASP.NET AJAX server controls

Figure 21-4 describes the five ASP.NET AJAX server controls that you can use to enable and manage asynchronous postbacks on a web page. These controls allow the other controls on the page to participate in an asynchronous postback. You'll find these controls in the AJAX Extensions group of the Toolbox in Visual Studio.

The ScriptManager control is the primary control that enables asynchronous postbacks, and it must be on a page for ASP.NET AJAX to work. It is often placed on a Master page so all the pages that use the Master page are AJAX-enabled. The other AJAX controls can then be placed on either the Master page or content pages.

In addition to enabling asynchronous postbacks, the ScriptManager control provides for loading and managing additional JavaScript files. It also provides for registering web services or WCF services so they can be accessed by JavaScript code on the client. *Web services* and *WCF services* both provide a way for one web site to communicate with another web site. Because WCF is a newer technology, it's the technology Microsoft recommends you use. You can learn more about creating and using WCF services in chapter 23. For the purposes of this chapter, though, you can think of web services and WCF services as essentially interchangeable. Because of that, I'll use the term *services* in this chapter to refer to either type of service.

Note that you can have only one ScriptManager control on a page. In addition, if you add a ScriptManager control to a Master page, you can't also add one to a content page that uses the master page. However, you can add a ScriptManagerProxy control to the content page. This control lets you load additional JavaScript files or register additional services needed by the content page but not by all the pages that use the Master page.

In this context, a *proxy* is an object that's created on the client that you can use to access a service that's running on the server. When you use the ScriptManagerProxy control, it automatically creates the proxy for you.

After you add a ScriptManager control to a page, you can use the UpdatePanel control to enclose standard ASP.NET server controls. Then, the controls inside the UpdatePanel control are updated in place when an asynchronous postback occurs. Note that you can have multiple UpdatePanel controls on a page. You can also have controls outside the UpdatePanel controls. If an event occurs on one of those controls, a full postback occurs on the web page.

Although an asynchronous postback is faster than a full postback, there may be times when an asynchronous postback takes more than a few seconds to perform. In that case, you may want to provide a visual indication that the postback is in progress. To do that, you can use the UpdateProgress control.

If you want to trigger an asynchronous postback at a set time interval, you can use the Timer control. This can be useful if you want to poll the server for any updates that need to be displayed. Keep in mind, however, that if an asynchronous postback is triggered too often, the load on the server can increase dramatically.

ASP.NET AJAX server controls

Control	Description
ScriptManager	Enables the use of the other ASP.NET AJAX controls, loads the ASP.NET AJAX client-side framework, and manages client-side JavaScript code.
ScriptManagerProxy	Extends the scripting services provided by a ScriptManager control.
UpdatePanel	Identifies a set of server controls to be updated using an asynchronous postback.
UpdateProgress	Provides visual feedback that an asynchronous postback is in progress.
Timer	Periodically triggers an asynchronous postback on an UpdatePanel control.

The ScriptManager control

- You can only have one ScriptManager control on a page. This includes master and content pages. If you put a ScriptManager control on a master page, you can't use one on a content page. If there is more than one ScriptManager control on a page, an Invalid Operation exception is generated.

- The ScriptManager control can also be used to load and manage additional JavaScript files and to register *web services* or *WCF services* so they can be accessed by JavaScript code on the client. See figure 21-6 for details.

The ScriptManagerProxy control

- The ScriptManagerProxy control lets you load JavaScript files and register WCF services or web services. It can be used in a content page if the master page contains a ScriptManager control.

The UpdatePanel control

- The UpdatePanel control is a container control that holds other server controls that will be updated during an asynchronous postback. All controls inside an UpdatePanel control will be updated at the same time. A page can contain multiple UpdatePanel controls, each with a different set of controls.

The UpdateProgress control

- The UpdateProgress control provides a visual indication that an asynchronous postback is in progress. Then, the user will know to wait until the postback completes before doing anything else on the page.

The Timer control

- When one or more UpdatePanel controls need to be updated automatically, you can use the Timer control to trigger partial-page updates at a set time interval.

Figure 21-4   The ASP.NET AJAX server controls

The ASP.NET AJAX Control Toolkit

The ASP.NET AJAX Control Toolkit provides more dynamic, visually appealing user interface controls. It is not a required component of ASP.NET AJAX and it is not built into Visual Studio 2010. Instead, it's an open source project hosted at Microsoft's Codeplex web site that you can download and use for free.

Figure 21-5 lists some of the most common controls in the toolkit. These controls extend the functions of existing ASP.NET controls. For example, the Calendar control extends the function of a TextBox control.

The toolkit currently contains over forty control extensions, and more are being added with every release. To view descriptions of these controls along with live examples, you can go to the first web site listed in this figure. To download the toolkit, you can go to the second web site.

The ASP.NET AJAX Control Toolkit is developed by volunteers and is not supported by Microsoft. Because of that, developers are responsible for checking for security updates related to the toolkit. If you publish a web page that uses an extension from the toolkit that is later found to have a security weakness, you must download the updated toolkit and republish the web page. You may also want to check the toolkit periodically for new features and bug fixes.

Common ASP.NET AJAX Control Toolkit controls

Control	Description
Accordion	Contains multiple panes of content, but only displays one at a time.
Animation	Adds methods to change the position, size, opacity, and color of a control. They can be combined to create many dynamic effects.
Calendar	Shows a calendar in a pop-up window for easy date entry.
CollapsiblePanel	Provides a one-click, hide/show effect for a control.
DragPanel	Lets the user move a panel of content around on the page.
DropShadow	Adds a drop shadow to a control.
HoverMenu	Displays a menu when the user hovers over a control.
ModalPopup	A pop-up control that hides the page until the user selects an option.
NumericUpDown	Adds up and down arrows to a text box for changing the value.
PagingBulletedList	Displays a long list of items across multiple pages.
PopupControl	Hides a set of controls until they are displayed in a pop-up window.
RoundedCorners	Adds rounded corners to a control.
Slider	Lets the user enter a value by dragging a slider.
SlideShow	Shows multiple images in one image tag. The images can change automatically or the user can manually scroll back and forth.
TabContainer	Shows multiple panes of content in a tabbed format.
TextBoxWatermark	Displays a message in an "empty" text box with a custom style. The text goes away when the user clicks in the text box.
ToggleButton	Replaces a check box with two images that indicate whether the check box is checked or not.

A web site that has live examples of the toolkit

`http://www.asp.net/ajax/ajaxcontroltoolkit/samples/`

A web site that provides downloads of the toolkit

`http://ajaxcontroltoolkit.codeplex.com/`

Description

- The ASP.NET AJAX Control Toolkit provides extensions to ASP.NET controls that enable animations, special effects, and dynamic data bindings through asynchronous postbacks.

- The toolkit is not an official part of ASP.NET. It is an open source project developed by the community at Microsoft's Codeplex web site.

- The toolkit is constantly being updated. You should check the toolkit site often for new features, bug fixes, and security vulnerabilities.

Figure 21-5   The ASP.NET AJAX Control Toolkit

How to use the ASP.NET AJAX server controls

The ASP.NET AJAX server controls can be added to almost any page to manage asynchronous postbacks. In the topics that follow, you'll learn the details of using each of the five controls.

How to use the ScriptManager control

As you know, you must add a ScriptManager control to a web page to enable asynchronous postbacks. Figure 21-6 presents some common attributes of this control along with some code examples. Note that this code must be added inside a Form element before any other ASP.NET AJAX controls.

By default, all the JavaScript code for a page is loaded before the user interface is displayed. This ensures that the user interface is fully functional when it's displayed, which is usually what you want. In some cases, though, the user interface takes too long to display. Then, you should consider setting the LoadScriptsBeforeUI attribute to False so the user interface is displayed before the JavaScript is loaded. If you do that, keep in mind that the user interface may not be fully functional when it's first displayed.

The AsyncPostBackTimeout attribute determines how long the ASP.NET AJAX client-side framework waits for a response after triggering an asynchronous postback. If a response isn't received within the specified time period, an exception is raised and the postback is cancelled. If the value of this attribute is set to a time interval that's too short, users will see a larger number of errors. If it's set to a time interval that's too long, users will wait too long to find out that there's a problem with the request.

The IsInAsyncPostBack attribute is a read-only Boolean value that is set to True while an asynchronous postback is in progress. This attribute can be examined by either client-side or server-side code. In most cases, you'll use it in the Load event handler for a web page. Because this event handler is executed for full postbacks as well as asynchronous postbacks, you can use the IsInAsyncPostBack attribute to execute code depending on which type of postback is being performed. For example, code that initializes a control would not run during an asynchronous postback.

In addition to setting attributes of the ScriptManager control, you can add Scripts and Services child elements. You use the Scripts element to load additional JavaScript code. Within this element, you code asp:ScriptReference elements that identify the files that contain the code.

You use the Services element to create service proxies that allow the use of WCF services and web services in client-side JavaScript code. Within this element, you code asp:ServiceReference elements that specify the location of the svc file for each WCF service or the asmx file for each web service.

Common attributes of the ScriptManager control

Attribute	Description
AsyncPostBackTimeout	Sets the time in seconds before an asynchronous postback times out if there is no response. The default is 90.
EnablePageMethods	Determines if shared methods on an ASP.NET page that are marked as web methods can be called from client scripts as if they're part of a service. The default is False.
EnableScriptLocalization	Determines if the server looks for localized versions of script files and uses them if they exist. The default is True.
IsInAsyncPostBack	A read-only Boolean value that is True if the page is currently processing an asynchronous postback.
LoadScriptsBeforeUI	Determines if scripts are loaded before or after user interface elements. If False, the user interface may load more quickly but not be functional at first. The default is True.

Aspx code for a ScriptManager control

```
<asp:ScriptManager ID="ScriptManager1" runat="server">
</asp:ScriptManager>
```

Aspx code for a ScriptManager control that registers scripts

```
<asp:ScriptManager ID="ScriptManager1" runat="server">
    <Scripts>
        <asp:ScriptReference Path="~/Scripts/SampleScript.js" />
        <asp:ScriptReference Assembly="SampleAssembly"
            Name="SampleAssembly.SampleScript.js" />
    </Scripts>
</asp:ScriptManager>
```

Aspx code for a ScriptManager control that registers a WCF service

```
<asp:ScriptManager ID="ScriptManager1" runat="server">
  <Services>
    <asp:ServiceReference
        Path="http://www.example.com/Services/SampleService.svc" />
  </Services>
</asp:ScriptManager>
```

A path that registers a web service

```
Path="~/Services/SampleService.asmx" />
```

Description

- The Scripts element of a ScriptManager control can contain asp:ScriptReference elements that cause the ScriptManager control to load and manage additional scripts. The asp:ScriptReference elements can load JavaScript code from a file using the Path attribute or from an assembly using the Assembly and Name attributes.

- The Services element of a ScriptManager control can contain asp:ServiceReference elements that cause the ScriptManager to create service proxies. To create a WCF service proxy, code a Path attribute that points to the svc file for the service. To create a web service proxy, the Path attribute should point to the asmx file for the web service.

Figure 21-6   How to use the ScriptManager control

How to use the ScriptManagerProxy control

The ScriptManagerProxy control is used to extend the capabilities of a ScriptManager control. The most common scenario for using a ScriptManagerProxy control is when you use a ScriptManager control on a Master page and you want to add either JavaScript code or a service proxy to a content page that uses that master page. This is illustrated in figure 21-7. Here, you can see a content page that uses a master page that contains an image and a ScriptManager control.

Unlike the ScriptManager control, you can have more than one ScriptManagerProxy controls on a page. However, these controls can't be used to modify the properties of the ScriptManager control. They can only add additional asp:ScriptReference and asp:ServiceReference elements to a page. As you can see in the second and third examples in this figure, you code these elements just like you do for a ScriptManager control.

A content page with a ScriptManagerProxy control

The aspx code for the ScriptManagerProxy control

```
<asp:ScriptManagerProxy ID="ScriptManagerProxy1" runat="server">
</asp:ScriptManagerProxy>
```

Aspx code for a ScriptManagerProxy control that registers scripts

```
<asp:ScriptManagerProxy ID="ScriptManager1" runat="server">
    <Scripts>
        <asp:ScriptReference Path="~/Scripts/SampleScript.js" />
        <asp:ScriptReference Assembly="SampleAssembly"
            Name="SampleAssembly.SampleScript.js" />
    </Scripts>
</asp:ScriptManagerProxy>
```

Aspx code for a ScriptManagerProxy control that registers a WCF service

```
<asp:ScriptManagerProxy ID="ScriptManager1" runat="server">
    <Services>
        <asp:ServiceReference
            Path="http://www.example.com/Services/SampleService.svc" />
    </Services>
</asp:ScriptManagerProxy>
```

Description

- The ScriptManagerProxy control lets you extend the scripting services that are provided by a ScriptManager control. It's used most often on a content page whose master page contains a ScriptManager control.

- You can have multiple ScriptManagerProxy controls on a page. However, the ScriptManagerProxy controls can't override the properties of the ScriptManager control.

Figure 21-7   How to use the ScriptManagerProxy control

How to use the UpdatePanel control

The UpdatePanel control encloses other server controls that are updated during an asynchronous postback. These controls are placed inside the ContentTemplate element of the UpdatePanel control. Then, the controls within this element are updated as a group. Figure 21-8 shows how to use the UpdatePanel control.

When controls are added to an update panel, they are automatically made triggers for the panel. That means that if any of the controls cause an asynchronous postback, the panel is updated. In most cases, that's what you want. If you don't want the controls in an update panel to trigger an update, however, you can set the ChildrenAsTriggers attribute of the panel to False. Then, you'll need to identify the controls that trigger an update in the Triggers element of the UpdatePanel control. I'll describe this element in just a minute.

As you know, you can have as many UpdatePanel controls on a page as you need. In addition, UpdatePanel controls can be nested inside each other. If you nest UpdatePanel controls, you should know that server controls in a child update panel won't trigger the update of the parent panel. That's true even if the ChildrenAsTriggers attribute of the panels is set to True.

By default, a panel is updated any time an asynchronous postback occurs on the page. This behavior is controlled by the UpdateMode attribute of the UpdatePanel control, which is set to Always by default. If you want a panel to be updated only when an asynchronous postback is caused by one of the panel's triggers, you can set the UpdateMode attribute to Conditional. Note that if an UpdatePanel control is nested inside another UpdatePanel control, it is always updated when its parent UpdatePanel control is updated. Also note that if you set the ChildrenAsTriggers attribute to False, you must set the UpdateMode attribute to Conditional or an exception will occur.

You can specify the controls that cause a panel to be updated in the Triggers element of the control, as illustrated in the second example in this figure. Here, the Triggers element includes two asp elements. The first one, asp:AsyncPostBackTrigger, identifies a control that causes an asynchronous postback to occur. In this case, the control is defined outside the update panel. However, you can also use this element for a control that's defined within an update panel. Notice that, in addition to naming the control that causes the postback to occur, the EventName attribute names the event that causes the postback. This isn't required, however. If this attribute is omitted, the postback occurs for the default event of the control.

The second element, asp:PostBackTrigger, names a control inside the update panel that causes a full postback to occur rather than an asynchronous postback. In other words, instead of causing just the panel to be updated, it causes the entire page to be reloaded.

This figure also lists some compatibility issues you may encounter when you use certain controls within an UpdatePanel control. You'll want to review this list before you use the UpdatePanel control so you're aware of any potential problems when you use these controls.

Two attributes of the UpdatePanel control

Attribute	Description
ChildrenAsTriggers	Determines if the controls in a panel are treated as triggers that cause the content of the panel to be updated when a control causes a postback. The default is True.
UpdateMode	Determines when the content of a panel is updated. If set to Always, the panel is updated whenever a postback occurs. If set to Conditional, the panel is updated only when one if its own triggers causes a postback. A nested UpdatePanel control is always updated when its parent UpdatePanel control is updated. The default is Always.

The starting aspx code for an UpdatePanel control

```
<asp:UpdatePanel ID="UpdatePanel1" runat="server">
    <ContentTemplate>
    </ContentTemplate>
</asp:UpdatePanel>
```

The aspx code for an UpdatePanel control that specifies triggers

```
<asp:UpdatePanel ID="UpdatePanel1" runat="server">
    <ContentTemplate>
        <asp:Button ID="Button2" runat="server" Text="Add" />
    </ContentTemplate>
    <Triggers>
        <asp:AsyncPostBackTrigger ControlID="Button1" EventName="Click" />
        <asp:PostBackTrigger ControlID="Button2" />
    </Triggers>
</asp:UpdatePanel>
```

Description

- The ContentTemplate element of an UpdatePanel control contains the controls that are updated during an asynchronous postback. UpdatePanel controls can be nested.

- You can use the Triggers element to specify controls that cause the panel to be updated. The asp:AsyncPostBackTrigger element identifies a control inside or outside of the UpdatePanel control that triggers an asynchronous postback. The asp:PostBackTrigger element identifies a control inside the UpdatePanel control that triggers a full postback.

Compatibility issues with other controls

- The GridView and DetailsView controls can't be used in an update panel if you set their EnableSortingAndPagingCallbacks attributes to True.

- The TreeView control can't be used in an update panel if you enable callbacks that are not part of an asynchronous postback, set its styles directly as control attributes, or set the EnableClientScript attribute to False.

- The Menu control can't be used if you set its styles directly as control attributes.

- A FileUpload control can only be used as a postback trigger for an update panel.

- The Login, PasswordRecovery, ChangePassword, and CreateUserWizard controls can only be used if you convert their contents to editable templates.

Figure 21-8   How to use the UpdatePanel control

How to use the Timer control

The Timer control triggers a periodic asynchronous postback. This control is typically placed inside the ContentTemplate element of the UpdatePanel control that's updated when the postback occurs. If it isn't placed inside an UpdatePanel control, it triggers a full postback of the entire page.

Figure 21-9 illustrates how the Timer control works. To start, you can determine how often an asynchronous postback occurs by setting the Interval attribute of the control. This attribute is measured in milliseconds (1/1000th of a second). In the example in this figure, the Interval attribute is set to 10,000, or 10 seconds.

When you set the Interval attribute, you should be careful not to specify a value that's too small. If you do, it can cause a severe load on the server, particularly when many people have the page displayed. A value of 5,000 to 10,000 milliseconds is probably the smallest value you would want to use under most circumstances.

Also, you shouldn't expect the timer to be very accurate. That's because it's controlled by the timing mechanisms available to JavaScript in the web browser, and these mechanisms can be off by several hundred milliseconds.

If you need to, you can have two or more Timer controls on the same page. In most cases, you'll place these controls in different update panels. Then, you'll typically set the UpdateMode attribute of the UpdatePanel controls to Conditional so that the Timer in one panel won't trigger the update of another panel.

Although you can use two or more Timer controls in the same update panel, there's usually no need to do that. Instead, if you need an update panel to refresh at different rates depending on what's happening in the web page, you can use a single Timer control and change its Interval attribute. If you want to use two or more Timer controls with preset intervals, however, you can use the Enabled attribute of the controls to determine which control is used at any given time.

A Timer control in Design view

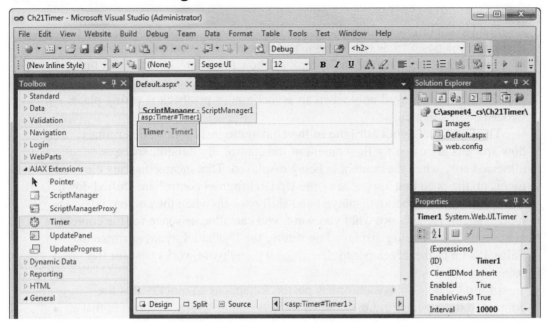

Two attributes of the Timer control

Attribute	Description
Interval	Determines how often in milliseconds the control triggers an asynchronous postback. The default value is 60,000 milliseconds (60 seconds).
Enabled	Determines whether a postback occurs when the time specified by the Interval attribute elapses. The default is True. You might set this attribute to False if you include more than one Timer control in the same panel, but you want only one to initiate a postback at any given time.

The aspx code for an UpdatePanel control with a Timer control

```
<asp:UpdatePanel ID="UpdatePanel1" runat="server">
    <ContentTemplate>
        <asp:Timer ID="Timer1" runat="server" Interval="10000">
        </asp:Timer>
    </ContentTemplate>
</asp:UpdatePanel>
```

Description

- The Timer control should be placed inside the ContentTemplate element of the UpdatePanel control that is updated when the timer triggers an asynchronous postback.

- Setting the value of the Interval attribute too small can cause an increase in the load on the web server and an increase in the amount of traffic to the web server.

- The accuracy of the Timer control is determined by the accuracy of the JavaScript implementation in the user's web browser.

Figure 21-9   How to use the Timer control

How to use the UpdateProgress control

The UpdateProgress control displays information to the user when an asynchronous postback is in progress. You code this information within the ProgressTemplate element of the control as shown in figure 21-10. Here, the information consists of simple text, but you can include controls as well. Note that this text is displayed only when an asynchronous postback is taking place. Otherwise, it's hidden.

The DynamicLayout attribute of the UpdateProgress control determines how space is allocated for the content of the control. By default, space is allocated only when the content is being displayed. That means that any elements on the page that appear after the UpdateProgress control are shifted down when the content is being displayed and shift back up when the content is hidden again. If that's not what you want, you can allocate space for the content even when it isn't being displayed by setting the DynamicLayout attribute to False. It's up to the developer to determine which layout works best for the page.

In some cases, an asynchronous postback happens so quickly that the content of the UpdateProgress control flickers on the screen. To prevent that from happening, you can set the DisplayAfter attribute to determine how long the control should wait after the asynchronous postback starts to display its content. By default, this attribute is set to 0.5 seconds. Then, if the postback takes longer than that to complete, the content of the UpdateProgress control is displayed on the page.

In most cases, you'll code the UpdateProgress control within an UpdatePanel control as shown in this figure. Then, its content is displayed only when an asynchronous postback occurs on that panel. However, you can also code an UpdateProgress control outside an UpdatePanel control. Then, you can set its AssociatedUpdatePanelID attribute to the ID of the panel you want to use it with. Or, you can omit this attribute, in which case its content is displayed anytime an asynchronous postback occurs.

An UpdateProgress control in Design view

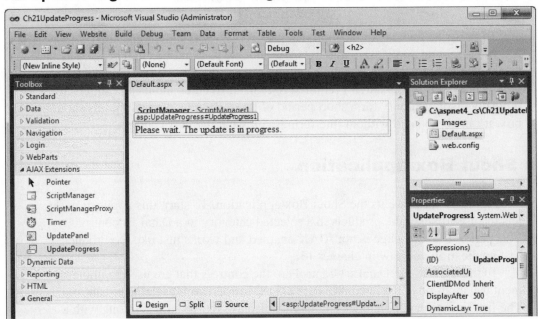

Three attributes of the UpdateProgress control

Attribute	Description
DynamicLayout	Determines whether space is allocated on the page for the content of the control when it isn't displayed. The default is True, which means that space is dynamically allocated. If set to False, space is allocated for the content even though it won't be seen until an asynchronous postback occurs.
DisplayAfter	Determines how long in milliseconds after the asynchronous postback has started to display the content. The default is 500 milliseconds (0.5 seconds). This value can prevent the content from flickering when the postback happens quickly.
AssociatedUpdatePanelID	The ID of the UpdatePanel control that the control is associated with.

The aspx code for an UpdatePanel control with an UpdateProgress control

```
<asp:UpdatePanel ID="UpdatePanel1" runat="server">
    <ContentTemplate>
        <asp:UpdateProgress ID="UpdateProgress1" runat="server">
            <ProgressTemplate>
                Please wait. The update is in progress.
            </ProgressTemplate>
        </asp:UpdateProgress>
    </ContentTemplate>
</asp:UpdatePanel>
```

Description

- An UpdateProgress control must contain a ProgressTemplate element that defines the content of the control. This content is displayed only while an asynchronous postback is in progress. It is hidden after the asynchronous postback is complete.

Figure 21-10   How to use the UpdateProgress control

An application that uses AJAX

To illustrate how an application that uses AJAX works, the topics that follow present an application that uses a shout box. A shout box can be used to implement an informal comment system on a web site. Unlike traditional comment systems, users aren't required to register to enter shouts and shouts are typically displayed only for a short period of time. By AJAX-enabling this shout box, it can be updated without interfering with what the user is doing.

The Shout Box application

Figure 21-11 presents the Shout Box application. To start, this application lets the user display the products in a selected category in a DataList control. This part of the web page is not AJAX-enabled and works just like the Product List application you saw in chapter 13.

To the right of the DataList control are the controls that are used to implement the shout box. These controls are placed inside two UpdatePanel controls. The first update panel includes a label that displays the shout box, along with a Timer control that causes the shout box to be updated every five seconds. The second update panel includes two text boxes that let the user enter the information for a shout, labels that identify the text boxes, required field validators for the text boxes, a button that submits the shout, and an UpdateProgress control.

Notice that the shouts in the shout box are displayed in reverse chronological order. In other words, they're displayed from the newest shout to the oldest shout. That way, if there are many shouts being displayed, the user won't have to scroll down to see the newest ones.

The shouts for this application are displayed in the shout box for three minutes. The shouts that are currently displayed are stored in a list in application state. That makes sense since the shouts are temporary. If you wanted to have a permanent record of the shouts, however, you could store them in a database and then display just the most recent shouts in the shout box.

The Shout Box application

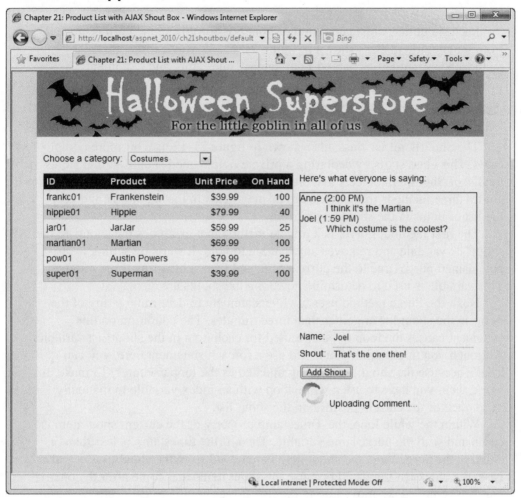

Description

- The Shout Box application is a variation of the Product List application you saw in chapter 13. It lets users post short messages, called shouts, which are then displayed in a shout box for other users to see.

- A list of the shout items that are currently displayed is stored in an application state variable. Shout items that are over three minutes old are deleted from this list whenever the shout box is updated or displayed.

- To implement the shout box, this page uses two UpdatePanel controls. The first one contains a label that's used to display the shout items and a Timer control that updates the panel every five seconds. The second one contains the controls that are used to submit a shout and display a progress indicator. It also contains required field validators for the two text boxes.

Figure 21-11   The Shout Box application

The ShoutItem class

Each shout that's displayed in the shout box for this application is created from the ShoutItem class shown in figure 21-12. As you can see, this class includes three properties named UserName, Timestamp, and Comment.

The ShoutItemList class

The ShoutItemList class, also shown in figure 21-12, is a bit more complicated. This class starts by declaring a private field named shoutList that stores the list of ShoutItem objects that are displayed in the shout box. Then, it includes three methods that are used to display items in the shout box and keep the list of items in the shout box current.

The first method, Purge, is a private method that examines the shouts in the shoutList variable and removes any that are too old. It starts by setting a variable named purgeTime to the current time and then subtracting three minutes. This variable is used to determine how long the shouts are displayed.

Next, the Purge method uses a while statement to determine if any of the items in the shout list are older than three minutes. The condition on this statement causes the loop to be executed for each item in the shoutList variable. Although you might think you could use a foreach statement here, you can't. That's because the shout list is being updated as the loop executes. To make this work, then, you have to use a while loop with an index variable to manually keep track of the current position in the shout list.

Within the while loop, the Timestamp property of the current shout item is compared with the purgeTime variable. Then, if the timestamp is less than or equal to the purge time, the shout item is removed from the shout list. In that case, the index isn't updated because the shout items that come after the one that was removed are moved up in the list. If the shout item isn't removed from the list, however, the index variable is increased by one so the next item can be checked.

The public Add method adds the shout item that's passed to it to the beginning of the shout list. But first, it calls the Purge method to remove any old shout items. In addition, it executes the Sleep method of the current thread to delay the Add method by two seconds. I included this method to ensure that the UpdateProgress control is displayed. Of course, you wouldn't want to include code like this in a production application.

The public Display method returns a text string that contains the contents of the shout box. Like the Add method, it starts by calling the Purge method. Then, it creates a StringBuilder object that will store the shout box text.

If the shout list contains at least one item, the Display method continues by adding a <dl> tag to the StringBuilder object. This tag defines a definition list, which can contain a formatted list of text items. Then, it uses a foreach loop to add the information for each shout item to this list. In this case, the user name

The ShoutItem.cs file

```csharp
using System;

public class ShoutItem
{
    public string UserName { get; set; };
    public DateTime Timestamp { get; set; };
    public string Comment { get; set; };
}
```

The ShoutItemList.cs file

```csharp
using System;
using System.Collections.Generic;
using System.Text;

public class ShoutItemList
{
    private List<ShoutItem> shoutList = new List<ShoutItem>();

    private void Purge() {
        DateTime purgeTime = DateTime.Now;
        purgeTime = purgeTime.AddMinutes(-3);
        int i = 0;
        while (i < shoutList.Count)
        {
            if (shoutList[i].Timestamp <= purgeTime)
                shoutList.RemoveAt(i);
            else
                i += 1;
        }
    }

    public void Add(ShoutItem shout) {
        Purge();
        System.Threading.Thread.Sleep(2000);
        shoutList.Insert(0, shout);
    }

    public string Display() {
        Purge();
        StringBuilder shoutBoxText = new StringBuilder();
        if (shoutList.Count > 0)
        {
            shoutBoxText.AppendLine("<dl>");
            foreach (ShoutItem shout in shoutList)
            {
                shoutBoxText.Append("<dt>" + shout.UserName + " (");
                shoutBoxText.Append(shout.Timestamp.ToShortTimeString() +
                    ")</dt>");
                shoutBoxText.AppendLine("<dd>" + shout.Comment + "</dd>");
            }
            shoutBoxText.AppendLine("</dl>");
        }
        return shoutBoxText.ToString();
    }
}
```

Figure 21-12   The ShoutItem and ShoutItemList classes

and timestamp are coded within a <dt> tag, which defines a definition term, and the comment is coded within a <dd> tag, which defines a definition. The <dt> tag causes the text to be left-aligned with no space above or below it. The <dd> tag causes the text to be indented. If you look back at the shout box in figure 21-11, you'll see how this works.

The aspx file

Figure 21-13 presents the aspx file for this application. Since you've already seen code like much of what's presented here, I'll just focus on the code that implements the AJAX controls. This code starts near the bottom of page 2 of this listing.

To start, a ScriptManager control is used to AJAX-enable the page. This control is followed by an UpdatePanel control that contains the label that displays the text of the shout box and the Timer control that's used to refresh the shout box. Because the Interval attribute of this control is set to 5000, it causes an asynchronous postback of the panel to occur every five seconds.

This panel also needs to be refreshed when the user adds a new shout. Because the UpdateMode attribute of the update panel has been left at its default of Always, this happens automatically. In case this attribute is ever changed, though, I included a Triggers element in the UpdatePanel control. This element contains a trigger that causes an asynchronous postback to occur when the user clicks the Add Shout button.

The second UpdatePanel control starts on page 3 of this listing. It contains the controls for submitting a shout. Notice that the UpdateMode attribute of this control is set to Conditional. That way, the panel is updated only when one of its own controls causes a postback.

This update panel contains an UpdateProgress control. Because the DynamicLayout attribute of this control has been set to False, space is reserved for it on the page even when it's not displayed. The content of this control includes a simple animated gif and a text comment.

The Default.aspx file   Page 1

```
<%@ Page Language="C#" AutoEventWireup="true" CodeFile="Default.aspx.cs"
Inherits="_Default" %>

<!DOCTYPE html PUBLIC "-//W3C//DTD XHTML 1.0 Transitional//EN"
"http://www.w3.org/TR/xhtml1/DTD/xhtml1-transitional.dtd">

<html xmlns="http://www.w3.org/1999/xhtml">
<head runat="server">
    <title>Chapter 21: Product List with AJAX Shout Box</title>
    <link href="Main.css" rel="stylesheet" type="text/css" />
</head>
<body>
  <form id="form1" runat="server">
  <div id="page">
    <div id="header">
      <asp:Image ID="Image1" runat="server" ImageUrl="~/Images/banner.jpg" />
    </div>
    <div id="main">
      <p>Choose a category: 
        <asp:DropDownList ID="Category" runat="server" AutoPostBack="True"
            Width="130px" DataSourceID="SqlDataSource1"
            DataTextField="LongName" DataValueField="CategoryID">
        </asp:DropDownList>
        <asp:SqlDataSource ID="SqlDataSource1" runat="server"
            ConnectionString=
                "<%$ ConnectionStrings:HalloweenConnectionString %>"
            SelectCommand="SELECT [CategoryID], [LongName]
                          FROM [Categories] ORDER BY [LongName]">
        </asp:SqlDataSource>
      </p>
      <div id="datalist">
        <asp:DataList ID="ddlProducts" runat="server"
            DataKeyField="ProductID" DataSourceID="SqlDataSource2"
            CellPadding="3" GridLines="Vertical">
          <HeaderTemplate>
            <table>
              <tr>
                <td class="col1">ID</td>
                <td class="col2">Product</td>
                <td class="col3">Unit Price</td>
                <td class="col4">On Hand</td>
              </tr>
            </table>
          </HeaderTemplate>
```

Figure 21-13   The aspx file for the Shout Box application (part 1 of 3)

The Default.aspx file

```
<ItemTemplate>
  <table>
    <tr>
      <td class="col1">
        <asp:Label ID="lblID" runat="server"
            Text='<%# Eval("ProductID") %>' />
      </td>
      <td class="col2">
        <asp:Label ID="lblName" runat="server"
            Text='<%# Eval("Name") %>' />
      </td>
      <td class="col3">
        <asp:Label ID="lblUnitPrice" runat="server"
            Text='<%# Eval("UnitPrice", "{0:C}") %>' />
      </td>
      <td class="col4">
        <asp:Label ID="lblOnHand" runat="server"
            Text='<%# Eval("OnHand") %>' />
      </td>
    </tr>
  </table>
</ItemTemplate>
<AlternatingItemStyle BackColor="#CCCCCC" />
<HeaderStyle BackColor="Black" Font-Bold="True" ForeColor="White" />
</asp:DataList>
<asp:SqlDataSource ID="SqlDataSource2" runat="server"
    ConnectionString=
        "<%$ ConnectionStrings:HalloweenConnectionString %>"
    SelectCommand="SELECT [ProductID], [Name], [UnitPrice], [OnHand]
                   FROM [Products]
                   WHERE ([CategoryID] = @CategoryID)
                   ORDER BY [ProductID]">
    <SelectParameters>
      <asp:ControlParameter Name="CategoryID" Type="String"
          ControlID="Category" PropertyName="SelectedValue" />
    </SelectParameters>
</asp:SqlDataSource>
</div>
<div id="shoutbox">
  <asp:ScriptManager ID="ScriptManager1" runat="server">
  </asp:ScriptManager>
  <p>Here's what everyone is saying:</p>
  <p>
    <asp:UpdatePanel ID="ShoutBoxPanel1" runat="server">
      <ContentTemplate>
        <asp:Label ID="lblShoutBox" runat="server"></asp:Label>
        <asp:Timer ID="Timer1" runat="server" Interval="5000">
        </asp:Timer>
      </ContentTemplate>
      <Triggers>
        <asp:AsyncPostBackTrigger ControlID="btnAddShout"
            EventName="Click" />
      </Triggers>
    </asp:UpdatePanel>
  </p>
```

Figure 21-13   The aspx file for the Shout Box application (part 2 of 3)

The Default.aspx file   **Page 3**

```
<p>
    <asp:UpdatePanel ID="ShoutBoxPanel2" runat="server"
        UpdateMode="Conditional">
    <ContentTemplate>
        <p class="label">Name:</p>
        <p class="entry">
            <asp:TextBox ID="txtUserName" runat="server"
                MaxLength="15" Width="100px"></asp:TextBox>
            <asp:RequiredFieldValidator ID="RequiredFieldValidator1"
                runat="server" ErrorMessage="Name is required."
                ControlToValidate="txtUserName" Display="Dynamic"
                CssClass="error">
            </asp:RequiredFieldValidator>
        </p>
        <p class="label">Shout:</p>
        <p class="entry">
            <asp:TextBox ID="txtShout" runat="server"
                MaxLength="255" Width="220px"></asp:TextBox>
            <asp:RequiredFieldValidator ID="RequiredFieldValidator2"
                runat="server" ErrorMessage="Shout is required."
                ControlToValidate="txtShout" Display="Dynamic"
                CssClass="error">
            </asp:RequiredFieldValidator>
        </p>
        <asp:Button ID="btnAddShout" runat="server" Text="Add Shout" />
        <asp:UpdateProgress ID="UpdateProgress1" runat="server"
            DynamicLayout="False">
        <ProgressTemplate>
            <img src="Images/spinner.gif" alt="Please Wait" />
            Uploading Comment...
        </ProgressTemplate>
        </asp:UpdateProgress>
    </ContentTemplate>
    </asp:UpdatePanel>
</p>
        </div>
    </div>
    </div>
    </form>
</body>
</html>
```

Figure 21-13   The aspx file for the Shout Box application (part 3 of 3)

The code-behind file

Figure 21-14 presents the code-behind file for the Shout Box application. This file consists of two event handlers. The first one is executed each time the page is posted back to the server, and the second one occurs when the user clicks the Add Shout button.

The Page_Load event handler starts by declaring a shout box object from the ShoutItemList class. Then, it checks if the application state object contains an item named ShoutBox. If it doesn't, a new shout box object is created from the ShoutItemList class, and this object is added to application state. Otherwise, the ShoutBox item in application state is assigned to the shout box object, the Display method of that object is used to get the text for the shout box, and that text is assigned to the Text property of the label that displays the shout box.

Finally, the Load event handler checks if the page is being processed as the result of an asynchronous postback. If it isn't, the focus is moved to the User Name text box to make it easy for the user to enter a shout.

If the user enters data into the Name and Shout text boxes and then clicks the Add Shout button, the Click event handler for that button is executed. This event handler starts by creating a new shout from the ShoutItem class. Then, it assigns the text in the Name and Shout text boxes to the UserName and Comment properties of the shout item, and it assigns the current time to the Timestamp property.

Next, this method locks application state so another user can't modify it at the same time. Then, it gets a reference to the ShoutBox item in application state, stores it in a ShoutItemList variable named shoutBox, adds the shout to the shout box, and unlocks application state.

Finally, the Display method of the shout box is called to get the updated text for the shout box, and this text is assigned to the Text property of the label for the shout box. In addition, the Text property of the Shout text box is cleared and the focus is moved to that text box to prepare for the user's next entry.

The Default.aspx.cs file

```
using System;
using System.Collections.Generic;
using System.Web;
using System.Web.UI;
using System.Web.UI.WebControls;

public partial class _Default : System.Web.UI.Page
{
    protected void Page_Load(object sender, EventArgs e)
    {
        ShoutItemList shoutBox;
        if (Application["ShoutBox"] == null)
        {
            shoutBox = new ShoutItemList();
            Application.Add("ShoutBox", shoutBox);
        }
        else
        {
            shoutBox = (ShoutItemList)Application["ShoutBox"];
            lblShoutBox.Text = shoutBox.Display();
        }
        if (ScriptManager1.IsInAsyncPostBack != true)
            txtUserName.Focus();
    }

    protected void btnAddShout_Click(object sender, EventArgs e)
    {
        ShoutItem shout = new ShoutItem();
        shout.UserName = txtUserName.Text;
        shout.Comment = txtShout.Text;
        shout.Timestamp = DateTime.Now;

        Application.Lock();
        ShoutItemList shoutBox = (ShoutItemList)Application["ShoutBox"];
        shoutBox.Add(shout);
        Application.UnLock();

        lblShoutBox.Text = shoutBox.Display();
        txtShout.Text = "";
        txtShout.Focus();
    }
}
```

Figure 21-14   The code-behind file for the Shout Box application

An introduction to jQuery

Like the ASP.NET AJAX client-side framework, *jQuery* is a JavaScript library that provides support for AJAX. In addition, jQuery contains functions that make it easier to modify documents, handle events, and apply effects and animations. In 2008, Microsoft adopted jQuery as part of its official application development platform and announced that it would provide official support for jQuery. Microsoft has included jQuery as part of ASP.NET 4, and it has included IntelliSense support for jQuery in Visual Studio 2010. In addition, Microsoft has contributed code to the jQuery project.

The core jQuery library

Figure 21-15 begins by summarizing some of the features of jQuery that have made it so popular. To start, jQuery makes it easy to write client-side JavaScript code that's compatible with all modern web browsers. In addition, it makes it easy to select and manipulate the DOM and the CSS for the DOM. This allows you to use JavaScript to change the appearance of the web page. jQuery takes this one step further by including some popular animations and effects such as having a control fade in or fade out.

In other words, jQuery can do a lot on the client side without ever needing to make a trip to the server. However, jQuery also includes AJAX capabilities that allow it to send an AJAX request to the server and to process the AJAX response that's returned from the server as shown in the next figure.

If you start a web site from the ASP.NET Web Site template, you will find three versions of the jQuery library in the Scripts folder. The jquery-1.4.1.js file contains the core library in a format that's easy for developers to read. The jquery-1.4.1.min.js file contains the core library in a condensed format that should be used when the application is deployed. And the jquery-1.4.1-vsdoc.js file contains the core library with comments that support Visual Studio IntelliSense.

The jQuery UI library

One additional feature of jQuery is its extensibility. This means that developers can develop plug-ins that are built on top of jQuery. Some of the most popular jQuery plug-ins can be found in the *jQuery UI* library. This library provides a wide range of user-interface controls, also known as *widgets*.

Many of the controls in the jQuery UI library duplicate functionality that's provided by the controls in the ASP.NET AJAX Control Toolkit. For example, jQuery UI contains a Calendar control that's similar in function to the Calendar control in the ASP.NET AJAX Control Toolkit. As a result, if you want to use a Calendar control, you'll need to decide which control to use. The use of each one has its pros and cons.

Features of jQuery

Feature	Description
Cross-browser compatibility	Makes it easy to write code that is compatible with all modern web browsers.
Event handling	Makes it easy to register functions as event listeners.
DOM selection	Makes it easy to select DOM elements.
DOM manipulation	Makes it easy to modify DOM elements.
CSS manipulation	Makes it easy to modify the CSS for a DOM element.
Effects and animations	Makes it easy to apply special effects and animations to DOM elements such as fading in or out, sliding up or down, and so on.
AJAX	Makes it easy to send an AJAX request to the server and use the data in the AJAX response to update the DOM for a web page.
Extensibility	Allows jQuery to work with plug-ins such as the controls in the jQuery UI library.

The jQuery web site

`http://jquery.com/`

The jQuery UI web site

`http://jqueryui.com/`

Description

- *jQuery* is a JavaScript library that simplifies working with the DOM, event handling, animation, special effects, AJAX, and plug-ins that provide for complex user-interface controls.

- Microsoft has adopted jQuery as part of its official application development platform, and it has included jQuery as part of ASP.NET 4.

- If you start a web site from the ASP.NET Web Site template, you'll find three versions of the jQuery library in the Scripts folder that will help you as you use and deploy this library.

- Visual Studio 2010 includes IntelliSense support for jQuery, which makes it easy to write code that uses the jQuery library.

- *jQuery UI* is a JavaScript library that's built on top of the core jQuery library. It provides a wide range of user-interface controls known as *widgets*. It also provides a wide range of low-level effect and interaction APIs such as drag and drop, resizing, selection, and sorting.

- Many of the jQuery UI controls provide functionality similar to controls in the ASP.NET AJAX Control Toolkit.

- Microsoft is actively contributing code and bug fixes to jQuery and developing widgets for JQuery UI.

Figure 21-15   jQuery and jQuery UI

How jQuery AJAX works

Figure 21-16 shows that jQuery AJAX works similarly to ASP.NET AJAX. As you would expect, however, jQuery AJAX uses the jQuery library instead of the ASP.NET AJAX client-side framework. Then, the JavaScript code uses jQuery AJAX to call a WCF service or web service that's running on the server. When a response is received from the server, the JavaScript code in the response uses jQuery to process the data and update the DOM accordingly.

Earlier in this chapter, you learned how to use ASP.NET AJAX to create a simple AJAX-enabled web application. The advantage of that approach is that the JavaScript code that works with the ASP.NET AJAX client-side framework is generated automatically when the page is rendered. This allows the developer to quickly develop web pages that use AJAX by dragging and dropping server controls onto the page, and it shields the developer from having to understand the details of what's going on under the hood. The disadvantage of this approach is that the developer gives up control over how the JavaScript code works.

The advantage of using jQuery AJAX is that the developer has more control over how the client-side controls and code work. The disadvantage of this approach is that it has a steeper learning curve. To start, the developer must have a solid understanding of HTML and CSS. Then, the developer must learn how to write JavaScript code that uses jQuery to work with the DOM and AJAX. Finally, the developer must manually write most of the client-side code.

So which approach should you use? If the ASP.NET AJAX approach shown in this chapter is adequate for your web pages, there's no reason to move to the jQuery AJAX approach. However, if your web pages require improved functionality or performance, the jQuery AJAX approach is probably what you want. In that case, you can get more information about jQuery AJAX in the ASP.NET environment by searching the Internet.

The architecture of jQuery AJAX

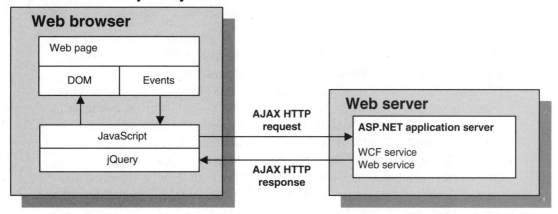

ASP.NET AJAX

Pros

- It allows the developer to quickly develop AJAX-enabled web pages by dragging and dropping server controls onto the page.
- It automatically generates the JavaScript code that works with the ASP.NET AJAX client-side framework. As a result, the developer doesn't need to know how to write this code.

Con

- It doesn't give the developer control over the client-side controls, which limits the developer's ability to improve the functionality and performance of these controls.

jQuery AJAX

Pro

- It gives the developer control over the client-side controls, which can lead to improved functionality and performance.

Con

- It requires the developer to manually write the client-side code. As a result, the developer must understand HTML and CSS, how to write JavaScript code, and how to use jQuery to manipulate the DOM and work with AJAX.

Description

- To use jQuery, you add JavaScript code to your web pages that accesses the various functions that jQuery provides.
- You can use jQuery to make an AJAX request to the server. Then, you can use the jQuery library to process the data in the AJAX response and update the DOM accordingly.

Figure 21-16   How jQuery AJAX works

Perspective

In this chapter, you've learned how AJAX works and how it's implemented in ASP.NET. At this point, you should be able to use the ASP.NET AJAX server controls to develop AJAX-enabled web applications of your own.

Of course, there's a lot more to learn about AJAX than what's presented here. For example, you may want to learn more about the controls that are available in the ASP.NET AJAX Control Toolkit. The best way to do that is to go to the web site listed in figure 21-5 and review the controls it contains. Then, you can download this toolkit and use any of these controls in your own applications.

On the other hand, you may want to take a more cutting edge approach and learn more about using jQuery to work with AJAX. To do that, you might want to start by searching the Internet for tutorials that show you how to use jQuery to do some client-side effects and animations. Then, once you feel comfortable using jQuery to work with the DOM, you can search the Internet for information about using jQuery and AJAX to work with ASP.NET.

Terms

rich Internet application (RIA)
Asynchronous JavaScript and XML (AJAX)
JavaScript
Document Object Model (DOM)
JavaScript Object Notation (JSON)
Dynamic HTML (DHTML)
asynchronous postback
ASP.NET AJAX client-side framework
ASP.NET AJAX Control Toolkit
web service
WCF service
service
proxy
jQuery
jQuery UI
widget

22

How to configure and deploy ASP.NET applications

This chapter presents the ways that ASP.NET applications can be configured and deployed. After this chapter presents two tools for configuring an application, it presents three general ways to deploy an application. Then, it presents four specific deployment techniques.

How to configure an ASP.NET application

As you know, the web.config file for an ASP.NET application contains configuration information. As a result, you usually need to change this file not only during the development of an application but also when it is deployed. For example, you need to create a connection string to access the application's database when you develop the application. But if you move the database to another server when the application is deployed, you need to adjust the connection string to point to the correct database.

Although you can edit the web.config file for an application manually, this technique is error prone. Because of that, you'll want to use one of the GUI tools for working with an application's configuration. These tools are presented in the topics that follow.

How to use the Web Site Administration Tool

As figure 22-1 shows, the Web Site Administration Tool is a web-based editor that lets you specify certain configuration options. This tool uses a tabbed interface that lets you switch between the home page and the pages that configure security, application, and provider settings.

The Security and Provider tabs let you configure the ASP.NET authentication and provider features. You can refer to chapter 19 for more information on using the Security tab. And if you ever create your own custom providers, you shouldn't have any trouble using the Provider tab.

The Application tab lets you create custom application settings that appear in the appSettings element of the web.config file and can be accessed in code by using the System.Configuration.ConfigurationManager class. In chapter 18, for example, you saw how to add a setting that specifies the path for an application. To enter this infomation using the Web Site Administration Tool, you can click the Create Application Settings link on the Application tab. Then, you can use the page that's displayed to enter the key and value for the setting.

The Application tab also lets you configure a web site to work with an SMTP server so it can send and receive email. You saw how this works in chapter 20. It also lets you configure debugging options for the site. And it lets you start and stop the site.

When you use the Web Site Administration Tool, you need to remember that it has two limitations. First, it doesn't let you set all of the configuration options that are available via the web.config file. For example, you can't use it to change the connection strings stored in the file or specify custom error pages. To edit these configuration settings, you must manually edit the web.config file or use the IIS Management Console that's described in the next two figures.

The second limitation is that you can only use the Web Site Administration Tool from within Visual Studio. As a result, you can't use this tool for a web site that's been deployed to a production server unless you can open the web site in Visual Studio.

The home page of the Web Site Administration Tool

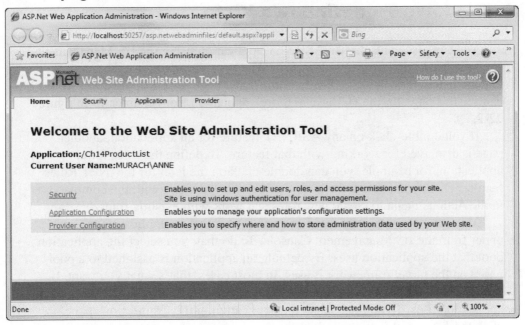

The four tabs of the Web Site Administration Tool

- **Home:** Displays the home page.
- **Security:** Lets you configure users, roles, and access rules. For more information, see chapter 19.
- **Application:** Lets you create custom application settings, configure SMTP email support (see chapter 20), control debugging and tracing settings, and start or stop the application.
- **Provider:** Lets you configure providers for features such as membership and roles.

Description

- The Web Site Administration Tool lets you configure certain web.config settings using a browser-based interface.
- To start the Web Site Administration Tool, open the project in Visual Studio 2010 and choose Website→ASP.NET Configuration.

Figure 22-1   How to use the Web Site Administration Tool to configure an ASP.NET application

How to use the IIS Management Console with Windows 7 or Windows Vista

You can also configure an ASP.NET application using the IIS Management Console. To do that from Windows 7 or Windows Vista, you use the features that are listed in the ASP.NET area of the home page for the application. You can see this page for the Halloween Store application from chapter 18 in figure 22-2.

If you double-click on any ASP.NET feature for an application, another page is displayed for working with that feature. To define the roles for an application, for example, you can double-click on the icon for the .NET Roles feature. Then, you can use the page that's displayed along with the commands in the Actions menu to create new roles and work with existing roles.

You can also change the version of ASP.NET that an application will run under from the IIS Management Console. To do that, you select the application pool that the application uses. By default, an application is assigned to a pool based on the target framework it uses. In most cases, that's what you want. If you define custom application pools, though, you can easily change the pool an application uses. To do that, select the application in the Connections pane, click the Advanced Settings link in the Actions pane, and then select an appropriate application pool.

Unfortunately, if an application targets .NET Framework 4 and is configured to use a .NET 4 application pool, you won't be able to use the IIS Management Console to configure roles, users, and providers. That's because the IIS Management Console is a .NET 2.0 application. If you want to use it to configure roles, users, or providers, then, you will need to temporarily change the target framework for your application as well as the application pool it uses.

The IIS Management Console for an ASP.NET application

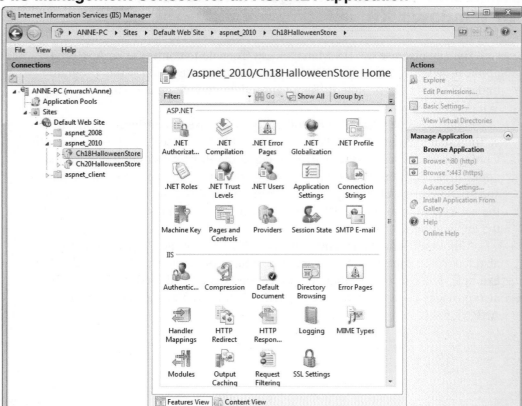

Description

- You can configure the web.config file for an ASP.NET application from the Home page for the application in the IIS Management Console. To do that, you work with the features that are available from the ASP.NET area of this page.

- To configure an ASP.NET application, highlight it in the Connections pane, and then double-click on a feature in the Home page to display a page for working with that feature.

- To change the version of ASP.NET that an application runs under, highlight the application in the Connections pane, click the Advanced Settings link in the Actions Pane, and then select an application pool that uses the appropriate .NET Framework version. To learn more about application pools, please see appendix B.

Figure 22-2   How to use the IIS Management Console to configure an ASP.NET application with Windows 7 or Windows Vista

How to use the IIS Management Console with Windows XP

You can also use the IIS Management Console to configure an ASP.NET application under Windows XP. However, the user interface for this program under Windows XP is quite different from the interface under Windows 7 and Windows Vista.

Figure 22-3 describes the dialog box you can use to configure application settings under Windows XP. You can access this dialog box by clicking the Edit Configuration button on the ASP.NET tab in the Properties dialog box for the application. With this dialog box, you can configure most of the settings that are specified via the web.config file. However, to use this dialog box, you must have the authorization to run the IIS Management Console on the server that hosts the application.

Although it's not shown here, the ASP.NET tab of the Properties dialog box also lets you set the ASP.NET version that an application should run under. For example, you can specify that an application created with ASP.NET 2.0 (which also provides the core features for ASP.NET 3.0 and 3.5) should run under ASP.NET 4.0.

The ASP.NET Configuration Settings dialog box

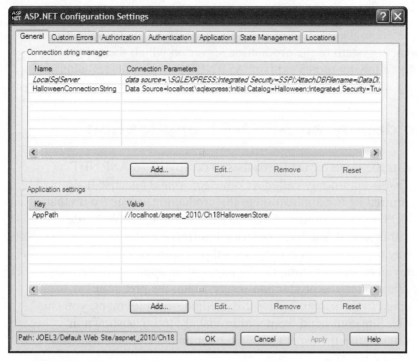

The seven tabs of the ASP.NET Configuration Settings dialog box

- **General:** Creates connection strings and application settings.
- **Custom Errors:** Configures custom error pages.
- **Authorization:** Creates authorization rules.
- **Authentication:** Specifies the authentication mode and configures membership and role providers.
- **Application:** Configures application settings such as the default master page and theme.
- **State Management:** Configures session state settings.
- **Locations:** Adds Location elements to the web.config file that let you apply configuration settings to specific parts of the application.

Description

- The IIS Management Console includes an ASP.NET Configuration Settings dialog box that lets you configure the web.config file for an ASP.NET application.
- The ASP.NET Configuration Settings dialog box lets you configure more web.config settings than the Web Site Administration Tool, but it only works for IIS-based applications.
- To open the ASP.NET Configuration Settings dialog box, open the IIS Management Console, right-click the web site, and choose Properties. Then, click the ASP.NET tab and click the Edit Configuration button.

Figure 22-3   How to use the IIS Management Console to configure an ASP.NET application with Windows XP

How to deploy an ASP.NET application

Deployment refers to the process of copying an ASP.NET web application from the development system to the production server on which the application will be run. As the following topics explain, ASP.NET provides several alternatives for deploying web applications.

Three ways to deploy an ASP.NET application

Figure 22-4 lists the three basic approaches to deploying an ASP.NET application. The first is commonly called *XCopy deployment* because it simply copies the files required by the application to the production server. To do that, you can use the DOS XCopy command, or you can use the Copy Web Site command from within Visual Studio as described in figure 22-5.

The second way to deploy a web site is called *precompiled deployment*. This type of deployment lets you compile the pages of an application before deploying the application to the production server. Then, the precompiled assemblies are copied to the server. To use this method of deployment, you can use the Publish Web Site command from within Visual Studio as shown in figure 22-6. Or, you can use the aspnet_compiler command from a command prompt as shown in figure 22-7.

The third way to deploy a web application is to develop a Web Setup project that creates a Windows *Setup program* for the application. Then, you can run this Setup program on the production server to install the application. This approach is described in figures 22-8 and 22-9.

Which of these deployment alternatives is the best choice depends on the particular needs of each application. XCopy deployment is the easiest, and it's often used during development to create copies of an application on different servers for testing purposes. For small applications, XCopy deployment may also be the best choice for production deployment.

Precompiled deployment has several advantages over XCopy deployment. For example, precompiled deployment provides better performance for the first users that access the site. In addition, it provides increased security because you don't have to copy the application's source files to the server.

For applications that are deployed to one or just a few servers, precompiled deployment is usually the best choice. However, if you're distributing an application to many different servers, you should consider creating a Setup program for the application. Although creating this program can involve considerable work, the effort will be repaid each time you use the program to install the application.

XCopy deployment

- To manually copy the files of an ASP.NET web site to a server, you can use the XCopy command from a command prompt. Then, you can use the IIS Management Console to create a virtual directory that's mapped to the directory that you copied the web site to.
- To automate the deployment, you can create a batch file for the XCopy command. Then, you can run the batch file any time you make changes to the application and want to deploy the updated code.
- You can also do XCopy deployment from Visual Studio by using the Copy Web Site command (see figure 22-5).

Precompiled deployment

- Deploys precompiled assemblies to the specified server.
- Lets you deploy the web site with or without the source files.
- Can be done from within Visual Studio using the Publish Web Site command (see figure 22-6) or from a command prompt using the aspnet_compiler command (see figure 22-7).

Setup program deployment

- Uses a Web Setup project to build a Windows Setup program that can be run to deploy a web application to a server (see figures 22-8 and 22-9).
- Useful if you want to distribute a web application to multiple servers.
- Can be used to deploy precompiled assemblies and can be configured to include or omit the source files.
- An application that's installed by a Setup program can be removed by using the Uninstall or Change a Program window (Windows 7 or Windows Vista) or the Add or Remove Programs window (Windows XP) that can be accessed from the Control Panel.

Description

- There are three general methods for deploying ASP.NET applications: *XCopy deployment*, *precompiled deployment*, and *Setup program deployment*.
- The method you should use for deployment depends on how often the application will need to be deployed and whether you want to include the source code with the deployed application.

Note

- Setup program deployment isn't available with Visual Web Developer Express Edition, and precompiled deployment is available only by using the aspnet_compiler command.

Figure 22-4   Three ways to deploy an ASP.NET application

How to use the Copy Web Site command for XCopy deployment

To implement XCopy deployment from within Visual Studio, you use the Copy Web Site command shown in figure 22-5. This command lets you copy a web site to a file system, local IIS, FTP, or remote IIS web site. In addition, it lets you copy all of the files in the web site or just selected files, and you can use it to synchronize web sites so that both sites have the most recently updated versions of each file.

To use this command, open the web site you want to copy and start the command to display the window shown in this figure. Here, the Source Web Site section lists the files in the current web site. Next, click the Connect button to display an Open Web Site dialog box that lets you pick the location you want to copy the web site to. If you're copying to a local or remote IIS server, you can also use this dialog box to create a new IIS application or virtual directory on the server if the directory doesn't already exist.

Once you select the remote web site, its files will appear in the Remote Web Site section of the dialog box. You can then select the files you want to copy in the Source Web Site list and click the right-arrow button that appears between the lists to copy the files from the source web site to the remote web site. You can use the other buttons to copy files from the remote web site to the source web site, to synchronize files in the web sites, or to stop a lengthy copy operation.

The Copy Web Site window

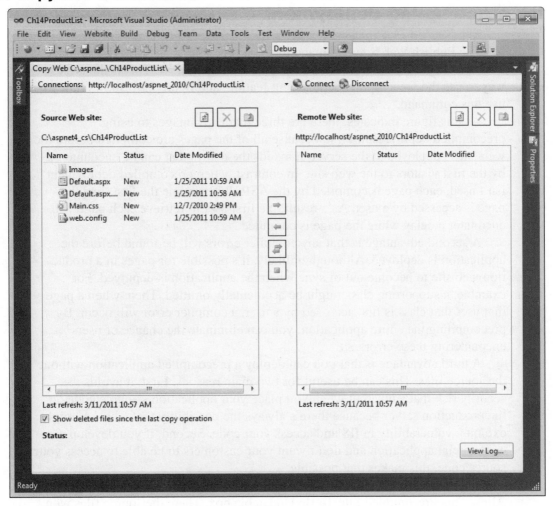

How to use the Copy Web Site command

1. In Visual Studio, open the web site you want to deploy and choose the Website→Copy Web Site command.
2. Click the Connect button to display an Open Web Site dialog box that lets you choose the destination you want to copy the web site to.
3. Select the files you want to copy. (Press Ctrl+A to select all of the site's files.)
4. Click the → button to copy the files from the source web site to the remote web site.

Description

- You can use the Copy Web Site command to deploy an ASP.NET application with XCopy deployment.

Figure 22-5   How to use the Copy Web Site command for XCopy deployment

How to use the Publish Web Site command for precompiled deployment

The Publish Web Site command lets you precompile an ASP.NET application and copy the precompiled assemblies to a target server. This is the easiest way to use the precompiled deployment feature, and figure 22-6 shows how to use this command.

As this figure indicates, there are three main advantages to using precompiled deployment. First, because all of the pages are compiled before the web site is deployed to the server, it avoids the delays that can be encountered by the first visitors to the web site. In contrast, when precompiled deployment isn't used, each page is compiled by the ASP.NET runtime the first time the page is accessed by a user. As a result, the first user to retrieve each page will encounter a delay while the page is compiled.

A second advantage is that any compiler errors will be found before the application is deployed. Although unlikely, it's possible for pages in a production web site to become out of sync when the application is deployed. For example, a supporting class might be accidentally omitted. Then, when a page that uses that class is first accessed by a user, a compiler error will occur. By precompiling the entire application, you can eliminate the chance of users encountering these errors.

A third advantage is that you can deploy a precompiled application without the source files. This can be useful for two main reasons. First, it avoids the security risk that's inherent when you place your application's source code on the production server because there's always the possibility that a hacker might exploit a vulnerability in IIS and access your code. Second, if you develop a commercial application and don't want your customers to be able to access your source code, this makes that possible.

To omit the source code from a precompiled application, you uncheck the Allow This Precompiled Site To Be Updatable box. Then, the source files won't be copied to the production server. Instead, dummy files with the same names as the source files will be copied to the server. If you open one of these files, you'll find that it contains a single line with the following text:

```
This is a marker file generated by the precompilation tool,
and should not be deleted!
```

Although these dummy files are required for the application to work, their contents are ignored by the ASP.NET runtime.

The Publish Web Site dialog box

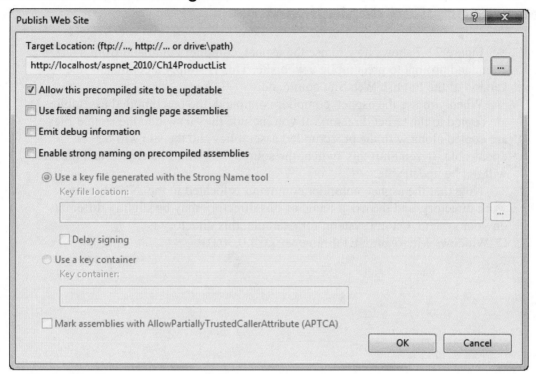

Advantages of precompiling a web site

- Avoids delays caused by compiling web pages when they are first accessed by a user.
- Finds compile errors before the site is deployed.
- Can copy just the executable files and not the source files to the server.

Description

- The Build→Publish Web Site command compiles all of the files that make up an ASP.NET application, and then deploys the compiled assemblies to the location you specify.
- If you check the Allow This Precompiled Site To Be Updatable box, the source files are deployed along with the executable files. If you leave this box unchecked, the source files aren't deployed.

Figure 22-6   How to use the Publish Web Site command for precompiled deployment

How to use the aspnet_compiler command for precompiled deployment

Figure 22-7 shows how to use the aspnet_compiler command from a command prompt to precompile a web site. This is simply a command-line version of the Publish Web Site command.

When you use the aspnet_compiler command, the precompiled assemblies are copied to the target directory. If you include the –u switch, the source files are copied along with the precompiled assemblies and the site will be updateable. If you omit this switch, the source files won't be copied and the site will not be updateable.

Note that the aspnet_compiler command is located in the .NET Framework directory, and the exact name of this directory may be slightly different on your system. On my system, for example, this directory is C:\Windows\Microsoft.NET\Framework\v4.0.30319.

The syntax of the aspnet_compiler command

```
aspnet_compiler -v virtual-directory [-u] [-d] [-f] [target-directory]
```

Switches

Switch	Description
-v	Precedes the name of the virtual directory of the existing web site to be precompiled.
-u	The precompiled web site will be updateable.
-d	Debug information will be included in the compiled assemblies.
-f	Overwrites the target directory if it already exists.

Examples

Precompiles an existing web site

```
aspnet_compiler -v Ch14ProductList c:\Deploy\Ch14ProductList
```

Precompiles a web site in place

```
aspnet_compiler -v Ch14ProductList
```

Creates an updateable precompiled web site with debugging information

```
aspnet_compiler -v Ch14ProductList -u -d c:\Deploy\Ch14ProductList
```

Description

- You can use the aspnet_compiler command to precompile a web site from a command prompt.
- If you specify a target directory, the precompiled web site is stored in the directory you specify. If you don't specify a target directory, the web site is precompiled in place.
- If the target directory isn't the final destination for an application, you can use XCopy deployment to move the precompiled web site to that destination.

Note

- The aspnet_compiler command is located in the .NET Framework 4 directory, which is %systemroot%\Microsoft.NET\Framework\v4.0.xxxxx, where *%systemroot%* is the root directory for Windows and *xxxxx* is the five-digit build number.

Figure 22-7   How to use the aspnet_compiler command for precompiled deployment

How to create a Web Setup project

Another way to deploy a web application is to develop a *Web Setup project* that creates a standard Windows *Setup program* that you can use to install the web application on an IIS server. As figure 22-8 shows, you start by adding a Web Setup project to an existing web site. Then, you configure the Web Setup project so it installs the files required by the web application. You can also use the setup editors to configure many custom options that control how the application will be installed.

You can use the File System Editor shown in this figure to add files and folders to the setup project. To add a Readme file, for example, you can right-click the Web Application Folder in the left pane of the File System Editor and then select Add→File. Note that the Web Application Folder represents the virtual directory where the web application will be installed, and it has properties that define that virtual directory. The two properties you're most likely to change are VirtualDirectory, which specifies the name of the virtual directory, and DefaultDocument, which specifies the page that's displayed by default.

You can use the Registry Editor to specify the keys and values that should be added to the registry on the target computer. And you can use the File Types Editor to establish a file association between a file extension and an application on the target computer. Since most web applications don't need to adjust registry settings or create file type associations, you shouldn't need either of these editors. However, the other three editors can be useful.

The User Interface Editor lets you customize the dialog boxes that are displayed when you run the Setup program to install a web application. For example, you can change the BannerBitMap property of any dialog box to display your company's logo in that dialog box. This editor also lets you change the text that's displayed in the dialog boxes, and it lets you add your own dialog boxes to those that are displayed by the Setup program.

The Custom Actions Editor lets you specify actions that are performed on the user's computer at the end of the install, commit, rollback, or uninstall phase of the installation. Visual Studio provides five predefined actions that install various components. In addition, you can create your own custom actions by developing a program or component that performs that action. For example, you can use a custom action to create a SQL Server database when the application is installed. Note, however, that a custom action can be difficult to develop.

Finally, the Launch Conditions Editor lets you set conditions that must be met before the application can be installed. For example, you can use a launch condition to check the operating system version or to see if a particular file exists on the target system. If the condition isn't met, the Setup program aborts the installation.

In addition to using the setup editors, you can set properties of the Setup project. Some of those properties provide support information and are displayed in the Uninstall or Change a Program window (Windows 7 and Windows Vista) or the Support Info dialog box that's available from the Add or Remove Programs window (Windows XP). Other properties provide additional information about the application, such as the product name that's displayed by the Setup program.

A Web Setup project with the File System Editor displayed

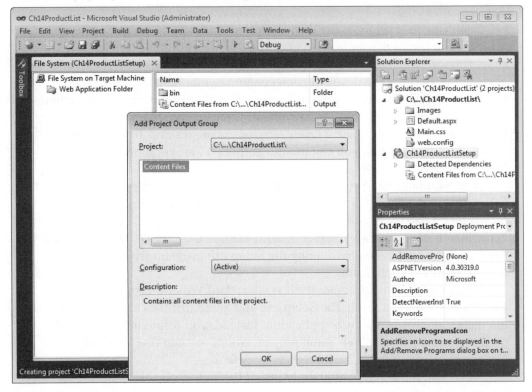

How to create a Setup project

- Choose the File→Add→New Project command to display the Add New Project dialog box. Then, expand the Other Project Types and Setup and Deployment groups, select the Visual Studio Installer option, select the Web Setup Project template, enter a name for the Web Setup project, and click OK.

- In the Solution Explorer, right-click the Web Setup project and choose the Add→Project Output command to display the Add Project Output Group dialog box. Then, click OK to add the content files from your web site to the Web Setup project.

- Use the buttons that are displayed at the top of the Solution Explorer when the Web Setup project is selected to access setup editors that let you customize various aspects of the Web Setup project.

Description

- A *Web Setup project* creates a standard Windows *Setup program* that installs the web application on an IIS server. To create a Web Setup project, add a Web Setup project to the web site you want to deploy and then configure it using the setup editors.

- You can set project properties that provide support and other information for the application. You can also set properties that provide information about the virtual directory where the application will be installed, which is represented by the Web Application Folder in the File System Editor shown above.

Figure 22-8   How to create a Web Setup project

How to create and use a Setup program

Once you've configured the Web Setup project, you can create the Setup program and install the application as described in figure 22-9. To start, you should choose whether you want to create a debug or release version of the application. Because the debug version contains symbolic debugging information that you don't typically need in a production application, and because this version isn't optimized, you'll usually create a release version. On the other hand, you may want to create a debug version during testing. To determine which version is created, you can use the Solution Configurations drop-down list as described in this figure.

Next, you build the Setup project. This creates the setup files (Setup.exe and Setup.msi) in the Debug or Release folder of the Web Setup project, depending on whether a debug or release version is created. Then, in most cases, you'll copy these files to a network server or burn them to a CD or DVD. Finally, you can install the application by running the Setup.exe program from the server that will host the application.

Note that the Setup program itself is a standard Windows application, not a web application. As a result, the Setup.exe and Setup.msi files aren't found in the same directory as the web application. Instead, you'll find these files in the project directory for the Web Setup project, which you can find under My Documents\Visual Studio 2010\Projects by default.

When you run a Setup program to install the web application on the host server, it steps you through the installation process. In this figure, for example, you can see the screen for one of the steps of a typical Setup program. Here, the application will be deployed to the default web site in a virtual directory named HalloweenProductList.

The Select Installation Address step of a typical Setup program

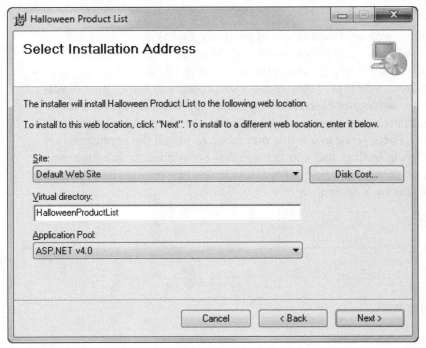

Description

- To create a Setup program, right-click the setup project in the Solution Explorer and then use the Build command. When you do, Visual Studio creates files named Setup.exe and Setup.msi. Setup.exe is the file you will run to install the application, and Setup.msi contains all of the files to be installed.

- The Setup.exe and Setup.msi files are stored in the Web Setup project's Debug or Release folder, depending on whether Visual Studio is configured to create a debug or release version of the Setup project. In most cases, you'll want to create a release version because it's fully optimized and contains no debugging information.

- To change the version of the Setup program that Visual Studio creates, highlight the Setup project in the Solution Explorer and then select the version you want to create from the Solution Configurations drop-down list in the Standard toolbar.

- To install the web application, copy the Setup.exe and Setup.msi files to a network server or burn them to a CD or DVD. Then, run the Setup program on the server that will host the application.

Figure 22-9   How to create and use a Setup program

Perspective

As you develop a web application, you'll probably find yourself working with both the Web Site Administration Tool and the IIS Management Console. In addition, you'll often find yourself editing the web.config file directly.

As for deployment, you'll probably spend a surprising amount of time developing procedures for deploying even relatively small applications. So for a large application, I recommend that you develop a procedure early in the application's development cycle. Then, you can use this procedure to install the application on multiple servers during testing, and you can use that experience to fine-tune the procedure as you go along. As a side benefit, you may discover installation issues that affect the application's design.

Terms

deployment
XCopy deployment
precompiled deployment
Web Setup project
Setup program

23

An introduction to WCF services

If you've used previous versions of ASP.NET, you may be familiar with web services, also called ASMX web services. Simply put, a web service is a class that resides on a web server and can be accessed via the Internet or an intranet. Web services provide a way to make common processing routines available to other programmers.

WCF (Windows Communication Foundation) services are similar to web services, but they provide more power and flexibility. WCF is part of a movement by Microsoft and other businesses towards service-oriented development, an approach that has gained wide acceptance in recent years. Service-oriented development focuses on developing services rather than objects. Then, a host can provide a service, and a client can consume the service. In this chapter, you'll learn the basic concepts and skills you need to create and use WCF services.

Basic concepts and terms

WCF (Windows Communication Foundation) was first released as part of .NET Framework 3.0, but it was updated with .NET Framework 3.5 and again with .NET Framework 4. WCF unifies all older .NET Framework communication technologies, including web services, advanced web service specifications, .NET Remoting, and more. In addition, WCF services provide interoperability with applications built on other technologies and platforms, such as web services built using Java EE and older .NET technologies.

Service-oriented development allows applications developed by different companies or organizations to interact with one another by using *services*. For example, the United States Postal Service has services that are available from its web site that let you calculate shipping rates, correct addresses, and track packages. You can use services like these to incorporate the features they provide into your applications.

How WCF services work

Figure 23-1 illustrates how WCF services work. In this case, the service is part of a web site that's hosted by IIS. Although this is a common scenario, you should realize that WCF services can also be hosted by a Windows Forms application, a Console application, or a Windows service. This is one of the advantages that WCF services have over ASMX web services. In this chapter, though, I'll focus on WCF services that are hosted by IIS.

As this figure shows, a WCF service exposes one or more *endpoints*. Then, the WCF client uses *SOAP (Simple Object Access Protocol)* over HTTP to communicate with one of these endpoints. Note that for this to work, both the client and the server must be running a version of the .NET Framework that supports WCF.

If you're using Windows Vista, Windows 7, or Windows Server 2008, you can also use *Windows Process Activation Service (WAS)* to host your WCF services. WAS provides a light-weight option for hosting that's also more powerful since it supports protocols in addition to HTTP. You'll learn more about these protocols in the next figure.

A WCF service that's hosted by IIS

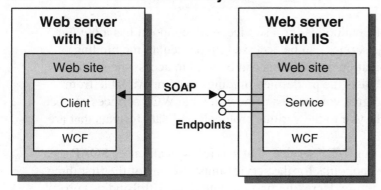

Description

- Prior to the release of .NET Framework 3.0, *web services* (also known as *ASMX web services*) were used to provide common processing routines through the web.

- *Windows Communication Foundation* (*WCF*) unifies all older .NET Framework communication technologies including web services, advanced web service specifications (the WS-* specifications), .NET Remoting, and more.

- WCF provides explicit support for *service-oriented development*. Service-oriented development focuses on developing *services*, not objects.

- When you use service-oriented development, a host *provides* a service and a client *consumes* the service.

- WCF services provide interoperability with applications built on other technologies and platforms, including ASMX web services and web services built on Java EE.

- A WCF service can be hosted by a Windows Forms application, a Console application, a Windows service, IIS, or *Windows Process Activation Service* (*WAS*).

- The IIS hosting option is integrated with ASP.NET and can take advantage of the features that IIS and ASP.NET have to offer. Because of that, it's common to use IIS to host a WCF service.

- A WCF service has one or more *endpoints* that determine how the service can be accessed.

- WCF provides support for *SOAP* (*Simple Object Access Protocol*). If a service runs under IIS, it typically uses SOAP over HTTP to pass data between the client and the service. SOAP wraps an XML message in other protocols to transmit the message.

- If a service runs under WAS, it can use protocols other than HTTP.

Figure 23-1   How WCF services work

An introduction to bindings

When you define the endpoints for a service, each endpoint has a *binding* that determines how the service can be accessed. In particular, the binding determines what combination of protocols can be used to access the service. The table in figure 23-2 lists the predefined bindings that are available from WCF. This table should give you an idea of how flexible WCF services can be. In addition, it introduces you to the various protocols and data formats that are supported by WCF.

If you use IIS to host a WCF service, that service typically uses SOAP over HTTP. In that case, the endpoints for the service must use one of the first three bindings shown in this figure. Here, the first binding (basicHttpBinding) provides support for *MTOM* (*Message Transmission Optimization Mechanism*), a web standard for efficiently sending binary data to and from web services. In contrast, the second binding (wsHttpBinding) provides support for the advanced web service specifications, which allow a WCF service to work with a web service on any platform that also supports these specifications.

The third binding (mexHttpBinding) works the same as the second binding, but with security disabled. This allows the endpoint and the client to exchange metadata, which contains information about how the service works. This type of binding is called a *metadata exchange (mex) binding*, and an endpoint that uses this binding is called a *mex endpoint*. This binding is useful for development but is often disabled for the final release of a service.

The fourth binding (webHttpBinding) can be used for any situation where SOAP isn't needed, such as if you use *REST* (*Representational State Transfer*). This binding supports several data formats including *JavaScript Object Notation* (*JSON*) or XML that isn't wrapped in SOAP, which is sometimes referred to as *plain old XML* (*POX*). Since this binding supports JSON, it's useful for creating services for AJAX clients.

The last three bindings aren't typically used by WCF services that are hosted by a web server and accessed through the Internet or an intranet. Instead, they're typically used by WCF services that are hosted on a Windows server and accessed through a private network.

By the way, you shouldn't be concerned if you don't understand all the terminology presented in this topic. Instead, just realize that WCF is a powerful and flexible technology that supports many communication protocols and data formats.

Types of bindings for endpoints

Binding	Description
`basicHttpBinding`	Uses SOAP over HTTP. Also supports HTTPS and optimizing data transmission using MTOM.
`wsHttpBinding`	Uses SOAP over HTTP. Also supports advanced web specifications such as reliable message transfer with WS-ReliableMessaging, security with WS-Security, and transactions with WS-AtomicTransaction. This binding allows interoperability with other web services that also support these specifications.
`mexHttpBinding`	Works the same as wsHttpBinding, but it has security disabled. As a result, this binding can provide information about the service (metadata) to its clients.
`webHttpBinding`	Uses HTTP or HTTPS without SOAP. It can be used in any situation where SOAP isn't needed, such as if you use REST. This binding provides for several data formats including POX and JSON.
`netTcpBinding`	Uses binary-encoded SOAP directly over TCP. This binding can be used only for WCF-to-WCF communication.
`netNamedPipesBinding`	Uses binary-encoded SOAP over named pipes. This binding can only be used for WCF-to-WCF communication between processes on the same machine.
`netMsmqBinding`	Uses binary-encoded SOAP over MSMQ (Microsoft Message Queuing). This binding can only be used for WCF-to-WCF communication.

Description

- Each endpoint that's exposed by a WCF service has a *binding* that determines how the service can be accessed. In particular, the binding determines what combination of protocols can be used to access the service.

- WCF provides support for *MTOM* (*Message Transmission Optimization Mechanism*), a web standard for efficiently sending binary data to and from services.

- WCF provides support for communication protocols such as HTTP, *TCP* (*Transmission Control Protocol*), *named pipes*, and *MSMQ* (*Microsoft Message Queuing*).

- WCF provides support for *Representational State Transfer* (*REST*). REST has gained widespread acceptance as a simpler alternative to SOAP-based web services.

- WCF provides support for multiple data formats including *JSON* (*JavaScript Object Notation*) and *POX* (*plain old XML*).

Figure 23-2   An introduction to bindings

How to create a WCF service

Now that you've been introduced to some of the basic concepts and terms for working with a WCF service, you're ready to create a WCF service. To do that, you can create a WCF service library. Then, you can add one or more services to that library, you can write the code for the services, and you can test the code.

How to start a WCF service library

To create a WCF service, you typically start by creating a WCF service library. To do that, you use the New Project dialog box shown in figure 23-3. Note that a WCF service library isn't a web site, it's a special type of project. As a result, you don't use the New Web Site and Open Web Site commands to work with it. Instead, you use the New Project and Open Project commands.

Before I go on, you should realize that you can't create a WCF service library if you're using Visual Web Developer 2010 Express. However, you can still create a WCF service. To do that, you add the WCF service directly to the web site that will host the service. You'll learn more about that later in this chapter.

The New Project dialog box

Description

- To start a WCF service library, select the File→New Project command, select the WCF template group, and select the WCF Service Library template. Then, enter a name and location for the service library and click OK.

Note

- You can't create a WCF service library with Visual Web Developer 2010 Express. Instead, you'll have to add the WCF services directly to the web site that will host the services as described later in this chapter.

Figure 23-3   How to start a WCF service library

How to develop the code for a WCF service library

Figure 23-4 shows the starting files that Visual Studio generates for a WCF service library. The code for the IService1.cs file is shown in the Code Editor in this figure. Here, you can see that this file contains an interface named IService1, along with a class named CompositeType. The interface defines the *operations* that the service can perform, and the class defines the data that can be used by the service.

To indicate that the interface defines a service, the statement that declares the interface is preceded by a ServiceContract *attribute*. Similarly, to indicate that a method defines an operation for a service, the statement that declares the method is preceded by the OperationContract attribute. By default, the IService1 interface includes two operations named GetData and GetDataUsingDataContract.

Notice that the second operation, GetDataUsingDataContract, accepts a parameter of type CompositeType and returns a value of the same type. This type is defined by the CompositeType class, which is identified as a composite data type by the DataContract attribute. By default, this class includes a Boolean property named BoolValue and a string property named StringValue. These properties are identified as *members* of the data type by the DataMember attribute.

In addition to the IService1.cs file, Visual Studio generates a file named Service1.cs. Although it isn't shown in this figure, this file defines a class named Service1 that implements the IService1 interface. In the next figure, you'll learn more about how this works.

The easiest way to get started developing a service is to rename the IService1.cs and Service1.cs files. Then, you can edit the starting code for these files. For example, you'll want to change the name of the Interface so it's the same as the name of the file that contains it, and you'll want to change the operations that are defined by the interface so they're appropriate for the service you're creating. You'll also want to change the name of the class that defines the data used by the service, and you'll want to define the appropriate properties. Finally, you'll want to change the name of the class that implements the interface, and you'll want to implement the methods defined by the interface.

Note that when you change the name of an interface or class, you should use the Rename command to change other occurrences of the interface or class name in the project. To use this command, place the mouse pointer over the bar that's displayed beneath the last character of the new name, click the drop-down arrow that appears, and select the Rename command from the smart tag menu that's displayed. If you don't use the Rename command, you'll have to rename each occurrence manually or use search-and-replace to locate and change them. That includes the occurrences in the App.config file.

In this chapter, you'll learn how to create a WCF service library that contains a single service. Since a single service can provide for multiple operations and data types, that should be enough to get you started. However, if you develop multiple operations and data types that aren't related, you may want to store them in different services. In that case, you can add a WCF service to the library as described in this figure.

The starting code for a WCF service library

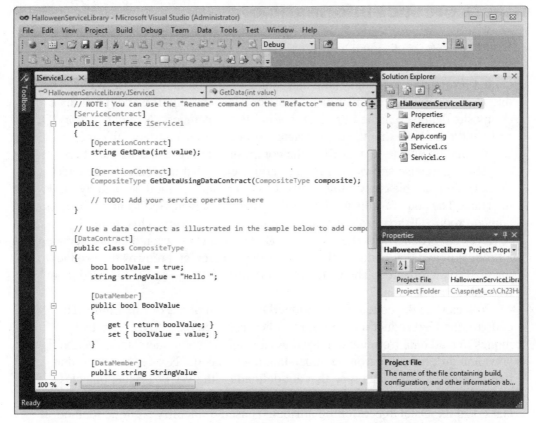

Description

- By default, a new WCF service library includes two files named IService1.cs and Service1.cs. The IService1.cs file contains an interface named IService1, along with a class named CompositeType that defines a composite data type. The Service1.cs file contains a class named Service1 that implements the IService1 interface.

- To define the operations of a service, you code an interface that has the ServiceContract *attribute*. Then, you can code one or more methods that have the OperationContract attribute.

- To define the data that's used by a service, you code a class that has the DataContract attribute. Then, you code one or more properties that have the DataMember attribute.

- To implement the operations of a service, you code a class that implements the interface for the service.

- To add a WCF service to the library, select the Project→Add New Item command. Then, select the WCF Service item from the resulting dialog box, enter a name for the service, and click Add.

Figure 23-4   How to develop the code for a WCF service library

The code for a WCF service that gets product information

To help you understand how WCF services work, figure 23-5 shows the code for a service named ProductService. To start, this code defines an interface named IProductService that contains a single operation named GetProduct. This operation accepts a string parameter that contains a productID, and it returns a composite data type named Product that has three members: Name, CategoryID, and UnitPrice. Note that the appropriate attributes are used to identify the service and its operation as well as the composite data type and its members.

This figure also shows the ProductService class that implements the interface. To do that, this class implements the GetProduct method defined by the interface. The code for this method calls a method named GetProduct in a class named ProductDB that's also included in the service library. This method retrieves the product with the specified ID from the Halloween database, creates a Product object that contains the data for the product, and returns the product to the GetProduct method. The GetProduct method, in turn, returns the product to the calling application.

You can see the code for the ProductDB class in part 2 of this figure. The code for the GetProduct method of this class uses standard ADO.NET techniques to read data from the database. As a result, if you understand ADO.NET, you shouldn't have any trouble understanding this code. Notice, however, that like the interface and data type that are defined by the WCF service, this class includes attributes. The DataObject attribute is used to identify a data object class, and the DataObjectMethod attribute is used to identify a public method. If you've read chapter 17 on object data sources, you'll realize that these are the same attributes you use to mark data access classes for an object data source. For more information, please see figure 17-10.

The configuration file for the WCF service

Figure 23-6 shows the App.config file for the service in figure 23-5. The starting code for this file is generated when you create a project from the WCF Service Library template. Then, when you change the names of the interface and class, any occurrences of those names in this file are changed automatically if you use the Rename command. As a result, you don't need to enter or modify any of this code yourself.

If you review the code in the service element of this file, you should get a general idea of how the file works. In particular, you should notice that it defines two endpoints. The first endpoint is a wsHttpBinding endpoint that uses SOAP over HTTP and supports the advanced web services specifications. The second endpoint is a mexHttpBinding endpoint that enables the metadata exchange between the service and the client. This endpoint has an address of "mex" that's appended to the base address for the service, which is also defined in this configuration file.

The IProductService interface

```
using System.Runtime.Serialization;
using System.ServiceModel;

namespace HalloweenServiceLibrary
{
    [ServiceContract]
    public interface IProductService
    {
        [OperationContract]
        Product GetProduct(string productID);
    }

    [DataContract]
    public class Product
    {
        string name = "";
        string categoryID = "";
        decimal unitPrice = 0;

        [DataMember]
        public string Name
        {
            get { return name; }
            set { name = value; }
        }

        [DataMember]
        public string CategoryID
        {
            get { return categoryID; }
            set { categoryID = value; }
        }

        [DataMember]
        public decimal UnitPrice
        {
            get { return unitPrice; }
            set { unitPrice = value; }
        }
    }
}
```

The ProductService class

```
namespace HalloweenServiceLibrary
{
    public class ProductService : IProductService
    {
        public Product GetProduct(string productID)
        {
            Product p = ProductDB.GetProduct(productID);
            return p;
        }
    }
}
```

Figure 23-5   The code for a WCF service that gets product information (part 1 of 2)

The ProductDB class

```
using System;
using System.ComponentModel;
using System.Data;
using System.Data.SqlClient;

namespace HalloweenServiceLibrary
{
    [DataObject]
    class ProductDB
    {

        [DataObjectMethod(DataObjectMethodType.Select)]
        public static Product GetProduct(string productID)
        {
            SqlConnection con = new SqlConnection(GetConnectionString());
            string sel = "SELECT * " +
                "FROM Products WHERE ProductID = '" + productID + "'";
            SqlCommand cmd = new SqlCommand(sel, con);
            con.Open();
            SqlDataReader rdr =
                cmd.ExecuteReader(CommandBehavior.CloseConnection);
            Product p = new Product();
            if (rdr.Read())
            {
                p.CategoryID = rdr["CategoryID"].ToString();
                p.Name = rdr["Name"].ToString();
                p.UnitPrice = Convert.ToDecimal(rdr["UnitPrice"]);
            }
            rdr.Close();
            return p;
        }

        private static string GetConnectionString()
        {
            return "Data Source=localhost\\sqlexpress;" +
                    "Initial Catalog=Halloween;Integrated Security=True";
        }

    }
}
```

Figure 23-5   The code for a WCF service that gets product information (part 2 of 2)

The App.config file

```xml
<?xml version="1.0" encoding="utf-8" ?>
<configuration>

  <system.web>
    <compilation debug="true" />
  </system.web>

  <!-- When deploying the service library project,
  the content of the config file must be added to the host's app.config file.
  System.Configuration does not support config files for libraries. -->
  <system.serviceModel>

    <services>
      <service name="HalloweenServiceLibrary.ProductService">
        <endpoint address="" binding="wsHttpBinding"
                  contract="HalloweenServiceLibrary.IProductService">
          <identity>
            <dns value="localhost" />
          </identity>
        </endpoint>

        <endpoint address="mex" binding="mexHttpBinding"
                  contract="IMetadataExchange" />

        <host>
          <baseAddresses>
            <add baseAddress=
              "http://localhost:8732/Design_Time_Addresses/ProductService/" />
          </baseAddresses>
        </host>
      </service>
    </services>

    <behaviors>
      <serviceBehaviors>
        <behavior>

          <!-- To avoid disclosing metadata information,
          set the value below to false and remove the metadata
          endpoint above before deployment -->
          <serviceMetadata httpGetEnabled="True"/>

          <!-- To receive exception details in faults for debugging purposes,
          set the value below to true.  Set to false before deployment
          to avoid disclosing exception information -->
          <serviceDebug includeExceptionDetailInFaults="False" />

        </behavior>
      </serviceBehaviors>
    </behaviors>

  </system.serviceModel>
</configuration>
```

Figure 23-6   The configuration file for the WCF service

How to test a WCF service

Figure 23-7 shows how to test a WCF service. To do that, you can press F5 or click the Start Debugging button in the Standard toolbar. When you do, Visual Studio displays a WCF Test Client window like the one shown in this figure. Then, you can test any operation in any service in the library by double-clicking on the operation, entering any required parameters, and clicking the Invoke button.

Although you can't see it in this figure, the WCF Test Client accesses the service with this URL:

```
http://localhost:8732/Design_Time_Addresses/ProductService/mex
```

Here, the /mex at the end of the URL indicates that the metadata exchange endpoint is used to access the service. If you look back to the App.config file, you can see that this URL corresponds with the address for the mexHttpBinding endpoint.

When you test a WCF service, it's automatically compiled into a dll file. This file contains debugging information by default so you can debug the service using the Visual Studio debugger. When you finish testing a service, you'll typically want to remove this debugging information so the service is more efficient. To do that, you can create a release build of the library as described in this figure.

The WCF Test Client window

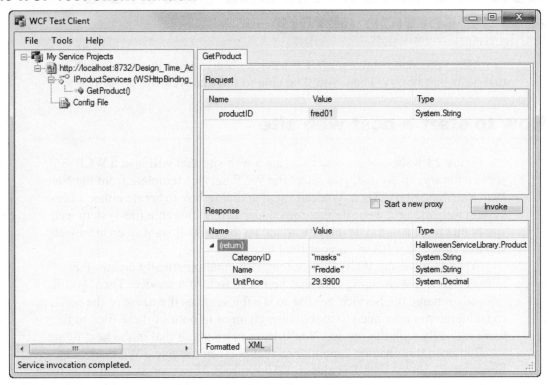

Description

- To test a WCF service, you can press F5 or click the Start Debugging button in the Standard toolbar. When you do, Visual Studio displays a WCF Test Client window for the service library.

- To test a service operation, double-click on the operation in the left pane of the window to display a tab for the operation in the right side of the window. Then, enter any required parameters for the operation in the Request section of the tab and click the Invoke button. When you do, the Response section will show the data that's returned by the operation.

- When you test a service, a dll file that contains debugging information is created and stored in the bin\Debug directory subordinate to the project directory. Then, you can use the Visual Studio debugger to debug the service.

- When you're done testing a service, you can create a release build for the service that doesn't contain debugging information. To do that, you can select the Release option from the Solution Configurations drop-down list in the Standard toolbar. Then, you can build or run the project to create a dll file that's stored in the bin\Release directory subordinate to the project directory.

Figure 23-7   How to test a WCF service

How to create a web site that hosts a WCF service library

After you create and test a WCF service library, you can create a web site that hosts that library. Then, you'll be able to run that web site under IIS.

How to start a host web site

Figure 23-8 shows you how to create a web site that will host a WCF service library. To do that, you select the WCF Service template from the New Web Site dialog box. Then, you can use that dialog box to create either a file-system web site or a web site that runs under IIS. Although a file-system web site is fine for the initial development and testing, you'll want to create a web site that runs under IIS to do your final testing.

When you use the WCF Service template, it automatically creates the Service.svc and Web.config files that you need to host a service. Then, you'll typically rename the Service.svc file so it's the same as the name of the service. In addition, you may need to make some changes to both of these files so they work correctly with the service. You'll learn more about that in the next figure.

Earlier in this chapter, I mentioned that you can't create a WCF service library using Visual Web Developer 2010 Express. However, you can still create a WCF service. To do that, you use the IService.cs and Service.cs files that are added to the App_Code folder of a WCF service web site by default. (This folder, along with the App_Data folder that's also added by default, has been deleted from the web site shown in this figure since it's not needed.) You write the code for these files just as you would for any other WCF service.

Unfortunately, when you create a WCF service directly in a WCF service web site, you can't test the service as shown earlier in this chapter. Instead, you have to test it from a client application that uses the service. In addition, you won't be able to host the web service in any other environments, such as a Windows application or WAS. Because of that, the service is much less flexible.

How to add a reference to a service library

If you create a WCF service in a service library, you need to add a reference to that library to the host web site. To do that, you use the Add Reference dialog box shown in figure 23-8. From this dialog box, you can use the Browse tab of the Add Reference dialog box to navigate to the dll file for the WCF service library. In this case, I navigated to the HalloweenServiceLibrary.dll file in the bin\Debug directory of the project directory so I could debug the service from a client that uses the service. When I added a reference to this file, the files shown in the Bin directory in this figure were added to the project.

A WCF service web site with a reference to a WCF service library

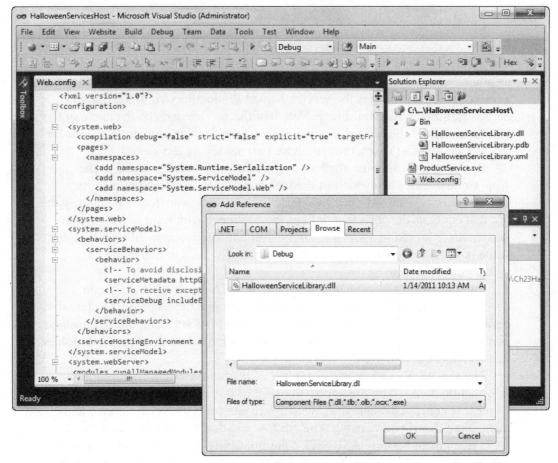

Description

- To start a web site that can host a WCF service library, select the File→New Web Site command. Then, select the WCF Service template and create a new file-system or HTTP web site.

- By default, a WCF service web site contains Service.svc and Web.config files. You typically rename the Service.svc file to correspond to the name of the service, and you modify both files as shown in the next figure.

- A WCF service web site also includes an App_Code folder by default that contains IService.cs and Service.cs files. You can use these files to create a web service as described earlier in this chapter. This is particularly useful if you're using Visual Web Developer 2010 Express and can't create a WCF service library.

- If you're creating a web site that will host an existing WCF service, you can delete the App_Code folder as well as the App_Data folder that's also added by default.

- To add a reference to a WCF service library, you can select the Website→Add Reference command to display the Add Reference dialog box. Then, you can use the Browse tab to navigate to and select the dll file for the WCF service library.

Figure 23-8   A WCF service web site that hosts a WCF service library

The configuration files for the host web site

Figure 23-9 shows the two configuration files for the host web site. The first file, ProductService.svc, contains a ServiceHost directive that identifies the web site as the host for a service. The main attribute to notice here is the Service attribute, which identifies the service that's being hosted. In this case, the Service attribute identifies the service named ProductService in the library named HalloweenServiceLibrary. Note that the service name is the name of the class that defines the service, not the name of the file that contains the code for the service. In most cases, though, these two names are the same.

By default, the Service attribute names the service that's added to the App_Code folder when you start the web site, which is defined by a class named "Service". In addition, a CodeBehind attribute is included to identify the file that contains the class that defines the service. If you want to host a web service that's stored in a service library, you will need to manually change the value of the Service attribute. In addition, you will need to delete the CodeBehind attribute.

You will also need to change the value of the Service attribute if you develop a service within the web site and you change the name of the class that defines the service. You won't delete the CodeBehind attribute, though. Instead, you will need to change its value so it identifies the file in the App_Code folder that contains the code for the service.

The second file shown in this figure, Web.config, contains configuration information required by the application. All of this code except for the services element is generated when you create a web site from the WCF Service template. Note that if you're using ASP.NET 4, you don't need to include the services element because ASP.NET 4 automatically defines default endpoints for the service. If you're using an earlier version of ASP.NET, though, you need to explicitly define the endpoints as shown in this figure.

The easiest way to add the services element is to copy it from the App.config file of the service library. Then, you can delete any elements that you don't need. And, of course, if you want to use an endpoint other than the default, you'll need to include a services element with the appropriate information.

In addition to adding and modifying the services element, you may want to modify elements within the behavior element. The first element, serviceMetadata, determines whether metadata information is disclosed. You should set the httpGetEnabled attribute of this element to false before deploying the web service. For this to work, you must also delete the endpoint element for the mex endpoint, if one exists. The second element, serviceDebug, determines whether exception information is made available for debugging purposes. You may want to change this value to true during testing, but it should be set to false before the web service is deployed.

The ProductService.svc file

```
<%@ ServiceHost Language="C#" Debug="true"
                Service="HalloweenServiceLibrary.ProductService" %>
```

The Web.config file

```xml
<?xml version="1.0"?>
<configuration>
  <system.web>
    <compilation debug="true" strict="false" explicit="true"
                 targetFramework="4.0"/>
    <pages>
      <namespaces>
        <add namespace="System.Runtime.Serialization"/>
        <add namespace="System.ServiceModel"/>
        <add namespace="System.ServiceModel.Web"/>
      </namespaces>
    </pages>
  </system.web>

  <system.serviceModel>

    <!-- You can copy this element from the App.config file of the library -->
    <services>
      <service name="HalloweenServiceLibrary.ProductService">
        <endpoint address=""
                  binding="wsHttpBinding"
                  contract="HalloweenServiceLibrary.IProductService" />

        <endpoint address="mex"
                  binding="mexHttpBinding"
                  contract="IMetadataExchange" />
      </service>
    </services>

    <behaviors>
      <serviceBehaviors>
        <behavior>
          <!-- To avoid disclosing metadata information,
          set the value below to false and remove the metadata
          endpoint above before deployment -->
          <serviceMetadata httpGetEnabled="true"/>

          <!-- To receive exception details in faults for debugging purposes,
               set the value below to true.  Set to false before deployment
               to avoid disclosing exception information -->
          <serviceDebug includeExceptionDetailInFaults="false"/>
        </behavior>
      </serviceBehaviors>
    </behaviors>

    <serviceHostingEnvironment multipleSiteBindingsEnabled="true"/>
  </system.serviceModel>

  <system.webServer>
    <modules runAllManagedModulesForAllRequests="true"/>
  </system.webServer>
</configuration>
```

Figure 23-9   The configuration files for the web host

How to display information about the service in a browser

After you create and configure the web site that hosts the service, you can display information about the service in a web browser. To do that, you should start by setting the svc file for the web site as the start page. Then, you can run the web site just as you would any other web site. If the host web site is configured properly, a Service page like the one shown in figure 23-10 is displayed.

As you can see, this page includes information about how to use the svcutil.exe tool to create files that you include in a client application to make the service available to the application. If you'll be developing the client application in Visual Studio, though, you can use the skills you'll learn in the next figure instead. The Service page also shows some basic C# and Visual Basic code that you can use to work with the service from a client application. You'll learn more about that in figure 23-12.

The WCF service displayed in a browser

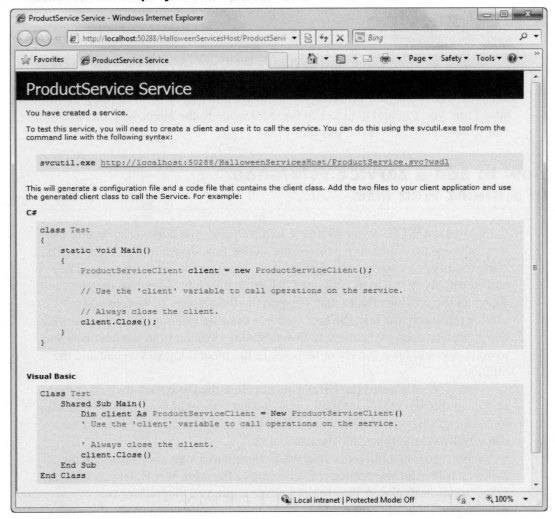

Description

- To display information about a WCF service in a browser, start by setting the start page for the web site to the svc file. Then, press F5 or click the Start Debugging button in the Standard toolbar to display a Service page like the one shown above.

- The Service page contains information about creating a client that consumes the service. In addition, it contains C# and Visual Basic code that illustrates how to use the service in a client.

- If an error is displayed instead of the Service page, it indicates that the web site that hosts the service isn't configured properly.

Figure 23-10   How to display information about the WCF service in a browser

How to create a web site that consumes a WCF service

After you create a web site that hosts a WCF service, you can create a client web site that consumes the service. Because any web site can be a client web site, you can use any of the skills you've learned in this book to develop the web site. Then, you can add a reference for the service to the client web site, and you can write code that uses the service.

How to add a service reference to a client web site

To make a WCF service available to a web site, you add a reference to the service using the Add Service Reference dialog box shown in figure 23-11. To start, you need to enter a URL that points to the .svc file for the service. The easiest way to do that is to copy the URL from a web browser like the one shown in the previous figure that's displaying the service. In fact, to add a service reference like this, the host web site must be running. For this to work, you'll need to open two copies of Visual Studio, open and run the host web site in one copy, and open the client web site in the other copy so you can add the reference.

Once you've entered the URL, you can click the Go button to display the service in the Services list. Finally, you can enter the namespace name you want to use for the service and click the OK button. In this example, I entered the name HalloweenServices for the namespace.

When you add a reference to a WCF service to a web site, Visual Studio creates a folder for the service reference under the App_WebReferences folder in the Solution Explorer. This folder has the name you entered for the namespace in the Add Service Reference dialog box. If you expand this folder, you can see the configuration files for the service. Since these files are generated for you automatically, you don't need to understand the code they contain. If you're curious about how these files work, though, you can display them in the Text Editor.

Before I go on, you should realize that if the port number for the development server that's used to run the host web site is different from the port number that's used for the service reference, the client web site won't be able to locate the service. For example, if you try to run the client web site for this chapter that you can download from our web site, it won't work. To fix that, you need to delete the folder for the service reference from the App_WebReferences folder. Then, you need to start the host web site and use its URL to add a service reference back to the client web site.

A web site after a reference to a WCF service has been added to it

Description

- To start a web site that will consume a WCF service, you can use any of the techniques you've learned throughout this book.

- To make a WCF service available to a web site, you add a reference to the service. To do that, you use the Website→Add Service Reference command to display the Add Service Reference dialog box. Then, you enter the URL for the service, click the Go button, enter a namespace name for the service, and click the OK button.

- When you add a reference to a WCF service, Visual Studio creates a folder for the service reference under the App_WebReferences folder in the Solution Explorer. If you expand this folder, you can see the configuration files for the service.

Figure 23-11   How to add a service reference to a client web site

How to consume a WCF service

Figure 23-12 shows how to consume a WCF service from a client web site. The application shown here consists of a simple web page that lets the user display information for a selected product. To do that, the user enters a product code and clicks the Get Product Data button. Then, the application uses the ProductService service you saw in figure 23-5 to get the name, unit price, and category for the product. Finally, the application displays the retrieved values in the labels on the form.

To code an application like this, you typically start by adding an using statement for the namespace that contains the service so it's easier to refer to. The name you specify here is the same as the name you entered in the Add Service Reference dialog box. In this case, it's HalloweenServices.

Next, you create a client object for the service. Since this object provides access to the operations and data types that are defined by the service, it is known as a *proxy* for the service. To create a proxy, you use a type name that consists of the name of the class that defines the service, appended with "Client". For example, the type name for the service named ProductService is ProductServiceClient.

Once you create the proxy, you can use it to call the operations the service provides. To do that, you use the same techniques that you use to execute a method of an object. In this figure, for example, the code calls the GetProduct operation of the proxy and passes the product ID the user entered in the text box. Then, it stores the Product object that's returned by this operation in a variable of the Product type. Next, it closes the proxy. Finally, it displays the properties of the Product object in the labels on the web page.

The web page in a browser

The code-behind file for the web page

```csharp
using System;
using HalloweenServices;

public partial class _Default : System.Web.UI.Page
{
    protected void btnGetProduct_Click(object sender, EventArgs e)
    {
        // Create a proxy for the service
        ProductServiceClient client = new ProductServiceClient();

        // Get the data from the service
        Product p = client.GetProduct(txtProductID.Text);

        // Close the proxy
        client.Close();

        // Display the data
        lblName.Text = p.Name;
        lblUnitPrice.Text = p.UnitPrice.ToString("c");
        lblCategory.Text = p.CategoryID;
    }
}
```

Description

- To consume a WCF service, you create a client object, or *proxy*, for the service. To do that, you use a type with the name of the class that defines the service, appended with "Client".

- After you create an object for the service, you can execute its operations using the same techniques you use to execute a method of any object.

- To make it easier to work with a service, you can include a using statement for the namespace that contains the service.

Figure 23-12   How to consume a WCF service

Perspective

Although the WCF service presented in this chapter is simple, it demonstrates the techniques you can use to develop more substantial WCF services. As a result, the basic skills you've learned here are enough to get you started developing your own WCF services. In addition, you'll be prepared to learn the more complicated aspects of WCF services programming when the need arises.

For example, before you deploy a WCF service, you may want to learn more about configuring its endpoints to improve the functionality or security of the service. Or, if you want to use REST instead of SOAP, you can learn more about creating WCF services that support REST. Or, if you don't want to use a web site as the host or client for a WCF service, you can learn more about the other options for providing and consuming web services.

* * *

In this book, we've done our best to present all of the skills that you need for developing ecommerce web applications. Now, if you've read all 23 chapters, we hope you feel that you're adequately prepared for doing that. You should also feel like you have the concepts, skills, and perspective to learn whatever else you need to know as you develop web applications. If that's the case, this book has done its job. And we thank you for reading it.

Terms

web service
ASMX web service
WCF (Windows Communication
    Foundation)
service-oriented development
service
provide a service
consume a service
WAS (Windows Process Activation
    Service)
endpoint
SOAP (Simple Object Access Protocol)
binding
MTOM (Message Transmission
    Optimization Mechanism)

TCP (Transmission Control
    Protocol)
named pipes
MSMQ (Microsoft Message
    Queuing)
metadata exchange (mex) binding
mex endpoint
REST (Representational State
    Transfer)
JSON (JavaScript Object Notation)
POX (plain old XML)
operation
attribute
member
proxy

Appendix A

How to install and use the software and downloadable files

To develop ASP.NET 4 applications, you need to have Visual Studio 2010 or Visual Web Developer 2010 Express Edition installed on your PC. Both of these products include a development web server that you can use to run your applications. However, because of the limitations of this server, you'll also want to test your applications using IIS. The easiest way to do that is to install IIS on your own PC.

If you're going to develop applications that use databases that are stored on your own PC rather than on a remote server, you also need to install SQL Server on your PC. The easiest way to do that is to install SQL Server 2008 Express Edition. In fact, this edition of SQL Server is installed by default when you install most editions of Visual Studio 2010.

This appendix shows you how to install both Visual Studio and IIS. In addition, it shows you how to install SQL Server 2008 Express Edition and how to create the SQL Server database that's used in this book. But first, it describes the files for this book that are available for download from our web site and shows you how to download, install, and use them. We recommend you read these topics before you start developing your first web application so you can be sure that you have all the software and files you need.

How to download and install the files for this book

Throughout this book, you'll see complete applications that illustrate the material presented in each chapter. To help you understand how these applications work, you can download the source code and databases for these applications from our web site at www.murach.com. Then, you can open and run them in Visual Studio. These files come in a single download, as summarized in figure A-1. This figure also describes how you download and install these files.

When you download the single install file and execute it, it will install all of the files for this book in the Murach\aspnet4_cs directory on your C drive. Within this directory, you'll find a directory named book_applications that contains all the applications in this book. You can open and run these applications in Visual Studio as file-system applications as described in figure A-7. The exceptions are the applications for chapters 8 and 21, which must be run under IIS because they use application state, and the application for chapter 18, which must be run under IIS because it requires a digital secure certificate. The procedure for running a file-system web site under IIS is also presented in figure A-7. For more information on application state, see chapter 8. And for more information on digital secure certificates, see chapter 18.

The download also includes an Access version of the Halloween database that's used by some of the applications in the first two sections of this book. Since the Access database is small, we've included it in the App_Data folder of each application that uses it so you can run these applications without any trouble.

To use the SQL Server version of the Halloween database, you'll need to use the create_database.bat and create_database.sql files in the C:\Murach\database directory to create the database. You may also need to use some of the other files in this directory to grant ASP.NET access to the database. You'll learn more about all of these files in figure A-6.

To help you practice the skills you'll learn in the first three sections of this book, we've included exercises at the end of these chapters. We also provide starting points for many of these exercises in the C:\Murach\aspnet4_cs\exercise_starts directory. When you execute the setup file, the contents of this directory are copied to the C:\aspnet4_cs directory (creating this directory if necessary). This makes it easy to locate the exercise starts as you work through the exercises.

What the downloadable application file for this book contains

- The source code for all of the applications presented in the book
- Access and SQL Server Express versions of the Halloween database used in these applications
- Files you can use to work with the SQL Server Express version of the Halloween database
- The starting points for the exercises in this book

How to download and install the files for this book

1. Go to www.murach.com, and go to the page for *Murach's ASP.NET 4 Web Programming with C# 2010*.
2. Click on the link for "FREE download of the book applications." Then, download "All book files." This will download one file named a4cs_allfiles.exe to your C drive.
3. Use Windows Explorer to find the downloaded file on your C drive. Then, double-click on this file and respond to the dialog boxes that follow. This installs the files in directories that start with C:\Murach\aspnet4_cs.

How your system is prepared for doing the exercises

- Some of the exercises have you start from existing applications. The source code for these applications is in the C:\Murach\aspnet4_cs\exercise_starts directory. After the setup file installs the files in the download, it runs a batch file named exercise_starts_setup.bat that copies the contents of the exercise_starts directory to the C:\aspnet4_cs directory. Then, you can find all of the starting points for the exercises in directories like C:\aspnet4_cs\Ch01Cart and C:\aspnet4_cs\Ch04Cart.

How to prepare your system for using the SQL Server database

- To use the database that comes with this book on your PC, you need to make sure that SQL Server 2008 Express is installed as described in figure A-5. Then, you need to run the batch file we provide to create the database and attach it to SQL Server Express as described in figure A-6.

Note

- The Access version of the Halloween database is included in the App_Data folder of each application that uses it.

Figure A-1   How to download and install the files for this book

How to install IIS under Windows 7 or Windows Vista

When you run an ASP.NET web application from Visual Studio, it runs under the built-in development server by default. Because of that, you don't have to have IIS installed to develop the applications in this book or to run the applications that you download from our web site (with the exceptions noted in the previous topic). Keep in mind, however, that the built-in server has some limitations, which you'll learn about in chapter 4. Because of that, you'll want to install IIS so that you can thoroughly test the applications you develop. (Note that the versions of IIS that come with the Home Basic Edition and the Starter Edition of Windows Vista and Windows 7 can't be configured for ASP.NET development. Because of that, you'll have to use the development server that comes with ASP.NET to test your applications, or you'll need to have access to a separate web server.)

Figure A-2 shows how to install IIS under Windows 7 or Windows Vista. To start, you display the Windows Features dialog box as described here. This dialog box lists all the available Windows features. If all of the features of a component are installed, the check box in front of the component will have a check mark in it. If only some of the features are installed, the check box for the component will be shaded.

To install the default features of IIS, you simply check its box and then click the OK button. If you want to install features other than the defaults, you can expand the Internet Information Services node and any of its subordinate nodes to select the features you want. By default, the features listed in step 3 of this figure should be selected. However, in some cases they aren't, so you need to select them. Similarly, if you want to use IIS as an FTP server so you can develop applications over the Internet, you need to select the FTP Server feature as described in step 4.

Note that the versions of IIS that come with Windows Vista (IIS 7.0) and Windows 7 (IIS 7.5) don't include FrontPage Server Extensions (FPSE). Because of that, you can't work with web sites on a remote server. Since the release of IIS 7.0, however, an edition of FPSE that works with IIS 7.0 and later has become available. You can download this product from the IIS web site as described in this figure.

The Windows Features dialog box

How to install IIS

1. Display the Control Panel and click the Programs link. Then, click the Turn Windows Features On or Off link in the Programs and Features category to display the Windows Features dialog box.

2. Select Internet Information Services from the list of features that are displayed.

3. Expand the Internet Information Service nodes and make sure to select these features:
    *   Web Management Tools ➔ IIS 6 Management Compatibility
    *   Web Management Tools ➔ IIS Management Console
    *   World Wide Web Services ➔ Application Development Features ➔ ASP.NET

4. If you want to configure IIS as an FTP Server, expand the Internet Information Services node and select the FTP Server feature.

5. Click the OK button to complete the installation.

Description

*   If you want to run applications from a local IIS server, install IIS before you install Visual Studio.

*   Windows Vista comes with IIS 7.0 and Windows 7 comes with IIS 7.5, which don't include FPSE. As a result, before you can create or access a web site on a remote computer, you must download FPSE. To do that, go to www.iis.net/downloads, click the link for the Administration category, and click the link for FrontPage 2002 Server Extensions for IIS 7.0.

*   If the check box for a component is shaded, it means that only some of the features of that component are installed. To see all features, you can expand the component.

Figure A-2   How to install IIS under Windows 7 or Windows Vista

How to install IIS under Windows XP

If you want to be able to test the web applications you develop under IIS on a Windows XP machine, you'll need to use the procedure in figure A-3 to install IIS. (Note that you can't install IIS if you're using Windows XP Home Edition. In that case, IIS isn't available to you, and you'll have to use the development server or you'll have to have access to a separate web server.) To start, you display the Add/Remove Programs dialog box and then click the Add/Remove Windows Components button at the left side of the dialog box that's displayed. When you do, the Windows Components Wizard starts and the first dialog box shown in this figure is displayed. This dialog box lists all the available Windows components. The components that are currently installed have a check mark in front of them. To install another component (in this case, IIS), just check it, click the Next button, and complete the dialog boxes that are displayed.

In this book, you'll learn how to develop ASP.NET applications using a local IIS server. You should know, however, that you can also use Visual Studio to develop ASP.NET applications on a remote serve or over the Internet. To develop applications on a remote server, you'll need to install FrontPage Server Extensions. And to develop applications over the Internet, you can use IIS as an FTP server.

To use either of these features, you must install components of IIS that aren't installed by default. To install these components, select IIS in the Windows Components Wizard and then click the Details button to display the Internet Information Services (IIS) dialog box shown here. Then, if you want to use IIS as an FTP server, select the File Transfer Protocol (FTP) Service component. And, if you want to create remote IIS web sites, select the FrontPage 2000 Server Extensions component. When you're done, click OK and then continue with the Windows Components Wizard.

The Windows Components Wizard

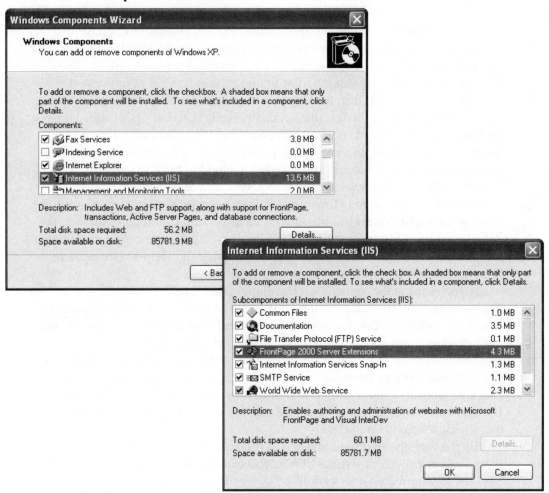

How to install IIS

1. Double-click Add or Remove Programs in the Control Panel. Then, click on Add/ Remove Windows Components to display the Windows Components Wizard, and select Internet Information Services (IIS) from the list of components that are displayed.

2. If you want to install FPSE, or if you want to configure IIS as an FTP Server, click the Details button, select the appropriate options from the Internet Information Services (IIS) dialog box that's displayed, and click OK.

3. Click the Next button to complete the installation.

Description

*   If you want to run applications from a local IIS server, install IIS before you install Visual Studio.

*   To create or access an IIS web site on a remote computer, that computer must have FPSE installed. To use IIS as an FTP server, the FTP Service must be installed.

Figure A-3   How to install IIS under Windows XP

How to install Visual Studio 2010

If you've installed Windows applications before, you shouldn't have any trouble installing Visual Studio 2010. You simply insert the DVD or the first CD and the setup program starts automatically. This setup program will lead you through the steps for installing Visual Studio as summarized in figure A-4.

When you click the Install Microsoft Visual Studio 2010 link, the setup program starts loading the installation components it needs. Then, after you click the Next button and accept the license terms, the program lets you select the type of installation. In most cases, you'll perform a full installation so the most commonly used features are installed, including .NET Framework 4, Visual Studio, C#, the development web server, and SQL Server Express.

When the installation is finished, you will have the opportunity to install the documentation for Visual Studio on your local system. If you don't do that, the default will be to use the documentation that's available online. You can change this default later from within Visual Studio by using the Help→Manage Help Settings command.

If you're using the Visual Web Developer 2010 Express Edition, you have to download and install Web Developer 2010 and SQL Server Express separately. But if you follow the directions on the Microsoft web site when you download these products, you shouldn't have any trouble installing them.

The final setup step is to apply any updates that have become available since the product was released. If you don't perform this step, though, you can check for updates from within Visual Studio by using the Help→Check for Updates command. In fact, you should use this command periodically to be sure that Visual Studio is up-to-date.

By the way, the first time you start Visual Studio, you'll be asked to select the default environment settings. Then, you can choose Web Development Settings so your menus will look like the ones in this book.

If you install Visual Studio before installing IIS and then later decide to install IIS, you should know that you will need to register ASP.NET with IIS. To do that, you run this command from the command prompt:

```
aspnet_regiis -i
```

You'll find this command in the %systemroot%\Microsoft.NET\Framework\ v4.0.xxxxx directory, where %systemroot% is the root directory for Windows and xxxxx is the last .NET build number. On my system, for example, the root directory for Windows is just "Windows", and the .NET build number is 30319.

To find the build number you need, you can first enter a cd\ command to return to the root directory of the C drive. Then, you can run this command:

```
C:\>cd %systemroot%\Microsoft.NET\Framework
C:\Windows\Microsoft.NET\Framework>
```

This shows you what the root directory is so you can use Windows Explorer to find the last build number in the Framework directory. Then, you can use the cd command to change to the appropriate directory so you can run the aspnet_regiis program.

The Visual Studio 2010 Setup program

How to install Visual Studio 2010

1. Insert the DVD or Disc 1 of the installation CDs. The setup program will start automatically.

2. Click the Install Microsoft Visual Studio 2010 link and follow the instructions. When the Options page is displayed, you can accept the Full option unless you have special requirements. When the Finish page is displayed, you can click the Install Documentation button to install the Visual Studio documentation on your local system.

3. To install any updates that are available, click the Check for Service Releases link.

How to install Visual Web Developer 2010 Express Edition

1. Go to the page on Microsoft's web site for the download of Visual Web Developer 2010 Express Edition and follow the instructions to download the setup program.

2. Run the setup program. It works similarly to the setup program for Visual Studio 2010, but fewer options are available.

Description

*   The Visual Studio 2010 Setup program installs not only Visual Studio, but also .NET Framework 4, the development web server, and SQL Server Express.

*   The setup program for Visual Web Developer 2010 Express Edition does not install SQL Server 2008 Express. As a result, if you want to use SQL Server 2008 Express to work with databases, you'll need to download and install it as described in figure A-5.

*   If you're using Visual Web Developer 2010 Express Edition, you must register it within 30 days.

Figure A-4   How to install Visual Studio 2010

How to install and use SQL Server 2008 Express

SQL Server 2008 Express Edition is a free, lightweight version of SQL Server 2008 that you can install on your PC to test database applications. By default, the original release of SQL Server 2008 Express is installed when you install Visual Studio. If you choose not to install SQL Server Express with Visual Studio, however, or if you install Visual Web Developer 2008 Express Edition, you can download and install SQL Server 2008 Express Edition R2 (Release 2) from Microsoft's web site.

Note that when you download SQL Server Express, you can choose from one of four options. For this book, you only need the database engine, so you can choose the Database Only option. If you also want to download a graphical tool that you can use to work with the database, though, you can choose the Database with Management Tools option. Then, the SQL Server Management Studio Basic tool will be installed along with the database engine. Although this tool isn't covered in this book, you should find it easy to use.

After you download SQL Server Express, you can install it by running the setup program. This program starts the SQL Server 2008 R2 Setup Wizard, which takes you through a series of steps. Figure A-5 describes these steps and indicates how you should respond to each one.

If you already have SQL Server 2005 installed on your computer, you should know that you don't need to install SQL Server 2008. That's because the script we provide that creates the database for this book works with both SQL Server 2005 and 2008. You'll learn about this script in the next figure.

If you prefer to use the newest release of SQL Server, you can install it alongside another instance of SQL Server. Each instance must have a different name, though. So if you have a 2005 instance named SQLEXPRESS, you'll need to give the 2008 instance another name like SQLEXPRESS2008. In that case, you'll need to modify the applications in this book to use this name since they assume you're using an instance named SQLEXPRESS. You'll also need to modify the batch files that we provide for working with the database as described in the next figure.

After you install SQL Server Express, you can use the SQL Server Configuration Manager shown at the top of this figure to work with the server. In particular, you can use it to start, continue, pause, or stop the SQL Server engine. By default, SQL Server is started each time you start your PC. If that's not what you want, you can display the Properties dialog box for the server, click the Services tab, and then select Manual for the Start Mode option. Then, you can start SQL Server whenever you need it using the Configuration Manager.

The SQL Server Configuration Manager

How to install SQL Server 2008 Express

- Run the setup program. When the SQL Server Installation Center dialog box is displayed, select the Installation option, select the "New installation or add feature to an existing installation" option to start the SQL Server 2008 R2 Setup Wizard, and respond to the resulting dialog boxes.
- At the Feature Selection step, select all available features.
- At the Instance Configuration step, create a named instance with a name of SQLEXPRESS.
- At the Server Configuration step, select NT AUTHORITY\SYSTEM as the account name for the SQL Server Database Engine service to run SQL Server on your computer.
- At the Database Engine Configuration step, you can accept the default setting of Windows Authentication Mode. You can also click the Add Current User button to add the current user as a SQL Server administrator.

How to use SQL Server Express

- After you install SQL Server Express, it will start automatically each time you start your PC. To start or stop this service or change its start mode, start the SQL Server Configuration Manager (Start→All Programs→Microsoft SQL Server 2008 R2→Configuration Tools→SQL Server Configuration Manager), select the server in the right pane, and use the buttons in the toolbar.
- The setup program creates a copy of SQL Server with a name that consists of your computer name followed by \SqlExpress. You can use this name to define connections to the databases that you use with this server.

Description

- If you're using Visual Studio 2010, you can install SQL Server 2008 Express at the same time that you install Visual Studio.
- If you're using Visual Web Developer 2008 Express Edition, you can download the setup file for SQL Server 2008 Express Edition Release 2 from Microsoft's web site for free. Then, you can run the setup file to install SQL Server Express.

Figure A-5   How to install and use SQL Server 2008 Express

How to create the Halloween database

If you want to use the database that's available with the download for this book, you can do that without much trouble. First, you'll need to download and install the book files as described in figure A-1. Then, you can run the batch file named create_database.bat that's in the C:\Murach\aspnet4_cs\database directory. This batch file runs a SQL Server script named create_database.sql that creates the Halloween database and attaches it to the SQL Server Express database server that's running on your computer.

Note, however, that if the database server on your system has a name other than the computer name appended with SQLEXPRESS, the batch file we provide won't work. But you can easily change it so it will work. To do that, just open the file in a text editor such as NotePad. When you do, you'll see a single command with this server specification:

```
sqlcmd -S localhost\SQLExpress -E /i create_database.sql
```

Then, you can just change this specification to the name of your server. You'll also need to make this change to the other batch files that we provide.

Figure A-6 shows the beginning of the create_database.sql file. Although you don't need to understand all the details of this script, you may want to have a general idea of how it works.

To start, this script checks if the Halloween database already exists. If it does, the database is deleted. In either case, the database is created. This makes it possible to use this script to create the database initially and to restore the database to its original state if you ever need to do that.

After it creates the database, this script creates each table in the database and then inserts the required rows into that table. In this figure, for example, you can see the Create Table statement that creates the States table. This statement is followed by four Insert statements that insert the first four rows into the table. Similar statements are used for each of the other tables. Finally, it creates the foreign key constraints that define the relationships between the tables.

If you'll be running the database applications under IIS, you'll also need to grant ASP.NET access to the database. To do that under Windows XP, you can run the grant_access_windows_xp.bat file in the database directory. But first, you must modify the grant_access_windows_xp.sql file that this batch file runs so it uses the name of your computer. To do that, open the file in a text editor, and replace each occurrence of [machineName] with the name of your computer. Then, save and close this file, and run the grant_access_windows_xp.bat file to grant ASP.NET access to the Halloween database.

You use a similar technique to grant ASP.NET access to the database under Windows 7 and Windows Vista. Specifically, you run the grant_access_windows_7_vista.bat file, which runs the grant_access_windows_7_vista.sql file. If you open this file, you'll see that it actually grants access to the ASP.NET 4 application pool. This is the application pool that your ASP.NET 4 applications will run in by default if you run them under IIS. You'll learn more about application pools in appendix B.

The beginning of the script for creating the Halloween database

```
IF DB_ID('Halloween') IS NOT NULL
    DROP DATABASE Halloween

CREATE DATABASE Halloween
GO


USE [Halloween]
GO
/****** Object:  Table [dbo].[States]    Script Date: 01/11/2011 17:06:16
******/
SET ANSI_NULLS ON
GO
SET QUOTED_IDENTIFIER ON
GO
SET ANSI_PADDING ON
GO
CREATE TABLE [dbo].[States](
    [StateCode] [char](2) NOT NULL,
    [StateName] [varchar](20) NOT NULL,
 CONSTRAINT [PK_States] PRIMARY KEY CLUSTERED
(
    [StateCode] ASC
)WITH (PAD_INDEX  = OFF, STATISTICS_NORECOMPUTE  = OFF, IGNORE_DUP_KEY =
OFF, ALLOW_ROW_LOCKS  = ON, ALLOW_PAGE_LOCKS  = ON) ON [PRIMARY]
) ON [PRIMARY]
GO
SET ANSI_PADDING OFF
GO
INSERT [dbo].[States] ([StateCode], [StateName]) VALUES (N'AK', N'Alaska')
INSERT [dbo].[States] ([StateCode], [StateName]) VALUES (N'AL', N'Alabama')
INSERT [dbo].[States] ([StateCode], [StateName]) VALUES (N'AR', N'Arkansas')
INSERT [dbo].[States] ([StateCode], [StateName]) VALUES (N'AZ', N'Arizona')
    .
    .
    .
```

Description

- To create the Halloween database, you can use Windows Explorer to navigate to the C:\Murach\aspnet4_cs\database folder and double-click the create_database.bat file. This runs the create_database.sql file that creates the database objects and inserts the rows into each table.

- The create_database.sql file starts by deleting the Halloween database if it already exists. That way, you can use it to recreate the database and restore the original data if you ever need to do that.

- When you create the Halloween database, two files named Halloween.mdf and Halloween_log.ldf are created and stored in the default data directory for your instance of SQL Server. For SQL Server 2008, for example, that directory is C:\Program files\Microsoft SQL Server\MSSQL10.SQLEXPRESS\MSSQL\DATA.

- To grant ASP.NET access to the database under Windows XP, you modify the grant_access_windows_xp.sql file so it uses your computer name and then run the grant_access_windows_xp.bat file. To do that under Windows 7 or Windows Vista, you just run the grant_access_windows_7_vista.bat file.

Figure A-6   How to create the Halloween database

How to use the downloaded web applications

You can use two techniques to run the downloaded web applications for this book. First, you can open the applications in Visual Studio and then run them using the built-in development server. Second, you can run them under a local IIS server. Figure A-7 describes both of these techniques.

Before you can run an application under a local IIS server, you must create a virtual directory for the application within IIS. A virtual directory is a directory that contains a pointer to the directory that actually contains the files for a web site. To create a virtual directory, you can use the procedure shown in this figure. But first, if you're using Windows 7, you should set the application pool that IIS will use when you create a virtual directory for an existing application from Visual Studio. To do that, you use the IIS Management Console as shown in figure B-4 of appendix B.

Once you create a virtual directory for a web application, you can also run the application from outside of Visual Studio. To do that, open a browser window and specify //localhost/ followed by the virtual directory name and the starting page. For example, if the virtual directory name is Ch03Cart and the starting page is Order.aspx, you can run the application by entering //localhost/Ch03Cart/Order.aspx in the browser's address bar.

The dialog box for working with a local IIS web site

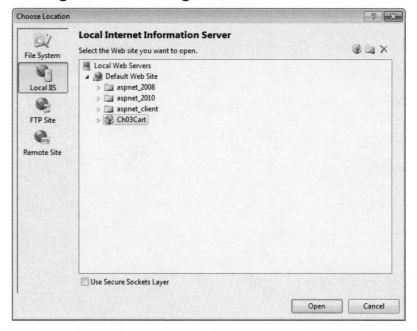

How to run a file-system web site under the development web server

1. Start Visual Studio and open the web site using the File→Open Web Site command.

2. Right-click the starting page for the application and select Set As Start Page.

3. Run the application using the Debug→Start Debugging command.

How to run a file-system web site under IIS

1. Start Visual Studio and display the New Web Site dialog box using the File→New Web Site command.

2. Click the Browse button to display the Choose Location dialog box.

3. Select the Local IIS button at the left side of the dialog box, select the Default Web Site node (or a directory that's subordinate to that node) from the tree that's displayed, and then click the Create New Virtual Directory button near the upper right corner of the dialog box. This displays the New Virtual Directory dialog box.

4. Enter the name for the virtual directory you want to create, enter the path where the files for the web site are stored, and click OK to return to the Choose Location dialog box.

5. Select the virtual directory you just created, and click Open to return to the New Web Site dialog box.

6. Click OK. A warning will be displayed indicating that there is already a web site at the location you specified. Select the Open the Existing Web Site option, and click OK.

7. Right-click the starting page for the application and select Set As Start Page.

8. Run the application using the Debug→Start Debugging command.

Figure A-7   How to use the downloaded web applications

Appendix B

How to work with web applications using IIS under Windows 7 and Windows Vista

In several places throughout this book, we've indicated that you can perform certain operations on a web application using IIS. You'll learn how to perform those operations under Windows 7 and Windows Vista in the topics that follow. Then, in appendix C, you'll learn how to perform many of the same operations under Windows XP.

Please note that you don't need to understand the material in these topics to develop web applications as described in this book. But as a professional programmer, you'll probably need these skills. So if you're using Windows 7 or Windows Vista, we recommend that you read these topics when we refer to them in the book or after you've completed the book.

If you've used a previous version of IIS, you'll see that the IIS Management Console for the versions of IIS that come with Windows Vista (IIS 7.0) and Windows 7 (IIS 7.5) is quite different from the IIS Management Console that came with earlier versions of IIS. In addition, the IIS Management Console has changed slightly from IIS 7.0 to IIS 7.5. In this appendix, I'll show the Management Console for IIS 7.5. You shouldn't have any trouble applying the same skills presented here to IIS 7.0, though.

How to create an IIS virtual directory or application

In appendix A, you learned how to create a virtual directory for a file-system web site from within Visual Studio. But if you prefer, you can create a virtual directory from the IIS Management Console. In figure B-1, for example, you can see the dialog box for creating a virtual directory named Ch03Cart that points to the web site stored in the C:\aspnet4_cs\Ch03Cart directory. Notice in this figure that the virtual directory is being created in the aspnet_2010 directory of the Default Web Site node. You can also create a virtual directory directly under the Default Web Site node.

After you create a virtual directory, you can use Visual Studio to open the web site from this directory. When you do that, Visual Studio will display a dialog box indicating that the web site isn't marked as an application and asking you if you want to open it. After you do that, you can run the application under IIS. But first, Visual Studio will display a dialog box that asks you if you want to configure the web site as an IIS application. Since this is necessary to run the application under IIS, you'll want to click Yes when this dialog box is displayed. Visual Studio may also display an error indicating that the web server isn't configured correctly. If you get this error, click the OK button to close the dialog box, then set the start page for the application and run it again.

If you want to run the application from outside of Visual Studio, you'll need to convert the virtual directory to an application from the IIS Management Console as described in this figure. Alternatively, you can create an application without first creating a virtual directory. The technique for doing that is also presented in this figure. Note that when you create an IIS application, you must specify the application pool you want it to run in. You'll learn more about application pools later in this appendix.

If you run an application from outside of Visual Studio under Windows Vista, you may run into a problem that's caused by insufficient permissions for the directory that contains the web site. In that case, you can use Windows Explorer to add the required permissions. To do that, right-click on the directory, choose Properties to display the Properties dialog box, and then display the Security tab. Then, review the list of groups and users to see if it includes Users (<computer name>\Users) and IIS_IUSRS (<computer name>\IIS_IUSRS) where <computer name> is the name of your computer. If not, you will need to add these two groups.

To add these groups, click the Edit button and then the Add button. In the dialog box that's displayed, enter the group name, including the computer name. For example, because the name of my computer is Anne-PC, I would enter Anne-PC\Users to add the Users group. To be sure you've entered the name correctly, click the Check Names button. Then, click the OK button and make sure that the Read & Execute, List Folder Contents, and Read permissions are selected. Repeat this process for the IIS_IUSRS group.

The dialog box for creating a virtual directory in IIS

How to create an IIS virtual directory for a file-system web site

1. Open the Control Panel, click the System and Security link, followed by the Administrative Tools link. Then, double-click Internet Information Services (IIS) Manager to open the IIS Management Console.

2. Use the tree to locate the Default Web Site node, right-click Default Web Site (or a directory that's subordinate to that node), and choose Add Virtual Directory to display the Add Virtual Directory dialog box.

3. Enter the name you want to use for the virtual directory, enter the path for the directory that contains the web site, and click the OK button.

Two ways to create an IIS application for a file-system web site

*   If a virtual directory already exists for the web site, right-click on it, select Convert to Application, select an application pool from the Add Application dialog box that's displayed, and click OK.

*   If a virtual directory doesn't exist for the web site, use the procedure above for creating a virtual directory, but choose Add Application to display the Add Application dialog box and select an application pool in addition to entering a name and path.

Description

*   In chapter 4, you can learn how to create a virtual directory for a new or existing web site using Visual Studio. When you do that, the directory is automatically configured as an IIS application. You can also create a virtual directory or application for a web site from IIS.

Figure B-1   How to create an IIS virtual directory or application

How to set the default page for a web site

To run a web application from outside of Visual Studio, you typically enter the URL of the application and the starting page in a browser. If you don't enter a starting page, however, IIS will look for a page with a name in the default document list for the application. Figure B-2 shows the file names that are in this list by default.

The last file name in the default document list, default.aspx, is the default name of the first page added to a new ASP.NET web site from Visual Studio. If you don't change the name of this page, you don't need to change the default document list. However, you may want to move the default.aspx file to the beginning of the list so IIS looks for it first.

In most cases, you'll use a more meaningful name for the first page of a web site. Then, you can add the name of that page to the default document list for the application. That way, the users of the application will be able to omit the starting page from the URL for the application.

The Default Document window of the IIS Management Console

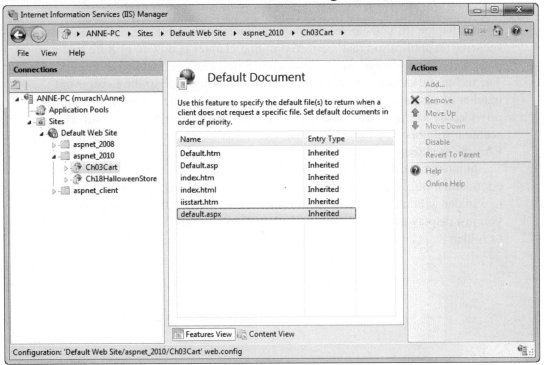

How to work with the list of default documents for a web site

- To display the list of default documents for a web site, display the IIS Management Console, and locate and select the web site. Then, double-click Default Document in the IIS group on the Home page for the web site to display the Default Document page.

- To add a file name to the list of default documents, click the Add link in the Actions pane, enter the file name in the dialog box that's displayed, and click OK.

- To change the order in which IIS looks for the file names, use the Move Up and Move Down links in the Actions pane.

- To remove a file name from the list, select the file and click the Remove link in the Actions pane.

Description

- By default, if you run a web application from a browser outside of Visual Studio and you don't include the name of the page you want to display in the URL, IIS looks for a file with the name Default.htm, Default.asp, index.htm, index.html, iisstart.asp, or default.aspx. If you want IIS to look for a file with a different name, you can use the procedure above to add that file name to the list of default file names.

- You can also add a file to the list of default file names for all your web sites. To do that, use the procedure above, but select the Default Web Site node instead of a specific web site.

Figure B-2   How to set the default page for a web site

How to force a page to use a secure connection

In chapter 18, you can learn how to secure a web application. One aspect of securing an application that's covered in that chapter is how to be sure that a page that should always use a secure connection can't be displayed without one. The technique shown in that chapter involves adding code to the Load event handler of the page. That way, if a user tries to bypass the navigation features provided by an application and access a page directly, the page will still be secured. Another way to provide that security is to use the IIS Management Console as shown in figure B-3.

In most cases, you'll only secure the pages of a web site that contain confidential information. If you need to, however, you can secure all the pages in a folder within the web site or all of the pages within the web site. To do that, you just display the SSL Settings window shown in this figure for the web site or folder.

Two IIS windows for securing a web page

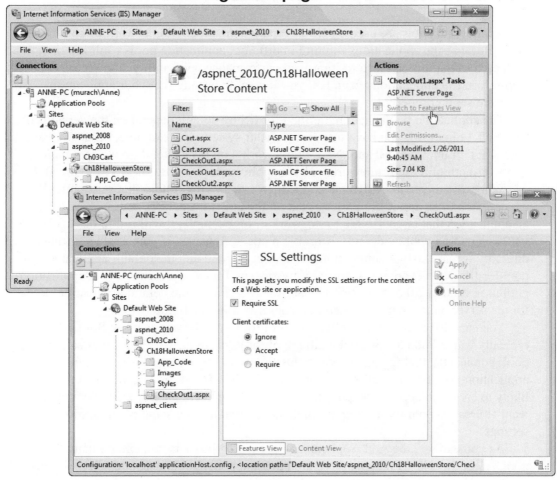

How to set the security for a web page

1. Display the IIS Management Console, and then locate and select the web site that contains the page you want to secure.

2. Click the Content View tab on the Home page for the web site, select the page you want to secure, and then click the Switch to Features View link in the Actions pane.

3. Double-click SSL Settings in the IIS group of the Home page to display the SSL Settings page. Then, select the Require SSL option and click the Apply link in the Actions pane.

Description

*   In chapter 18, you can learn how to add C# code to a page to be sure that it uses a secure connection. Another way to do that is to use the IIS Management Console.

*   You can also set the security for all the pages within a folder of a web site or for all the pages of a web site. To do that, select the folder or web site, display the SSL Settings window, and then set the appropriate options.

Figure B-3   How to force a page to use a secure connection

How to work with application pools

Application pools are used by IIS to separate the processing of various applications. Because the applications running in different application pools can't interact with each other, this can lead to improved performance, availability, and security. Before you run applications from IIS, you'll want to be sure that your application pools are set up properly.

The application pools that are defined for IIS by default depend on the versions of the .NET Framework you have installed on your system. For example, because I have both .NET Framework 2.0 and .NET Framework 4 on my system, I have application pools for both of these frameworks. These application pools are shown in figure B-4.

When you create an ASP.NET application from Visual Studio that runs under IIS, it's assigned to an application pool based on the target framework it uses. If you create an application that targets .NET Framework 4, for example, it will run in the ASP.NET v4.0 application pool by default. A problem arises, however, if you create a virtual directory for an existing application from Visual Studio and the default application pool for IIS isn't set appropriately. On my system, for example, the default application pool uses version 2.0 of the .NET Framework. To change the default application pool for the server, you can use the technique described in this figure.

You can also change the application pool for a specific application. But first, you'll typically want to add a new application pool for it to run in. To add an application pool, you use the dialog box shown in this figure. In this example, I'm creating an application pool for the Halloween Store application. However, you're much more likely to create an application pool for a group of applications. For example, you might want to create a pool for a group of applications that use the same configuration settings.

As you can see, the Add Application Pool dialog box lets you enter a name for the pool, select the .NET Framework version that the pool should use, and select a managed pipeline mode. This dialog box also lets you choose whether you want the application pool to start immediately. If you don't start the application pool when you create it, you can start it by highlighting the pool in the Application Pools page and then clicking the Start link in the Actions pane.

By default, IIS runs ASP.NET applications in integrated mode. This mode allows ASP.NET features, such as authentication and authorization, to be used with any content that can run under IIS. That includes static web pages as well as applications developed with other frameworks. Because this mode gives you maximum flexibility, you'll use it most of the time. In some cases, though, you may need to use classic mode for compatibility with existing applications.

If you're using a 64-bit operating system, you should know that a complication can arise if you try to run an application that uses an Access database under IIS 7. That's because the Jet OLE DB provider that's used to work with Access databases is 32-bit, and 32-bit processing is disabled in IIS by default for 64-bit operating systems. To enable 32-bit processing, select the application pool that the application uses and then click the Advanced Settings link in the Actions pane to display the Advanced Settings dialog box. Then, set the Enable 32-Bit Applications option in the General category to True.

IIS application pools

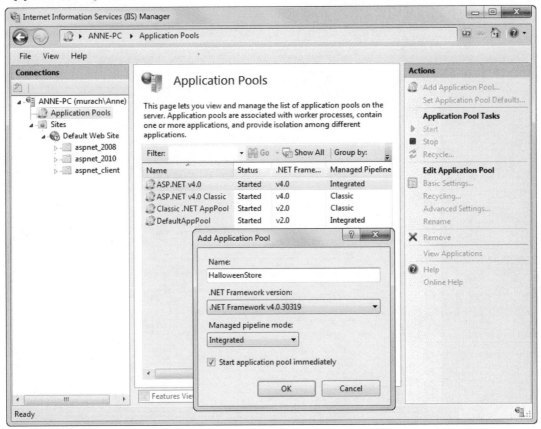

Description

- After you install ASP.NET 4, four application pools will be defined for IIS. To display these pools, click the Application Pools node in the Connections pane.

- If you create a new IIS application or virtual directory from Visual Studio, it's assigned to an application pool based on the target framework you specify. If you create an IIS application from the IIS Management Console, you specify the pool you want to use.

- To add an application pool, click the Add Application Pool link in the Actions Pane to display the dialog box shown above. Then, enter a name for the pool, select the .NET Framework the application uses, and click OK.

- To change the application pool that an application runs in, select the application in the Connections pane, click the Basic Settings link in the Actions pane, click the Select button in the Edit Application dialog box that's displayed, and select the pool from the Application Pool drop-down list.

- To change the default application pool for the server, select the Default Web Site node instead of a specific application.

- You can also perform a variety of operations on individual application pools by selecting a pool in the Application Pool page and then using the links in the Action pane.

Figure B-4   How to work with application pools

Appendix C

How to work with web applications using IIS under Windows XP

In several places throughout this book, we've indicated that you can perform certain operations on a web application using IIS. Although you don't need to know how to use IIS to perform these operations to develop web applications as described in this book, you'll probably need these skills as a professional programmer. So if you're using Windows XP, we recommend that you read these topics when we refer to them in the book or after you've completed the book.

How to create a virtual directory

In appendix A, you learned how to create a virtual directory for a file-system web site from within Visual Studio. But if you prefer, you can create a virtual directory from the IIS Management Console. In figure C-1, for example, you can see two of the dialog boxes for creating a virtual directory named Ch03Cart that points to the web site stored in the C:\aspnet4_cs\Ch03Cart directory.

After you create a virtual directory, it will appear under the Default Web Site node in the IIS Management Console. Then, you can use Visual Studio to open the web site from this directory so you can run the application under IIS. You can also run the application from outside of Visual Studio. Note that you can also create a virtual directory in a subdirectory of the Default Web Site node. In the illustration in this figure, for example, the virtual directory is being created in the aspnet_2010 directory.

The dialog boxes for creating a virtual directory in IIS

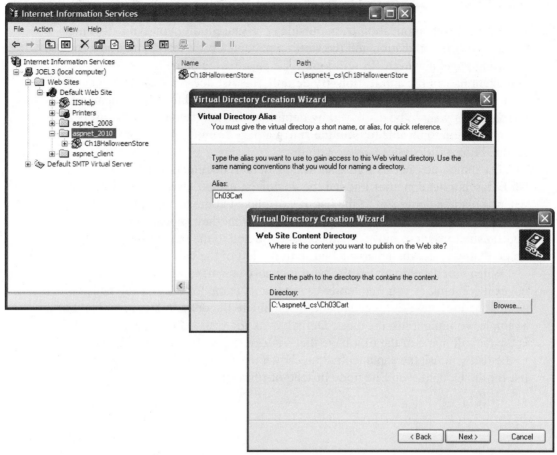

How to create a virtual directory for a file-system web site

1. Open the Control Panel, double-click Administrative Tools, and double-click Internet Information Services to open the IIS Management Console.

2. Use the tree to locate the Default Web Site node, right-click Default Web Site (or a directory that's subordinate to that node), and choose New→Virtual Directory to start the Virtual Directory Creation Wizard.

3. Enter the name you want to use for the virtual directory on the Virtual Directory Alias page of the wizard, enter the path for the directory that contains the web site on the Web Site Content Directory page, and accept the defaults on the Access Permissions page.

Description

- In chapter 4, you can learn how to create a virtual directory for a new or existing web site using Visual Studio. You can also create a virtual directory for a web site from IIS. Then, you can use Visual Studio to open the web site from the virtual directory, and you can run the web site under IIS.

Figure C-1   How to create a virtual directory

How to set the default page for a web site

To run a web application from outside of Visual Studio, you typically enter the URL of the application and the starting page in a browser. If you don't enter a starting page, however, IIS will look for a page with a name in the default document list for the application. By default, this list doesn't include a document with the aspx extension. Because of that, you'll need to add the name of the page you want to be displayed by default to this list if you want the users of the application to be able to omit the starting page from the URL for the application. Figure C-2 shows how you do that.

The dialog box in this figure shows the default document list for the Ch03Cart application after I added the document named Order.aspx. Note that when you add a document to the list, it's displayed at the end of the list. Because IIS will check for documents in the order that they appear in the list, you'll usually want to move the document you add to the beginning of the list. To do that, you use the up arrow button to the left of the list.

When you develop a web site, you typically use meaningful names for the pages it contains. If you frequently use the same name for the starting page of an application, however, you can add this name to the default document list. For example, you might use the name Default.aspx for your starting pages since this is the default name of the first page that's added to a web site. To add this name to the list, you use the same technique shown in this figure, but you change the list for the Default Web Site node instead of for a specific web site.

The Documents tab of the Properties dialog box

How to work with the list of default documents for a web site

- To display the list of default documents for a web site, display the IIS Management Console, and locate the web site. Then, right-click on the web site, select Properties from the shortcut menu, and click the Documents tab in the Properties dialog box that's displayed.
- To add a document to the list of default documents, click the Add button, enter the document name in the dialog box that's displayed, and click OK.
- To change the order in which IIS looks for the documents, use the up and down arrow buttons to the left of the document list.
- To remove a document from the list, select the document and click the Remove button.

Description

- By default, if you run a web application from a browser outside of Visual Studio and you don't include the name of the page you want to display in the URL, IIS looks for a document with the name Default.htm, Default.asp, index.htm, or iisstart.asp. If you want IIS to look for a document with a different name, you can use the procedure above to add that document to the list of default documents.
- You can also add a document to the list of default documents for all your web sites. To do that, use the procedure above, but right-click the Default Web Site node instead of a specific web site. For example, you might want to add Default.aspx to the list since this is the default name of the first page that's added to a new web site in Visual Studio.

Figure C-2   How to set the default page for a web site

How to force a page to use a secure connection

In chapter 18, you can learn how to secure a web application. One aspect of securing an application that's covered in that chapter is how to be sure that a page that should always use a secure connection can't be displayed without one. The technique shown in that chapter involves adding code to the Load event handler of the page. That way, if a user tries to bypass the navigation features provided by an application and access a page directly, the page will still be secured. Another way to provide that security is to use the IIS Management Console as shown in figure C-3.

In most cases, you'll only secure the pages of a web site that contain confidential information. If you need to, however, you can secure all the pages in a folder within the web site or all of the pages within the web site. To do that, you use the same technique shown in this figure, but you display the properties of the folder or the web site.

The dialog boxes for securing a web page

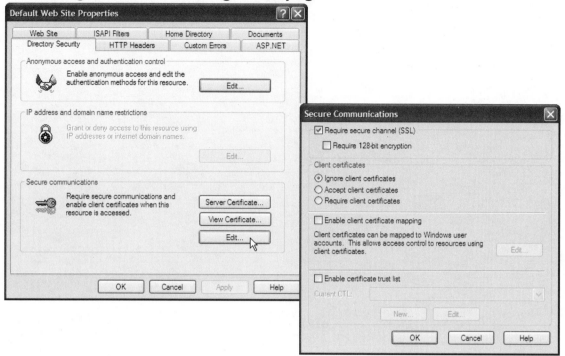

How to set the security for a web page

1. Display the IIS Management Console, locate the web site that contains the page you want to secure, and select the web site or the folder within the web site that contains the page.

2. Right-click the page (.aspx) in the right pane of the IIS Management Console, select the Properties command from the shortcut menu, and display the Directory Security tab of the Properties dialog box that's displayed.

3. Click the Edit button in the Secure Communications section to display the Secure Communications dialog box. Then, select the Require Secure Channel (SSL) option. If you want the page to be displayed only if 128-bit encryption is used, select the Require 128-bit Encryption option.

Description

- In chapter 18, you can learn how to add C# code to a page to be sure that it uses a secure connection. Another way to do that is to set IIS security properties for the page.

- You can also set the security for all the pages within a folder of a web site or for all the pages of a web site. To do that, display the properties for the folder or web site, display the Directory Security tab, and then set the appropriate options.

Figure C-3   How to force a page to use a secure connection

Index

X

Y

For more on Murach products, visit us at
www.murach.com

Books for .NET developers

Murach's C# 2010	$54.50
Murach's ASP.NET 4 Web Programming with C# 2010	54.50
Murach's ADO.NET 4 Database Programming with C# 2010	54.50
Murach's Visual Basic 2010	$54.50
Murach's ASP.NET 4 Web Programming with VB 2010	54.50
Murach's ADO.NET 4 Database Programming with VB 2010	54.50
Murach's SQL Server 2008 for Developers	$52.50

Books for web developers

Murach's HTML, XHTML, and CSS	$44.50
Murach's JavaScript and DOM Scripting	54.50
Murach's PHP and MySQL	54.50

Books for Java developers

Murach's Java SE 6	$52.50
Murach's Java Servlets and JSP, Second Edition	52.50
Murach's Oracle SQL and PL/SQL	52.50

Prices and availability are subject to change. Please visit our website or call for current information.

Our unlimited guarantee...when you order directly from us

You must be satisfied with our books. If they aren't better than any other programming books you've ever used...both for training and reference...you can send them back within 90 days for a full refund. No questions asked!

Your opinions count

If you have any comments on this book, I'm eager to get them. Thanks for your feedback!

To comment by

E-mail:	murachbooks@murach.com
Web:	www.murach.com
Postal mail:	Mike Murach & Associates, Inc.
	4340 North Knoll Ave.
	Fresno, California 93722-7825

To order now,

 Web: www.murach.com

 Call toll-free:
1-800-221-5528
(Weekdays, 8 am to 4 pm Pacific Time)

 Fax: 1-559-440-0963

 Mike Murach & Associates, Inc.
Professional programming books

What software you need for this book

- Any edition of Microsoft Visual C# 2010 or the free Visual Web Developer 2010 Express Edition.

- These editions include everything you need for developing ASP.NET 4 applications, including .NET Framework 4, ASP.NET 4, C# 2010, a built-in web server, and a scaled-back version of SQL Server called SQL Server Express.

- If you want to use IIS (Internet Information Services) instead of the built-in web server to run web applications on your own PC, you also need to install IIS. You need to do this to test some aspects of web applications.

- For information about installing these products, please see appendix A.

The downloadable files for this book

- The source code for all of the applications presented in this book.

- Files for creating the SQL Server version of the Halloween database that's used by some of the applications, along with an Access version of this database.

- Starting points for the exercises in the book so you can get more practice in less time.

- For more information about downloading and installing these applications and databases, please see appendix A.

The VB edition of this book

- If this book looks interesting but you're a Visual Basic developer, please see *Murach's ASP.NET 4 Web Programming with VB 2010*. It covers all of the same features but uses Visual Basic coding examples.

www.murach.com